Managerial Accounting

John Y. Lee
Schaeberle Professor of Accounting
Pace University
New York

Hampton House
Santa Fe Springs, CA 90670

Pictures and information have been provided by AFLAC, JPMorganChase, Motorola, MetLife, Daimler-Chrysler, Southwest Airlines, Pitney Bowes, Kellogg, Northwest Airlines, AES, Union Pacific, Marriott Hotel, DTE, GM, DIRECTV, Airborne Express, Olive Garden, Timken, Pizza Hut, Harnischfeger, Cisco Systems, Ritz-Carlton, FedEx, UPS, Sara Lee, PepsiCo, Sempra Energy Solutions, Edison Development, First Union, AEP, Avis, Hannaford, Electrocom, P&H, Baldor Electric, Amoco, Union Electric Steel, John Deere, Morton International, Tellabs, and Merck. The cover photography by J.C. Hong, The K.T., Los Angeles.

ISBN 1-891666-08-8

Printed in Hong Kong

10 9 8 7 6 5 4 3 2 1

To My Colleagues

John Y. Lee is the Schaeberle Professor of Accounting at Lubin School of Business, Pace University, New York. He is also editor of *Advances in Management Accounting*, a refereed academic journal, and has taught at the State University of New York at Buffalo, University of Southern California, and California State University, Los Angeles, where he was selected as the 1990 University Outstanding Professor.

The author of *Managerial Accounting Changes for the 1990s* (Addison-Wesley), he has written three books and has contributed chapters to two books. He has published numerous articles in accounting and business journals, and taught continuing education courses in cost accounting for eleven state CPA societies. For his contribution to the education of CPAs, Dr. Lee received Instructor Excellence Award in 1992 from the California State CPA Society. A Ph.D. in accounting from Louisiana State University, he has served as Director of the Western Region, Management Accounting Section, American Accounting Association.

BRIEF CONTENTS

CONTENTS

5 Process-Costing and Hybrid-Costing Systems

9 Standard Costs and Flexible Budgets

10 Performance in the New Environment

13 Capital Budgeting

14 Capital Budgeting: Taxes, Inflation and Technology

15 Constraints and Relevant Costs

16 Statement of Cash Flows [In the Supplement]

Appendix B Pricing Products and Services

Glossary

Index

This text is intended to introduce students to the concepts and roles of cost in the new environment of managerial accounting. It is designed for a one-term course in managerial accounting.

The book is structured around the topics managers in the manufacturing and service environments have to deal with for their planning and control activities. The arrangement of chapters reflects that. The approach to teaching the traditional and new concepts in managerial accounting, however, is unique in this book.

A Unique Approach to Teaching the Traditional and New Concepts

Managerial accounting instructors would find that the book is unique in the way it organizes traditional topics and the new paradigm in managerial accounting. The following illustrates how it does that:

The book starts from a discussion of the concepts and behavior patterns of cost in various environments of manufacturing and service to help students understand the basic cost behavior (chapters 1,2, and 3). A coverage of cost systems follows that (chapters 4 and 5).

Cost-activity relationships are then explained in the context of understanding and estimating cost-activity relationships (chapter 6). This will reinforce the basic understanding of cost concepts and behavior, and introduce students to cost estimation. The coverage of activity-based costing becomes an easy task after these (chapter 7).

The author is firmly convinced that the best approach to teaching the ABC paradigm is to teach it using the cost estimation framework. Several different attempts at teaching ABC in the classroom over several years have led the author to reach this conclusion.

This is distinctly different from the approach used in most other texts in which ABC is covered in connection with service department cost allocation. Many instructors would agree with me that the whole coverage of ABC becomes so mundane and static if it is conducted this way. ABC is a lot more than using just additional cost drivers in service department cost allocation.

Gordian Knot. This textbook takes a pragmatic approach to the coverage of budgeting and standard costing (chapters 8 and 9). Despite various criticisms leveled against it, standard costing is still a widely used cost accounting methodology. It deserves an adequate coverage in a basic managerial accounting course. The coverage, however, is not extended to the discussion of recent attempts at improving standard costing as a cost management technique. Vollman's use of the Gordian Knot analogy can explain the author's approach. An oracle had prophesied that whoever loosed the massive knot on the yoke of King Gordius's chariot would rule the world. Ancient warriors made countless, but futile, attempts to untie the knot until Alexander the Great came up to it with his sword and cut it in two.

Companies can use standard costing as an efficient cost accounting methodology in a mass-production environment. Making serious attempts at connecting any improved standard costing methodology to cost management would not be fruitful in the new environment. Chapter 10 discusses new methodologies for such cost management purposes.

In chapter 11, this textbook approaches variable and absorption costing using the product costing format that is consistent with previous chapters. Segmented reporting is covered here since the reporting format is consistent with the main topic of the chapter. Chapter 12 discusses responsibility accounting and decentralized operations. Chapters 13 and 14 discuss capital budgeting from various perspectives. Constraints and issues of non-routine decision making based on relevant costs are discussed in chapter 15. Cash flow statement (chapter 16) and financial statement analysis (chapter 17) represent the coverage of the analysis of individual firms' financial performance. Service department cost allocation and pricing of products and services are discussed in appendixes A and B.

Changes in the Second Edition

Relying on comments and suggestions from users of the first edition, I have maintained the positive features in the second edition while improving upon them by increasing the number of real-world applications. The primary reason why the first edition was so well received was the ease with which the traditional as well as new paradigm topics were integrated throughout the textbook. That was the strength of a newly designed book compared with established textbooks that have to introduce new materials tacked onto the existing structure.

Numerous additional actual stories and scenarios have been added to make management accounting discussions even more lively and interesting throughout the second edition. Existing users would notice that early chapters have more cross-section connections that keep students focused on each topic being discussed while affording to consider different perspectives from other parts of the textbook. The balanced scorecard section has been beefed up with actual examples from practice and introduced early in Chapter 10.

The second edition has added the following new sections and projects:

E-Business. A section on e-business has been added in Chapter 1, Chapter 4, Chapter 6, and Chapter 9.

Internet Project. Interesting websites have been selected and meaningful assignments have been designed to provide students an opportunity to relate what they learn in each chapter to the real-world information available on the Internet.

Chapter 16 and Chapter 17 have been moved to separate Supplements. Schools that desire to cover either one or both of the two chapters can order the supplements based on their needs.

Student's CD-ROM now has a List of Check Figures and Excel Spreadsheet Templates. The templates help students learn Excel on their own and are intended for easy and meaningful application to solving selected exercises and problems.

Acknowledgments

The author would like to thank those users of the first edition who have provided valuable comments and suggestions that have been instrumental in the revision process. They are from all over the world and too numerous to mention but they will recognize their impact in various parts of the second edition.

The author acknowledges the support and encouragement received from the following colleagues during the revision process: Rudy Jacob, Pat Healy, Anne Fosbre, Lee Tagliaferri, Roberta Cable, Tony Pustorino, Bob Zwicker, Joan Magratten, Charles Tang, Arnie Berman, Joe DiBenedetto, Phil Finn, Mike Ulinski, Joe Russo, Mary Ellen Oliverio, John McKenna, Kam Chan, Bairj Donabedian, and Dean Centonze. The author owes the former colleague Chor Lau for valuable advice and support.

Appreciation also goes to The Institute of Certified Management Accountants for their generous permission to use or adapt problems and unofficial answers from past CMA examinations, and Jim Moran and Jerry McLendon of GraphicType for their outstanding artistic work to make the second edition a truly useful learning tool.

And, finally, I would like to thank my wife Jungmi and my children Patti, Hanie, and Howard for their love, support, and encouragement during the revision process.

John Y. Lee

MANAGERIAL ACCOUNTING: AN OVERVIEW

After studying this chapter, you should be able to:

1. Define managerial accounting.

2. Identify and describe the basic managerial functions and explain how managerial accounting helps management perform those functions.

3. Illustrate the importance of cost concepts and systems, planning and control, nonroutine and special decisions, and financial reporting and analysis.

4. Distinguish between line and staff positions in an organization.

5. Contrast financial accounting and managerial accounting.

6. Identify the nature of service industries and outline the differences between manufacturing and service organizations.

7. Explain recent changes in the competitive environment of manufacturing and service companies, including e-business.

8. Describe the balanced scorecard, activity-based cost management and the lean production paradigm.

9. Understand the meaning of strategic cost management and value chain analysis.

10. Explain the implications of ethical behavior for managers and management accountants.

WHAT IS MANAGERIAL ACCOUNTING?

Managerial accounting is a branch of accounting that is concerned with providing information to the managers in an organization to help them in making decisions, planning and controlling operations, and evaluating the performance of subordinates.

In general, the major objective of any accounting system is to provide information that is useful in decision making. If we apply this statement to **financial accounting,** we can say that the major objective of financial accounting is to provide persons outside the organization (such as investors, creditors and others, e.g., government agencies) with information that is useful to them in making investment, lending, or other decisions about the organization. If we apply the same statement to **managerial accounting,** then we can say that the major objective of managerial accounting is to provide managers of all levels inside the organization with information that is useful to them in making all kinds of decisions. The **managerial accounting information** generated from a managerial accounting system is helpful to managers in making strategic decisions, in planning and controlling routine day-to-day activities, and in evaluating the performance of individuals, departments, and divisions.

AFLAC's chairman and president are shown here with the company's marketing symbol in the background. Management accounting information needs to be useful to them in their efforts to accomplish one of their organizational objectives of becoming the best provider of supplemental insurance in the global marketplace.

MANAGERIAL DECISION MAKING

But what type of information would be helpful to management in making the kinds of decisions mentioned above? Management is the process of setting strategies for the organization, drawing plans to achieve these strategies, organizing people to carry out these plans, directing these people by showing them how to implement the plans, monitoring and evaluating whether their performance was in accordance with plans, and if not, investigating the reasons for lack of conformity with plans, and finally making decisions to correct the situation, or modify the plans if correction is not possible.

Planning represents the outlining of specific steps to be taken and rules to be followed by the people in the organization to achieve the organizational objectives. While the organizational objectives are usually long-run in nature, the plans are more short-term. For example, one of the strategic objectives of an organization may be to capture a twenty five percent share of the market for a particular product within five years. To achieve that objective, plans must be made to show the sales volume or sales value required in the first year, as well as the expected rate of growth in sales volume or value every year after that so that the sales volume or value in the fifth year will represent a twenty five percent market share.

Controlling is the process of making sure that plans are being implemented and that everyone in the organization is performing the job effectively and efficiently. Controlling also involves seeing that the company's general policies and specific rules are adhered to by everybody within the organization. **Performance**

evaluation involves comparison of actual performance to planned objectives to assess how plans are being achieved.

Decision making represents selecting one approach to solve the problem indicated by the investigation. The corrective action may be an effort to remove the causes of the variance between actual performance and plans or may be an effort to change the original plans. For instance, if a shortfall in the units sold is determined to be due to lack of advertising, lack of trained salespeople, or both, the corrective action may be to increase advertising, train the sales force, or do both. However, if the shortfall is due to tough competition in the marketplace that was not properly evaluated or anticipated at the time plans were drawn, the plans may have to be revised downward.

MANAGERIAL ACCOUNTING INFORMATION

Decision making exists in almost all managerial functions. Since decisions are based on information, the quality of the decisions cannot exceed the quality of the information on which the decisions are based. That is, good information will probably lead to good decisions, and bad or wrong information will probably lead to poor decisions. In order to make the right decisions, management needs to obtain the most appropriate managerial accounting information. This explains the importance of a course in managerial accounting to managers or to those who would someday be managers.

While the purpose of managerial accounting is to provide information to help management in making decisions and in performing required functions, managerial accounting focuses particularly on the planning and controlling functions of management. These are the most frequent and perhaps the most important functions of management. Besides the basic objective of minimizing costs and planning and controlling routine operations, the management of an organization is faced with a myriad of nonroutine and special decisions such as capital investment decisions, make or buy decisions, pricing products and services sold to outside customers or transferred among divisions or departments within the organization, and so forth. These decisions may be even more difficult to make than minimizing costs or planning and controlling routine operations. Providing management with the right information for making nonroutine decisions is an important aspect of managerial accounting as well.

MANAGERIAL ACCOUNTING FUNCTIONS IN AN ORGANIZATION

Line and Staff Positions

Some of the positions in an organization are considered **line** positions while others are considered **staff** positions. The distinction between line and staff positions is made on the basis of whether the functions of the positions relate directly to the basic objective of the organization. If they relate directly, they are line positions; otherwise they are staff positions. For example, the basic objective of a company like General Motors is the manufacturing and selling of motor vehicles. Thus, all positions that are engaged directly in these functions, e.g., manufacturing vice president, marketing vice president, and sales vice president, are considered line positions. Other positions, e.g., controller, treasurer, personnel vice president, and public relations manager are considered staff positions. These staff positions exist only to provide services to the line positions.

Line positions are said to have line authorities whereas staff positions are said to have staff authorities. **Line authority** means that direct authority is exerted over subordinates. Line authority exists within both line and staff positions. For example, controller holds a staff position in the organization as a whole, but has line authority over his/her subordinates. **Staff authority** is the authority to give guidance, consultation, or advice, but not to command. Thus, staff authority can be exerted laterally, downward, or upward.

Controller

The **controller** is the chief accountant and belongs to top management of an organization. Since accounting is a staff function, the controller does not exercise line authority in the context of the whole organization. The controller is responsible for maintaining data and reporting information needed in decision making. These responsibilities include: overseeing that the accounting system functions properly and generates the amount of detail required for internal and external purposes; designing and maintaining the organization's internal control system; and helping management interpret accounting information. The controller exercises the technical abilities and has a unique influence on decisions by providing and interpreting accounting information for managerial decisions.

In today's environment, many organizations expect the controller to move beyond the traditional role of number crunching to instead play a more active role in the strategic planning process. The strategic planning process receives input from all operating units, such as production, marketing, finance, engineering, human resource, accounting, and other support services. Top management is heavily involved in this process, and the role of controller is to coordinate planning, formulate and select strategies, translate strategies into operational plans and budgets, and monitor past plans and their implementations.

Treasurer

The **treasurer** is responsible for financing and investment activities. Since the treasurer handles the real resources, he or she is not allowed to have access to the accounting records. The specific functions of the treasurer include, for example, raising funds through either short-term or long-term borrowing from banks or by issuing bonds or stocks to the public. The treasurer's functions may also include investor relations, banking relations, setting credit and collection policies, making various short-term and long-term investments, and insurance.

Internal Audit

The **internal audit** department is usually responsible for auditing internal control systems and procedures to determine whether they are appropriate and functioning properly. The department also makes recommendations to top management as to any improvements deemed necessary to the internal control system in light of its audit. The internal audit department also usually assists external auditors in their audit function.

The internal audit department may not exist in some organizations depending on the size and nature of the organization. Also, it may be under the direct supervision of the controller, finance vice president, or the president of the organization depending on (a) the importance of the internal audit function as perceived by top management and (b) the potential conflict between the controller's record-keeping role and the internal audit function. In large organizations, such as General Motors or General Electric, the internal audit department does not report to the controller and usually the director of internal audit has the authority to communicate directly with the audit committee of the board of directors.

FINANCIAL AND MANAGERIAL ACCOUNTING CONTRASTED

Exhibit 1-1 contrasts financial accounting and managerial accounting from various perspectives. Managerial accounting, unlike financial accounting, is not constrained by Generally Accepted Accounting Principles (GAAP). It provides detailed information to all managerial levels to help them in evaluating the performance of all segments of the organization in frequent (hourly, daily or weekly) intervals by comparing actual results to predetermined plans. In this process, managerial accounting emphasizes relevance over reliability and qualitative and nonmonetary over quantitative and monetary data. Managerial accounting thus draws heavily on other disciplines such as economics, marketing, management, behavioral, and decision sciences. Furthermore, managerial accounting is not mandatory; only the **cost-benefit** concept determines how much managerial information is required. That is, management will likely continue to demand more information as long as the benefits of such information exceed the costs of acquiring it.

As indicated in Exhibit 1-1, managerial accounting emphasizes relevance over reliability because managers need more timely information that has the capacity to confirm or correct management's earlier expectations and that helps management in planning for the future. Management also needs this information more frequently (hourly, daily, weekly, and monthly, rather than quarterly, semi-annually or annually). Internal managers are not so concerned with reliability because it may be too costly to get an independent verification for all kinds of information that is continually flowing within the organization.

On the other hand, financial accounting usually emphasizes reliability over relevance because financial accounting information is used by various external users. Hence, it must be verifiable and, in most cases, certified by an independent auditor. It must be neutral and must represent exactly what it purports to represent since there is no immediate two-way communication between the organization and the external users of its financial statements. In financial accounting, organizational performance is evaluated by comparing current year actual results with those of the prior year or with those of other organizations for the current year. However, in managerial accounting, a segment's or a division's performance is usually evaluated by comparing current period actual results with planned and predetermined expectations for the period.

EXHIBIT 1-1 Financial and Management Accounting Contrasted

Perspective	Financial Accounting	Managerial Accounting
Major Users	External users: Primarily present and prospective investors and their analysts; creditors; and others, e.g., government agencies	Internal users: Managers of all levels
GAAP Constraints	Constrained by GAAP	Not constrained by GAAP
Data Characteristics	Emphasizes reliability over relevance and usually reports only monetary data.	Emphasizes relevance over reliability and reports both monetary and nonmonetary data
Performance Evaluation	Compares current actual data to historical data	Compares current actual data to expected plans
Types of Reports	Summary reports about the organization as a whole	Detailed reports about the different segments and managerial levels
Frequency of Reports	Less frequent: primarily every quarter or every year	More frequent: could be hourly, daily or weekly; but mostly monthly
Quantity of Information Required	Certain minimum quantity of information required by regulatory authorities or financial accounting standard setters	No specified minimum: cost-benefit analysis determines quantity of information required

Both financial accounting and managerial accounting rely on the same accounting information system and on the stewardship concept. The actual results generated by the financial accounting system may be used by the managerial accountant to evaluate performance by comparing these actual results with predetermined plans. Also, while financial accounting is concerned with management's stewardship over the organization as a whole, managerial accounting is concerned with the stewardship of different managerial levels over the different parts or segments of the organization.

SERVICE ORGANIZATIONS

Due to the differences in the nature of service businesses from manufacturing, managerial accounting practices may be applied a little differently depending on whether the organization in question is in service or manufacturing. In service businesses, inventory does not exist. Service is mostly intangible, and generating and rendering service in personal service businesses occur at the same time. For service entities, operations are labor intensive, and people are the most crucial factor in competing against others in the market. The nature of service capacity, compared to production facility in manufacturing, is unique. This is because of the people factor. Measuring service volume and quality is difficult, and evaluation of performance tends to be more subjective than in manufacturing. In manufacturing, it is not too difficult to standardize products when manufacturing reaches the mass-production stage. Service organizations, however, cannot standardize their services so easily, because no service may be duplicated exactly the way management wants.

The basic implication in making any distinction between service and manufacturing is that all businesses have service components. It is a matter of the *extent* of the service component of a business, rather than the *kind*, that determines whether a business is in manufacturing or service. For example, a hotel, which is in a typical service business, prepares food in its restaurant in exactly the way a product is manufactured, using materials, labor, and other items called overhead, such as electricity. Similarly, a manufacturer of mainframe computer also provides operational support service of its software specialists to its customers.

There are many more companies whose primary business is service than manufacturing. A few examples of service industries are: communications, transportation, health care, education, financial services, retail and wholesale trading,

entertainment, food and lodging, consulting, and other personal services. As service industries are deregulated and the rules and mode of competition change to a more global nature, today's service companies face the same need to know and understand their costs that manufacturing companies have long faced. Knowing what the costs of providing services to customers are and how those costs are incurred, is of paramount importance to all service companies.

In service industries, the traditional cost patterns of manufacturing companies cannot be applied without some modification. We will discuss the slight differences in Chapter 4.

CHANGING ENVIRONMENT AND THE NEW MANAGERIAL ACCOUNTING

Although the economic laws have not changed, the world economy has in recent years seen two broad trends: the **globalization** of commerce and the revolution in **information technology (IT).** The globalization of commerce has transformed business perspectives in almost every phase of business. Market forces have been introduced around the whole world. The revolution in information technology is not confined to cellular phones, modems, and the Internet. It has digitized all the information that businesses use, not just pictures, words, and data.

As the environment of managerial accounting undergoes tremendous change, managerial accounting must change to continue to be useful and relevant. The fundamental structure, concepts, and procedures of managerial accounting are still useful and relevant and will continue to be the backbone of managerial accounting. Changes in the competitive environment, however, dictate some changes in the way managerial accounting information functions. In this section, we will look at those functional changes in managerial accounting.

The day dot-coms enjoyed the blind confidence of venture capitalists is gone. The Internet has not turned out to be the "disruptive technology" that would give unlimited advantages to new entrants to industries once dominated by major existing players. The Internet, however, has changed business forever. So many corporations have been and currently are Webifying their business models to enjoy the enormous benefits of the Net. The virtual companies are seeking sound business models that would produce profits and the physical companies are seeking to attain the benefits of the virtual companies. Management accounting has changed forever as the Net has changed business, from cost movements to the view of efficiency to performance and profit expectations. Our discussions in chapters 4, 6, 9, and 12 will provide a new perspective management accountants need in their efforts to be effective in the brave new world.

Globalization and Market Forces

The globalization of commerce has transformed the perspectives of almost every competitor in today's market. At the turn of the century, for instance, Microsoft's structure was changed. Its four divisions are no longer organized around the products it makes but the markets it serves as follows:

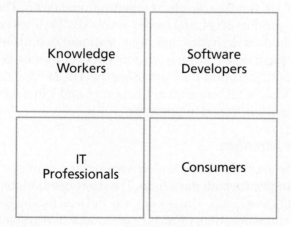

Customer focus is the theme of the competitive environment. Executives must listen carefully to customers to survive as a competitor. Bill Gates, Chairman of Microsoft, has stated that Microsoft's new president Steve Ballmer is on "a customer-satisfaction jihad." The management accounting aspects of the changes in the business perspectives and the introduction of market forces on the global scale are discussed in Chapter 10.

Multiple Measures of Performance–The Balanced Scorecard

As organizations reorganize to deal with increasing pressures from global competition, they have eliminated the traditional hierarchy based on functional areas such as development, manufacturing, marketing, accounting, and finance. Instead, individuals in organizations usually work in cross-functional teams. For example, at Ford Motor Company's Premier Automotive Group, now based in California, the new product development teams have designers, engineers, and cost accountants working together on new models of Jaguar and Volvo. Accordingly, competitive organizations are increasingly reliant on a mix of quantitative and qualitative measures. The **balanced scorecard** is a measurement system that translates an organization's strategy into transparent objectives, measures, targets, and initiatives. We will discuss the balanced scorecard in Chapter 10.

A New View of Cost-Activity Relationships

In order to plan and control managerial accounting activities, managers need reliable cost figures. The costs are measured, estimated, and must reflect the relationships between costs and activities. In the process of identifying cost-activity relationships, companies can either rely on a very simple concept of cost behavior or a more realistic, dynamic concept of cost behavior. The simple concept of cost behavior is based on the notion that, within a relevant range, variable costs increase (decrease) as production volume increases (decreases). The more realistic, dynamic concept, called **activity-based cost management (ABCM),** regards the conventional understanding of the dichotomous structure of variable and fixed costs as too unrealistic. Under ABCM, organizational costs are understood in a more comprehensive, hierarchical structure. According to ABCM's cost hierarchy, there are four, not two, levels of organizational costs. The four are: unit-level, batch-level, product-level, and facility-level. ABCM views costs through the prism of organizational activities, not organizational departments. ABCM has become a very popular cost management concept over the last decade. Currently about a third of all U.S. corporations are using the ABCM concept in one form or another. We will look at this concept in Chapters 6 and 7 in a coherent managerial accounting framework used in this book.

Lean Production Paradigm

In the last decade, manufacturing and service organizations in the world have embraced the **lean production paradigm.** The way organizations do business has changed drastically as a result. The reason why the lean production paradigm has become so powerful is that Henry Ford's mass-production system, which was the guiding concept of the auto industries of North America and Europe up until the mid-1980s, was not as efficient or effective as the lean production paradigm developed and practiced by the Japanese auto makers. American and European auto makers could not compete, in product cost and quality, with their Japanese counterparts, who subsequently gained a considerable share of the global market. Ultimately, American and European auto makers have transformed their manufacturing and related operating systems into more competitive ones based on the new paradigm. The lean production paradigm soon became the standards of operations and guiding philosophy in all sorts of manufacturing industries. The paradigm has subsequently found its way into all areas of business, both manufacturing and service alike. We look at how accounting for managerial decisions is influenced as organizations go lean in Chapter 10.

Strategic Cost Management and Value Chain Analysis

In order to be effective, managerial accounting information should involve more than just the manufacturing function of the organization. It should involve product design and development, marketing, and customer service as well. **Strategic cost management** relies on managerial accounting information to develop and choose organizational strategies that will ensure a long-term competitive advantage for the organization.

A long-term competitive advantage comes from an organization's ability to create better customer value for the same cost charged by competitors. Customer value is the excess of what a customer receives over what the customer pays in various forms. In order to focus on the customer's view of value, an organization identifies the **value chain,** the linked set of value-creating activities ranging from material procurement to product and service delivery to customers. Value chain analysis uses an external focus, while managerial accounting usually uses an internal focus. We will discuss value chain analysis in Chapter 10.

ETHICS IN MANAGEMENT ACCOUNTING

Ethics is related to judgment and behavior. In management accounting, as in many other fields, ethics matter when managers of all levels are tempted to cut corners, or take an easy way out of a difficult situation. Business periodicals report numerous stories on unethical behavior that has led to undesirable outcomes for organizations and people. We realize that ethics cannot be taught in a single course, even when the course is devoted entirely to ethics. The purpose of this section is to look at the long run implications of unethical behavior in the business environment. We hope that, when future managers are sensitized to those long-term implications, making ethical decisions would become easier at all levels of organizations.

Ethics and Managers

Consider the case of a divisional manager of a computer manufacturer whose performance is evaluated based on manufacturing cost reductions. The manager has an opportunity to reduce computer manufacturing costs substantially because a foreign parts manufacturer can supply a key component at a price which is 40 percent lower than the regular, domestically produced part. The cheaper, imported part can function almost as well as the regular part, except that it has

The Enron debacle has resulted in the destruction of America's seventh-largest corporation. Top executives' unethical behavior mixed with their arrogance, deceit, and greed turned Enron's $60 billion stock market valuation into a fraction. Enron's control systems virtually collapsed when the executives used off-balance-sheet transactions to hide Enron's true financial structure.

1400 Smith Street

a history of malfunction after three years. The manager has an excellent chance of getting promoted very soon to the position of general manager if this kind of significant cost reduction is realized. Once he gets promoted to general manager, a head hunter has almost guaranteed recently, that he would be offered a president's job in another comparable-size company. The manager would be gone in less than a year.

Long-Term Consequence   What would you do if you were the divisional manager? You have a very tempting incentive to procure the cheaper import. Reduce cost; show the record; get promoted to general manager; and leave the company. Nice and easy way out, isn't it? But is it right? Would it be ethical? Usually, unethical behavior seems to lead to a more profitable consequence in the short run. In the long run, however, the implications are more complicated. How long do you think you can hide from the malfunctioning computers that you helped produce? Quite often, there is no clear-cut answer to a question involving a business reality. Considering long-term consequences, however, helps managers decide which course of action to choose.

Codes of Ethical Conduct   Various organizations have developed their own codes of ethical conduct to guide the organization's stakeholders, especially, employees. These codes usually state the organization's responsibilities in a broad context, and describe what stakeholders are expected to do. These codes, of course, do not have specific enforcement clauses and are largely symbolic and educational.

Ethics and Management Accountants

As a group of professionals, management accountants have a code of ethical conduct, called **Standards of Ethical Conduct for Management Accountants.** The code outlines the following four areas of the highest standards of ethical conduct management accountants are expected to follow:

Competence   Under the standards, management accountants have a responsibility to maintain an appropriate level of professional competence, follow proper rules, and prepare complete and clear reports and recommendations.

Confidentiality   Management accountants have a responsibility to refrain from improperly disclosing their work-related confidential information, inform subordinates regarding the confidentiality, and refrain from using the confidential information for unethical gain.

Integrity   Management accountants have a responsibility to avoid conflicts of interest, refuse any gift or favor that would influence their actions in fact or in appearance, recognize and communicate professional limitations, and refrain from engaging in any discreditable act.

Objectivity   Management accountants have a responsibility to communicate information fairly and objectively and make a full disclosure of all relevant information for an intended user's proper understanding.

These standards just outlined lack enforcement power, however, so management accountants are advised to consider the following course of action in order to resolve any further ethical conflict: (a) Discuss the difficulty of conflict resolution with the immediate superior. (b) Report to the next higher managerial level, if the immediate superior is involved. (c) Resign and submit an informative memorandum to the representative of the organization after exhausting all levels of internal review.

SUMMARY

Managerial accounting is concerned with providing information that is useful to management in minimizing costs and expenses, planning and controlling routine operations, evaluating performance, and making nonroutine and special decisions. Managerial accounting helps management in performing its basic functions of setting strategies, planning, organizing, controlling, evaluating performance, investigating, and decision making.

Line positions in an organization are those positions engaged directly in achieving the basic objective of the organization. Staff positions are those positions which provide services to line positions and do not engage directly in achieving the basic objective of the organization. Line authority is authority that is exerted downward from supervisors to subordinates, whereas staff authority is advisory in nature and thus is exerted laterally, upward, or downward.

Managerial accounting differs from financial accounting in that it is not constrained by GAAP. It provides detailed information to all managerial levels to help them evaluate the performance of all segments of the organization on a more frequent basis. Managerial accounting also emphasizes relevance over reliability. It reports both monetary and nonmonetary data and thus draws more heavily on other disciplines, such as economics and the behavioral and decision sciences. Management accounting is also not mandatory and is constrained only by cost-benefit analysis.

The nature of business is different between manufacturing and service. All businesses have service components. It is a matter of the extent of the service component of a business, rather than the kind, that determines whether a business is in manufacturing or service. In service businesses, inventory does not exist. Service is mostly intangible and generating and rendering service in personal service businesses occur at the same time. Service operations are labor-intensive, and the nature of service capacity is unique. Service organizations cannot standardize their services so easily. As service industries are deregulated and the rules and mode of competition change to a more global nature, service companies are in need of more relevant managerial accounting information.

As the environment of managerial accounting undergoes tremendous changes, managerial accounting must change to continue to be useful and relevant. The globalization of commerce has transformed business perspectives and market forces have been introduced around the world. The revolution in information technology has digitized all information businesses use, not just pictures, words, and data. The virtual companies are seeking sound business models that would produce profits and the physical companies are seeking to attain the benefits of the virtual companies. Management accounting changes as the Net has changed business, from cost movements to the view of efficiency to performance and profit expectations.

As organizations reorganize to deal with increasing pressures from global competition, they have eliminated the traditional hierarchy based on functional areas and introduced cross-functional teams. Accordingly, competitive organizations are increasingly reliant on a mix of quantitative and qualitative measures. The balanced scorecard is a measurement system that translates an organization's strategy into transparent objectives, measures, targets, and initiatives.

In the process of identifying cost-activity relationships, companies can either rely on a very simple concept of cost behavior or a more realistic, dynamic concept of cost behavior. Under the more realistic, dynamic concept, called activity-based cost management (ABCM), organizational costs are understood in a more comprehensive, hierarchical structure. ABCM views costs through the prism of organizational activities, not organizational departments.

In the last decade, manufacturing and service organizations in the world have embraced the lean production paradigm. Lean organizations have replaced traditional organizations. The lean production paradigm has become the standard of operations and guiding philosophy in all sorts of manufacturing industries. The paradigm has subsequently found its way into all areas of business, both manufacturing and service alike. Value chain analysis is another very important concept in dealing with the challenges in the new environment.

Ethics is related to judgment and behavior. In management accounting, as in many other fields, ethics matters when managers of all levels are tempted to cut corners or take an easy way out of a difficult situation. We look at the implications of unethical behavior in the business environment in the long run. We hope that when future managers are sensitized to those long-term implications, making decisions leading to ethical behavior will become easier.

BASIC CONCEPTS AND TERMS FOR SELF REVIEW

Activity-based cost management	Information Technology (IT)
Balanced scorecard	Internal audit
Budgets	Internet
Controller	Lean production paradigm
Controlling	Line position or function
Cost-benefit concept	Line authority
Customer value	Management accounting
dot-coms	Organization Structure
e-business	Planning
Ethics	Performance evaluation
Financial accounting	Staff authority
GAAP	Staff position or function
Globalization	Value chain analysis

Required:

You are asked to have access to *Fortune* (December 24, 2001, pp.58-68) and read the in-depth story, "Why Enron Went Bust," by Bethany McLean. After you have read the story, answer the following questions:

1. Do you find Skilling's response ethical? Why or why not?

2. People around Enron were reported to be asking the question, "Is someone going to wind up in jail?" What difference is there between "winding up in jail" and being unethical from the management accounting perspective?

COST CONCEPTS AND BEHAVIOR PATTERNS

After studying this chapter, you should be able to:

1. Classify costs into different types from the following perspectives:
   a. Elements of costs
   b. Functions or activities of an organization
   c. Ease of traceability to a final product or a segment of the organization
   d. Relationship to a product or period
   e. Appearance in financial statements
   f. Behavior of cost in relation to changes in volume or level of activity
   g. Controllability by a certain managerial level
   h. Time of spending or method of determination or estimation

2. Give examples of each type of costs as classified in (1) above.

3. Define and give examples of differential (or incremental) costs and of opportunity cost.

4. Explain how cost of goods sold is computed in a merchandising firm and in a manufacturing firm and differentiate between the balance sheets of these two types of firms.

5. Prepare a schedule of cost of goods manufactured.

6. Distinguish between variable costs, fixed costs, and mixed costs.

7. Differentiate among, and give examples of, true (or proportionately) variable costs, step-variable costs, and semi-variable costs.

8. Distinguish between, and give examples of, committed fixed costs and discretionary fixed costs.

9. Explain the relevant range and its significance to the definition of variable costs and fixed costs.

A **cost** may be defined as resources given up to generate some services or to obtain goods. Such resources are frequently measured in cash, but may be measured in other assets transferred or services provided. The recorded costs may be classified in many different ways depending on management needs or on the perspective from which we look at costs.

In this chapter, we look at some of those different cost concepts, including cost terms and types, and cost behavior patterns. We will discuss various ways in which managers classify costs for their use in planning and controlling activities.

VARIOUS COST CLASSIFICATIONS

Table 2-1 summarizes various cost classifications according to different perspectives. In examining Table 2-1, note that these various cost classifications are not mutually exclusive. That is, one cost item can be classified according to more than one perspective.

For example, the plastics used by Motorola in manufacturing a cellular phone is

Motorola's cellular phone

Cost Classification	Perspective
a material cost	1
a manufacturing cost	2
a direct cost	3
a product cost	4
an income statement (balance sheet) cost if the cell phone is sold (still on hand)	5
a variable cost	6
a controllable cost to a first-line supervisor	7
a historical cost (since it is already used in production)	8

You may ask why is one cost element classified in accordance with so many different perspectives? The reason is that management may need to make various internal decisions in relation to that cost from various perspectives. In most cases,

TABLE 2-1 Various Cost Classifications From Different Perspectives

Perspective	Cost Classifications
1. Elements of cost	Material, Labor, Other expenses
2. Functions or activities of an organization	Manufacturing (or Production) costs, Non-manufacturing (selling or administrative) costs
3. Traceability to a product or a segment of the organization	Direct costs, Indirect costs
4. Relationship to a product or period	Product costs, Period costs
5. Appearance on financial statements	Income statement costs, Balance sheet costs
6. Behavior in relation to changes in volume or level of activity	Variable costs, Fixed costs, Mixed costs
7. Controllability by a certain managerial level	Controllable costs, Noncontrollable costs
8. Time of spending or method determination or estimation	Historical (actual or sunk) costs, Future (budgeted or standard) costs
9. Other cost concepts or terms	Differential (or incremental) costs, Opportunity costs, Imputed costs, Common costs

the major reason for classification is to be able to manage the cost so that it is kept at the most efficient minimum.

The remainder of this chapter provides some further explanations and examples of each cost classification presented in Table 2-1.

COST CLASSIFICATIONS

Elements and Activities

To manufacture or create any product or service, one needs three elements of costs: material, labor, and other expenses. If these cost elements are associated with the manufacturing of a product they are considered **manufacturing costs;** otherwise they are considered **non-manufacturing costs.**

Usually, manufacturing costs are also considered **product costs** because they are associated with or attached to the product. Non-manufacturing costs are considered **period costs** because they are not attached to the creation of the product and are matched against the sales revenue generated during the period in which these period costs are incurred.

Direct and Indirect Costs

If the three cost elements (material, labor, and other expenses) can be easily traced to the final product, they are considered **direct costs.** If they can be traced to the final product only at a great cost and inconvenience, they are considered **indirect costs.**

For example, the plastics used by Motorola in making a cellular phone can be physically and easily traced to the final product (the phone), since it is an integral part of the phone. Thus, the plastics are considered a **direct material.** While the paint and glue that are used in assembling a phone can also be traced physically to the phone, this can only be done at a great cost and inconvenience and thus we classify them as **indirect materials.**

Another reason for this classification is that the cost of the paint and glue assigned to the phone is so insignificant in relation to the total manufacturing cost that the benefit of its separate identification does not outweigh the cost and effort expended in that identification. In managerial accounting, this is called the **cost-benefit** concept.

Also, the labor costs that can be easily traced to the manufacturing of the phone, such as the wages paid to fabrication workers and phone assemblers, are classified as **direct labor costs.** The salaries and wages of supervisors, janitors, and security guards in the factory are considered **indirect labor costs,** again because they either cannot be traced to the final product or can be traced, but only at a great cost, inconvenience, and effort. All other manufacturing expenses, such as factory rent, insurance, depreciation, property taxes, and utilities, cannot be conveniently traced to the final product and are thus considered indirect.

Manufacturing Costs

Now, if we add direct material and direct labor, we obtain what is called **prime cost.** The total of all the indirect elements, including indirect material, indirect labor, and other manufacturing expenses, is referred to as **manufacturing overhead.** If we add prime cost and manufacturing overhead, we obtain total manufacturing costs.

If we add direct labor and manufacturing overhead, we obtain what is called **conversion cost,** i.e., the cost of converting direct material into finished goods. These cost terms are illustrated in Exhibit 2-1, assuming direct material cost of $10,000, direct labor cost of $15,000, indirect material cost of $5,000, indirect labor cost of $3,000, and other indirect costs of $4,000.

EXHIBIT 2-1 Manufacturing Cost Terms

Direct Materials	Direct Labor	Indirect Materials	Indirect Labor	Others	Total Manufacturing Costs
$10,000 +	$15,000 +	$5,000 +	$3,000 +	$4,000 =	$37,000

Prime Cost		Manufacturing Overhead		
$25,000	+	$12,000	=	$37,000

Direct Materials	Conversion Cost		
$10,000 +	$27,000	=	$37,000

Nonmanufacturing Costs

Nonmanufacturing costs are those material, labor, and overhead expenses associated with other functions or activities besides manufacturing, such as selling and administrative activities. All organizations, whether they are manufacturing, merchandising, or service organizations, have both selling and administrative costs. Exhibit 2-2 illustrates some examples of manufacturing, selling, and administrative costs classified by cost element (material, labor, and other expenses).

EXHIBIT 2-2 Examples of Manufacturing, Selling and Administrative Cost Classified by Cost Elements

Cost Element	Manufacturing Costs	Selling Costs	Administrative Costs
Material	Direct material (plastic, steel) Indirect material	Shipping, advertising material (carton boxes, billboards)	Office supplies
Labor	Direct factory payroll (wages of assembly-line workers, machine operators) Indirect factory payroll (factory supervisors' salaries)	Salespersons' salaries Sales commissions	Administrative salaries Executive compensation
Other Expenses	Rent, insurance and utilities of factory Factory building depreciation, property taxes, repairs and maintenance	Rent, insurance and utilities of sales offices Sales travel costs Warehouse and sales offices depreciation, property taxes, and maintenance	Rent, insurance and utilities of administrative offices Executive travel costs Administrative offices depreciation, property taxes, and maintenance

The major purpose of classifying costs by functions is to allow management to have proper and adequate control over the costs of these different functions. In many cases, some expenses (such as rent, insurance, and property taxes) may have to be allocated among the manufacturing, selling, and administrative functions using some allocation criteria.

Product Costs and Period Costs

If the costs are incurred in the creation of the products, they are called **product costs.** All manufacturing costs (direct materials, direct labor, and manufacturing overhead) are product costs. When the units of the product are sold, the product costs of the units sold become expenses (cost of goods sold) and are matched, in the income statement, against the revenue generated from the sale of the units. Before the sale, product costs are carried on the balance sheet as inventory.

Period costs are those that are incurred during the period, but are not directly related to the creation of the products. All nonmanufacturing (selling and administrative) costs are period costs and are shown on the income statement for the period in which they are incurred.

Manufacturing costs are product costs, and nonmanufacturing costs are period costs. Product costs do become period costs if and when the units of products to which they are attached are sold. This point is perhaps the most important reason why we differentiate between product and period costs.

Motorola provides summer learning programs for children. The costs of these programs are period costs which are not directly related to the creation of products.

CLASSIFICATION OF COSTS ON THE FINANCIAL STATEMENTS

In the above discussion of product and period costs we explained that product costs would appear on the balance sheet as inventory until they are sold, at which time they appear on the income statement as a part of cost of goods sold. Period costs are shown directly on the income statement as expenses for the period. In this section, we will show what types of product costs are shown on the balance sheet, how each type is determined, and how the cost of goods manufactured is transferred to the income statement when these goods are sold.

Types of Product Costs on the Balance Sheet

The balance sheet of a merchandising firm, one that has no manufacturing activities, contains only one type of product cost called merchandise inventory. The cost of this merchandise inventory represents the purchase cost plus any transportation costs incurred to bring these goods to the point where they are ready for sale.

The balance sheet of a manufacturing firm, on the other hand, contains three types of product costs, (a) Raw Materials (RM) inventory: the cost of raw materials purchased for use directly in production (direct material) and for use in other activities (indirect material); (b) Work-in Process (WIP) inventory: the cost of goods partially completed by the end of the period (including cost of materials, labor, and manufacturing overhead spent so far), and (c) Finished Goods (FG) inventory: the cost of finished goods manufactured but not yet sold by the end of the period.

Determination of Cost of Goods Sold on the Income Statement

In a merchandising firm, cost of goods sold equals beginning inventory plus purchases minus ending inventory as in the equation below:

$$COGS = BI + Purchases - EI$$

For such a firm, beginning and ending inventory as well as purchases represent finished goods. In a manufacturing firm, cost of goods sold is computed in the same way except instead of adding purchases, we add **cost of goods manufactured** as shown in the equation below:

$$COGS = BI + Cost\ of\ Goods\ Manufactured - EI$$

The cost of goods manufactured simply equals the cost of raw material used plus direct labor cost plus manufacturing overhead incurred. If there is any work in process at the beginning and/or at the end of the period, we simply add beginning WIP and subtract ending WIP to and from the total of the above three elements of production. These adjustments for beginning and ending WIP are required because the beginning WIP is completed during the period and is part of cost of goods manufactured, but the ending WIP is not completed during the period and is not part of cost of goods manufactured. The equation for cost of goods manufactured is thus as shown below:

$$COGM = RM\ used + DL\ cost + Mfg\ OH + Beg.\ WIP - End.\ WIP$$

The cost of raw materials used in production equals beginning raw materials plus raw materials purchased minus ending raw materials as shown in the equation below:

$$RM\ used = Beg.\ RM + RM\ Purchased - End.\ RM$$

Another way to compute the cost of raw materials used, cost of goods manufactured, and cost of goods sold, in addition to the equations above, is to analyze T-accounts as illustrated below:

Raw Materials			Work in Process			Finished Goods		
BB	X		BB	X		BB	X	
Purchased	X	X Used	RM Used	X	X COGM	COGM	X	X COGS
			DL Cost	X				
			Mfg OH	X				
EB	X		EB	X		EB	X	

BB	Beginning balance	Mfg OH	Manufacturing overhead
EB	Ending balance	COGM	Cost of goods manufactured
RM	Raw materials	COGS	Cost of goods sold
DL	Direct labor		

ILLUSTRATION 2-1

Assume the following information is available from the records of Lone Star Toy Company for Year 6: (All raw materials in this example are direct materials.)

Direct materials inventory, January 1	$10,000
Direct materials inventory, December 31	12,000
Work in process inventory, January 1	8,000
Work in process inventory, December 31	6,000
Finished goods inventory, January 1	20,000
Finished goods inventory, December 31	18,000
Direct material purchases during Year 6	30,000
Rent, factory building	5,000
Rent, office building*	10,000
Insurance, factory building and equipment	3,000
Insurance, office building and equipment*	2,000
Factory property taxes	1,000
Indirect labor cost	5,000
Direct labor cost	15,000
Depreciation, factory building and equipment	4,000
Depreciation, office building and equipment*	3,000
Repairs and maintenance, factory equipment	2,000
Repairs and maintenance, office equipment*	1,000
Salespersons salaries	10,000
Administrative salaries	12,000
Sales for Year 6	115,000

*Office expenses are allocated equally between selling and administrative expenses.

In this toy manufacturing company, the direct materials are primarily plastic components of various shapes and sizes. The cost of the direct materials used for production is a product cost, and whatever is left over is direct materials inventory. The cost of the plastic toys that are completed and moved to the finished goods warehouse represent the cost of goods manufactured. The cost of the pieces left on the factory floor unfinished (at the end of the period) represents the work-in-process inventory. The cost of toys shipped to retailers represents the cost of goods sold; whereas, the cost of those toys remaining in the finished goods warehouse represents the finished goods inventory.

Exhibit 2-3 illustrates the schedule of cost of goods manufactured, Exhibit 2-4 illustrates the income statement for Year 6, and Exhibit 2-5 presents comparative balance sheet inventory accounts at January 1 and December 31, Year 6. **NOTE:** All manufacturing overhead costs are included in the cost of goods manufactured, cost of goods sold, and ending work in process and finished goods inventory.

EXHIBIT 2-3

Lone Star Toy Company
Schedule of Cost of Goods Manufactured
For the Year Ended December 31, Year 6

Direct materials:		
Direct materials, January 1	$10,000	
Direct material purchases during year	30,000	
Available for use	40,000	
Direct materials, December 31	(12,000)	
Direct materials used in production		$28,000
Direct labor cost		15,000
Manufacturing overhead:		
Indirect labor cost	5,000	
Rent, factory building	5,000	
Insurance, factory building & equipment	3,000	
Depreciation, factory building & equipment	4,000	
Repairs & maintenance, factory equipment	2,000	
Factory property taxes	1,000	
Total manufacturing overhead costs		20,000
Total manufacturing costs		63,000
Work in process, January 1		8,000
		71,000
Work in process, December 31		(6,000)
Cost of goods manufactured		$65,000

EXHIBIT 2-4

Lone Star Toy Company
Income Statement
For the Year Ended December 31, Year 6

Sales			$115,000
Cost of goods sold:			
Finished goods inventory, January 1		$20,000	
Cost of goods manufactured (Exhibit 2-3)		65,000	
Finished goods available for sale		85,000	
Finished goods inventory, December 31		(18,000)	
Cost of goods sold			67,000
Gross profit			48,000
Selling expenses:			
Salespersons' salaries	$10,000		
Rent*	5,000		
Insurance*	1,000		
Depreciation*	1,500		
Repairs and maintenance*	500		
Total selling expenses		18,000	
Administrative expenses:			
Administrative salaries	$12,000		
Rent*	5,000		
Insurance*	1,000		
Depreciation*	1,500		
Repairs and maintenance*	500		
Total administrative expenses		20,000	
Total selling and administrative expenses			38,000
Income before tax			10,000
Income tax expense at 30%			3,000
Net income			$7,000

*Office expenses are allocated equally between selling and administrative activities.

EXHIBIT 2-5

Lone Star Toy Company
Partial Comparative Balance Sheets

| | Year 6 | |
	December 31	January 1
Assets		
Current Assets		
Inventory:		
Direct materials	$12,000	$10,000
Work in process	6,000	8,000
Finished goods	18,000	20,000
Total inventory	$36,000	$38,000

Cost Flows and Classifications

Product costs are shown on the balance sheet as inventory until the units to which they relate are sold. For that reason, they are called **inventoriable costs.** When units are sold, their costs are released ★ from the product and become expenses to be matched against the revenues generated by the sale. Period (nonmanufacturing) costs are charged against the revenue for the period. Exhibit 2-6 illustrates these cost flows and classifications using Illustration 2-1 information.

COST BEHAVIOR PATTERNS

Cost Driver

For each activity of an organization, there is a factor which will be the best indicator of the cost increase or decrease. This factor is called **cost driver.** The costs of purchasing materials and parts (activity) may depend on how many times the company handles purchases (cost driver). The costs of operating machines (activity) may depend on how many hours the machine is used (cost driver). The costs of inspecting finished products (activity) may depend on how many units of finished products are produced (cost driver).

Cost drivers are used for many important purposes in management accounting. For calculating costs of activities, cost drivers are used. Those activity costs become the bases of calculating product costs, determining product prices, and managing costs for many other purposes. For these reasons, it is important to understand the relationships between cost drivers, activities, and products.

Variable Costs and Fixed Costs

Different cost elements behave differently in relation to changes in the organization's volume of output or level of activity, however measured. Certain cost elements increase or decrease by exactly the same percent as the increase or decrease in volume or activity level. For example, if output or activity level increases by 10%,

EXHIBIT 2-6

Illustration of Cost Flows & Classification Using Information in Illustration 2-1 and Exhibits 2-3 to 2-5

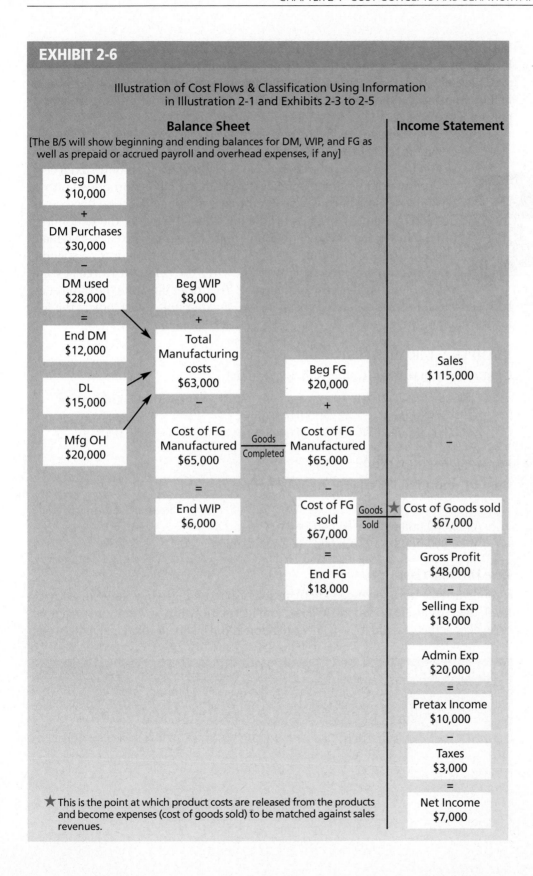

Balance Sheet

[The B/S will show beginning and ending balances for DM, WIP, and FG as well as prepaid or accrued payroll and overhead expenses, if any]

Beg DM
$10,000

+

DM Purchases
$30,000

–

DM used
$28,000

=

End DM
$12,000

DL
$15,000

Mfg OH
$20,000

Beg WIP
$8,000

+

Total Manufacturing costs
$63,000

–

Cost of FG Manufactured
$65,000

=

End WIP
$6,000

Goods Completed

Beg FG
$20,000

+

Cost of FG Manufactured
$65,000

–

Cost of FG sold
$67,000

=

End FG
$18,000

Goods Sold

Income Statement

Sales
$115,000

–

Cost of Goods sold
$67,000

=

Gross Profit
$48,000

–

Selling Exp
$18,000

–

Admin Exp
$20,000

=

Pretax Income
$10,000

–

Taxes
$3,000

=

Net Income
$7,000

★ This is the point at which product costs are released from the products and become expenses (cost of goods sold) to be matched against sales revenues.

the total of these cost elements will increase by exactly 10%. If volume or activity level decreases by 5%, the total of these cost elements will decrease by exactly 5%. Therefore, these costs are called **variable costs.** While total variable costs vary in the same percentage of variation in volume or level of activity, the variable cost per unit is constant.

Fixed costs behave exactly the opposite of variable costs. Their total remains constant regardless of the changes in volume or level of activity. As a result, if the company produced a lot of units during a month, fixed cost per unit would be much smaller than if the company produced only a few units. This is because the fixed cost per unit equals total fixed costs divided by number of units produced. Thus, the higher the denominator, the lower the fixed cost per unit and vice versa. Fixed costs remain constant in total only during a specified period of time or for a specific range of output or level of activity known as the **relevant range** beyond which they may increase or decrease. To further illustrate the difference between variable costs and fixed costs, in total and per unit, let us look at the following examples:

Shown here is MetLife's tribute to Mr. Charles M. Schulz who passed away in 2000. Snoopy and the gang still enliven the image of MetLife. The payments made by the insurance company for the use of the cartoon characters are fixed costs. How many life insurance policies MetLife writes (activity level) for a period are not related to the amount of the fixed costs.

EXAMPLE A: VARIABLE COST

Cost of raw material (Unit cost is $2 per unit)

			Total variable costs
At 10,000 units:	$2 × 10,000 units	=	$20,000
At 20,000 units:	$2 × 20,000 units	=	$40,000

EXAMPLE B: FIXED COST

Cost of rent (Total fixed cost is $5,000 per period)

			Fixed cost per unit
At 10,000 units:	$5,000 ÷ 10,000 units	=	$ .50
At 20,000 units:	$5,000 ÷ 20,000 units	=	$ .25

True Variable Cost

If total variable costs change exactly in relation to changes in volume or activity level, the cost is a **true variable cost,** and its relationship to variation in volume or level of activity is said to be a linear relationship. The linear relationship between

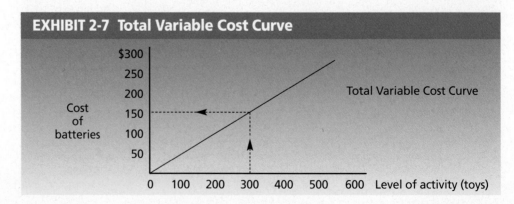

EXHIBIT 2-7 Total Variable Cost Curve

total variable cost and volume or level of activity is illustrated by a straight line as shown in Exhibit 2-7.

The reason the total variable cost curve in Exhibit 2-7 is a straight line is that the variable cost per unit of output or level of activity is *constant.* Assume that a toy factory uses one size C, 9-volt battery for each toy and each unit of the battery costs the factory $.50. Now we can see that the higher the number of battery-operated toys produced, the higher the total cost of batteries used and vice versa. As Exhibit 2-7 illustrates, if no toys were produced, the total cost of batteries would be zero. Exhibit 2-7 also indicates that if 300 toys were produced, total cost of batteries would be $150 (300 batteries at $.50 each). Similar lines can be drawn to show the cost of batteries for any number of toys produced.

Volume or Activity Base

In Exhibit 2-7, we assumed that the volume of production is the base that determines the total variable cost of batteries used. However, this base is not limited to volume of units. Organizations can use any base to measure the **level of activity** on which total variable costs may be determined. A trucking company may use the number of miles driven as the activity base; a merchandising company may use the number of units sold; an advertising firm may use the number of hours spent on a client's account; a hospital may use the number of beds occupied; an airline may use the number of passengers flown certain miles; a university may use the number of students enrolled; and so on.

These activity bases are not the only possible bases for measuring the activity level of the types of organizations indicated. Any of the above organizations may use other bases instead of, or in addition to, these bases to measure their activity level. A single organization may find it necessary to use several different measures of activity, depending upon what "drives the cost."

Because there is more than one base for measuring activity level, a cost may vary with one base but not with another. If the total cost varies with the variation in the activity level selected by management, the cost is a variable cost. Thus, before making a decision that will affect the future cost structure (total variable, fixed, and mixed costs) of the company, a prudent manager must analyze carefully the relationships of these types of costs to the activity base or bases selected.

Variable Costs and the Relevant Range

While the assumption of constant unit variable cost may be valid within a certain normal range of activity, it may not be valid at abnormally high or low ranges of activity. Assume that the toy factory referred to earlier has a normal range of between 200 and 400 toys per month. Within that level of activity, the factory can obtain the batteries at $.50 per battery. That level of activity (200-400 toys) is referred to as the **relevant range.**

This range is called the relevant range because within that range the assumption that the cost per battery will be constant at $.50 is a valid assumption. If, however, production in one month is increased to 700 or 800 toys, it is possible that the factory can obtain the batteries at lower than $.50 per battery due to quantity discounts, lower shipment cost per unit, and/or other similar savings that economists refer to as "economies of scale." On the other hand, if production of battery-operated toys is reduced to only a few toys, say 5 or 10, it is possible that the factory pays $1 or $1.50 per battery.

Thus, we can say that abnormally high or low levels of activity are outside the relevant range, and therefore, the cost per unit may not be constant. In making a decision that will significantly increase or decrease future costs, a prudent manager should hence carefully consider whether the company will still be operating within the relevant range. Since organizations are expected to grow in the long run, the variable costs, and, for that matter, fixed costs to be discussed later, are short-run rather than long-run concepts.

Step-Variable Costs

Assume that a factory supervisor, who makes $50,000 a year, supervises five factory workers. If the demand for the factory's products increases, the factory may hire one additional worker. The supervisor's salary will remain at $50,000 a year even though he or she is now supervising six workers. If demand increases further, the factory may hire a seventh worker, again without increasing the supervisor's salary. Note that production and direct labor cost (a true variable cost) may have increased by 40% (wages of two additional workers, assuming the wage rate per hour is the same for all workers), whereas the indirect labor cost (the supervisor's salary) remained constant.

If demand increases even further and the factory hires an eighth worker, the supervisor will probably have had it by then and will either require that the factory hire an additional supervisor or ask for a significant salary increase. In either case, the indirect labor cost will no longer remain constant, but will increase by a big chunk, either $50,000 (if an additional supervisor is hired) or, say, $10,000 (if the existing supervisor's salary is increased by that amount).

Thus, while direct labor cost (which is a true variable cost) was increasing proportionately with demand and production increases, indirect labor cost (supervisors' salaries) would only increase in steps, with each step representing a significant increase. Such costs are called **step-variable costs,** since their total varies with production in steps.

Semi-Variable Costs

Semi-variable (or mixed) costs are those costs that include both fixed and variable portions. For example, a salesperson's compensation may be computed as $30,000 a year plus 10% of sales. Utility costs (telephone, electricity, gas, water, etc.) usually equal a minimum monthly charge plus an additional charge based on the number of units used.

While variable costs at two different levels of activity yield a constant unit cost, semi-variable costs yield a varying unit cost (because of the effect of the fixed cost component). This may be illustrated by the following examples:

Variable Costs (e.g., direct material)
Level 1 (10,000 units): $20,000 ÷ 10,000 units = $2/unit
Level 2 (20,000 units): $40,000 ÷ 20,000 units = $2/unit

Semi-Variable Costs (e.g., maintenance)
Level 1 (10,000 units): $15,000 ÷ 10,000 units = $1.50/unit
Level 2 (20,000 units): $22,000 ÷ 20,000 units = $1.10/unit

Of course, fixed costs also yield *varying* unit cost at two different volumes of activity.

Exhibit 2-8 compares true variable, step-variable, and semi-variable costs. All types of semi-variable costs start from point X, which is greater than zero. The fixed portion of this cost is equal to O-X. In part C1, the variable portion of the semi-variable cost is true variable. In part C2, the variable portion increases slowly first, and then rapidly as volume increases. In part C3, the variable portion increases rapidly first, and then slowly as volume increases.

EXHIBIT 2-8 True Variable, Step-Variable and Semi-Variable Costs

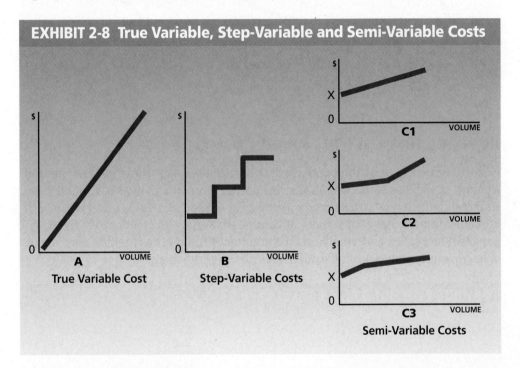

Other Types of Variable Costs

Other variable costs behave differently from the types indicated above. In one case, the variable cost per unit, instead of staying constant, decreases as activity level increases. This happens, for example, when materials are obtained at a lower cost per unit as quantity purchased increases and/or when labor cost per unit decreases as employees become more efficient with experience (this concept is referred to as the **learning curve**).

In another case, variable cost per unit may increase as activity level increases. This may happen when materials are obtained at a special discount under or from a government support program which puts a limit on the quantity purchased under the program; any excess quantities must be purchased at the regular higher price. This may also happen when workers become tired or perhaps bored at higher levels of activity and their productivity starts to decrease. These costs are referred to as **curvilinear variable costs** because the total cost curve is not a straight line, but rather a curving line as shown in Exhibit 2-9.

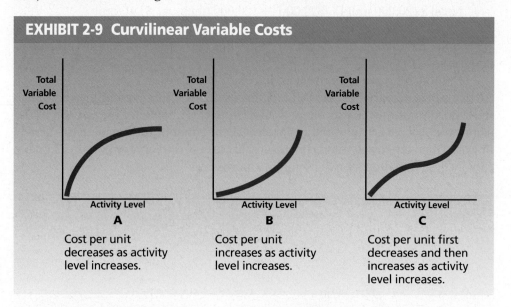

EXHIBIT 2-9 Curvilinear Variable Costs

A
Cost per unit decreases as activity level increases.

B
Cost per unit increases as activity level increases.

C
Cost per unit first decreases and then increases as activity level increases.

FURTHER DISCUSSIONS ON FIXED COSTS

Fixed costs are exactly the opposite of true variable costs; they remain constant, *in total*, regardless of the variation in volume or level of activity (see Exhibit 2-10). As a result, the fixed costs on a *per unit basis* varies in a reverse order of the variation in volume or level of activity; if volume or activity level increases, fixed cost per unit decreases and vice versa. Examples of fixed costs include rent, insurance, property taxes, administrative salaries, and the like.

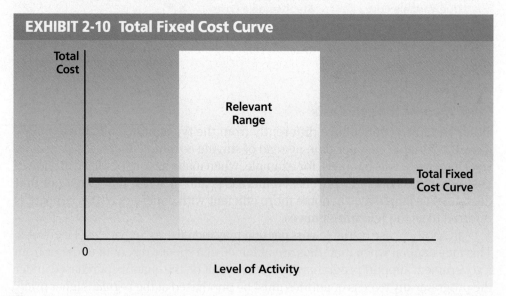

EXHIBIT 2-10 Total Fixed Cost Curve

Fixed costs may be classified into two types: capacity (or committed) and discretionary. These two types are explained below.

Committed Fixed Costs

Committed, or **capacity, fixed costs** are those costs that the organization must incur if it is to have the capacity to be in business. Some of these capacity costs may be eliminated if the operations are shut down temporarily though the company is still in business. For example, if a manufacturing company decided to close the factory for a month, the fixed cost of security guards may be eliminated during that month. This type of capacity costs must be incurred in full if operations resume at any level.

Other capacity costs, such as rent, property taxes, insurance, straight line depreciation, executive salaries and compensations and the like, cannot be eliminated even during a temporary shut down. Such capacity cost is referred to as committed fixed cost. They are considered committed because they are long-term in nature and cannot be eliminated, even for a short time, without seriously impairing the future prospects of the company. As a result, a prudent manager should carefully study these long-range costs before committing itself to such costs. Construction of a factory building that will last for many years, for example, is one of those important decisions that management has to evaluate carefully.

Discretionary Fixed Costs

Discretionary fixed costs are those costs over which management has some choice as to whether they should be incurred during a short period of time. Management's discretion in this case stems from the fact that these discretionary costs can be eliminated temporarily without seriously impairing the long-term goals of the organization. These costs are also referred to as *managed* or *programmed costs* in the sense that top management can program or plan when such costs may or may not be spent. Examples of discretionary costs include research and development, employee training programs, company name or image building advertising, and perhaps major repairs and overhauls of company's facilities. These discretionary costs become fixed once management makes a commitment to spend them during a particular year. Thus, these costs are fixed in the short run.

Fixed Costs and the Relevant Range

Fixed costs remain constant, in total, within the relevant range. For example, assume a company pays $5,000 factory rent per month, and the factory capacity is to produce 10,000 units per month in one 8-hour shift. This factory rent expense will remain fixed whether the company operates the factory for one additional shift to produce a total of 20,000 units or operates the factory for three shifts (24 hours a day) to produce a maximum of 30,000 units. Thus, we say that the relevant range for the fixed factory rent expense of $5,000 is 0-30,000 units.

If, however, the demand for the company's product increases above 30,000 units a month, this excess volume puts the company beyond the relevant range for the $5,000 fixed rent expense. The company will have to rent additional space, get additional equipment, and hire additional factory supervisors if it is to meet the demand of over 30,000 units. Thus, the fixed costs will not remain constant at the original level. Once the company expands the factory facilities, a new relevant range will be established within which the new level of fixed costs will remain constant.

The factory rent expense may increase, for example, after a year or two above the original $5,000 a month without expanding factory facilities if the lease term has expired and a new lease is negotiated at a higher level. In this case, we say that the original lease term was the relevant range. Thus, the relevant range with respect to fixed costs may be expressed in terms of the level of activity or the time period within which these fixed costs are expected to remain constant.

ADDITIONAL COST CLASSIFICATIONS

Controllable Costs

If a supervisor of a shop, a manager of a department, or a director of a division has complete authority as to whether certain costs should be incurred or not, such costs are said to be **controllable** by that person. Usually, the higher the level of management, the broader the range of costs that are controllable by that level and vice versa. For example, top management usually has control over most costs because it has the authority and power to expand or contract operations, open up new branches or close existing ones. Lower levels of management, however, may have limited control because they are usually given the power to authorize the spending of costs up to a certain limit, beyond which they have to get authority or approval from higher levels of management.

Uncontrollable Costs

Uncontrollable costs are those costs that cannot be authorized by a particular managerial level. For example, if depreciation is computed on a straight line basis and top management decides to replace the existing factory equipment with new equipment, the depreciation expense on factory equipment will increase, but the factory superintendent has no control over that increase.

Once the replacement decision has been made, however, even top management will not have control over depreciation expense in the short run. This is because the company is committed to the equipment until it is sold. Thus, the controllability concept has a time dimension. A cost that may be controllable in the long run may not be controllable in the short run.

Historical Costs

Historical (also known as **sunk**) **costs** are those costs that have already been spent. They are a product of a past decision, and no present action can change that decision. Other than their tax effects, such costs are not useful in making decisions since decisions made now concern the present or the future and not the past.

For example, assume that you bought a Model A personal computer for $1,000. A month later, the manufacturer came out with a new Model B that is twice

---

Sylvester Stallone and Sunk Costs

Some sunk costs are related to high-stakes risks. Savoy Pictures Entertainment, Inc. closed its movie operations and sold all remaining operations in late 1995. Among the company's problems was an agreement to pay actor Sylvester Stallone $20 mil-lion to agree to appear in a future film. Is the $20 million a sunk cost to the company that acquired Savoy's movie operations?

For more details please refer to "Lights! Camera! Check-books! Costs Menace Movie Makers," *The Wall Street Journal*, December 21, 1995, B1,3

---

as powerful as Model A but sells for only $1,200. The historical cost of $1,000 spent on Model A has nothing to do with whether you should buy Model B. This is true whether the price for Model A was $1,000, $5,000, or any other amount. That is why these costs are referred to as sunk costs.

Future Costs

Future costs are those costs that are expected or projected to be spent in the future for a specific purpose. They could be either **budgeted costs** or **standard costs.** Budgeted costs are those that are planned to be spent for a specific purpose where their estimate is a total dollar amount. For example, a company may plan to spend $100,000 on advertising next year. This $100,000 is considered budgeted advertising expense.

If the cost to be spent in the future for a specific purpose is based on a per unit estimate (usually determined based on a scientific research or precise chemical formula), it is considered standard cost. For example, if it is already estimated that each unit of final output requires 2 pounds of raw material at a cost of $1 per pound, then the standard raw material cost required for producing 1,000 units of output is $2,000. Both budgeted and standard costs are used for control purposes through comparing actual cost of production to budgeted or standard cost of production to determine whether actual cost exceeded budgeted or standard cost.

Differential Costs

Differential (or **incremental**) **costs** represent differences in the costs of alternative courses of action. Consider the following: You live in Chicago and you want to spend a two-week vacation in Los Angeles, but you are undecided as to whether you go by plane or by car. In order to make your decision, you must consider various factors. If you assume that the factors that are hard to quantify (including the length of travel time, the opportunity to see the Rocky Mountains and Las Vegas, etc.) offset each other, you may want to determine the out-of-pocket cash expenses for each alternative.

The cost of each alternative and differential costs are shown below:

	Traveling by Plane	Traveling by Car	Differential Costs
Airline ticket	$ 250	$ —	$ 250
Gasoline	—	200	(200)
Hotel in L.A.	700	300	400
Motels on the road	—	240	(240)
Car rental	350	—	350
Food in L.A.	490	210	280
Food on the road	—	320	(320)
Other expenses	150	250	(100)
Total	$1,940	$1,520	$ 420

Differential costs are sometimes referred to as **incremental costs** since they represent the increase in cost as a result of going from one alternative to another.

Opportunity Cost

Opportunity cost is the benefit sacrificed as a result of choosing one alternative compared to another. If you choose alternative B rather than A, the opportunity cost of B is the benefit that you gave up by not choosing A. Because a person may be able to choose one alternative from among many alternatives, some people prefer to define opportunity cost as the benefit foregone of the next-best alternative. Opportunity cost is an economic, rather than an accounting, concept, and it is not usually entered in financial accounting records. Once the decision has been made, the alternative is foregone, and hence the opportunity disappears.

Examples of opportunity costs include the following. A college student may choose to spend the summer vacation visiting Europe instead of working and earning $5,000. The opportunity cost of visiting Europe is the $5,000 of lost earnings that could have been gained if the student decided to work instead. In the business world, a company may decide to sell a building to realize a current capital gain of $200,000 instead of keeping it and renting it out for $50,000 a year for many years to come. The opportunity cost of selling the building is the positive cash flow (the annual rent income) for all the future years that the company would have to give up.

Every alternative course of action has an opportunity cost attached to it. In the above examples, if the other alternative were chosen, each would have had an opportunity cost. If the student worked in the summer instead of visiting Europe, the opportunity cost would be all the enjoyment given up by not going to Europe. And if the company decided to keep the building, the opportunity cost would have been the capital gain lost and the income that could have been generated in the future by investing the money from the sale of the building.

Imputed Costs

Imputed costs are those costs that are not obvious, stated, or paid directly for a specific purpose even though they do exist. A good example of imputed costs is the interest expense included in the maturity value of a non-interest bearing note. If a wholesaler offers to sell a product for $10,000 cash now or $11,000 for a note receivable one year from now, the dealer is imputing interest of $1,000 in the maturity value of the note even though the note does not bear interest. A car dealer who advertises zero percent financing when the prevailing interest rate is 10 percent is probably imputing the difference in the sales price of the car.

Common Costs

Common costs are those costs that cannot be directly traced to any one segment or any one product of the organization. Sometimes indirect costs are called common costs. Common fixed costs persist even if one of the segments to which they are common is eliminated. Examples of common costs include plant depreciation and the salary of the sales manager. Elimination of one product line will not eliminate these common costs.

SUMMARY

This chapter covered various cost concepts and terminology. A cost may be classified as either materials, labor, or other expenses if viewed from the perspective of nature or cost elements. If categorized according to functions or activities, costs may be identified as either a manufacturing (production) cost or a nonmanufacturing (selling or administrative) cost. When analyzed according to the ease of traceability to a final product or segment of an organization, costs may be classified as either direct or indirect. Finally, costs may be either product costs or period costs when viewed according to their relationship to a product or period.

With respect to their presentation in the financial statements, costs may appear on the income statement as expenses or on the balance sheet as assets. Usually manufacturing costs are product costs, and nonmanufacturing costs are period costs. Furthermore, product costs are known as inventoriable costs and appear on the balance sheet as inventory before the product is sold. When the product is sold, product costs become expenses and appear on the income statement as costs of goods sold. We have also discussed how to compute cost of goods sold for a merchandising firm and both cost of goods manufactured and cost of goods sold for a manufacturing firm.

When considering how costs behave in relation to changes in volume of output or level of activity, costs may be classified as variable, fixed, or mixed. Variable costs vary, either proportionately, in steps, or in other ways. Fixed costs may be classified into capacity and discretionary.

Both variable and fixed costs behave in the ways just described only within the relevant or normal range of activity. Note that because total true variable cost varies proportionately with the variation in the level of activity, variable cost per unit must be constant. For the opposite reason, fixed cost per unit varies in reverse order with the variation in volume. If the organization operates beyond the relevant range, variable cost per unit and total fixed cost per period may not stay constant.

With respect to controllability by a certain managerial level, costs may be controllable or noncontrollable. With respect to time of spending or method of determination or estimation, costs may be classified into historical or future costs. Other cost concepts include differential costs and opportunity cost.

BASIC CONCEPTS AND TERMS

Activity base	Indirect manufacturing expenses
Administrative costs	Indirect materials
Budgeted costs	Inventoriable costs
Committed fixed costs	Managed fixed costs
Controllable costs	Manufacturing costs
Conversion costs	Manufacturing overhead
Cost of goods manufactured	Mixed costs
Curvilinear costs	Opportunity costs
Differential costs	Period costs
Direct cost	Prime cost
Direct labor	Product costs
Direct materials	Programmed fixed costs
Discretionary fixed costs	Relevant range
Factory overhead	Semi-variable costs
Finished goods	Standard costs
Fixed costs	Step-variable costs
Historical costs	Sunk costs
Incremental costs	Variable costs
Indirect costs	Work in process
Indirect labor	

■ SELF-REVIEW PROBLEM 1:
Cost Classifications

Given the following list of costs, classify them in a table as follows:

Product Cost			Period Cost		Cost Behavior		
Direct		**Indirect**					
Material	Labor	Mfg OH	Marketing	Admin.	Variable	Fixed	Mixed

Monthly fees paid to Internet provider (Internet used to publicize products), rent on factory building, advertising expense, raw materials used in production, wages of assembly line workers, factory supervisory salaries, straight line depreciation on administrative buildings, utilities used in factory, maintenance and repairs for sales warehouse building, janitorial services for company headquarters building, lubricants for factory machines, straight line depreciation on factory equipment, sales persons' commissions, glue used in toy factory, utilities used in sales offices, tires used in an automobile factory, wood used in a furniture factory, salaries of an HMO's customer service representatives, salaries of an HMO's physicians (in the short-term).

SOLUTION

| | PRODUCT COST | | | PERIOD COST | | COST BEHAVIOR | | |
| | DIRECT | | INDIRECT | MARKET- | ADMINI- | VARI- | | |
	MAT.	LABOR	MFG. OH	ING	STRATIVE	ABLE	FIXED	MIXED
Monthly fees paid to Internet provider (Internet used to publicize products)				X			X	
Rent on factory building			X				X	
Advertising expense				X			X	
Raw materials used in production	X					X		
Wages of assembly line workers		X				X		
Factory supervisors' salaries			X				X	
Straight-line depreciation on administrative buildings					X		X	
Utilities used in factory			X					X
Maintenance and repairs for sales warehouses				X				X
Janitorial services for company headquarters building					X		X	
Lubricants for factory machines			X			X		
Straight-line depreciation on factory equipment			X				X	
Salespersons' commissions				X		X		
Glue used in toy factory			X			X		
Utilities used in sales offices				X				X
Tires used in an auto factory	X					X		
Wood used in a furniture factory	X					X		
Salaries of HMO's customer service reps.					X		X	
Salaries of HMO's physicians (short-term)		X					X	

Note: Part of the mixed costs could have been classified either as variable (e.g., utilities) or fixed (e.g., maintenance and repairs).

■ SELF-REVIEW PROBLEM 2: Schedule of Cost of Goods Manufactured and Income Statement

The following is a list of selected accounts of LST Manufacturing, Inc. for the year ended December 31, Year 6:

Direct materials inventory, January 1	$ 70,000
Direct materials inventory, December 31	30,000
Purchases of direct materials	760,000
Factory payroll, direct labor	200,000
Factory payroll, indirect labor	50,000
Selling expenses	160,000
Administrative expenses	110,000
Factory supplies	40,000
Property taxes, factory	100,000
Depreciation, factory	250,000
Utilities, factory	27,000
Repairs and maintenance, factory	19,000
Sales	2,300,000
Work in process inventory, January 1	120,000
Work in process inventory, December 31	130,000
Finished goods inventory, January 1	220,000
Finished goods inventory, December 31	240,000

Based on the given information, prepare the following statements for the management:

1. Schedule of cost of goods manufactured for Year 6.
2. Income statement for Year 6. Show the computation of the cost of goods sold in the proper section.

SOLUTION

1.

LST Manufacturing, Inc.
Schedule of Cost of Goods Manufactured
For Year 6

Direct materials:		
DM inventory, January 1	$ 70,000	
DM purchases during year	760,000	
DM available for use	830,000	
DM inventory, December 31	(30,000)	
DM used in production		$ 800,000
Direct labor cost		200,000
Manufacturing overhead:		
Indirect labor cost	50,000	
Factory supplies	40,000	
Property taxes	100,000	
Depreciation, factory	250,000	
Utilities, factory	27,000	
Repairs & maintenance, factory	19,000	
Total manufacturing overhead		486,000
Total manufacturing costs		1,486,000
Work in process inventory, January 1		120,000
		1,606,000
Work in process inventory, December 31		(130,000)
Cost of goods manufactured		$1,476,000

2.

LST Manufacturing Inc.
Income Statement for Year 6

Sales		$2,300,000
Cost of goods sold:		
Finished goods inventory, January 1	$ 220,000	
Cost of goods manufactured	1,476,000	
Finished goods available for sale	1,696,000	
Finished goods inventory, December 31	(240,000)	
Cost of goods sold		1,456,000
Gross profit		844,000
Selling and administrative expenses:		
Selling expenses	160,000	
Administrative expenses	110,000	270,000
Net income		$ 574,000

■ REVIEW QUESTIONS

2-1 Given the following perspectives what is the proper classification of the cost of fine leather used in the manufacturing of designer shoes?
   a. Element of cost:
   b. Functions of the organization:
   c. Traceability to the final output:
   d. Behavior in relation to changes in volume of output:
   e. Controllability by first line supervisor:

2-2 Refer to question 2-1. Give the classification of each of the following costs from the perspectives indicated in question 2-1:
   a. Cost of electricity used in a fax-modem manufacturing facility.
   b. Straight line depreciation on factory robots.
   c. Administrative executive salaries.
   d. Hourly wages of camera operators in a motion picture company.
   e. Glue and nails used in a furniture factory.
   f. Advertising costs.

2-3 Differentiate between product costs and period costs and give examples of each. Why are product costs sometimes referred to as inventoriable costs?

2-4 Define and give an example of an opportunity cost.

2-5 How is the cost of goods sold computed in a merchandising firm and in a manufacturing firm?

2-6 How is the cost of goods manufactured computed?

2-7 How is the cost of raw materials used computed?

2-8 Differentiate between prime cost and conversion cost.

2-9 What is meant by "relevant range"? Why is the concept important to the definition of variable costs and fixed costs?

2-10 Explain why variable cost is constant per unit whereas fixed cost is variable per unit?

2-11 Differentiate between historical costs and future costs.

2-12 Why are historical or sunk costs irrelevant in decision making?

2-13 Define and give an example of differential (or incremental) costs.

2-14 Distinguish between step-variable costs and semi-variable costs.

2-15 Not all variable costs are truly variable, and not all fixed costs are truly fixed. Explain.

2-16 Why is variable cost per unit constant whereas fixed cost per unit varies with volume or level of activity?

2-17 Differentiate between true variable costs and step-variable costs.

2-18 Distinguish between, and give examples of, committed fixed costs and discretionary fixed costs.

2-19 Is volume of business the only activity base for variable costs? If there are other bases, give examples for various organizations.

🌐 INTERNET PROJECT

Web 2-1:

Websites: www.chrysler.com
www.MBUSA.com
www.Lexus.com

Marilyn's Pride, a design swimsuit manufacturer, wants to buy an SUV to use 30% for picking up fabrics for urgent uses in the plant, 50% for delivering finished swimsuits to its customers, and 20% for the company's general administrative purposes. The company has narrowed the choices down to three vehicles: Jeep Grand Cherokee, ML-320 of Mercedes, or RX-300 of Lexus.

Required:

1. Which SUV would cost the least? Can the vehicle costs be compared for different vehicles with different capacities and functions? Use the information gathered from the websites to determine the costs.

2. Assume the company has bought the least expensive SUV among the three. How would the purchase costs appear (a) on the schedule of cost of goods manufactured, and (b) on the income statement? Use Exhibit 2-3 and Exhibit 2-4 as your reference.

■ EXERCISES

E2-1 Various Cost Classifications

The following costs are associated with manufacturing operations:
1. Monthly payments on rented machine center equipment.
2. Sugar in cookies.
3. Laser disc players installed in automobiles.
4. Salaries paid to "knowledge workers" in a flexible manufacturing systems environment.
5. Property taxes on factory buildings.
6. Insurance premiums paid for factory automobiles.
7. Plastic cans used in the packaging of tennis balls.
8. Payments on leased drinking water containers for factory employees.
9. Salaries paid to process engineers.
10. Wages paid to assemblers of mountain bikes.
11. Production supervisors' salaries.
12. Monthly lease payments of $5,000 on new color printing machines at a printing facility.
13. Depreciation on exercise equipment in the factory gymnasium.
14. Health insurance premiums paid on behalf of plant janitors.

Required:

Classify each cost as being either variable **(V)** or fixed **(F)** with respect to volume or level of activity. Also classify each as being either direct **(D)** or indirect **(I)** with respect to units of product.

E2-2 Product Cost vs. Period Cost

Classify the following costs of a manufacturer as either product (inventoriable) costs or period (noninventoriable) costs:

1. Rent on an automatic materials handling system used to move materials and parts.
2. Engine oil used for maintenance of computerized machine tools.
3. Depreciation on the company's three Porsches assigned to three consultants who are working on redesigning the administrative offices' procedures.
4. Salaries paid to the security guards at the finished goods warehouse.
5. Electricity used to power the conveyor belt in a plant.
6. Special containers used for shipping finished products to overseas customers.
7. $500,000 paid to a major TV network for a 15-second spot during the halftime of this year's Superbowl. It promotes the company's new product.
8. Health insurance premiums paid on behalf of plant workers.
9. Wages paid to janitors in the factory.

10. Personal property tax on the company's yacht used by top executives of the company.
11. Rent on a conference room at a Palm Springs resort used for product quality improvement workshops attended by plant workers.
12. Fee paid to an outside designer for a new design of cereal packaging box. The new design has been used.
13. Monthly payments for the drinking water used by employees in the assembly plant.
14. Payments to a customs agent for services on the shipments of the company's new product to importers in Italy.

E2-3 Determining Specific Balance Sheet and Income Statement Items

RCX, Inc. was organized on May 2, Year 6. On that date the company purchased 10,000 plastic emblems showing the company's name and logo. The company purchased each emblem at a cost of $2.50. During May, 8,000 emblems were removed from the inventory. Of these, 600 were taken by the sales manager to a convention in San Francisco and handed out as product promotion.

The remaining emblems drawn from the inventory were affixed to units of the company's product. Of the units of product having emblems affixed during May, 85% were fully completed during the month and were transferred from work in process to finished goods. Of the goods fully completed, 60% were sold during the month.

Required:

1. Determine the cost of emblems that would be reported as the following at May 31, Year 6:
   a. Raw Materials Inventory.
   b. Work in Process Inventory.
   c. Finished Goods Inventory.
   d. Advertising Expense.
   e. Cost of Goods Sold.
2. Indicate whether each item should appear on the balance sheet or the income statement at May 31.

E2-4 Costs Appearing on the Income Statement and the Balance Sheet

Hillary School Supply Company has a student's supply kit in its product line. The kit includes a color marker in a case that bears the company logo. On September 1, Year 2, the company had 10,000 of these color markers in inventory, which were originally purchased at 75 cents per color marker. During September, 4,000 color markers were taken from the inventory. The sales manager used 1,000 of these for product promotion at a national convention of school teachers. The remaining 3,000 color markers drawn from the inventory were used in producing students supply kits. Of these kits, 80% were completed and transferred to finished goods during September. Of the completed kits, 60% were sold during the month.

Required:

1. Determine the cost of color markers that would be reported as the following at September 30, Year 2:
   a. Raw Materials Inventory.
   b. Work in Process Inventory.
   c. Finished Goods Inventory.
   d. Selling (Promotion) Expense.
   e. Cost of Goods Sold.
2. Indicate whether each item should appear on the balance sheet or the income statement at September 30.

E2-5 Cost of Goods Manufactured and Cost of Goods Sold

The White Corporation submits the following information on December 31, Year 6:

Direct labor cost	$14,000
Indirect labor cost	8,000
Purchase of raw materials	12,000
Repairs to factory equipment	1,000
Insurance, factory equipment	700
Insurance, office equipment	200
Light and power, factory facilities	5,000
Rent, factory facilities	4,000
Depreciation, office equipment	500
Property taxes, factory	1,000
Depreciation, factory equipment	1,300
Raw materials, December 31, Year 5	7,000
Work in process inventory, December 31, Year 5	10,000
Finished goods inventory, December 31, Year 5	20,000
Raw materials, December 31, Year 6	9,000
Work in process inventory, December 31, Year 6	17,000
Finished goods inventory, December 31, Year 6	14,000

Required:

1. Prepare a schedule of cost of goods manufactured for Year 6.
2. Prepare the cost of goods sold section of the company's income statement for Year 6.

E2-6 Cost of Goods Manufactured; Cost of Goods Sold

The accounting records of Miami Company show the following data for the year ended December 31, Year 4:

Purchases of raw materials	$10,500
Beginning raw materials inventory	9,000
Ending raw materials inventory	8,000
Beginning work in process inventory	10,000
Ending work in process inventory	12,000
Beginning finished goods inventory	15,000
Ending finished goods inventory	18,000
Direct labor	11,000
Indirect labor	7,000
Depreciation, office equipment	1,000
Depreciation, factory equipment	6,000
Insurance, office equipment	800
Insurance, factory equipment	1,500
Factory maintenance	3,000
Factory rent	6,000
Factory property taxes	13,000

Required:

1. Prepare a schedule of cost of goods manufactured for Year 4.
2. Prepare the cost of goods sold section of the company's income statement for Year 4.

E2-7 Cost of Goods Manufactured and Cost of Goods Sold

The accounting records of JTK, Inc. show the following information as of June 30, Year 6:

	July 1, Year 5	June 30, Year 6
Inventories:		
Raw materials	$15,000	$10,000
Work in process	21,000	26,000
Finished goods	40,000	32,000

Costs incurred:	
Direct labor	$90,000
Rent, factory	50,000
Sales salaries	45,000
Purchase of raw materials	120,000
Indirect labor	25,000
Utilities, factory	8,000
Advertising expense	80,000

Property taxes, factory	12,000
Repairs, factory equipment	9,000

Required:

1. Prepare a schedule of cost of goods manufactured for the year ended June 30, Year 6.
2. Prepare the cost of goods sold section of the company's income statement for the year ended June 30, Year 6.

E2-8   Variable and Fixed Costs; Differential Costs and Revenues

John Barker operates a retail store. Product A costs John $16 per unit and sells for $24 per unit. The store sells 500 units of Product A each year. John is considering dropping Product A and selling Product B instead. Product B would cost $20 per unit and sell for $30 per unit. John thinks that he could sell 600 units of product B each year. Product B would require special display equipment which can be rented at a cost of $700 per year. John would no longer have to pay $500 per year in repair costs to support Product A. Product A requires $300 per year and Product B requires $1,000 per year in advertising.

Required:

1. Compute the differential costs and revenues between Product A and Product B in terms of total annual costs, revenues, and profits. Mark each cost as being either variable (V) or fixed (F).

2. Is there an opportunity cost associated with eliminating Product A? Explain.

E2-9   Differential Costs; Opportunity Costs

Sally Rand owns and operates a decorative accessory store that specializes in ceiling fans. The Columbian model ceiling fan costs Sally $35 per unit; she sells it for $80. Sally currently sells 300 units of the Columbian model per year. She is considering replacing the Columbian model with the Chicago model in hopes that she will sell 250 of the Chicago model. The Chicago model costs $45 per unit and would sell for $95. Advertising costs are $2,000 and $2,500 per year for the Columbian and the Chicago models, respectively. Shipping costs for the Columbian and the Chicago models are $4 and $3 per unit, respectively.

Required:

1. Compute the differential costs and revenues between the Columbian and the Chicago models in terms of total annual costs, revenues, and profits. Indicate whether each cost is variable (V) or fixed (F).

2. Is there an opportunity cost associated with dropping the Columbian model? Explain.

E2-10   True Variable Costs; Step-Variable Costs; Semi-Variable Costs

Refer to Exhibit 2-8 showing different types of variable costs. Classify the following costs as being *true variable* costs, *step-variable* costs, or *semi-variable* costs:

1. Salaries paid to knowledge workers assigned to semi-automatic metal fabrication machines. Each knowledge worker can handle up to 3 machines.
2. Wages paid to direct labor workers.
3. Compensation paid to manufacturing systems consultants who are paid a base fee of $20,000 per year plus $50 per hour of working time.
4. Cost of factory electricity which is $200 per month plus $10 per Kilowatt-hour.
5. Salaries paid to assembly line supervisors. Each supervisor is responsible for eight workers.
6. Costs of operating the automatic material handling system. The costs represent depreciation of the system plus the hourly cost of the manpower needed to handle the volume of materials and parts.
7. Purchasing department's operating costs, which represent fixed salaries of regular employees and wages for temporary order-processing employees who are hired on an hourly basis.
8. Cost of parts used in assembling hand-held calculators.
9. Salaries paid to shift-managers. There are two shifts at the present time, but the plant is adding one more shift next month.
10. Costs of operating the quality assurance department. The costs represent the salaries paid to the regular full-time staff members and hourly product quality inspectors who are paid based on the number of pieces inspected.
11. Payments to an outside firm for performing repair and maintenance of computer-operated machine centers. There is a basic charge per month and charges for each service visit to the plant by the firm's specialists.
12. Salaries paid to product quality inspectors. The amount of work depends on the production quantity, but each inspector can handle up to 25 units of product a day.

■ PROBLEMS

P2-11   Ethics and Managers' Actions: An International Context

Jennifer Langdon was appointed general manager of a European subsidiary of an American auto maker as of July 1, Year 6. In order to minimize the income tax expense paid to the host country, Ms. Langdon has decided that the subsidiary will pay the highest prices legally possible for the automobile parts imported from the head office in Detroit. Procurement and accounts payable managers were subsequently instructed to follow the new policy.

The high cost of purchased parts would certainly inflate the cost of goods manufactured, reducing gross margin and taxable income for the subsidiary. The earnings reported by the subsidiary would be deflated but Ms. Langdon thinks she can contribute to top management's efforts to maximize shareholder wealth in a no-nonsense, professional manner.

Required:

Are the actions taken by Ms. Langdon ethical? Discuss her actions from the perspectives of various stakeholders of the company.

P2-12   Various Cost Classifications

The following are the items of costs incurred in operations of manufacturing companies in different industries:

1. Electricity used to power "shower" machines in a micro-chip manufacturing facility. The machines are used only when employees and visitors enter the manufacturing area. The employees enter the area twice a day.
2. Depreciation on dust control systems at a CD-ROM facility.
3. Plastics used in the production of television sets.
4. Peaches in a cannery.
5. Property taxes on factory buildings.
6. Wages paid to workers assembling laser printers.
7. Salaries of technicians maintaining automatic material handling systems.
8. Factory cafeteria food costs.
9. Wages of skilled technicians assembling stop-watches.
10. Gold solution used in tap-plating circuit boards.
11. Rent on a factory building.
12. Fees paid to CPAs auditing financial statements of a manufacturer.
13. Lease payments on welding robots.
14. Fees paid to reengineering consultants.
15. Payments to a Colorado hotel which was used to train office employees in productivity improvement.
16. Billing department expenses.
17. A factory supervisor's salary.
18. Insurance premium covering a computerized manufacturing facility.

Required:

Classify each cost item as shown in the example below:

	Cost Behavior		Selling and Administrative Cost	Product Cost	
	Variable	Fixed		Direct	Indirect
Raw materials	x			x	

P2-13   Cost Identification; Total and Per-Unit Costs

T&D, Inc., a manufacturing company with a set of related metal products, has incurred the following costs in the administrative offices and the factory:

Wages of assembly line workers	$259,000
Payments to a local TV station for a commercial on a new product	25,000
Night-shift supervisor's salary	50,000
Property taxes on the factory building	3,000
Commissions paid to product salespeople	90,000
Fire insurance premium on the factory	2,200
Depreciation on sales office computers	4,000
Payments on leased factory robots	65,000
Indirect materials used in production	7,000
Depreciation on machine cells	115,000
Papers for administrative office copiers	2,500
Salaries paid to office secretaries	130,000
Direct materials used in production	147,000
Electricity used in machine cells	15,000

Required:

1. Classify each cost item as either variable or fixed, and calculate the following:
    a. What is the total variable cost?
    b. What is the total fixed cost?
2. a. Calculate the total product cost, and break it down to the direct cost and the indirect cost.
    b. Calculate the total period cost.
3. Due to the current recession, the sales and production of the set of related metal products have decreased to 60% of the usual level. Explain, without actual calculations, whether each of the following costs would increase, decrease, or remain at the same level in the near future:
    a. Total cost of goods manufactured.
    b. Per-unit cost of goods manufactured.
    c. Total cost of goods sold.
    d. Per-unit cost of goods sold.

P2-14   Cost Behavior Patterns

Various types of cost behavior patterns are depicted in the graphs presented below.

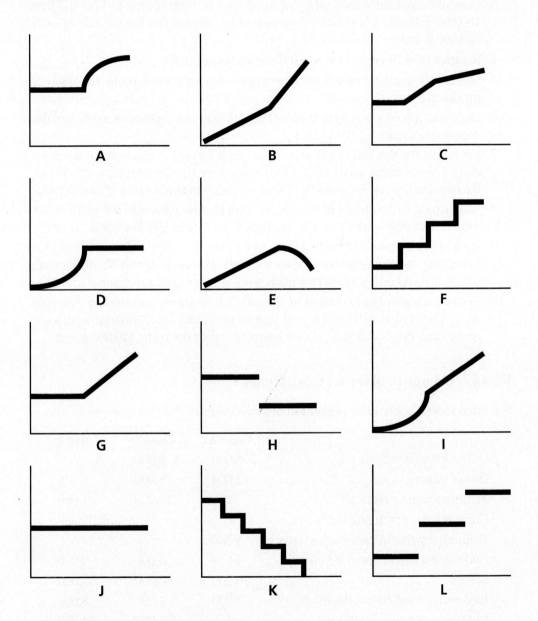

Required:

Indicate which graph best depicts the cost behavior patterns described below. A graph may be used more than once.

1. A computer manufacturer's cost of memory chips. The 5-year contract requires the company to buy a minimum of 1,000 chips a year at a specific price. For the next 1,000 additional chips purchased, the unit price decreases 10%. After 2,000 chips, the unit price decreases 15%.

2. A printed circuit board manufacturer's cost of waste disposal. The disposal cost increases by 1% of the initially agreed-upon amount per gallon of waste for each of the first 200 gallons, after which the per-gallon cost stays at $5.

3. Cost of industrial water, where a fixed cost of $500 is charged for the first 100,000 gallons. After that 1 cent per gallon is charged for the use of over 100,000 gallons.

4. Salaries of shift-supervisors. All three shifts are used.

5. Salaries of quality inspectors. One inspector can handle up to 100 units of products a day.

6. Depreciation of a machine center. The straight-line method is used, and the depreciation rate is 20% a year.

7. Payments for the direct labor workers' memberships in a private aerobics club. The company pays a fixed fee for the first 10 memberships. After that, the membership fee decreases by 5% per worker for each additional membership.

8. Wages paid to assembly line workers. Due to downsizing in the plant, overtime is normally expected. The overtime pay rate is 150% of the base rate.

9. Rent on a city-owned building in an inner-city area. The building is used for recruiting and training direct labor workers. The basic rent is $60,000 a year, which is reduced by $1,000 for each worker hired for more than 6 months.

10. Rent on a tract of land owned by the city. The company is building a factory on it. The rent is $100,000 a year unless and until 500,000 labor hours are generated. Beyond 500,000 labor hours, the rent drops to $40,000 a year.

P2-15 Compute Missing Cost Items

For each independent case presented below, compute the missing cost items.

	Case a	Case b	Case c
Direct materials used	$ 5,000	$ 6,000	$?
Direct labor	12,000	8,000	6,000
Manufacturing overhead	?	18,000	21,000
Current manufacturing costs	?	?	36,000
Beginning work in process inventory	5,000	?	?
Ending work in process inventory	4,000	6,000	9,000
Sales	70,000	80,000	53,000
Beginning finished goods inventory	3,000	4,000	8,000
Cost of goods manufactured	?	35,000	34,000
Goods available for sale	39,000	?	?
Ending finished goods inventory	5,000	7,000	?
Cost of goods sold	?	?	?
Gross margin	36,000	?	?
Operating expenses	?	30,000	10,000
Net income	8,000	?	6,000

P2-16 Cost of Goods Manufactured; Cost of Goods Sold; Unit Cost vs. Total Cost

Hampton Company's sales and cost data for Year 2 are given below:

Raw materials inventory, beginning	$ 2,000
Raw materials inventory, ending	3,000
Raw material purchases	10,000
Direct labor cost	18,000
Factory depreciation	27,000
Administrative expenses	8,000
Factory utilities	3,000
Factory maintenance	2,000
Factory repairs	2,000
Factory insurance	1,500
Indirect labor	5,500
Advertising	1,500
Selling expenses	10,000
Work in process, beginning	12,000
Work in process, ending	9,000
Finished goods, beginning	10,000
Finished goods, ending	9,000

Required:

1. Prepare a schedule of cost of goods manufactured for Year 2.
2. Prepare the cost of goods sold section of the income statement for Year 2.
3. If the above costs represent the data for the production of 1,000 units of product during Year 2, what was the unit cost of direct materials? What will be the total cost of materials if the production increases to 1,500 units?

P2-17 Connecting Manufacturing Operations to Income Statement Data; Calculating Missing Data Items

For each independent case presented below, compute the missing items.

	Case 1	Case2	Case 3	Case 4
Direct materials used	$ 4,000	$ 2,000	$ 5,000	$ 3,000
Direct labor	2,000	?	3,000	?
Manufacturing overhead	5,000	6,000	5,000	4,000
Current manufacturing costs	?	?	?	9,000
Work in process, beginning	3,000	4,000	?	2,000
Work in process, ending	2,000	5,000	4,000	?
Cost of goods manufactured	?	14,000	11,000	8,000
Sales	?	?	20,000	10,000
Finished goods, beginning	?	3,000	6,000	2,000
Finished goods, ending	4,000	?	7,000	?
Cost of goods sold	13,000	11,000	?	7,000

Gross margin	?	4,000	?	3,000
Operating expenses	2,000	?	5,000	?
Net income.	4,000	3,000	5,000	2,000

P2-18 Schedule of Cost of Goods Manufactured; Variable Cost vs. Fixed Cost

Zyzex Company is a manufacturer of plastic keyboards used for different types of computer products. The company's data on operations and cost are provided below:

Raw materials, January 1, Year 2	$ 4,000
Raw material purchases	18,000
Raw materials, December 31, Year 2	3,000
Work in process, January 1, Year 2	8,000
Work in process, December 31, Year 2	12,000
Finished goods, January 1, Year 2	13,000
Finished goods, December 31, Year 2	12,000
Wages of direct labor workers	23,000
Factory depreciation	30,000
Factory electricity	7,000
Repairs and maintenance	5,000
Rent on factory robots	6,000
Factory insurance	4,000
Factory supervision	8,000

Required:

1. Prepare a schedule of cost of goods manufactured for Year 2.
2. Prepare the cost of goods sold section of the income statement for Year 2.
3. If the above data represent the production of 2,000 equivalent units of product during Year 2, what was the per-unit cost of direct materials? What was the per-unit cost of rent on factory robots?
4. Assume the company produces 1,000 equivalent units of product during a different year. Calculate the per-unit and total cost of (a) direct materials and (b) rent on factory robots.
5. Compare the per-unit costs of rent on factory robots in (3) and (4). Explain any difference in the per-unit cost figures of rent on factory robots, in comparison to any change in the per-unit cost of raw materials.

P2-19 Relating Costs to Physical Units in Manufacturing and Sales

FutureTerm, Inc. is a manufacturer of unique, state-of-the-art medical equipment used in hospitals. The following records reflect the operations of the calendar year Year 7:

Sales in dollars	$990,000
Physical units:	
Finished goods sold	?
Finished goods produced	?
Finished goods inventory, December 31, Year 6	1,760
Finished goods inventory, December 31, Year 7	2,760
Cost and other information:	
Indirect labor	40,000
Raw materials, December 31, Year 6	23,000
Purchases of raw materials	190,000
Rent on the building (60% used by manufacturing;	
40% used by sales and administration)	50,000
Gross margin	440,000
Direct labor	150,000
Factory utilities	85,000
Repairs and maintenance	65,000
Total current period manufacturing costs	570,000
Work in process, December 31, Year 6	35,000

The company's product is sold for $45 per unit. Per-unit manufacturing cost stayed the same in Year 6 and Year 7.

Required:

1. Calculate the following for Year 7:
   a. Units of finished goods sold.
   b. Cost of goods sold.
   c. Per-unit cost of goods manufactured.
   d. Year 7 ending finished goods inventory.
   e. Year 7 beginning finished goods inventory.
   f. Cost of goods manufactured.
   g. Number of units produced.
   h. Manufacturing overhead cost.
   i. Direct materials used.
   j. Year 7 ending work in process inventory.
   k. Year 7 ending raw materials inventory.
2. Prepare a schedule of cost of goods manufactured for Year 7.
3. Prepare the cost of goods sold section of the income statement for Year 7.

P2-20 Relating Manufacturing Operations to Cost and Sales Data

BuenaProda, Inc. is a manufacturer of a single product. The company uses the lean production concept to manage finished goods inventories and maintains minimum amounts of finished goods inventories. The following records reflect the operations of the calendar year Year 2:

Sales in dollars	$940,500
Physical units:	
Finished goods sold	?
Finished goods produced	?
Finished goods inventory, December 31, Year 1	400
Finished goods inventory, December 31, Year 2	300
Cost and other information:	
Selling expenses	$ 50,000
Factory depreciation	120,000
General administration	110,000
Property taxes, factory	42,000
Raw materials, December 31, Year 1	4,000
Miscellaneous factory overhead	20,000
Purchases of raw materials	140,000
Gross margin	256,500
Direct labor	240,000
Factory utilities	70,000
Repairs and maintenance	55,000
Total current period manufacturing costs	671,000
Work in process, December 31, Year 1	40,000
Work in process, December 31, Year 2	?

The single product is sold for a unit price of $55. Per-unit cost of finished products stayed the same in Year 1 and Year 2.

Required:

1. Calculate the following for Year 2:
   a. Units of finished goods sold.
   b. Cost of goods sold.
   c. Per-unit cost of goods manufactured.
   d. Year 2 ending finished goods inventory.
   e. Year 2 beginning finished goods inventory.
   f. Cost of goods manufactured.
   g. Number of units produced.
   h. Manufacturing overhead cost.
   i. Direct materials used.
   j. Year 2 ending work in process inventory.
   k. Year 2 ending raw materials inventory.
2. Prepare a schedule of cost of goods manufactured for Year 2.
3. Prepare the cost of goods sold section of the income statement for Year 2.

■ CASES

C2-21 Part 1 Changing Environment; Service Firm's Variable, Fixed, Product, Period, and Differential Costs

Architects-R-Us is a medium-sized architectural firm involved in designing and developing shopping malls. As is the case with most service firms, the firm's operation is labor-intensive. The labor cost represents salaries paid to architects and support staff and is a major part of project costs. The firm has, in the past, billed clients based on the following formula:

$$\text{Amount billed} = \text{Labor} + \text{Overhead} + \text{Guaranteed markup}$$

Recently, stiff competition in the market has changed the environment of the firm, and the pricing and billing formula has also changed. Now architectural contracts involve a lump sum fee paid to the lowest bidder, which has forced firms to strive for higher efficiency and lower cost in order to avoid sustaining losses. They have turned to new technologies to increase efficiency and reduce cost.

The newest technology available in the industry is computer-aided design and drafting (CADD), which can help the firm perform various new functions that were not available in traditional processes, such as storing hundreds of figures and shapes in memory.

The firm installed a miniature version of CADD in Year 7. It was a stand-alone PC system which required the following first-year investment:

Hardware	$30,000
Software	10,000
Training of employees	7,000
Total	$47,000

The hardware and software are depreciated 25% each year. Training costs are expensed 100% in the first year. The stand-alone PC system requires the following annual CADD operating costs in addition to the above depreciation and training expenses:

Direct labor costs	$10,000
Hardware support and maintenance	4,000
Software support and maintenance	3,000
Utilities	2,000
Supplies	1,000
	$20,000

The $20,000 of CADD operating costs represent an annual cost savings of $24,000, primarily in labor costs, compared to the old way of designing and drawing. Accordingly, the firm recovered the investment of $47,000 in a little less than two years.

Required:

1. Compared to a manufacturing company, what is the major difference in operating cost characteristics of this service firm?
2. Classify each of the annual CADD operating cost items as either variable (V) or fixed (F).
3. In Year 7, what is the differential cost between the old system and the stand-alone PC system?
4. Products of this service firm are the architectural drawings and designs produced in the office. Which items in (2) are product costs? Which items are period costs?

Part 2   Service Firm; Changing Technology; Differential Costs; Sunk Costs

In Year 9, Architects-R-Us lost three bids, primarily because the competition used far more advanced generation technologies, such as the leading edge CADD with 3-D capability which allows the designer to see the drawing from different angles. The competitors' presentations look more sophisticated and impressive when state-of-the-art technologies are used.

The third defeat persuaded Architects-R-Us to upgrade its present equipment, which is a scaled-down version of CADD with limited quality and flexibility in meeting the demands of potential clients. The firm received the following quote on an advanced CADD system:

Initial outlays:	Hardware	$400,000
	Software	80,000
	Training	20,000
		$500,000

(The hardware and software are depreciated 25% each year. Training costs are expensed 100% in the first year.)

Estimated annual CADD system operating costs:

Maintenance & upgrades of hardware	$ 55,000
Maintenance & upgrades of software	12,000
System operation	10,000
Training	15,000
Utilities	4,000
Insurance	5,000
Supplies	3,000
	$104,000

The advanced CADD system is a minicomputer-based system with full line graphics capabilities. It can generate drawings and designs of far superior quality and can utilize the labor force to the maximum. Architects-R-Us could even explore and develop new markets in fields of other specialties, which the firm has not been able to penetrate because of the limited technology.

The firm estimates that the advanced CADD system will generate additional revenues of $200,000. Other benefits, such as productivity improvements, are also expected.

Required:

1. Calculate the differential revenue (including savings) and costs between the stand-alone PC system and the advanced CADD system in Year 9. If the advanced system is installed, the stand-alone PC system will be donated to an urban youth program. The tax savings from the donation will be $4,000.
2. Assume that Architects-R-Us has decided to install the advanced CADD system. Is there any sunk cost involved in the decision to replace the stand-alone PC system with the new system?
3. Assume that it takes five years to recover the investment in the new system, and top management's opinion is that five years is too long to justify the big cash investment of half a million dollars. As the management consultant of the firm, how would you advise top management?

3

COST-VOLUME-PROFIT ANALYSIS

After studying this chapter, you should be able to:

1. Explain the basic concepts of cost-volume-profit analysis.

2. Compute and explain the contribution margin in total, on a per unit basis and as a percentage of sales.

3. Compute the break-even point in units and in dollars using both an equation and a graph.

4. Describe operating leverage and compute the degree of operating leverage at different sales levels.

5. Explain and compute the margin of safety.

6. Apply cost-volume-profit analysis and the contribution margin concept to various internal managerial decisions.

7. Apply cost-volume-profit analysis to multi-product organizations and to nonprofit organizations.

8. Describe the assumptions and limitations of cost-volume-profit analysis.

When managers know the cost behavior patterns that are applicable to a situation, they can make planning and control decisions based on the relationships between output volume, costs, revenue, and profit. The study of these relationships is called **cost-volume-profit (CVP) analysis.** CVP analysis can provide answers to such questions as:

- How many units must the firm sell to at least cover the fixed costs?
- How many units must it sell to achieve a given amount of profit?
- Should the firm increase or decrease the selling price for its products?
- Should the firm increase variable cost per unit in order to decrease fixed costs, or should it do the opposite?
- Should the firm expand or contract its production facilities?
- Should the firm drop a product line and/or add a new one?

This chapter deals with managerial decisions involving CVP relationships.

BASIC COST-VOLUME-PROFIT ANALYSIS

For our discussion of basic CVP analysis, we use the following scenario:

Ann, Bob, and Cecil, three recent college graduates, have started a new company, called ABC Enterprises. Their company produces and sells a single product known as the "ABC card," which enhances the graphics capability of lap-top computers. ABC estimates the following cost and sales relationships:

Chrysler Technology Center where new cars and trucks are designed. A project like this requires a high level of fixed costs that should be recovered through the sales of cars and trucks.

	Per Unit	Percentage to Sales
Sales price	$10	100%
Variable cost	6	60
Sales price less variable cost	$ 4	40%
Fixed costs per year	$80,000	

Break-Even Point

The three entrepreneurs can see that ABC's sales price provides a $4 margin over its variable costs. But they still need to know how many units they must sell to cover their fixed costs. Managers also need to understand the effects of changes in business volume on costs, revenues, and profits.

The point at which revenues exactly equal expenses is called the **break-even point** because at that point the company makes neither profits nor losses. If the company sells more than the break-even point, it makes a profit. If it sells less than the break-even point, it incurs a loss.

The break-even point can be computed in two ways: the contribution margin method and the equation method.

Contribution-Margin Method

In the above example, ABC Enterprises earns a $4 margin on every computer graphics card it sells. This margin, representing the unit sales price of $10 less the unit variable cost of $6, is called **contribution margin.** Each unit sold contributes $4 toward the recovery of the $80,000 fixed costs. Once the fixed costs are covered, each unit sold contributes $4 toward profits.

How many units must ABC sell to break even? To break even, ABC Enterprises must accumulate a total contribution margin of $80,000 to cover the fixed costs. The number of units that must be sold can be computed as follows:

Total contribution margin	=	$4 per unit × _?_ units
	=	$80,000
	=	Fixed costs
Break-even point in units sold	=	$80,000 ÷ $4 per unit
	=	20,000

The sales of 20,000 units would produce the following operating results:

		Ratio to Sales
Sales price per unit	$ 10	100%
Variable cost	6	60
Contribution margin	$ 4	40%
Units sold	× 20,000	
Total contribution margin	$80,000	
Fixed costs per year	(80,000)	
Operating income	$ 0	

The break-even point of 20,000 units generates sales revenues of $200,000 (20,000 units × $10 per unit). This break-even point in sales dollars can also be calculated using the 0.4 **contribution margin ratio** (1 − 0.6 **variable cost ratio**) to sales:

Break-even point in sales dollars = $80,000 ÷ 0.4 = $200,000

Once the break-even point is reached, the fixed costs are fully recovered. Each additional unit sold contributes $4 to profit. Accordingly, if 20,001 units are sold, the operating profit will be $4, which is equal to the unit contribution margin. If you prepare an income statement, such as the one previously presented, you can confirm this result yourself.

The Equation Method

We have seen that total revenues equal total expenses at the break-even point. In an equation form, we can write this as:

$$\text{Total revenues} = \text{Total expenses} \tag{1}$$

Total revenues equal the quantity of output sold times the selling price per unit. Total expenses equal total fixed costs plus total variable costs. Thus, Equation (1) may be rewritten as:

$$\text{Quantity sold} \times \text{Price per unit}$$
$$= \text{Total fixed costs} + \text{Total variable costs} \tag{2}$$

We know that the variable cost per unit, within the relevant range, is constant. Therefore, total variable costs equals the quantity sold times the variable cost per unit. We can rewrite Equation (2) as:

$$Q \times P = F + Q \times V, \tag{3}$$

where:

Units sold:	Q
Price per unit:	P
Total fixed costs for the period:	F
Variable cost per unit:	V

Since Equation (3) is the break-even point equation, all we have to do to compute the number of units to break even is to solve the above equation for Q. This can be done in the following steps:

$$QP - QV = F \tag{4}$$

Now, we factor out Q to obtain

$$Q(P - V) = F \tag{5}$$

The final break-even point (in quantity) equation is:

$$Q = \frac{F}{P - V} \tag{6}$$

Note that "P − V" is the contribution margin per unit.

Using Equation (6) above, we can calculate ABC's break-even point in units as follows:

$$Q = \frac{\$80,000}{\$10 - \$6} = \frac{\$80,000}{\$4} = 20,000 \text{ units}$$

Based on what we have seen thus far, we can generalize the break-even point calculation as follows:

$$\text{Break-even point in units} = \frac{\text{Fixed costs}}{\text{Contribution margin per unit}}$$

Graphical Presentation of CVP Relationships

CVP relationships can also be presented in graphical form. A **cost-volume-profit graph** shows the level of activity on the horizontal (X)-axis and the dollar amount on the vertical (Y)-axis. The CVP graph shows two curves: one for total revenue (TR) and one for total cost (TC).

We draw the TR curve as follows:

(1)   Select a given volume (say 40,000 units) and multiply it by the selling price per unit ($10 in the ABC example) to get TR ($400,000) at that volume;

(2)   Plot the point for that TR and connect it with the zero point using a straight line on the chart.

We draw the TC curve by showing the total fixed cost (F) curve first and adding the total variable cost curve to it. Exhibit 3-1 illustrates the CVP graph. The TC curve starts from $80,000 of fixed costs and not from the origin, because TC equals fixed costs even if the company sells zero units.

The TR curve intersects the TC curve at the break-even point. At that point, 20,000 units are sold at the total sales of $200,000, which we have already calculated.

Volume-Profit Graph

A **volume-profit graph** shows how much profit or loss would be made at each level of sales volume. A volume-profit graph does not show any cost curves. It instead shows a break-even line and a profit-loss line as illustrated in Exhibit 3-2.

Profits and losses are shown on the vertical axis. The break-even line is drawn horizontally at the zero point on the vertical axis since at the break-even point there is no profit or loss. We draw the profit and loss line as follows:

1.   Plot a point on the vertical axis (below zero) representing the total fixed cost for the period ($80,000 in our example). The loss will equal the fixed costs if no units were sold.

2.   Then, plot a point representing total profit at a high sales volume, say 35,000 units. If 35,000 units were sold, the total revenue would be $350,000 and total variable costs would be $210,000 but fixed costs remain at $80,000. Thus, the operating profit would be $60,000 ($350,000 − $210,000 − $80,000).

3.   Connect the two points.

To determine how much profit or loss would be made at a given volume, a manager can draw a vertical line from the desired volume until it intersects the profit-loss line. At that point the manager can draw a horizontal line toward the vertical axis to determine the profit or loss. For illustration, two lines are drawn on Exhibit

EXHIBIT 3-1 Determining the Break-Even Point Using Graph

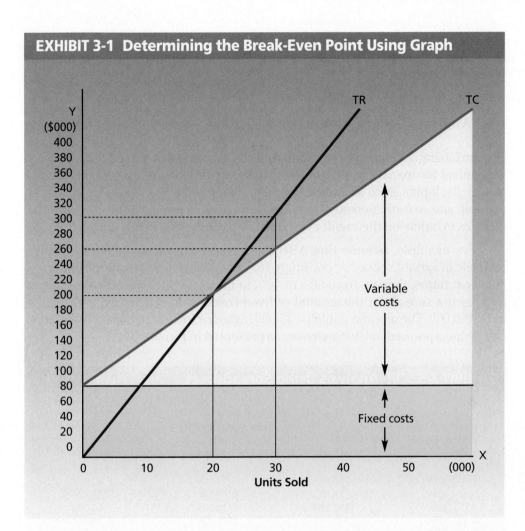

EXHIBIT 3-2 Volume-Profit Graph

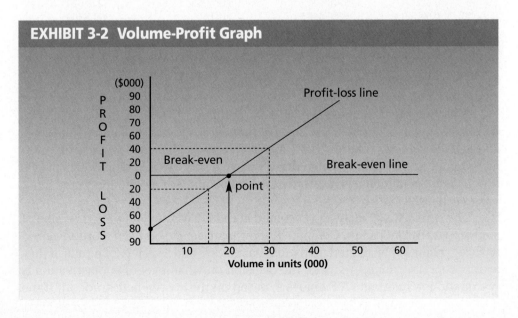

3-2: At 30,000 units, the profit is $40,000, and at 15,000 units, the loss is $20,000. Profits or losses always equal the vertical distance between the profit-loss line and the break-even line.

CVP Analysis Using Computers

The availability of computers and spreadsheet software has made CVP analysis very convenient for managers. For various planning purposes, managers can simply change the inputs, such as number of units, selling price, fixed cost, variable cost per unit, and so forth. Sensitivity analyses can be performed on the effects of the changes in inputs on the break-even point or any other CVP decisions.

For example, assume that ABC Enterprises' managers suspect a future increase in variable costs. Accordingly, they are interested in using various variable cost ratios, ranging from 60% to 70%, in their CVP analyses. The managers also are not sure about the amount of fixed costs, which currently is estimated to be $80,000. The amount could be $5,000 higher or lower. All these possibilities can be incorporated in CVP analyses, as presented in Exhibit 3-3.

EXHIBIT 3-3 CVP Analysis Using Spreadsheet

	A	B	C	D
1			**Break-Even Point in $ Sales**	
2	Variable		If the Total Fixed Cost is	
3	Cost Ratio	*$80,000*	*$75,000*	*$85,000*
4				
5	0.70	$266,667 *	$250,000	$283,333
6	0.68	$250,000	$234,375	$265,625
7	0.66	$235,294	$220,588	$250,000
8	0.64	$222,222	$208,333	$236,111
9	0.62	$210,526	$197,368	$223,684
10	0.60	$200,000 ¶	$187,500	$212,500
11				
12	* B3/(1 − A5) = $80,000 / (1 − 0.70)			
13	¶ B3/(1 − A10) = $80,000 / (1 − 0.60)			

The computer calculates the 18 (6 × 3) different break-even points in sales dollars, based on six different estimates of variable cost ratios (Column A) and three levels of fixed costs (columns B, C, and D on Row 3). Managers can use different input values to investigate the **sensitivity** of each decision outcome, which means how a decision outcome is affected as an input value (or a combination of input values) changes.

The spreadsheet analysis, presented in Exhibit 3-3, is a simplified version of studying CVP relationships. Computers allow managers to perform more advanced analyses, using sophisticated mathematical models and a variety of inputs, if they are appropriate. Managers make the decision on what level of sophistication is warranted for a certain CVP analysis, based on the cost-benefit tradeoff. If the benefits from employing a more sophisticated model outweigh the costs of doing it, managers would decide to use a more sophisticated CVP analysis.

Contribution Approach and Incremental Analysis

The format we have used in the CVP analyses so far in this chapter is based on contribution margin, rather than gross margin (sales minus cost of goods sold). Using the same ABC Enterprises data, and assuming a sales level of 25,000 units in Year 7, an income statement using the contribution approach is shown in Exhibit 3-4 below.

EXHIBIT 3-4

ABC Income Statement for Year 7
Contribution Approach

	Total	Per Unit
Sales (25,000 Units × $10)	$250,000	$10
Variable costs (25,000 × $6)	(150,000)	6
Contribution margin	100,000	$ 4
Fixed costs	(80,000)	
Operating income	$ 20,000	

The **contribution approach** to income statement presentation helps managers find operating characteristics of the company more clearly. The contribution margin of $100,000 here is greater than the total fixed costs of $80,000, and the company has an operating income of $20,000. This income is generated because ABC sold 5,000 units more than the break-even point of 20,000 units. At the break-even point of 20,000 units, the contribution margin of $80,000 (20,000 units × $4 contribution margin per unit) will only cover fixed costs of $80,000, and operating income will be zero.

If ABC operates below the break-even point (say, 15,000 units), the contribution margin of $60,000 (15,000 units × $4 contribution margin per unit) will not be enough to cover total fixed costs of $80,000. The company will end the year with an operating loss of $20,000 ($60,000 contribution margin − $80,000 fixed costs).

The contribution approach also helps managers clearly see the effect on operating income of an increment in sales. Analysis of the effect of an increment in a factor on final results is widely used in accounting and is called **incremental analysis.** Incremental analysis, for example, can be applied to such questions as, "What will be the increase in operating income if there is one additional unit sold in excess of the break-even point?" We have already discussed how to approach this issue.

Target Income and Desired Volume

If managers want to know how many units must be sold to earn a certain amount of target income, they can use the same method as was used in the computation of the break-even point. The amount of the target income is simply added to the fixed costs in the break-even formula, which was presented in Equation (6). Assume that ABC Enterprises would like to earn an income of $40,000 for the year. How many units must be sold? What is the amount of dollar sales? We can find the answers as follows:

$$\begin{aligned} \text{Break-even point in units} &= \frac{\text{Fixed costs}}{\text{Contribution margin per unit}} \quad (6) \\[2ex] \text{Target Sales in units} &= \frac{\text{Fixed costs} + \text{Target income}}{\text{Contribution margin per unit}} \quad (7) \\[2ex] &= \frac{\$80,000 + \$40,000}{\$10 - \$6} = \frac{\$120,000}{\$4} \\[2ex] &= 30,000 \text{ units} \\[1ex] \text{Target sales in dollars} &= 30,000 \text{ units} \times \$10 = \$300,000 \end{aligned}$$

The following income statement confirms the accuracy of the above answer:

Sales (30,000 units × $10)	$300,000
Variable costs (30,000 units × $6)	(180,000)
Contribution margin (CM)	120,000
Fixed costs	(80,000)
Operating income	$ 40,000

Operating Leverage

The ratio of a firm's fixed costs to variable costs is known as **operating leverage.** Managers are interested in this ratio because operating leverage explains the percentage change in operating income associated with a given percentage change in sales. How? The comparison of a product line with a high CM ratio to one with a low CM ratio provides a good example.

Airlines have high operating leverage because fixed costs, such as expenditures on aircrafts and terminals, are very high compared to variable costs, such as costs of meals and tickets for passengers.

Terminal operations at Southwest Airlines are shown here. Airlines have high operating leverage that is compared to supermarkets' low operating leverage.

A low variable cost ratio means a high CM ratio. This in turn means that even one percent increase in sales of an airline yields a big increase in CM and profit.

In contrast, a supermarket has low operating leverage. Its fixed costs, such as the cost of renting a building space, are low compared to high variable costs of buying grocery items. A high variable cost ratio means a low CM ratio. One percent increase in sales of a supermarket does not yield a significant increase in CM and profit.

Which is more desirable: high operating leverage with high fixed cost and high CM, or low operating leverage with low fixed cost and low CM? This is not a very relevant question, because the choice of an industry pretty much defines the operating leverage of a company. But the issue of operating leverage becomes relevant when a company considers how to deal with changing economic conditions, or such business alternatives as whether to advertise heavily (thereby increasing fixed costs) to increase sales and profits. The decision depends on whether the sales level is expected to increase or decrease in future years with no additional changes in fixed costs.

Let's consider the two companies illustrated in Exhibit 3-5.

EXHIBIT 3-5 High Operating Leverage vs. Low Operating Leverage

	Airline A		Supermarket K	
	Amount	%	Amount	%
Sales	$200,000	100	$200,000	100
Variable Costs	80,000	40	180,000	90
Contribution Margin	120,000	60	20,000	10
Fixed Costs	110,000	55	10,000	5
Operating Income	$ 10,000	5	$ 10,000	5

Managers of Hannaford Bros. Co., a multi-regional food retailer operating Shop'n Save, Wilson's and Sun Foods, review the new format store layout. The new format store markets everyday low grocery prices in combination with good-quality products and services. A supermarket has low operating leverage. Its variable cost ratio is high and fixed cost ratio is low.

While both Airline A and Supermarket K have the same sales amount and same operating income, Airline A's CM ratio is 60% whereas Supermarket K's CM ratio is only 10%. Since operating income to sales is 5% for both companies, we cannot say that one company performed better than the other. If the sales level is expected to increase, Airline A's profits will improve much more rapidly than Supermarket K's. This is because A's CM ratio is much higher than K's CM ratio. If, on the other hand, the sales level is expected to decrease, Supermarket K will not suffer as much loss as Airline A would. This is because K's CM ratio and fixed costs are much lower than A's CM ratio and fixed costs.

This is illustrated in Exhibit 3-6. Assume (1) sales will increase 20%, and (2) sales will decrease 20%.

EXHIBIT 3-6 Changing Sales Level and Operating Income

	(1) Sales increase 20%				(2) Sales decrease 20%			
	Airline A		Supermarket K		Airline A		Supermarket K	
Sales	$240,000	100	240,000	100	$160,000	100	$160,000	100
Variable costs	96,000	40	216,000	90	64,000	40	144,000	90
Contribution margin	144,000	60	24,000	10	96,000	60	16,000	10
Fixed costs	110,000	46	10,000	4	110,000	69	10,000	6
Operating income	$ 34,000	14	$14,000	6	($ 14,000)	(9)	$ 6,000	4

Let's compare Exhibit 3-5 and Exhibit 3-6(1). A 20% increase in sales level results in a $24,000 increase (from $10,000 to $34,000) in the operating income of Airline A but only $4,000 increase (from $10,000 to $14,000) in the operating income of Supermarket K. As a result, the percentage of operating income to sales for Airline A increased from 5% to 14%, whereas for Supermarket K, it increased from 5% to only 6%. In a strong economy and with rising sales levels, companies with high operating leverage (high fixed costs and high CM ratio) will perform better than companies with low operating leverage (low fixed costs and low CM ratio).

Now compare Exhibit 3-5 and Exhibit 3-6(2). A 20% decrease in sales level results in a $14,000 operating loss for Airline A, a decrease of $24,000 (from $10,000). In the meantime, Supermarket K's operating income is $6,000, only a $4,000 decrease (from $10,000). The percentage of operating income to sales becomes a 9% loss, instead of a 5% profit for Airline A, and becomes a 4% profit instead of a 5% profit for Supermarket K. In a weak economy and with falling sales levels, companies with low operating leverage (low fixed costs, low CM ratio, low risk) will not suffer as badly as companies with high operating leverage (high risk).

Using the above definition, the **degree of operating leverage** at a given level of sales is computed as follows:

$$\text{Degree of operating leverage} \ = \ \frac{\text{Contribution margin}}{\text{Operating income}}$$

For example, at the sales level presented in Exhibit 3-5, the degrees of operating leverage for Airline A and Supermarket K are:

For Airline A: $\dfrac{\$120,000}{\$10,000} \ = \ 12$

For Supermarket K: $\dfrac{\$20,000}{\$10,000} \ = \ 2$

We can use the concept of the degree of operating leverage to estimate by how much operating income will increase or decrease if sales increased or decreased by any percentage other than 20%. For example, if the sales level in Exhibit 3-5 increased by 30%, operating income for Airline A would increase by 30% × 12, or 360%, to $46,000. Operating income for Supermarket K would increase by only 30% × 2, or 60%, to $16,000. Exhibit 3-7 provides a proof of these results.

EXHIBIT 3-7 Increasing Sales Level and Operating Income

| | (30% Increase in sales per Exhibit 3-5) | | | |
| | Airline A | | Supermarket K | |
	Amount	%	Amount	%
Sales	$260,000	100	$260,000	100
Variable Costs	104,000	40	234,000	90
Contribution Margin	156,000	60	26,000	10
Fixed Costs	110,000	42	10,000	4
Operating Income	$ 46,000	18	$ 16,000	6

The closer the level of operations is to the break-even point, the higher the degree of operating leverage and vice versa. This is so because, at the break-even point, the operating income (the denominator in the formula) is zero. Companies operating near the break-even point usually face higher degrees of risk than companies operating at above the break-even level. A competent manager can benefit from the concept of operating leverage by quickly estimating the expected impacts of various changes in the existing sales level.

Margin of Safety

The **margin of safety** is the excess of a given sales level over the break-even point. It can be expressed in sales dollars, sales units, or as a percentage. It indicates the safety cushion above the break-even point, or the possible decrease in sales revenue or sales units before the company starts to incur operating losses. The margin of safety in its three forms can be computed as follows:

(1) Margin of safety in dollars = Actual sales − Break-even point in sales dollars

(2) Margin of safety in units = Actual units sold − Break-even point in units

(3) Margin of safety in percentage = (1) ÷ Actual sales
  = (2) ÷ Actual units sold

Managers can replace *actual* sales in (1) and *actual* number of units sold in (2) with *budgeted* (or *estimated*) sales and *budgeted* (or *estimated*) number of units sold, depending on the decision making needs. Exhibit 3-8 illustrates the computation of the margin of safety in its three forms for Airline A and Supermarket K for the sales level of $260,000 as per Exhibit 3-7, assuming the selling price per unit of output (an airline ticket or a weekly basket of groceries) is $200.

EXHIBIT 3-8 Margin of Safety Computations

	Airline A		Supermarket K	
	Amount	*Units*	*Amount*	*Units*
Sales (selling price per unit $200) [A]	$260,000	1,300	$260,000	1,300
Break-even point	183,333	917	100,000	500
Margin of safety [B]	$76,667	383	$160,000	800
Margin of safety (%) [B/A]	29.5%	29.5%	61.5%	61.5%

Break-even point in sales dollars = Fixed costs ÷ CM ratio

For Airline A: $110,000 ÷ 0.60 = $183,333
For Supermarket K: $ 10,000 ÷ 0.10 = $100,000

Break-even point in units = BEP in sales dollars ÷ Selling price per unit

For Airline A: $183,333 ÷ $200 = 917 Units
For Supermarket K: $100,000 ÷ $200 = 500 Units

The break-even point in units in Exhibit 3-8 can also be computed using Equation (6) as follows:

For Airline A:

Selling price per unit	$200
CM ratio	× 60%
CM per unit	$120
Fixed costs	$110,000
CM per unit	÷ $120
Break-even point in units	917 units

For Supermarket K:

Selling price per unit	$200
CM ratio	× 10%
CM per unit	$20
Fixed costs	$10,000
CM per unit	÷ $20
Break-even point in units	500 units

An examination of Exhibit 3-8 reveals the following:

Companies with high fixed costs, such as airlines, have higher break-even points than companies with low fixed costs, such as supermarkets. For the same level of sales, the former type of companies will have lower margins of safety in terms of sales dollars, units, or percentage than the latter type of companies. Accordingly, the former type of companies have a higher degree of risk than does the latter type of companies.

Managers find the margin of safety a very helpful indicator of whether they need to take a certain action. What the managers will actually do if the margin of safety is too low will depend on the circumstances. Possible courses of action include decreasing the level of fixed expenses, increasing the level of sales, or a combination of both.

Mirage Building

A Las Vegas Casino and CVP Analysis

A web-based research study reveals that about 40% of all U.S. residents visit Las Vegas in their lifetime. About 85% of all people who visit Las Vegas gamble. The average (not median) gambling budget for each visitor who gambles is about $600. On an average, the gamblers gamble about 4 hours a day. More than 20% of the visitors to Vegas are in the age group of 65 and older. In a recent quarter, Mirage Resorts, the owner of Bellagio Hotel, among others, charged a depreciation expense of about $55 million, reflecting the increase in the fixed costs due to expansion in the casino facilities. Casino revenues increased by about $100 million. What items from the financial statements do you need to figure out how many gamblers Mirage needs to attract in order to at least break even on its casino expansion?

CVP ANALYSIS: VARIATIONS

The elements of CVP analysis can change. The changes can take place in fixed costs, selling prices, variable costs, and sales volume. We can deal with any types of changes using the basic concepts and applications we have discussed thus far. In this section, we will discuss variations of CVP analysis. We will use ABC Enterprises' data. For ease of reference, ABC's data are repeated below:

	Per Unit	Ratio to Sales
Sales price	$10	100%
Variable cost	6	60
Contribution margin	4	40
Fixed costs per year		$80,000

Assume that the current sales volume is 25,000 units.

The operating results from the sales of 25,000 units vs. 20,000 units (breakeven point) are shown below:

	25,000 Units	20,000 Units	Ratio to Sales
Sales price per unit (P)	$10	$10	100%
Variable cost per unit	6	6	60
Contribution margin (CM)	$ 4	$ 4	40%
Units sold (Q)	× 25,000	× 20,000	
Total contribution margin	$100,000	$80,000	
Fixed costs per year	(80,000)	(80,000)	
Operating income (I)	$20,000	0	

All of the following variations are independent of each other and refer back to this situation.

Changes in Fixed Costs

(a) If ABC's fixed costs increase from $80,000 to $100,000, what is the new break-even point in units and in sales dollars?

Solution: At the break-even point, fixed costs = Total CM.
$$\$100,000 = \$4Q$$
$$Q = \$100,000 \div \$4 = 25,000 \text{ units}$$
$$QP = 25,000 \times \$10 = \$250,000$$

(b) If fixed costs decrease to $70,000, what would be the new break-even point in units and in sales dollars?

Solution: $\$70,000 = \$4Q$
$$Q = \$70,000 \div \$4 = 17,500 \text{ units}$$
$$QP = 17,500 \times \$10 = \$175,000$$

Change in Target Income (Before and After Tax) and Desired Volume

(a) Assume ABC would like to increase the target operating income to $30,000. How many units must be sold if no other variables change?

$$\begin{aligned} \textit{Solution: } \$30,000 &= \$4Q - \$80,000 \\ \$110,000 &= \$4Q \\ Q &= \$110,000 \div \$4 = 27,500 \text{ units} \end{aligned}$$

(b) The operating income of $30,000 in (a) above was before taxes. What if the tax rate is 40%, and ABC would still like to achieve a target income of $30,000 after taxes? How many units must be sold if no other variables will change?

Solution: Since the tax rate is 40%, the income after taxes equals operating income $\times$ (1 − 0.40). If the target income after taxes is $30,000, then:

Operating income before taxes $\times$ 0.60 = $30,000
Operating income before taxes = $30,000 $\div$ 0.60 = $50,000

Now,

$$\begin{aligned} \$50,000 &= \$4Q - \$80,000 \\ \$130,000 &= \$4Q \\ Q &= \$130,000 \div \$4 = 32,500 \text{ units} \end{aligned}$$

Determination of New Selling Price

(a) Assume ABC cannot sell more than the current volume of 25,000 units, but it still would like to achieve $30,000 operating income before taxes. What selling price must it charge per unit if the demand for ABC products is not sensitive to changes in price (i.e., it is not price-elastic) and no other variables will change?

$$\begin{aligned} \textit{Solution: } \$30,000 &= 25,000(P - \$6) - \$80,000 \\ \$30,000 &= 25,000P - \$150,000 - \$80,000 \\ \$260,000 &= 25,000P \\ P &= \$260,000 \div 25,000 = \$10.40 \end{aligned}$$

(b) Assume the same facts as in (a) above except that ABC would like to achieve $30,000 net income after 40% taxes.

Solution: We know that, to achieve $30,000 income after 40% taxes, we need $50,000 income before taxes. Thus,

$$\begin{aligned} \$50,000 &= 25,000(P - \$6) - \$80,000 \\ \$50,000 &= 25,000P - \$150,000 - \$80,000 \\ \$280,000 &= 25,000P \\ P &= \$280,000 \div 25,000 = \$11.20 \end{aligned}$$

Higher Fixed Costs and Sales Volume

Assume that the marketing manager of ABC suggests spending $20,000 on a television advertising campaign to increase sales volume by 4,000 units to 29,000 units. No other variables will change. Should this suggestion be implemented?

Solution: We will determine whether the advertising will increase or decrease operating income.

$$\text{Operating income (I)} = Q \times CM - \text{Fixed costs}$$
$$= 29,000(\$10 - \$6) - \$100,000$$
$$= \$116,000 - \$100,000 = \$16,000$$

The new operating income of $16,000 is below the original operating income of $20,000. The suggestion should be rejected.

Alternative solution using incremental analysis:

$$\text{Incremental I} = \text{Incremental CM} - \text{Incremental fixed costs}$$
$$\text{Incremental I} = 4,000(\$10 - \$6) - \$20,000$$
$$= \$16,000 - \$20,000 = -\$4,000$$

Since the incremental income is a negative $4,000, the suggestion should be rejected. By using an incremental analysis, we did not have to deal with the existing sales volume, fixed costs, or operating income. We only used the incremental portions: the incremental CM and fixed costs.

Higher Fixed Costs, Lower Selling Price, and Higher Sales Volume

(a) The marketing manager predicts that a $20,000 advertising campaign and a reduction of the selling price by 5%, from $10 to $9.50, will increase the sales volume by 20%, from 25,000 units to 30,000 units. Should this suggestion be implemented?

Solution: $I = 30,000(\$9.50 - \$6) - \$100,000$
$$= \$105,000 - \$100,000 = \$5,000$$

Since the new operating income is lower than the original income of $20,000, this suggestion should be rejected.

(b) Refer to (a). By what percentage must sales volume increase to make the marketing manager's suggestion (of increasing advertising expenses by $20,000 and reducing selling price by $0.50) acceptable?

Solution: For the suggestion to be acceptable, operating income must exceed $20,000. Find the sales volume that will yield at least $20,000 of income.

$$\$20,000 = Q(\$9.50 - \$6) - \$100,000$$
$$\$20,000 = \$3.50Q - \$100,000$$
$$\$120,000 = \$3.50Q$$
$$Q = \$120,000 \div \$3.50 = 34,286 \text{ units}$$

Thus, at least 34,286 units must be sold. This represents a 37% increase [(34,286 ÷ 25,000) − 1].

Lower Variable Cost and Lower Sales Volume

Assume the purchasing manager of ABC suggests that the company buy its raw materials from a new supplier whose raw materials are cheaper. Despite the lower quality of the materials, this will reduce variable cost to $4.80. The lower quality will lead to a lower sales volume, but the volume reduction is expected to be at most 10%, or 2,500 units. Should this suggestion be accepted?

> *Solution:* Determine the new operating income for the expected sales volume of 22,500 units and compare to the current level.

$$I = 22,500(\$10 - \$4.80) - \$80,000$$
$$= \$117,000 - \$80,000 = \$37,000$$

The new income is higher than the current income of $20,000. Accept the suggestion. However, management may want to consider the impact of lower quality products on the company's reputation and the competitive position in the market before implementing the suggestion.

Replacing Fixed Costs with Variable Costs; Point of Indifference

Assume the sales manager of ABC suggests that salespersons' compensation be changed from fixed salaries to strictly commissions. Fixed costs will decrease $30,000, and salespersons will be paid 20% commissions on sales. Sales volume will increase by 40%, from 25,000 to 35,000 units. Should the suggestion be accepted?

> *Solution:* The new variable costs will be $6 + 20% of $10 selling price, or $8. Fixed costs decrease from $80,000 to $50,000.

$$I = 35,000(\$10 - \$8) - \$50,000$$
$$= 35,000 \times \$2 - \$50,000 = \$20,000$$

The new income is the same as the existing income of $20,000. It makes no difference whether the suggestion is implemented. If sales volume increases more than 40%, the suggestion would be attractive. An increase of exactly 40% produces a situation to which management is **indifferent.**

Changes in Selling Price and Volume; CM-Related Variable Costs

The sales manager suggests that instead of paying salespersons 20% commissions on sales, the company should pay them commissions equivalent to 30% of contribution margin. Salespersons will have the authority to reduce selling price per unit (as long as it does not fall below a certain minimum specified by the company) to increase sales volume and total contribution margin.

If this is implemented, salespersons will decrease selling price to $9.90, and the sales volume is expected to increase by 50% to 37,500 units. Should this suggestion be implemented?

Solution: I = CM × Q × (1 − 0.30) − $80,000

I = ($9.90 − $6) × 37,500 units × 0.7 − $80,000

I = $102,375 − $80,000 = $22,375

The new income is higher than the current income of $20,000. The suggestion should be accepted.

Basing salespersons commissions on the contribution margin, rather than on sales, may be particularly beneficial, if the company sells more than one product. Salespersons will focus on selling the products that will maximize the contribution margin, and their commissions. Some companies may also deduct salespersons' travel and/or entertainment expenses from contribution margin before calculating the commission. This may encourage salespersons to minimize their own expenses.

Special Order; Incremental Analysis

Assume that a foreign importer is willing to order 10,000 units from ABC if the price is right. Accepting this order will have no impact on the domestic sales. ABC does not want to deal with the complexities of foreign trade unless it can earn at least $5,000 in operating income from the deal. What is the right price?

Solution: Incremental I = Incremental CM − Incremental fixed costs

$5,000 = 10,000(P − $6) − $0

$5,000 = 10,000P − $60,000

$65,000 = 10,000P

P = $65,000 ÷ 10,000 = $6.50

Nonprofit Entities

Making profit is not the objective of such organizations as universities, churches, and governmental units. However, some of those organizations may have activities for which CVP analysis is useful.

For example, a university may use CVP analysis to determine what tuition to charge based on student enrollments and the variable and fixed costs of operating the university. A church planning a fund-raising dinner may use CVP analysis to determine the number of people who must attend, given the price per ticket and the variable and fixed costs of this function. A state government may use CVP analysis to decide how much toll to charge per car to recover the costs of a planned highway in a given number of years.

(a) Assume a university has a dormitory of 500 rooms for student housing. Fixed costs associated with the dormitory (repairs and maintenance, depreciation, etc.) are $10,000 per month. Variable costs (electricity, gas, water, food, etc.) are $200 per occupied room per month. How much monthly rent per room should the university charge to break even?

Solution: Let R be the monthly rent. To break even,

$$500(R - \$200) - \$10{,}000 = 0$$
$$500R - \$100{,}000 - \$10{,}000 = 0$$
$$500R = \$110{,}000$$
$$R = \$110{,}000 \div 500 = \$220$$

(b) Assume a church is planning a fund-raising event to raise $50,000. The organizers estimate that a reasonable price per ticket is $50. They can get entertainers for $2,500, and a restaurant is willing to provide as many meals as they need for $15 each. How many tickets must be sold to raise the $50,000?

Solution: Let Q be the number of tickets.

$$\$50{,}000 = Q(\$50 - \$15) - \$2{,}500$$
$$\$50{,}000 = \$35Q - \$2{,}500$$
$$\$52{,}500 = \$35Q$$
$$Q = \$52{,}500 \div \$35 = 1{,}500 \text{ tickets}$$

(c) Assume a state government is planning to build a toll highway that is estimated to cost $50 million to construct. Of these $50 million, the state will pay $30 million, and the federal government is willing to pay $20 million, provided the toll does not exceed $0.30 per car, of which the federal government will get back $0.05 per car. The fixed costs of toll collection are estimated at $100,000 a year. It is estimated that about 7 million cars per year will pass through the only toll booth to be built on the planned highway. The governor has made it clear that she will veto the project if it will take more than 20 years for the state to recover its $30 million.

1. Would the governor approve the project, assuming the toll is $0.30? Assume that the time value of money is not considered in this analysis.
2. What is the lowest toll that can be charged?

Solution:

1. The governor will approve the project if it will take 20 years or less to recover $30,000,000.

Amount of the fund to be accumulated per year
= Number of cars × (Toll − Federal government's take) − Fixed costs
= 7,000,000($0.30 − $0.05) − $100,000
= $1,750,000 − $100,000
= $1,650,000

Years to take to recover the $30,000,000
= $30,000,000 ÷ $1,650,000 = 18.18 years

The governor will approve the project because the state will be able to get its $30 million back in less than 20 years.

2. The lowest toll (T) should still generate enough fund every year to recover $30,000,000 in 20 years.

Amount of fund that is generated every year
$$= 7{,}000{,}000(T - \$0.05) - \$100{,}000$$

Amount of fund that must be generated every year
$$= \$30{,}000{,}000 \div 20 \text{ years}$$

Now,

$$
\begin{aligned}
7{,}000{,}000(T - \$0.05) - \$100{,}000 &= \$30{,}000{,}000 \div 20 \text{ years} \\
7{,}000{,}000T - \$350{,}000 - \$100{,}000 &= \$1{,}500{,}000 \\
7{,}000{,}000T &= \$1{,}950{,}000 \\
T &= \$1{,}950{,}000 \div 7{,}000{,}000 \\
&= \$0.2786
\end{aligned}
$$

Thus, the lowest toll is $0.28 per car.

PRODUCT MIX AND CVP ANALYSIS

For simplicity, we have assumed so far that the company produces and/or sells one product. In reality, most companies produce and/or sell more than one product. A company with multiple products can use CVP analysis if the **product mix,** the relative proportion of each product to total sales in units or in dollars, remains constant.

Product Mix in Units

Generation X's Corner, a snack shop for young people, sells Snack X and Drink X. Monthly operating data follow:

	Snack X	Drink X
Quantity (Q)	200,000	100,000
Selling price per unit (P)	$.55	$.50
Variable cost per unit (V)	.33	.18
Contribution margin per unit	$.22	$.32
Fixed costs per month	$57,000	

EXHIBIT 3-9

Generation X's Corner
Contribution Income Statement

	Snack X		Drink X		Total	
	Amount	%	Amount	%	Amount	%
Quantity (in units)	200,000	67	100,000	33	300,000	100
Sales	$110,000	100	$50,000	100	$160,000	100
Variable costs	66,000	60	18,000	36	84,000	52.5
Contribution margin	$ 44,000	40	$32,000	64	76,000	47.5
Fixed costs					57,000	
Operating Income					$ 19,000	

A contribution income statement, shown by product and for the combined operating results, are presented in Exhibit 3-9.

Computation of the Break-Even Point

When a company sells more than one product, the break-even point may be computed in different ways as discussed below:

Using an Average CM Ratio: Exhibit 3-9 indicates that the average (or overall) CM ratio is 47.5%. Thus, we calculate the *break-even point in sales dollars* as:

$$\frac{\text{Fixed costs}}{\text{CM Ratio}} = \frac{\$57,000}{0.475} = \$120,000$$

Using a Weighted Average CM: If the product mix is assumed to be constant at two snacks for every glass of drink sold, a weighted average CM may be computed as follows:

	Product Mix	CM Per Unit	Weighted Average CM
Snack	2/3	$0.22	$0.1467
Drink	1/3	$0.32	0.1066
			$0.2533

The break-even point in units is then computed as:

$$\frac{\text{Fixed costs}}{\text{Weighted average CM}} = \frac{\$57,000}{\$0.2533} = 225,000$$

Of these, 150,000 (2/3) would be snacks and 75,000 (1/3) would be glasses of drink.

Proof: At the break-even point: Total CM = Total fixed costs

Snacks:	150,000 × $0.22	=	$33,000
Drinks:	75,000 × $0.32	=	24,000
			$57,000

Change in Product Mix and CVP Analysis

If the product mix does not remain constant, some confusing changes in operating profits may result. Depending on how many units of high CM and low CM products are sold, operating profits could change in any direction.

Refer to Exhibit 3-9. Assume a decrease in the total number of units sold, by 10% from 300,000 to only 270,000. Also assume a product mix of 1 snack and 4 glasses of drink instead of a product mix of 2 snacks and one glass of drink. Despite the decrease in sales units and sales dollars, profits will increase as shown in Exhibit 3-10.

EXHIBIT 3-10

Generation X's Corner
Contribution Income Statement

	Snack X		Drink X		Total	
	Amount	%	Amount	%	Amount	%
Quantity (in units)	54,000	20	216,000	80	270,000	100
Sales	$29,700	100	$108,000	100	$137,700	100
Variable costs	17,820	60	38,880	36	56,700	41.2
Contribution margin	$11,880	40	$ 69,120	64	$ 81,000	58.8
Fixed costs					57,000	
Operating Income					$ 24,000	

Let's compare the operating results presented in Exhibits 3-9 and 3-10. While sales volume in units decreased by 10% and dollar sales decreased by about 14% (from $160,000 to $137,700), operating income increased by 26% (from $19,000 to $24,000). This is a result of a preferable change in the product mix from 2-to-1 to 1-to-4 between snacks and drinks .

If there is an unfavorable change in product mix, such as to 4 snacks to 1 drink, profits will go down, even when there is an increase in the number of units sold and dollar sales.

CVP ANALYSIS: ASSUMPTIONS AND LIMITATIONS

Throughout our discussion of CVP analysis in this chapter, we have made certain simplifying assumptions. We summarize all these assumptions below so that managers would be careful about them:

1. Total costs for the company can be reliably broken down into variable and fixed components.

2. All variables of the CVP analysis, i.e., variable cost per unit, selling price per unit, and fixed costs per period, do not change within the relevant range of activity.

3. The efficiency of workers and equipment remains constant throughout the relevant range of activity.

4. Product mix remains constant throughout the relevant range of activity.

5. Inventory remains constant throughout the period. That is, there should be no significant difference between beginning and ending inventories.

6. Technology, such as input/output ratio, remains constant throughout the relevant period and relevant range.

While the above simplifying assumptions differ somewhat from reality, they make CVP analysis easy to understand and use. Some of these assumptions may be relaxed. However, this can be done only at the expense of making CVP analysis more complex and more difficult to understand and use. Competent managers could keep these assumptions in mind and use a range of values for every variable. Then they can compare the results.

SUMMARY

In this chapter, we discussed the basic concept of CVP analysis, the contribution margin concept, some applications of CVP analysis and contribution margin concept, product mix and CVP analysis, and assumptions and limitations of CVP analysis.

The concept of CVP analysis and the contribution margin approach are useful in many planning and decision making situations. While CVP analysis is easy to use when dealing with a single product, it may still be used in multi-product cases, if we know the product mix and the CM per unit of each product. We assume the product mix will remain constant. While CVP analysis is useful, it is subject to certain limiting assumptions that the user must keep in mind.

BASIC CONCEPTS AND TERMS

Break-even point	Margin of safety
Contribution margin concept	Operating leverage
Contribution margin ratio	Product mix
Cost-volume-profit graph	Profit-loss line
Degree of operating leverage	Volume-profit graph
Indifference	

■ SELF-REVIEW PROBLEM

GP, Inc. sells a type of cellular phone. The operating data are presented below:

	Per Unit
Sales price	$20
Variable cost	12
Contribution margin	$?
Fixed costs per year	$120,000
Current sales volume	20,000 units

Answer the following questions based on the provided data:

1. a. What is the company's variable cost ratio?
   b. What is the contribution margin ratio?
2. What is the break-even point in units and in sales dollars?
3. What is the current operating income? Use the contribution approach.

4. How many units must be sold to achieve the following:
   a. Operating income of $60,000 before tax?
   b. Operating income of $60,000 after tax? Tax rate is 40%.
5. If fixed costs increase to $160,000, what will the new break-even point be in units and in sales dollars?
6. If variable cost per unit increases to $15, what will the new break-even point be in units and in sales dollars?
7. If GP spends $80,000 for advertising per year, volume will increase by 50%. Should the money be spent for advertising?
8. If GP changes its policy on salespersons' compensation from $30,000 fixed salaries to 20% commissions on sales, sales volume will increase by 50%. Should GP make the change?
9. Refer to (8) above. If GP wants to set the sales commission rate so that income increases by 50%, what should the commission rate be? Assume that volume will increase by 50% regardless of the rate.
10. Compute GP's margin of safety in dollars, units, and percentage, given the current level of sales.
11. a. What is the degree of operating leverage, given the current level of sales?
    b. Using the result of (a), answer the following:
       An advertising campaign is expected to increase the sales by 10%. By what percentage would operating income increase?
    c. Prepare a brief income statement, showing the 10% increase in sales. Does the income statement confirm the result of (b)?

Solution:

1. a. Variable cost ratio $= \$12 \div \$20 = 0.60$
   b. Contribution margin ratio $=$ CM $\div$ Sales price
      $= (\$20 - \$12) \div \$20 = 0.40$

2. BEP in units $= \dfrac{\text{Fixed costs}}{\text{CM}} = \dfrac{\$120,000}{\$20 - \$12} = 15,000$ units

   BEP in sales dollars $= 15,000$ units $\times \$20 = \$300,000$, or
   $\dfrac{\text{Fixed costs}}{\text{CM ratio}} = \dfrac{\$120,000}{0.40} = \$300,000$

3. Operating income $=$ Total CM $-$ Fixed costs
   $= 20,000 \times \$8 - \$120,000$
   $= \$160,000 - \$120,000 = \$40,000$

4. a. Units to be sold $= \dfrac{\$120,000 + \$60,000}{\$8} = 22,500$ units
   b. If the tax rate is 40%,
      Income after tax $= (1 - 0.4) \times$ Pre-tax income
      $\$60,000 = 0.6 \times$ Pre-tax income
      Thus,
      Pre-tax income $= \$60,000 \div 0.6 = \$100,000$.
      Units to be sold $= \dfrac{\$120,000 + \$100,000}{\$8} = 27,500$ units

5. $\text{BEP in units} = \dfrac{\text{Fixed costs}}{\text{CM}} = \dfrac{\$160,000}{\$8} = 20,000 \text{ units}$

$\text{BEP in sales dollars} = 20,000 \text{ units} \times \$20 = \$400,000$

6. $\text{BEP in units} = \dfrac{\$120,000}{\$20 - \$15} = 24,000 \text{ units}$

$\text{BEP in sales dollars} = 24,000 \text{ units} \times \$20 = \$480,000$

7. If \$80,000 is spent for advertising:

$$\text{New fixed costs} = \$120,000 + \$80,000 = \$200,000$$
$$\text{New sales volume} = 20,000 \text{ units} \times 1.50 = 30,000 \text{ units}$$
$$\text{New income} = \text{Total CM} - \text{Fixed costs}$$
$$= 30,000 \times \$8 - \$200,000 = \$40,000$$

Since the current income is also \$40,000, the company would be indifferent to the advertising campaign.

8. If the change is made:

New fixed costs	$= \$120,000 - \$30,000 = \$90,000$
New variable cost per unit	$= \$12 + (20\% \times \$20) = \$16$
New volume	$= 20,000 \times 1.50 = 30,000 \text{ units}$
New income	$= \text{Total CM} - \text{Fixed costs}$
	$= 30,000 \times (\$20 - \$16) - \$90,000$
	$= \$120,000 - \$90,000 = \$30,000$

Since the new income is less than the current income of \$40,000, the change should not be made.

9.
New volume	$= 20,000 \times 1.50 = 30,000 \text{ units}$
New fixed costs	$= \$120,000 - \$30,000 = \$90,000$
New income	$= \$40,000 \times 1.50 = \$60,000$

Income $= \text{Total CM} - \text{Fixed costs}$

Now let X = new variable cost per unit. Then,

$$\$60,000 = 30,000(\$20 - X) - \$90,000$$
$$\$60,000 = \$600,000 - 30,000X - \$90,000$$
$$30,000X = \$600,000 - \$90,000 - \$60,000$$
$$30,000X = \$450,000$$
$$X = \$450,000 \div 30,000 = \$15$$

The new variable cost per unit should be \$15. Since the current variable cost is \$12, the increase of \$3 represents sales commission. Three dollars out of the price per unit of \$20 represents 15% (\$3 ÷ \$20).

10. Margin of safety in dollars

$$= \text{Sales} \qquad - \text{Break-even sales}$$
$$= \$20 \times 20,000 - \$300,000$$
$$= \$400,000 \qquad - \$300,000 = \$100,000$$

Margin of safety in units

$$= \text{Units sold} - \text{BEP in units}$$
$$= 20,000 \qquad - 15,000 = 5,000 \text{ units}$$

Margin of safety in %

$$= \$100,000 \div \$400,000 = 25\%, \text{ or}$$
$$5,000 \div 20,000 = 25\%$$

11. a. Degree of Operating Leverage $= \dfrac{\text{Contribution Margin}}{\text{Operating Income}}$

$$= \dfrac{\$160,000}{\$40,000} = 4$$

b.

Increase in sales.................	10%
Degree of operating leverage......	× 4
Increase in operating income	40%

c. A total of 22,000 units will be sold after a 10% increase.

	Total	Per Unit
Sales (22,000 units)	$440,000	$20
Variable costs	264,000	12
Contribution margin	176,000	$ 8
Fixed costs	120,000	
Operating income	$ 56,000	

The new operating income of $56,000 represents a 40% increase from the previous $40,000, since the $16,000 increase is 40% of $40,000. Accordingly, we have confirmed the result of (b).

■ REVIEW QUESTIONS

3-1 Explain the basic concept of cost-volume-profit analysis.

3-2 What is meant by break-even point in units and in dollars, and how is each computed?

3-3 Describe what is meant by the contribution margin, and explain how it is computed in total, per unit, and as a percentage of sales.

3-4 What is the significance of the contribution margin ratio?

3-5 If you have to choose between two companies, one with a high CM ratio and high fixed costs and another with a low CM ratio and low fixed costs, which one would you choose?

3-6 What is meant by operating leverage, and how is the degree of operating leverage computed?

3-7 Why is the degree of operating leverage highest when the level of operations is closest to the break-even point, and vice versa?

3-8 What is meant by margin of safety? Present three forms of computing margin of safety.

3-9 What kinds of actions can management take when the margin of safety is too low?

3-10 Cost-volume-profit analysis can be used in a variety of internal decision making situations. Present an equation that can be used to calculate operating income and for making those decisions. Use the following symbols:

Operating income:	I
Quantity sold:	Q
Selling price per unit:	P
Variable cost per unit:	V
Fixed costs for the period:	F

Explain how a decision can be made using such an equation and how such an equation can be used to derive the break-even point.

3-11 Can break-even point be computed when an organization sells more than one product? If yes, explain how the computation works.

3-12 If a company sells more than one product, is it possible that total units sold and total sales revenue decrease while total operating income increases? Why or why not?

3-13 What are the major assumptions and limitations of CVP analysis?

🌐 INTERNET PROJECT

Web 3-1:

Websites: www.parkplace.com
              www.treasureislandcasino.com
              www.trump.com

The websites listed above represent entertainment companies that own casinos, resorts, and hotels.

Required:

Choose one of the websites. Search the site for information on its recent expansion of an existing casino or an acquisition of a new one. Using the statistics on casinos provided in the chapter, construct your own CVP scenario. You need to formulate a CVP case and find a solution to the case question(s).

■ EXERCISES

E3-1   Basics of CVP Analysis

D&D Company manufactures a single toy product and sells it to kindergartners.
The toy manufacturing and sales data for one recent period are presented below:

Selling price per unit	$ 40
Variable cost per unit	$ 16
Fixed costs for the period	$180,000
Sales volume	12,000 units

Required:

1. What is the break-even point in units and in sales dollars?
2. What is the total contribution margin at the break-even point? Answer the question without any computations.
3. At the given sales level of 12,000 units, what is the contribution margin? What is the operating income?
4. The company has set a target operating income of $60,000 for the next period. How many units should be sold to achieve the target?
5. Prepare a contribution income statement based on the target sales level you computed in (4).

E3-2   Margin of Safety

Refer to the original data in E3-1. A recession hits the economy, and D&D is expecting a decrease in sales.

Required:

1. How much decrease in sales units can the company have to experience before it incurs operating losses?
2. What is the margin of safety (MS) in dollars and percentage?
3. Due to the recession, the company's sales have decreased by $150,000. Does the company still make a profit? Answer the question without any new computations.
4. Due to the recession, the company's sales have decreased 30% from the original level. Does the company still make a profit? Answer the question without any new computations.

E3-3   Operating Leverage

Refer to the original data in E3-1. Thanks to the growing population of kindergartners, the sales of D&D's toy are expected to increase 10% for the next period.

Required:

1. Compute the degree of operating leverage for the original data.
2. If the toy sales increase 10% from the original 12,000 units, what is the company's new operating income? Answer the question using the operating leverage concept.
3. Prepare a contribution income statement to prove that your answer in (2) is correct.
4. Assume that the company's sales decrease 20% from the original 12,000 units. What is the company's new operating income? Answer the question using the operating leverage concept.
5. Prepare a contribution income statement to prove that your answer in (4) is correct.

E3-4 Change in Variable Costs and CVP Analysis

Cerritos, Inc. manufactures and sells a single product. The product sells for $50 per unit. Its variable cost ratio is 60%, and fixed costs are $150,000 per year.

Required:

1. What is the contribution margin (CM) per unit?
2. What is the break-even point in units and in sales dollars?
3. What is the total CM at the break-even point? Answer the question without any computations.
4. At the given sales level of 8,000 units, compute the total CM and the operating income.
5. How many units must be sold to earn an operating income of $50,000?
6. Refer to (4). How much can sales (in units) decrease from the given level before the company incurs any operating loss?
7. Due to wage increases, the company's variable costs increase $3 per unit from the previous level. Other conditions remain the same.
   a. What is the new break-even point in units?
   b. How many units must the company sell to earn an operating income of $50,000?

E3-5 Changes in Costs and CVP Analysis

Ecobag, Inc. manufactures and sells a reusable grocery shopping bag. The following are selected sales and cost data for the last quarter:

Selling price	$ 40 per unit
Number of units sold	12,000 units
Contribution margin ratio	55%
Fixed costs	$180,000

Required:

1. Compute the total variable costs incurred for the quarter.
2. What is the quarterly break-even point in units sold and in sales dollars?
3. Prepare a contribution income statement for the quarter.
4. The company wants to earn an operating income of $60,000. How many units must be sold to achieve the desired income?
5. The company has decided to automate its sewing process. The automation will reduce direct labor costs by $2 per bag produced and increase fixed costs by $60,000 per quarter.
   a. Compute the new break-even point in units sold and sales dollars.
   b. How many units must be sold to achieve an operating income of $60,000 when automation is implemented?

E3-6   Changing Sales and CVP Analysis

Refer to the original data of Ecobag, Inc. in E3-5. Answer each of the following questions independently.

1. Due to a weakening economy in the region, the company's sales have been declining. How much decrease in sales units can the company experience before it incurs an operating loss?
2. Assume that Ecobag's sales actually decrease 15% from the original 12,000 units. What is the new operating income? Answer the question using the operating leverage concept. Other conditions remain the same as the original data.
3. Prepare a contribution income statement to prove that your answer in (2) is correct.
4. The regional economy has recovered from the recession. Now sales show an increase of 10% over the original level of 12,000 units. Compute the new operating income. Use the operating leverage concept.
5. Prepare a contribution income statement to prove that your answer in (4) is correct.

E3-7   Determination of Selling Price

Gamma Chapter of a national business students society is planning its annual fundraising dinner. The following are relevant cost data for this year's dinner:

Hotel dinner cost per person..............................	$ 22
String trio...	500
Program printing and mailing	400
Travel expenses for the guest speaker	1,300

Gamma Chapter has tentatively set the dinner ticket price at $50.

Required:

1. How many tickets must be sold to at least break even?

2. The chapter estimates that about 250 seats will be sold. What will be the net profit from the dinner if the estimate turns out to be correct?

3. The chapter management is rethinking whether the dinner ticket price should be lower to make it more affordable to students. The dinner should still make a profit of $3,000, which has already been budgeted as income in this year's chapter activity plan. What price should be charged for each ticket? Assume that 250 seats will be sold and the target profit is $3,000.

 E3-8   Changing Sales Price and Volume; Changing Costs

FL Company's income statement for the last quarter is presented below:

	Total	Per Unit
Sales (10,000 units)	$250,000	$25
Variable costs	100,000	10
Contribution margin	150,000	$15
Fixed costs	80,000	
Operating income.	$ 70,000	

Required:

1. Prepare a new income statement under each of the following changing conditions. Each case (a, b, and c) is independent of the others.

2. For each case, indicate which of the five items (sales, variable costs, CM, fixed costs, and operating income) changes in the same percentage and direction as the changing condition.
   a. The number of units sold increases 20%.
   b. The selling price decreases 20%.
   c. Variable costs per unit increase 10%.

E3-9   Product Mix and CVP Analysis

Aerobics-R-Us, Inc. sells two fitness-related products, Alpha and Beta. Quarterly operating data are shown below:

	Product	
	Alpha	Beta
Units sold	8,000	12,000
Selling price per unit	$25	$20
Variable cost ratio	55%	50%
Fixed costs	$130,000	

Required:

1. Prepare a quarterly contribution income statement showing the results by each product and for the company.

2. Compute the break-even point in sales dollars using the company's average CM ratio.
3. Compute the break-even point in units using the weighted average CM. Specify units for each product.

■ PROBLEMS

P3-10   Basics of CVP Analysis; Graphing

Smart Kids, Inc. has developed a manual, called Smart K, which is intended for use by parents of kindergartners for early development of children's analytical skills.

Initial estimates on the sales and costs of the company's first year operations follow:

	Per Unit
Selling price.	$ 50
Variable costs	$ 20

	Per Year
Fixed costs:	
Rent	$ 9,000
After-sale teaching support	12,000
Advertising	30,000
Other office expenses	6,000
Total fixed costs	$57,000

The advertising cost of $30,000 (presented above) is estimated for advertisements on the World Wide Web (WWW). The ads in the online magazine are expected to generate sales of 4,000 units in the first year.

Required:

1. What is the break-even point in units and in sales dollars?
2. Draw a CVP graph presenting cost and sales estimates from a zero-sales level up to 6,000 manuals sold for the first year. Mark the break-even point on the graph.
3. At the given sales level of 4,000 units, what is the total contribution margin? What is the operating income?
4. The company has set a target operating income of $100,000 for the next period. How many units must be sold to achieve the target?
5. Prepare a contribution income statement based on the target sales level computed in (4).
6. In addition to the ads on the WWW, the company is considering advertisements in newspapers around the state. The newspaper ads would cost $15,000 and generate additional sales of 800 manuals in the first year. Should the com-

pany try the promotion through newspapers? Assume no other changes in the variables and limit your consideration to the first year.

P3-11 Basic CVP Analysis

Each of the following situations is independent.
1. Data for a single-product company:

Selling price per unit	$30
Contribution margin ratio	40%
Fixed expenses per year	$120,000

    a. What are the variable costs per unit?
    b. What is the break-even point in units and in dollar sales?
    c. What sales level in units and in dollar sales is required to achieve a target income of $24,000?
2. ETech, Inc. sells golf equipment at a price of $12. The variable costs of producing and selling the product are $8 per unit. Fixed costs per year amount to $24,000. The sales volume for the current year is 9,000 units. ETech pays sales commissions of 5% of sales.
    a. Compute the contribution margin per unit.
    b. Compute the operating income for the current year. Do not prepare an income statement.
3. Flashlights, Inc. sold 25,000 flashlights last quarter and produced a contribution margin of $3 on each flashlight sold. Fixed costs amounted to $60,000 last quarter and are expected to increase by $30,000 in the current quarter. This quarter the company wants to earn the same income as last quarter. How many units will have to be sold in the current quarter? Assume the CM per unit remains the same.

P3-12 CVP Analysis; Global Market

Soothe, Inc. manufactures and sells a medical product that helps control arthritis pain. Price and cost data regarding the single product are provided below:

Selling price per unit	$20
Variable costs per unit:	
Raw materials	$ 8
Direct labor	4
Manufacturing overhead	2
Marketing	1
	$15
Annual fixed costs	$400,000
Forecasted annual domestic sales volume	100,000 units

Consider each situation independently, unless stated otherwise.
1. What is the break-even point in units and in sales dollars?

2. The company estimates that its direct labor costs will increase by $1 per unit next year. How many units will it have to sell next year to break even?

3. Refer to the original data. If the company wants to make a profit of $90,000, how many units does it have to sell?

4. With some help from the U.S. Commerce Department, Soothe, Inc. has entered the Japanese market. The product will be imported from the U.S. plant, but will be packaged in a local facility in Japan which is rented for $140,000 per year. The same selling price will be quoted, and variable costs will remain the same for the product, except that overseas shipping will add $2 per unit to the product cost. No fixed costs of the U.S. plant will be charged to the Japanese operations. A market analyst predicts first-year sales of 12,000 units in the Japanese market. How many units does the company have to sell in the U.S. market if its company-wide target income is $90,000?

5. Refer to the data in (4). Assume that the company's product has a tremendous appeal in the Japanese market, and 12,000 units can still be sold even at a much higher price. What selling price should be quoted in order to break even in the Japanese operations? Also assume that the company does not charge its fixed costs of the U.S. plant to the Japanese operations.

P3-13   Variable vs. Fixed Costs; Point of Indifference

Informkids, Inc. produces and sells an educational video which it developed five years ago. Since the company's sales in the U.S. have been static in recent months, it is considering opening a sales outlet in Canada. Thanks to NAFTA, the company foresees no problem in establishing a store in Toronto.

The following cost and revenue estimates are based on a typical store's operations with some necessary adjustments for the Canadian operation:

	Per Video
Selling price	$20
Variable costs:	
Video duplication cost	$ 3
Other variable costs	5
Total variable costs	$ 8

	Per Quarter
Fixed costs:	
Rent	$15,000
Salaries	44,000
Advertising, etc.	10,000
Total fixed costs	$69,000

Required:

1. What is the quarterly break-even point in units and in dollar sales?

2. If 9,000 units are sold, what is the Canadian operation's total CM and operating income?

3. The company wants to provide more performance-based incentives to its Canadian sales force by reducing fixed salaries to $30,000 per quarter and paying sales commissions of 5% of sales.

   a. What is the new quarterly break-even point in units?

   b. Assume a sales level of 9,000 units. Would the performance-based incentive policy generate more profit than the original policy?

4. Compare the original policy and the performance-based incentive policy in (3) above.

   a. At which sales level does the company make the same amount of profit under either plan?

   b. What you computed in (a) is called the point of indifference. Explain why it is called the point of indifference.

5. Refer back to the incentive policy in (3) above. In order to provide an extra incentive to the Canadian sales force, the company considers paying an additional 5% commission (making the total commission 10%) on each video sold in excess of the break-even point. What is the operating income if 6,500 units are sold?

P3-14   CVP Analysis; Multiple Choice

Villa Olivia Ski Company recently expanded its manufacturing capacity which will allow it to produce up to 15,000 pairs of cross country skis of the mountaineering model or the touring model. The sales department assures management that it can sell between 9,000 and 13,000 of either product this year. Because the models are very similar, Villa Olivia will produce only one of the two models.

The following information was compiled by the accounting department:

	Model	
	Mountaineering	**Touring**
Selling price per unit	$88.00	$80.00
Variable cost per unit	$52.80	$52.80

Fixed costs will total $369,600 if the mountaineering model is produced, but will be only $316,800 if the touring model is produced. Villa Olivia Ski Company is subject to a 40% income tax rate.

1. The contribution margin ratio of the touring model is
   a. 40.0%.
   b. 66.0%.
   c. 51.5%.
   d. 34.0%.
   e. Some amount other than those given above.

2. If the Villia Olivia Ski Company sales department could guarantee annual sales of 12,000 skis of either model, Villia Olivia would
   a. Produce touring skis because they have a lower fixed cost.

    b. Be indifferent as to which model is sold because each model has the same variable cost per unit.

    c. Produce mountaineering skis because they have a lower breakeven point.

    d. Be indifferent as to which model is sold because both are profitable.

    e. Produce mountaineering skis because they are more profitable.

3. How much would the variable cost per unit of the touring model have to change before it had the same breakeven point in units as the mountaineering model?

    a. $2.68/pair decrease.

    b. $4.53/pair increase.

    c. $5.03/pair decrease.

    d. $2.97/pair decrease.

    e. Some amount other than those given above.

4. If the variable cost per unit of touring skis decreases by 10%, and the total fixed cost of touring skis increases by 10%, the new breakeven point will be

    a. Unchanged from 11,648 pairs because the cost changes are equal and offsetting.

    b. 10,730 pairs.

    c. 13,007 pairs.

    d. 12,812 pairs.

    e. Some amount other than those given above.

5. Which one of the following statements is not an assumption made when employing a cost-volume-profit study for decision analysis?

    a. Volume is the only relevant factor affecting costs.

    b. Changes in beginning and ending inventory levels are insignificant in amount.

    c. Sales mix is variable as total volume changes.

    d. Fixed costs are constant over the relevant volume range.

    e. Efficiency and productivity are unchanged.

(CMA, adapted)

P3-15   Profit Objectives and Decision Alternatives; Limiting Assumptions

Almo Company manufactures and sells adjustable canopies that attach to motor homes and trailers. The market covers both new unit purchasers as well as replacement canopies. Almo developed its Year 9 business plan based on the assumption that canopies would sell at a price of $400 each. The variable costs for each canopy were projected at $200, and the annual fixed costs were budgeted at $100,000. Almo's after-tax profit objective was $240,000; the company's effective tax rate is 40%.

    While Almo's sales usually rise during the second quarter, the May financial statements reported that sales were not meeting expectations. For the first five months of the year, only 350 units had been sold at the established price, with variable costs as planned, and it was clear that the Year 9 after-tax profit projection would not be reached unless some actions were taken. Almo's president assigned a management committee to analyze the situation and develop several alternative courses of action. The following mutually exclusive alternatives were presented to the president.

Alternative 1: Reduce the sales price by $40. The sales organization forecasts that with the significantly reduced sales price, 2,700 units can be sold during the remainder of the year. Total fixed and unit variable costs will stay as budgeted.

Alternative 2: Lower variable costs per unit by $25 through the use of less expensive raw materials and slightly modified manufacturing techniques. The sales price will also be reduced by $30, and sales of 2,200 units for the remainder of the year are forecast.

Alternative 3: Cut fixed costs by $10,000 and lower the sales price by 5%. Variable costs per unit will be unchanged. Sales of 2,000 units are expected for the remainder of the year.

Required:

1. If no changes are made to the selling price or cost structure, determine the number of units that Almo Company must sell
   a. in order to break even.
   b. to achieve its after-tax profit objective.
2. Determine which one of the alternatives Almo Company should select to achieve its annual after-tax profit objective. Be sure to support your selection with appropriate calculations.
3. The precision and reliability of cost-volume-profit analysis are limited by several underlying assumptions. Identify at least four of these assumptions.

(CMA, adapted)

 P3-16 Product Mix and CVP Analysis

The Mix Company sells three products: X, Y, and Z. Budgeted sales by product and in total for the coming month are shown below:

	Product									
	X		Y		Z		Total	
Percentage of total sales	40%		35%		25%		100%	
Sales...............	$32,000	100%	$28,000	100%	$20,000	100%	$80,000	100%
Variable expenses....	20,800	65	11,200	40	12,000	60	44,000	55
Contribution margin..	$11,200	35%	$16,800	60%	$ 8,000	40%	36,000	45%
Fixed expenses........							26,325	
Operating income......							$ 9,675	

Break-even sales are budgeted as follows:

$$\frac{\$26,325}{0.45} = \$58,500$$

Operating income is budgeted at $9,675. Assume the following actual sales for the month:

Product	Actual Sales
X	$48,000
Y	8,000
Z	24,000
Total	$80,000

Required:

1. Prepare a contribution income statement for the month based on actual sales. Show the results by each product and for the company.
2. Compute the break-even point in dollar sales for the month based on the actual sales.
3. The company met its $80,000 sales budget for the month. Why are the operating income and break-even sales different from what was budgeted?
4. Assume that sales of the three products show an increase of 10% over the budgeted level of $80,000 and the product mix is maintained at the budgeted ratio of 40% X, 35% Y, and 25% Z. Compute the new operating income. Use the operating leverage concept.

P3-17   Comprehensive CVP Analysis; Variations in Price and Cost Structure; Graphing

MAZE, Inc. has developed a computer game, called Maze-in-the-City, which is based on a true story of an inner-city kid who overcomes adversities in his violent environment under the guidance of a priest who once was a gang member himself. Early tests have confirmed the game's appeal to teenagers and also revealed instructional values.

Initial estimates on the sales and costs of the company's first year operations follow:

	Per Unit
Selling price	$20
Variable costs	$14
Fixed costs:	Per Year
Rent	$12,000
Online customer support	25,000
Advertising	35,000
Other office expenses	8,000
Total fixed costs	$80,000

The computer games are duplicated and delivered to MAZE, Inc. by another multi-media company in West Hollywood, California. The advertising cost of $35,000 is estimated for advertisements in local newspapers, which are expected to generate sales of 15,000 units in the first year.

Required:

1. What is the break-even point in units and in sales dollars?
2. Draw a CVP graph presenting cost and sales estimates from a zero-sales level up to 20,000 units sold for the first year. Mark the break-even point on the graph.
3. At the given sales level of 15,000 units, what is the total contribution margin? What is the operating income?
4. The company wants to earn a target income of $50,000 in the first year. How many units should be sold to achieve the target income?
5. Assume the first year's sales were 15,000 units. It is now the second year of operations. The region's economy is entering a recession, and the company expects some decrease in sales. What percentage decrease in dollar sales can the company experience before it incurs an operating loss?
6. Refer to the original data. Because of the immense popularity, the sales of Maze-in-the-City increase by 60% from the original 15,000 units. What would be the new operating income? Answer the question using the operating leverage concept.
7. Refer to the original data. A marketing study reveals that a 30-second spot on educational TV, which costs $40,000, in addition to the $35,000 newspaper advertising, would increase sales 60%. Should the company buy the time on TV?
8. Refer to the original data. Another market study indicates that a 10% reduction in selling price would increase sales by 60%. Should the company lower the selling price?
9. Refer to the original data. Higher duplication costs increase variable costs by $2 per unit. The company, however, wants to maintain the same break-even point in units that was originally computed in (1). What will be the new selling price?

P3-18 Comprehensive CVP Analysis; Computations and Concepts

Beauty Care, Inc. produces and sells a single product called BC-1, which was first developed for stroke rehabilitation and later has been marketed as a beauty-aid. BC-1 tightens the face and chin, making people look younger. The product is sold for $45, and variable costs are $18 per unit.

The company's contribution income statement for the last year is as follows:

Sales (8,000 units)	$360,000
Variable costs	144,000
Contribution margin	216,000
Fixed costs	150,000
Operating income	$ 66,000

Required:

1. Compute the following based on last year's performance:
    a. Break-even point in units and in sales dollars
    b. Margin of safety in dollars and as a percentage
    c. Degree of operating leverage
2. Assume that the company's target operating income was only $30,000. How many units were required to be sold?
3. The company expects a temporary shortage in the market of unique plastics used in the production of BC-1 next year. This will increase the raw material cost by $2 per unit. All other conditions remain the same as last year.
    a. Compute next year's break-even point in sales dollars using the CM ratio.
    b. Compute next year's target sales volume in units if the company wants to earn $4,000 more in operating income than last year.
    c. The company still wants to maintain the same contribution margin ratio next year despite the increased raw material cost. What action will the company have to take? Be specific.
4. Assume that next year's performance will be the same as last year's, except that a $40,000 advertising campaign is expected to increase the number of units sold by 25%.
    a. What will be the difference between next year's CM ratio and last year's?
    b. Indicate whether next year's break-even point in units and in sales dollars will be higher, lower, or unchanged, compared to last year's. Answer the question without actual calculations.
    c. Will there be any change in the degree of operating leverage next year from last year?
5. Refer to last year's original data. Assume that next year's unit sales of BC-1 increase 60% from last year's due to the product's popularity among women of all ages. What will next year's operating income be? Answer the question using the operating leverage concept. All other conditions remain unchanged from last year.

P3-19   Breakeven Point; Operating Income; Optimal Production Plan; Capacity*

The PTO Division of the Galva Manufacturing Company produces power take-off units for the farm equipment business. The PTO Division, headquartered in Peoria, has a newly renovated, automated plant in Peoria and an older, less automated plant in Moline. Both plants produce the same power take-off units for farm tractors that are sold to most domestic and foreign tractor manufacturers.

The PTO Division expects to produce and sell 192,000 power take-off units during the coming year. The division production manager has the following data available regarding the unit costs, unit prices, and production capacities for the two plants.

	Peoria		Moline	
Selling price		$150.00		$150.00
Manufacturing costs:				
Variable	$72.00		$88.00	
Fixed	30.00		15.00	
Commission (5%)	7.50		7.50	
Administrative expenses	25.50		21.00	
Total unit cost		135.00		131.50
Unit profit		$ 15.00		$ 18.50
Production rate				
per day		400 units		320 units

1. All fixed costs are based on a normal year of 240 working days. When the number of working days exceeds 240, variable manufacturing costs increase by $3.00 per unit in Peoria and $8.00 per unit in Moline. Capacity for each plant is 300 working days.
2. Galva Manufacturing charges each of its plants a per unit fee for administrative services such as payroll, general accounting, and purchasing, as Galva considers these services to be a function of the work performed at the plants. For each of the plants at Peoria and Moline, the fee is $6.50 and represents the variable portion of administrative expenses.

Wishing to maximize the higher unit profit at Moline, PTO's production manager has decided to manufacture 96,000 units at each plant. This production plan results in Moline operating at capacity and Peoria operating at its normal volume. Galva's corporate controller is not happy with this plan as he does not believe it represents optimal usage of PTO's plants.

Required:

1. Determine the annual break-even units for each of PTO's plants.
2. Calculate the operating income that would result from the division production manager's plan to produce 96,000 units at each plant.
3. Determine the optimal production plan to produce the 192,000 units at PTO's plants in Peoria and Moline, and calculate the resulting operating income for the PTO Division. Be sure to support the plan with appropriate calculations.

(CMA)

* Before attempting this problem, students are suggested to read Appendix 4A, Capacity (presented at the end of Chapter 4).

P3-20   Breakeven Point; Selling Strategies; Income Tax

Marston Corporation manufactures pharmaceutical products that are sold through a network of sales agents located in the U.S. and Canada. The agents are currently paid an 18% commission on sales, and this percentage was used when Marston prepared the following Pro Forma Income Statement for the fiscal year ending June 30, Year 5.

Marston Corporation
Pro Forma Income Statement
For the Year Ending June 30, Year 5
($000 omitted)

Sales		$26,000
Cost of goods sold:		
Variable	$11,700	
Fixed	2,870	14,570
Gross profit		11,430
Selling and administrative costs:		
Commissions	4,680	
Fixed advertising cost	750	
Fixed administrative cost	1,850	7,280
Operating income		4,150
Fixed interest cost		650
Income before income taxes		3,500
Income taxes (40%)		1,400
Net income		$ 2,100

Since the completion of the above statement, Marston has learned that its agents are requiring an increase in the commission rate to 23% for the upcoming year. As a result, Marston's president has decided to investigate the possibility of hiring its own sales staff in place of the network of sales agents and has asked Tom Ross, Marston's controller, to gather information on the costs associated with this change.

Ross estimates that Marston will have to hire eight sales people to cover the current market area. The annual payroll cost of each of these employees will average $80,000, including fringe benefit expense. Travel and entertainment expense is expected to total $600,000 for the year, and the annual cost of hiring a sales manager and sales secretary will be $150,000. In addition to their salary, the eight sales people will each earn commissions at the rate of 10% on the first $2 million in sales and 15% on all sales over $2 million. For planning purposes, Ross expects that all eight sales people will be at the level previously projected. Ross believes that Marston should also increase its advertising budget by $500,000.

Required:

1. Calculate Marston Corporation's break-even point in sales dollars for the fiscal year ending June 30, Year 5, if the company hires its own sales force and increases its advertising costs.
2. If Marston Corporation continues to sell through its network of sales agents and pays the higher commission rate, determine the estimated volume in sales dollars for the fiscal year ending June 30, Year 5, that would be required

to generate the same net income as projected in the Pro Forma Income Statement presented above.

3. Describe the general assumptions underlying break-even analysis that limit its usefulness.

(CMA, adapted)

P3-21 Target Income; Variable and Semi-Variable Costs

Hugh Darren, a college student in Hawaii, wants to earn some money this summer by selling T-shirts which show a recent solar eclipse in the Big Island of Hawaii. His uncle will let Hugh use some space in his shop, and no facility cost is expected for the T-shirt sales. Hugh will hire part-time sales people who will work on a commission basis.

The T-shirts would cost Hugh $11.50 each with a minimum initial order of 100 units. Any additional units would have to be ordered in increments of 25. No leftover T-shirts can be returned to the manufacturer. The unit selling price of the T-shirts would be $16.50. The sales commission would be $3 for each unit sold.

Required:

1. What level of sales in units and in dollars would be required, assuming a target income of $750 for the first six months?
2. If an order of 100 T-shirts is placed, what would be the break-even point in units and in sales dollars?
3. Assume that Hugh will be able to order only the minimum inventory he will need within the constraints in purchasing.
   a. What net income will result if 80 T-shirts are sold?
   b. What net income will result if 110 T-shirts are sold?

P3-22 CVP Analysis; More Complex Cost Structure

Gen-X Snack, Inc. has just developed a new product, a snack called G-X. A just completed market test indicated a significant appeal of the snack among young, health-conscious urban consumers. The company has a G-X production capacity of 15,000 units each month.

The sales and cost data are provided below:

	Per Unit
Selling price.	$ 2.50
Variable costs	1.60
	Per Month
Fixed costs	$16,000

The market test also predicted that the demand for the product will exceed the monthly production capacity of 15,000 units. Additional production capacity can be rented in the neighborhood at a fixed cost of $3,500 per month. Direct labor costs in the rented facility would be 15 cents per unit higher than those in Gen-X Snack's own facility.

Required:

1. Compute the monthly break-even point in units and in dollar sales.
2. Compute the sales volume in units that are required to make a target profit of $3,750 each month.
3. The sales manager receives an incentive bonus of 10 cents per unit on the sales in excess of the break-even point. How many units must be sold each month in order to earn a return of 10% on the monthly investment (fixed costs)?

P3-23   Effect of Fixed Costs on Profits

Fixed Co. and Variable Co. compete in the same market with an identical product which sells for the same price. Fixed Co.'s operations are more automated, and all its manufacturing and most of the sales personnel are paid fixed salaries. Variable Co.'s operations are more manual, and most of its manufacturing personnel are hourly workers. Its sales personnel are paid on a commission basis.

Two companies' cost and operating data for the last two years are presented below:

	Fixed Co.		Variable Co.	
	Year 1	Year 2	Year 1	Year 2
Sales.................	$100,000	$125,000	$100,000	$150,000
Costs	90,000	95,000	90,000	130,000
Operating income	$ 10,000	$ 30,000	$ 10,000	$ 20,000
Fixed costs included....	$ 70,000	$ 70,000	$ 10,000	$ 10,000

Required:

1. Prepare the contribution income statement for both years for each company.
2. a. Compute the break-even point for each company.
   b. Compute the degree of operating leverage for each company for Year 1.
3. Variable Co.'s sales in Year 2 were higher than Fixed Co.'s. Explain why Variable Co.'s operating income was lower.
4. Fixed Co. made a profit of $30,000 in Year 2. What sales volume would Variable Co. have to achieve to make the same profit?
5. Assume that all other conditions remain unchanged in Year 1, except that the sales decreases 20% from the original Year 1 levels. What is each company's new operating income in Year 1? Answer the question using the operating leverage concept.
6. a. Which company would fare better in a strong economy?
   b. Which company would do better in a weak economy?

P3-24   CVP Analysis and Income Tax

The following income statement for Sandra Company represents the operating results for the fiscal year just ended. Sandra had sales of 1,800 tons of product during the current year. The manufacturing capacity of Sandra's facilities is 3,000 tons of product.

Sandra Company

Income Statement

For the Year Ended December 31, Year 4

Sales	$900,000
Variable costs:	
Manufacturing	315,000
Marketing	180,000
Total variable costs	495,000
Contribution margin	405,000
Fixed costs:	
Manufacturing	90,000
Marketing	112,500
Administration	45,000
Total fixed costs	247,500
Income before income taxes	157,500
Income taxes (40%)	63,000
Net income	$ 94,500

1. If the sales volume is estimated to be 2,100 tons in the next year, and if the prices and costs stay at the same levels and amounts next year, the after-tax net income that Sandra can expect for Year 5 is
   a. $135,000.
   b. $110,250.
   c. $283,500.
   d. $184,500.
   e. Some amount other than those shown above.

2. Sandra plans to market its product in a new territory. Sandra estimates that an advertising and promotion program costing $61,500 annually would need to be undertaken for the next two or three years. In addition, a $25 per ton sales commission over and above the current commission to the sales force in the new territory would be required. How many tons would have to be sold in the new territory to maintain Sandra's current after-tax income of $94,500?
   a. 307.5 tons
   b. 1,095.0 tons
   c. 273.333 tons
   d. 1,545.0 tons
   e. Some amount other than those shown above.

3. Assume that Sandra estimates that the per-ton selling price would decline 10% next year. Variable costs would increase $40 per ton and the fixed costs

would not change. What sales volume in dollars would be required to earn an after-tax net income of $94,500 next year?

    a. $1,140,000.

    b. $825,000.

    c. $1,500,000.

    d. $1,350,000.

    e. Some amount other than those shown above.

(CMA, adapted)

P3-25 CVP Analysis and Tax

Crayon-Crayon, Inc. is a wholesaler of crayons used by schoolchildren. The company's sales have been growing at a healthy pace for the last several years. The company is planning its operations for next year, which include projected sales of 400,000 cases at $2,400,000 and a projected after-tax income of $108,000. The current year's data on cost and operations follow:

	Per Case
Selling price (average)	$6.00
Variable costs:	
Crayon purchase cost	$3.00
Marketing	0.60
Total	$3.60
Fixed costs:	**Per Year**
Marketing	$150,000
Others	300,000
Total	$450,000

The company's tax rate is 40%. The company estimates that the crayon manufacturers will increase the crayon cost an average of 8% next year. The company expects no other changes in operations.

Required:

1. Compute the company's break-even point in cases of crayon and in sales dollars for the current year.

2. What selling price per case must the company charge to maintain the current contribution margin ratio even after the 8% increase in the purchase cost of crayon?

3. Assume that the selling price of crayon remains at $6 per case and the purchase cost of crayon increases 8%. How much sales in dollars must the company achieve next year to earn the target income after taxes of $108,000?

P3-26 Sales Mix and CVP Analysis

AV 2000 Inc. has developed a laser disc and a compact disc which have become popular among young adults. Last year's cost and operating data for the two audio-visual products are presented below:

	Per Unit	
	Laser Disc	**Compact Disc**
Selling price	$50	$10
Variable costs.	20	8
	Per Year	
Sales volume in units	5,000	15,000
Fixed costs.		$99,000

Required:

1. Prepare last year's contribution income statement showing both amount and percent columns for each product and for the company as a whole.
2. a. Compute the break-even point in dollars.

   b. Compute the margin of safety in both dollars and percent.
3. The company has developed a third product, and expects to sell 4,000 units of the new product. It will be sold at $25 each, and the variable costs would be $17.50 per unit. A market study indicates that the sales of the first two products would not be affected by the new product. Annual fixed costs will remain unchanged. Prepare a contribution income statement for each product and in total.
4. Refer to (3) above. Compute the new break-even point in dollars and the margin of safety in both dollars and percent.

 ## P3-27 CVP and Sensitivity Analysis

Bryan Adams, a college business major, has just been hired as a part-time employee of the planning department of Con-E, Inc., a consumer electronics firm. Con-E sells a single product that is highly price-sensitive. As the first major assignment, Bryan is performing a sensitivity analysis of selling price, sales volume, and profit.

Based on the initial market analysis, Bryan believes that Con-E can increase sales by 5,000 units for each $2 reduction in unit selling price. Con-E currently sells 30,000 units a year at $80 per unit. Variable costs are $50 per unit. Fixed expenses are $600,000 per year.

Required:

1. Compute the current net income per year.
2. What is the break-even point in units and in dollar sales?

3. Assume Bryan's market analysis is correct. What is the maximum annual profit that the company could generate? At how many units and at what selling price per unit would the company generate this profit?
4. What is the new break-even point in units and in dollar sales using the selling price you have determined in (3) above?
5. Would the information on the new break-even point affect the answer in (3) above?

P3-28   CVP Analysis; Change in Sales Mix; Income Taxes

Packard Electronics manufactures two products (TR and EC) and sells them nationally to wholesalers and retailers. The Packard management is very pleased with the company's performance for the current fiscal year. Projected sales through December 31, Year 4, indicate that 70,000 TR's and 140,000 EC's will be sold this year. The projected earnings statement, which appears below, shows that Packard will exceed its earnings goal of 9% on sales (after taxes).

Packard Electronics
Projected Earnings Statement
For the Year Ended December 31, Year 4
(dollars in thousands except per-unit amounts)

	TR		EC		
	Total Amount	Per Unit	Total Amount	Per Unit	Total
Sales...................	$1,050	$15.00	$3,150	$22.50	$4,200.00
Production costs:					
Materials.............	$ 280	$ 4.00	$ 630	$ 4.50	$ 910.00
Direct labor	140	2.00	420	3.00	560.00
Variable overhead.....	140	2.00	280	2.00	420.00
Fixed overhead	70	1.00	210	1.50	280.00
Total..............	630	9.00	1,540	11.00	2,170.00
Gross margin	$ 420	$ 6.00	$1,610	$11.50	2,030.00
Fixed marketing and administrative costs.......................					1,040.00
Net income before income taxes....................					990.00
Income taxes (55%)...........................					544.50
Net income					$ 445.50

The TR business has been fairly stable the last few years, and the company does not intend to change the TR price. However, competition among manufacturers of EC's has been increasing. Packard's EC has been very popular with consumers.

In order to sustain this interest in its EC and to meet the price reduction expected from competitors, management has decided to reduce the wholesale price of its EC from $22.50 to $20.00 per unit, effective January 1, Year 5. At the same time, the company plans to spend an additional $57,000 on advertising during the next fiscal year.

As a consequence of these actions, management estimates that 80% of its total revenue will be derived from EC sales, as compared to 75% in Year 4. As in the prior year, the sales mix is assumed to be the same at all volume levels.

The total fixed overhead costs and the variable overhead cost rates will not change in Year 5. However, the cost of materials and direct labor is expected to change. Packard estimates that material costs will drop 10% for TR and 20% for EC in Year 5. However, direct labor costs for both products will increase 10% in the coming year.

Required:

1. How many TR and EC units did Packard Electronics have to sell in Year 4 to break even?
2. What volume of sales is required if Packard Electronics is to earn a profit in Year 5 equal to 9% of sales (after taxes)?

(CMA, adapted)

P3-29   Ethics and CVP Analysis

Don Donovan works for Facial Care Products, Inc. as manager of business planning. Currently he is working on a CVP analysis involving a possible acquisition of a new technology from an R&D lab. The company is considering the technology acquisition to launch a new product called the facial exerciser.

Initially developed for those who go through stroke rehabilitation, the facial exerciser can be a substitute for cosmetic surgery among people who want a face lift. The facial exerciser has been known to tighten the facial skin of its users. Top management has hinted that Donovan would probably head the new product team if the acquisition becomes a reality. Donovan likes the prospect very much.

Donovan's initial CVP analysis indicates a break-even point of 95,000 units of sales. The company's marketing team has projected the annual sales at below 100,000 units, leaving a very small margin of safety for the new product.

Concerned about the possibility that top management may reject the project, Donovan is considering making a small change in the assumptions he used for the CVP analysis. He thinks that the benefit from the projected advertising on the World Wide Web (WWW) is doubtful and that the related budget item could be eliminated, leaving the advertising in a national news magazine as the only primary advertising campaign.

Required:

1. Assume that Donovan has made the change in the advertising plan. How would the change affect the outcome of the CVP analysis?
2. Is it ethical to make the change that Donovan is considering? Why or why not?
3. Identify the stakeholders involved in this ethics-related situation.

■ CASES

C3-30   A Confusing Change in Sales Mix and CVP Analysis

Sonoma Valley Winery, located midway between Sonoma and Santa Rosa, California, was founded in Year 3 by a winemaking family. The winery occupies a building at the foot of a hill. Winemaking started in Year 4 from grapes provided by the winery's own 700-acre vineyard.

Mature vineyards are generally known to produce superior quality grapes and wines. Sonoma Valley Winery's vineyards are at least twice as old as most of the vineyards in Sonoma Valley, which are 15 to 20 years old. Winemaking and grape quality are also affected by the varied exposures from the microclimate of the location, grape harvest date, and variables in the wine production process.

The winery's winemaking process consists of grape harvest; crush and fermentation in tanks; aging in oak barrels; blending of various lots; filtering; bottling; and bottle aging. Bottle aging takes about two months for white wines, and more than a year for red wines.

The wines made in Year 4 were Cabernet Sauvignon, Chardonnay, and Sauvignon Blanc. Of the three wines that were made in Year 4, only the two white wines were released in Year 6. The selling prices per gallon at the wholesale level were $25 for Chardonnay and $24 for Sauvignon Blanc. The first vintage of Cabernet Sauvignon was still in the aging process at the end of Year 6.

The cost and sales data for May, Year 6 are given below:

	Chardonnay	Sauvignon Blanc
Gallons sold	18,200	12,100
Manufacturing costs:		
Variable	$250,250	$130,680
Fixed	$90,000	
Variable selling expenses:	5% of sales	
Fixed administrative expenses:	$230,000	

The grape costs are $1,500 per ton for Chardonnay and $860 per ton for Sauvignon Blanc, reflecting the usually higher cost for Chardonnay grapes.

Required:

1. Prepare a contribution income statement for May Year 6 showing amount and percentage for each product. Fixed expenses should appear only in the Total column.

2. In May, Year 7, the sales of Chardonnay increased 20%, while the sales of Sauvignon Blanc decreased 20%, compared to May Year 6. Per-unit variable costs and total fixed costs remained unchanged. Prepare a contribution income statement for May, Year 7 using the same format as in (1).

3. Explain the reason for the increase (decrease) in the net income of May, Year 7 from the same period in Year 6. Include in your explanation a comment on favorable (unfavorable) change in sales mix.

4. Compute the break-even point in sales dollars for white wines for (a) May, Year 6 and (b) May, Year 7.

5. Cabernet Sauvignon was released in January, Year 8 at the selling price of $28 per gallon. Thanks to the media hype about the value of red wine to reduce the risk of heart disease, the sales of Cabernet Sauvignon have been phenomenal. In January, Year 8 the winery sold 20,200 gallons of the red wine.

   There was no change in the costs and sales of the two white wines in January, Year 8 from the data of May, Year 6. Per-unit variable costs of manufacturing the red wine are $12.60. Variable selling expenses remain unchanged at 5% of sales. Fixed expenses remain unchanged from May, Year 6.

   a. Compute the weighted average CM per unit for all wines using the figures of January, Year 8.

   b. Compute the break-even point in units for all three wines (total and each wine) using the figures of January, Year 8.

C3-31 CVP and Projection of Future Business

Joe Fix and Art Varia graduated from the same college. Instead of becoming employees of big corporations, they wanted to succeed as entrepreneurs. Joe established a company called Salt Lake Aerial Tramway, and Art opened a 24-hour convenience store in Las Vegas.

This is the second year of their operations. Both ventures performed at the same level of sales in the first quarter growing at the same rate each month as follows:

	January	February	March
Sales	$200,000	$240,000	$260,000

While the sales are at the same level, the cost structures of the two companies are different, as represented by the following variable cost ratios and fixed costs:

	Joe's Tramway	Art's Store
Variable cost ratio	0.4	0.9
Fixed costs (per month)	$110,000	$10,000

On May 8, Joe was visiting with Art on his way back from a promotional campaign in Las Vegas. While discussing their respective businesses, they came to some disagreement about who will do better in good times and bad times. The following is part of their conversation:

Joe: "At least I know we can use the operating leverage concept we learned in our managerial accounting course to find out whose business will do better in good times and bad."

Art: "You are right. If we calculate degrees of operating leverage for high and low sales levels, we will be able to see."

Joe: "We will see how much income the degree of operating leverage for my business will get out of my sales."

Art: "I've lost you. What do you mean by the degree?"

Joe: "Have you forgotten? A company's cost structure determines the degree of operating leverage for that company."

Art: "Cost structure? You mean the relative proportions of fixed and variable costs?"

Joe: "Yes. The proportion is determined for each company and stays at the level as long as the structure doesn't change."

Art: "I beg to differ, Joe. That's not what I remember. If I remember correctly, as sales level changes, so does the degree of operating leverage."

Joe: "I believe you are mistaken about that."

Art: "No, I don't think so. I remember, although a little vaguely, that in one case analysis we did in the class, the degree of operating leverage was highest near the break-even point and decreased as the level of operations moved farther and farther away from the break-even point."

Joe: "Art, I think the desert heat has gotten to you. It has had quite an effect on your brain. Take a break, and come up to Utah for a breath of cool air. Your brain needs a break."

Required:

1. Compute the break-even point in sales dollars for Joe's Tramway and Art's store.
2. What do you think about Art's statement on the degree of operating leverage being highest near the break-even point and so forth? Prepare a contribution income statement for both companies for the first quarter in order to prove whether Art is right or wrong. Show four columns, with the first column for a sales level near the break-even point (sales of $10 above the break-even point) and one column for each of the three months. Show the degree of operating leverage at the bottom of each column.
3. For the same level of sales, which company has the higher degree of operating leverage?
4. Which company's break-even point is higher? Why? Explain in terms of the two companies' cost structures.
5. Who is right with respect to sales level and degree of operating leverage?

Job-Costing Systems for Manufacturing and Service Industries

After studying this chapter, you should be able to:

1. Explain the basic purpose of costing systems and concepts.

2. Differentiate between, and give examples of, job-order costing systems and process costing systems.

3. Explain how materials and labor are measured and accumulated in a job-order costing system.

4. Illustrate how a predetermined manufacturing overhead rate is developed and how overhead is applied to each job.

5. Prepare journal entries and T-accounts to record the flow of costs through a job-order costing system.

6. Determine ending balances in Raw Materials, Manufacturing Overhead, Work in Process, and Finished Goods accounts, and explain how to dispose of the overapplied or underapplied overhead.

7. Explain the mechanism of job-costing systems for service and nonprofit organizations.

8. Explain how the two-stage cost assignment works.

9. Explain how costs change in an e-business.

Managers rely on cost accounting systems to measure costs of performing activities for an organization. Cost accounting systems assign costs to departments, teams, or any other business units for planning and control of the business units and/or costing products or services.

Purpose of Costing Systems – Campus Printing Shop

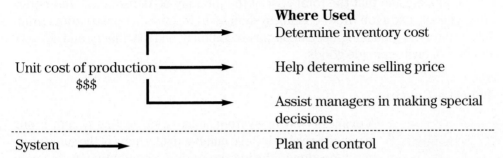

Where Used

Determine inventory cost

Unit cost of production — Help determine selling price
$$\$

Assist managers in making special decisions

System — Plan and control

DISTINCTION BETWEEN JOB-ORDER COSTING AND PROCESS COSTING SYSTEMS

Unit cost of production is the result of an averaging process. The total cost of production during a period is averaged over the number of units produced during that period. Because of the variation in the production process from one industry to another, two costing systems have emerged to meet such variations. One is known as **job-order costing** (or **job costing**) and the other is known as **process costing.**

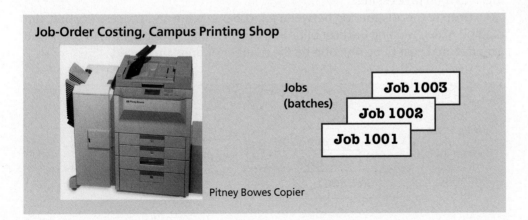

Job-Order Costing, Campus Printing Shop

Jobs (batches)

Job 1003

Job 1002

Job 1001

Pitney Bowes Copier

Job-Order Costing

A **job-order costing system** is characterized as one in which many different jobs, products, or batches of products are produced during the period, each of which requires varying degrees of attention and skills. For example, Campus Printing Shop may have several jobs (batches) to be completed during one day. Student Government Association may need 100 color posters for its publicity campaign (Job 1001). Beta

Gamma Sigma may need 500 flyers for its activities (Job 1002). Campus Fitness Center may need 200 programs for its fundraising banquet.

Each of these customer orders is different. Each must be treated as a separate job order. Each job order is entered manually or electronically on a **job-cost sheet** (or **job-cost record**) which contains information about the customer, type and class of product, type of job needed, parts (or materials) used, labor hours spent on the job, etc., so that the total cost of the job may be determined. Industries that typically use a job-order costing system include aircraft, construction, printing, furniture, shipbuilding, special-purpose equipment and machinery, and any production of custom-made goods.

Process Costing

Process Costing, Kellogg Company

Kellogg's packing line at its Battle Creek plant.

A **process costing system,** unlike a job costing system, is one in which a relatively large number of like units of the same product is produced during the period, usually by passing continuously through a series of uniform production steps or processes. Since the output of such processes is alike, it is usually sold to customers in small or large quantities as the customer needs. For example, paint is produced by paint companies through a process that mixes certain materials and chemicals together. Different customers buy basically the same type of paint in the quantities needed: one gallon, five gallons, one hundred gallons, etc. Industries that typically use a process costing system include chemicals, gasoline, plastics, textiles, flour, sugar, cereal, rubber, glass, lumber, mining, electricity, cement, brick, meat packing, and food processing.

Despite this distinction between job-order costing and process costing, the method of determining the cost of production per unit is basically the same: divide accumulated cost of production by the number of units produced.

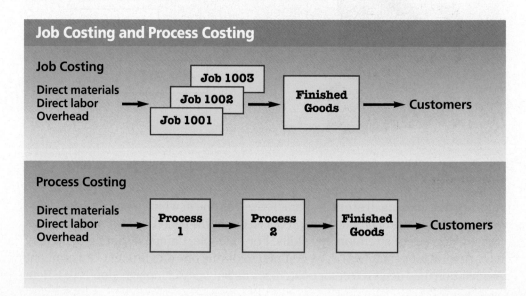

JOB-ORDER COSTING: THE SYSTEM AND PROCESS

The major objective of a job-order costing system is to measure and accumulate the three cost elements of producing the job or the order:

1. The quantities and costs of materials and parts used;
2. The numbers and costs of labor hours used;
3. The costs of manufacturing overhead allocated to the particular job.

Job Cost Sheet

A job cost sheet contains the cost of direct materials, direct labor, and overhead charges, and is completed for each job for internal costing purposes. As illustrated in Exhibit 4-1, the job cost sheet contains detailed information about the job including the job number and description; direct materials, direct labor, and manufacturing overhead assigned to the job; total job cost; and cost per unit if the job contains more than one unit.

The job cost sheet is used not only for accumulating costs of materials, labor, and overhead per job, but also for determining unit cost. The unit cost then is used to determine inventory cost for the balance sheet and the cost of goods sold for the income statement. If job No. 1001 passes through other departments in addition to Department A, another job cost sheet may be prepared for the costs

---

EXHIBIT 4-1 Job Cost Sheet

Campus Printing Shop

Job No. **1001**
Date Started _____ 10/1/x9 _____
Department **A**

Job Cost Sheet No. _10-01_
Job Description _Poster_
Date Completed _10/1/x9_

Direct Materials	Quantity or Hours	Unit Cost or Rate	Total Cost	Job Summary
Materials Requisition No. 5	100	$5	$500	
Materials Requisition No. 7	50	6	300	
				$ 800
Direct labor				
Time Card 1	4	10	40	
Time Card 2	10	30	300	
				340
Overhead				
Applied	30	8	240	240
Total Job Cost				$1,380
Units Completed				100
Cost Per Unit				$13.80

From Exh. 4-2 →

From Exh. 4-3 →

of these departments assigned to job 1001. In that case, a job cost summary sheet must be prepared to show all costs assigned to job 1001 in one place.

Direct Materials

Materials are purchased from suppliers, and delivered directly to the manufacturing floor, or stored in a storeroom until requested. The invoice received for the materials is used as a basis for recording the journal entry for purchases as well as for recording each type of material received. In a typical computer system, each type of material is assigned a special magnetic code number, and the entry for the purchase as well as the addition of each material on the stock card is made in one step.

When materials are issued for production, a special materials requisition form, such as the one illustrated in Exhibit 4-2, must be filled out. The form contains detailed information about the materials issued, total cost, department and job number to be charged. It is used to control the flow of materials from the storeroom to the production departments, and is the basis for recording such transactions in the cost accounting records.

Direct Labor

Similar to direct materials, direct labor hours must be accumulated and the costs charged to the particular job. A time card or time ticket is used for each employee in the factory (manufacturing) or office (service). The time card contains detailed information about the worker, the number of hours spent on each job, wage rate per hour and total labor cost charged to each job. The time card is used for measuring total wages to be paid to each worker and for accumulating direct labor cost for each job. A time card is illustrated in Exhibit 4-3.

Manufacturing Overhead

Manufacturing overhead includes all factory cost except direct material and direct labor. Examples are indirect materials, indirect labor, factory rent, insurance, utilities, and depreciation. These expenses are usually charged monthly whereas jobs may be completed on a daily basis. For example, Campus Printing Shop can complete a printing job in 30 minutes or less. While jobs or orders can be completed that fast, total actual manufacturing overhead is not known until the end of the month or the end of the year. Depreciation, for example, is recorded annually.

Then, how do we assign a portion of each of these overhead items to each job? One of the easiest ways to assign manufacturing overhead to each job is to use an **overhead application rate.** This overhead application rate usually is determined before the start of the year. The manager selects an activity base (number of direct labor hours, number of machine hours, cost of direct material, or cost of direct labor), estimates total manufacturing overhead expected to be incurred during the coming year, and divides the cost driver into the overhead costs.

EXHIBIT 4-2 Materials Requisition Form

Campus Printing Shop Date ___10/1/x9___ Requisition No. ___5___
Requesting Dept. ___Printing___ Job No. to be charged ___1001___

Material Code	Description	Quantity Issued	Unit Cost	Total Cost
CD	Poster paper	100	$5	$500

→ To Exh. 4-1

Requesting Department
Authorized Signature ___*T. Cruise*___

EXHIBIT 4-3 Time Card

Campus Printing Shop Date ___10/1/x9___ Time Card # ___1___
Worker's Name ___R. Kent___ Worker's # ___124___ Worker's Dept ___#2___

Time Started	Time Stopped	No. of Hours	Wage Rate per Hour	Total Labor Cost	Job # to be Charged
8:00	12:00	4	10	$40	1001
1:00	3:00	2	10	$20	1002
3:00	5:00	2	10	$20	1003
TOTALS		8	10	$80	

→ To Exh. 4-1

Authorized Signature ___*M. Gibson*___
(Supervisor)

For example, the manager selects the number of machine hours as the activity base. For the forthcoming year, the machine hours and the total manufacturing overhead are estimated to be 100,000 hours and $500,000 respectively. The predetermined manufacturing overhead rate is $5.00 per machine hour, calculated as follows:

$$\text{Predetermined Overhead Rate} = \frac{\text{Estimated total manufacturing overhead}}{\text{Estimated total machine hours}}$$

$$= \frac{\$500,000}{100,000} = \$5 \text{ per machine hour}$$

Once the overhead rate is determined, the assignment of overhead to products becomes very simple and straight-forward. A job that takes 10 machine hours is assigned $50 for overhead (10 MHs x $5), a product that takes 50 MHs would be charged $250 for overhead, and so forth.

Estimating Overhead Application Rates

While both the numerator and denominator of the predetermined overhead rate are estimates, these estimates usually are quite accurate. Managers develop estimation skills as they gain experience. Managers consider the following in estimating predetermined overhead rates:

1. The activity or application base selected should be one that best reflects the relationship between products (services) and overhead expenses. For example, in most service operations and labor-intensive manufacturing operations, direct labor hours may best reflect that relationship, whereas in capital-intensive or highly automated industries, machine hours may best reflect that relationship.

2. No one single predetermined overhead application rate must be used throughout the whole company. Each department may use its own application rates for different activity bases or cost drivers. Chapters 6 and 7 discuss these more fully.

3. Overhead application rates need not be changed from day to day or month to month, even if actual activity levels fluctuate from day to day and from month to month. Checking the overhead application once or twice a year for possible revisions is a reasonable policy.

4. Since a predetermined overhead application rate is an estimate, differences between total actual overhead and total applied overhead for each period occur. Such differences may be carried over from month to month since they tend to offset each other during the year. Any remaining over-applied or under-applied overhead at the end of the year may be disposed of either by adjusting cost of goods sold for the year or, if significant, by adjusting work in process inventory, finished goods inventory, and cost of goods sold. This process will be illustrated in a later example.

Machine Hour As a Base

A machining operation at a plant of Harnischfeger Industries, Inc., Milwaukee, Wisconsin. Machine hour is a good indicator of the activity level here.

Direct labor workers at Electrocom Automation Inc. are building sub-assemblers on a production line.

Labor Hour As a Base

COST FLOW THROUGH JOB-ORDER COSTING SYSTEM

The three cost elements used in the manufacturing process are Direct Material, Direct Labor, and Manufacturing Overhead. The costs of these elements flow through a job costing system through Work in Process (WIP) and Finished Goods, and arrive at the end as the Cost of Goods Sold. Exhibit 4-4 illustrates the flow of costs through a job-order costing system in a typical production cycle.

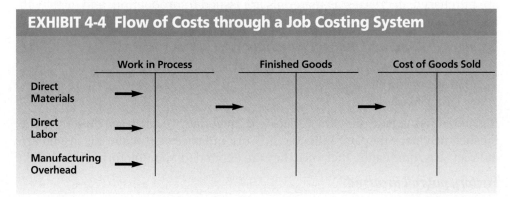

EXHIBIT 4-4 Flow of Costs through a Job Costing System

Illustration of the Flow of Costs (Including Journal Entries)

Assume that on October 1, Year 9, XYZ Company had the following balances:

Raw Materials	$10,000
Work in Process	5,000
Finished Goods	20,000

During October Year 9, the following transactions took place:

Materials purchased	$35,000
Direct materials issued to production	20,000
Indirect materials used	3,000
Total factory payroll	45,000
Direct labor charged to production	30,000
Indirect labor incurred	15,000
Additional manufacturing overhead incurred (including factory rent, insurance, utilities, depreciation, etc.)	12,000
Cost of finished goods manufactured	77,000
Cost of goods sold	82,000

Other information:

1. Manufacturing overhead is applied to production at the rate of $11 per machine hour. Three thousand machine hours were charged to production for the month.
2. Over- or under-applied overhead is carried forward from month to month until the end of the year.

The journal entries and the T-accounts related to the above illustration are as follows:

Journal Entries

Purchase of materials

1. Raw Materials.................................35,000
         Accounts Payable (or Cash)...........................35,000

Raw Materials account starts with beginning balance (BB), increases as materials are purchased, decreases as materials are issued to production, and ends with ending balance (EB).

Issuance of direct and indirect materials

2. Work in Process.............................20,000
    Manufacturing Overhead.................... 3,000
         Raw Materials..23,000

If materials issued are direct materials (e.g., materials we can trace directly to the finished product), they are reflected in Work in Process. If materials issued are indirect (e.g., lubricants, fuel, oil), they are debited to Manufacturing Overhead.

Factory payroll incurred

3. Work in Process.............................30,000
    Manufacturing Overhead.....................15,000
         Wages Payable (or Cash)..............................45,000

Factory payroll incurred during the period of $45,000 represents either direct labor (e.g., wages of workers directly involved in the manufacturing process, excluding shift or overtime premium which is usually treated as overhead) or indirect labor (e.g., salaries of factory supervisors). The entire payroll account is allocated as direct labor ($30,000) or indirect labor ($15,000). Unlike materials and other inventory accounts that follow, there is no end-of-the-period balance.

Additional manufacturing overhead incurred

4. Manufacturing Overhead....................12,000
         Various Accounts (cash, accounts
         payable, accrued liabilities,
         accumulated depreciation, etc.).......................12,000

In addition to indirect materials and indirect labor, manufacturing overhead includes other expenses such as factory rent, factory insurance, depreciation of factory equipment, and factory utilities.

Application of manufacturing overhead using the predetermined overhead rate

5. Work in Process.............................33,000
         Manufacturing Overhead..............................33,000
         (3,000 MHs x $11 = $33,000)

As discussed earlier, some of the actual manufacturing overhead expenses may not be known until year end, and thus, manufacturing overhead is applied to production using a predetermined overhead rate of $11 per MH.

If the amount of applied overhead (debited to Work in Process) is found at the end of the period to be less than actual overhead, there will be a debit balance in Manufacturing Overhead representing underapplied overhead. On the other hand, if applied overhead is found to be greater than actual overhead, the credit balance in Manufacturing Overhead represents overapplied overhead.

Transfer From Work in Process to Finished Goods

6. Finished Goods 77,000
    Work in Process 77,000

Direct materials, direct labor, and applied overhead are added to the beginning balance of Work in Process ($5,000). From that total ($88,000) the cost of finished goods manufactured (and transferred to finished goods warehouse) of $77,000 is subtracted to determine the balance remaining at the end of the period in WIP. This balance represents the cost of goods still in process at the end of the period.

Cost of Goods Sold

7. Cost of Goods Sold 82,000
    Finished Goods 82,000

In Finished Goods, the cost of goods manufactured of $77,000 is added to the beginning balance ($20,000) of Finished Goods. This total ($97,000) represents the goods that are available for sale. From this total, the cost of goods sold of $82,000 is subtracted to find the balance of Finished Goods remaining unsold at the end of the period.

At the end of October, the ending balances in the inventory accounts are:

Raw Materials $22,000
Work in Process 11,000
Finished Goods 15,000

Overapplied or Underapplied Manufacturing Overhead

At the end of October, the Manufacturing Overhead account has total debits of $30,000. This represents total actual overhead costs for the period. However, the journal entry (5) applied $33,000 to Work in Process. Accordingly, the manufacturing overhead for October is overapplied in the amount of $3,000.

Applied manufacturing overhead $33,000
Actual manufacturing overhead 30,000
Overapplied manufacturing overhead .... $ 3,000

The overapplied or underapplied overhead is carried over from month to month, and closed out at the end of the year to Cost of Goods Sold.

Assume that, by the end of December, Year 9, a net overapplied overhead of $3,000 exists. (Remember that this is not the overapplied overhead of $3,000 for October.) Cost of Goods Sold would be adjusted by the following entry:

8. Manufacturing Overhead 3,000
    Cost of Goods Sold 3,000

General Ledger

After the above journal entries are made and posted, the T-accounts of the general ledger will reflect the flow of costs as shown in Exhibit 4-5. The numbers refer to journal entries.

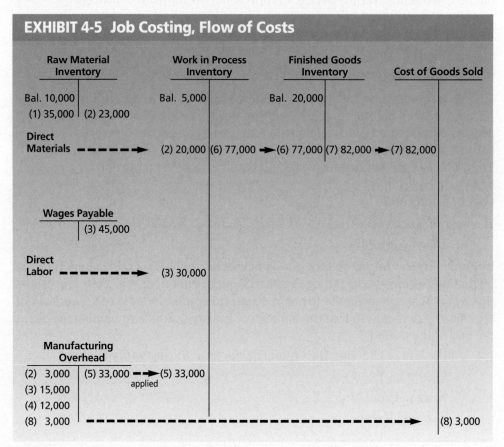

EXHIBIT 4-5 Job Costing, Flow of Costs

Proration of Underapplied or Overapplied Overhead

In the previous disposition of overapplied overhead of $3,000, we adjusted Cost of Goods Sold, as the journal entry (8) shows. If the amount of overapplied or underapplied overhead is significant, it may be apportioned among the ending balances of Work in Process, Finished Goods, and Cost of Goods Sold. The ending balances of Raw Materials, Work in Process, and Finished Goods accounts appear in the current assets section of the balance sheet.

To close out overapplied overhead for the year by prorating between WIP, Finished Goods, and Cost of Goods sold, simply follow the ratio of the balances in those three accounts. For example, assume that by the end of December, Year 9, the balances of these accounts were as follows:

Work in Process	$ 12,000
Finished Goods	24,000
Cost of Goods Sold	120,000
Total	$156,000

The $3,000 overapplied overhead would be prorated among the above three accounts as follows:

$$\text{Work in Process} = \frac{\$12,000}{\$156,000} \times \$3,000 = \$231$$

$$\text{Finished Goods} = \frac{\$24,000}{\$156,000} \times \$3,000 = \$462$$

$$\text{Cost of Goods Sold} = \frac{\$120,000}{\$156,000} \times \$3,000 = \$2,307$$

The following journal entry results:

Manufacturing Overhead	3,000	
Work in Process		231
Finished Goods		462
Cost of Goods Sold		2,307

COST DRIVERS AND OVERHEAD APPLICATION

Manufacturing overhead is comprised of various cost items that are not directly traceable to individual jobs as direct materials and direct labor can be. How then is overhead applied to jobs?

Overhead is applied indirectly to jobs, based on cost drivers (discussed in Chapter 2) that serve as indicators of resource usage by those jobs. **Cost drivers** are the factors that serve as the best measures of the cost increases or decreases for any activities in an organization. Managers must find the right cost driver that best establishes the cost-activity relationship. We will discuss the cost-activity relationship in more detail in Chapter 6. In this part, we examine how to apply manufacturing overhead indirectly to jobs using cost drivers.

Assume that a factory uses two departments: Cutting and Finishing. The Cutting Department's operations are capital-intensive, incurring heavy depreciation, repairs, and maintenance expenses. The Finishing Department's operations are labor-intensive, incurring heavy direct labor costs.

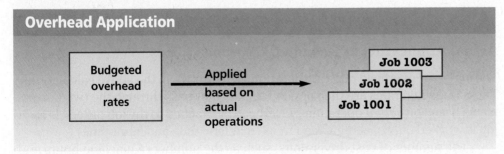

The following are operations forecasts and a labor and overhead budget for a forthcoming month:

	Department	
	Cutting	Finishing
Operations forecasts:		
Machine hours	55,200	9,000
Direct labor hours	6,000	58,000
Labor and overhead budget:		
Direct labor cost	$ 96,000	$928,000
Manufacturing overhead costs:		
Indirect materials	$ 9,000	$ 2,000
Indirect labor	24,000	43,000
Depreciation	185,000	20,000
Repairs and maintenance	24,000	3,000
Utilities	18,000	8,000
Factory rent	10,000	7,000
Other overhead costs	6,000	4,000
Total overhead costs	$276,000	$ 87,000

Determination of Budgeted Overhead Rates

It is reasonable to assume that the Cutting Department chooses machine-hours as the cost driver for its machine-focused operations, and the Finishing Department chooses direct-labor hours or direct-labor cost as the cost driver for its labor-intensive operations. Assume that the factory decides to use machine-hours and direct-labor cost as the two departments' respective cost drivers.

The overhead rates are computed as follows:

	Department	
	Cutting	Finishing
Budgeted manufacturing overhead	$276,000	$ 87,000
Budgeted machine-hours	55,200	
Budgeted direct-labor cost	00,000	$928,000
Budgeted overhead rate:		
$276,000 ÷ 55,200 MHs = ... $5 per MH		
$ 87,000 ÷ $928,000 = ... 00,000		9.375% of
		DL cost

Actual Application of Budgeted Overhead Rates

The *budgeted* overhead rates are determined as shown in the above calculations. These budgeted rates are then applied to jobs that pass through the two departments based on *actual* operations. Overhead is attached to the job orders as each job is worked on, consuming resources (machine time and labor time).

The number of cost driver units, such as the number of machine-hours and the amount of direct-labor cost, consumed by each job is used for actual overhead application as follows:

$$\begin{array}{lll} \text{Actually} \\ \text{applied} & = & \textit{Budgeted} \text{ overhead rate} & \times & \textit{Actual} \text{ cost driver units} \\ \text{overhead} & & & \text{(machine hours, labor hours)} \end{array}$$

Assume that Job 104 was started and completed during the period. The job cost sheet showed the following:

	Cutting	Finishing
Machine-hours	54	6
Direct-labor hours	110	500
Direct-labor cost	$1,760	$8,000
Materials requisitioned	$2,300	$1,700

The following illustrates the *actual* application of overhead to job 104:

	Cutting	Finishing	Total
Budgeted overhead rate	$5 per MH	9.375%	
Actual machine hours	× 54		
Actual direct labor cost		× $8,000	
Overhead actually applied	$270	$ 750	$1,020

Work in Process, as seen in previous journal entries, is charged for direct materials, direct labor, and manufacturing overhead consumed by all jobs, including job 104.

NORMAL COSTING

The job costing system described thus far uses actual costs of materials and labor. The system, however, did not use actual overhead costs. It used applied overhead that was estimated or budgeted. If the overhead application rate is based on the long-run average level of activity observed over a number of years rather than on the expected activity level of any given year, it is called a **normalized** overhead rate.

The cost of goods manufactured, accordingly, is composed of actual direct material, actual direct labor, and normal applied overhead. This is a **normal costing system.**

If a company could wait until all actual overhead costs were available, then actual average overhead costs could be applied to jobs. The overhead costs incurred would be the same as the overhead costs applied to Work in Process as follows:

Manufacturing Overhead (Actual Costing)	
Incurred	Applied
(Actual)	(Actual)

Actual costing is compared to normal costing as follows:

Manufacturing Overhead (Normal Costing)	
Incurred	Applied
(Actual)	(Normal)

In an actual costing system, there would be no need for adjusting for underapplied or overapplied overhead. Actual overhead costs incurred would be offset by the same amount of overhead costs applied to WIP. However, as explained earlier, it is not possible to use the actual costs for overhead because some overhead costs (such as depreciation) are not recorded until year-end. Businesses cannot wait until year-end to cost and price their products.

TWO-STAGE COST ALLOCATION

In manufacturing or service operations, there are two-stage cost assignments which consist of stage 1 assignment and stage 2 assignment.

Stage 1 cost assignment: Stage 1 cost assignment occurs when overhead cost items from the general ledger are assigned to manufacturing departments, such as cutting, finishing, machining, and assembly. In the previous example of overhead application, we assumed that stage 1 assignment of overhead items, such as indirect labor, depreciation, utilities, repairs and maintenance, had already been made to cutting and finishing departments.

Stage 2 cost assignment: Stage 2 cost assignment takes place when those costs that were assigned in stage 1 are charged to products. The cutting department used machine hours to apply overhead to jobs, and eventually to individual products. The finishing department used direct labor cost to apply overhead to jobs and products.

The following diagram illustrates the two-stage cost assignment process:

	Stage 1		Stage 2	
Overhead	- - - - - →	Manufacturing	- - - - - →	Jobs
Items		Departments		(Products)

The two-stage cost assignment will be discussed in more detail in Chapter 7.

JOB-ORDER COSTING IN SERVICE AND NONPROFIT ORGANIZATIONS

We started our discussion of job costing in this chapter with an example from an auto service center. The job costing approach can be used in other service and nonprofit organizations also. When service or nonprofit organizations use job costing, however, other names may be used to indicate the nature of *job*.

Overhead Allocation and Research Universities

Direct costs of conducting research at a university are easy to determine. The annual costs of graduate assistants, lab supplies and equipment, and travel expenses to conferences represent a professor's direct costs. Overhead costs, however, are difficult to compute. How much does it cost to supply him with an office, library, mowed grass and all the other extras that make a university function? Harvard Medical School charges 88 cents for every dollar of direct costs. Yale and Johns Hopkins ask for a little over 60 cents. MIT's rate is 57.5 cents. This lucrative practice runs into trouble when federal auditors question some overhead items, such as flowers, depreciation on a yacht, and a 19th-century Italian fruitwood commode for the president's house.

From "Milking the Laboratories for Dollars: The 'Overhead' Mess," *Newsweek*, May 6, 1991, p.58.

The following list illustrates the names that indicate "job" in other service and nonprofit organizations:

Organization	Names of Job
Research lab	R&D project
Finance company	Loan programs
Movie studio	Movie production
Moving company	Customer account
University	Research project, student program
Hospital	Case
School district	Education program
CPA firm	Audit (consulting) engagement
Community agency	Program
Welfare agency	Case
Law firm	Case

In all these services, materials and labor may be assigned to a particular job, called account, case, program, or project. Overhead is applied based on cost drivers that are similar to cost drivers in manufacturing.

Unlike manufacturing, however, service firms' direct materials costs account for a small portion of total costs. Labor and overhead costs are very significant in the cost structure.

Service Job Costing

Service industries are very diverse in the nature of business, as the above listing of service organizations and job names indicate. Each service firm must design its own job costing system based on the unique characteristics of its own business.

We now use a consulting firm to illustrate the process of service job costing. The firm employs 8 partners and 12 assistants who provide design and registration services involving the construction of plants producing environmentally sensitive materials. The firm uses a job costing system to accumulate operating costs of its two departments—Design Department and Registration Department.

The consulting firm's forecasts for Year 8 are presented below:

	Department	
	Design	Registration
Consulting-hours (partners)	15,000	10,000
Consulting-hours (assistants)	18,000	12,000
Design-hours	8,000	—
Documents and materials	$ 14,000	$ 16,000
Department overhead cost	$420,000	$280,000

The firm charges the budgeted overhead rates to its jobs, called cases, using the following cost drivers for two departments:

Department	Cost Driver
Design	Design-hours
Registration	Consulting-hours of partners

The service costs are composed of the following:

1. Costs of documents and materials
2. Costs of consulting-hours and design-hours
    Labor rate:
    Per design-hour .... $ 120
    Per consulting-hour (partner) 200
    Per consulting-hour (assistant) 80
3. Applied department overhead costs

Budgeted department overhead rates are determined as follows:

	Department	
	Design	Registration
Budgeted department overhead	$420,000	$280,000
Cost driver units:		
Design-hours	÷ 8,000	
Consulting-hours (partners)		÷ 10,000
Budgeted overhead rate per hour	$ 52.50	$ 28

The firm has spent the following costs and time on case A-516, which was started and completed in the current period:

	Department	
	Design	Registration
Documents and materials	$ 218	$ 264
Design-hours	32 hours	–
Consulting-hours (partner)	38 hours	24 hours
Consulting-hours (assistant)	42 hours	22 hours

The overhead costs are applied to case A-516 as follows:

Design department overhead:
    32 Hours × $52.50 = $1,680

Registration department overhead:
    24 Hours × $28 = $ 672

    Total department overhead charged $2,352

The total cost is charged to case A-516 as follows:

| | Department | | |
	Design	Registration	Total
Documents and materials . . . .$	218	$ 264	$ 482
Labor costs:			
Design-hours cost:			
32 hours × $120 =	3,840	–	3,840
Consulting-hours (partner):			12,400
38 hours × $200 =	7,600		
24 hours × $200 =		4,800	
Consulting-hours (assistant):			5,120
42 × $80 =	3,360		
22 × $80 =		1,760	
Overhead applied	1,680	672	2,352
Total job cost . . . .$	$16,698	$7,496	$24,194

As can be seen, the job costing process for manufacturing and service firms are very similar. The costing system, however, should be designed for each firm according to its particular needs.

E-BUSINESS AND COSTS

Overhead costs we discuss in this chapter change as e-business is introduced. Once a corporation installs an e-business infrastructure, most costs associated with the infrastructure tend to be *fixed* in the nature of cost behavior. The primary expenditures for installing the infrastructure on both hardware and software do not increase as e-business volume increases, within a certain range. Accordingly, corporations would try their best to maximize the output in their efforts to reduce costs per unit.

Would those fixed costs of e-businesses stay fixed for a long time? The answer to this question is a definite "no." Many e-consultants who have worked with e-tailers have realized that as e-tailers expand their businesses, the supposedly fixed costs move up at about the same rate at which business expands. The infrastructure hardware and software installation and operating costs increase as e-business expands. This has been a nasty surprise for e-businesses and e-consultants.

Has the nature of e-business-specific costs shown dramatic changes from the costs we have observed in the pre-Net period? No, it hasn't changed because fixed costs we used to know from the pre-Net era start to increase once the business expands beyond a certain range, called relevant range. Fixed costs become unfixed beyond that range.

SUMMARY

The basic purpose of costing systems is to measure the cost of production per unit and to provide some mechanism for controlling costs within an organization. Per-unit cost is required for costing ending inventory and goods sold, in pricing, and in making various special decisions.

Job-order costing systems are used in industries where many different products are produced during the period such as auto repair and service, customized construction, printing, and furniture. Process costing systems are used in industries where many like units of the same product are produced during the period such as gasoline, rubber, flour, sugar, and food processing. In either costing system, however, the cost per unit is derived by dividing total cost of production by the number of units produced.

In job-order costing systems, the three cost elements of production (materials, labor, and overhead) must be measured and accumulated on a job by job basis. Materials assigned to a job are measured by a materials requisition form; labor is measured by time tickets; and manufacturing overhead is applied to each job using a predetermined overhead application rate. Such a rate is determined by dividing estimated total manufacturing overhead for the coming year by an estimated activity base (such as direct labor hours, machine hours, or direct labor cost).

Because the predetermined manufacturing overhead rate is based on estimates, total actual manufacturing overhead for a period is likely to differ from applied overhead. Such differences, known as over- or under-applied overhead, may be carried forward from month to month until the end of the year when they are closed to cost of goods sold for the year, or, if significant, apportioned between Work in Process, Finished Goods, and Cost of Goods Sold, in the ratio of ending balances for those accounts. When the overhead rates are normalized rates, normal costing replaces actual costing.

Overhead is applied to jobs and products through a two-stage assignment process, first to manufacturing departments and then to jobs. The job costing process can work in both manufacturing and service environments in a similar fashion.

BASIC CONCEPTS AND TERMS

Actual costing	Predetermined overhead
Cost driver	application rate
Full absorption costing	Process costing system
Job cost sheet	Service job costing
Job-order costing system	Stage 1 cost assignment
Materials requisition form	Stage 2 cost assignment
Normal costing	Time card
Overapplied overhead	Two-stage cost assignment
Overhead application rate	Underapplied overhead

■ SELF-REVIEW PROBLEM 1:
Job Costing (Manufacturing)

Shelves, Inc. is a manufacturer of steel shelves used by supermarkets. The company uses job costing, and applies overhead cost to jobs using machine-hours. The company's estimates for Year 8 and the inventory balances on January 1, Year 8 were as follows:

Estimates for Year 8:
Estimated machine-hours. 54,000
Estimated manufacturing overhead costs $378,000

Inventory balances, January 1, Year 8:
Raw materials . . . . $ 8,000
Work in process 6,000
Finished goods 12,000

During Year 8, the following transactions took place:

a. Raw materials were purchased on account, $230,000.
b. Raw materials were issued to production, $220,000 ($200,000 direct and $20,000 indirect).
c. Payroll costs were incurred as follows: direct labor, $46,000; indirect labor, $94,000; sales commissions $44,100; administrative salaries, $120,000.
d. The following costs were incurred: factory utilities, $28,000; factory depreciation, $180,000; factory building property taxes, $31,000; factory insurance, $15,000.
e. Manufacturing overhead was applied to production. Machine-hours recorded for the period were 56,000.
f. As shelves were completed, they were transferred from manufacturing to the finished goods area. Work-in-process inventory balance of December 31, Year 8 was $11,000.

g. Finished shelves costing $630,000 were sold for $882,000 to customers during the year.

Required:

1. Prepare journal entries to record the transactions listed above. Some transactions require calculations before they are recorded as journal entries.
2. Post the appropriate journal entries to the following T-accounts: Raw Materials, Work in Process, Finished Goods, and Cost of Goods Sold.
3. Calculate the inventory balances of Raw Materials and Finished Goods on December 31, Year 8.
4. What is the amount of underapplied or overapplied manufacturing overhead for the year? Prepare a journal entry to close any balance in the Manufacturing Overhead account to Cost of Goods Sold.
5. Prepare an income statement for the year.

Solution to Self-Review Problem

1. a. Raw Materials.................... 230,000
        Accounts Payable   230,000

    b. Work in Process................. 200,000
       Manufacturing Overhead. 20,000
           Raw Materials   220,000

    c. Work in Process................. 46,000
       Manufacturing Overhead.......... 94,000
       Administrative Salaries........... 120,000
       Selling Expenses 44,100
           Wages and Salaries Payable.....   304,100

    d. Manufacturing Overhead.......... 254,000
           Accrued Expenses.............   28,000
           Accumulated Depreciation 180,000
           Property Taxes Payable   31,000
           Prepaid Insurance   15,000

    e. The applied overhead is computed as follows:

$$\text{Predetermined overhead rate} = \frac{\text{Estimated total manufacturing overhead}}{\text{Estimated total machine hours}}$$

$$= \frac{\$378,000}{54,000} = \$7 \text{ per machine hour}$$

$$\text{Overhead applied} = \text{Predetermined overhead rate} \times \text{Actual MHs}$$
$$= \$7 \times 56,000 \text{ hours} = \$392,000$$

The journal entry to record the applied overhead would be:

Work in Process 392,000
    Manufacturing Overhead....................... 392,000

f. The cost of goods manufactured (completed) is calculated as follows:

Direct materials used	200,000
Direct labor	46,000
Manufacturing overhead applied	392,000
Current manufacturing costs	638,000
Beginning WIP inventory	6,000
Manufacturing costs to account for	644,000
Ending WIP inventory	(11,000)
Cost of goods manufactured	633,000

The journal entry to record the cost of goods manufactured would be:

Finished Goods	633,000	
Work in Process		633,000

g.
Cost of Goods Sold	630,000	
Finished Goods		630,000
Accounts Receivable	882,000	
Sales		882,000

2.

Raw Materials			Work in Process		
BB 8,000			BB 6,000		
(a) 230,000	(b) 220,000		(b) 200,000		
			(c) 46,000		
			(e) 392,000	(f) 633,000	
EB 18,000			EB 11,000		

Finished Goods			Cost of Goods Sold		
BB 12,000				(g) 630,000	
(f) 633,000					
	(g) 630,000				
EB 15,000					

3. Raw Materials balance, December 31, Year 8:

Beginning raw material	8,000
Raw material purchases	230,000
RM available for use	238,000
RM used	220,000
Ending raw materials	18,000

Finished Goods balance, December 31, Year 8:

Beginning finished goods	12,000
Cost of goods manufactured	633,000
Goods available for sale	645,000
Cost of goods sold	630,000
Ending finished goods	15,000

4. Applied overhead 392,000

    Actual overhead:

Indirect materials.................	20,000	
Indirect labor.....................	94,000	
Factory utilities...................	28,000	
Factory depreciation	180,000	
Factory property taxes	31,000	
Factory insurance..................	15,000	368,000
Overapplied overhead		24,000

    Journal entry to close overapplied overhead to Cost of Goods Sold:

Manufacturing Overhead	24,000	
Cost of Goods Sold		24,000

5.

Shelves, Inc.
Income Statement
For the Year Ended December 31, Year 8

Sales..............................		$882,000
Cost of Goods Sold (adjusted):		
Cost of Goods Sold...............	$630,000	
Overapplied overhead	(24,000)	606,000
Gross margin		276,000
Selling and administrative expenses:		
Sales commissions	44,100	
Administrative salaries	120,000	164,100
Net income........................		$111,900

■ SELF-REVIEW PROBLEM 2: Job Costing (Service)

Trade-Info, Inc. provides trade-related consulting services for small businesses that are first-time exporters to foreign customers. The firm uses a job costing system to accumulate operating costs of its two departments—Research Department and Practice Department.

    The consulting firm's forecasts for Year 9 are presented below:

	Department	
	Research	Practice
Consulting-hours	.21,000	14,000
Research-hours	.7,000	–
Materials	.$ 11,000	$13,000
Department overhead cost	.$280,000	$140,000

The Research Department performs research services for (1) outside customers and (2) Practice Department. Hours spent for outside customers are directly billed to customers as consulting-hours. Hours spent for research at the request of the Practice Department are recorded as research-hours, and the research-hours portion of the Research Department's overhead is charged to the Practice Department before the departmental overhead rates are calculated. Predetermined overhead rates are charged to the jobs based on consulting-hours of each department.

The service costs are composed of the following:
1. Costs of materials
2. Costs of consulting-hours
   Labor rate: $90 per hour
3. Applied department overhead costs

Required:
1. Calculate each department's overhead after adjusting for inter-departmental service transactions.
2. Calculate each department's budgeted overhead rate.
3. The firm has spent the following costs and time on the case of a client, L.A. Apparel, which was started and completed in the current period:

	Department	
	Research	Practice
Materials.....................	$ 268	$ 327
Consulting-hours	63 hours	45 hours

   a. What is the amount of overhead charged to the L.A. Apparel account?
   b. What is the total job cost charged to the L.A. Apparel account?

Solution to Self-Review Problem
1. Inter-departmental service is provided by the Research Department for the Practice Department. Accordingly, that portion (7,000/28,000) of the Research Dept.'s overhead ($280,000) is allocated to the Practice Dept. as follows:

   Adjustment for inter-departmental service:

   $$\$280,000 \times \{7/(21 + 7)\} = \$280,000 \times 7/28 = \$70,000$$

	Department	
	Research	Practice
Overhead before adjustment for inter-departmental service	$280,000	$140,000
Adjustment	(70,000)	70,000
Overhead after adjustment.............	$210,000	$210,000

2. Budgeted department overhead rates are determined as follows:

	Department	
	Research	Practice
Budgeted department overhead ..... (after adjustment)	$210,000	$210,000
Cost driver units:		
Consulting-hours..............	÷ 21,000	÷ 14,000
Budgeted overhead rate per hour....	$ 10	$ 15

3. a. The overhead costs are applied to the L.A. Apparel account, which is a job, as folllows:

> Research department overhead:
>   63 Hours × $10 = $ 630
> Practice department overhead:
>   45 Hours × $15 = $ 675
> Total department overhead charged $1,305

b. The total cost is charged to the L.A. Apparel account as follows:

	Department		
	Research	Practice	Total
Materials	$ 268	$ 327	$ 595
Labor costs:			
63 hours × $90 =	5,670		
45 hours × $90 =		4,050	9,720
Overhead applied	630	675	1,305
Total job cost	$6,568	$5,052	$11,620

APPENDIX 4A

CAPACITY

In Chapter 2, we defined **capacity costs** as those costs that the organization must incur if it is to stay in business, i.e., if it is to have the capacity to produce or sell or both. In Chapter 4, we computed predetermined overhead rates based on the activity levels, which reflected the **levels of capacity** to produce.

The concept of capacity is very imporatant in product costing and managerial planning. We will discuss capacity and capacity costs in this appendix.

Baseline Capacity Defined

Managers use four different capacity measures:

Maximum Capacity. Maximum capacity, also called **theoretical** or **ideal capacity,** is 100% of total capacity. The required conditions for maximum capacity is 24-hour, seven-day operations of plant, equipment, and people at perfect efficiency. It does not make any allowance for unavoidable interruptions, such as setups, preventive maintenance, vacations, weekend time off, or downtime.

Practical Capacity. If we subtract unavoidable interruptions from maximum capacity, we obtain practical capacity.

Normal Capacity. The three-to-five-year average of the utilized capacity is considered normal capacity.

Expected Capacity. This is management's short-term estimate of capacity utilization, which fluctuates around normal capacity.

We can show a company's levels of capacity as follows:

100%	- - - - - →	Maximum capacity
− 20%		Unavoidable interruptions
80%	- - - - - →	Practical capacity
− 10%		Avoidable or planned interruptions (5-year average)
70%	- - - - - →	Normal capacity ▲▼ Expected capacity

Which Capacity Should We Use?

We use different capacity measures for different purposes in managerial accounting, as illustrated below:

Northwest cargo capacity has been increasing. How does the capacity cost per unit of cargo change?

For Aggressive Implementation of Value-Creating Activity Plans. In today's competitive market, companies need to eliminate any kind of waste in planning and control of operations. The use of maximum capacity will show how successful the company has been in creating values in all areas.

For Overhead Rate Computation. In computing overhead rates, the budgeted or actual overhead costs are divided by activity levels. For this activity level, practical, normal, or expected capacity is used.

For Short- or Medium-Term Capacity Cost Management. In order to manage the cost of capacity in the short- or medium-term period, companies use maximum capacity to measure the utilization of capacity.

For Normalized Costing. In the application of the normalized costing approach, companies use normal capacity.

For Use with Short-Term Market Demand Forecast. In matching market demand forecasts with the company's capacity in a particular year, use that year's expected capacity level. Normal capacity is not appropriate because it is based on average.

Choice of Capacity Measure and Overhead Rates

We already know that the variable cost per unit remains unchanged, regardless of the level of capacity. Only fixed cost per unit will be influenced by the level of capacity, as demonstrated in Exhibit 4A-1.

Consider a company with a single plant whose maximum capacity is 10,000 units of its single product. Using the percentages of utilization given in the above discussion of capacity measures, we can derive the following total costs and overhead rates per unit:

EXHIBIT 4A-1 Capacity Measure and Overhead Rates

	Maximum Capacity 100%	Practical Capacity 80%	Normal Capacity 70%	Expected Capacity 68%
Units produced	10,000	8,000	7,000	6,800
Total costs:				
Variable	$ 20,000	$ 16,000	$ 14,000	$ 13,600
Fixed	68,000	68,000	68,000	68,000
Total	$ 88,000	$ 84,000	$ 82,000	$ 81,600
Cost per unit:				
Variable	$ 2.00	$ 2.00	$ 2.00	$ 2.00
Fixed	6.80	8.50	9.71	10.00
Total	$ 8.80	$10.50	$11.71	$12.00

As the level of capacity decreases from maximum capacity of 10,000 units to practical capacity of 8,000 units, the fixed cost per unit increases from $6.80 to $8.50. At normal capacity of 7,000 units, the fixed cost increases even further to $9.71 per unit. Accordingly, we can generalize that the higher the capacity level, the lower the fixed overhead rate per unit. Variable cost per unit stays at $2 per unit, regardless of capacity level.

Unused Capacity

Unused capacity could result from three different situations:

1. **Excess Capacity.** For the example presented in Exhibit 4A-1, the 10% excess of practical capacity (80%) over normal capacity (70%) is excess capacity. The excess capacity is usually caused by inaccurate capacity planning, and managers cannot eliminate excess capacity in the short run.

2. **Idle Capacity.** For the same example, the 2% difference between normal capacity (70%) and expected capacity (68%) is idle capacity. Expected capacity fluctuates around normal capacity, depending on the demand forecast. Idle capacity, accordingly, will disappear when the customer demand increases.

3. **Unused Capacity Created by Continuous Improvement.** Some capacity will be relieved when the company's efforts to make continuous improvement in its operations become successful. The use of lean production, including the application of just-in-time (JIT) and total quality management (TQM), activity-based management (ABM), and other continuous improvement techniques would leave some capacity free without lowering the company's ability to perform at the same level. We will discuss these concepts in future chapters.

■ REVIEW QUESTIONS

4-1 Why is the unit cost of production important?

4-2 Differentiate between the job-order costing system and the process costing system and give examples of industries likely to use each system.

4-3 How are material costs measured and accumulated on a job in a job-order costing system?

4-4 What is the purpose of a time ticket in a job-order costing system?

4-5 How is a predetermined manufacturing overhead application rate developed and why?

4-6 How is manufacturing overhead applied to each job in a job-order costing system?

4-7 State some of the factors that should be considered in the development of a manufacturing overhead application rate.

4-8 What is a normalized overhead rate, and why is it so called?

4-9 What is the purpose of a job cost sheet in a job-order costing system?

4-10 Briefly explain, using T-accounts without figures, how costs flow through a job-order costing system.

4-11 Distinguish between overapplied and underapplied overhead.

4-12 Explain two possible methods of disposing of overapplied or underapplied overhead at year-end.

4-13 Company A applies overhead to production at 150% of direct labor cost. Job number 1001 had direct materials cost of $20,000 and direct labor cost of $30,000. During the period, 100 units of the product were produced. What would be the cost of production per unit?

4-14 Refer to question 4-13. If actual overhead was $50,000 and Company A closes overapplied or underapplied overhead to cost of goods sold, what is the cost of sales of one unit of job 1001 if only 80 units were sold?

4-15 Is it possible to use a job-order costing system in a service organization or non-profit organization? Explain.

4-16 Explain how costs are allocated in Stage 2 cost assignment of the two-stage cost assignment?

4-17 (Appendix 4A) If the level of capacity decreases from maximum capacity of 100,000 units to practical capacity of 85,000 units, what is the effect on fixed cost per unit? Why?

4-18 (Appendix 4A) What happens to the variable cost per unit when the capacity level decreases? Why?

4-19 (Appendix 4A) What would create unused capacity?

⊕ INTERNET PROJECT

Web 4-1:

Websites: www.starbucks.com
             www.jpmorganchase.com

The websites listed above represent two famous companies. Search the sites for information on their product and operating characteristics.

Required:

1. Which product and operating characteristics indicate that a job-order costing would be appropriate?

2. Which product and operating characteristics indicate that a job-order costing would *not* be appropriate?

Web 4-2:

Websites: www.oracle.com
             www.pfizer.com

The websites listed above represent two famous companies. Search the sites for information on their overhead costs.

Required:

1. What kinds of major overhead items do they have?
2. How should they allocate overhead costs to their products?

■ EXERCISES

E4-1   Job Costing vs. Process Costing

Indicate whether job-order costing (J) or process costing (P) would be the proper method of costing products in the following cases:

a. A campus printing shop.
b. An antique car restorer.
c. A perfume manufacturer.
d. An oil refinery.
e. A glass manufacturer.
f. A copper mining company.
g. A local electric utility.
h. A Hawaiian pineapple juice manufacturer.
i. An oil tanker manufacturer.
j. A home security consulting firm.
k. A public relations firm.
l. A lumber company in the Pacific Northwest.

E4-2 Predetermined Overhead Rate; Job Cost Sheet

Furniture, Inc. uses a job order costing system. Overhead is applied on the basis of direct labor cost in department A and machine-hours in department B. At the start of Year 6, the company made the following estimates:

	Department A	Department B
Direct labor-hours	15,000	5,000
Machine-hours	2,500	20,000
Manufacturing overhead cost	$80,000	$72,000
Direct labor cost	$64,000	$42,000

Required:

1. Compute the predetermined overhead rate to be used in Department A and in Department B.
2. The cost sheet for Job X-101 showed the following:

	Department A	Department B
Direct labor-hours	30	5
Machine-hours	10	60
Materials requisitioned	$550	$150
Direct labor cost	$120	$35

Compute the overhead applied to Job X-101.

3. Compute the total job cost charged to X-101.

E4-3 Automation and the Nature of Actual Product Costs

Flex Forever, Inc. is a small manufacturer of physical fitness equipment. The company had relied heavily on manual labor in the manufacturing process until the first quarter of Year 6. In the second quarter of Year 6, the company introduced robotics in the manufacturing operations. The employees had been fully trained in working in the automated environment by the end of Year 6.

The operations and cost data for the first quarter of Year 6 and Year 7 follow:

	First Quarter	
	Year 6	Year 7
Direct labor-hours	24,580	13,610
Machine-hours	6,874	10,658
Units produced	8,540	9,135
Materials costs	$ 86,459	$ 92,376
Direct labor costs	$442,440	$272,200
Manufacturing overhead	$456,270	$474,087

The company uses a job-order costing system based on actual costs.

Required:

1. Compute the actual product cost per unit for the first quarter of each year.
2. Which period shows the lower unit cost? Why? [Hint: Compute unit cost of each cost element and compare.]
3. In Year 7, the company's sales showed only a slight increase over Year 6. The sales in Year 8, however, increased significantly over the sales of prior years. During the first quarter of Year 8, the company produced 15,500 units. The unit costs of materials and labor remained unchanged from Year 7. Total overhead cost incurred was $653,325 in the first quarter of Year 8. Compute the total and unit product costs for the first quarter of Year 8. Also show the unit cost of each of the three cost elements.
4. Refer back to the costs in the first quarter of Year 8. What would be the reason for the change in the unit product cost?

E4-4   Normal Costing vs. Actual Costing

Refer to E4-3. The manufacturing overhead costs shown above are actual costs. In practice, most companies use predetermined overhead rates based on estimated costs and levels of activity such as direct labor-hours, machine-hours, or number of units produced.

Required:

1. Explain why a company, such as Flex Forever, Inc., would want to use estimated overhead cost instead of actual cost.
2. Which overhead allocation basis would you recommend for each of the three periods (Year 6, Year 7, and Year 8), if the company decided to use estimated overhead costs instead of actual costs?
3. At the beginning of Year 6 and Year 7, the company made the following estimates for the operations of the first quarter of Year 6 and Year 7:

	First Quarter	
	Year 6	**Year 7**
Direct labor-hours	22,000	15,000
Machine-hours	7,000	12,000
Manufacturing overhead.	$420,000	$500,000

Compute the predetermined overhead rate for each period using the overhead allocation bases you selected in part 2 of E4-4.

4. In which case, actual costing or normal costing, does a company need to adjust for under- or overapplied overhead cost at the end of the period? Why?

E4-5   Journal Entries; Actual vs. Applied Overhead

The Premier Manufacturing Company uses a job order costing system. The following data relate to the month of July:

a. Raw materials purchased on account, $94,000.

b. Raw materials issued to production, $79,000
c. Direct labor cost incurred, $61,000 (credit Wages Payable).
d. Actual manufacturing overhead costs totaled $42,700 for the month (credit Accounts Payable).
e. Overhead is applied on a basis of $3.50 per machine-hour. For the month, 12,000 machine-hours were recorded.
f. Production orders costing $175,000 were completed during the month.
g. During the month, sales invoiced were $178,750. The company uses a 25% mark-up above cost.

Required:

1. Prepare journal entries to record the information above.
2. Compute the ending balance of work in process. The beginning balance was $23,000.
3. Compute the overapplied or underapplied manufacturing overhead.

E4-6 Under- or Overapplied Overhead; Cost of Goods Manufactured

Cabinets, Inc. provides the following data for Year 6:

Work in process inventory, December 31, Year 5	$ 6,000
Work in process inventory, December 31, Year 6	7,500
Insurance, factory	6,000
Depreciation, factory	24,000
Depreciation, general office	2,000
Indirect labor cost	10,000
Utilities, factory	8,000
General office supplies	7,500
Purchases of raw materials	30,000
Raw materials inventory, December 31, Year 5	7,000
Raw materials inventory, December 31, Year 6	4,000
Direct labor cost	40,000

Manufacturing overhead is applied to production at the rate of $5 per machine hour. Production records reveal that a total of 10,000 machine hours were used for Year 6.

Required:

1. Compute the amount of under- or overapplied overhead.
2. Prepare a schedule of cost of goods manufactured for Year 6.

E4-7 Predetermined Overhead Rate; Job Cost Sheet

CDI, Inc. started its operations in Year 1. In Year 1, the company started its work on 18 jobs. The first 17 jobs were completed by the end of Year 1. The following

T-account shows the activities of Year 1 in the Work in Process account with respect to the 18 jobs:

Work in Process			
Direct materials	30,000	Transferred to finished	
Direct labor	60,000	goods	125,000
Manufacturing overhead	45,000		

The company uses a job order costing system and applies manufacturing overhead to work in process on the basis of direct labor cost. Job 18, the last job in Year 1 and the only remaining job at the end of Year 1, has been charged with $5,000 in direct labor cost.

Required:

1. Compute the predetermined overhead application rate.
2. Refer to Job 18, and complete the job cost sheet.

Job Cost Sheet-Job 18

Direct materials	$	?
Direct labor	$ 5,000	
Manufacturing overhead		?
Total cost...............................	$	?

E4-8 Predetermined Overhead Rate; Disposition of Over- or Underapplied Overhead; Proration

Singer Inc. uses a job order costing system. The company's records revealed the following actual cost and operating data at the end of Year 6:

Machine-hours recorded	40,000
Direct labor cost.....................................	$250,000
Factory overhead cost	163,000
Raw materials inventory..............................	9,000
Work in process inventory	24,000
Finished goods inventory.............................	45,000
Cost of goods sold	171,000

The company uses predetermined overhead rates based on machine-hours in applying manufacturing overhead to jobs. Estimated cost and operating data for Year 6 are given below:

Estimated machine-hours	50,000
Estimated direct labor cost	$300,000
Estimated factory overhead...........................	200,000

Required:

1. Compute the company's predetermined overhead rate for Year 6.
2. How much is the under- or overapplied overhead?
3. There are two options the company has for disposing of its under- or over-applied overhead. Prepare a journal entry under each of these options.
4. What is the difference in net income under these two options?

E4-9   Two-Stage Cost Assignment

There are two-stage cost assignments in manufacturing or service operations before final product or service cost is determined. For the following activities, indicate whether each activity takes place in Stage 1 or Stage 2 of the two-stage cost assignments:

a. Machine-hours are used for the allocation of cost to products.
b. Indirect labor cost is allocated to the assembly department.
c. Direct labor cost is used to allocate finishing department costs to 46 different jobs completed for the period.
d. Repairs and maintenance cost is taken from the general ledger.
e. Fabrication department's cost is allocated to various jobs.
f. Depreciation expense of robots is charged to machining department.
g. Finishing department's cost is assigned to products.
h. Material handling cost is charged to machining department.

 ### E4-10   Overhead Applied; Unit Cost

Hang-Nine Inc., which has just completed one full month of operations, uses a job-order costing system. The production team worked on the following three jobs:

	Job Number		
	H1	**H2**	**H3**
Units of product in the job	1,800	1,500	2,000
Direct labor-hours worked	1,000	600	1,200
Direct materials cost	$3,980	$1,200	$3,200
Direct labor cost	5,000	3,000	6,000

The company incurred actual overhead costs of $5,500 during the month and applied manufacturing overhead to production on a basis of direct labor-hours at a predetermined rate of $2 per hour. Jobs H1 and H3 were completed during the month. Job H2 was not completed.

Required:

1. Compute the amount of overhead applied to each job.
2. Compute the unit cost of jobs H1 and H3.

3. Prepare a journal entry to transfer the completed jobs to Finished Goods.
4. What is the balance in Work in Process at the end of the month?

 ## E4-11 Service Job Costing

Market-Info, Inc. provides market research services to small businesses that cannot perform their own in-house market research. The firm uses a job costing system to accumulate operating costs of its two departments: Foreign Market Department and Domestic Market Department.

The firm's estimates for the operations of Year 9 are presented below:

	Department	
	Foreign Market	Domestic Market
Research hours............................	16,000	14,000
Data retrieval cost	$49,000	$27,000
Department overhead cost................	$215,000	$165,000

The firm charges departmental overhead costs to jobs using predetermined overhead rates on the basis of research hours spent. The service job costs include data retrieval cost, labor cost for research time, and applied departmental overhead cost. The firm's average labor rate is $80 per hour.

Required:

1. Compute each department's predetermined overhead rate.
2. BPI, Inc. is a client of Market-Info, Inc. In the current period, BPI received services from both departments of Market-Info. The time and costs spent on the BPI account are presented below:

	Department	
	Foreign Market	Domestic Market
Research hours............................	86	78
Data retrieval cost	$273	$192

a. What is the amount of overhead charged to the BPI account?
b. What is the total job cost charged to the BPI account?

E4-12 Capacity (Appendix 4A)

Assume the following data relative to a company's capacity utilization:

Unavoidable interruptions in operations.....................	15%
Planned interruptions based on a 5-year average	8%

Management plans to operate at three percentage points below normal capacity next year.

Required:

Determine each of the following capacity levels:

1. Maximum capacity
2. Practical capacity
3. Normal capacity
4. Expected capacity for next year

E4-13 Capacity (Appendix 4A)

Consider each of the following situations:

1. A company wants to compute overhead rates.
2. A company has undertaken an aggressive plan of value creation, and wants to measure the success of the plan.
3. A company wants to apply the normalized costing approach.
4. A company wants to match market demand forecasts with the company's capacity in a year.
5. A company wants to manage the capacity cost for a trial period of two years.

Required:

Which capacity measure should be used in each of the above situations?

■ PROBLEMS

P4-14 Ethics in Job Order Costing

Cal Mac, Inc. is a subcontractor providing precision machining services to major defense contractors located in southern California. Cal Mac's work involves both governmental and commercial projects. The company tries to keep its productive capacity and overhead as low as possible, since governmental and commercial orders can disappear very quickly.

Due to a series of cutbacks in defense spending, Cal Mac's customers have decreased their orders over the last several years. This has put a strain on Cal Mac's operations, because the smaller number of jobs completed in each period has led the company to allocate higher manufacturing overhead costs to the jobs.

Jennifer Dito, assistant controller, has recently been pressured by Frank Passet, vice president-finance, to recognize job No. 164 as the last job completed in Year 8. Ms. Dito checked the preliminary compilation of jobs completed around the year-end, which revealed the following:

Jobs	Date Completed	Total Job Cost	Contract Price
No. 162	12/22/x8	$84,000	$134,000
No. 163	12/27/x8	63,000	100,000
No. 164	1/03/x9	91,000	140,000

Job No. 164, according to the records, was completed in the early afternoon of January 3, the first day of operations in Year 9. Dito informed Mr. Passet that job

No. 164 belonged to Year 9, not to Year 8. Passet responded that it was only a few days' difference, and the exclusion of the job would substantially increase the amounts of overhead applied to other Year 8 jobs.

Passet emphasized the importance of maximizing the number of jobs completed and profit for Year 8 and said everyone involved should be a team player for the organization.

Required:

1. Discuss the ethical implications of the situation Jennifer Dito faces.
2. What are the consequences of following the course of action suggested by the vice president-finance?
3. Identify desirable courses of action Jennifer Dito can take.

P4-15 Job Order Cost Concepts; Multiple Choice

Beginning work in process in Department 203:

Job No.	Material	Labor	Overhead	Total
1376.............	$17,500	$22,000	$33,000	$72,500

Department 203 costs for Year 9:

Incurred by

Jobs	Material	Labor	Other	Total
1376	$ 1,000	$ 7,000	--	$ 8,000
1377	26,000	53,000	--	79,000
1378	12,000	9,000	--	21,000
1379	4,000	1,000	--	5,000

Not Incurred by Jobs:

	Material	Labor	Other	Total
Indirect materials ..	15,000	--	--	15,000
Indirect labor	--	53,000	--	53,000
Employee benefits..	--	--	$23,000	23,000
Depreciation.......	--	--	12,000	12,000
Supervision........	--	20,000	--	20,000
Total...........	$58,000	$143,000	$35,000	$236,000

Department 203 overhead rate for Year 9:

Budgeted overhead:		
Variable:	Indirect materials......................	$ 16,000
	Indirect labor	56,000
	Employee benefits.......................	24,000
Fixed:	Supervision.............................	20,000
	Depreciation............................	12,000
Total	....	$128,000
Budgeted direct labor dollars........................		$ 80,000
Rate per direct labor dollar ($128,000 ÷ $80,000)......		160%

1. The actual overhead for Department 203 for Year 9 was
   a. $156,000.
   b. $123,000.
   c. $70,000.
   d. $112,000.
   e. Not shown above.
2. Department 203 overhead for Year 9 was
   a. $11,000 underapplied.
   b. $11,000 overapplied.
   c. $44,000 underapplied.
   d. $44,000 overapplied.
   e. Not shown above.
3. Job No. 1376 was the only job completed and sold in Year 9.
   What amount was included in cost of goods sold for this job?
   a. $72,500.
   b. $91,700.
   c. $80,500.
   d. $19,200.
   e. Not shown above.
4. The value of work in process inventory at the end of Year 9 was
   a. $105,000.
   b. $180,600.
   c. $228,000.
   d. $205,800.
   e. Not shown above.

(CMA, adapted)

P4-16 T-accounts; Disposition of Under- or Overapplied Overhead; Proration

Tech Inc. uses a job-order costing system. The company's inventory balances at the beginning of the period are shown below:

Raw materials	$15,000
Work in process	9,000
Finished goods	40,000

During the year, the following transactions were recognized:

1. Raw materials were purchased on account, $100,000.
2. Raw materials were issued for production, $95,000 (80% direct; 20% indirect).
3. Factory payrolls were accrued, $150,000 (75% direct; 25% indirect).
4. Cash payments were made:

   To suppliers, $80,000
   To employees for payrolls, $145,000
   For factory utilities, $12,000
   For factory rent, $25,000
   For miscellaneous factory costs, $36,600

5. Overhead was applied to jobs on a basis of 120% of direct labor cost. This reflects the labor-intensive nature of the work.
6. The ending balance in the Work in Process inventory account was $32,500.
7. The ending balance in the Finished Goods inventory account was $50,000.

Required:

1. Enter the above transactions directly into T-accounts.
2. Complete the following schedule:

Direct materials	$	?
Direct labor		?
Manufacturing overhead		12,000
Work in Process (ending balance)		$32,500

3. Compute the under- or overapplied factory overhead for the year.
4. What two options does the company have for disposing of its under- or overapplied overhead? Prepare a journal entry under each of these options showing disposition of the under- or overapplied overhead for the year.

P4-17   T-Accounts; Job Costing Process; Income Statement

Home Entertainment Inc.'s trial balance as of January 1, Year 5 is as follows:

Cash	$ 20,000	
Accounts Receivable	24,000	
Raw Materials	15,000	
Work in Process	35,000	
Finished Goods	40,000	
Property, Plant and Equipment	450,000	
Accumulated Depreciation		$ 90,000
Accounts Payable		60,000
Capital Stock		300,000
Retained Earnings		134,000
	$584,000	$584,000

The company manufactures home entertainment center display sets and uses a job-order costing system. During Year 5, the following transactions took place:

a. Raw materials purchased, $90,000.
b. Raw materials used in production, $80,000 (90% direct materials; 10% indirect materials).
c. Wages and salaries incurred were:

Direct labor	$82,000
Indirect labor	34,000
Selling and administrative salaries	70,000

d. Depreciation recorded on property, plant and equipment, $45,000 (80% related to factory; 20% related to selling and administrative offices).

e. Insurance paid, $6,000 (80% related to factory; 20% related to selling and administrative functions).

f. Factory utilities incurred, $22,000.

g. Manufacturing overhead was applied to production at the rate of 150% of direct materials cost.

h. Cost of goods manufactured and transferred to finished goods warehouse, $252,000.

i. The balance in the Finished Goods account at December 31, Year 5 was $30,000.

j. Sales revenues from goods sold on account were $400,000.

k. Other selling and administrative expenses incurred were $34,000.

Required:

1. Prepare T-accounts for Raw Materials, Work in Process, Finished Goods, Manufacturing Overhead, and Cost of Goods Sold. Record the above transactions directly into those T-accounts. Find the ending balance in each account.

2. Prepare a journal entry to close over- or underapplied overhead into Work in Process, Finished Goods, and Cost of Goods Sold. Post to T-accounts and find new ending balances of the accounts.

3. Prepare a schedule of cost of goods manufactured for Year 5 using (a) applied overhead costs and (b) actual overhead costs.

P4-18 Job-Order Costing Concepts; Multiple Choice

Blue Star Manufacturing Company's fiscal year runs from July 1 to June 30. Blue Star uses a job-order costing system for its production costs.

A predetermined overhead rate based upon direct labor-hours is used to apply overhead to individual jobs. A budget of overhead costs was prepared for the fiscal year as shown below:

Direct labor-hours	120,000
Variable overhead costs	$390,000
Fixed overhead costs	216,000
Total overhead	$606,000

The information presented below is for November. Jobs x6-50 and x6-51 were completed during November.

Inventories, November 1:

Raw materials and supplies.........................	$10,500
Work in process (Job x6-50)	54,000
Finished goods....................................	112,500

Purchases of raw materials and supplies:

Raw materials....................................	$135,000
Supplies	15,000

Materials and supplies requisitioned for production:

Job x6-50	$ 45,000
Job x6-51	37,500
Job x6-52	25,500
Supplies	12,000
Total	$120,000

Factory direct labor-hours:

Job x6-50	3,500 DLH
Job x6-51	3,000 DLH
Job x6-52	2,000 DLH

Labor costs:

Direct labor wages...............................	$51,000
Indirect labor wages (4,000 hours).................	15,000
Supervisory salaries	6,000

Building occupancy cost:
(heat, light, depreciation, etc.):

Factory facilities	$6,500
Sales offices....................................	1,500
Administrative offices............................	1,000
Total	$9,000

Factory equipment costs:

Power...	$4,000
Repairs and maintenance..........................	1,500
Depreciation	1,500
Other...	1,000
Total	$8,000

1. The predetermined overhead rate to be used to apply overhead to individual jobs during the fiscal year is
   a. $3.25 per DLH.
   b. $4.69 per DLH.
   c. $5.05 per DLH.
   d. $5.41 per DLH.
   e. Some rate other than those shown above.

   Note: Without prejudice to your answer to item 1, assume the predetermined overhead rate is $4.50 per direct labor-hour. Use this amount in answering items 2 through 6.

2. The total cost of job x6-50 is
   a. $81,750.
   b. $135,750.
   c. $142,750.
   d. $146,750.
   e. Some amount other than those shown above.

3. The manufacturing overhead costs applied to job x6-52 during November were
    a. $9,000.
    b. $47,500.
    c. $46,500.
    d. $8,000.
    e. Some amount other than those shown above.
4. The total amount of overhead applied to jobs during November was
    a. $29,250.
    b. $38,250.
    c. $47,250.
    d. $56,250.
    e. Some amount other than those shown above.
5. Actual factory overhead incurred during November was
    a. $38,000.
    b. $41,500.
    c. $47,500.
    d. $50,500.
    e. Some amount other than those shown above.
6. At the end of the last fiscal year, Blue Star Company had the following account balances:

Overapplied overhead	$ 1,000
Cost of goods sold	980,000
Work in process inventory	38,000
Finished goods inventory	82,000

   The most common treatment of the overapplied overhead would be to
    a. Prorate it between work in process inventory and finished goods inventory.
    b. Prorate it between work in process inventory, finished goods inventory, and cost of goods sold.
    c. Carry it as a deferred credit on the balance sheet.
    d. Carry it as miscalleneous operating revenue on the income statement.
    e. Credit it to cost of goods sold.

                                        (CMA, adapted)

P4-19   Journal Entries; T-accounts

On January 1, Year 6, AMP Company had the following balances:

Finished goods	$45,000
Work in process.	30,000
Raw materials	25,000

The following transactions were recognized during Year 6:
    a. Raw materials purchased on account, $80,000.
    b. Raw materials issued to production, $90,000 ($5,000 of this amount was for indirect materials).

   c. Salaries and wages incurred:
       Direct labor (20,000 hours). $120,000
       Indirect labor.   30,000
       Sales commission.   35,000
       Administrative salaries   40,000

   d. Factory utilities, $12,000 (to support 15,000 hours of machine opera-
       tion).
   e. Depreciation recorded for the year, $30,000 ($5,000 on office equip-
       ment; $25,000 on factory equipment).
   f. Factory insurance, $2,000.
   g. Advertising, $12,000.
   h. Other manufacturing overhead costs incurred, $14,000.
   i. Manufacturing overhead was applied to production at a rate of $6 per
       machine-hour.
   j. The cost of goods completed for the year, $310,000.
   k. Goods that had cost $300,000 to manufacture were sold on account for
       $450,000.

Required:

   1. Prepare journal entries to record the information given above.
   2. Prepare T-accounts for Raw Materials, Work in Process, Manufacturing Over-
       head, Finished Goods, and Cost of Goods Sold. Post the appropriate parts of
       the above journal entries to these selected T-accounts. Show the ending bal-
       ance in each T-account.
   3. Prepare a journal entry to close any balance in Manufacturing Overhead to
       Cost of Goods Sold.

P4-20   Normal Costing; Statement of Cost of Goods Manufactured and Sold

The beginning inventory balances are given below for MCR Company:

       Raw Materials $76,000
       Work in Process.   23,000
       Finished Goods   49,000

   The following information and transactions are related to the operations of
MCR Company for the year:

   a. Purchases of raw materials amounted to $233,000.
   b. Issuances of raw materials amounted to $241,000 for direct materials and
       $1,300 for indirect materials.
   c. Payroll for the year amounted to $161,000 for direct labor and $45,000
       for indirect labor.
   d.   Manufacturing overhead is applied to production at 80% of direct
       labor cost.

e. Other manufacturing overhead for the year amounted to $104,300. Credit Sundry Credits.

f. Goods costing $516,000 were completed for the year.

g. Sales on account for the year were $842,000. The cost of these sales amounted to $498,000.

h. The company's policy is to close any underapplied or overapplied manufacturing overhead to cost of goods sold.

Required:

1. Prepare journal entries to record the information given above.
2. Prepare T-accounts for Raw Materials, Work in Process, Manufacturing Overhead, Finished Goods, and Cost of Goods Sold. Post the appropriate parts of the above journal entries to these selected T-accounts. Show the ending balance in each T-account.
3. Prepare a statement of cost of goods manufactured. Use applied overhead (not actual overhead).

P4-21   Service Costing; Overhead Allocation Basis

College Auxiliary Services, Inc. (CAS) is a nonprofit, tax-exempt organization that provides administrative support services to various units of a local college. CAS uses a job-order costing system, and charges its service costs to the college units (clients) using predetermined overhead rates of its two departments—the personnel services department and the financial services department.

CAS planners made the following estimates for the year at the beginning of Year 7:

	Department	
	Personnel Services	*Financial Services*
Service hours..........................	16,000	18,000
Clients' personnel size...................	310	--
Direct manpower cost...................	$364,000	$357,000
Departmental overhead cost	489,000	326,000

CAS charges each client its share of direct manpower cost and departmental overhead cost at the predetermined rates. Personnel services department applies its departmental overhead cost based on the number of employees of each client. Financial services department uses the number of service hours each client's jobs require to apply overhead to clients. The direct manpower cost is charged to clients at the average hourly rate of each department based on the service hours consumed.

Required:

1. Compute the predetermined overhead rates to be used in the two service departments.

2. The college's Contract and Grants Office, with five employees, consumed 3,280 service hours of the personnel services department and 1,070 service hours of the financial services department during the year. How much departmental overhead cost should be applied to Contract and Grants Office?

3. Compute the total service cost charged to Contract and Grants Office for the year. Show the charges by department and in total.

4. The year-end records provided the following actual results for the entire operations of CAS for Year 7:

	Department	
	Personnel Services	*Financial Services*
Service hours...........................	16,870	17,250
Clients' personnel size...................	287	–
Direct manpower cost...................	$358,260	$343,980
Departmental overhead cost	472,430	306,590

What is the amount of over- or underapplied overhead cost in each department for Year 7?

5. The manager of Contract and Grants Office complained about the high overhead cost CAS charged. She claimed that those overhead numbers were "pulled out of the air." How would the manager of CAS have to justify the overhead allocation bases that were used?

P4-22 Predetermined Overhead Rate; Job Cost Sheet; Over- or Underapplied Overhead

CPI Inc. employs a job-order costing system, and uses predetermined overhead rates in applying manufacturing overhead to individual jobs. The predetermined overhead rate in Department A is based on direct labor cost, and the rate in Department B is based on machine-hours.

At the beginning of Year 6, the company's management made the following estimates for the year:

	Department	
	A	*B*
Machine-hours..........................	12,000	50,000
Direct labor-hours.......................	30,000	15,000
Direct labor cost........................	$180,000	$ 80,000
Manufacturing overhead..................	225,000	162,000

Job 1001, containing 10 units of product, was started into production and completed during the month of September. The company's cost records show the following information on the job:

	Job 1001	
	Department A	*Department B*
Machine-hours.........................	20	75
Direct labor-hours......................	40	22
Materials used	$250	$450
Direct labor cost	$175	$120

Required:

1. Compute the predetermined overhead rate for each department.
2. Compute the total overhead cost applied to job 1001.
3. Compute the total cost of job 1001 and the unit cost of product.
4. Actual cost and operating data at the end of Year 6 are presented below:

	Department A	Department B
Machine-hours	13,000	48,000
Direct labor-hours	32,000	14,500
Direct labor cost	$180,000	$ 78,000
Manufacturing overhead	216,000	160,000

What was the amount of under- or overapplied overhead in each department at the end of Year 6?

 P4-23   Service Job Costing; CPA Firm

Cable & Healy, CPAs, use a service job-costing system, and charges overhead cost to client accounts at predetermined rates that vary according to the actual relationships between direct chargeable professional cost and indirect/support cost of the immediately preceding year. Professional cost (both direct chargeable and indirect nonchargeable) includes the compensation paid to partners, managers, senior accountants, and staff accountants. Support cost represents office expenses and the compensation paid to paraprofessionals and secretaries.

At the beginning of Year 8, management of the firm present the following data of Year 7 and the estimates for Year 8:

Year 7 Data:
    Professional hours (weekly average):

Direct chargeable hours	32
Indirect nonchargeable hours	8
Total professional hours	40

Billing rates:

Partners	$200
Managers	130
Senior accountants	80
Staff accountants	50

Year 8 Estimates:

Professional staff compensation	$6,300,000
Support cost	2,500,000
Total compensation	$8,800,000

Other information:
a. Due to the competitive environment, the Year 7 billing rates will remain unchanged in Year 8.
b. Average rates will be used to compute compensation cost.

Required:

1. Compute the predetermined overhead rate per dollar of direct chargeable cost (direct labor cost) of professional staff.
2. The job-cost sheet for Efram Bailey, a client, shows the following for January, Year 8:

	Chargeable Hours				Total
	Week 1	*Week 2*	*Week 3*	*Week 4*	Hours
Partners...........	3	4	4	2	13
Managers...........	2	4	3	4	13
Seniors...........	22	24	20	24	90
Juniors...........	52	64	76	80	272
Total...........	79	96	103	110	388

Compute the total job cost of the Efram Bailey account for January, Year 8. The average professional staff compensation is 50% of the billing rate for each professional employee class.

P4-24 Normal Cost and Actual Cost; Journal Entries Prepared from Statement of Cost of Goods Manufactured and Sold

JSN Company
Statement of Cost of Goods Manufactured and Sold
For the Year Ended December 31, Year 6

Direct materials:		
Raw materials, January 1..................	$280,000	
Purchases of raw materials...............	610,000	
Raw materials available.................	$890,000	
Raw materials, December 31..............	(228,750)	
Raw materials used.....................	661,250	
Indirect materials used..................	(3,750)	
Direct materials used in production......		$ 657,500
Direct labor................................		825,000
Manufacturing overhead:		
Indirect materials........................	3,750	
Indirect labor	162,500	
Miscellaneous factory costs	586,250	
Actual overhead costs	752,500	
Underapplied overhead	(10,000)	
Overhead applied to work in process		742,500
Total manufacturing costs...............		2,225,000
Work in process, January 1		100,000
Costs to account for		2,325,000
Work in process, December 31		(87,500)

Cost of goods manufactured at normal........	$2,237,500
Finished goods, January 1	212,500
Goods available for sale	2,450,000
Finished goods, December 31	(175,000)
Cost of goods sold at normal.................	2,275,000
Underapplied manufacturing overhead	10,000
Cost of goods sold at actual..................	$2,285,000

Required:

1. Some transactions and entries are implicit in the statement presented above. Show those journal entries and indicate which transaction each of the journal entries represents.
2. The company applies its overhead using a predetermined rate per machine-hour. Was the actual number of machine-hours higher or lower than the estimated number of machine-hours?

P4-25 A Service Firm's Disposition of Under- or Overapplied Overhead; Missing Numbers

Cartoons-R-Us Inc. creates animated cartoons for use in motion pictures produced by a major entertainment company in Burbank, California. Cartoons-R-Us uses a job-order costing system for its operations that require many hours of animators' time, although the animators rely heavily on computer graphics. The company uses predetermined overhead rates based on operating hours in applying manufacturing overhead to jobs.

At the beginning of Year 6, management prepared the following projections on estimated cost and operating data for the year:

Estimated operating hours............................	25,000
Estimated direct labor cost	$320,000
Estimated overhead....................................	100,000

At the end of Year 6, the company's records revealed the following actual cost and operating data:

Operating hours	28,000
Direct labor cost.......................................	$360,000
Factory overhead cost.................................	125,000
Cost of goods sold	408,000
Ending balance, work in process	?
Ending balance, finished goods........................	?

The company's policy is to prorate under- or overapplied overhead between work in process, finished goods, and cost of goods sold in proportion to their ending balances.

Required:

1. Compute the company's predetermined overhead rate for Year 6.
2. How much is the under- or overapplied overhead?
3. The adjustment for under- or overapplied overhead under the stated company policy represented an increase of $11,050 in the cost of goods sold account balance. Compute the ending balances of Work in Process and Finished Goods, before the adjustment is made. Assume that the work-in-process ending balance is only 50% of the finished goods ending balance.
4. Make a journal entry to close under- or overapplied overhead according to the company's policy.

P4-26 Nonprofit Job Costing

A social service agency of a municipal government has a cost-accounting system that tracks costs by department (for example, family counseling, general welfare, and foster children) and by case.

The condensed line-item budget for the general welfare department of the agency for Year 4 showed the following:

Annual professional compensation:

	Staff Size	Salary	Total	
Level 7	7	$30,000	$210,000	
Level 5	20	20,000	400,000	
Level 3	35	15,000	525,000	$1,135,000
Other operating costs for Year 4				408,600
Total departmental operating costs				$1,543,600

For costing various cases (jobs), the department uses a single overhead application rate based on direct labor costs. Direct labor cost is defined as the professional salaries assigned to specific cases. The hours spent on each case by professional workers are available on weekly case-time reports. Unassigned time is listed separately on the reports.

About 20% of the available time of professionals is not assigned to specific cases and is typically used for professional development purposes. The unassigned time becomes a part of overhead.

Required:

1. Compute the predetermined overhead rate as a percentage of the assignable professional salaries (direct labor).
2. A welfare case, Client No. 427, required three hours of Level 7 time, five hours of Level 5 time, and seven hours of Level 3 time last week. What is the job cost that must be allocated to Client No. 427 for the week? Assume that all professional employees work a 1,750-hour year.

P4-27 Multiple Jobs; Actual Cost of Goods Manufactured; Over- and Underapplied Overhead

Valport Company employs a job-order cost system based on the full absorption of actual costs. Manufacturing overhead is applied on the basis of machine-hours (MH) using a predetermined overhead rate. The current fiscal year overhead rate is calculated as follows:

Estimated manufacturing overhead costs.......	$1,200,000
Estimated activity level......................	80,000 MH
Overhead rate	$15 per MH

Valport's policy is to close the over/under application of manufacturing overhead to the Cost of Goods Sold.

Operations for the year ended November 30, Year 9 have been completed. All of the accounting entries have been made for the year except the application of manufacturing overhead to the jobs worked on during November, the transfer of costs from Work in Process to Finished Goods for the jobs completed in November, and the transfer of costs from Finished Goods to Cost of Goods Sold for the jobs that have been sold during November.

Summarized data that have been accumulated from the accounting records as of October 31, Year 9 and for November, Year 9 are presented below:

Work in Process:

Job No.	Balance 10/31/x9	November Activity Direct Materials	Direct Labor	Machine Hours
N11-007	$ 87,000	$ 1,500	$ 4,500	300
N11-013	55,000	4,000	12,000	1,000
N11-015	-0-	25,600	26,700	1,400
D12-002	-0-	37,900	20,000	2,500
D12-003	-0-	26,000	16,800	800
Totals	$142,000	$95,000	$80,000	6,000

Operating Activity:

	Activity Through 10/31/x9	November Activity
Manufacturing overhead incurred:		
Indirect materials	$ 125,000	$ 9,000
Indirect labor	345,000	30,000
Utilities	245,000	22,000
Depreciation................	385,000	35,000
Total overhead incurred ...	$1,100,000	$96,000
Other items:		
Material purchases*	$965,000	$98,000
Direct labor costs	$845,000	$80,000
Machine hours..............	73,000	6,000

Account balances at the beginning of the fiscal year:

	12/01/x8
Materials inventory*	$105,000
Work-in-process inventory	60,000
Finished goods inventory	125,000

* Material purchases and materials inventory consist of both direct and indirect materials. The balance of the Materials Inventory account as of November 30, Year 9, is $85,000.

Jobs N11-007, N11-013, and N11-015 were completed during November. All completed jobs except Job N11-013 had been turned over to customers by the close of business on November 30, Year 9.

Required:

1. Valport Company uses a predetermined overhead rate to apply manufacturing overhead to its jobs. When overhead is accounted for in this manner, there may be over- or underapplied overhead.

   a. Explain why a business uses a predetermined overhead rate to apply manufacturing overhead to its jobs.

   b. How much manufacturing overhead would Valport have applied to jobs through October 31, Year 9?

   c. How much manufacturing overhead would be applied to jobs by Valport during November, Year 9?

   d. Determine the amount by which the manufacturing overhead is over- or underapplied as of November 30, Year 9. Be sure to indicate whether the overhead is over- or underapplied.

   e. Over- or underapplied overhead must be eliminated at the end of the accounting period. Explain why Valport's method of closing over- or underapplied overhead to the Cost of Goods Sold is acceptable in this case.

2. Determine the balance in Valport's Finished Goods Inventory at November 30, Year 9.

(CMA, adapted)

P4-28   Analysis of Cost Flows; Missing Numbers

You are the new assistant controller of VLS, Inc. On a rainy day in May, you are trying to compile some information on manufacturing cost flows for top management while the controller is on sabbatical leave. The controller left incomplete data, but you certainly do not want to disturb her during her leave.

The folllowing data are available:

Raw Materials				Manufacturing Overhead		
Bal. April 1,	12,000			Actual costs for April	14,800	

Work in Process		
Bal. April 1,	4,500	

Finished Goods				Cost of Goods Sold	
Bal. April 1	11,000				
Bal. April 30	16,000				

Additional information:

a. You remember that the predetermined overhead rate was based on 60,000 direct labor-hours to be worked on during the year and $180,000 in estimated manufacturing overhead costs.

b. The production cost sheets showed only one job in process on April 30. Materials of $2,600 had been added to the job and 300 direct labor-hours had been worked at $6 per hour.

c. Raw material purchases during April amount to $42,000.

d. You know that 5,200 direct labor-hours were recorded for the month. There are no variations in pay rates among employees.

e. The cost of goods manufactured for April was $89,000.

Required:

You want to show that you can handle the task without bothering the controller. Determine the following amounts:

1. Predetermined overhead rate for the period.
2. Work in process, April 30.
3. Manufacturing overhead applied to production during April.
4. Under- or overapplied overhead for the period.
5. Raw materials issued to production during April.
6. Raw materials, April 30.
7. Cost of goods sold for April.

P4-29   Overall Process of Job Costing (at Normal)

SPK Inc. uses a job-order costing system and applies overhead to jobs on a basis of 120% of direct labor cost. The beginning balances of Year 6 in the inventory accounts were as follows:

Raw Materials	$ 3,000
Work in Process	7,250
Finished Goods	12,000

The following transactions took place during Year 6:

a. Raw materials purchased on account, $16,500.

b. Direct materials requisitioned for use in production, $17,000.

c. Wages and salaries incurred during the year, $30,000 (70% direct labor, 10% indirect labor, and 20% selling and administrative salaries).

d. Factory utilities paid, $4,200.

e. Depreciation, $10,000 (80% on factory machinery and 20% on office equipment).

f. Other factory overhead costs incurred, $11,500.

g. Advertising expense incurred, $20,000.

h. Manufacturing overhead was applied to production.

i. The cost of jobs completed during the year is recognized. The ending balance in the Work in Process inventory account for Year 6 was $14,750.

j. Sales for the year totaled $98,000.

k. Cost of goods sold for the year totaled $60,000.

Required:

1. Prepare journal entries to record the above transactions.

2. Post your entries to T-accounts. Show the ending balances in the inventory accounts and in the Manufacturing Overhead account.

3. Prepare a schedule of cost of goods manufactured. Use normal costing to show the cost of goods manufactured.

■ CASES

 C4-30 Comprehensive Analysis of Cost Flows; Job-Order Costing

SCG, Inc. manufactures space communications equipment and uses a job-order costing system. SCG claims that its operations are efficient and it applies manufacturing overhead in a fair manner.

SCG started operations on January 1, Year 8. Manufacturing overhead is applied to jobs on the basis of machine-hours. For Year 8, management estimated the following:

Estimated machine-hours...........................	300,000
Estimated direct labor-hours	90,000
Estimated direct labor cost	$5,500,000
Estimated manufacturing overhead.................	$3,300,000

The first 11 months of operations (January-November) used 290,000 machine-hours and resulted in the following balances in selected accounts:

Raw Materials

Bal. 38,000	

Work in Process

Bal. 835,000	

Finished Goods

Bal. 674,000	

Cost of Goods Sold

Bal. 14,541,000	

Manufacturing Overhead

Costs incurred (1/1 through 11/30) 3,212,000	?
Bal. ?	

Additional information on the ending inventory balances at November 30:

a. The ending work in process inventory represents the following two jobs:

Job No.	Product	Units	Cost as of 11/30
8111	Space com-T1	3	$420,000
8112	Space com-S1	5	415,000
			$835,000

b. The ending finished goods inventory represents the following items in stock:

Product	Units	Product Cost
Space com-T1	1	$150,000
Space com-S1	2	180,000
Space com-S2	2	240,000
Wave DST	1	104,000
		$674,000

The following items, (c) through (h), represent the activity of the company during December, Year 8:

c. Raw materials of $765,000 were purchased.
d. Raw materials were issued to production as follows:

Inc. The contract required TMP to create an Internet advertisement on a new CD-ROM targeted for the Gen-X market. TMP spent the following costs and time to service the contract:

	Department	
	Market Information	Internet Advertising
Consulting-hours	42 hours	125 hours
Materials	$278	$1,926

a. Compute the amount of overhead applied to the CD-ROM USA, Inc. account.

b. Compute the total cost of servicing the CD-ROM USA, Inc. contract.

CHAPTER 5

PROCESS-COSTING AND HYBRID-COSTING SYSTEMS

After studying this chapter, you should be able to:

1. Distinguish between process-costing and job-costing systems.

2. Give an overview of a process-costing system.

3. Trace the flow of costs through a process-costing system using journal entries.

4. Prepare a production cost report for each processing department.

5. Distinguish between production cost reports under the weighted-average method and the first-in, first-out (FIFO) method.

6. Understand the effects of recent developments in management accounting and today's business environment on process costing.

7. Explain how operation costing works as a hybrid-costing system.

In chapter 4, we learned that in job-order costing many different products or jobs are worked on during the period. In **process costing** many like units are completed by going through various processing stages or departments in a continuous fashion.

This chapter discusses process-costing systems in more detail. Using journal entries and T-accounts, we will see how costs flow through a process-costing system. We also learn how production cost reports may be prepared under the weighted-average and first-in, first-out (FIFO) method.

In reality, very few companies actually use a pure job-costing or process-costing system. Most companies use a **hybrid-costing** system which takes characteristics from both job-costing and process-costing systems. Each company, whether it is in manufacturing or service, designs its own costing system that suits the company's needs for cost information. We will discuss **operation costing,** a form of a hybrid-costing system, in this chapter.

JOB COSTING VERSUS PROCESS COSTING

At plants that process many like products, such as chemicals, food, metal, and paper, production flows differently in comparison to the job shop environment we saw in chapter 4. Production and resources flow continuously in multiple stages, as illustrated in Exhibit 5-1.

These polypropylene units of Amoco Corporation's Belgian plant show an environment of process costing. Polypropylene replaces metal, paper and other plastics in a variety of uses.

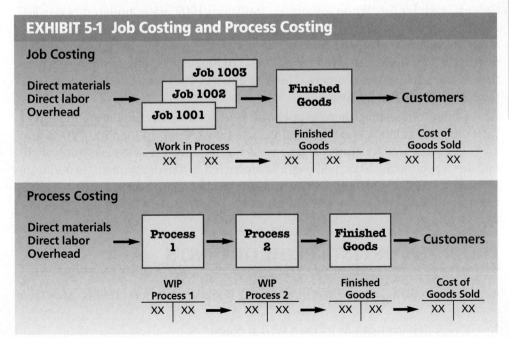

EXHIBIT 5-1 Job Costing and Process Costing

Job Costing

Direct materials
Direct labor → Job 1001 / Job 1002 / Job 1003 → Finished Goods → Customers
Overhead

Work in Process / Finished Goods / Cost of Goods Sold
XX | XX → XX | XX → XX | XX

Process Costing

Direct materials
Direct labor → Process 1 → Process 2 → Finished Goods → Customers
Overhead

WIP Process 1 / WIP Process 2 / Finished Goods / Cost of Goods Sold
XX | XX → XX | XX → XX | XX → XX | XX

Objectives Are Similar

Process-costing systems and job-costing systems are similar in their objectives as the following shows:

1. Determine an average production cost per unit for the purpose of computing the cost of ending inventory (for balance sheet) and the cost of goods sold (for income statement).

2. Provide a mechanism for managing costs assigned to products or departments and total costs of production.

Production Flows Are Different

On the other hand, the two systems are different basically because production flows are different. Observe the following:

1. In job costing, costs are accumulated by individual jobs whereas in process costing, costs are accumulated by departments.

2. In job costing, the cost of one job is usually not transferred to another job, so each job has a job cost sheet within each department and for all departments. In process costing, the costs of units processed in one department are usually transferred to the next processing department, thus each department has a department production report.

3. In job costing, the costs of all individual jobs are usually reflected in one Work in Process account. In process costing, each department has its own subsidiary ledger WIP account. Of course, in the general ledger and on the balance sheet, all these subsidiary WIP accounts are combined in one account for the company as a whole.

Refer to Exhibit 5-1. When jobs 1001, 1002, and 1003 are completed under job costing, they are transferred separately to the finished goods warehouse where they await delivery to customers. However, under process costing, the units processed in Process 1 are transferred to Process 2 and to Finished Goods warehouse where they await delivery to customers. The cost flows in T-accounts under the two systems are different as follows:

Under job costing, there is only one WIP account accumulating the direct materials, direct labor, and overhead from the cost sheets of jobs 1001, 1002, and 1003. Under process costing, each process has its own WIP account which accumulates all materials, labor, and overhead incurred in that department. In addition, Process 2 has transferred-in costs from the preceding process, Process 1. Finished Goods and Cost of Goods Sold are used in the same way under both systems.

PROCESS COSTING: FLOW OF COSTS

In process costing, costs flow in a similar fashion as in job costing with two exceptions:

1. Every department has its own WIP account.

2. In addition to its own materials, labor, and overhead, a process may receive costs from a preceding process.

There are multiple WIP accounts in process costing, but cost accumulation is much simpler than in job costing. This is because there is no need to trace costs to hundreds of jobs each day. We simply trace costs to a few processing departments for a relatively longer period (weeks, months, quarters).

A numerical example of a process-costing system for ABC Company, which has two processing departments, A and B, is presented to illustrate the process.

The following is a summary of transactions that took place during the month of September, the first month of operations:

1. Costs incurred:

	Processing Dept. A	Processing Dept. B	Company Total
Materials	$10,000	—	$10,000
Labor	20,000	$16,000	36,000
Overhead	7,000	9,900	16,900
Total	$37,000	$25,900	$62,900

2. Costs transferred:
   a. From Department A to Department B, $32,000.
   b. From Department B to the finished goods warehouse, $52,500.

3. Cost of goods sold for September, $42,000.

Journal Entries

1. a. Materials used in Department A:

| Work in Process-Dept. A............ | 10,000 | |
| Raw Materials................. | | 10,000 |

   b. Labor costs incurred in Department A:

| Work in Process-Dept. A............ | 20,000 | |
| Salaries & Wages Payable ...... | | 20,000 |

   c. Overhead incurred in Department A:

| Work in Process-Dept. A............ | 7,000 | |
| Various Accounts.............. | | 7,000 |

   d. Labor and overhead costs incurred in Department B:

| Work in Process-Dept. B............ | 16,000 | |
| Salaries & Wages Payable ...... | | 16,000 |

| Work in Process-Dept. B............ | 9,900 | |
| Various Accounts.............. | | 9,900 |

2. a. Costs transferred from Department A to Department B:

| Work in Process-Dept. B............ | 32,000 | |
| Work in Process-Dept. A .... | | 32,000 |

b. Costs of finished units transferred from Department B to the finished goods warehouse:

Finished Goods.	52,500	
Work in Process-Dept. B		52,500

3. Cost of goods sold to customers:

Cost of Goods Sold	42,000	
Finished Goods		42,000

T-Accounts and Ending Balances

Exhibit 5-2 illustrates the related T-accounts after the above journal entries are posted:

EXHIBIT 5-2 ABC Company's Manufacturing Cost Flows

	Work in Process Department A			Work in Process Department B			Finished Goods	
Bal.	0		Bal.	0		Bal.	0	
Raw Materials	10,000	32,000 →		32,000	52,500 →		52,500	42,000
Labor	20,000		Labor	16,000				
Overhead	7,000		Overhead	9,900				
Bal.	5,000		Bal.	5,400		Bal.	10,500	

Manufacturing Process

Union Electric Steel's forged hardened steel rolls are manufactured in multiple processes, such as the melting, forging, and finishing processes shown in these pictures.

We assume that manufacturing overhead costs are incurred uniformly throughout the period. This is different from a job-order costing system where there may be hundreds of heterogeneous jobs being worked on at the same time, each requiring a different amount of overhead costs. For that reason, predetermined overhead rates had to be developed for applying overhead to jobs.

If, in a process-costing system, overhead is not incurred uniformly throughout the period or if output levels vary significantly from period to period, predetermined overhead rates should be developed and used in applying overhead to processes just as we did in a job costing system. In that case, over- or underapplied overhead would result and should be disposed of.

Simple Production Cost Reports

In our previous example, a production cost report for each processing department would include the total costs incurred during the period, the costs of completed units, and the costs of ending WIP. If we ignore the number of units completed in each department for a moment, these production cost reports would be prepared as shown in Exhibit 5-3.

EXHIBIT 5-3 Simple Production Cost Reports

Department A		Department B	
Materials	$10,000	Transferred-in costs	$32,000
Conversion costs	27,000	Conversion costs	25,900
Total costs	$37,000	Total costs	$57,900
Cost of units completed	$32,000	Cost of units completed	$52,500
Cost of ending WIP	5,000	Cost of ending WIP	5,400
Total costs	$37,000	Total costs	$57,900

As we learned in chapter 2, **conversion costs** include all manufacturing costs except direct materials. The nature of operations of most process industries is material-intensive, and direct labor is not a major portion of total costs. Accordingly, only the two major classifications, materials and conversion costs, are used in process costing.

Department A's total costs of $37,000 equal the total costs incurred in that department as given in the example. Department B's total costs of $57,900 exceed the costs incurred of $25,900. While total costs incurred by ABC Company during September were only $62,900, the two production cost reports in Exhibit 5-3 show a total of $94,900 (= $37,000 + $57,900). The difference of $32,000 represents the costs transferred from Department A to Department B. When ABC Company prepares its financial statements, interdepartmental cost transfers will be eliminated.

The $62,900 costs incurred equal the $52,500 cost of units completed in Department B plus the $10,400 ending WIP in Departments A ($5,000) and B ($5,400). However, each department must prepare its own production cost report which reflects all the costs that pass through the department whether they were incurred directly by the department or transferred in from a preceding department. The department manager must account for all such costs.

The reason the production cost reports in Exhibit 5-3 were so simple to prepare is that we were told how much the costs of units completed were and how much the costs of ending WIP were in each department. Now, suppose we were not given that cost information, but were given instead information about the units started, units completed, and units still in process at the end of the period in each department. Can we still prepare a production cost report for each department?

If there is no WIP at the end of the period, all the costs in each department will be included in the costs of the units completed. The cost per unit will simply equal total costs divided by the number of units completed. If there is unfinished WIP at the end of the period, the ending WIP cost will depend on the percentage of its completion.

Because materials can be added either at the beginning, or at the end of the process, or perhaps at some point between these two points, we also need to know at what point of the process the materials are added. We will now discuss how production cost reports are prepared based on those additional considerations.

Percentage of Completion and Production Costs

Refer back to the original example and assume that materials are added at the beginning of the process in Department A. Also assume the following additional information is available:

	Dept. A	Dept. B
Units started (or transferred in)	10,000	8,000
Units completed and transferred out	8,000	7,000
Units still in process, ending	2,000	1,000
Ending WIP, percentage of completion (with respect to conversion costs)	50%	40%

Because materials are added at the beginning of the process, ending WIP already contains all the materials that are needed (100 percent complete as to materials). If materials are added only at the end of the process, ending WIP would be zero percent complete as to materials. If materials are added at some point during the process, the ending WIP percentage of completion with respect to materials will depend on whether the materials have already been added or not.

For example, if materials are added in Department A when WIP is 30 percent complete, then ending WIP in Department A would be 100 percent complete as to materials because it was already 50 percent complete as to labor and overhead. If, however, materials are added in Department A when work is 60 percent complete, then ending WIP in Department A would be zero percent complete as to materials.

Equivalent Units

The ending WIP percentage of completion discussed above is important for the computation of *equivalent units*. **Equivalent units** represent the number of units that could have been produced from all materials, labor, and overhead used in production. If all units started during a period are completed by the end of the period, equivalent units equal physical units. If there is WIP at the end, equivalent units are less than physical units.

Equivalent units can be written as follows:

$$\begin{array}{c} \text{Equivalent} \\ \text{units of} \\ \text{production} \end{array} = \begin{array}{c} \text{Number of physical} \\ \text{units completed} \\ \text{during the period} \end{array} + \begin{array}{c} \text{Number} \\ \text{of ending} \\ \text{WIP units} \end{array} \times \begin{array}{c} \text{Percentage} \\ \text{of} \\ \text{completion} \end{array}$$

Now refer to the above example.

> Equivalent units of ending WIP in Department A:
>
> As to conversion costs: 2,000 units × 50% = 1,000
> As to materials: 2,000 units × 100% = 2,000

Remember that materials are added at the beginning of the process. Although the ending WIP units are 50% complete, all the materials required are 100% included.

The computation of equivalent units is needed to determine the cost per equivalent unit. The unit cost is used to determine the cost of units completed and the cost of ending WIP appearing on each department's production cost report.

Referring to the previous example, the equivalent units of each department's ending WIP would be computed as shown below:

	Dept. A	Dept. B
Physical units, ending	2,000	1,000
Percentage of completion:		
As to materials.	100%	100%
As to conversion cost.	50%	40%
Equivalent units:		
As to materials.	2,000	1,000
As to conversion costs.	1,000	400

Equivalent Units and Service Organizations

The concept of equivalent units is used in service and nonprofit organizations as well. For example, when a school wants to compute the cost of instruction, it looks at the number of students per full-time equivalent faculty.

If a full-time faculty is defined as one who teaches six courses per year, then two part-time faculty who teach three courses each would be equivalent to one full-time faculty. Three part-time faculty teaching two courses each would be equivalent to one full-time faculty.

Service Process
The AES Company provides a fun workplace. Would an advanced ballet class (advanced process) look different from a beginner ballet class (first process)? In service processes, we may not see the advanced nature of operation as we saw in manufacturing.

Production Cost Reports for Individual Departments

Department A's production cost report is illustrated in Exhibit 5-4.

Section 1 shows the number of physical units to be accounted for, how they are accounted for during the period, and the percentage of completion of the ending WIP. Since there was no beginning WIP, the number of units to account for is the number of units started during the period, or 10,000 units. These units were accounted for as follows:

8,000 units were completed during the period.

2,000 were still in process at the end of the period.

These 2,000 ending WIP units were 100% complete as to materials, but only 50% complete as to conversion cost.

Section 2 provides a computation of equivalent units. The ending WIP equivalent units equal the physical units multiplied by the percentage of completion. Since they are 100% complete as to materials, the equivalent units equal the physical units, or 2,000. For conversion costs, equivalent units are only 1,000 (or 2,000 physical units x 50%).

Section 3 presents the costs of production to account for during the period. Since there was no beginning WIP cost, the cost of production to account for equals the costs added during the month, or $10,000 materials plus $27,000 conversion costs. A total of $37,000 has to be accounted for.

Section 4 presents a computation of cost per equivalent unit. We compute unit cost by dividing "total cost to account for" in Section 3 by "equivalent units" in Section 2 for material and conversion costs. The total cost per equivalent unit of $4 represents the material cost of $1 plus the conversion cost of $3. Be careful not to divide "total costs to account for" of $37,000 by "total units to account for" of 10,000 units. This is because the total column for units does not equal the total units for material plus the total units for conversion cost.

Section 5 provides an explanation of how the costs of production are accounted for. We multiply the numbers in Section 2 by Section 4 for material and conversion costs, and then add them up. The result is "total costs accounted for." "Total costs accounted for" (Section 5) equal "total costs to account for" (Section 3).

Exhibit 5-5 illustrates a production cost report for department B. It is prepared in the same way as the production cost report for department A. The only difference between the two is that department B has "Transferred-in Costs" instead of "Materials".

EXHIBIT 5-4 Production Cost Report - Department A

	Total	Materials	Conversion Costs
Section 1: Accounting for Physical Units		**Percent Completed**	
Beginning WIP units	0		
Units started during period	10,000		
Total units to account for	10,000		
Units completed during period	8,000	100%	100%
Ending WIP units	2,000	100%	50%
Total units accounted for	10,000		
Section 2: Equivalent Units			
Units completed during period	8,000	8,000	8,000
Ending WIP units	2,000	2,000	1,000
Total units accounted for	10,000	10,000	9,000 [A]
Section 3: Costs of Production to Account for			
Beginning WIP costs	—	—	—
Costs added (or transferred-in)	$37,000	$10,000	$27,000
Total costs to account for	$37,000	$10,000	$27,000 [B]
Section 4: Cost per Equivalent Unit			
Cost per equivalent unit	$4.00	$1.00	$3.00 B ÷ A
Section 5: Costs of Production Accounted for			
Cost of units completed	$32,000	$ 8,000	$24,000
Ending WIP cost	5,000	2,000	3,000
Total costs accounted for	$37,000	$10,000	$27,000

Computations:
   Cost of units completed:

Materials	8,000 units × $1 = . .	$ 8,000	
Conversion costs	8,000 units × $3 = . .		$24,000
Ending WIP cost:			
Materials	2,000 units × $1 = . .	2,000	
Conversion costs	1,000 units × $3 = . .		3,000

EXHIBIT 5-5 Production Cost Report - Department B

	Total	Transferred-in Costs	Conversion Costs
Section 1: Accounting for Physical Units		**Percent Completed**	
Beginning WIP units	0		
Units transferred in	8,000		
Total units to account for	8,000		
Units completed during period	7,000	100%	100%
Ending WIP units	1,000	100%	40%
Total units accounted for	8,000		
Section 2: Equivalent Units			
Units completed	7,000	7,000	7,000
Ending WIP units	1,000	1,000	400
Total units accounted for	8,000	8,000	7,400 [A]
Section 3: Costs of Production to Account for			
Beginning WIP costs	—	—	—
Costs added (or transferred-in)	$57,900	$32,000	$25,900
Total costs to account for	$57,900	$32,000	$25,900 [B]
Section 4: Cost per Equivalent Unit			
Cost per equivalent unit	$7.50	$4.00	$3.50 B ÷ A
Section 5: Costs of Production Accounted for			
Cost of units completed	$52,500	$28,000	$24,500
Ending WIP cost	5,400	4,000	1,400
Total costs accounted for	$57,900	$32,000	$25,900

Computations:
   Cost of units completed:

Transferred-in costs 7,000 units × $4.00 =	$28,000	
Conversion costs 7,000 units × $3.50 =		$24,500
Ending WIP cost:		
Transferred-in costs 1,000 units × $4.00 =	4,000	
Conversion costs 400 units × $3.50 =		1,400

EXISTENCE OF BEGINNING WIP; TWO PERIODS

If beginning WIP exists in a department, we need to know the following to complete the production cost report:

    a.   The number of beginning WIP units.
    b.   The percentage of completion of those units as to transferred-in costs, materials, and conversion costs.
    c.   The total beginning WIP costs.

There are two methods of accounting for cost flows when beginning inventory exists: weighted-average method and first-in, first-out (FIFO) method. The weighted-average method is described here. The FIFO method is described later.

    Refer to the first example and assume that the following information is available for the next month, October:

	Department A
Beginning WIP units (a)	2,000
Percentage completion of beginning	
WIP (as to conversion costs) (a)	50%
Units started (or transferred-in)	8,000
Units completed/transferred out	9,000
Percentage completion of ending	
WIP (as to conversion costs)	30%
Costs:	
Beginning WIP:	
Materials (a)	$ 2,000
Conversion costs (a)	3,000
Incurred during the period:	
Materials (b)	36,800
Conversion costs (c)	24,993

(a)   These are the same as the ending WIP figures of September.
(b)   Added at the beginning of the process in Department A.
(c)   Incurred uniformly throughout the process.

Weighted-Average Method

Under the weighted-average method, the cost of production in the current period is averaged with, and added to, the cost of production in the previous period that is reflected in the current period's beginning WIP. The computation of equivalent units is the same as explained above, because the percentages of completion of beginning WIP units are completely ignored under this method. Exhibit 5-6 presents the production cost report of Department A using the weighted-average method.

The production cost report in Exhibit 5-6 is prepared in exactly the same way as in Exhibits 5-4 and 5-5, with one exception. In Section 3, we added the beginning WIP costs to costs added during the period. This means that under the weighted-average method, the percentages of completion of beginning WIP units are completely ignored.

EXHIBIT 5-6 Production Cost Report - Department A

For October
Weighted-Average Method

	Total	Materials	Conversion Costs	
Section 1: Accounting for Physical Units		**Percent Completed**		
Beginning WIP units	2,000	100%	50%	
Units started during period	8,000			
Total units to account for	10,000			
Units completed during period	9,000	100%	100%	
Ending WIP units	1,000	100%	30%	
Total units accounted for	10,000			
Section 2: Equivalent Units				
Units completed during period	9,000	9,000	9,000	
Ending WIP units	1,000	1,000	300	
Total units accounted for	10,000	10,000	9,300	[A]
Section 3: Costs of Production to Account for				
Beginning WIP costs	$ 5,000	$ 2,000	$ 3,000	
Costs added (or transferred-in)	$61,793	$36,800	$24,993	
Total costs to account for	$66,793	$38,800	$27,993	[B]
Section 4: Cost per Equivalent Unit				
Cost of production per equivalent unit	$6.89	$3.88	$3.01	B ÷ A
Section 5: Costs of Production Accounted for				
Cost of units completed	$62,010	$34,920	$27,090	
Cost of ending WIP	4,783	3,880	903	
Total costs accounted for	$66,793	$38,800	$27,993	

Computations:
  Cost of units completed:

Materials	9,000 units × $3.88 =		$34,920	
Conversion costs	9,000 units × $3.01 =			$27,090

  Ending WIP cost:

Materials	1,000 units × $3.88 =		3,880	
Conversion costs	300 units × $3.01 =			903

First-In, First-Out (FIFO) Method

Under the FIFO method, the cost of production in the current period is not averaged with, or added to, the cost of production in the previous period that is reflected in the current period's beginning WIP. Accordingly, equivalent units are calculated differently from the weighted-average method, or when beginning WIP does not exist.

The difference, however, is very simple to understand. The beginning WIP equivalent units are deducted from the equivalent units as calculated under the weighted-average method. Exhibit 5-7 presents the production cost report for Department A under the FIFO method using the same information as the weighted-average method example.

Under the FIFO method, the equivalent units in beginning WIP (the work done in the previous period) is deducted from the weighted average equivalent units to obtain the equivalent units for the current period (the work done in the current period). This number of equivalent units is divided into the cost of production for the current period (in Section 3) to obtain the cost per equivalent unit for the current period (in Section 4).

In Section 5, the cost of units completed during the period is made up of two components: (1) the cost of beginning WIP completed during the period, and (2) the cost of units started and completed during the period.

(1) The cost of beginning WIP completed during the period represents the costs in beginning WIP and the additional costs needed to complete these units. The additional costs needed is equal to beginning WIP units multiplied by (1 - percentage of completion at the beginning) at the current period cost per equivalent unit.

(2) The cost of units started and completed during the period is equal to units started and completed during the period (9,000 — 2,000)multiplied by the cost per equivalent unit for the current period. The cost of ending WIP is equal to the ending equivalent units multiplied by the cost per equivalent unit for the current period.

Comparison of Weighted-Average and FIFO Methods

A comparison of Exhibits 5-6 and 5-7 showing the production cost reports of Department A under the weighted-average and FIFO methods, respectively, indicates that the basic difference is in Section 2: Equivalent Units. Under the weighted-average method, the equivalent units calculation completely ignores the percentages of completion of the beginning WIP. Under the FIFO method, the beginning WIP equivalent units are deducted from the equivalent units computed under the weighted-average method, to obtain the current period's equivalent units.

This basic difference between the two methods in calculating equivalent units, combined with the fact that under FIFO the current period's costs of production are not added to the costs of beginning WIP, produce different costs of production per equivalent unit. This difference in cost per equivalent unit results in different

EXHIBIT 5-7 Production Cost Report - Department A

For October
FIFO Method

	Total	Materials	Conversion Costs
Section 1: Accounting for Physical Units		**Percent Completed**	
Beginning WIP units	2,000	100%	50%
Units started during period	8,000		
Total units to account for	10,000		
Units completed during period	9,000	100%	100%
Ending WIP units	1,000	100%	30%
Total units accounted for	10,000		
Section 2: Equivalent Units			
Units completed during period	9,000	9,000	9,000
Ending WIP units	1,000	1,000	300
Weighted average equivalent units	10,000	10,000	9,300
Beginning WIP equivalent units	(2,000)	(2,000)	(1,000)
Work done in the current period	8,000	8,000	8,300 [A]
Section 3: Costs of Production to Account for			
Beginning WIP costs	$ 5,000	$ 2,000	$ 3,000
Current period production costs	61,793	36,800	24,993 [B]
Total costs to account for	$66,793	$38,800	$27,993
Section 4: Cost per Equivalent Unit			
Cost per equivalent unit for current period	$7.6112	$4.6000	$3.0112 B÷A
Section 5: Costs of Production Accounted for			
Cost of beginning WIP completed during the period (2,000 units):			
Beginning WIP costs	$5,000	$2,000	$3,000
Additional costs to complete beginning WIP . . .	3,011	—	3,011
Subtotal	8,011	2,000	6,011
Cost of units started and completed during the period (7,000 units)	53,278	32,200	21,078
Total costs of units completed during the period . .	61,289	34,200	27,089
Ending WIP costs	5,504	4,600	904
Total costs accounted for	$66,793	$38,800	$27,993

Computations:

Additional conversion costs to complete
beginning WIP = (1 − 0.50) × 2,000 units × $3.0112 = $3,011

Additional 50% of processing has to be done to
complete beginning WIP with respect to conversion costs.

Ending WIP cost:

(Materials)   100% × 1,000 units × $4.6000 = $4,600

(Conversion costs)   30% × 1,000 units × $3.0112 = $904

EXHIBIT 5-8 Comparison of Weighted-Average and FIFO Methods Department A

	Weighted Average Method (Exhibit 5-6)	FIFO Method (Exhibit 5-7)	Difference
Cost of units completed	$62,010	$61,289	$721
Ending WIP cost	4,783	5,504	(721)
Total costs accounted for	$66,793	$66,793	$ 0

costs allocated to the units completed during the period and the ending WIP. These differences are illustrated in Exhibit 5-8 for Department A.

Thus, the cost of units completed during the period is $721 higher under the weighted-average method than under the FIFO method. This difference is offset in the ending WIP cost, since total costs accounted for in Department A are the same under both methods.

Which method is preferred by companies? The FIFO method seems to be somewhat more complicated than the weighted-average method. Perhaps this is the reason that most companies use the weighted-average method. However, for planning and control purposes, the FIFO method is more accurate than the weighted-average method, since the performance of each period may be evaluated separately from prior periods.

PROCESS COSTING AND TODAY'S ENVIRONMENT

In connection with recent developments in management accounting and today's business environment, we can make two observations on process costing that are relevant to today's practice.

They are related to the following two aspects of managerial accounting:

1. The level of overhead support activities.
2 The classification of materials and conversion costs.

The level of overhead support activities: The process-oriented manufacturing environment, for which process costing is appropriate, differs significantly from the job-shop environment. The job-shop environment requires many different levels of overhead support activities, such as procurement of materials and parts, changing engineering and process routines, and inspecting different WIP and finished products according to the requirements.

Accordingly, the costs of overhead support activities can be very significant, compared to direct materials and direct labor, in a job-shop environment. Sometimes overhead costs can be almost as high as direct materials cost. Chapters 6 and 7 will address those overhead support activities and their costs.

In a process-oriented environment, operations are material-intensive. If the manufacturing facilities require heavy capital expenditures, overhead costs can be significant in a process-oriented plant also, as discussed later in this book. The manufacturing operations in a process-oriented environment, however, do not require a high level of coordination or overhead support activities. The major part of complex overhead support activities may take place during the machine operation, automatically inside the machines.

Because of the above reason, new methods such as activity-based costing (ABC) are not as appealing in process costing as they have been in an environment in which high levels of overhead support activities take place. Some modifications may, in some cases, be desirable, but the framework of process costing discussed in this chapter would be appropriate in today's practice. Chapters 6 and 7 will discuss the concepts of ABC.

The classification of materials and conversion costs: In a lean production environment of today's industry, operating methods such as just-in-time (JIT) systems would require a different type of cost accounting. Many JIT firms have adopted a system called backflush costing which assigns costs to products upon completion of production process. Lean production, JIT, and backflush costing will be discussed in chapter 10.

In such new costing systems, manufacturers have used only two cost categories: materials and conversion costs, as we have discussed in this chapter. Direct labor is not significant enough to be tracked separately and has been combined with overhead. The process-costing framework, which we have discussed in this chapter, is very convenient to apply to efficiency-oriented costing systems of today's industry.

OPERATION COSTING AS A HYBRID SYSTEM

We have discussed job costing and process costing as the two major costing methodologies. In reality, very few companies actually use pure job costing or pure process costing. Most companies use some form of a **hybrid system** that fits the manufacturing activities of the company. Hybrid systems blend features from job costing and process costing.

Characteristics of Operation Costing

The most frequently used hybrid-costing system is operation costing. In an **operation-costing system,** different batches of like products go through individual and common processing stages.

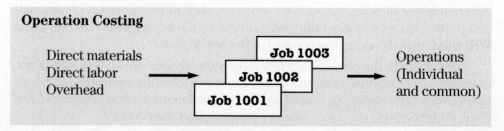

Operation Costing

Direct materials
Direct labor
Overhead → Job 1003 / Job 1002 / Job 1001 → Operations (Individual and common)

Work orders represent the production orders for proper batches of products. The products may be based on variations of one representative product design. The first design may require a certain sequence of standardized processing routines, called **operations.** Those variations in product design, however, may require different sequences of operations.

Assume a manufacturer of printed circuit (PC) boards, which are needed in every electronic product, produces two lines of PC boards. The standard boards use standard panel and go through four operations. The special boards use non-standard panel and go through five operations as presented below:

	Standard PC Board	Special PC Board
Direct materials:	18′ by 24′ panel	18′ by 12′ panel
Operations:	1. Inner layer	1. Inner layer
	2. Outer layer	2. Outer layer
	3. Solder mask	3. Solder mask
	4. —	4. Component legend
	5. Tab plate	5. Tab plate

The costs are compiled as follows:
Direct materials:

Each work order identifies different materials used.
Conversion costs:

Each operation's costs are compiled separately, and are assigned to products based on each operation's cost driver, the factor by which costs vary most. The cost driver of the first two operations, operations 1 and 2, is the number of units produced. The cost driver of the last three operations, operations 3, 4, and 5, is the number of sides to be processed.

The Process of Operation Costing

We now look at how operation costing actually works in a costing system. Assume the PC board manufacturer has the two work orders, 701 and 702, with the following details:

A direct labor worker is soldering on a printed circuit board at Electrocom Automation Inc.

	Work Order 701	Work Order 702
Product	Standard board	Special board
Number of units	450	150
Sides per unit of product	2	4
Costs:		
Direct materials	$ 8,100	$ 2,250

The conversion cost is assigned to products in a manner that is similar to overhead application in job costing. At the beginning of this year the company estimated the following costs and operations for the year:

Estimated production volume:

Standard PC boards	22,500 units	×	2	=	45,000 sides
Special PC boards	7,500	×	4	=	30,000
Total	30,000 units				75,000 sides

Estimated labor and overhead costs:

	Total	Units of Cost Driver	Cost per Driver
1. Inner layer	$ 750,000	30,000 units	$25
2. Outer layer	600,000	30,000 units	20
3. Solder mask	75,000	75,000 sides	1
4. Component legend	30,000	30,000 sides	1
5. Tab plate	37,500	75,000 sides	0.50
	$1,492,500		

Note: Only special PC boards go through operation 4.

As PC boards go through each operation, they accumulate conversion costs at the estimated rates, such as $25 per unit in operation 1, $1 per side in operation 3, and so forth. Each unit of standard board has two sides and each unit of special board has four sides. Thus, work order 701 will accumulate $11,250, or $25 per unit multiplied by 450 units, from operation 1, inner layer. Work order 702 will be charged $600, or $1 per side multiplied by 600 (4 x 150) sides from operation 3, solder mask.

After the conversion costs are assigned to products, the two jobs would show the following costs:

	Work Order 701	Work Order 702
Units	450	150
Sides	900	600
Costs:		
Direct materials	$ 8,100	$ 2,250
Conversion costs:		
1. Inner layer	11,250	3,750
2. Outer layer	9,000	3,000
3. Solder mask	900	600
4. Component legend	—	600
5. Tab plate	450	300
Total manufacturing costs	$29,700	$10,500
Per-unit cost	$66	$70

Journal Entries

Journal entries for the transactions that take place in connection with work order 702 follow.

1. Direct materials are issued to production:

Work in Process	2,250	
Direct Materials		2,250

2. Various actual conversion costs are incurred:

Conversion Costs.	8,250	
Accounts Payable, Wages Payable,		
Accrued Expenses, etc.		8,250

3. Conversion costs are applied to production in operations 1, 2, 3, 4, and 5:

Work in Process	8,250	
Conversion Costs.		8,250

After the above entries have been posted, the Work-in-Process account will show the following:

Work in Process – Special PC Board

Bal.	0	
Direct materials	2,250	
Conversion costs (applied)	8,250	
Bal.	10,500	

4. Production of 150 units of special PC boards (work order 702) is completed, and the finished boards are transferred to the finished goods area:

Finished Goods	10,500	
Work in Process		10,500

5. Out of the 150 special PC boards finished in the current period, 140 boards are shipped to the customers:

Cost of Goods Sold (140 × $70).	9,800	
Finished Goods		9,800

After the above entries are posted, the Finished-Goods account will show the following:

Finished Goods – Special PC Board

Bal.	0		
Current production	10,500	To customers	9,800
Bal.	700		

Since estimated rates of conversion costs are applied to production in each operation, there will be under- or overapplied conversion costs at the end of the year. The difference between the actual and applied conversion costs will be disposed of in the same manner as under- or overapplied overhead in job costing.

SUMMARY

Process costing and job-order costing systems are similar in (a) their basic objective (to determine cost per unit of output and control the flow of costs of production), (b) cost flow through the system and related journal entries, and (c) manufacturing accounts used. The two systems are different in the following respects: (a) In a process costing system, costs are accumulated by department and not by job. Each department has its own separate WIP account and its production cost report, as opposed to a job cost sheet in a job-order system. (b) Costs may be transferred from one department to another.

A production cost report should be prepared for each department showing five sections: (1) accounting for physical units (i.e., units in process at beginning plus units started must equal units completed plus units in process at end), (2) equivalent units, (3) costs of production to account for, (4) cost per equivalent unit, and (5) costs of production accounted for.

If beginning WIP exists, the production cost reports may be prepared using either the weighted-average method or the FIFO method. While the difference in cost of production per unit is usually not significant under the two methods, the FIFO method is superior to the weighted-average method for control purposes.

Although job costing and process costing are the two major costing methodologies, very few companies actually use a pure job-costing or a pure process-costing system. Most companies use some form of a hybrid system that fits the manufacturing activities of the company. Hybrid systems blend features from job costing and process costing.

The most frequently used hybrid-costing system is operation costing. In an operation-costing system, different batches of like products go through individual and common processing stages. Work orders represent the production orders for proper batches of products.

BASIC CONCEPTS AND TERMS

Equivalent units	Production cost report
First-in, first-out (FIFO) method	Transferred-in costs
Hybrid-costing system	Weighted-average method
Operation costing	

■ SELF-REVIEW PROBLEM

TS Plastics Company has two departments: Mixing-Forming (MF) and Firing-Cooling (FC). Materials are added at the beginning of the process in MF Department. No materials are added in FC Department. Units completed in MF Department are transferred to FC Department. Units completed in FC Department are transferred to the finished goods warehouse. Conversion costs are assumed to be incurred uniformly as the work progresses in each department.

The two departments' costs and other data for August follow:

	MF Department	FC Department
Units in process, beginning	30,000	20,000
Percentage of completion (as to conversion costs)	20%	30%
Beginning inventory costs:		
Transferred in..........................	—	$5,000
Materials	$10,000	—
Conversion costs......................	44,000	10,000
	MF Department	FC Department
Units started into production during August	270,000	?
Units completed and transferred out during August....................	255,000	?
Costs added during the period:		
Materials............................	$ 95,000	—
Conversion costs	256,300	$156,750
Ending WIP units	?	75,000
Percentage of completion (as to conversion costs) of ending WIP	40%	20%

Required:

1. Prepare a production cost report for MF Department using the weighted-average method.
2. Prepare a production cost report for FC Department using the FIFO method. (Use the costs of units transferred in from MF Department and assume they were based on FIFO.)

Solution to Self-Review Problem

Ending WIP units in MF Department:

Beginning WIP units	30,000
Units started during month	270,000
Units to account for	300,000
Units completed during the month	(255,000)
Ending WIP units.............................	45,000

$$\begin{array}{ccccc} \text{Units started in} \\ \text{FC Department} \end{array} = \begin{array}{c} \text{Units completed in} \\ \text{MF Department} \end{array} = \begin{array}{c} 255{,}000 \\ \text{units} \end{array}$$

Units completed in FC Department:

Beginning WIP units	20,000
Units started during month	255,000
Units to account for	275,000
Ending WIP units.	(75,000)
Units completed	200,000

1. See Exhibit 5-9.
2. See Exhibit 5-10.

■ REVIEW QUESTIONS

5-1 Job-order costing and process-costing systems are similar in some respects and different in others. Explain.

5-2 Give a brief overview of a process-costing system. You may use T-accounts for illustration.

5-3 What is the basic purpose of a production cost report?

5-4 What are the components of a production cost report?

5-5 What is the meaning of an equivalent unit of production?

5-6 Can the concept of equivalent units be used in service and nonprofit organizations? Explain.

5-7 Consider the weighted-average and FIFO methods. What is the basic difference between these two methods with respect to beginning work in process?

5-8 What sections of a production cost report would change most significantly when the method switches from the weighted-average method to the FIFO method?

5-9 It is believed that most companies use the weighted-average method, even though the FIFO method is superior from a cost control standpoint. How would you explain that situation?

5-10 Why is a hybrid-costing system needed?

5-11 How is operation costing related to job costing and process costing?

5-12 Do recent developments in management accounting and today's business environment have an impact on process costing? Explain the impact with respect to the level of overhead support activities.

EXHIBIT 5-9

TS PLASTICS CO.
MF Department
Production Cost Report for August
Weighted-Average Method

	Total	Materials	Conversion Costs
Section 1: Accounting for Physical Units		**Percent Completed**	
Beginning WIP units	30,000	100%	20%
Units started	270,000		
Units to account for	300,000		
Units completed	255,000	100%	100%
Ending WIP units	45,000	100%	40%
Units accounted for	300,000		
Section 2: Equivalent Units			
Units completed	255,000	255,000	255,000
Ending WIP units	45,000	45,000	18,000
Total	300,000	300,000	273,000 [A]
Section 3: Costs of Production to Account for			
Beginning WIP costs	$ 54,000	$ 10,000	$ 44,000
Costs added during month	351,300	95,000	256,300
Costs to account for	$405,300	$105,000	$300,300 [B]
Section 4: Cost per Equivalent Unit			
Cost per equivalent unit	$1.45	$0.35	$1.10 B ÷ A
Section 5: Costs of Production Accounted for			
Cost of units completed	$369,750	$ 89,250	$280,500
Ending WIP costs	35,550	15,750	19,800
Costs accounted for	$405,300	$105,000	$300,300

Computations:
  Cost of units completed:

(Materials)	255,000 units × $0.35 =	$89,250	
(Conversion costs)	255,000 units × $1.10 =		$280,500

  Ending WIP cost:

(Materials)	100% × 45,000 units × $0.35 =	$15,750	
(Conversion costs)	40% × 45,000 units × $1.10 =		$ 19,800

EXHIBIT 5-10

TS PLASTICS CO.
FC Department
Production Cost Report for August
FIFO Method

	Total	Transferred-in Costs	Conversion Costs
Section 1: Accounting for Physical Units		Percent Completed	
Beginning WIP units	20,000	100%	30%
Units transferred in	255,000		
Units to account for	275,000		
Units completed	200,000	100%	100%
Ending WIP units	75,000	100%	20%
Units accounted for	275,000		
Section 2: Equivalent Units			
Units completed	200,000	200,000	200,000
Ending WIP units	75,000	75,000	15,000
Weighted average equivalent units	275,000	275,000	215,000
Beginning WIP	(20,000)	(20,000)	(6,000)
FIFO equivalent units	255,000	255,000	209,000 [A]
Section 3: Costs of Production to Account for			
Beginning WIP costs	$15,000	$ 5,000	$10,000
Costs added during period	526,500	369,750	156,750 [B]
Costs to account for	$541,500	$374,750	$166,750
Section 4: Cost per Equivalent Unit			
Cost per equivalent unit for current period	$2.20	$1.45	$0.75 B ÷ A
Section 5: Costs of Production Accounted for			
Cost of beginning WIP completed during the period (20,000 units):			
Beginning WIP costs	$15,000	$5,000	$10,000
Additional costs to complete beginning WIP . . .	10,500	—	10,500
Subtotal	25,500	5,000	20,500
Cost of units started and completed during period (180,000 units)	396,000	261,000	135,000
Costs of units completed (200,000 units)	421,500	266,000	155,500
Cost of ending WIP (75,000 units)	120,000	108,750	11,250
Total costs accounted for	$541,500	$374,750	$166,750

Computations:

Additional costs to complete
  beginning WIP = 20,000 units × 70% × $0.75 = $10,500

Cost of units started/completed:

(Transferred-in)	180,000 units × $1.45 =	$261,000	
(Conversion costs)	180,000 units × $0.75 =		$135,000

Ending WIP cost:

(Transferred-in)	75,000 units × $1.45 =	$108,750	
(Conversion costs)	75,000 units × 20% × $0.75 =		$11,250

⊕ INTERNET PROJECT

Web 5-1:

> Websites: www.exxonmobil.com
>   www.ford.com

The websites listed above represent two famous companies. Search the sites for information on their product and operating characteristics.

Required:

1. Which product and operating characteristics indicate that a process costing would be appropriate?

2. Which product and operating characteristics indicate that a process costing would *not* be appropriate?

Web 5-2:

> Websites: www.att.com
>   www.verizon.com

The websites listed above represent two famous companies. Search the sites for information on their conversion costs.

Required:

1. What would be the largest conversion cost items you can actually find?
2. Define their products.
3. Would a typical process costing work for each company? Why or why not?

■ EXERCISES

E5-1   Equivalent Units; Weighted-Average Method

Gen-X Scent, Inc. is a manufacturer of perfume which is popular among young women and uses a process-costing system. Department A's production data for July are presented below:

		Percent Completed	
	Ounces	**Materials**	**Conversion**
Work in process, July 1	6,000	70	50
Work in process, July 31	3,000	60	40

Department A started 87,000 ounces into production during the month of July. A total of 90,000 ounces were transferred to the next processing department.

Required:

Compute the equivalent units of production for July. Use the weighted-average method of accounting for costs and units.

E5-2   Equivalent Units; FIFO Method

Refer to E5-1. Use the same data for the computations.

Required:

Use the FIFO method of accounting for costs and units and compute the equivalent units of production for July.

E5-3   Equivalent Units; Weighted-Average Method

EST Paint Company uses process costing. In the first processing department, materials are put into the production process at the beginning of the process. Labor and overhead costs are incurred uniformly throughout processing. The department's data relating to units and costs are presented below for May:

	Units	Percent Completed
Work in process, May 1	3,000	40
Started into production during May	27,000	–
Work in process, May 31	2,000	70

Required:

Compute the equivalent units of production for May. Use the weighted-average method.

E5-4   Equivalent Units; FIFO Method

Refer to E5-3. Use the same data for the computations.

Required:

Use the FIFO method of accounting for costs and units and compute the equivalent units of production for May.

E5-5   Cost Flows in Process Costing; Journal Entries

Alchemy Company, a manufacturer of a unique chemical product, uses a process-costing system. T-accounts containing cost flows through the company's two processing departments, mixing and finishing, for March follow:

Work in Process–Mixing

March 1	4,000	Transferred out	74,000
Direct materials	35,000		
Direct labor	18,000		
Overhead	26,000		

Work in Process–Finishing

March 1	3,000	Transferred out	110,000
Transferred in	74,000		
Direct labor	21,000		
Overhead	30,000		

Required:

Prepare journal entries for the above cost flows during March.

E5-6   Accounting for Physical Units

The Clonex Company uses a process-costing system. The following data are available for two processing centers for May:

Process 1:	Units
Beginning inventory......................................	15,000
Ending inventory..	20,000
Started into processing during the month.................	127,000

Process 2:	
Beginning inventory......................................	8,000
Ending inventory..	15,000
Received during the month from Process 1	?

Materials are added at the beginning of Process 1. No materials are added in Process 2.

Required:

Prepare a schedule accounting for physical units.

E5-7   Service Industry and Equivalent Units

Lake Tahoe Ski School has various divisions and uses process costing. Its beginners division takes novices and teaches them to be advanced beginners in the following three processes:

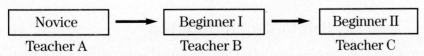

No students will be admitted as transfer students. All novice skiers entering the beginners division start in the Novice process and go through the same three processes to reach the level of advanced beginners.

The following "inventory" of students was in each process on February 28:

Process	Number of Students	Percent Completed
Novice	125	60
Beginner I	110	80
Beginner II	90	50

Required:

Prepare schedules showing the following at the end of February:
1. Equivalent units of teacher A's labor included in all inventories of students.
2. Equivalent units of teacher B's labor included in all inventories of students.
3. Equivalent units of teacher C's labor included in all inventories of students.

E5-8   Total and Unit Costs; Weighted-Average Method

Agua-Paint, Inc. produces an environmentally correct paint that goes through two processing departments. Department A's data on units and costs for the last month are presented below:

	Units	Percent Completed Materials	Conversion
Work in process, beginning.....	3,000	60	30
Units started..................	37,000		
Units transferred out..........	36,000		
Work in process, ending.......	4,000	80	40

	Cost Materials	Conversion
Work in process, beginning	$ 10,000	$ 6,000
Current period costs	187,000	220,200

Required:

The company uses the weighted-average method of accounting for production and costs.
1. Compute the equivalent units for the period.
2. Compute the materials and conversion costs per equivalent unit for the period.
3. Compute the cost of goods completed.
4. Compute the cost of ending work in process.

E5-9   Total and Unit Costs; FIFO Method

Refer to E5-8. Use the same data and FIFO method of accounting for production and costs.

Required:

1. Compute the equivalent units for the period.
2. Compute the materials and conversion costs per equivalent unit for the period.
3. Compute the cost of goods completed.
4. Compute the cost of ending work in process.

E5-10 Operation Costing

Anna Karen of L.A., Inc. (AKLA) is a designer swimsuit manufacturer and uses operation costing. The company produces two lines of swimsuits, Kathie and Rachel, in its four operations. Kathie goes through operations 1, 2, and 3. Rachel goes through operations 1, 2, and 4. Cost drivers used to compile and assign conversion costs to products are: the number of units produced for operations 1 and 2; and direct labor hours for operations 3 and 4.

At the beginning of Year 8 AKLA estimated the following production and costs for the year:

	Product	
	Kathie	**Rachel**
Units to be produced	22,000	30,000

Estimated hours and costs:

	Operations			
	1	2	3	4
Direct labor hours	25,000	36,000	28,000	37,000
Direct labor cost	$250,000	$360,000	$280,000	$370,000
Overhead	175,000	295,000	365,000	282,000
Conversion costs	$425,000	$655,000	$645,000	$652,000

Required:

1. Compute the predetermined conversion cost application rates per unit of driver for each operation.
2. In Week 17, AKLA had the following two work orders:

	Work Order 1701	Work Order 1702
Product	Kathie	Rachel
Number of units	480	710
Direct labor-hours charged:		
Operation 1	15	21
Operation 2	17	19
Operation 3 (120 hours)	?	?
Operation 4 (124 hours)	?	?
Total direct labor-hours	152	164
Costs:		
Direct materials	$2,960	$2,865

a. Compute the conversion costs applied to each work order.
b. Compute the total and unit manufacturing costs of the two products covered by the two work orders.

■ PROBLEMS

P5-11   Production Cost Report; No Beginning Work in Process

Sam's Cement Manufacturing Company produces a high-quality cement that goes through five processing departments. Department A's data on production and costs for the first month of operation are presented below:

	Units	Percent Completed	
		Materials	Conversion
Work in process, beginning.....	–		
Units started..................	65,000		
Units transferred out	?		
Work in process, ending	7,000	80	40

	Costs	
	Materials	Conversion
Current period costs	$69,000	$78,000

Required:

1. Compute the equivalent units for the period.
2. Compute the materials and conversion costs per equivalent unit for the period.
3. Compute the costs of units completed and ending work in process.

 ### P5-12   Production Cost Report; No Beginning Work in Process

Chem-Eco, Inc. manufactures a chemical product that goes through two processing stages before completion. The following is the information on the first department's production and costs for June, the first month of operation:

Production:	
Units started	47,000
Units transferred out to the next department............	42,000
Units in process, June 30 (60% complete)...............	?
Current period cost:	
Materials..	$75,000
Conversion costs	42,000

All materials are added at the beginnng of work in the first department. Conversion costs are incurred uniformly during processing. No units are lost in the process.

Required:

1. Compute the equivalent units for the period.
2. Compute the materials and conversion costs per equivalent unit for the period.
3. Compute the costs of units completed and ending work in process.

P5-13 Production Cost Report; Weighted-Average Method

F-Scent Inc. manufactures one brand of cologne for women that goes through four processing stages before completion. The following is the information on the first department's production and costs for June:

Production:

Units in process, June 1; 100% complete as to materials and 90% complete as to conversion costs....................................	3,000
Units started in June	15,000
Units transferred out to the next department............	?
Units in process, June 30; 80% complete as to materials and 40% complete as to conversion costs	2,000

Costs:

Work in process, June 1:	
Materials...	$ 2,900
Conversion costs	2,600
Current period cost:	
Materials	15,000
Conversion costs.................................	14,500

Required:

Use the weighted-average method.
1. Compute the equivalent units and unit costs for June.
2. Compute the total cost of units completed and transferred to the next department. Also compute the ending WIP cost.

P5-14 Production Cost Report; FIFO Method

Refer to P5-13. Use the same data and FIFO method of accounting for production and costs.

Required:

1. Compute the equivalent units for the period.
2. Compute the materials and conversion costs per equivalent unit for the period.
3. Compute the cost of goods completed.
4. Compute the cost of ending work in process.

P5-15   First Department; Weighted-Average Method

Exeter Products Co. manufactures an industrial-grade glue that goes through two processing departments, mixing and finishing, prior to completion. Information on work in the mixing department for the month of May is provided below:

Production:

Units in process, May 1; 60% complete.	20,000
Units started into production.	200,000
Units transferred to finishing	190,000
Units in process, May 31; 80% complete	?

Costs:

Work in process, May 1:

Materials cost	$ 4,000
Conversion cost	6,000

Costs incurred during May:

Materials cost	86,000
Conversion cost	105,000

Materials are added at the beginning of the processing in the mixing department. Conversion costs are incurred uniformly throughout the process.

Required:

Use the weighted-average method of accounting for production and costs for the following:

1. Compute the equivalent units for the period.
2. Compute the materials and conversion costs per equivalent unit for the period.
3. Compute the costs of units completed and ending work in process.

P5-16   First Department; FIFO Method

Refer to P5-15. Use the same data for computations.

Required:

The company uses the FIFO method of accounting for production and costs.

1. Compute the equivalent units for the period.
2. Compute the materials and conversion costs per equivalent unit for the period.
3. Compute the costs of units completed and ending work in process.

P5-17 Two Processing Departments; Second Department; Weighted-Average Method

Sander Chemical Company manufactures a product that requires processing in two departments. All units from Department A are transferred to Department B. No additional materials are added in Department B. Conversion costs are added continuously throughout the process.

The following data pertain to the operations of Department B for the month of July:

Transferred from Department A during July:

12,000 units, Department A costs	$75,000
Conversion costs incurred during July..................	$162,000

In process, July 1, 3,000 units, 60% complete:

Department A costs	$17,300
Department B conversion costs	25,100

In process, July 31, 4,000 units, 80% complete.

Required:

Use the weighted-average method of accounting for production and costs for the following:
1. Compute the equivalent units for the period.
2. Compute the transferred-in cost and conversion cost per equivalent unit for the period.
3. Compute the costs of units completed and ending work in process.

P5-18 Two Processing Departments; Second Department; FIFO Method

Refer to P5-17. Use the same data for computations.

Required:

The company uses the FIFO method of accounting for production and costs.
1. Compute the equivalent units for the period.
2. Compute the transferred-in cost and conversion cost per equivalent unit for the period.
3. Compute the costs of units completed and ending work in process.

P5-19 Equivalent Units; Additional Materials

Marlan Manufacturing produces a product that passes through two departments. The units from the Molding Department are completed in the Assembly Department. The units are completed in Assembly by adding the remaining direct materials when the units are 60% complete with respect to conversion costs. Conversion costs are added proportionately in Assembly. The production activity in the Assembly Department for the current month is presented below. Marlan uses the FIFO (first-in, first-out) inventory method in its process cost system.

Beginning inventory units (25% complete with respect to conversion costs)	8,000
Units transferred in from the Molding department during the month.	42,000
Units to account for	50,000
Units completed and transferred to finished goods inventory	38,000
Ending inventory units (40% complete with respect to conversion costs)	12,000
Units accounted for	50,000

Required:

1. The equivalent units transferred from the Molding Department to the Assembly Department for the current month would be
    a. 30,000 units.
    b. 38,000 units.
    c. 40,800 units.
    d. 42,000 units.
    e. 50,000 units.
2. The equivalent units in the Assembly Department for direct materials for the current month would be
    a. 30,000 units.
    b. 38,000 units.
    c. 40,800 units.
    d. 42,000 units.
    e. 50,000 units.
3. The equivalent units in the Assembly Department for conversion costs for the current month would be
    a. 36,800 units.
    b. 40,800 units.
    c. 42,800 units.
    d. 43,200 units.
    e. 45,200 units.

(CMA)

P5-20 Two Types of Materials; Weighted-Average Method vs. FIFO Method

Kristina Company, which manufactures quality paint sold at premium prices, uses a single production department. Production begins with the blending of various chemicals, which are added at the beginning of the process, and ends with the canning of the paint. Canning occurs when the mixture reaches the 90% stage of completion. The gallon cans are then transferred to the Shipping Department for crating and shipment. Labor and overhead are added continuously throughout the process. Factory overhead is applied on the basis of direct labor hours at the rate of $3.00 per hour.

Prior to May, when a change in the process was implemented, work-in-process inventories were insignificant. The change in the process enables greater production but results in material amounts of work-in-process for the first time. The company has always used the weighted-average method to the first-in, first-out method.

The following data relate to actual production during the month of May.

Costs for May:

Work-in-process inventory, May 1
(4,000 gallons 25% complete):

Direct materials - chemicals.	$ 45,600
Direct labor ($10 per hour).	6,250
Factory overhead	1,875

May costs added:

Direct materials - chemicals.	228,400
Direct materials - cans.	7,000
Direct labor ($10 hour)	35,000
Factory overhead	10,500

Units for May:

	Gallons
Work-in-process inventory, May 1 (25% complete)	4,000
Sent to Shipping Department.	20,000
Started in May	21,000
Work-in-process inventory, May 31 (80% complete)	5,000

Required:

1. Prepare a schedule of equivalent units for each cost element for the month of May using the
   a. weighted-average method.
   b. first-in, first-out method.
2. Calculate the cost (to the nearest cent) per equivalent unit for each cost element for the month of May using the
   a. weighted-average method.
   b. first-in, first-out method.
3. Discuss the advantages and disadvantages of using the weighted-average method versus the first-in, first-out method, and explain under what circumstances each method should be used.

(CMA)

■ CASES

C5-21 Operation Costing; Total Costs and Unit Costs

Gregg Industries manufactures a variety of plastic products including a series of molded chairs. The three models of molded chairs, which are all variations of the same design, are Standard (can be stacked), Deluxe (with arms), and Executive (with arms and padding). The company uses batch manufacturing and has an operation costing system.

Gregg has an extrusion operation and subsequent operations to form, trim, and finish the chairs. Plastic sheets are produced by the extrusion operation, some of which are sold directly to other manufacturers. During the forming operation, the remaining plastic sheets are molded into chair seats and the legs are added; the Standard model is sold after this preparation. During the trim operation, the arms are added to the Deluxe and Executive models and the chair edges are smoothed. Only the Executive model enters the finish operation where the padding is added. All of the units produced receive the same steps within each operation.

The May production run had a total manufacturing cost of $898,000. The units of production and direct material costs incurred were as follows.

	Units Produced	Materials for Extrusion	Form	Trim	Finish
Plastic sheets........	5,000	$ 60,000			
Standard model......	6,000	72,000	$24,000		
Deluxe model	3,000	36,000	12,000	$ 9,000	
Executive model.....	2,000	24,000	8,000	6,000	$12,000
	16,000	$192,000	$44,000	$15,000	$12,000

Manufacturing costs applied during the month of May were:

	Operation Extrusion	Form	Trim	Finish
Direct labor	$152,000	$60,000	$30,000	$18,000
Factory overhead	240,000	72,000	39,000	24,000

Required:

1. For each product produced by Gregg industries during the month of May, determine the
   a. unit cost.
   b. total cost.

   Be sure to account for all costs incurred during the month, and support your answer with appropriate calculations.

2. Without prejudice to your answer in (1), assume that 1,000 units of the Deluxe model remained in work-in-process at the end of the month. These units were 100% complete as to material costs and 60% complete in the trim operation. Determine the value of the 1,000 units of the Deluxe model in Gregg Industries' work-in-process inventory at the end of May.

(CMA)

CHAPTER 6

COST-ACTIVITY RELATIONSHIPS: COST DRIVER, HIERARCHY, AND ESTIMATION

After studying this chapter, you should be able to:

1. Understand the relationships between costs and activities based on cost drivers.

2. Explain how typical manufacturing support activities are related to manufacturing overhead costs.

3. Differentiate between volume-related measures and activity-related measures to explain variations in overhead costs.

4. Understand the cost hierarchy, and explain how the four levels of costs and activities are used in cost measurement and estimation.

5. Estimate cost-activity relationships in manufacturing and service operations, and determine appropriate cost functions.

6. Estimate cost-activity relationships using the high-low method, the scattergraph method, or the least squares method.

7. Compare the high-low, scattergraph, and least squares methods as to simplicity and accuracy.

8. Explain how cost estimation changes in e-business.

Many different types of **activities** are performed by an organization's personnel. In a manufacturing company, product designers design new products, process engineers write process routines for manufacturing products, purchasing agents purchase raw materials and parts, material handlers move materials and parts to where they are needed, manufacturing department personnel produce products using those materials and parts, and packaging and shipping personnel prepare finished products to be delivered to dealers and customers.

In order to plan and control costs for short- and long-run operations, managers must understand how those activities affect costs. This means they must understand **cost behavior** not just for the past periods, but for future periods as well. In this chapter, we will look at cost behavior in detail, and discuss how to estimate cost-activity relationships.

ACTIVITIES AND COST DRIVERS

For each activity of an organization, there is a factor which will be the best measure of the cost increase or decrease. This factor is called a **cost driver.** The costs of purchasing materials and parts (activity) may depend on the number of purchases (cost driver). The costs of operating machines (activity) may depend on the number of hours of machine operation (cost driver). The costs of inspecting finished products (activity) may depend on the number of units of finished products (cost driver).

The manufacturing floor of John Deere & Co. is shown here. John Deere has performed an excellent study on cost-acitivty relationships.

Cost drivers serve many important functions in management accounting. For calculating costs of activities, such as those we saw in the previous examples, cost drivers are used. Those activity costs become the bases of calculating product costs, determining product prices, and managing costs for many other purposes in manufacturing and service organizations. That is why it is important to understand the relationships between cost drivers, activities,, and products. These relationships are the subject of this and subsequent chapters.

Typical Manufacturing Support Activities

The kinds of activities performed in a manufacturing company are related closely to the nature of the operations of the company. Each company must identify the appropriate activities for each shop or business segment. There are, however, certain common activities found in typical manufacturing environments.

Engineering Most manufactured products consist of many components. A component is defined by a drawing, called an **engineering drawing,** which illustrates the dimensions, materials, and finishes of the component. An engineering drawing is also listed on a **bill-of-material (B-O-M),** which shows the components and the quantity of each required for a finished product unit. When an engineering drawing is modified, an **engineering change notice (ECN)** is used to notify the appropriate personnel. Engineering costs would include: salaries of engineers and supervisors; costs of analyzing materials; and costs of examining component tolerances.

Setup   Setup costs are incurred when there are multiple jobs to run on machines. For example, Job #121, which consists of processing 10,000 units of blue markers, is run first on a machine. If Job #122, which calls for processing 25,000 units of green markers, follows Job #121, then the machine must be re-set for a run of Job #122. Setup costs include: setup workers' labor for actual setup; engineers' salaries; maintenance of machines and tools; depreciation of related machines, tools, etc.; and other supporting costs, such as supervision of setup activities.

Material Handling   Material handling overhead costs are incurred moving materials and parts from one area to the next. Costs in this pool include: indirect labor connected to material handling; and repairs and maintenance for equipment used for this purpose.

Purchasing   Various products require the use of different types and combinations of materials. The purchasing patterns of these materials would also be different, depending on the order frequency and size, delivery mode, receiving room activities, and so forth. Purchasing department costs include: salaries of purchasing agents, order clerks, and receiving room employees; order processing costs, including supplies, postage, telephone, etc.; and receiving room operating costs.

Scheduling   Scheduling resolves conflict in the use of production resources. Different jobs on the factory floor often compete for the same resources (materials, labor, and overhead) or jobs may have different levels of priorities with some more urgent than others. Reliable schedules ensure scheduled work will be performed in the proper sequence by assigning dates to specific jobs. Scheduling costs consist of salaries of schedulers and supervisors.

Other Activities   There are other activities that a manufacturing company performs. They are: direct labor-related activities; machine operation activities; inventory control activities; data management activities; quality inspection activities; and general factory administration activities.

COST-ACTIVITY RELATIONSHIPS

In order to plan and control management accounting activities, managers need reliable cost figures, which are measured for past periods, and estimated for future periods. The measured and estimated costs must reflect the relationships between costs and activities through cost drivers. In order to estimate costs, a company can observe of its actual cost performance in past periods, or use the results of activity analyses. Estimation of costs can be a very challenging task, and we discuss various methods of cost estimation in this chapter. Many factors are involved in the cost-activity relationships. In our discussions in this chapter, we examine the relationships between costs and activities to further understand the various types of cost behavior.

Simple Cost Functions

The relationship between a cost driver and the cost it drives can be formulated in a **cost function.** A cost function with only one cost driver is the simplest type. Consider the following example:

In the finishing department of a toy manufacturing company, a worker puts the company label on each completed toy, using an automatic sticker dispenser. Each label costs 25 cents. The automatic dispenser has been rented from a local industrial equipment rental company at $150 per month. The monthly cost of the label attaching operation is

$$\text{Monthly cost} = \$150 \text{ Rent} + (\$0.25 \times \text{Number of toys produced})$$
$$= \text{Fixed cost} + \text{Variable cost}$$

Let

$$Y = \text{total cost of the label attaching operation}$$
$$a = \text{fixed rent cost}$$
$$b = \text{variable cost of label (per unit)}$$
$$X = \text{number of toys produced}$$

The above can be rewritten as

$$Y = a + bX, \text{ or}$$
$$Y = \$150 + \$0.25X$$

Exhibit 6-1 shows the mixed cost of the label attaching operation. The straight line, displaying a **linear** cost function, starts at $150 of the **Y-intercept,** and shows an increase of 25 cents of cost per each additional unit of toys — i.e., the **slope** of the cost function. If 1,000 units of toys are produced, the variable cost of the labels will be $250 (= $0.25 × 1,000). The total monthly cost of the label attaching operation amounts to $400, which includes the fixed rental cost of $150 per month plus the $250 variable cost.

EXHIBIT 6-1 The Behavior of Variable and Fixed Costs

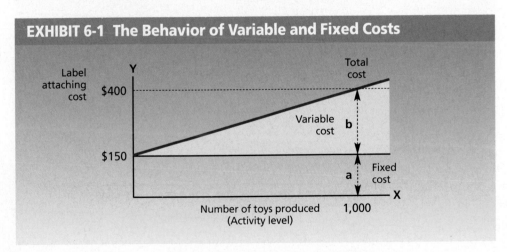

Identifying Simple Cost-Activity Relationships

A simple and easy method of identifying a linear cost-activity relationship is called the **high-low method.** Consider the finishing department operation of the previous toy manufacturer. The monthly activities, number of toys produced, and finishing department's operating costs for the past year are shown in the following table:

	Finishing Department Data, Year 5	
Month	Operating Cost Y	Number of Toys X
January	$46,000	8,300
February	48,000	9,000
March	47,000	8,600
April	45,000	7,600
May	43,000	6,600
June	39,000	4,500
July	38,000	4,000
August	40,000	4,900
September	49,000	9,500
October	48,000	9,100
November	46,000	8,200
December	45,000	7,700

If these cost-activity data are plotted on a graph, a visual scanning of whether there exists a general pattern of cost-activity relationship can be done. The high-low method relies on two points on the graph (Exhibit 6-2) for the estimation of cost-activity relationship: the highest and lowest values of the cost driver (number of toys produced) within the relevant range.

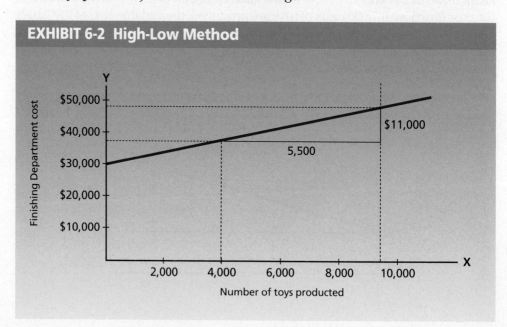

EXHIBIT 6-2 High-Low Method

Using the two points in the above example:

	Cost Driver: Number of Toys	Finishing Department Operating Cost
High point	9,500	$49,000
Low point	4,000	38,000
Difference	5,500	$11,000

$$\text{Slope coefficient} = \frac{\text{Cost difference}}{\text{Cost driver difference}} \quad \frac{\$11,000}{5,500}$$

$$= \$2 \text{ per unit of toy}$$

Since $\qquad$ $Y = a + bX,$

then $\qquad$ $a = Y - bX$

$$\text{Y-intercept} = \text{Total cost} - (\text{Slope coefficient} \times \text{Number of cost driver units})$$

If the high point is used:

$$\text{Y-intercept} = \$49,000 - (\$2 \times 9,500)$$
$$= \$30,000$$

If the low point is used:

$$\text{Y-intercept} = \$38,000 - (\$2 \times 4,000)$$
$$= \$30,000$$

Accordingly, the cost-activity relationship can be expressed as

$$Y = a + bX$$
$$= \$30,000 + \$2(\text{number of toys})$$

COMPLEX COST-ACTIVITY RELATIONSHIPS

In Chapter 2, we learned the difference between variable and fixed costs. Within a relevant range, variable costs increase (decrease) as production volume increases (decreases). Production volume is a cost driver, just as the number of purchases and the number of machine operating hours were cost drivers in the previous example.

The discussion of variable and fixed costs in Chapter 2 was based on a very simple concept of cost behavior. When the number of units produced increases, costs increase as well. But the number of units produced is just one type of cost driver. There are many different types of cost drivers and activities in manufacturing. We will look at the complex patterns of cost behavior in this chapter.

KAPLAN'S TALE OF TWO FACTORIES[1]

Imagine there are two factories. They both have the same physical facilities, and so they look the same after the people who work there have cleaned up the floor and have gone home at night. Other characteristics are:

	Factory A	Factory B
Products	Blue markers only	100 different color markers
Production volume	100,000 units a year	100,000 units a year

What would you see in factory B that you wouldn't see in factory A?

Two factories produce and sell the same number of units, 100,000 markers a year. The production volume as a cost driver is the same for both factories. In order to support the production of the 100,000 markers of 100 different colors, however, factory B should incur significantly higher overhead costs. Why? Please consider the following:

In Factory A, they produce only blue markers. This means that a production scheduling department is not needed. However, Factory B does need a production scheduling department to schedule the production of 100 different products. Factory B needs many material handling people to move and prepare many different types of materials. Factory B needs more purchasing department people to handle many more purchase orders and related documents for different color materials. Factory B requires more people to do more setups and engineering changes to support the production of 100 different products. Accordingly, Factory B incurs much higher costs of scheduling, material handling, purchasing, setup, and engineering, all of which represent *activities* and are manufacturing *overhead* costs.

Volume-Based Measures Don't Tell the Whole Story

Now, answer this question: Would you be able to explain the higher overhead costs of Factory B based on **volume-related measures,** such as direct labor hours (or costs), machine hours, or number of units produced? Can you answer how much the overhead costs increased as direct labor workers put in one additional hour of work, as machines were operated for one additional hour, or as one more unit of markers was produced?

The answer is a definite **no.** The direct labor workers in the two factories should work the same direct labor hours to produce 100,000 markers. The machines should be operated for the same machine hours (run time) to process 100,000 markers. The number of units produced is the same 100,000 for both factories.

---

[1] Adapted from the presentation, "Strategic Cost Analysis," made by R.S. Kaplan at the Cost Accounting for the '90s Conference, National Association of Accountants (now Institute of Management Accountants), Boston (April 29, 1986).

These volume-related measures cannot account for the higher demands of Factory B for more *activities* which represent overhead support services. The facts are summarized below:

	Factory A	Factory B
Volume-related measures:		
Direct labor hours	Same	Same
Machine hours	Same	Same
Number of units	Same	Same
Activity-related measures:		
Scheduling	Less	More
Purchasing	Less	More
Material handling	Less	More
Setup	Less	More
Engineering	Less	More

The Reality of Manufacturing

Of course, there are volume-related overhead costs that are directly tied to direct labor time and/or machine run time. The cost of supplies used in production is the best example of volume-related overhead costs. The longer direct labor workers operate, the more supplies are used. The cost of supplies is a variable overhead item, and the overhead costs will increase as more are used. Repairs and maintenance costs are similar. As production increases, these volume-related overhead costs also increase.

But the reality is that, for the last several decades, the proportion of the activity-related overhead costs, such as scheduling, purchasing, material handling, etc., has increased to a greater extent than that of the volume-related overhead costs. This is the result of the development of more product lines and more sophisticated manufacturing processes by businesses in their efforts to become more competitive.

We have observed, in the above example, Factory B with its more diverse products demands more *activities* to support those products. The reality of manufacturing in today's business world is a lot closer to Factory B than the single-product Factory A.

COST HIERARCHY

The conventional understanding of the dichotomous structure of variable and fixed costs has recently been developed into a more comprehensive understanding of the dynamic, hierarchical structure of organizational costs. Based on the observations of cost accounting and management systems of various manufacturers in recent years, Robin Cooper and Robert S. Kaplan have formulated a hierarchy of manufacturing costs. The Cooper-Kaplan's hierarchy of costs (called cost hierarchy) has now become the conceptual foundation of understanding manufacturing cost behavior.

According to the **cost hierarchy,** there are four levels of factory operating expenses that correspond with the four levels of activities. The four levels are the following:

(1) Unit level
(2) Batch level
(3) Product level
(4) Facility level

The four levels of activities and the factory operating expenses which the activities create provide organizations with a new perspective on the costs of producing products and services. This also represents a step forward in understanding cost behavior in general, from the traditional dichotomous structure of variable versus fixed costs. The cost hierarchy is discussed in detail here.

(1) *Unit-level activities and factory operating expenses*

The traditional view of cost accounting regards all variable costs as volume-driven. According to the traditional view, as a manufacturer operates longer in terms of direct labor hours or machine hours, and produces more units of products, variable costs increase in proportion to the increases in those volume-related measures. According to the cost hierarchy concept, this type of cost behavior is defined as just one level of cost hierarchy, rather than as a general cost behavior pattern.

If the production volume of a product changes 10%, and the related resource consumption changes 10% as a result, the activity and expense are unit-level. Examples of those resources are: materials, direct labor, supplies, repairs and maintenance, fuel, and electricity. But not all variable costs are volume-driven, as illustrated below.

(2) *Batch-level activities and factory operating expenses*

Certain activities are not volume-related, but batch-related. The activity of setting up a machine, for example, is related to the number of batches and production runs. The setup cost varies according to the number of batches, but is fixed for all the items in the batch. That is, once a machine is set up to run, there is no incremental setup cost regardless of how many items are processed on the machine.

Examples of batch-level activities include setting up machines to process batches, moving loads of materials and parts, ordering and receiving materials and parts for certain batches, and inspecting inputs and outputs that come in and go out of production lines.

(3) *Product-level activities and factory operating expenses*

Certain activities are performed to sustain different types of products in a product line. These activities are not directly related to the number of units or the number of batches. Examples of product-level activities include maintaining required parts on the computer system, maintaining other product specifications on materials and routing sequences, and making engineering changes on products and processes.

Assigning the product-level costs to units or batches of products requires some linear allocations, usually based on the volume. The product-level costs are fixed as to all units and batches of each different product, regardless of the number of units or batches involved.

(4) *Facility-level activities and factory operating expenses*

Some activities are performed to maintain the facility. They are independent of the numbers of units, batches, or products. This fixed cost category is used to deal with the expense items that relate to factory management, building and grounds, and other items that are of the facility-level.

For this level of activities and factory operating expenses, it is difficult to find logical drivers that can be used for assigning the expenses to products. Usually, arbitrary allocations are made.

VARIABLE VS. FIXED: A TRANSITORY DISTINCTION

According to the traditional view of cost behavior, variable costs are those costs that change in proportion to production volume changes. Fixed costs are viewed as those that stay the same as production volume changes. The only expansion of this unit-level view of cost behavior has been the coverage of the time dimension: Given enough time, almost every cost item becomes variable. For example, rent on the factory building is a fixed cost item. The rent, however, increases if a new building is added to meet higher demands for the company's products in a future period.

The cost hierarchy concept changes the view of cost behavior in general. The variable/fixed distinction is a transitory concept that varies according to the level at which the cost is viewed. The previous discussion of the four levels of activities and factory operating expenses leads to the following understanding of the behavior of costs:

(1) If viewed at the unit-level,

    Unit-level costs   are   variable costs.

    Batch-level costs
    Product-level costs   are   fixed costs.
    Facility-level costs

(2) If viewed at the batch-level,

    Unit-level costs
    Batch-level costs   are   variable costs.

    Product-level costs
    Facility-level costs   are   fixed costs.

(3) If viewed at the product-level,

Unit-level costs
Batch-level costs $\Big\}$ are variable costs.
Product-level costs

Facility-level costs are fixed costs.

(4) If viewed at the facility-level,

All costs are variable costs.

Of course, those costs that are viewed as variable may not always be purely variable, and may be step-wise variable. For example, setup costs (batch-level) may be fixed only for those product items that belong to the specific batch, and not for other items outside the batch. But the cost hierarchy concept allows cost accountants to escape from the confines of the traditional dichotomy of variable vs. fixed costs, and to gain a new perspective on cost behavior.

MORE COMPLEX COST FUNCTIONS

The cost function is simple when only one cost driver, typically unit-level, is used. Cost functions become more complex when batch-level and product-level cost drivers are involved, which usually is the case in the real world.

A quality inspector is performing a final test on a sorter module at Electrocom Automation Inc., Arlington, Texas.

Cost-Activity Relationship at the Batch-Level

Consider a company's quality assurance department operations. The activities in that department are primarily concerned with inspecting products to maintain the quality standard. Defects should be prevented from occurring, or, at least, must be detected before customers are exposed to them.

Assume the toy company has determined that its quality inspection costs are driven by two activities: The first activity is the output production level, and its cost driver is the number of units produced. The second activity is the frequency of new production runs. Each production run requires more intensive first-item inspection work after the new setup. The cost driver for the second activity is the number of production runs, or batches.

The implication of those two cost drivers is the following: The inspection cost is related not only to the number of units produced, but also to the number of first-item inspection needs. This is because the first items of a new production setup are more likely to have defects before necessary adjustments are made.

The cost function for the inspection costs thus needs two explanatory variables (cost drivers), and is

$$Y = a + bX_1 + cX_2$$

where

Y	=	total cost of the inspection department
a	=	fixed cost of the department
b	=	variable cost of inspecting each unit of product
X_1	=	number of toys inspected
c	=	variable inspection cost per each batch of products
X_2	=	number of batches

It is true that X_1 and X_2 are not entirely independent of each other. Number of toys inspected, X_1, would usually increase as more batches, X_2, are processed. This is because a larger number of batches would mean not only more first-item inspection but also a higher volume of toys. The toy company may want to look at the separate effects of the two cost drivers because there are distinct effects of each cost driver on the inspection cost.

Assume the following for the quality assurance department:

On an average, 10% of the production volume is chosen as the sample for inspection. The average size of each batch is 1,000 units of toys.

Variable cost (b)	=	$22 per unit inspected
Fixed cost (a)	=	$25,000
Variable cost (c)	=	$900 per batch

Now, can you estimate the quality inspection cost for the July operation?

The production volume of July in the above example was 4,000. The number of units inspected is 10% of 4,000, or 400. Therefore,

$$bX_1 = \$22 \times 400 = \$8,800$$

Number of batches processed is 4, since

Production volume ÷ Average batch size = 4,000 ÷ 1,000 = 4

Now,

$$cX_2 = \$900 \times 4 = \$3,600$$

Total cost is

$$Y = a + bX_1 + cX_2$$
$$= \$25,000 + \$8,800 + \$3,600 = \$37,400$$

Cost-Activity Relationship at the Product-Level

Earlier in this chapter, an engineering change notice (ECN) was mentioned, as a means of notifying appropriate personnel of modifications or corrections to an engineering drawing for a product. Consider the toy company's engineering department operations. As consumer tastes change, the company must continually develop new toys to stay competitive in the toy market. Product engineers must prepare new engineering drawings, and process engineers must write new routines for processing newly-designed products.

Engineering costs, such as the salaries of engineers and supervisors, costs of analyzing materials, and costs of examining toy component tolerances, are product-level costs. The behavior of engineering costs would certainly depend on the number of different toys produced, rather than on the number of units or batches of toys processed.

Accordingly, the engineering department's cost function would most likely be

$$Y = a + bX$$

where

Y	=	total cost of the engineering department
a	=	fixed cost of the department
b	=	variable cost of servicing each engineering change notice
X	=	number of engineering change notices handled

Estimating costs for the engineering department would require the information on how many engineering change notices are serviced. Let's assume the following for the engineering department:

Variable cost (b) = $4,700 per engineering change notice
Fixed cost (a) = $250,000

Now, total cost estimated for a period, in which 24 ECN's are handled, is

$$Y = a + bX$$
$$= \$250,000 + \$4,700 \times 24 = \$362,800$$

Cost-Activity Relationship When All Three Levels Are Involved

In reality, manufacturing operations usually involve all three levels of activities and costs that have been discussed thus far. When unit-level, batch-level, and product-level activities and costs are all involved, there are three different levels of cost drivers present in the cost functions.

The cost function, with three levels of activities and costs involved, looks like the following:

Total cost = Fixed cost + Unit-level cost + Batch-level cost + Product-level cost

The calculations of costs for each level would be performed as discussed thus far in this chapter.

Cost-Activity Relationship at the Facility-Level

When activities and costs are viewed at the facility-level, and enough time is allowed for all activities to be performed, every cost item may become variable. Consider the toy company's operations as an example. If the business becomes very successful, the company may want to add one more plant to double its capacity to produce and sell toys.

If one more plant is added, fixed costs, such as depreciation and property tax on the plant buildings and machineries, plant managers' salaries, etc., may double. Accordingly, the fixed costs become variable costs. There may not be any fixed cost remaining if we expand our horizon to look at long time and wide range of activities.

COSTS AND ACTIVITIES IN SERVICE INDUSTRY

In a service firm,, we can apply most of the concepts and techniques discussed in this chapter in the same manner as we would in a manufacturing company. Of course, some adjustments must be made for the unique characteristics of a specific service firm, as variations exist and adjustments are needed for a particular type of service operation.

Definition of Activity

Activities usually are defined for each major stage of operations in service industry. Consider a finance company's operations.

In stage 1, loan applications are received and recorded by the receptionist. The first loan processor sorts and batches new loan applications according to the type of loan. The processor sends out and collects confirmations of employment and bank balances; acquires credit reports on the applicants through credit bureaus; and collects other loan related documents and reports as they come in.

In stage 2, loan analysts examine the credit and loan files and other information. They draw their conclusions and write recommendations to approve or reject the loan applications.

In stage 3, the loan committee meets to evaluate and make the final decision on each loan. The committee usually meets once a week. The loan committee members are paid a fee for each meeting they attend.

At certain intervals (stage 4), the finance company reviews its loan review and approval policies and procedures; evaluates the efficiency of operations; and reviews the appropriateness of documents and forms used.

For each of the four stages described in this example, various activities are defined. For instance, stage 1 activities are receiving and recording of loan applications, as are sorting and batching applications.

A New Service Activity
Chase's new financial services include a 21st century safe deposit box. Now an electronic image archive enables a customer to store and retrieve financially related documents and data. The service is web-based.

Service Activity and Cost

If the four levels of cost and activity hierarchy are used in this finance company, the following cost-activity relationships can be established:

Unit-level: Most of the activities and costs that are related to stage 1. For example, the costs of sending confirmations and printing credit reports would depend on how many applications are handled.

Batch-level: Sorting and batching applications in stage 1 would be batch-related. If loan committee members are paid for each meeting they attend, the loan committee-related costs would be batch-related. It doesn't matter how many applications are decided on at each meeting. One day's meeting in stage 3 is a batch-related activity for the company.

Product-level: Most of the costs in stage 4 may be product-related. The loan forms may be designed according to the types of loans. The loan review policies may be formulated according to the types of loans also.

Facility-level: President's salary, rent and office maintenance expenses, and credit bureau annual membership fee would be facility-related.

As this finance company example demonstrates, many concepts and practices previously discussed for the manufacturing industry can be applied to the service industry also. The concepts and procedures, of course, should be modified to suit the particular operating characteristics of the company which is being analyzed.

A Numerical Example

Suppose the above finance company recorded the following costs and activities for the first year of their operations:

Number of loan applications	184
Number of loan committee meetings	40
Types of loans (commercial, residential, etc.)	5
Personnel expenses:	
Receptionist	$ 28,000
Loan processor	35,000
3 Loan analysts	121,000
Management personnel	176,000
Total	360,000
Fees paid to 5 loan committee members	94,000
Loan forms and policy-related expenses	32,000
Facility-related expenses	175,000
Total expenses for the first year	$661,000

A cost-activity study indicates the following:

The activities and costs of the receptionist, loan processor, and 3 loan analysts are unit-level. Loan committee-related costs are batch-level. Loan forms and policy-related costs are product-level. Costs of management personnel and other operating expenses are facility-level.

Cost rates for different activities are calculated below:

Unit-level cost rate:		
Unit-level costs ($28,000 + $35,000 + $121,000)		$184,000
Number of applications	÷	184
Cost rate per application		$ 1,000

Batch-level cost rate:

Batch-level costs (loan committee expenses)	$ 94,000
Number of loan committee meetings	÷ 40
Cost rate per meeting	$ 2,350

Product-level cost rate:

Product-level costs (loan forms and policy-related costs)	$ 32,000
Types of loans	÷ 5
Cost rate per loan type	$ 6,400

Facility-level costs (fixed):

Management personnel expenses	$176,000
Other fixed operating expenses	175,000
Total	$351,000

The total operating cost of the finance company for the first year can be summarized as

Unit-level costs	$1,000	×	Number of applications
Batch-level costs	$2,350	×	Number of committee meetings
Product-level costs	$6,400	×	Types of loans
Facility-level costs	$351,000		
Total operating costs	$661,000		

Now we can estimate future costs of operating this finance company. Suppose other conditions stay the same except the following changes for the second year:

Number of loan applications increases 25%.

Loan committee holds 5 more meetings to handle increased business volume.

The total cost of the second-year operations will be

$$
\begin{aligned}
& \$1,000 \times (184 \times 1.25) \\
+\ & \$2,350 \times (40 + 5) \\
+\ & \$6,400 \times 5 \\
+\ & \$351,000 \\
=\ & \$718,750
\end{aligned}
$$

Similar calculations can be made for cost-activity relationships that are found in other service industry applications.

COST ESTIMATION METHODS

Previously in this chapter, we briefly discussed the high-low method of estimating the cost-activity relationships. The high-low method is a simple, but crude, method that is used to identify cost-activity relationships. There are other methods of estimating cost-activity relationships, which we discuss here. Assume the toy manufacturer incurred the following repairs and maintenance costs during the first six months of Year 7:

Month	Number of Toys Produced	Total Repairs and Maintenance Cost
January	6,000	$ 8,500
February	10,500	11,500
March	7,000	9,500
April	4,500	7,000
May	8,000	10,000
June	9,000	10,500

From the above data, we can estimate the variable and fixed components of repairs and maintenance costs, and express the cost-activity relationship as a cost function, using various cost estimation methods.

HIGH-LOW METHOD

The high-low method, as previously discussed, relies on two points of the observation data: the highest and lowest values of the cost driver (number of toys produced) within the relevant range. Using the two points in the example, 10,500 units (highest) and 4,500 units (lowest), we can estimate the cost-activity relationship as follows:

$$\text{Variable cost per unit} = \frac{\text{Cost difference}}{\text{Cost driver difference}}$$

$$= \frac{\$11,500 - \$7,000}{10,500 - 4,500} = \frac{\$4,500}{6,000} = \$0.75$$

Total variable cost = Number of units × Variable cost per unit

(Using the highest level of activity)

= 10,500 units × $0.75 = $7,875

(Using the lowest level of activity)

= 4,500 units × $0.75 = $3,375

Total fixed cost = Total cost − Total variable cost

(Using the highest level of activity)

= $11,500 − $7,875 = $3,625

(Using the lowest level of activity)

= $7,000 − $3,375 = $3,625

Cost Estimation, Hollywood Style

Estimating the costs of making movies is becoming ever more difficult for movie makers. "Costs are way up." The high costs are attributed to various factors. The studios need big stars to attract crowds at the box office. Actors like Tom Cruise, Jim Carrey, and Harrison Ford demand and get $20 million for a single movie. Film rights to books by unknown authors can cost $3 million and popular directors ask $10 million. The total manufacturing cost of an average movie is $50 million now. Hollywood, meanwhile, is producing many more movies than before and movie makers need to spend large sums on advertising. Can you see which costs are variable and which costs are fixed?

From "Lights! Camera! Checkbooks! Costs Menace Movie Makers," *The Wall Street Journal*, December 21, 1995, B1, B3.

Note that whether we use the highest level or the lowest level of activity, the total fixed cost is the same: $3,625. Now that we know total fixed costs and the variable cost per unit, the total cost of repairs and maintenance may be expressed in a cost formula as follows:

Total repairs and maintenance cost

$$= \quad \$3,625 \quad \text{fixed cost per month}$$
$$+ \quad \$0.75 \quad \text{per unit of output produced.}$$

Statisticians prefer to present the above equation in terms of the Y-axis (representing total cost) and the X-axis (representing total units produced) as follows:

$$Y = a + bX$$

where Y is total cost, a is fixed cost per period, b is variable cost per unit, and X is the number of units produced.

In our example, the highest (lowest) value of the cost driver coincided with the highest (lowest) value of the cost. Quite often, nevertheless, this may not be the case. What if the highest value of the cost driver or the cost does not coincide with the highest value of the other? Choose the highest value and the lowest value of the *cost driver* for the estimation. Why not the highest value and the lowest value of the *cost?* It is because the cause-and-effect relationship starts from the cost driver and runs to the cost.

Advantage and Disadvantage of the High-Low Method

The advantage of the high-low method is its simplicity; its major disadvantage is that it ignores all the different levels of activity, since it uses the two extremes only. The above possibility that the highest value of the cost driver will not coincide with the highest value of the cost is real. There apparently are dangers of estimating the cost-activity relationship based on only two observations of the data. One such danger is the **outlier** problem. In Exhibit 6-3, the estimated cost function based only on the highest and lowest values of the data, obviously does not represent the cost-activity relationship you can see on the graph. The highest and the lowest points on the graph are outliers, rather than the representative data items. The relationship between the cost driver and repairs and maintenance cost for the company should be estimated using a different cost estimation technique.

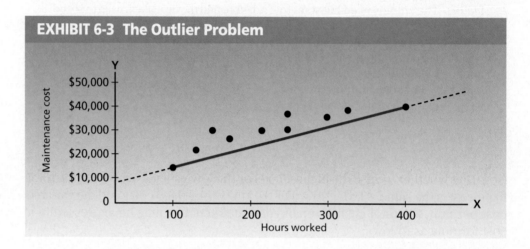

EXHIBIT 6-3 The Outlier Problem

SCATTERGRAPH METHOD

Instead of using only the highest point and the lowest point of activity, the **scattergraph** (or **scatterdiagram**) method uses all activity levels. A graph is constructed with the activity level on the horizontal (X) axis and the total cost on the vertical (Y) axis. Then all the activity levels are plotted on the graph where each activity level would be represented by one point which is placed at the intersection of the volume of activity and the total cost corresponding to that volume of activity. Then a line is fitted through these points where approximately equal num-

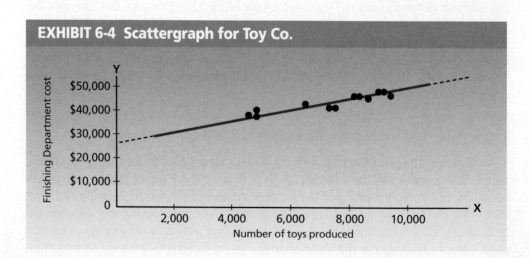

EXHIBIT 6-4 Scattergraph for Toy Co.

ber of points fall above and below the line. Statisticans refer to this line as a **cost estimation line.** The scattergraph method is illustrated in Exhibit 6-4 using the same data for the toy manufacturer's finishing department which was used in Exhibit 6-2.

The scattergraph can be used to estimate the total operating cost for any future level of activity visually and quickly. The *visual fit* obtained here can indicate whether the cost-activity relationship to be estimated is linear or not. In Exhibit 6-4, a straight line could be fitted. The scattergraph often ignores the extreme levels of activity or outliers.

LEAST-SQUARES METHOD

Rather than visually fitting the cost estimation line through the points, as we did using the scattergraph method, statisticians prefer a more accurate method known as the **least-squares method.** The name is derived from the fact that this method produces a cost estimation line where the sum of the squared differences between each point and that line is the least possible. We call this line the **regression line,** because the least-squares method is a method of regression analysis.

Previously, we presented the total cost equation as:

$$Y = a + bX, \tag{1}$$

where

$$
\begin{aligned}
Y &= \text{total cost,} \\
X &= \text{the number of units,} \\
a &= \text{fixed cost per period (Y-intercept), and} \\
b &= \text{the variable cost per unit (slope of the total cost curve).}
\end{aligned}
$$

Since the least-squares method considers all activity levels, each level represented by an equation, if we have a number of activity levels, say n, and we add all of them, we obtain the following equation:

$$\text{Sum of } Y = \text{Sum of } a + b\,(\text{Sum of } X) \tag{2}$$

Since b (variable cost per unit) is the same in all equations, only X for each activity level is summed, and the sum of X is multiplied by b. Since a, the fixed cost, is the same for all activity levels, the sum of a equals n times a. Thus, we can write equation (2) above statistically as follows:

$$\Sigma Y = na + b\Sigma X \tag{3}$$

where Σ (pronounced Sigma) is the Greek symbol for "sum of."

If we also multiply equation (1) by X, we get

$$XY = aX + bX^2 \tag{4}$$

If we sum equation (4) for all activity levels, we get

$$\Sigma XY = a\Sigma X + b\Sigma X^2 \tag{5}$$

Since a and b are the same for each equation, they are multiplied by ΣX and ΣX^2, respectively. The least-squares method requires solving equations (3) and (5) simultaneously. We use the following data to show the process:

Data:

	Number of Toys Produced	Total Operating Cost
January	6,000	$ 8,500
February	10,500	11,500
March	7,000	9,500
April	4,500	7,000
May	8,000	10,000
June	9,000	10,500

Calculations:

Month	Number of Activity Levels n	Number of Units X (000)	Total Costs Y	XY	X^2
January	1	6.0	8,500	51,000	36.00
February	2	10.5	11,500	120,750	110.25
March	3	7.0	9,500	66,500	49.00
April	4	4.5	7,000	31,500	20.25
May	5	8.0	10,000	80,000	64.00
June	6	9.0	10,500	94,500	81.00
Totals →		45.0	57,000	444,250	360.50
	↑	↑	↑	↑	↑
	n	ΣX	ΣY	ΣXY	ΣX^2

Now, we substitute the above numbers in equations (3) and (5) above, and solve them simultaneously to derive b and then a, as follows:

$$\Sigma Y = na + b\Sigma X \quad \rightarrow \quad 57,000 = 6a + 45b \quad (3)$$
$$\Sigma XY = a\Sigma X + b\Sigma X^2 \quad \rightarrow \quad 444,250 = 45a + 360.5b \quad (5)$$

To solve for b, we make the a portion the same in both equations (3) and (5), and subtract one from the other to eliminate a. To do that, we multiply equation (3) by 45 and equation (5) by 6 as follows:

$$45 \times \text{equation (3)} \quad \rightarrow \quad 2,565,000 = 270a + 2,025b \quad (6)$$
$$6 \times \text{equation (5)} \quad \rightarrow \quad 2,665,500 = 270a + 2,163b \quad (7)$$

Subtract equation (6)
from equation (7) → $\quad 100,500 = 0 + 138b$

$$b = 100,500 \div 138 = \$728.26$$

Substitute b
in equation (3) → $\quad 57,000 = 6a + 45(728.26)$
$$= 6a + 32,772$$
$$57,000 - 32,772 = 6a$$
$$a = (57,000 - 32,772) \div 6 = 4,038$$

The variable cost is $728.26 per 1,000 units or $.728 per unit, and the fixed cost is $4,038 per month. Thus, the cost formula for operating costs is

Total operating cost
= $4,038 (fixed cost per month)
+ $.728 (variable cost per unit) × Number of units.

The advantage of the least-squares method is that it is the most statistically sound method among the cost estimation methods. The only disadvantage is its apparent difficulty. With the widespread use of personal computers, this disadvantage is not serious.

Regression Analysis and Cost Hierarchy

We assumed in all the cost estimation methods discussed above that there is only one measure of activity level (X) that affects the behavior of the variable component of total cost. For example, we assumed that the variable component of operating cost is affected only by the number of units produced. However, we have learned in our discussion of cost hierarchy that there may be other levels of activity which influence costs. Operating costs may also be affected by the number of machines, capacity of machines, labor classes, and so forth. In this case, the equation $Y = a + bX$ will have to be extended to $Y = a + bX + cW + dZ$, and so on. The coefficients a, b, c and d of this equation can be estimated using **multiple regression analysis.** It involves the same principles as in the least-squares method, but is somewhat more complex and requires computer solutions.

OTHER ESTIMATION METHODS

Account Analysis

The **account analysis** approach relies on a review of each cost item to identify it as either fixed or variable, in order to determine cost-activity relationships. Since the review is performed by managers or accountants who are familiar with the particular operations which consume resources, the reliability of the account analysis approach is heavily dependent upon the expertise and judgment of the person making the estimate. Accordingly, more objective methods of cost estimation are often used even when the account analysis approach is used, in order to minimize the negative effect of its subjective nature.

Union Pacific's Dispatch Center in Omaha, Nebraska. Costs incurred in operations such as this require a combination of various estimation methods discussed here.

Engineering Approach

The **engineering approach** to the determination of cost-activity relationships involves a systematic study of materials, labor, services, and facilities needed at varying activity levels. Where no past experience is available, as with a new product, plant, or method, this approach can be very useful in estimating the changes in cost associated with changes in activity levels. As was true with the account analysis method, the engineering approach is also used in conjunction with other methods of cost estimation. This is because engineering estimates are required in the analyses of most activities that are performed in the process of determining cost-activity relationships.

E-BUSINESS AND COST ESTIMATION

Cost estimation we discuss in this chapter is affected as e-business is introduced. We learned in Chapter 4 that once a corporation installs an e-business infrastructure, most costs associated with the infrastructure tend to be *fixed* in the nature of cost behavior. The expenditures for installing the infrastructure on both hardware and software do not increase as e-business volume increases, within the relevant range. Those fixed costs of e-businesses do not stay fixed for a long time, according to many e-consultants who have worked with e-tailers. The infrastructure hardware and software installation and operating costs increase as e-business expands.

Has the nature of e-business-specific costs shown dramatic changes from the costs we have observed in the pre-Net period? We said "no" in our Chapter 4 discussions. No, the nature of e-business-specific costs hasn't changed because fixed costs start to increase once the business expands beyond the relevant range. In this chapter, however, we get more realistic about this issue. The answer can be "yes" from the cost estimation perspective. Yes, it has changed because where those changes occur is different. E-businesses have substantially reduced working capital requirements, cut inventories, eliminated the number of operating centers needed, and removed various paper-shuffling functions from the corporate operations. Management accountants should be aware of these changes when cost estimation is performed.

SUMMARY

In this chapter, we discussed cost-activity relationships, and how to estimate them. Starting from the concepts of variable and fixed costs, we examined the complex cost hierarchy. Costs are determined based on various levels of activity: unit-level, batch-level, product-level, and facility-level. Cost estimation should include the examination of different levels of activities, not just at the unit-level, but other levels also. The cost hierarchy is applicable to the manufacturing industry, and to the service industry in a similar fashion. The cost-activity relationships may be estimated using various methods, but the three least subjective methods are: (1) the high-low method, (2) the scattergraph method, and (3) the least squares method. The high-low method is the simplest but the least accurate; the least squares method is the most complex but the most accurate; and the scattergraph method is somewhere between the other two. Some managers prefer to use a combination of the results of more than one method.

BASIC CONCEPTS AND TERMS

Batch-level activities	Multiple regression analysis
Complex cost functions	Outlier problem
Cost driver	Product-level activities
Cost formula	Regression line
Cost hierarchy	Scattergraph or scatter diagram
Cost structure	method
Engineering approach	Service activity
Engineering change notice	Setup
Facility-level activities	Simple cost functions
High-low method	Unit-level activities
Least squares method	Volume-related measures
Material handling	

■ SELF-REVIEW PROBLEM

Problem 1: Measurement of Cost-Activity Relationships

United Engineering Company is in a new and innovative business of providing robotics-related engineering services for smaller manufacturers which cannot afford to carry an in-house engineering department. More specifically, the services provided are:

1. On-site machine repair service: During the client's operating hours, one of United's repair specialists will stand by on site to do repairs.
2. Machine setup service: According to the client's weekly production schedule, United's setup specialists will do the necessary setups and adjustments.
3. Processing routine re-writing service: When engineering change needs arise, United's process engineers will re-write processing routines.

This is the second year of operations. United has performed cost-activity analyses based on its first-year operating data. The following information has been obtained:

Cost drivers for services 1, 2, and 3 are operating hours, number of production runs (setups), and number of products, respectively. Most clients' operations require similar services. United's cost and operating data for the first year (technical personnel only) follow:

		Personnel Costs
10	Repair specialists	$ 400,000
12	Setup specialists	468,000
4	Process engineers	243,000
	Total technical personnel costs	$1,111,000

Number of clients	6	companies
Cumulative operating hours (for all clients)	12,500	hours
Cumulative production volume (for all clients)	20,960,000	units
Average number of setups (per client)	120	
Average number of products (per client)	15	

Required:

1. Calculate cost rates for
    (a) service #1 (unit-level activity),
    (b) service #2 (batch-level activity), and
    (c) service #3 (product-level activity)
    for cost estimation purposes.

2. United wants to estimate reliable costs of servicing new clients, so that more accurate prices can be quoted based on the costs. Calculate the estimated (a)unit-level, (b)batch-level, (c)product-level, and (d)total costs of servicing a new client, EMax Manufacturing, Inc., which has the following operations:

Annual production volume	2,100,000	units
Annual operating hours	2,100	hours
Average number of annual production runs per product	9	
Number of products (currently produced)	10	

Solution

1. (a) Unit-level activity cost rate (service #1):

Service #1 costs (repair personnel costs)	$400,000
Number of cost driver units (operating hours)	÷ 12,500 hours
Cost rate per hour	$32

   (b) Batch-level activity cost rate (service #2):

Service #2 costs (setup personnel costs)	$468,000
Number of cost driver units (number of setups)	÷ (120 × 6)
Cost rate per setup	$650

   (c) Product-level activity cost rate (service #3):

Service #3 costs (process engineering costs)	$243,000
Number of cost driver units (number of products)	÷ (15 × 6)
Cost rate per product	$2,700

2. (a) Estimated unit-level service cost (service #1):

Unit-level activity cost rate (per hour)	$32
Number of cost driver units (hours)	× 2,100
	$67,200

(b) Estimated batch-level service cost (service #2):

Batch-level activity cost rate (per setup)	$650
Number of cost driver units (setups)	
9 setups per product × 10 products =	× 90
	$58,500

(c) Estimated product-level service cost (service #3):

Product-level activity cost rate (per product)	$2,700
Number of cost driver units (products)	× 10
	$27,000

(d) Total cost of servicing the new client:

$$\$67,200 + \$58,500 + \$27,000 = \$152,700$$

Problem 2: Cost Estimation and the High-Low Method

Bill Gold, an accountant who has been hired to assist in financial reporting for United, thinks the way the company estimates costs, based on cost hierarchy, is too complicated. He wants to use the simple high-low method to estimate just the variable and fixed costs, using the following data for the first six months of the second year:

Month	Operating Cost	Number of Hours
January	$135,000	1,080
February	137,000	1,100
March	130,000	1,000
April	140,000	1,150
May	137,000	1,120
June	131,000	1,020

Required:

Use the high-low method to determine the company's operating cost function.

Solution

The highest and lowest points are in April (1,150 hours) and March (1,000 hours).

$$\text{Variable cost per hour} = \frac{\text{Difference in cost}}{\text{Difference in activity}}$$

$$= \frac{\$140,000 - \$130,000}{1,150 - 1,000}$$

$$= \frac{\$10,000}{150} = \$66.6667 \text{ per hour}$$

Fixed cost per month = Total cost − Variable cost

If the high point is used:

$$\text{Fixed cost per month} = \$140,000 - \$66.6667 \times 1,150$$
$$= \$63,333$$

If the low point is used:

$$\text{Fixed cost per month} = \$130,000 - \$66.6667 \times 1,000$$
$$= \$63,333$$

Accordingly, the operating cost function is:

$$\text{Y (Total cost per month)} = \$63,333 + \$66.6667 \times \text{Number of hours}$$

Problem 3: High-Low Method and Least Squares Method

The marketing costs of Plum Grove Co. for the last six months of 19x8 were as follows:

Month	Units Sold (000)	Marketing Costs
July	17	$46,000
August	21	51,000
September	23	54,000
October	19	49,000
November	14	42,000
December	12	41,000

Required:

1. Based on the above data, compute the variable marketing cost per unit and the fixed marketing costs per month and express them in a cost formula $(Y = a + bX)$ using the following methods:

   (a) High-Low Method
   (b) Least Squares Method

2. Using the cost formula in 1 above, estimate the marketing costs for the first quarter of Year 9 if the number of units sold are expected to be 10,000 in January, 13,000 in February, and 15,000 in March.

Solution

1. (a) High-Low Method

$$b = \frac{\$54,000 - \$41,000}{23,000 - 12,000} = \frac{\$13,000}{11,000} = \$1.18$$

$$a = \$54,000 - (23,000 \times \$1.18) = \$26,860$$

Thus, the cost formula is

$$Y = \$26,860 + \$1.18X$$

(b) Least Squares Method

Month	No.	X Units Sold (000)	Y Marketing Cost	XY	X^2
July	1	17	46,000	782,000	289
August	2	21	51,000	1,071,000	441
September	3	23	54,000	1,242,000	529
October	4	19	49,000	931,000	361
November	5	14	42,000	588,000	196
December	6	12	41,000	492,000	144

Totals $n = 6$ $\Sigma X = 106$ $\Sigma Y = 283,000$ $\Sigma XY = 5,106,000$ $\Sigma X^2 = 1,960$

$$\Sigma XY = a\Sigma X + b\Sigma X^2 \rightarrow \qquad 5,106,000 = 106a + 1960b \qquad (1)$$
$$\Sigma Y = \quad na + b\Sigma X \rightarrow \qquad 283,000 = \quad 6a + 106b \qquad (2)$$

Multiplying equation (1) by 6 $\rightarrow$ 30,636,000 = 636a + 11,760b   (3)
Multiplying equation (2) by 106 $\rightarrow$ 29,998,000 = 636a + 11,236b   (4)

Subtracting equation (4) from equation (3)
$$\rightarrow \qquad 638,000 = 524b$$

Thus,
$$b = 638,000 \div 524$$
$$= \$1,217.56 \text{ per 1,000 units}$$
$$\text{or} \quad \$1.22 \text{ per unit.}$$

By substitution in (2) above $\rightarrow$
$$283,000 = 6a + 106(1,217.56)$$
$$283,000 = 6a + 129,061$$
$$283,000 - \$129,061 = 6a$$
$$a = \$153,939 \div 6 = \$25,656.50$$

Thus, the cost formula is:

$$Y = \$25,656.50 + \$1.22X$$

2. (a) Estimated marketing costs for the first quarter of Year 9:

For January: $26,860 + $1.18(10,000) = $ 38,660
For February: $26,860 + $1.18(13,000) = 42,200
For March: $26,860 + $1.18(15,000) = 44,560

Total for the quarter $125,420

The total marketing costs for the first quarter may be estimated in one step using the following formula:

$$Y = 3a + \$1.18X$$
$$= 3(\$26,860) + \$1.18(10,000 + 13,000 + 15,000)$$
$$= \$80,580 + \$44,840 \qquad = \$125,420$$

(b) Estimated marketing costs for the first quarter of Year 9:

For January:	$25,656.50 +	$1.22(10,000) =	$ 37,856.50
For February:	$25,656.50 +	$1.22(13,000) =	41,516.50
For March:	$25,656.50 +	$1.22(15,000) =	43,956.50

Total for the quarter $123,329.50

The total marketing costs for the first quarter may be estimated in one step using the following formula:

$$
\begin{aligned}
Y &= \quad\quad 3a \quad + \$1.22X \\
&= \quad 3(\$25,656.50) + \$1.22(10,000 + 13,000 + 15,000) \\
&= \quad \$76,969.50 \quad + \$1.22(38,000) \quad\quad = \$123,329.50
\end{aligned}
$$

■ REVIEW QUESTIONS

6-1   Both activity and cost driver are related to cost. What is the difference between activity and cost driver?

6-2   What is a B-O-M? What is an ECN? How are these related to cost?

6-3   What is the relationship between setup and production run? Do they have the same effect on production cost in general?

6-4   What is the role of material handling in the calculation of product cost?

6-5   Why is the number of purchases more meaningful than the amounts of purchases in the calculation of batch-level costs?

6-6   Is a scheduling activity more affected by production volume than number of products? Why or why not?

6-7   Consider the "Kaplan's tale of two factories." If factory B's manufacturing costs are usually higher than those of factory A, why would a company want to build and maintain a factory such as B?

6-8   How has the proportion of volume-related overhead costs to total production cost changed from the 1930s to the 1990s?

6-9   How has the proportion of activity-related overhead costs to total production costs changed from the 1930s to the 1990s?

6-10 Why is cost hierarchy distinguished from cost behavior in general?

6-11 What is the relationship between variable costs and production volume in the traditional view of cost accounting?

6-12 How would the traditional view of cost accounting regard batch-level and product-level costs?

6-13 What would happen to the batch size (number of items in the batch) if managers try to minimize batch-related operating costs?

6-14 What would be the conflict between a controller and a marketing manager regarding the issue of the number of products to carry and the product-related costs?

6-15 Do facility-level costs always stay fixed?

6-16 If you draw a cost-activity graph, what would the horizontal axis depict, cost or activity? Why?

6-17 If all activities of a company were unit-level, would the high-low method have any value in cost estimation?

6-18 Why do you think batch-level activities and costs were ignored in the traditional view of management accounting?

6-19 Consider a company that has multiple plants in three different states. Are the facility-level costs fixed costs for the company? Are the facility-level costs fixed costs for each plant that computes its own operating costs?

6-20 Between manufacturing and service, which case would provide management accountants with more complex cost-activity issues? Why?

6-21 Describe, in your own words, how the high-low method is used to estimate cost-activity relationships.

6-22 Why is the least squares method called by that name?

6-23 Compare the high-low, scattergraph and least squares methods as to simplicity and accuracy.

6-24 Describe the engineering approach to the study of cost behavior.

🌐 INTERNET PROJECT

Web 6-1:

Websites: www.statefarm.com
              www.aig.com

The websites listed above represent two famous companies. Search the sites for information on their product and operating characteristics.

Required:

1. List three items of costs at each different level of cost hierarchy for the two companies.

2. What would be each company's cost estimation problems as reflected by the website information?

Web 6-2:

Websites: www.walmartstores.com
              www.sears.com

The websites listed above represent two famous companies. Search the sites for information on their operating characteristics.

Required:

1. List three items of costs at each different level of cost hierarchy for the two companies.

2. What would be each company's cost estimation problems as reflected by the website information?

■ EXERCISES

E6-1   Cost-Activity Levels and Hierarchy

Listed below are costs associated with common types of manufacturing support activities. Indicate with a U, B, P, or F whether the item would represent a unit-level (U), batch-level (B), product-level (P), or facility-level (F) cost. An item could represent two or more activities and costs.

1. Wages paid to workers who perform actual setups.
2. Salaries paid to process engineers.
3. Overtime portion of the wages paid to the employees who move purchased parts from the storeroom to the manufacturing floor.
4. Wages paid to direct labor workers in the assembly department.
5. Health insurance premiums paid on behalf of the factory superintendent.
6. Depreciation of fork-lift trucks used for material handling.
7. Purchase order processing costs, such as postage and telephone charges.
8. Wages paid to receiving room workers.
9. Personnel expenses related to schedulers who assign dates to specific jobs.
10. Salaries paid to work-in-process inventory management personnel.
11. Costs incurred in connection with the use of computers by new product designers.

E6-2   Simple Cost-Activity Relationship

Microchips Inc. wants to estimate quality inspection costs, consisting of variable and fixed costs. Relevant data for May are:

Variable cost:	$17 per unit
Fixed cost of quality inspection department	$15,000
Production volume in May	10,000 units

The company selects 5% of units produced for inspection.

Required:

1. Estimate the variable cost of inspection for May.
2. Estimate the total cost of inspection for May.

E6-3 Batch-Level Cost-Activity Relationship; Quality Inspection

Peggy's Toys, Inc. believes its quality inspection costs are driven by unit-level (number of units inspected) and batch-level (number of batches produced) activities. Cost and activity data for July are:

Variable cost per unit inspected	$ 12
Variable cost per batch	$ 300
Fixed cost of the department	$26,000
Units produced in July	7,000
Average batch size (in units)	350

The company selects 8% of the production volume for inspection.

Required:

1. Estimate the unit-level cost of inspection for July
2. How many batches were produced in July? Estimate the batch-level cost of inspection for July.
3. Estimate the total cost of inspection for July.

E6-4 Batch-Level Cost-Activity Relationship; Purchasing

Discount Stores, Inc. has performed a cost-activity study, which indicates that its purchasing department cost is driven by the number of purchase activities, rather than the purchase volume involved. Cost and activity data for February are:

Merchandise purchases	$23,460,000
Purchase volume	17,300 cases
Purchase order numbers used:	
(no interruption in sequence)	
The first P.O. number of February 1	#91267
The last P.O. number of February 28	#91476
Purchasing department cost	$77,910

Required:

1. Calculate the cost rate per unit of driver for February.
2. The company estimates a 10% decrease in all levels of purchase activities for March. Estimate the purchasing department cost for March.

E6-5   Batch-Level Cost-Activity Relationship; Setup

The fabrication department of Auto Engines, Inc. wants to estimate setup costs for Year 5. The company has determined that its setup costs are batch-related. Relevant data for the past five years are:

Annual setup costs (average):	
Personnel	$240,000
Other	$ 45,600
Number of production runs per year (average)	120
Annual production volume (average)	48,000 units

Required:

1. Determine the cost rate for each setup activity.
2. In Year 5 the company is planning on reducing the number of production runs by 20% from the previous five years level. Estimate the setup cost for Year 5.
3. Refer to the annual setup costs. Now assume that $45,600 (other setup costs) actually represents the costs of setup equipment. How would your answers to the above two questions change? What assumptions did you make with respect to the existing capacity and the increase (decrease) in the number of setups?

E6-6   Product-Level Cost-Activity Relationship; Process Engineering

Cal Circuits Company's management desires to have an estimate of the process engineering cost for Year 6. A cost-activity study has revealed that the company's process engineering cost is driven by the number of different products it designs and produces. Cost and activity data for the past five years reveal the following:

Annual process engineering cost	$124,800
Number of the company's products	12
Annual production volume (average)	1,278,000 units

Required:

1. Determine the cost rate for each process engineering activity.
2. In Year 6 the company is planning to add two new products to its product lineup. Estimate the process engineering cost for Year 6.

E6-7   Cost-Activity Relationship at a Service Firm; Unit-level

The Claim Processing Department of Tri-State Insurance Company wants to estimate its operating costs for Year 4 based on the actual cost-activity relationships of the past three years. The cost and activity data for the past three years (average per year) are:

Number of insurance claims handled (per year)	2,568
Department operating expenses:	
Variable portion	$267,072
Fixed portion	241,392
Total	$508,464

Required:

1. Assume the cost driver for insurance claim processing activity is number of claims handled. Determine the cost function for the department's operations.
2. Due to a natural disaster in the business region, Tri-State expects an increase of 40% in the number of claims filed for Year 4. Estimate the claims department operating expenses for Year 4.

E6-8 Cost-Activity Relationship at a Service Firm; Batch-Level and Product-Level

Refer to E6-7. Assume that total expenses remain at $508,464. A more detailed cost-activity study reveals the following:

Thirty percent of the variable expenses are more directly related to how claims are batched for processing. The remaining 70% of the variable expenses follow the typical variable cost behavior. Forty percent of the fixed expenses are insurance policy-related (product-level) expenses, while the remaining 60% are not related to any particular level of activity.

Additional data from the same period (3 years average):

Number of batches handled (per year)	152
Types of insurance policies Tri-State serves	8

Required:

1. Determine the new cost function for the department's operations. Consider the additional information on batch-level and product-level costs and activities.
2. The new product development team of Tri-State has proposed two new types of insurance policies to boost sales revenue. The company forecasts an increase of 5% in the number of insurance policies sold and subsequent claims. What would be the new total operating costs of the claims department per year if management approves the new plan? Assume the same batch size and fixed costs.

E6-9 Cost Estimation; High-Low Method

The following are the data on the days patrons stayed at Monterey Resort and Spa and the spa operating expenses for the most recent eight months:

	Patron-Days of Stay	Spa Operating Expenses
April.....................	3,000	$ 6,100
May......................	5,000	6,500
June	6,500	8,200
July.....................	8,000	10,500
August	10,000	10,560
September................	7,500	8,500
October..................	6,000	8,100
November.................	5,800	7,800

Required:

1. Present the cost formula for spa operating expenses, using the high-low method.
2. Estimate the amount of spa operating expenses for an activity level of 9,000 patron-days.

E6-10 Total Cost and Unit Cost

Dolls-R-Us, Inc. makes and sells a single-model doll. The company currently produces 25,000 dolls a year. The doll is very popular among young mothers, and the company expects that the sales will reach 35,000 units very soon. The current capacity will be able to handle the activity level of 35,000 units without changing the cost structure. Currently, the variable cost of producing the doll is $5 per unit and the per-unit fixed cost calculated is $6.

Required:

What will be the total cost of producing 35,000 dolls?

E6-11 High-Low Method; Multiple Stages

Aerobics School's operating costs have three components: facility cost (fixed), exercise supplies (variable), and manpower cost (mixed). Past records reveal that, at the activity level of 500 operating hours, the following overhead costs were incurred:

Facility cost...	$30,000
Exercise supplies......................................	10,000
Manpower cost...	24,000
Total	$64,000

The same records also reveal that, at the 700 operating-hour level, the total overhead was $76,000.

Required:

1. Estimate the cost of exercise supplies at the 700-hour level.
2. What is the facility cost at the 700-hour level?
3. Estimate the manpower cost at the 700-hour level.
4. What is the variable cost per hour of the manpower cost?
5. What is the fixed portion of the manpower cost?
6. Compute the total fixed cost of the school.
7. What is the variable cost per hour of operating the school?
8. Present the cost formula for operating the school.
9. Estimate the school operating costs at the 600-hour level.

E6-12   Cost Estimation; High-Low Method

ADL, Inc. produces gold earrings that are sold to young adults. The quality assurance department's data on the number of earrings inspected and inspection costs are presented below:

Month	Earrings Inspected	Inspection Cost
March	600	$3,500
April	1,000	4,500
May	700	3,200
June	900	4,000
July	1,400	4,400
August	1,500	5,000
September	400	2,200

Required:

Determine the cost formula for earrings inspection cost, using the high-low method.

E6-13   Service Industry; High-Low Method

Santa Monica Hotel's usual room occupancy rate is 85% for its 400 guest rooms. The usual daily operating costs, variable and fixed, at this level of activity are $40 per guest room. The hotel is busiest in the summer months with the California vacationers.

During November, the hotel incurred total operating costs of $357,000 at the occupancy level of 70%. The hotel uses the high-low method of cost estimation.

Required:

1. What is the variable cost of operating an occupied guest room per day?
2. What is the fixed cost per month of operating the hotel?
3. In December, the hotel's occupancy rate is expected to reach 75% because of winter vacationers. What will be the total December hotel operating costs?

E6-14   High-Low Method

Zern, Inc. produces digital versatile disks (DVDs) which are superior in data capacity to CD-ROMS, compact disks, and video players. The company's DVD processing costs for the last ten months of operations are presented below:

	DVDs Processed	Processing Costs
March	3,500	$30,000
April	9,000	40,000
May	10,000	45,000
June	4,000	30,000
July	7,000	38,000
August	8,500	40,000
September	6,000	35,000
October	4,000	31,000
November	9,000	42,000
December	4,500	35,000

There are more sophisticated cost estimation methods, but the company wants to estimate the approximate cost behavior.

Required:

Estimate the cost formula for processing DVDs, using the high-low method.

E6-15   High-Low Method

DTS, Inc. operates a fleet of watercraft, which are popular among water sports enthusiasts in Redondo Beach, California. The company's past records reveal the following costs for two different levels of activity:

Activity Level (kilometers)	Fleet Operating Cost Per Kilometer
40,000	$0.14
50,000	0.12

Required:

1. Present the cost formula for fleet operating costs.
2. If a watercraft is operated 45,000 kilometers, how much will the total operating cost be?

 ## E6-16   Least-Squares Method

The following are the data on the number of units of circuit boards that went through the soldering operation and soldering costs of PCB, Inc.:

	Units of Circuit Boards	Soldering Costs
Week 1	10	$65
Week 2	12	80
Week 3	18	105
Week 4	14	85
Week 5	15	90
Week 6	11	70
Total	80	$495

The company wants to use the estimates of variable and fixed costs for various cost management purposes.

Required:

1. Estimate the variable and fixed costs of soldering operation and present the cost formula. Use the least-squares method for cost estimation.
2. Estimate the expected soldering cost for Week 7 in which the company plans to process 13 units of circuit boards.

E6-17 Least-Squares Method; Multiple Choice

Boston Company is accumulating data to be used in preparing its annual profit plan for the coming year. The cost behavior pattern of the maintenance costs must be determined. The accounting staff has suggested that linear regression be employed to derive an equation in the form of $y = a + bx$ for maintenance costs. Data regarding the maintenance hours and costs for last year and the results of the regression analysis are as follows:

	Hours of Activity	Maintenance Costs
January	480	$ 4,200
February	320	3,000
March	400	3,600
April	300	2,820
May	500	4,350
June	310	2,960
July	320	3,030
August	520	4,470
September	490	4,260
October	470	4,050
November	350	3,300
December	340	3,160
Sum	4,800	43,200
Average	400	3,600
Average cost per hour ($43,200 ÷ 4,800) =		$9
a coefficient		684.65
b coefficient		7.2884

1. In the standard regression equation of $y = a + bx$, the letter b is best described as the
   a. Independent variable.
   b. Dependent variable.
   c. Constant coefficient.
   d. Variable coefficient.
   e. Coefficient of determination.

2. The letter y in the standard regression equation is best described as the
   a. Independent variable.
   b. Dependent variable.
   c. Constant coefficient.
   d. Variable coefficient.
   e. Coefficient of determination.

3. The letter x in the standard regression equation is best described as the
   a. Independent variable.
   b. Dependent variable.
   c. Constant coefficient.
   d. Variable coefficient.
   e. Coefficient of determination.

4. If Boston Company uses the high-low method of analysis, the equation for the relationship between hours of activity and maintenance cost would be
   a. $y = 400 + 9.0x$.
   b. $y = 570 + 7.5x$.
   c. $y = 3,600 + 400x$.
   d. $y = 570 + 9.0x$.
   e. Some equation other than those given above.

5. Based upon the data derived from the regression analysis, 420 maintenance-hours in a month would mean the maintenance costs would be budgeted at
   a. $3,780.
   b. $3,461.
   c. $3,797.
   d. $3,746.
   e. Some amount other than those given above.

(CMA, adapted)

■ PROBLEMS

P6-18   Cost-Activity Relationships; Unit-Level; Batch-Level; Product-Level

Metal Works, Inc. is a manufacturer of various machine tools which are sold to machining companies in the Great Lakes region. Its manufacturing support department does machine repairs and setups, and process engineering for manufacturing departments.

Joe Dineto, the manager of the manufacturing support department, wants to have a better understanding of his department's operating costs so that he can manage the costs better. He has asked the company's cost accountants to examine cost-activity relationships of the manufacturing support activities. The cost accountants, after a careful study, have identified the following cost drivers:

Cost Driver	Activity
Operating hours	Repair
Number of production runs	Setup
Number of engineering changes	Process engineering

Now the cost accountants are developing cost rates for the cost drivers based on the past three years data. The three-year average data are (per year):

Repair personnel costs (3 workers)	$102,328
Repair tools and equipment (depreciation, etc.)	67,400
Setup personnel costs (2 workers)	82,300
Other setup-related costs	12,340
Salaries of 3 process engineers	168,280
Salaries of Joe Dineto and his secretary	119,500
Total manufacturing support costs (per year)	$552,148
Annual operating hours (average)	2,496
Number of different products carried	14
Annual number of production runs per product (average)	4
Annual number of ECN's issued per product (average)	1.5

Required:

1. Calculate cost rates for (a) repair, (b) setup, and (c) process engineering activities. The rates are for cost estimation purposes.

2. The manager of the manufacturing support department wants to know what the total cost of his department's operations will be next year. Estimate the total cost for him. Higher demands for the company's products are anticipated, and operating hours will be increased by 10% next year. The higher demands are attributed to 12 of the company's 14 products. The two unpopular products will be discontinued next year. Other conditions remain the same. Use average runs and engineering changes for each product in your calculations.

P6-19 Cost-Activity Relationships; Unit-Level; Batch-Level; Product-Level

Hintendo, Inc. is in the business of processing one major segment of video-game production for one international company in the entertainment industry called

JJ & Co. The following relates to quality inspection, setup, and design-support operations of Hintendo:

Quality Inspection activity:
Cost driver 1 — Number of units inspected
Cost driver 2 — Number of batches processed
Setup activity:
Cost driver — Number of batches (runs) processed
Design support activity:
Cost driver — Number of products carried

Cost data:

Variable cost of quality inspection (per unit)	$	15
Variable cost of quality inspection (per batch)		450
Fixed cost of quality inspection per period		18,000
Setup personnel costs per period		220,000
Other setup-related costs per period		71,000
Design support personnel costs		198,000
Other design support-related costs		48,000

All costs, other than the designated fixed cost, are variable.

Products and production information:
Hintendo does processing for JJ's 4 products.
Each product is run 5 times a period.
The total processing volume for all four products is 14,600 units per period.
Hintendo selects 5% of its production for quality inspection.

Required:

1. What is the average batch size which Hintendo processes?
2. What is the total quality inspection cost for each period?
3. What is the setup cost per each processing run?
4. What is the design support cost per each product?
5. JJ & Co. has informed Hintendo that one more product will be added next period to the list of products Hintendo is doing processing for. Other conditions stay the same.
   a. What will be Hintendo's estimated setup cost next period if one more product is added?
   b. What will be Hintendo's estimated design support cost next period if one more product is added?

P6-20   High-Low Method; Multiple Levels of Costs

CTS Metalwork Company has recently performed a cost analysis of its operations and found that the overhead costs of its Machine Center A show three different components. The first component is facility cost which stays at a fixed level. The second is support supplies that vary with the level of activity very closely. All other costs have both variable and fixed components. Past records reveal that, at the activity level of 40,000 operating hours, the following overhead costs were incurred:

Facility cost...	$ 80,000
Support supplies.....................................	480,000
All other items......................................	180,000
Total	$740,000

When the company was operating at a lower level of 30,000 hours, the total overhead costs amounted to $580,000. The company has been experiencing sluggish sales recently, which has caused top management's concern. Top management wants to know how much cost reduction will be possible within the existing environment.

Required:

1. Estimate the cost of support supplies at the 30,000-hour level of operations.
2. What is the cost of all other items at the 30,000-hour level of operations?
3. Present the cost formula for the cost of all other overhead items.
4. Present the cost formula for operating Machine Center A, and estimate the machine center operating costs at the reduced level of 30,000-hours.

P6-21 High-Low Method; Cost Estimation at Multiple Levels

Over several years, the receiving area of BTW, Inc. has shown three different components of its operating costs. The first component is facility cost which stays at a fixed level. The second is supplies cost that varies exactly with the level of activity. Human resources costs have both variable and fixed components.

Past records reveal that, at the activity level of 40,000 operating hours, the following operating costs were incurred:

Facility cost	$ 80,000
Supplies cost.......................................	12,000
Human resources	33,000
Total..	$125,000

When the company was operating at a 60,000-hour level, the total operating costs amounted to $135,000.

Required:

1. Estimate the cost of supplies at the 60,000-hour level of operations.
2. What is the cost of human resources at the 60,000-hour level of operations?
3. Present the cost formula for the cost of human resources.
4. Present the cost formula for operating the receiving area, and estimate the operating costs at the 50,000-hour level of activity.

P6-22 Least-Squares Method

The State CPA Society operates continuing professional education (CPE) programs for its members. Past records on the CPE programs show the following:

Season	Number of CPE Courses Offered	Total Cost
Spring, Year 1	12	$16,500
Fall, Year 1	10	15,000
Spring, Year 2	15	18,000
Fall, Year 2	14	17,500
Spring, Year 3	13	17,000
Fall, Year 3	16	19,000

The costs include both variable costs and fixed costs. Variable costs represent honoraria paid to instructors. Fixed costs are the salaries of the society staff.

Required:

1. Determine the variable cost per CPE course and the total fixed cost per CPE season, using the least-squares method.
2. Present the cost formula for operating CPE courses.
3. The society will offer 20 CPE courses during the spring season of Year 4. What is the expected total cost of running the 20 CPE courses?

P6-23 Least-Squares Method

Computer Services Department of LCT, Inc. measures its services to other departments in service-units provided. The following data on service-units provided and department operating expenses are available:

Month	Service-Units Provided	Operating Expenses
March	24	$39,000
April	18	32,000
May	20	34,500
June	19	33,800
July	16	31,500
August	23	36,500

The department manager wants to estimate the relationship between service-units provided and department operating expenses, which are believed to have both variable and fixed components.

Required:

1. Determine the variable cost per service-unit and the fixed cost portion of operating expenses, using the least-squares method.
2. Present the cost formula for operating the Computer Services Department.

P6-24 Mixed Cost Analysis; Least-Squares Method; Scattergraph Method; High-Low Method

The Pistons Company manufactures a wide range of products at several different plant locations. The Franklin plant, which manufactures electrical components, has been experiencing some difficulties with fluctuating monthly overhead costs. The fluctuations have made it difficult to estimate the level of overhead that will be incurred for any one month.

Management wants to estimate overhead costs accurately in order to plan its operation and financial needs better. A trade association publication to which the Pistons Company subscribes indicates that, for companies manufacturing electrical components, overhead tends to vary with direct labor-hours.

One member of the accounting staff has proposed that the cost behavior pattern of the overhead costs be determined. The overhead costs could be predicted from the budgeted direct labor-hours.

Another member of the accounting staff sugggested that a good starting place for determining the cost behavior pattern of overhead costs would be an analysis of historical data. The historical cost behavior pattern would provide a basis for estimating future overhead costs. The methods proposed for determining the cost behavior pattern included the high-low method, the scattergraph method, simple linear regression, and multiple regression. Of these methods, Pistons Company decided to employ the high-low method, the scattergraph method, and simple linear regression. Data on direct labor-hours and the respective overhead costs incurred were collected for the past two years. The raw data are as follows:

	Direct Labor-Hours	Overhead Costs
Year 3:		
January.	20,000	$84,000
February.	25,000	99,000
March	22,000	89,500
April.	23,000	90,000
May	20,000	81,500
June.	19,000	75,500
July	14,000	70,500
August.	10,000	64,500
September	12,000	69,000
October.	17,000	75,000
November	16,000	71,500
December.	19,000	78,000
Year 4:		
January.	21,000	86,000
February.	24,000	93,000
March	23,000	93,000
April.	22,000	87,000
May	20,000	80,000
June.	18,000	76,500

7

ACTIVITY-BASED COSTING

After studying this chapter, you should be able to:

1. Explain why conventional cost systems cannot capture the demands of different products for overhead support services properly.

2. Discuss the meaning of activity-based costing in designing new cost systems.

3. Explain volume-related cost allocation measures and activity-related cost allocation measures, and use these in calculating overhead allocations to products.

4. Discuss the two-stage overhead allocation processes, and explain why it is necessary to identify activity-based allocation measures.

5. Explain what cost drivers are, and discuss the process of finding cost drivers in operations.

6. Determine the amounts of overhead allocations based on cost drivers, first to activities and then to products.

7. Explain how activity-based costing can be applied to both manufacturing and service sectors.

8. Explain the international aspect of activity-based costing.

As we observed in Chapter 6, cost behavior has evolved from the conventional dichotomous structure of variable and fixed costs to the dynamic, hierarchical structure of organizational costs. Conventional cost systems that rely heavily on volume-based measures for overhead cost allocations were intended for a production environment in which direct labor was the major focus of costing and control. The overhead component of manufacturing costs was not as significant as today.

In manufacturing industries today, overhead cost can be three or four times the size of direct labor cost. When manufacturing and other related functions undergo change, management accounting must change also. Otherwise, management accounting reports will not reflect the realities of how costs are incurred in manufacturing, customer service, distribution, and so forth.

In this chapter, we discuss **activity-based costing,** a cost management approach that employs cost drivers and activities. This approach helps the manager to have a better understanding of the dynamic, hierarchical structure of organizational costs than a traditional approach allows.

THE CONCEPT OF ACTIVITY-BASED COSTING

Activity-based costing (ABC) views costs through the prism of organizational activities, not organizational departments. This view is totally different from the conventional one. In an ABC structure, organizational departments, where costs are accumulated for assignment to products or services, are replaced by organizational activities through which costs are viewed. The gist of ABC is its relentless effort to trace and account for the pool of fixed overhead costs and show that most are really variable. The cost hierarchy we learned in Chapter 6 is a foundation for ABC.

Food service operations at a Marriott Hotel. ABC can help service organizations identify the costs of performing activities.

What Problems Can Conventional Cost Systems Create?

Conventional cost systems can create problems for decision making. Consider the following example.

Assume a color marker manufacturing plant produces color markers in one plant owned and operated by the company. There are now two product lines carried by the company: standard blue markers (product line 1) and "high value" markers of many different colors and shapes (product line 2). In one typical cost accounting period, the following sales records are revealed:

	Product Lines		
	1	**2**	**Total**
Sales volume (units)	600,000	100,000	700,000
Average selling price (per unit)	$1	$2	
Sales revenue	$600,000	$200,000	$800,000

About 86% of sales volume, measured by units sold (600,000 ÷ 700,000 = 0.86), is from the standard blue markers (product line 1). The remaining 14% of the business volume is from the "high value" markers of many different colors and shapes (product line 2). Because of the different colors and shapes, the "high value" markers command higher prices in the market than the standard blue markers ($2 a unit average price compared to $1 a unit).

For the same period, assume the following costs were incurred:

		Product Lines				
		1		**2**		**Total**
Units		600,000		100,000		700,000
Direct material	@$0.25	$150,000	@$0.26	$ 26,000		$176,000
Direct labor	@$0.07	42,000	@$0.08	8,000		50,000
Variable overhead	@$0.09	54,000	@$0.38	38,000		92,000
Fixed overhead	6/7	300,000	1/7	50,000		350,000
Total costs		$546,000		$122,000		$668,000

Materials and labor costs of the "high value" markers are virtually the same as those of the standard blue markers. The variable portion of manufacturing overhead required by the "high value" markers is $0.38 per unit (compared to $0.09 for the standard blue markers), reflecting the more specialized and diverse nature of the product line. Fixed manufacturing overhead is allocated at the rates of 6/7 versus 1/7, based on the production volume of 600,000 units compared to 100,000 units.

When manufacturing costs are subtracted from sales revenues, the following gross margins are generated for the two product lines:

	Product Lines					
	1		**2**		**Total**	
Sales revenue	$600,000	100%	$200,000	100%	$800,000	
Manufacturing costs	546,000	91%	122,000	61%	668,000	
Gross margin	$54,000	9%	$78,000	39%	$132,000	

Despite the lower sales revenue of $200,000, the "high value" markers generated a gross margin of $78,000. When compared to the $54,000 gross margin generated by the standard blue markers from sales revenue of $600,000, the performance is remarkable. The "high value" markers' gross margin ratio of 39% compares to a meager 9% shown for the standard blue markers. The result is that the low-volume, high-margin "high value" markers contributed 59% ($78,000/$132,000) of the company's gross margin. The high-volume, low-margin standard blue markers contributed only 41% ($54,000/$132,000) of the company's gross margin.

Based on these operating performance results, it is not difficult to imagine that top management of the company would value the profit contribution of the "high value" markers very highly. Management, as well as all others in the company, may believe that, without the "high value" markers, the profit would be very small, if any at all.

But, is it really the case? Or, is it a distorted reality produced by the company's poor cost accounting system?

Activity Analysis

In Chapter 6, we learned that the products requiring more activities in production cause the company to incur higher overhead costs. Accordingly, it is reasonable to assume that the "high value" markers of different colors and shapes would require more overhead support activities than their business volume (1/7 of the total) indicates. For example, they would require more design work, more setups (i.e., to change from a green marker production run to a red marker production run), more inspection work (after each new setup), and so forth.

Allocation of overhead support to the various product lines can be accomplished through **activity analysis.** It entails surveying the manufacturing and the support department personnel and analyzing the work performed by each support department.

Now the overhead cost items can be rearranged according to which activities the cost items support. Assume that the cost accountants have found the following activity-related cost pools and their costs with respect to fixed overhead:

Cost Pool	Related Overhead Costs
Engineering	$ 96,000
Setup	110,000
Purchasing	32,000
Plant administration	112,000
Total fixed overhead	$350,000

These cost pools do not represent overhead support departments. They represent particular **activities** created and performed to support the manufacturing function.

Activities and Drivers

Now, the cost accountants determine, for each cost pool, a factor which will be the best measure of the cost increase or decrease. This factor is the **cost driver.** Suppose the cost accountants' studies reveal the following cost drivers for the cost pools:

Cost Pool	Cost Driver
Engineering	Number of engineering change notices (ECN's)
Setup	Number of setups
Purchasing	Number of purchase orders
Plant administration	Number of units produced

With the exception of the plant administration cost pool, there are logical drivers that affect the costs in each pool most directly. Engineering costs change with the number of changes in the process routines (represented by the number of ECN's). Setup costs vary according to the number of setups. Purchasing costs contain the costs of handling purchase requisitions, locating vendors, placing orders, coordinating deliveries, and processing payments. It is mostly affected by how many purchase transactions are handled, rather than purchase volume or dollar value of purchases.

The cost accountants then gather data on the demands made by the two product lines for those activities. Assume the following data is obtained:

| | Demanded By | | |
Cost Drivers	Standard Blue Markers	High Value Markers	Total
ECN's	12	19	31
Setups	11	28	39
Purchase orders	20	58	78
Units produced	600,000	100,000	700,000

ABC and Fixed Overhead Allocation

To assign the fixed overhead costs of the four cost pools to the standard blue markers and the "high value" markers, the costs are divided by the number of cost driver units. The following per-driver unit, overhead cost rates are computed:

| | (a) | (b) | (a ÷ b) |
Cost Drivers	Overhead in the Pool	Number of Driver Units	Per-Driver Overhead Rate
ECN's	$ 96,000	31	$3,096.77
Setups	110,000	39	2,820.51
P.O.'s	32,000	78	410.26
Units produced	112,000	700,000	0.16

John Deere & Co. uses activity-based costing. The company's manufacturing floor, where different levels of activities take place, is shown here.

The overhead rate per unit of each cost driver is then multiplied by the number of drivers for each product line to produce fixed overhead costs, which are allocated to the standard blue markers and the "high value" markers. Using ECN's as an example, a fixed overhead cost of $37,161 is calculated, based on 12 ECN's required by the standard blue markers.

Per-driver overhead rate $3,096.77 × 12 ECN's = $37,161.

The amount is then allocated to the standard blue markers. The allocations between the two product lines appear as follows:

| | | Allocated to | |
Cost Pool	Total Cost in the Pool	Standard Blue Markers	High Value Markers
Engineering	$ 96,000	$37,161	$58,839
Setup	110,000	31,026	78,974
Purchasing	32,000	8,205	23,795
Plant administration	112,000	96,000	16,000
Total	$350,000	$172,392	$177,608

Now, manufacturing costs change to the following:

| | Manufacturing Costs of | | | | |
	Standard Blue Markers		High Value Markers		Total
Direct material	@$0.25	$150,000	@$0.26	$ 26,000	$176,000
Direct labor	@$0.07	42,000	@$0.08	8,000	50,000
Variable overhead	@$0.09	54,000	@$0.38	38,000	92,000
Fixed overhead		172,392		177,608	350,000
Total manufacturing costs		$418,392		$249,608	$668,000

When the cost driver-based manufacturing costs are subtracted from sales revenues, the gross margins produced look very different from the previous figures.

	Standard Blue Markers		High Value Markers		Total
Sales revenue	$600,000	100%	$200,000	100%	$800,000
Manufacturing costs	418,392	70%	249,608	125%	668,000
Gross margin	$181,608	30%	$(49,608)	(25%)	$132,000

The "high value" markers actually are losing money! As the highly specialized product line, the "high value" markers are sold at an average of twice the selling price of the standard blue markers. The amount of resources the "high value" markers consume, however, is greater than the sales revenue generated. The higher selling prices the company has been charging for the "high value" markers are not high enough to recover the resources needed to produce the products.

The standard blue markers incurred 49% ($172,392) of the total fixed manufacturing overhead costs, while the "high value" markers spent the remaining 51% ($177,608). This is surprising, since the production volume of the standard blue markers is 86% of the company total of 700,000 units produced. The "high value" markers, which represent only 14% of the production volume, consumed about half of the fixed manufacturing overhead support resources.

ABC AND PRICING DECISIONS

If the color marker manufacturer prices its products based on the real costs incurred, ABC would have impact on product prices. The marketing manager, in charge of the "high value" markers, would think about price increases. How much price increase is warranted depends on the cost information provided by the ABC system. In many mature industries, companies are not in a position to raise or lower their prices as they like. For well established products in the market, companies usually price their products according to what the competitive market allows.

However, for highly specialized products, market prices are not clearly stated. We simply do not know, for example, what the market price for a small, precision machined part should be. Economists can wait for six months or one year, and then they can state: "For that kind of precision machined part, the market prices were in the range of $1.50 to $2.40 in the first half of Year 1." They can wait to come up with reasonably reliable price information. But, accountants must provide cost-based pricing information to marketing personnel before the market prices are well known, so that sales people can go out in the market and compete with other companies. To do so, accountants need a relevant cost accounting system that explains how resources are consumed.

ABC AND PROFITABILITY ANALYSIS

What happens if the market conditions do not allow the color marker manufacturer to raise the prices of the "high value" markers? The ABC analysis indicates that the manufacturer cannot sustain its operations if the maximum price is the current price. This is where ABC analysis is useful. The results of ABC analysis can be used for profitability analyses of different products the company carries.

If the company cannot raise the prices of the "high value" markers, it should consider dropping some or all of those markers. Of course, the potential effect of dropping the "high value" markers on the sales of the standard blue markers should be examined, before such actions are taken. Some customers may not return if they have to purchase the "high value" markers needed from another full-line supplier. The company management, however, would certainly want to examine the possibility of dropping unprofitable products from the product lineup.

If the "high value" markers are dropped, without creating any adverse impact on the sales of the standard blue markers, the operating loss of $49,608 can be eliminated. This is based on the premise that the elimination of those products would lead to the corresponding reduction of the related costs. The company's overall gross margin then would increase by the same amount, from the current $132,000 to $181,608.

The fact is that the standard blue markers have been subsidizing the operations of the "high value" markers. ABC allows a company to look at the profitability of its products and product lines. The cost accounting system the company had been using thus far portrayed a distorted picture of how well each product or product line performed.

THE DESIGN OF AN ABC SYSTEM

ABC represents a general approach to the design of cost systems based on the product's (service's) demand for activities. Activities consume resources. Accordingly, ABC considers the consumption of resources by products and services. It is a general approach, because it does not cater just to specific decision making needs of an organization, such as pricing a special order of some products based on short-term, variable costs.

If properly designed, the ABC system can readily provide the relevant, full-cost information on products. Why is the full-cost information better? Please refer to "Kaplan's Tale of Two Factories" in Chapter 6. We can see that the demand for more activities in the second factory is not accounted for just by direct labor hours or number of units. These volume-based measures can explain short-term, variable costs, such as materials or labor costs, but do not explain full costs, including fixed costs.

In an ABC system, the distortion of product costs, which has been caused by the conventional process of cost assignment, is corrected. Next we look at how this is accomplished, and how an ABC system is designed.

Two-Stage Cost Allocation

Chapter 4 discussed how manufacturing overhead costs are allocated to production. In a manufacturing plant, there are two-stage cost assignments. The stage 1 assignment occurs when plant overhead costs, such as material handling, purchasing, utilities, and repairs and maintenance, are assigned to manufacturing departments, such as fabrication, assembly, and finishing. These manufacturing departments are called **cost centers** because costs are accumulated here, and they have control over the costs they incur. The stage 2 assignment takes place when those costs assigned in stage 1 are moved to products.

The stage 1 cost assignment has been accomplished by manufacturing companies with no difficulty. The problem is with the stage 2 cost assignment. This is because the manufacturing overhead costs lose their identity upon reaching the cost centers.

In Chapter 4, overhead costs were allocated to production based on direct labor hours, direct labor costs, machine hours, or number of units produced. We have allocated overhead costs based on these **volume-based** measures for the last several decades. The underlying premise is that if we produce more, we operate longer hours, in terms of direct labor or machine operating time. If we produce more, and operate longer hours, we must spend more overhead support resources. Therefore, we allocate more overhead costs.

The volume-based measures are appropriate as overhead allocation bases as long as operations are intensive in materials and labor usage. In other words, this is true if the operations consist mainly of **unit-level** activities. However, if operations become complex and products are diverse, these volume-based measures lose their relevance as the allocation bases.

The Conventional Process of Cost Assignment

Conventional cost assignment proceeds as follows: Plant overhead costs, taken from the general ledger, are first allocated to manufacturing departments called cost centers. The cause-and-effect relationships are used for the stage 1 allocations. For example, labor hours is used to measure the usage of supplies, number of employees for personnel administration costs and cafeteria operating costs, and square footage for plant maintenance costs.

The costs in the cost pools, which are allocated to products in stage 2, represent the manufacturing departments' own costs plus service department cost allocations. As products are routed through those manufacturing departments, the pool of costs, now traced to each manufacturing department, should be distributed to the products. The process is illustrated in Exhibit 7-1.

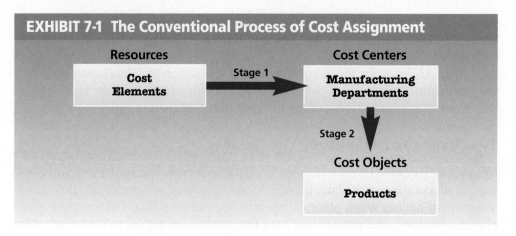

EXHIBIT 7-1 The Conventional Process of Cost Assignment

Resources

Cost Centers

Cost Elements

Stage 1 →

Manufacturing Departments

Stage 2 ↓

Cost Objects

Products

The ABC Process of Cost Assignment

In an ABC system, costs are viewed through the prism of organizational **activities**, not organizational departments. An activity can be a very simple action each worker performs, such as picking up a case of color marker plastic caps from the pallet. Or an activity can be a sequence of actions, such as picking up a case of materials, putting them on the color marker fabrication machine, and retrieving the fabricated pieces from the machine.

There is a high correlation between the scope of activity and the activity measurement cost. If we define the scope of an activity as a narrow one, there are many activities to measure. Accordingly, the measurement cost will be high. If our definition of an activity is wide in scope, i.e., the activity represents a whole series of plastic cap processing actions, there will be fewer activities to measure. The measurement cost will, therefore, be lower.

Stage 1 assignment actually represents tracing cost elements to proper activity cost pools in their activity centers. An **activity cost pool** is created to house all the costs incurred while a certain activity is performed. An **activity center** represents an area of operations for which a meaningful collection of activities is separately identified and reported. Exhibit 7-2 shows the overall process of ABC cost assignment.

Energy trading at DTE. The trading activities shown here can be identified in an activity center.

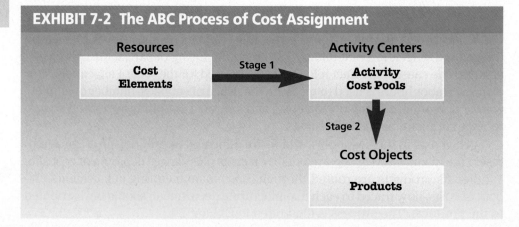

EXHIBIT 7-2 The ABC Process of Cost Assignment

Resources

Activity Centers

Cost Elements

Stage 1 →

Activity Cost Pools

Stage 2 ↓

Cost Objects

Products

The following example illustrates the use of activity cost pools and activity centers:

Procurement Activity Center

Activity	*Activity Cost Pool*
Order activity	**Order activity cost pool**

Get authorization for purchase requisition, locate the vendor, place a purchase order, and follow up on the order.

Receiving activity	**Receiving activity cost pool**

Receive the shipment, inspect it, and deliver to the operating area.

In this example, there are two activities, "order" and "receive," for which two activity cost pools are created and maintained in the activity center, called procurement activity center. If the organization desires to reduce the measurement and reporting costs, then the two activities (order and receive) could be combined into one activity (procurement).

Stage 2 assignment is performed to attribute costs in the activity cost pools to the products manufactured. Activities, identified in the ABC system design, are supposed to be capable of explaining most of the demands for actions made by all of the products.

Stage 1 Assignment of Costs

In stage 1 cost assignment, resources consumed are attributed to the activities identified. Usually, resources represent the cost elements contained in the company's general ledger. The information is downloaded from the computer files to the ABC system. Although ordinary general ledger systems do not provide the cost of activities directly, many items of information on activities and their costs could be obtained or estimated from the already existing data in the company. Exhibit 7-3 illustrates stage 1 cost assignment.

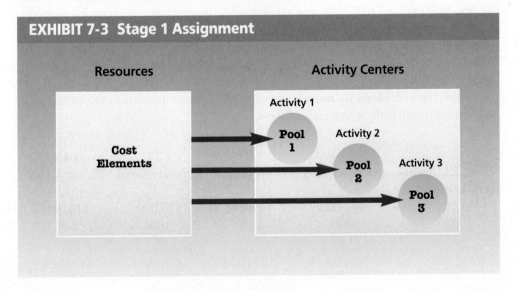

EXHIBIT 7-3 Stage 1 Assignment

How are cost elements attributed to activities? For the first attempts at ABC, past actual costs from the general ledger and the related information from procurement, production, inventory control, manufacturing support, etc. can be used as the bases. Suppose we examine only fixed overhead resources here, and the following four activities have been identified through plant-wide activity analyses: Engineering, setup, procurement, and plant administration.

Now, arrange the cost elements and activities as the following in a matrix:

	Activities			
	(1)	**(2)**	**(3)**	**(4)**
Cost Elements	**Engineering**	**Setup**	**Procurement**	**Plant Adm.**
Indirect labor →				
Supplies →				
Repairs →				
Utilities →				

Then, ask the following question for each of these cost elements: "Which activity demands the support of this cost element, and how much?" The first cost element is indirect labor. From the general ledger, we obtain the amount for the last period of $82,000. Through surveys and interviews with experienced personnel in the plant, the following information is gathered:

Costs	Incurred to Support:
$23,000	Process engineering work
18,000	Product engineering work
17,000	Setup and material movements
13,000	Receiving and inspecting materials
11,000	Other plant operations
$82,000	

The first two items, with combined costs of $41,000 ($23,000 + $18,000), are attributed to engineering activity (activity 1) as defined by the company. The third item, with a cost of $17,000, is attributed to setup and material movements in and around the plant (activity 2). The costs of $13,000 and $11,000 are attributed to procurement (activity 3) and plant administration (activity 4), respectively.

Now, the cost element, indirect labor, which shows an actual cost of $82,000, is assigned to the four activities as follows:

Quality inspectors at Electrocom Automation Inc. are testing a completed mail sorting system. Quality inspection usually is measured as a separate activity under activity-based costing.

	Activities			
	(1)	**(2)**	**(3)**	**(4)**
Cost Elements	**Engineering**	**Setup**	**Procurement**	**Plant Adm.**
Indirect labor				
$82,000 →	$41,000	$17,000	$13,000	$11,000
100%	50%	21%	16%	13%
••	•	•	•	•
Total	$96,000	$110,000	$32,000	$112,000

Similar assignments can be made for supplies, repairs, utilities, and so forth to complete the stage 1 assignment task, creating a matrix. The bottom-line figures for the completed matrix would be $96,000, $110,000, $32,000, and $112,000.

Now the four activity cost pools contain the costs which have been attributed to them according to the activities that characterize each cost pool. **Activity centers,** areas of operations for which meaningful collections of activities are separately identified and reported, can be determined and arranged according to the needs of the plant.

Stage 2 Assignment of Costs

After the resources consumed by the identified activities have been attributed to activity cost pools, they are finally assigned to cost objects, such as products, services, customer groups, and distribution channels. This is the stage 2 cost assignment, and links activities to cost objects through cost drivers. Exhibit 7-4 illustrates the linkage.

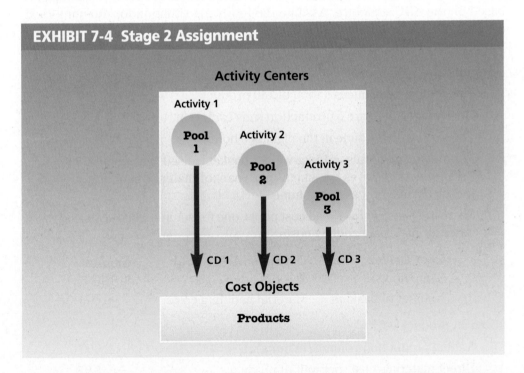

EXHIBIT 7-4 Stage 2 Assignment

Cost drivers should be the best possible measures of links between activities and cost objects (products in our example). Suppose, for the engineering cost pool, the analyses of activities and related costs reveal that engineering costs vary most directly with the number of changes in the process routines. Then the cost driver for the engineering cost pool is the number of ECN's, which represents the notices for changes in the process routines.

In the previous discussion of the stage 1 assignment of costs, cost elements were attributed to activities. Our example used indirect labor, which was attributed to four activities at the rates of 50%, 21%, 16% and 13%. This assignment can be based on labor hours or any other appropriate driver, which will correctly explain the relationships between cost elements and activities.

The cost drivers, used in the stage 2 assignment, can either be the same as the stage 1 drivers or different. The nature of the linkage is, however, a little unique for each of the two stages. For example, in Hewlett-Packard's ABC system, the process engineering resource consumption is directly linked to major processes (similar to activity centers), but indirectly to products. Accordingly, the varying levels of the process engineering resource consumption are identified in stage 1 at the activity center level, but not in stage 2 at the product level.

THE ABC APPLICATION: A NUMERICAL EXAMPLE

Chapter 6 discussed cost drivers, cost behavior and hierarchy, and how cost accountants use these concepts to understand costs better. In this part, we expand our scope to examine the allocation of overhead costs to products (cost objects) based on the ABC structure. Assume the following situation for the numerical analysis of Global Manufacturing Company's ABC process at its only manufacturing plant:

Overall data:

The company produces a total of 140 products.

On average, there are 5 production runs each year.

The average setup time in the plant is 6 hours.

For moving materials, a 15-kg-weight basket is used. On average, each of the products requires 8 baskets (per year) of material handling support for the normal processing volume.

There are only two overhead cost pools, one for setup-related costs and the other for material handling costs.

Cost Driver	Overhead Cost Pool	Amount
Setup hours	Setup-related costs	$185,000
Number of baskets	Material handling costs	96,000

Data on product 1001:

Annual production volume (in units)	2,000
Direct materials cost (per unit of product)	$10

This product is run 3 times a year.

The setup time for the specific operation for product 1001 is 7 hours.

The weight needed to be carried is 0.08 kilograms (kg) per unit.

Below, we look at the assignment of Global Manufacturing Company's overhead costs to product 1001 under ABC. Overhead costs are assigned to the remaining 139 products in a similar fashion.

Assignment of Setup-Related Overhead Costs

Based on the above data, the setup cost per unit of product 1001 is calculated in the ABC system as follows:

First, the setup overhead rate per hour is established in the system because setup hours is the cost driver. This is done by dividing the total setup-related overhead cost by the number of setup hours, as follows:

Total setup overhead cost	$185,000
Total number of setup hours:	
5 runs (setups) × 6 hours (average time	
per setup) × 140 products =	÷ 4,200 hours
Setup overhead rate per setup hour	$44

Next, the setup overhead is assigned to product 1001 based on the number of setup hours the product consumes.

Setup overhead rate per hour	$44
Number of setup hours demanded by product 1001:	
3 setups per year × 7 hours (setup time) =	× 21 hours
Setup overhead costs charged to product 1001	$924

$924 ÷ 2,000 units = $0.462 per unit

An ABC system recognizes the product's demand for a specific activity, setup in this case, to reflect the consumption of resource by a product. If the product line manager wants to reduce the cost of producing product 1001, efforts should be made to reduce setup hours and the number of runs and setups. Since ABC is based on activities, managers can focus on those activities to manage costs.

Assignment of Material Handling-Related Overhead Costs

The material handling cost per unit of product 1001 is calculated in the ABC system as follows:

First, the material handling overhead cost rate per 15-kg-weight basket should be established. In actual practice, management accountants need a detailed study to establish the rate. In this example, the average number of baskets the plant needs to handle for all materials and parts is assumed.

Total material handling overhead cost	$96,000
Number of baskets needed for all 140 products:	
140 × 8 baskets (average) =	÷ 1,120
Material handling overhead cost rate per basket	$85.71

Next, the material handling overhead cost is assigned to product 1001 based on the number of baskets needed for product 1001.

Volume of material handling per each run product 1001 requires:

2,000 (annual volume) ÷ 3 runs =	667 units
Weight per unit	× 0.08 kg
Weight of the total volume	53.36 kg
Weight a basket can handle	÷ 15 kg
Number of baskets needed per run	4*
Number of runs per year	× 3
Number of baskets handled per year	12
Material handling overhead rate per basket	× $85.71
Total material handling overhead charged	$1,028.52

$1,028.52 ÷ 2,000 units = $0.5143 per unit

*Use whole number 4 instead of 3.56, because one basket is needed for a load of 0.56.

The ABC system recognizes the product's demand for the material handling activity. If the product line manager desires to reduce the product cost, the manager should make efforts to control the demand for the material handling activity.

The ABC Application: Other Cost Drivers

In the previous numerical example, we looked at only two cost drivers, which were setup-related and material handling-related. When other cost drivers are involved, the process of ABC cost assignment works in a similar fashion. Some examples are presented below.

Direct Labor-Related Driver Direct labor hours or direct labor cost can be a cost driver. Personnel and payroll costs that are incurred in connection with direct labor-related activities can be pooled and assigned on the basis of the overhead rate per labor hour or the percentage ratio to labor cost dollar. For example, assume a direct labor-related overhead of $560,000 and 8,000 direct labor hours in a manufacturing area. Then, this overhead is assigned to products at a rate of $70 (= $560,000 ÷ 8,000 hours) per direct labor hour. If a product consumes 0.15 hours of direct labor time per unit, the assigned direct labor-related overhead cost is $10.50 per unit. ($70 per hour × 0.15 hour per unit = $10.50 per unit.)

Machine-Related Driver If a considerable amount of machine usage is involved in the operation, machine hours may be selected as a cost driver. The costs of maintaining and repairing machines, supporting equipment and tools, and facility can be pooled together. Those costs can be assigned to products according to the overhead cost rate per machine hour. For example, assume a machine-related overhead cost of $480,000 and 40,000 machine hours. Then, the overhead cost is charged to products at a rate of $12 (= $480,000 ÷ 40,000 hours) per machine hour. If a product consumes 0.25 hours of machine operation time per unit, the assigned machine overhead cost will be $3 per unit. ($12 per hour × 0.25 hour per unit = $3.00 per unit.)

Quality Assurance-Related Driver Quality inspection costs can be charged to different products according to the number of units produced or the number of setups each product requires, since each new setup would demand more-intensive-than-usual first-item inspection.

Waste Treatment-Related Driver As society becomes more environmentally conscious, the costs of treating wastes generated in the manufacturing process have increased significantly for most manufacturing companies. A suitable cost driver must be identified to charge waste treatment costs to proper products.

ABC: ADVANTAGES AND DISADVANTAGES

ABC allows managers to have a good understanding of how costs are incurred in connection with the activities the organization performs. As is true with any type of costing system, however, there exist advantages and disadvantages of using ABC.

Advantages of ABC

The advantages of ABC include the following:

First, ABC allows an organization to trace and account for the pool of fixed overhead costs and show that most are really variable, thereby increasing the accuracy of product costs. This is made possible by incorporating the cost hierarchy concept into the system of costing products. The cost hierarchy concept can explain four different categories (unit, batch, product, and facility-level) of activities and resource consumption of an organization, which is an improvement over the traditional understanding of variable and fixed costs.

Second, managers can use ABC to make better decisions related to products, customers, distribution channels, and product lines by focusing on causality and variability with respect to operations (activities) and resource consumption (expenses) in an organization. The causality and variability can be achieved by the linkage between activities and expenses in an ABC system.

Third, managers can use ABC to gather data on activities beyond the traditional boundaries of organizational functions. Unlike conventional costing systems, which rely entirely on department-based costs in collecting and allocating costs, ABC cuts across departments. Managers can see the cost of changing a product design, the cost of shifting a distribution channel, or the cost of performing an administrative activity, such as processing a purchase order.

Overall, ABC helps managers make better decisions by allowing them to see which activities generate costs. Managing activities that generate costs is much more effective than trying to manage costs through departments without the benefit of direct correlation between costs and causes of cost changes.

Disadvantage of ABC

Although arbitrary cost allocations are minimized and correlations between costs and activities are emphasized and achieved under ABC, there is a clear disadvantage of ABC that managers must be aware of. The disadvantage of ABC is its *high measurement costs.*

ABC requires the creation of multiple activity centers and cost pools. Accordingly, the costs of measurement are higher under ABC. In our discussions of ABC, we have assumed that the data on various cost drivers and their consumption by each product (or service) were available. For example, we looked at setup hours, number of material movements, number of purchase orders, direct labor hours, machine hours, waste treatment transactions, and so forth. In practice, the cost data must be tracked through various routing files and shop floor tracking systems. ABC requires the number of each of the above cost drivers, and the overhead application rate per each cost driver must be measured by each product and the related processes. The costs of implementing ABC can become significant for some organizations.

ACTIVITY-BASED COSTING AND SERVICE INDUSTRIES

Most of the concepts and techniques discussed in Chapter 6 and this chapter can be applied to service firms. Of course, some adjustments must be made for the unique characteristics of a specific service firm, as variations exist and adjustments are needed for a particular type of service operations.

Definition of Activity

GMAC Customer Service Center. The financial services can be analyzed at different levels of service activities discussed here.

Activities usually are defined for each major step of operations in a service industry. Consider a finance company's operations.

(1) Loan applications are received and recorded by the receptionist. The first loan processor sorts and batches new loan applications according to types of loans. The processor sends out and collects confirmations of employment and bank balances; acquires credit reports on the applicants through credit bureaus; and collects other loan related documents and reports as they come in.

(2) Loan analysts perform analyses based on credit and loan files and other information. They draw their conclusions and write recommendations regarding approval or rejection on the loan applications.

(3) The loan committee meets to evaluate and make the final decision on each loan. The committee meets once a week, and the loan committee members are paid a fee for each meeting they attend.

(4) At certain intervals, the finance company reviews its loan approval policies and procedures; evaluates the efficiency of operations; and reviews the appropriateness of documents and forms used.

For each of the above four steps, various activities are defined. In (1), for instance, receiving and recording of loan applications are activities. Sorting and batching applications are activities also.

Service Activity and Cost

If the four levels of cost and activity hierarchy are used, the following cost-activity relationships can be established:

Unit-level: Most of the activities and costs that are related to (1) are unit-level. For example, the costs of sending confirmations and printing credit reports would depend on how many applications are handled.

Batch-level: Sorting and batching applications in (1) would be batch-related. If loan committee members are paid for each meeting they attend, the loan committee-related costs would be batch-related. It doesn't matter how many applications are decided on at each meeting.

Product-level: Most of the costs in (4) may be product-related. The loan forms may be designed according to the types of loans. The loan review policies may be formulated according to the types of loans also.

Facility-level: President's salary, rent and office maintenance expenses, and credit bureau annual membership fee would be facility-related.

As this finance company example demonstrates, many concepts and practices previously discussed for manufacturing industries can be applied to service industries also. The concepts and procedures should be modified to suit the particular operating characteristics of the company being analyzed.

A Numerical Example

Suppose the above finance company recorded the following costs and activities for the first year of their operations:

Number of loan applications	184
Number of loan committee meetings	40
Types of loans (commercial, residential, etc.)	5
Personnel expenses:	
Receptionist	$ 28,000
Loan processor	35,000
3 Loan analysts	121,000
Management personnel	176,000
Total	360,000
Fees paid to 5 loan committee members	94,000
Other operating expenses:	
Loan forms and policy-related	32,000
Facility-related	175,000
Total expenses for the first year	$661,000

A cost-activity study indicates the following:

The activities and costs of receptionist, loan processor, and 3 loan analysts are unit-level. Loan committee-related costs are batch-level. Loan forms and policy-related costs are product-level. Costs of management personnel and other operating expenses are facility-level.

Cost rates for different activities are calculated below:

Unit-level cost rate:

Unit-level costs, $28,000 + $35,000 + $121,000 =	$184,000
Number of cost driver units (applications)	÷ 184
Unit-level cost rate per application	$1,000

Batch-level cost rate:

Batch-level costs (loan committee expenses)	$94,000
Number of cost driver units (committee meetings)	÷ 40
Batch-level cost rate per meeting	$2,350

Product-level cost rate:

Product-level costs (loan forms and policy-related)	$32,000
Number of cost driver units (types of loans)	÷ 5
Product-level cost rate per loan type	$6,400

Facility-level costs (fixed):

Management personnel expenses	$176,000
Other fixed operating expenses	175,000
Total	$351,000

The total operating cost of the finance company for the first year can be summarized as:

	$1,000 × Number of applications	(unit-level costs)
+	$2,350 × Number of committee meetings	(batch-level costs)
+	$6,400 × Types of loans	(product-level costs)
+	$351,000 Fixed operating expenses	(facility-level costs)
=	$661,000	

Now we can estimate future costs of operating this finance company. Suppose other conditions stay the same except the following changes for the second year:

Number of loan applications increases 25%.
Loan committee holds 5 more meetings to handle increased business volume.

The total cost of the second-year operations will be

	$1,000 × (184 × 1.25)
+	$2,350 × (40 + 5)
+	$6,400 × 5
+	$351,000
=	$718,750

Similar calculations can be made for cost-activity relationships that are found in other service industry applications.

Cost Assignment to Services (Cost Objects)

Activity costs that have been identified and measured can be assigned to *services*, which represent cost objects, just the same as activity costs have been assigned to *products*. This is accomplished, in the stage 2 cost assignment, by charging a certain service (for example, commercial loan type) for the resources the service has consumed.

For example, the finance company can calculate the total cost of its commercial loan service, as compared to other four loan types (residential, etc.). Let's assume the following:

> Information on commercial loan's resource consumption:
>
> Unit-level: Out of 184 applications, 102 are commercial loan applications.
>
> Batch-level: A total of 22.5 loan committee meetings are attributed to commercial loan service.
>
> Product-level: Commercial loan service is one of the five loan types.
>
> Facility-level: Facility-level costs are allocated to different loan types (services) on the basis of the number of applications.

Now the costs can be assigned to commercial loan service as follows:

Stage 2 cost assignment to commercial loan service:

Unit-level costs:
$1,000 per application $\times$ 102 applications = $102,000

Batch-level costs:
$2,350 per meeting $\times$ 22.5 meetings = 52,875

Product-level costs:
Charge for one loan type = 6,400

Facility-level costs:
$351,000 $\times$ 102/184 = 194,576

Total costs of commercial loan service = $355,851

$355,851 $\div$ 102 loan applications = $3,489 per application.

(Unit cost if most commercial loans require a similar amount of work.)

The ABC system for this finance company has recognized the product's (commercial loan service's) demand for company resources based on different levels of activities. Management can use the total cost information to determine how much profit commercial loan service generates by comparing the cost to the revenues from commercial loans. Many service firms have, thus far, implemented ABC in costing their services.

INTERNATIONAL ASPECT OF ACTIVITY-BASED COSTING

It is interesting to note that activity-based costing was first developed around 1985. This was just after new manufacturing technologies, such as just-in-time (JIT) and total quality management (TQM), were adopted by innovative companies in the United States. The early ABC installations included several manufacturing companies in the U.S. and Germany. A couple of years was just enough time for operating managers of those companies to experience frustration over conventional cost accounting reports that failed to fully explain the diversity in products and operations.

While those U.S. and German companies tried to explain and account for activities by taking a second look at cost accounting systems, Japanese companies abandoned cost accounting in their efforts to manage activities. The implication of the Japanese manufacturers' aversion to cost accounting is not that management accounting information is of limited usefulness to managers. Rather, the Japanese companies use a combination of cost management techniques, such as target costing and kaizen costing, which are different from ABC. The Japanese cost management techniques reflect a cost management philosophy that is made to work outside cost accounting systems. The Japanese cost management techniques function with the overall operating philosophy that helps companies rely on setup time, defect rate, and other direct performance measures. They believe their employees find those direct performance measures easier to understand than cost accounting information.

SUMMARY

Companies cannot explain the higher overhead costs of a plant, whose products are more diversified and processes are more complex, simply by concentrating on volume-based measures, such as direct labor hours, machine hours, or number of units produced. A plant that produces more diverse products demands more activities to support those products. The major manufacturing changes that have taken place in recent decades pay more attention to simplifying and improving business transactions or activities than before. When manufacturing and other related functions change, cost accounting was forced to change to be compatible with other functions of the organization.

Activity-based costing has emerged as the new cost accounting methodology that is compatible with the recent improvement in manufacturing. ABC is a cost accounting concept that views costs through the prism of organizational activities, not through organizational departments. Activity analysis is used to investigate which product line requires which resources under ABC. The issues are related to the questions asked of overhead support service functions: "Which product demands which support services?" "What activities do those services consist of?"

Activity analysis allows an organization to identify what activities are created and performed. For each of those activities, a cost pool is formed and a unique cost driver is identified. Data on the products' demands for those activities that are represented by the cost drivers are gathered. Then the costs in the cost pools are divided by the number of cost driver units, which yield the overhead rates per unit of cost driver. The overhead rates are then multiplied by the number of drivers for each product or product line, which yields overhead costs assigned under ABC.

The product costs generated under ABC can be drastically different from the costs produced from a conventional, volume-based cost accounting system. The implications can be very significant for the company's pricing decisions, profitability analyses, product decisions, and performance measurement.

BASIC CONCEPTS AND TERMS

Activity analysis	Facility-level cost
Activity-based costing	Pricing decision
Activity center	Product-level cost
Batch-level cost	Profitability analysis
Cost center	Two-stage cost assignment
Cost driver	Unit-level cost
Cost objects	

■ SELF-REVIEW PROBLEM

Global Enterprises Inc. uses activity-based costing. A study of costs and activities in the purchasing and receiving areas of the company for a certain cost accounting period reveals the following:

Information relating to the cost center (purchasing and receiving):

1. Total cost of materials and parts purchased for the period is $214,000.

2. For each production run, about four purchase orders are processed with various vendors.

3. A total of 360 purchase orders are processed for the period. Purchases and deliveries are scheduled as close to the time the lots are run as possible to minimize the inventory level. Accordingly, the products that are run more often require more purchasing transactions.

4. Overhead costs of the cost center:

Purchasing office costs	$10,000
Receiving room costs	15,000
Total	$25,000

5. Cost drivers:

   (a) Number of purchase orders is the driver for purchasing office activities.

   (b) For 40% of receiving room activities, the driver is the number of purchase orders, as more shipments from vendors require more work. For the remainder of the receiving room costs, the dollar value of purchases is the driver, because higher-value items require more attention and time in unpacking, inspection, etc.

6. Information regarding product #1001:

   (a) The product is run three times in each period.

   (b) Production volume for this period (in units)   2,000

   (c) Material purchases related to product #1001 $20,000

   (d) Materials cost per unit of product #1001 $10

Required:

1. Calculate the purchasing overhead rates for the two cost drivers in the ABC system.

2. Calculate the purchasing overhead cost per unit of product #1001 in the ABC system.

3. Assume you are the product #1001 manager. If you want to control purchasing overhead costs related to your product, what would you have to do?

Solution

1. Costs of overhead related to purchase order (driver 1):

Purchasing office costs		$10,000
Receiving room costs	$15,000	
Purchase order-related	× 40%	6,000
Total		$16,000

Purchasing overhead rate per unit of driver 1:

Costs of overhead related to purchase order	$16,000
Number of purchase orders	÷ 360
Purchasing overhead rate per purchase order	$44.44

Costs of overhead related to dollar value of purchases (driver 2):

Receiving room costs	$15,000	
Dollar value-related	× 60%	$9,000

Purchasing overhead rate per unit of driver 2:

Costs of purchasing overhead related to dollar value of purchases	$9,000
Total amount of material purchases	÷ $214,000
Purchasing overhead rate per dollar	0.0421

2. Purchasing overhead cost for product #1001:

Cost of driver 1 to be applied:

Purchasing overhead rate per each order	$44.44
Number of purchase orders for product #1001	× 12
Cost of driver 1	$533

Number of purchase orders for product #1001:

Number of orders processed per run	4
Number of runs	× 3
Number of purchase orders	12

(Remember that purchases are closely coordinated with each production run.)

Cost of driver 2 to be applied:

Purchasing overhead rate per dollar	0.0421

Dollar purchases for product #1001	× $20,000
Cost of driver 2	$842

Purchasing overhead cost per unit of product #1001:

Purchasing overhead costs charged to product #1001, $533 + $842 =	$1,375
Units of product #1001 produced	÷ 2,000
Purchasing overhead per unit	$0.6875

3. Product #1001 manager's focus to control purchasing overhead costs:

To control purchasing overhead costs, the product manager would have to focus his efforts on managing the number of production runs and number of purchase orders. An optimal decision, however, would require a careful consideration of trade-offs between the higher cost of carrying larger-size inventories and the lower number of orders. Cost driver 2 is primarily related to the total amount of materials used, and the effectiveness of the product manager's cost control efforts in this respect would be limited. Different companies use different sets of cost drivers in applying purchasing overhead costs. The decisions on cost pools, activities, and cost drivers depend upon the nature of operations and the needs of the organizational unit. For example, some divisions of Hewlett-Packard use the active part numbers products require rather than the number of purchase orders in the allocation of purchasing overhead. Of course, more parts in a product would require more purchase orders.

■ REVIEW QUESTIONS

7-1 Why is it important to view costs through the prism of organizational activities rather than through organizational departments?

7-2 Would activity-based costing be viewed as a significant cost management methodology in a business environment in which every cost item is variable cost?

7-3 Do you see any difference between activity analysis and time-and-motion study?

7-4 What is the difference between cost driver and activity? Don't they represent the same thing in an organization?

7-5 An economist remarks: "It doesn't matter what cost accounting method a firm employs as far as pricing of products is concerned. The firm simply has to accept the price the market allows based on demand and supply." How would you, as a cost accountant, respond to this?

7-6 Should performance measurement of a company be affected by the cost accounting approach it employs? Discuss the issue in relation to a manager's choice of a cost accounting system.

7-7 Why is activity-based costing called a general approach to the design of cost systems?

7-8 What is the role of cost centers in the stage 1 assignment of costs?

7-9 Are volume-based measures, as overhead allocation bases, the same as unit-level activities? Explain.

7-10 Explain the nature of the correlation between the scope of activity and the activity measurement cost. Indicate, as a part of your explanation, whether the correlation is positive or negative.

7-11 What is the difference between activity cost pools and activity centers?

7-12 If an organization wants to install an activity-based costing system, but does not like to incur high-level accounting expenses, how would it want to define activity?

7-13 Explain the stage 1 assignment of costs in terms of cost data flows.

7-14 Is the number of activity centers always smaller than the number of activity cost pools?

7-15 If engineering changes take different amounts of time, can you still use the number of engineering change notices as the cost driver for the engineering cost pool?

7-16 There are cost drivers in both "stage 1" and "stage 2" cost assignments. Should they be different?

7-17 What do you think is the strongest advantage of activity-based costing? Why?

7-18 What is the disadvantage of using an activity-based costing system?

7-19 What is so unique about defining activities in the implementation of activity-based costing for a service firm? How is it different from the activity definition for a manufacturing firm?

7-20 Why do you think Japanese manufacturers have abandoned managing costs within cost accounting systems?

INTERNET PROJECT

Web 7-1:

Websites: www.ups.com
www.fedex.com

The websites listed above represent two famous companies. Search the sites for information on their operating characteristics.

Required:

1. If you were the chief financial officer (CFO), where would you implement an ABC first? Why? Be specific as to which part of the website you refer to.

2. What would be the most difficult phase of ABC implementation based on what you decide to do in (1)? Why?

Web 7-2:

Websites: www.cisco.com
              www.xerox.com

The websites listed above represent two famous companies. Search the sites for information on their operating characteristics.

Required:

1. If you were the chief financial officer (CFO), where would you implement an ABC first? Why? Be specific as to which part of the website you refer to.

2. What would be the most difficult phase of ABC implementation based on what you decide to do in (1)? Why?

■ EXERCISES

E7-1   Classification of Cost Driver and Cost Pool

Indicate, for each item, whether it represents a cost driver(D) or a cost pool(P).

a. Receiving
b. Number of production runs
c. Units of production
d. Purchasing
e. Number of purchase orders
f. Engineering
g. Design
h. Number of weight baskets
i. Material handling
j. Direct labor

E7-2   Cost Assignment Stages

The following items are found in cost assignment stages of conventional or activity-based costing. Indicate whether each item is related to "stage 1" cost assignment (1), "stage 2" cost assignment (2), or both (3).

a. Cause-and-effect relationship
b. Activity center
c. Cost elements
d. Cost center
e. Cost object
f. Activity cost pool
g. Activity
h. Initial downloading of general ledger data
i. Activity cost driver
j. Customer classes

E7-3   Activity-Based Costing; Multiple Choice

1. The following statements have been made by a manager about cost allocation and activity-based costing (ABC). Which statement is *not* true?

a. ABC views costs through organizational activities, not through organizational departments.

b. In an ABC structure, the company's departments are replaced by activities for cost accumulation.

c. ABC's main thrust is its focus on fixed costs; ABC shows most fixed costs are really variable.

d. ABC is just a decision making tool; it can not be used as a formal cost accounting system.

2. Which of the following statements is *not* true?

a. Volume-based measures of cost allocation represent units of production or hours of operations.

b. In the early part of the 20th century the overhead component of the manufacturing costs was not as high as what we see today.

c. The conventional cost systems were intended for a production environment in which fixed cost was the major focus of attention.

d. Cost accounting changes when the environment changes.

3. Which of the following statements about cost and managerial accounting is *not* true?

a. ABC is a very reliable cost accounting methodology; it does not rely on estimation.

b. Understanding a hierarchical structure of organizational costs helps a manager control costs better.

c. The traditional cost accounting knowledge of cost behavior was based primarily on variable and fixed costs.

d. ABC is now used by a significant portion of U.S. manufacturers.

E7-4   Activity-Based Costing; Multiple Choice

1. The following statements are made about cost allocations in conventional or activity-based costing system. Which statement is *not* true?

a. Manufacturing departments of a plant usually serve as cost centers.

b. All manufacturing support department costs should ultimately be allocated to products.

c. The stage 1 cost assignment is about assigning cost center costs to products or services.

d. As far as the stage 1 cost assignment is concerned, there has been virtually no problem in the U.S. manufacturing industry in the past.

2. Which one of the following statements about activity-based costing (ABC) is *not* true?

a. There is a negative correlation between the scope of activity and the activity measurement cost.

b. The stage 1 cost assignment actually means tracing cost elements to appropriate activity cost pools.

c. An activity cost pool is formed to accommodate all the costs incurred by the performance of a certain activity.

    d. In order to implement an ABC system, a company must always bundle a series of activities together as a basis of cost assignment, since individual activities cannot be used as bases.

3.   Which one of the following *cannot* be used as an *activity* in an ABC system?

    a. A sequence of purchase order processing steps.

    b. Receiving a shipment, checking the contents, and delivering to the production floor.

    c. An agreement made by two production managers on processing sequence.

    d. An order clerk's simple task of locating a vendor.

E7-5   Activity (Setup) Cost Assignment to Products

A study on activity and cost of Ajax Company reveals the total setup-related overhead cost at $168,000 for a cost center. The data on production scheduling and control indicate the following:

For the cost center:
It takes an average of 5 hours to do a setup in this machine area.
The area has 80 different products under its responsibility.
On an average, products are run 4 times a year.
The cost driver is number of setup hours.

Required:

1.   Calculate the setup overhead rate per hour.
2.   Product JAX-1 of Ajax is run 3 times a year. Annual production volume is 2,500 units. The specific setup operation, which JAX-1 requires, takes an average of 6 hours. What is the setup cost per unit of JAX-1?

E7-6   Activity (Material Handling) Cost Assignment to Products

A study on activity and cost of Baker Company reveals the total material handling overhead cost at $124,000 for a cost center. The data on production scheduling and control indicate the following:

For the cost center:
It takes an average of 4 baskets per year of material handling support for each product.
The area has 80 different products under its responsibility.
The basket used for moving materials handles 10 kilograms.
The cost driver is number of baskets handled.

Required:

1.   Calculate the material handling overhead rate per 10-kg-weight basket.
2.   Each unit of a product, called Baker-1, requires materials the weight of which is 0.1 kilograms (kg). Annual production volume is 2,200 units. Baker-1 is

run 4 times a year. For each run, the number of baskets needed should be in whole numbers, which means workers cannot move a fraction of a basket, such as one-fifth of a basket. What is the material handling cost per unit of Baker-1?

E7-7 Activity (Purchasing) Cost Assignment to Products

Cedras Company's total purchasing overhead cost for a period is $48,000, which was incurred to process 128 purchase orders covering materials and parts purchases of $314,760. The cost-activity study indicates that the proper cost driver for purchasing activities is number of purchase orders.

Required:

1. Calculate the purchasing overhead rate per purchase order.
2. Among the 128 purchase orders were 6 orders for the materials and parts needed for producing a product, called Ced-1. The annual production volume of Ced-1 was 2,300 units. What is the purchasing overhead cost per unit of Ced-1?

E7-8 Activity (Receiving) Cost Assignment to Products

Dandy, Inc. performed a cost-activity study of its receiving area, which indicates the following:

Costs of Dandy's receiving activities are driven 50% by the number of purchase orders and 50% by the dollar value of purchases.

The total receiving area cost for the period was $38,688.

The total cost of materials and parts purchased for the period was $639,000, for which 124 purchase orders were processed.

On an average, 4 purchase orders are placed with various vendors for each production run. To minimize inventory, purchases are made right before each production run starts.

Required:

1. Calculate (a) the receiving overhead rate per purchase order, and (b) the receiving overhead rate per each dollar purchase.
2. A product of this company, DD-1, is run 3 times a year. Each unit of DD-1 requires a materials cost of $12. The production volume of DD-1 is 1,000 units a year. What is the amount of the receiving overhead charged to DD-1? Assume all other conditions stay at the average level.

E7-9 Activity (Direct Labor) Cost Assignment to Products

A circuit board manufacturing company assigns its assembly department cost based on the direct labor activity. The cost driver is direct labor hours. The direct labor activity cost pool had $876,375 for one period. The total number of direct labor hours recorded in the assembly department was 142,500, 57% of which was spent to assemble a product, called CB-1, and 43% was used to assemble another product, called CB-2.

An activity analysis of the assembly-related direct labor has revealed that, under normal circumstances, 6 minutes is the time required to assemble one unit of CB-1. CB-2 takes twice as much time for assembly. The production volume for the period was 808,692 units of CB-1 and 305,472 units of CB-2.

Required:

1. What is the direct labor activity cost rate per unit of cost driver, based on the actual hours spent?
2. How much direct labor activity costs should be assigned to product CB-1 and product CB-2 under normal circumstances for the actual output? Assume that the cost rate calculated in (1) is valid under normal circumstances also.
3. How much direct labor activity costs should be assigned to product CB-1 and product CB-2, based on the actual hours spent?

E7-10 Activity (Machine Operation) Cost Assignment to Products

Robotics, Inc. produces three types of parts, RT-1, RT-2, and RT-3, which are used as major components of industrial robots. The company assigns its fabrication operations costs based on the machine operation activity. The cost driver is machine hours. The activity and cost data for July follow:

The machine operations activity cost pool amount $901,876

The number of actual machine hours recorded in the plant routing file:

Used for Producing	Hours Used
RT-1	3,648
RT-2	1,769
RT-3	2,256
Total	7,673

Normal machine processing time required (per unit):

	Minutes
RT-1	15
RT-2	12
RT-3	20

Actual production volume:

	Units
RT-1	14,520
RT-2	8,625
RT-3	6,603

Required:

1. What is the machine operation activity cost rate per unit of cost driver, based on the actual hours spent?
2. How much machine operation activity costs should be assigned to products RT-1, RT-2, and RT-3, respectively, under normal circumstances, for the actual output? Assume that the machine operation activity cost rate per hour under normal circumstances is $120.
3. How much machine operation activity costs should be assigned to products RT-1, RT-2, and RT-3, respectively, based on the actual hours spent?

P7-11 Activity (Quality Inspection) Cost Assignment to Products

Genie-Video Inc., a producer of children's video games, uses activity-based costing in costing its products. The company's cost-activity study indicates that its quality inspection costs are driven by unit-level (number of units inspected) and batch-level (number of batches produced) activities. Quality assurance department's fixed costs, for which no proper driver can be found, are assigned to products based on the number of units produced.

Quality assurance department's cost and activity data for Year 7 are presented below:

Variable cost per unit inspected	$9
Variable cost per batch	$240
Fixed costs of the department	$338,670
Video game cassettes produced in 19x1	761,000 units
Average batch size	2,450 units

According to the company's experience, an average of 6% of actual output produced is selected for inspection.

Required:

1. Estimate the unit-level cost of inspection for Year 7.
2. How many batches were produced in Year 7? Estimate the batch-level cost of inspection for Year 7.
3. Estimate the total cost of inspection for Year 7.
4. "Ario Brothers" is one of the most popular video games the company produces. A total of 48,600 units of "Ario Brothers" were produced in Year 7 in

six production runs. How much of the quality assurance department's costs should be assigned to "Ario Brothers"?

P7-12 Activity (Purchasing and Receiving) Cost Assignment to Products

Purchasing and receiving activities of Computer Chips, Inc. are performed by the purchasing department. According to a recent cost-activity study, the two drivers of purchasing department costs are the number of purchase orders (for all purchasing and part of receiving activities) and the dollar amount of purchases (for part of receiving activities).

Monthly cost data:

Dollar amount of purchases	$700,000
Personnel costs:	
Purchasing - 2 agents ($3,500 each)	$ 7,000
Receiving - 4 workers ($2,500 each)	10,000
Department manager and secretary	9,000
Total personnel costs	$ 26,000
Office rent	$ 8,000

Cost-activity information:

a. Three hundred orders are processed in a typical month. Each purchase order takes about an equal amount of time and attention for processing.

b. One-third of the work receiving room workers perform is individual order-related. Two-thirds is related to dollar values.

c. The manager and the secretary divide their time equally among the six other employees.

d. The purchasing activities use 20% of the office space. The receiving activities use 80%.

Required:

1. Calculate cost rates for the two cost drivers of purchasing and receiving activities.

2. A product, Chip #A101, requires the purchasing department's support for the procurement (twice every month) of its raw materials. The monthly cost of raw materials is $160,000. How much is the monthly cost of supporting this product with purchasing and receiving activities?

3. Assume that, as the newly appointed manager, you are responsible for Chip #A101 as well as other products. You want to reduce the purchasing and receiving overhead costs assigned to Chip #A101. How would you do it?

P7-13 Comprehensive Cost-Activity Relationships at a Service Firm

Finances-R-Us, Inc. is a finance company, located in Westchester County, New York. Its customers are individual residents and small businesses in the region. The company is in the business of providing four different types of loans to its customers: commercial short-term, commercial medium-term, mortgage, and consumer loans. The company uses activity-based costing for its product costing and shows the following costs and activities for Year 5:

Loan packages handled		168
Number of loan committee meetings held		35
Fees paid to 6 loan committee members		$ 77,000
Personnel expenses:		
Secretary/receptionist	$ 29,000	
2 Loan analysts	74,000	
Management personnel	126,000	
Total		229,000
Expenses related to loan forms and procedures		28,000
Office expenses		92,000
Total expenses for Year 5		$426,000

A cost-activity study reveals the following:

The costs of secretary/receptionist and loan analysts are related to the number of loan packages handled. Loan committee members are paid based on the number of meetings they attend. Expenses incurred in connection with loan forms and procedures are related to the types of loans. Costs of management personnel and office expenses are facility-level and should be assigned to each loan package equally.

Required:

1. Calculate cost rates for unit-level, batch-level, product-level, and facility-level activities.
2. The following changes are expected for Year 6:
   The number of loan applications increases 10%, requiring 3 more loan committee meetings to be held. Other conditions stay the same. Estimate the total operating cost for Year 6.
3. Refer to the original data in Year 5. Assume that the company's loan fund is limited and management wants to eliminate either consumer loan or short-term commercial loan. The same interest rate is charged for both loans and the company can find enough customers for either loan. The resource requirements of and other information on the two loans for Year 5 follow:

	Consumer Loan	Short-Term Commercial Loan
Number of applications	100	40
Average loan amount	$15,000	$37,500

Of the 35 loan committee meetings, 24 are attributed to the two loan types. The ratio between the meeting time the loan committee spends on a consumer loan and on a commercial loan is 1 to 3, which means that a consumer loan takes only one-third of the meeting time the loan committee spends on a commercial loan. Assume that, as the manager in charge, you must decide which loan type to eliminate to maximize earnings. What is your decision? Disregard facility-level costs in this analysis.

P7-14 Determining Cost Driver Units Based on Already Assigned Overhead Costs

Printed Circuit Division of a large computer manufacturer is in the business of producing and selling personal computer components, called PC-S and PC-N. PC-S is the company's standard-size product, which sells for $120 per unit, and PC-N is a specialized product, which sells for $200 per unit. The company uses activity-based costing and has allocated fixed manufacturing overhead costs in Year 7 to the two products based on four cost drivers as follows:

	Fixed Overhead Costs Assigned to		
Cost Drivers	*PC-S*	*PC-N*	*Total*
Engineering changes	$ 79,876	$124,249	$204,125
Setups	72,275	159,004	231,279
Purchase orders	27,360	41,040	68,400
Production volume	225,694	48,361	274,055
			$777,859

The Year 7 routing files of the company reveal that 69 engineering change orders, 80 setups, 200 purchase orders, and a production volume of 8,500 were recorded for the period.

Required:

1. Determine how many units of each of the four cost drivers were required by each product.
2. For the first three cost pools, higher fixed overhead costs were assigned to PC-N. Why would a product, whose production volume is lower, be charged with higher fixed overhead costs? Explain.

P7-15 Cost and Profit Comparison Between Two Products with Different Activity Requirements

Gateway Manufacturing Inc. produces 14 types of truck rear bumpers for one of the Big Three auto makers. It takes 40 minutes to perform a setup for processing bumper GM-1, 20 minutes for bumper GM-2, and an average of 30 minutes for 12 other types of bumpers in the fabrication area. Bumper GM-1 is usually run 9 times, GM-2 is run 18 times, and each of the other bumpers is run 6 times a year.

Gateway's production volume is 35,000 units a year, which includes 8,000 units of GM-1 and 6,000 units of GM-2. GM-1 and GM-2 are sold for the same price and all other costs of processing the two bumpers are equal. There are 6 workers who are involved in setup operations and their total personnel cost is $240,000 per year. Gateway uses activity-based costing and setup hours is the cost driver for the setup activity.

Required:

1. What is the cost rate per setup hour?
2. Calculate the total and per-unit setup overhead costs charged to GM-1 and GM-2.
3. Which of the two products is more profitable?
4. Gateway has recently introduced a continuous improvement program into its manufacturing process, which has reduced the setup time for bumper processing by 50% and enabled the company to release two of the six setup workers. The continuous improvement program saved $90,000 a year in personnel costs. Repeat the requirements of (1) and (2) under the new conditions of continuous improvement.

P7-16 Finding Cost Driver Units Based on Assigned Activity Costs

Setup costs of Ajax Company, an automobile part manufacturer, are determined based on time and cost estimates. Ajax uses activity-based costing for product costing purposes. The following are this year's data on costs and production:

Cost data:

Wages for setup workers	$109,278
Setup-related salaries for engineers assigned	84,295
Maintenance costs for machines and tools dedicated to setup operations	10,024
The portion of the supervisor's salary identified to setup activities	9,751
The portion of the depreciation costs of machines, tools, etc. identified to setup in this area	22,392

Data of cost center CC-1 on production scheduling and control:

a. The cost driver for the setup-related overhead costs is number of setup hours.
b. Past production records indicate that a setup takes an average of 4 hours.
c. Cost center CC-1 is responsible for the processing of 68 different parts.
d. On an average, these parts are run 8 times a year.

Required:

1. Calculate the overhead application rate per hour for setup activities.
2. Part #59 requires a processing operation, called RT-R. A setup for each RT-R operation takes 6 hours. A total of 3,500 units of part #59 are produced this year. Based on the activity cost assignment, an annual setup overhead cost of $3,250 has been charged to part #59. How many times was part #59 run this year?
3. Refer to (2). A total setup overhead cost of $390 has been charged to the June cost accounting period this year for the production of part #59. How many units of part #59 were processed in June?

 P7-17   Stage 1 Cost Assignment to Activity Centers

Tompac Electronics, Inc., located in San Diego, California, is a manufacturer of computer components. The company uses activity-based costing, for the first time, in costing its products. In Stage 1 cost assignment, the company distributes its overhead support activity costs to five major activity centers based on first-level drivers as follows:

Support costs	Amount	Driver
Material handling	$42,500	Material movements
Process engineering	39,000	Engineering hours
Manufacturing support	56,500	Actual usage (%)

Rates of support costs used for assignment to major activity centers were: $50 per material movement; $32 per process engineering hour; and $565 per each actual usage percentage point.

Stage 1 cost assignment has produced the following costs which have been distributed to the five major activity centers in a certain period:

Support Costs	Major Activity Centers				
	(1)	*(2)*	*(3)*	*(4)*	*(5)*
Material handling	$30,000		$12,500		
Process engineering			5,000	$20,000	$14,000
Mfg. support	12,000	$10,000	2,000	3,000	29,500
Total support costs	42,000	10,000	19,500	23,000	43,500
Center's own costs	43,000	30,000	25,000	38,000	34,000
Total costs	$85,000	$40,000	$44,500	$61,000	$77,500

Required:

1. How many material movements were there in the period, in total and for each of the major activity centers?
2. How many process engineering hours were spent to support the operations of the five activity centers, in total and for each activity center?
3. What were the actual percentages of service each of the five activity centers received from manufacturing support?

P7-18   Stage 2 Cost Assignment to Products

Refer to P7-17. Tompac Electronics performs Stage 2 cost assignment to distribute costs of activity centers to products based on the following activity drivers and rates:

Activity Centers	Activity Drivers	Rate Per Driver
(1)	Number of parts required	$17.0000 per part
(2)	Number of service hours	$28.5714 per hour
(3)	Weight of workpieces	$ 0.1780 per pound
(4)	Number of insertions	$ 0.1525 per insertion
(5)	Labor hours	$20.3947 per hour

The costs of activity centers distributed to products have been calculated as follows:

Activity Centers	Costs Distributed to Products A	B	C	D	Total
(1)	$21,000	$14,000	$25,000	$25,000	$ 85,000
(2)	12,000	11,000	9,000	8,000	40,000
(3)	12,000	18,000	9,000	5,500	44,500
(4)	23,000	21,000	17,000		61,000
(5)	25,000		15,000	37,500	77,500
	$93,000	$64,000	$75,000	$76,000	$308,000

Required:

1. How many parts were required for the production of all four products? How many parts did each product require respectively?
2. How many service hours did Activity Center 2 generate in total for the period? How many service hours were used to support each product?
3. What was the total weight of all workpieces? What was the weight of the workpieces related to each product?
4. How many insertions were performed for the period in total and for each product?
5. How many hours did Activity Center 5 work in total and for each product?

P7-19   Making Product Decisions Based on Activity-Based Cost Information

Refer to P7-18. This is the first year Tompac uses activity-based costing. In addition to the costs distributed from five activity centers, materials costs were incurred for the production of products A, B, C, and D as shown below. The production volumes and sales prices of the four products are also shown for the same period.

	Products			
	A	B	C	D
Units produced	1,500	1,000	500	250
Materials cost per unit	$ 30	$ 26	$ 40	$ 42
Sales price per unit	$125	$120	$180	$300

According to the company's management, products C and D are highly specialized products and command substantially higher market prices than products A and B, which are standard products producing relatively low profit margins.

Required:

1. Calculate the unit manufacturing cost of each of the four products.
2. Calculate the gross margin earned on each of the four products.
3. Assume that the company's management has been using product profitability as the major criterion for measuring performance of product managers. Do you see any problem in the management's practice?
4. Product decisions involve dropping existing products and/or adding new products. What product decisions would you recommend to the management to improve profitability?
5. Is there any alternative to dropping any of the four products in order to increase profits?

P7-20   Cost and Profit Comparison Between Two Products with Different Activity Requirements

PT Parts, Inc. produces 10 types of car parts that are used in mid-size automobile manufacturing at an auto plant located in Tennessee. The information on last year's production is provided below:

Product	Setup Time(Hour)	Number of Runs Per Year	Production Volume
PT	0.5	6	20,000
QS	0.4	5	12,000
8 others	0.2 each	4 each	88,000 (all 8 products)
			120,000

Parts PT and QS are sold for the same price and all other costs of processing the two parts are equal. There are 5 workers who are involved in setup operations and their total personnel cost is $220,000 per year. The company uses activity-based costing and setup hours is the cost driver for setup activity.

Required:

1. What is the cost rate per setup hour?
2. Calculate the total and per-unit setup overhead costs charged to parts PT and QS.

3. Which of the two products, PT or QS, is more profitable?
4. The company has recently reduced setup time for part processing by 40%, which is expected to enable the company to decrease personnel costs by 40% next year. Repeat the requirements of (1) and (2) for next year.

P7-21   Product Profitability; Different Activity Requirements

Ace Wheels, Inc. is a manufacturer of aluminum wheels used on automobiles. The company's products, such as Ace One, have been especially popular among the younger drivers. The company regards continuous improvement efforts as very important in all areas of operations, including manufacturing and manufacturing support.

The company produces 12 different types of wheels. Ace One and Ace Two are the two most popular products among the 12 products. The operating records reveal the following information on average setups, number of runs, and production volume for each product:

Product	Required Setup Time	Number of Runs per Year	Annual Production Volume
Ace One	30 minutes	8	6,000 units
Ace Two	15	20	5,000
Other 10 wheels	20 each	9 each	27,000 (all 10)
			38,000 units

Ace One and Ace Two sell for the same price. Other manufacturing costs for the two wheels are equal. The setup operations require 4 workers who are paid $175,500 in total per year.

Ace Wheels, Inc. uses activity-based costing. The cost driver for the setup activity cost pool is the number of setup hours.

Required:

1. Compute the cost rate per setup hour.
2. Compute the total and per-unit setup overhead costs charged to products Ace One and Ace Two.
3. Which product's profitability is better, Ace One or Ace Two?
4. The continuous improvement efforts of Ace Wheels, Inc. have reduced the setup time by 40% and the setup personnel costs by $70,000 per year. Repeat the requirements of (1) and (2) under the new conditions of continuous improvement.

P7-22   Connecting Activity Costs to Cost Driver Units

The fabrication department of Ridefun, Inc. fabricates major parts used in the assembly process of all-terrain vehicles (ATVs). Thanks to the popularity of ATVs, especially in the west coast, the sales of the company's ATVs have been increasing at phenomenal rates.

In order to manage its manufacturing costs effectively, the company has adopted activity-based costing. One activity cost pool accommodates setup costs which are determined based on time and cost estimates. Some selected information on production and costs for this year is presented below:

a. Wages and salaries paid:

For	Wages and Salaries
Setup workers	$110,000
Engineers assigned to setup operations	83,000
	$193,000

b. The maintenance costs for the machines and tools dedicated to setup operations amounted to $9,000.
c. The portion of the supervisor's salary identified to setup activities was $9,500.
d. The portion of the depreciation costs of machines, tools, etc. identified to setup activities in this area was $20,000.
e. The production scheduling and control data on the operations of the Fabrication cost center indicate the following:

The cost driver for the setup-related overhead costs is the number of setup hours. Past production records indicate that a setup takes an average of 4 hours. The Fabrication cost center is responsible for the processing of 70 different parts. On an average, these parts are run 9 times a year.

Required:

1. Compute the overhead application rate per hour for setup activities.
2. A part, called fender, requires a processing operation, called fab-dent. A setup for each fab-dent operation takes 5 hours. A total of 4,000 units of fender are produced this year. Based on the activity cost assignment, an anual setup overhead cost of $3,675 has been charged to fender. How many times was fender run this year?
3. Refer to (2). A total setup overhead cost of $459 has been charged to the October cost accounting period this year for the production of fender. How many units of fender were processed in October?

P7-23 Cost Distribution and Cost Drivers; Stage 1 Cost Assignment

ADT, Inc., manufactures and sells various products used in cosmetic dentistry. The company's products are used to whiten and straighten teeth. Bill Paxon, president of the company, likes to use the number 150 billion to inspire his employees. The number approximates the number of teeth in people's mouths worldwide.

The company uses activity-based costing for the first time in costing its products. The company has identified three cost drivers for the Stage 1 cost assignment: number of setups, engineering hours, and actual usage of service. In the Stage 1 cost assignment, the company distributes its overhead support activity costs to five major activity centers based on those three first-level drivers as follows:

Support costs	Amount	Driver
Setup	$52,000	Number of setups
Process engineering	31,080	Engineering hours
Manufacturing support	60,000	Actual usage (%)

Number of setups is used in lieu of setup hours, because all setups take about the same amount of time. Rates of support costs, used to distribute costs to major activity centers, were $800 per setup, $28 per process engineering hour, and $600 per each actual usage percentage point.

The Stage 1 cost assignment has produced the following costs distributed to the five major activity centers in a certain period:

Support Costs	Major Activity Centers				
	(1)	(2)	(3)	(4)	(5)
Setup	$32,000	–	$20,000	–	–
Process engineering	–	–	4,480	$15,120	$11,480
Mfg. support	12,000	$ 9,000	3,000	6,000	30,000
Total support costs	44,000	9,000	27,480	21,120	41,480
Center's own costs	40,000	30,000	20,000	35,000	38,000
Total costs	$84,000	$39,000	$47,480	$56,120	$79,480

Required:

1. How many setups were performed in the period, in total and for each of the major activity centers?
2. How many process engineering hours were spent to support the operations of the five activity centers, in total and by activity center?
3. What were the actual percentages of service each of the five activity centers received from manufacturing support?

P7-24   Stage 2 Cost Assignment to Products

Refer to P7-23. ADT, Inc. performs Stage 2 cost assignment to distribute costs of activity centers to products. The company uses the following activity drivers and rates for the Stage 2 cost assignment:

Activity Centers	Activity Drivers	Rate Per Driver
(1)	Number of components required	$20 per component
(2)	Number of service hours	$25 per hour
(3)	Weight of workpieces	$0.42 per pound
(4)	Number of attachments	$0.20 per attachment
(5)	Labor hours	$18 per hour

The costs of the activity centers distributed to products have been calculated as the following:

Activity Centers	Costs Distributed to Products				
	P	Q	R	S	Total
(1)	$22,000	$16,000	$24,000	$28,000	$90,000
(2)	10,000	8,750	7,000	6,250	32,000
(3)	23,100	42,000	18,480	12,600	96,180
(4)	28,000	26,000	20,000	–	74,000
(5)	21,600	–	10,800	30,600	63,000
	$104,700	$92,750	$80,280	$77,450	$355,180

Required:

1. How many components were required for the production of all four products? How many components did each product require, respectively?
2. How many service hours did Activity Center 2 generate in total for the period? How many service hours were used to support each product?
3. What was the total weight of the workpieces related to all products? What was the weight of the workpieces related to each product?
4. How many attachments were performed for the period in total and for each product?
5. How many hours did Activity Center 5 work in total and for each product?

P7-25   Service Firm; Comprehensive Cost-Activity Relationships

Hancock Finance Company, located in the mid-Wilshire area of Los Angeles, has been in the commercial and consumer lending business for over 20 years. The company serves customers who are individual residents and small businesses. The company provides four types of loans to its customers: commercial loan I, commercial loan II, mortgage loan, and consumer loan.

The company uses activity-based costing for its product costing and shows the following costs and activities for Year 7:

Loan packages handled		154
Number of loan committee meetings held		20
Fees paid to 5 loan committee members		$71,000
Personnel expenses:		
Secretary/receptionist	$30,000	
Loan analyst	56,240	
Management personnel	141,000	
Total	$227,240	
Expenses related to loan forms and procedures		32,000
Office expenses		74,600

A cost-activity study reveals the following:

The number of loan packages directly affects the costs of secretary/receptionist and loan analysts. The company pays loan committee members based on the number of meetings the members attend. The expenses incurred in connection with loan forms and procedures are related to how many types of loans are involved. The costs of management personnel and office expenses are facility-level, and the same amount should be assigned to each loan package.

Required:

1. Compute cost rates for the unit-level, batch-level, product-level, and facility-level activities identified in the study.
2. For Year 8, the number of loan applications will increase 10%, requiring two more loan committee meetings to be held. Other conditions stay the same. Estimate the total operating cost for Year 8.
3. Refer to the original data in Year 7. Assume that the company's loan fund is limited and the management wants to eliminate either consumer loan or commercial loan I. The same interest rate is charged for both loans and the company can find enough customers for either loan. The resource requirements of and other information on the two loans for Year 7 follow:

	Consumer Loan	Commercial Loan 1
Number of applications	80	30
Average loan amount	$18,000	$36,000

Of the 20 loan committee meetings, 16 are attributed to the two loan types. The ratio between the meeting time the loan committee spends on a consumer loan and on a commercial loan is 1 to 3, which means that a consumer loan takes only one-third of the meeting time the loan committee spends on a commercial loan. Assume that you are the manager in charge. Which loan would you eliminate to maximize earnings? Disregard facility-level costs in this analysis.

■ CASES

C7-26   Determination of Cost Rate and Driver Units

Visions, Inc. manufactures and sells eyeglass lenses and special lenses. Special lenses are surgically implanted in the eye. The special lenses make the old method of correcting for cataracts look like a truly ancient method of eye care.

The market for both eyeglass lenses and special lenses is growing at healthy rates. The demand for eyeglasses will continue to be strong as baby-boomers age. Since special lenses replace the lost natural lenses in most cataract surgeries in the U.S., the demand for the special lenses of Visions, Inc. has been strong. Eyeglass lenses sell for $110 per case and special lenses sell for $280 per case. The company uses activity-based costing and has allocated fixed manufacturing overhead costs in Year 7 to the two products based on four cost drivers as shown below:

	Fixed Overhead Costs Allocated		
Cost Drivers	to Eyeglass Lenses	to Special Lenses	Total
Engineering changes	$ 30,000	$ 75,000	$105,000
Setups	33,600	43,200	76,800
Purchase orders	32,000	16,000	48,000
Production volume	112,000	56,000	168,000
	$207,600	$190,200	$397,800

The company's routing files of Year 7 revealed that 70 engineering change orders, 64 setups, 120 purchase orders, and a production volume of 6,000 were recorded for the period. Top management of the company has not seen actual results of how effective the new activity-based costing system can be, and is looking forward to the direction the new system will pinpoint in terms of cost incurrence and profitability.

Required:

1. Determine how many units of each of the four cost drivers were required by each product.
2. Higher fixed overhead costs were allocated to the special lenses for the first two cost drivers (engineering changes and setups), while the production volume for the eyeglass lenses was twice as large. How can this happen?

C7-27   ABC and Profitability Analysis

Electronic Circuits, Inc., located in San Jose, California, is a manufacturer of sub-assemblies used to assemble lap-top computers. In Year 4, the company's sales in units for the standard product line EC-S and the specialized product line EC-N were 4,000 units and 1,000 units, respectively. Due to the specialized nature, EC-Ns are sold at a higher price than EC-Ss, $200 a unit for EC-Ns compared to $100 a unit for EC-Ss. The company incurred operating losses for the year.

The following are the per-unit manufacturing cost data for Year 4 by product line:

	Product Lines	
	EC-S	EC-N
Direct material	$26	$27
Direct labor	7	8
Variable overhead	9	40

Fixed overhead costs for Year 4 amounted to $390,000 and were allocated to the two product lines on the basis of the production quantity (four-fifths for EC-S and one-fifth for EC-N). All units produced were sold in Year 4. When product-line operating statements were prepared, the results confirmed the belief of the company's management: only one product line, as usual, made a significant contribution toward the company's profit. Without that product line, the management believed, the company's loss would be much higher.

About a week after the release of the Year 4 operating statements, Pat Tealy, cost accounting manager, was visited by Jonathan Adams, the EC-S product line manager. Adams expressed his frustrations over the cost accounting process and stated: "My gut feeling tells me your overhead allocations are all messed up. I am not an accountant, thank God, but I do know that our product line does not use as much overhead resources as you pencil-pushers claim."

Tealy did not like the wholesale treatment she received from Adams, but she was also a little skeptical about the theoretical soundness of the way the company allocated overhead. After a preliminary study, Tealy decided to apply activity-based costing to fixed overhead allocation. Based on surveys of the manufacturing and the overhead support personnel and analysis of the work performed by each support department and their costs, the following cost drivers and cost data were determined:

	Number of Driver Units			Fixed Overhead Cost in the Pool
	Total	EC-S	EC-N	
Setups	40	12	28	$102,000
Engineering changes	35	13	22	126,000
Purchase orders	100	40	60	22,000
Production volume	5,000	4,000	1,000	140,000
				$390,000

Required:

1. What was the gross margin contributed by each product line in Year 4 before activity-based costing was used? Prepare an operating statement by product line to answer this question. Which product line, do you think, was management's favorite?
2. Determine the gross margin contributed by each product line based on the cost allocations under activity-based costing.
3. What is the main reason for the difference between the results obtained in (1) and (2)? When, do you think, activity-based costing would produce the same kind of result that the previous cost allocation method did?

C7-28   Activity-Based Costs vs. Standard Costs

Alaire Corporation manufactures several different types of printed circuit boards; however, two of the boards account for the majority of the company's sales. The first of these boards, a television (TV) circuit board, has been a standard in this industry for several years. The market for this type of board is competitive and, therefore, price-sensitive. Alaire plans to sell 65,000 of the TV boards in Year 3 at a price of $150 per unit. The second high-volume product, a personal computer (PC) circuit board, is a recent addition to Alaire's product line. Because the PC board incorporates the latest technology, it can be sold at a premium price; the Year 3 plans include the sale of 40,000 PC boards at $300 per unit.

Alaire's management group is meeting to discuss strategies for Year 3, and the current topic of conversation is how to spend the sales and promotion dollars for next year. The sales manager believes that the market share for the TV board could be expanded by concentrating Alaire's promotional efforts in this area. In response to this suggestion, the production manager said, "Why don't you go after a bigger market for the PC board? The cost sheets that I get show that the contribution from the PC board is more than double the contribution from the TV board. I know we get a premium price for the PC board; selling it should help overall profitability."

Alaire uses the following "standard" rates (per unit) in the determination of total and per-unit product costs:

	TV Board	PC Board
Direct material	$80	$140
Direct labor	1.5 hours	4 hours
Machine time	.5 hours	1.5 hours

Variable factory overhead is applied on the basis of direct labor hours. For Year 3, variable factory overhead and direct labor hours are estimated at $1,120,000 and 280,000 hours, respectively. The hourly rates for machine time and direct labor are $10 and $14, respectively. Alaire applies a material handling charge at 10% of material cost; this material handling charge is not included in variable factory overhead. Total Year 3 expenditures for material are estimated at $10,600,000.

Estimated cost		Cost Driver	Annual Activity For Cost Driver
Material handling overhead:			
Procurement	$ 400,000	Number of parts	4,000,000
Production scheduling	220,000	Number of boards	110,000
Packaging and shipping	440,000	Number of boards	110,000
	$1,060,000		
Variable overhead:			
Machine set-up	$ 446,000	Number of setups	278,750
Hazardous waste disposal	48,000	Pounds of waste	16,000
Quality control	560,000	Number of inspections	160,000
General supplies	66,000	Number of boards	110,000
	$1,120,000		
Manufacturing:			
Machine insertion	$1,200,000	Number of parts	3,000,000
Manual insertion	4,000,000	Number of parts	1,000,000
Wave soldering	132,000	Number of boards	110,000
	$5,332,000		

Required per unit	TV Board	PC Board
Parts	25	55
Machine insertions	24	35
Manual insertions	1	20
Machine set-ups	2	3
Hazardous waste	.02 lb.	.35 lb.
Inspections	1	2

Ed Welch, Alaire's controller, believes that before the management group proceeds with the discussion about allocating sales and promotional dollars to individual products, it might be worthwhile to look at these products on the basis of the activities involved in their production. As Welch explained to the group, "Activity-based costing integrates the cost of all activities, known as cost drivers, into individual product costs rather than including these costs in overhead pools." Welch has prepared the schedule shown above to help the management group understand this concept.

"Using this information," Welch explained, "we can calculate an activity-based cost for each TV board and each PC board and then compare it to the standard cost we have been using. The only cost that remains the same for both cost methods is the cost of direct material. The cost drivers will replace the direct labor, machine time, and overhead costs in the standard cost."

Required:

1. Identify at least four general advantages of using activity-based costing.
2. On the basis of "standard" costs, calculate the total contribution expected in Year 3 for Alaire Corporation's
   a. TV board.
   b. PC board.
3. On the basis of activity-based costs, calculate the total contribution expected in Year 3 for Alaire Corporation's
   a. TV board.
   b. PC board.
4. Explain how the comparison of the results of the two costing methods may impact the decisions made by Alaire Corporation's management group.

(CMA, adapted)

[Note: No prior knowledge of standard costs is needed to work this problem.]

C7-29 Activity-Based Costs; Market Strategy

Applewood Electronics manufactures two large-screen television models, the Monarch which has been produced since Year 1 and sells for $900, and the Regal, a new model introduced in early Year 4 which sells for $1,140. Based on the Income Statement at November 30, Year 5, presented below, a decision has been made to concentrate Applewood's marketing resources on the Regal model and begin to phase out the Monarch model.

Applewood Electronics
Income Statement
For the Fiscal Year Ended November 30, Year 5

	Monarch	Regal	Total
Sales	$19,800,000	$4,560,000	$24,360,000
Cost of goods sold	12,540,000	3,192,000	15,732,000
Gross margin	7,260,000	1,368,000	8,628,000
Selling and administrative expense	5,830,000	978,000	6,808,000
Net income	$ 1,430,000	$ 390,000	$ 1,820,000

Units produced and sold	22,000	4,000
Net income per unit sold	$65.00	$97.50

Presented below are the standard unit costs for the Monarch and the Regal.

	Monarch	Regal
Direct materials	$208	$584
Direct labor		
- Monarch (1.5 hours x $12)	18	
- Regal (3.5 hours x $12)		42
Machine usage		
- Monarch (8 hours x $18)	144	
- Regal (4 hours x $18)		72
Manufacturing overhead*	200	100
Standard cost per unit	$570	$798

*Manufacturing overhead was applied to machine hours at a predetermined rate of $25 per hour.

Applewood's controller is advocating the use of activity-based costing and has gathered the following information about the company's manufacturing overhead costs for the year ended November 30, Year 5.

Activity Center (Cost Driver)	Related Costs	Monarch	Regal	Total
Soldering (number of solder joints)	$ 942,000	1,185,000	385,000	1,570,000
Shipments (number of shipments)	860,000	16,200	3,800	20,000
Quality control (number of inspections)	1,240,000	56,200	21,300	77,500
Purchase orders (number of orders)	950,400	80,100	109,980	190,080
Machine power (machine hours)	57,600	176,000	16,000	192,000
Machine set-ups (number of set-ups)	750,000	16,000	14,000	30,000
Total related costs	$4,800,000			

Required:

Using activity-based costing, determine if Applewood Electronics should continue to emphasize the Regal model and phase out the Monarch model.

(CMA, adapted)

BUDGETING FOR OPERATIONS

After studying this chapter, you should be able to:

1. Explain what is meant by a budget, budgeting, and budgetary control.

2. Enumerate the major advantages of budgeting.

3. Describe the different types of budgets.

4. Briefly explain the budgeting process, including selection of a budget period, role of a budget committee, sales forecasting and expense and cash flow estimation.

5. Prepare all schedules that collectively make up the master budget.

6. Explain the importance of human behavior in the budgeting process.

7. Understand the limitation of budgeting in the new global environment of business.

8. Understand how budgeting changes in the new production environment.

Organizations, whether they are profit-oriented or not, need to plan for the future. Lack of short run planning may lead to failure to stock enough raw materials to meet production needs, or failure to produce enough finished products to meet customer demands. A company may fail to accumulate enough cash to pay its debts as they come due. Lack of long run planning may cause a company to make poor decisions on what product lines to pursue, or what manufacturing methods it should employ. Overall, planning is essential for a company to succeed in the marketplace. In this chapter, we look at budgeting and the budget process, which represents the first step in the planning and control of routine operations.

THE OPERATING BUDGET: WHAT IT IS AND WHY IT IS IMPORTANT

What is a Budget?

A **budget** is a plan of future activities, expressed in quantities and/or monetary values. A budget is not just a forecast, and it is not just a maximum limit on spending such as a government budget. It is a vehicle used to communicate performance expectations to everyone in the organization, and to measure the efficiency and effectiveness of actual performance against the targets set forth in the budget. The actual preparation of a budget is referred to as **budgeting.**

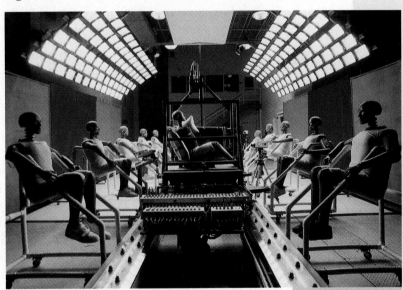

Profit Planning and Budgetary Control

In a profit-oriented organization, the budget will show how much profit is expected in a future period, such as a month, a quarter, or a year. The budget, accordingly, may be called a **profit plan** and budgeting may be referred to as **profit planning.** If the actual performance does not meet the budgeted or expected performance target, prudent managers will take action to correct the situation. This process of monitoring performance and taking corrective action is **control,** and the use of budgets as a part of this control process is called **budgetary control.**

Wait your turn! Lining up for side-impact sled tests at Morton International Inc.'s technical center in Rochester Hills, Michigan. For proper budgeting, the company must know how many tests will be performed.

The use of budgeted performance, rather than past performance, is more appropriate in evaluating actual performance, because past performance may conceal inefficiencies and usually does not reflect expected changes in economic or industry conditions or changes in the organization's goals. For example, assume that last year's sales were only $10 million because of various operational inefficiencies. This year's sales were $12 million, but should have been $15 million since new products were introduced this year and market conditions are favorable. Using last year's sales to evaluate this year's sales will indicate a favorable variance of $2 million, whereas using budgeted performance will indicate an unfavorable variance of $3 million. Sales managers should be asked to justify the unfavorable variance rather than be rewarded for what seems to be a favorable variance.

Budgeting in Nonprofit Organizations

The value of budgets and budgetary control is not limited to for-profit business applications. Nonprofit organizations, as well as individuals, can benefit as well. For example, a university can plan its activities and facilities, based on the number of expected students. Or it can set its criteria for admission based on the available facilities. A hospital plans for the number and types of patients to be admitted based on its available facilities and specialties. Individuals may have to make some budgets also. A prudent student will plan how many courses to take in any one term and how many study hours to be devoted to each course if the target grade is to be achieved. A family will look at its monthly income, make allowances for fixed expenses, such as mortgage, rent, utilities and food, and then plan its discretionary entertainment and vacation expenses.

Why Budgeting is Necessary

Budgeting is not just guesswork. Budgeting forces management to do some thinking and planning in advance on how to achieve certain sales, cost, and profit objectives based on the company's resources, past performance, and expected future conditions. If the budget is well thought of in that way, it will also serve as a benchmark against which future performance may be compared. Furthermore, in the process of preparing the budget, all units in the organization must simultaneously consider the company's resources and activities. This leads to coordination among units such as purchasing, production, sales, shipping, and so forth. The coordination efforts will provide opportunities that are conducive to detecting and eliminating any overlaps or repetitions in the activities. Once the budget is prepared for the company as a whole and for each of its divisions, departments, or activities, it serves as an official plan of what is expected of the managers of those units so there will be no guessing as to who is expected to do what.

If the budgeting process is well implemented, the budget will clarify expectations and will serve as a motivating force for everyone. While budgeting will not by itself eliminate impending problems, it will make management aware of them in time to do something about them.

We can summarize the reasons why budgeting is necessary and important as follows:

1. Budgeting forces managers to think about and plan ahead for future activities.

2. A budget serves as a vehicle of resource allocation as well as a benchmark against which future actual performance may be measured.

3. Budgeting requires coordination of all activities in the organization. This may lead to elimination of repetitions, conflicts, overlaps, or bottlenecks among the various activities.

4. A budget serves as a written formal plan of expectations that is communicated to every managerial level in the organization.

5. Budgeting may serve as a motivating force for employees within the organization and this may lead to better performance.

6. Budgeting forewarns managers of impending problems before it is too late to do something about them.

Signs of Successful Budgeting

How do we know whether budgeting in an organization has been successfully performed? The following indicators can be used:

1. *Understanding and commitment.* In order for an organization to achieve the above benefits of budgeting, everyone involved must fully understand the importance of budgeting and make a commitment to meeting the budgeted targets. Management should manifest the commitment by making substantial resources available to accomplish the budgeting process.

2. *Involvement in the process.* Everyone in the organization should be involved in the budgeting process. In order to nurture involvement, management must demonstrate that it truly believes in the importance of budgeting. How? The budgetary targets should be set in a bottom-up fashion. A top-down assignment of budgetary targets is not conducive to generating everyone's commitment to achieving targets.

3. *Linkages with long-term plans.* An organization's long-term strategic plans are implemented through actual programs that usually span a period of longer than one year. Operating budgets cover a period of one year or the operating cycle of the organization, and should be linked with strategic plans and programs to be effective.

4. *Identification with managers.* Budgets represent short-term targets derived from longer-term plans and programs. The targets should be identified with individual managers, and the managers should be held responsible for actual deviations from the targets.

5. *Minimum dysfunctional aspects.* In the budgeting process, the human aspects and interpersonal relationships should be considered to minimize the dysfunctional aspects budgeting can create. People can play budget games, such as requesting more resources than needed for performing func-

DIRECTV broadcast operations center receives programming from movie studios, cable companies, and entertainment programmers, routes it to satellites, and then beams it directly to subscribers. Budgeting forces managers here to think about and plan ahead for future activities.

tions, or spending the entire budget allocated so that more can be asked for in the following periods without trying to find ways to reduce spending levels. Interdepartmental frictions can arise since budgeting entails setting targets and allocating resources, and every unit is motivated to lower its targets and get as much resources as possible.

Management must value the importance of human relations in budgeting. This means that top management gives its whole-hearted support to the budgeting system and that middle management and employees actively participate in the budget preparation and are convinced that the budgeting system is intended to achieve the organization's goals by helping each one of them perform better and be rewarded. This also requires that expense budgets be regarded as an outline of available resources and not as a restriction on organizational units' activities.

Types of Budgets

Budgets take on different names for their intended uses. For example, budgets that relate to the organization's operating activities, such as the sales budget, purchase budget, production budget, operating expenses budget, and budgeted income statement are called **operating budgets.** Budgets that relate to financial activities, such as the cash budget, capital budget, and budgeted balance sheet are called **financial budgets.**

Budgets that relate to long-term investment projects are called **capital budgets** or **capital investment budgets.** When all operating, financial, and capital budgets are put together in one master plan, it is called the **master budget.** If operating budgets are presented at various possible levels of activity (e.g. units produced and/or sold), and actual results are compared with the operating budget for the actual level of activity, that budget is called a **flexible budget.** If an organization adds one future month to the master budget as the month just ended is dropped, and applies this process in a continuous fashion, the master budget may be called a **continuous** or **perpetual budget.**

THE BUDGETING PROCESS

The budgeting process includes all the procedures and activities involved in the preparation of a master budget for the entire organization. This may include the selection of a budget period, the establishment of a budget committee if there is no permanent budgeting department, the sales forecast, and the integration of the budgets for all activities into one master budget.

Selection of a Budget Period

Budgets can be prepared for daily, weekly, monthly, or annual periods. They may also be prepared for longer periods such as five, ten, or even thirty years. Daily or

NBC, "Seinfeld," "Cheers," and Budgeting

For a broadcasting company such as NBC, the budgeted price for TV commercials represents a part of its forecasted sales receipts. NBC didn't get its $2 million asking price for commercials on the final "Seinfeld" episode from its advertisers. The price was about $1.5 million. NBC, however, was happy about this price because it didn't repeat the disaster of "Cheers," whose final episode (underpriced at only $650,000) sold out within hours in 1993.

From "NBC May Get Only $1.5 Million for Ad Spots on 'Seinfeld' Finale," *The Wall Street Journal*, March 4, 1998, B6.

weekly budgets are quite rare and may be used only by individual managers as a plan for a small task within the overall monthly or quarterly budget. The master budget is usually prepared for one year but is then broken down into quarters and months. Sometimes, management will prepare monthly budgets for only the first quarter of the fiscal year and quarterly budgets for the remaining three quarters of the year. As the end of the first quarter approaches, monthly budgets would be prepared for the second quarter, and so on. In continuous or perpetual budgets, a new month is added as the month just ended is dropped. This helps management to have an updated 12-month budget at all times.

Budget Department or Committee

Large organizations may have a permanent department for budgets and financial analysis. Such a department is responsible for starting the budget process and for the preparation and modification of the master budget. The department sends the organizational units the budget forms together with detailed instructions of how the forms are to be filled out. This would take place around August for a calendar year company. The forms are usually returned during October after the different departments have looked at the actual results from the first three quarters, which are usually helpful in estimating the budget figures for the coming year.

The budget department compiles these individual budgets into a master budget which is presented during November to top management for review and approval. If top management makes some changes, the department incorporates these into the budget and resubmits it to top management for approval. The finalized budget should be available to all units well before the new fiscal year begins.

If there is no permanent department for budgets and financial analysis, a budget committee must be established to carry out the above functions. Such a committee usually includes the chief executive officer and vice presidents of production, sales, purchasing, and finance. Since the budget committee includes most of top management, the committee itself approves the budget.

EXHIBIT 8-2

Budget Stores, Inc.
Balance Sheet
December 31, Year 6

Assets

Cash		$ 25,000
Accounts receivable		581,000
Inventory:		
Raw materials	$ 7,350	
Finished goods	84,000	91,350
Total current assets		697,350
Property, plant and equipment	768,000	
Accumulated depreciation	(230,400)	
Property, plant and equipment, net		537,600
Total assets		$1,234,950

Liabilities and Stockholders' Equity

Accounts payable	$ 15,190
Total current liabilities	15,190
12% Long-term notes payable	600,000
Total liabilities	615,190
Common stock, par	500,000
Paid-in capital	100,000
Retained earnings	19,760
Total stockholders' equity	619,760
Total liabilities & stockholders' equity	$1,234,950

The following additional information is available:

1. **Sales**

	Year 6 Actual		Year 7 Estimated				
	Nov.	Dec.	Jan.	Feb.	March	Apr.	May
Units	11,000	10,000	12,000	13,000	15,000	14,000	16,000

The selling price per unit has remained constant at $50 for the past year and is expected to remain unchanged throughout the first quarter of Year 7.

2. **Cash Collection Policy**

Thirty percent of total sales are cash sales and 70% are credit sales. Of the 70% credit sales, the company collects 40% in the month after the month of sale and 60% in the month following that. Budget Stores, Inc. has not had any bad debts during the first quarter of Year 7.

3. **Production Policy**

The company's policy is to produce, during each month, enough units to meet the following month's sales as well as the desired inventory at the end of the month which is equal to 25% of next month's estimated sales. At the end of December, Year 6, the finished inventory was 3,000 units at a cost of $28 each.

4. **Raw Materials Purchasing Policy**

In each month the company purchases enough raw materials to meet that month's production requirements and to maintain raw materials at the end of each month equivalent to 30% of next month's production requirements. Each unit of finished product requires four pounds of raw materials. Raw materials are purchased at a cost of 50 cents per pound. On December 31, Year 6, there was enough raw materials inventory to meet 30% of Year 7's January production requirements.

The company pays 30% of the cost of raw materials purchased in the month of purchase and the remaining 70% in the following month. The accounts payable balance of $15,190 on December 31, Year 6 represents 70% of purchases made in December, Year 6 to be paid in January, Year 7.

5. **Direct Labor Cost**

Each unit of finished product takes an average of two labor hours. The average wage rate per hour is $8.

6. **Manufacturing Overhead**

The company applies variable manufacturing overhead cost to production at the rate of 50% of direct labor cost. In addition, the company has the following fixed overhead expenses per month:

Factory supervisor's salary	$20,000
Factory rent	6,000
Factory insurance	600
Depreciation of factory equipment	400

All manufacturing overhead costs, except depreciation, are paid for in cash during the month in which they are incurred.

7. **Selling and Administrative Expenses**

Variable selling expenses are:

Freight out	$1 per unit
Sales commission	5% of sales

Fixed selling and administrative expenses per month are:

Salaries	$2,500
Rent	300
Advertising	200
Insurance	100
Depreciation, excluding depreciation of personal computers to be purchased in January, Year 7 (see below)	6,000

8. Capital Expenditures

The company expects to buy new personal computers for use in the administrative and sales offices at a cost of $250,000 which will be paid for by the end of January, Year 7. The monthly depreciation expense will be $4,000 for these PCs.

9. Financing Policy

On March 31, Year 7, the company is scheduled to pay $300,000 of the long-term notes payable plus the interest expense on the December 31, Year 6 balance of $600,000 for the first quarter at the rate of 12% per year.

With respect to short-term borrowing, the company's policy is to borrow at the beginning of a month with anticipated cash deficiency. A minimum cash balance of $20,000 is required at the end of each month. The company repays such short-term borrowing plus interest thereon at the end of the first month with anticipated excess cash. The company's bank is willing to lend the company what it needs at 12% per year, provided the borrowing and repayment (except interest expense) is in a multiple of $1,000.

List of Budgets and Schedules

Based on the above information, Budget Stores decided to prepare the following budgets and schedules that collectively make up the master budget for the first quarter of Year 7 broken down by month and in total:

1. Sales budget.
2. Production budget.
3. Direct materials budget.
4. Direct labor budget.
5. Manufacturing overhead budget.
6. Cost of goods sold and ending finished goods inventory budget.
7. Selling and administrative expenses budget.
8. Cash receipts schedule.
9. Cash disbursements schedule.
10. Cash budget.
11. Budgeted income statement for the first quarter, Year 7.
12. Budgeted balance sheet at March 31, Year 7.

We will now prepare each of the above budgets.

1. Sales Budget

The **sales budget** is the starting point in preparing the master budget. The sales budget shows units sold and total dollar amount of sales. The sales budget should also differentiate between cash sales and credit sales to facilitate the preparation of the cash receipts schedule. Schedule 1 presents the sales budget on a monthly basis for the first quarter of Year 7.

Schedule 1
Budget Stores, Inc.
Sales Budget
For First Quarter, Year 7

	January	February	March	Total First Quarter
Budgeted sales in units	12,000	13,000	15,000	40,000
Selling price per unit	× $50	× $50	× $50	× $50
Budgeted sales	$600,000	$650,000	$750,000	$2,000,000
Cash sales (30%)	$180,000	$195,000	$225,000	$ 600,000
Credit sales (70%)	420,000	455,000	525,000	1,400,000
Budgeted sales	$600,000	$650,000	$750,000	$2,000,000

2. Production Budget

The **production budget** presents the number of units of finished goods to be produced during the budget period. The number of units to be produced during a month simply equals the budgeted sales units for the month plus desired units on hand at the end of the month, less the units the company has on hand at the beginning of the month. Schedule 2 presents the production budget on a monthly basis, for the first quarter of Year 7.

Schedule 2
Budget Stores, Inc.
Production Budget (in Units)
For First Quarter, Year 7

(In units)	January	February	March	Total First Quarter
Budgeted sales (Schedule 1)	12,000	13,000	15,000	40,000
Desired ending inventory*	3,250	3,750	3,500	3,500
Total needs	15,250	16,750	18,500	43,500‡
Beginning inventory†	(3,000)	(3,250)	(3,750)	(3,000)
Required production	12,250	13,500	14,750	40,500

* 25% of next month's budgeted sales. April budgeted sales were 14,000 units. The desired ending inventory for March is thus 25% of 14,000, or 3,500 units.
† 25% of the current month's budgeted sales. It is also the same as the prior month's ending inventory. Ending inventory at December 31, Year 6 was 3,000 units, which also equals 25% of January, Year 7 budgeted sales, and represents the beginning inventory for the first quarter.
‡ This amount does not equal the total for the three months because each month's amount includes ending inventory whereas total first quarter needs includes only the ending inventory for March, Year 7.

3. Direct Materials Budget

The production budget now shows the number of units to be produced each month. This allows us to prepare a **direct materials budget** showing the quantity and costs of raw materials to be used in production and to be purchased each month.

Actual computations are performed as follows:

Raw materials units to be used in production
= Units of finished goods to be produced
× Units of raw materials required for each unit of finished goods

Raw materials units to be purchased
= Raw materials units to be used in production
+ Desired raw materials ending inventory
− Raw materials beginning inventory

If we assign the unit cost of raw materials to the above units, we can compute the dollar amounts of raw materials to be used and to be purchased. The total cost of purchases will be used later to determine cash payments for purchases. Schedule 3 presents the direct materials budget for the first quarter, 19x7.

In a merchandising firm, neither the production budget nor the direct materials budget will be required since the firm does not purchase raw materials for production. It instead purchases finished goods. As a result, a purchases budget will be needed which would be very similar to the production budget in Schedule 2.

Schedule 3
Budget Stores, Inc.
Direct Materials Budget
For First Quarter, Year 7

	January	February	March	Total First Quarter
Required production (Schedule 2) ..	12,250	13,500	14,750	40,500
Pounds of direct material per unit of output	× 4	× 4	× 4	× 4
Direct materials needed for production (X)	49,000	54,000	59,000	162,000
Desired ending inventory of direct materials *	16,200	17,700	17,400	17,400
Total needs	65,200	71,700	76,400	179,400
Direct materials beginning inventory†	(14,700)	(16,200)	(17,700)	(14,700)
Required purchases (Y)	50,500	55,500	58,700	164,700
Cost per pound (Z)	× $0.50	× $0.50	× $0.50	× $0.50
Total cost of direct material purchases (Y x Z)	$25,250	$27,750	$29,350	$ 82,350
Total cost of direct materials needed for production (X x Z) ..	$24,500	$27,000	$29,500	$ 81,000

* 30% of the next month's production needs.

April production requirement

= Budgeted April sales of 14,000

+ Desired ending inventory (25% of May sales of 16,000 units)

− Beginning inventory (3,500 units)

= 14,000 units + 4,000 units − 3,500 units = 14,500 finished units.

Direct materials needed for April production

= 4 pounds x 14,500 = 58,000 pounds.

Thus, 30% of 58,000 pounds is 17,400 pounds.

† 30% of the current month's production requirements. Same as the ending inventory of the prior month.

The beginning inventory of the first quarter is the beginning inventory for January. The ending inventory of the first quarter is the ending inventory for March.

4. Direct Labor Budget

The **direct labor budget** simply shows the finished units to be produced, the number of direct labor hours required, and the total cost of the direct labor hours. Schedule 4 presents the direct labor budget for the first quarter of Year 7.

Schedule 4
Budget Stores, Inc.
Direct Labor Budget
For First Quarter, Year 7

	January	February	March	Total First Quarter
Required production (Schedule 2)	12,250	13,500	14,750	40,500
Direct labor hours per unit	× 2	× 2	× 2	× 2
Total hours needed	24,500	27,000	29,500	81,000
Direct labor cost per hour	× $8	× $8	× $8	× $8
Total direct labor cost	$196,000	$216,000	$236,000	$648,000

5. Manufacturing Overhead Budget

The **manufacturing overhead budget** includes all manufacturing costs other than the costs of direct materials and direct labor. If we list the overhead costs according to cost behavior, as variable and fixed, it would be more useful. Since depreciation does not require a cash outlay, it is subtracted from the total manufacturing overhead for use in preparing the cash disbursements schedule. Schedule 5 presents the manufacturing overhead budget for the first quarter, Year 7.

Schedule 5
Budget Stores, Inc.
Manufacturing Overhead Budget
For First Quarter, Year 7

	January	February	March	Total First Quarter
Budgeted direct labor cost (Schedule 4)	$196,000	$216,000	$236,000	$648,000
Variable overhead rate	× 50%	× 50%	× 50%	× 50%
Budgeted variable overhead	$ 98,000	$108,000	$118,000	$324,000
Budgeted fixed overhead:				
Supervisors' salaries	$ 20,000	$ 20,000	$ 20,000	$ 60,000
Factory rent	6,000	6,000	6,000	18,000
Factory insurance	600	600	600	1,800
Factory depreciation	400	400	400	1,200
Budgeted fixed overhead	27,000	27,000	27,000	81,000
Total manufacturing overhead	125,000	135,000	145,000	405,000
Depreciation expense	(400)	(400)	(400)	(1,200)
Cash disbursement for manufacturing overhead	$124,600	$134,600	$144,600	$403,800

6. **Cost of Sales and Ending Finished Goods Inventory Budgets**

It is preferable, though not necessary, to prepare a **cost of sales budget** to use in preparing the budgeted income statement and an **ending finished goods inventory budget** to use in preparing the budgeted balance sheet. Schedule 6 presents both for the first quarter of Year 7.

Schedule 6
Budget Stores, Inc.
Cost of Sales and Ending Finished Goods Inventory Budgets
For First Quarter, Year 7

Budgeted Cost of Production Per Unit	Quantity Required Per Finished Unit	Cost Per Unit	Total Cost
Direct materials (Schedule 3)	4 pounds	$0.50	$ 2.00
Direct labor (Schedule 4)	2 hours	8.00	16.00
Manufacturing overhead (Schedule 5)	2 hours	5.00*	10.00
Cost of sales per unit			$28.00
Budgeted cost of sales: 40,000 Units (Schedule 1) × $28 =			$1,120,000
Budgeted ending inventory: 3,500 Units (Schedule 2) × $28 =			$ 98,000

* Total manufacturing overhead (Schedule 5) ÷ Number of labor hours
(Schedule 4) = \$405,000 ÷ 81,000 hours = \$5.00.

7. **Selling and Administrative Expenses Budget**

The **selling and administrative expenses budget** includes all expenses other than manufacturing expenses. As in the manufacturing overhead budget, selling and administrative expenses are classified into variable and fixed expenses. Here too, we subtract depreciation expense (already calculated for you) from the total selling and administrative expenses for use in preparing the cash disbursements schedule. Schedule 7 presents the selling and administrative expenses budget for the first quarter of Year 7.

Schedule 7
Budget Stores, Inc.
Selling and Administrative Expenses Budget
First Quarter, Year 7

	January	February	March	Total First Quarter
Budgeted variable selling expenses:				
Freight (\$1 per unit sold)	\$ 12,000	\$ 13,000	\$ 15,000	\$ 40,000
Sales commission				
(at 5% of sales)	30,000	32,500	37,500	100,000
Total	42,000	45,500	52,500	140,000
Budgeted fixed selling and administrative expenses:				
Advertising	200	200	200	600
Salaries	2,500	2,500	2,500	7,500
Rent	300	300	300	900
Insurance	100	100	100	300
Depreciation (given)	6,000	10,000	10,000	26,000
Total	9,100	13,100	13,100	35,300
Total selling and				
administrative expenses	51,100	58,600	65,600	175,300
Depreciation expense	(6,000)	(10,000)	(10,000)	(26,000)
Cash disbursements for selling				
and administrative expenses ...	\$ 45,100	\$ 48,600	\$ 55,600	\$149,300

8. **Cash Receipts Schedule**

The **cash receipts schedule** includes cash sales, collections on credit sales, and other cash receipts from stock issuance, borrowing, dividends, interest, or rent income. For simplicity, the cash receipts schedule in Schedule 8 includes only cash sales and collections on credit sales.

Sony's $120 Million Budget for *Godzilla*

Preparing a cash budget for the block-buster movie, *Godzilla*, must have been a real challenge to the management accountants working for Sony. According to the Los Angeles-area news media reports in the spring of 1998, the movie's $120 million production budget was dwarfed by the $200 million committed to promoting the entire operation of the *Godzilla* project, which included marketing and sales of records, T-shirts, tickets to theme parks, spinoffs, etc. Sony dealt with a very unique forecasting problem: the marketing had to be done without showing the consumers what they were supposed to buy (the monster's face wasn't revealed until the movie's release).

Schedule 8
Budget Stores, Inc.
Cash Receipts Schedule
For First Quarter, Year 7

	January	February	March	Total First Quarter
Cash sales (Schedule 1)	$180,000	$195,000	$225,000	$ 600,000
Collections on credit sales:				
November, Year 6				
$385,000* × 60%	$231,000			$ 231,000
December, Year 6				
$350,000† × 40%, 60%	140,000	$210,000		350,000
January, Year 7				
$420,000 × 40%, 60%		168,000	$252,000	420,000
February, Year 7				
$455,000 × 40%			182,000	182,000
Total collections on credit sales	$371,000	$378,000	$434,000	$1,183,000
Total cash receipts	$551,000	$573,000	$659,000	$1,783,000

* 11,000 Units × $50 × 70% = $385,000
† 10,000 Units × $50 × 70% = $350,000

9. Cash Disbursements Schedule

Now that we have prepared the direct materials, direct labor, manufacturing overhead, and selling and administrative expenses budgets, we are ready to prepare a **cash disbursements schedule.** The schedule simply includes all budgeted cash payments from all of the above budgets, and other cash payments of interest or principal, taxes, dividends, or capital expenditures. For simplicity, we ignore dividends and income taxes here.

It was mentioned under financing policy that the company is scheduled to pay $300,000 of the long-term notes payable plus interest on the December 31, Year 6 balance for the first quarter of Year 7 at the rate of 12%. The borrowing and repayment of short-term debt plus interest thereon will be accounted for in the cash budget. Schedule 9 presents the cash disbursements schedule for the first quarter of Year 7.

Schedule 9
Budget Stores, Inc.
Cash Disbursements Schedule
For First Quarter, Year 7

	January	February	March	Total First Quarter
Payments for direct material purchases:				
December, Year 6 purchases	$ 15,190*			$ 15,190
January, Year 7 purchases				
$25,250† × 30%, 70%	7,575	$ 17,675		25,250
February, Year 7 purchases				
$27,750† × 30%, 70%		8,325	$19,425	27,750
March, Year 7 purchases				
$29,350† × 30%			8,805	8,805
Subtotal	22,765	26,000	28,230	76,995
Payments for direct labor (Schedule 4)	196,000	216,000	236,000	648,000
Payments for manufacturing overhead (Schedule 5)	124,600	134,600	144,600	403,800
Payments for selling and administrative expenses (Schedule 7)	45,100	48,600	55,600	149,300
Purchase of personal computers	250,000			250,000
Payment of long-term notes payable			300,000	300,000
Payment of interest on long-term notes payable			18,000‡	18,000
Total cash disbursements ...	$638,465	$425,200	$782,430	$1,846,095

* Given.
† Per Schedule 3.

‡ $600,000 × $\dfrac{12}{100}$ × $\dfrac{3}{12}$ = $18,000.

10. Cash Budget

The **cash budget** is a combination of the cash receipts schedule, the cash disbursements schedule, and any necessary short-term borrowings or repayments plus interest thereon. The cash budget indicates whether short-term borrowing will be necessary, in what month, and in what amount. Borrowing will be necessary in any month with anticipated cash deficiency. Repayment of borrowing will be possible in any month with anticipated excess cash. Cash deficiency will occur if the total of the beginning cash balance plus cash receipts is less than cash disbursements. Cash excess will occur if the opposite is true. The amount to borrow is equal to the cash deficiency plus the minimum cash balance desired.

A study of the cash budget in Schedule 10 indicates that cash disbursements in January will exceed the cash available (beginning cash balance plus January cash receipts) by $62,465. As a result, the company will have to borrow that amount plus the desired minimum cash balance of $20,000, or a total of $82,465. Since the bank requires borrowing to be made in multiples of $1,000, a short-term loan of $83,000 will be borrowed in January. The February cash receipts will exceed the cash disbursements by $168,335, and the company will be able to pay the $83,000 borrowed at the beginning of January plus the interest thereon at 12% for two months, January and February. Remember the payment is assumed to occur at the end of the month. In March, the company will have another cash deficiency of $39,755. It will borrow $60,000 to cover that deficiency plus the $20,000 minimum cash balance.

Schedule 10
Budget Stores, Inc.
Cash Budget
For First Quarter, Year 7

	January	February	March	Total First Quarter
Beginning cash balance*	$ 25,000	$ 20,535	$ 83,675	$ 25,000‡
Cash receipts (Schedule 8)	551,000	573,000	659,000	1,783,000
Total cash available	576,000	593,535	742,675	1,808,000
Cash disbursements (Schedule 9)	(638,465)	(425,200)	(782,430)	(1,846,095)
Excess (deficiency) of cash available over disbursement ...	(62,465)	168,335	(39,755)	(38,095)‡
Financing:				
Borrowing (at beginning) ...	83,000	—	60,000	143,000
Repayments (at end)	—	(83,000)	—	(83,000)
Interest on borrowing (at 12% per year)	-	(1,660)†	-	(1,660)
Total financing	83,000	(84,660)	60,000	58,340
Ending cash balance	$ 20,535	$ 83,675	$ 20,245	$ 20,245‡

* Ending cash balance of the prior month. January balance is from the 12/31/x6 balance sheet.

† $83,000 × 12% × 2/12 = $1,660.

‡ This amount does not equal the total of the three months because balances cannot be added across.

While the majority of firms prepare the cash budget on a monthly or quarterly basis, some firms prepare it for a shorter period. The cash budget is a very useful planning tool for the following two reasons:

First, it identifies, in advance, the month or months in which borrowing will be necessary and the amount of such borrowing. This information is critical for planning, since most banks require advance notice of such information and there will be lead time between the loan application and the use of the funds. Second, the cash budget preparation allows the company to select the appropriate timing of major capital expenditures. Let's take a look at schedules 9 and 10. Budget Stores, Inc. could have avoided the borrowing of $83,000 in January and paying the $1,660 interest on such borrowing by simply postponing the payment of $83,000 of the $250,000 purchase price of personal computers, if possible. The company could also consider purchasing computers in February.

11. Budgeted Income Statement

The **budgeted income statement** uses information from the sales budget, all expense-related budgets, the cash disbursements schedule, and the cash budget. The budgeted income statement indicates whether or not the company's operations will be profitable in the forthcoming period. Any budgeted operating profit or loss depends on the sales budget. Overestimated sales will yield higher operating profit. Assuming the sales forecasts are reasonable, the budgeted income statement may be used as a benchmark against which future operating performance may be measured.

Schedule 11 presents the budgeted income statement for Budget Stores, Inc. for the first quarter of Year 7.

Schedule 11
Budget Stores, Inc.
Budgeted Income Statement
For First Quarter, Year 7

Sales (Schedule 1)	$2,000,000
Cost of sales (Schedule 6)	1,120,000
Gross profit	880,000
Selling and administrative expenses (Schedule 7)	175,300
Operating income	704,700
Interest expense	20,260*
Net income	$ 684,440

* $18,000 (Schedule 9) + $1,660 (Schedule 10) + $600 interest on $60,000 borrowed at the beginning of March ($60,000 × 12% × 1/12) = $20,260.

12. Budgeted Balance Sheet

The **budgeted balance sheet** is prepared from the information presented in the schedules prepared above. For example, the budgeted cash balance at the end of the period is from the cash budget. The accounts receivable balance at

Zero-base budgeting, however, is cumbersome and time consuming, and in many cases, its benefits may not outweigh its costs. It is often introduced as part of a cost-cutting or reengineering exercise. Employees frequently feel threatened by zero-base budgeting since they (often rightly) perceive that this analysis increases the chances that their jobs will be cut or that they will be required to take on more duties. Some companies use it once every five years or so in order to avoid or reduce organizational inertia and bureaucracy.

BUDGETING IN THE NEW PRODUCTION ENVIRONMENT

The implicit assumption we made in our discussion of estimated production in this chapter was that we operate in a **mass-production** environment. A mass-producer's budgeting process starts with the product demand forecast. All other budgets depend, more or less, on the sales budget. In algebraic form, the production requirement is calculated as follows:

Production requirement (in mass-production)

= Sales forecast + desired ending inventory − beginning inventory

In such a system, the reliability of the whole cycle of operations and budgets depends heavily on the accuracy of the demand forecast. If the demand forecast is greater than actual demand, the manufacturer will produce more than necessary. This will leave excess inventories in storage. If the demand forecast is smaller than actual demand, the manufacturer produced less than needed. Stockouts result, and contribution margins are lost.

When a manufacturer becomes a **lean producer** in the new manufacturing environment, it manufactures based on actual demand, not based on demand forecast. It may seem impossible to accomplish this. How can a company plan manufacturing in such a way? We will discuss this in more detail in Chapter 10.

SUMMARY

This chapter introduced an overview of budgeting and the budget process. A budget is a formal written plan of what is expected from every function, activity, individual, or a department in an organization. The process of comparing actual performance to the budget and taking the necessary actions to correct deviations (particularly those that are unfavorable) from the budget is known as budgetary control.

The master budget represents a network of interrelationships among all operating, financial and investments budgets. It is usually prepared for one year but is broken down into months or quarters. The most important part of the master budget is the sales budget because all other budgets depend on the sales budget in one way or another. The chapter presented an illustration of how all schedules of the master budget are prepared. A review and an understanding of all these schedules should be considered an integral part of this summary.

The matter of human relations in budgeting is extremely important. This requires that top management gives its whole-hearted support to the budgeting system and that middle management and employees actively participate in the budget preparation and be convinced that the budgeting system is intended to achieve the organization's goals through helping each one of them achieve better performance and better rewards. This also requires that expense budgets be looked at as providing an outline of available resources and not a restriction on managers' freedom of action.

BASIC CONCEPTS AND TERMS

Budget	Direct Materials Budget
Budget Committee	Ending Finished Goods
Budgetary Control	Inventory Budget
Budgeted Balance Sheet	Financial Budgets
Budgeted Income Statement	Flexible Budgets
Budgeted Statement of Cash Flows	Manufacturing Overhead Budget
Budgeting and Human Relations	Master Budget
Capital Budgets	Operating Budgets
Capital Investment Budgets	Production Budget
Cash Budget	Profit Planning
Cash Disbursements Schedule	Sales Budget
Cash Excess or Deficiency	Sales Forecasting
Cash Receipts Schedule	Selling and Administrative
Continuous or Perpetual Budget	Expense Budget
Cost of Sales Budget	Zero-Base Budgeting
Direct Labor Budget	

■ SELF-REVIEW PROBLEM

Ship-Laptops, Inc. is a manufacturer of a new type of reusable plastic case used to package lap-top computers. The following information pertains to sales forecasts and other operating data for the next year, Year 5, and for the first two quarters of Year 6:

a.   The price of plastic case is $35 per unit. Budgeted sales in units for the six quarters follow:

	Year 5				Year 6	
Quarter	1	2	3	4	1	2
Budgeted sales (in units)	2,000	3,000	4,500	2,500	3,500	4,000

b. Estimated collections from sales: 80% in the quarter the sales are made, and 20% in the following quarter. The accounts receivable balance as of January 1, Year 5 was $15,000. The company's customers are carefully screened, and bad debts are almost zero.

c. Required finished goods inventory on hand: 25% of the expected sales for the following quarter should be in stock at the end of each quarter. This requirement was met as of December 31, Year 4.

d. Raw materials requirement for production: Three pounds (costing $1.50 per pound) of plastics per unit of finished product are required.

e. Required raw materials inventory on hand: 10% of the expected usage of the following quarter should be in stock at the end of each quarter. This requirement was met as of December 31, Year 4.

f. Estimated payments for raw material purchases: 70% in the quarter the purchases are made, and 30% in the following quarter. The accounts payable balance as of January 1, Year 5 was $3,240 for raw material purchases.

Required:

For each of the four quarters and the year, Year 5, prepare the following:

1. A sales budget.
2. A schedule of expected cash collections.
3. A production budget. You may need to include part of Year 6 in the process.
4. A direct materials budget. You may need to include part of Year 6 here also.
5. A schedule of expected cash payments for raw material purchases.

Solution

1. The sales budget shows units sold and dollar amounts of sales as follows:

| | Year 5 Quarter | | | | Year 5 |
	1st	2nd	3rd	4th	Total
Budgeted sales in units	2,000	3,000	4,500	2,500	12,000
Selling price per unit	$35	$35	$35	$35	$35
Budgeted sales	$70,000	$105,000	$157,500	$87,500	$420,000

2. The schedule of expected cash collections shows a part of the cash receipts schedule, and would be prepared as follows:

| | Year 5 Quarter | | | | Year 5 |
	1st	2nd	3rd	4th	Total
Accounts receivable, 1/1/x5	$15,000				$ 15,000
Sales and collections:					
1st Q. $ 70,000 × 80%, 20%	56,000	$14,000			70,000
2nd Q. $105,000 × 80%, 20%		84,000	$ 21,000		105,000
3rd Q. $157,500 × 80%, 20%			126,000	$ 31,500	157,500
4th Q. $ 87,500 × 80%				70,000	70,000
Total cash collections	$71,000	$98,000	$147,000	$101,500	$417,500

3. The production budget would be prepared based on the budgeted sales in units as follows:

(In units)	Year 5 Quarter				Year 5 Total	Year 6 Qtr. 1st
	1st	2nd	3rd	4th		
Budgeted sales	2,000	3,000	4,500	2,500	12,000	3,500
Desired ending inventory*	750	1,125	625	875	875	1,000
Total needs	2,750	4,125	5,125	3,375	12,875	4,500
Beginning inventory†	(500)	(750)	(1,125)	(625)	(500)	(875)
Required production	2,250	3,375	4,000	2,750	12,375	3,625

* 25% of the budgeted sales units for the following quarter.
† 25% of the budgeted sales units of the current quarter.

4. The direct materials budget shows quantity and costs of raw materials to be used in production and to be purchased, and would be prepared as follows:

	Year 5 Quarter				Year 5 Total	Year 6 Qtr. 1st
	1st	2nd	3rd	4th		
Required production	2,250	3,375	4,000	2,750	12,375	3,625
Pounds of direct material per unit of output	× 3	× 3	× 3	× 3	× 3	× 3
Production materials needed (X)	6,750	10,125	12,000	8,250	37,125	10,875
Desired materials ending inventory*	1,013	1,200	825	1,088	1,088	
Total needs	7,763	11,325	12,825	9,338	38,213	
Beginning inventory † ...	(675)	(1,013)	(1,200)	(825)	(675)	
Required direct material purchases (Y)	7,088	10,312	11,625	8,513	37,538	
Cost per pound of direct material (Z)	× $1.50	× $1.50	× $1.50	× $1.50	× $1.50	
Total cost of direct material purchases	$10,631	$15,469	$17,438	$12,769	$56,306	(Y × Z)
Total cost of direct materials needed for production	$10,125	$15,188	$18,000	$12,375	$55,688	(X × Z)

* 10% of the expected usage of the following quarter.
† 10% of the expected usage of the current quarter. The beginning inventory of the first quarter is the beginning inventory of the year.

5. A schedule of expected cash payments for raw material purchases is a part of cash disbursements schedule, and would be prepared based on the raw material purchases above.

| | Year 5 Quarter | | | | Year 5 |
	1st	2nd	3rd	4th	Total
Accounts payable, 1/1/x5	$ 3,240				$ 3,240
Material purchases:					
1st Q. $10,631 × 70%, 30%	7,442	$ 3,189			10,631
2nd Q. $15,469 × 70%, 30%		10,828	$ 4,641		15,469
3rd Q. $17,438 × 70%, 30%			12,207	$ 5,231	17,438
4th Q. $12,769 × 70%				8,938	8,938
Total cash disbursements	$10,682	$14,017	$16,848	$14,169	$55,716

■ REVIEW QUESTIONS

8-1 Differentiate between a budget, budgeting, and a budgetary control system.

8-2 Can a budgeting system be applied in a not-for-profit organization? Explain.

8-3 Why is budgeted performance, rather than past performance, more appropriate in evaluating actual performance?

8-4 Discuss the advantages of budgeting.

8-5 List the major types of budgets.

8-6 What are the major functions of a budget department or committee?

8-7 Why is sales forecasting important in a successful budgeting system? What factors enter into sales forecasting?

8-8 What is the difference between sales forecasting and a sales budget?

8-9 What are the incentives for sales managers to forecast sales accurately?

8-10 What is a master budget? Are the contents of a master budget the same in every organization?

8-11 Give two important factors that enter into the preparation of each of the following budgets:
  a. Sales budget
  b. Production budget
  c. Direct labor budget
  d. Cash receipts budget
  e. Cash disbursements budget

8-12 In what way can the cash budget assist management in planning its investments and financing policies?

8-13 Why are human relations important in budgeting?

8-14 What is zero-base budgeting and what are its advantages and disadvantages?

8-15 Why is product demand forecast so important in a mass-production environment?

8-16 Does a lean producer manufacture based on forecast also?

⊕ INTERNET PROJECT

Web 8-1:

Websites: www.circuitcity.com
www.bestbuy.com

The websites listed above represent two famous companies. Search the sites for information on their operating characteristics.

Required:

1.   Do you find any signs of successful budgeting for the companies? Why? Why not?

2.   Which budgets of the companies would be related to long-term investment projects?

Web 8-2:

Websites: www.msdw.com
www.ml.com

The websites listed above represent two famous companies. Search the sites for information on their operating characteristics.

Required:

1.   If zero-base budgeting is introduced to a particular business segment, where would you apply that first? Why?

2.   Who would object to the introduction of zero-base budgeting the most? Why?

■ EXERCISES

E8-1   Budgeting Process

A listing of various budgets is presented below. Rearrange the budgets according to the order of preparation so that "1" is assigned to the first budget that should be prepared, and so forth.

a. ___ Production budget
b. ___ Cost of goods sold budget
c. ___ Direct materials budget
d. ___ Budgeted balance sheet
e. ___ Cash budget
f. ___ Sales budget

E8-2   Types of Budgets

Assign each of the budgets listed below (a-g) to one of the following types:

(1) Operating budget
(2) Financial budget
(3) Capital budget
(4) Flexible budget

a. Cash budget
b. Production budget
c. Long-term investment budget
d. Purchase budget
e. Actual level of activity achieved shown with various planned levels of activity
f. Budgeted balance sheet
g. Budgeted income statement

E8-3   Budgeted Sales and Collections

PLR, Inc. makes electromechanical crash sensors for car airbag systems. The sales show seasonal fluctuations that follow automakers' manufacturing patterns. Actual and budgeted sales for a part of Year 5 are presented below:

Month	Actual Sales	Budgeted Sales
May	$190,000	
June	210,000	
July		$240,000
August		400,000
September		180,000

The company has experienced the following pattern of receivables collections:

Percentage	Collected in
30%	the month of sale
50%	the month following sale
20%	the second month following sale
100%	

Required:

1. Present a schedule of budgeted collections for the third quarter (July, August, and September).
2. What will be the balance of receivables at September 30?

E8-4   Production Budget

TLC, Inc. is preparing a production budget for the third quarter of Year 7. The company maintains as its ending inventory an amount equal to 20% of the following month's sales. This requirement was met at the end of June also. The budgeted sales for July through October are presented below:

Month	Budgeted Sales
July	40,000
August	62,000
September	70,000
October	65,000

Required:

Present a production budget for the third quarter, showing the monthly production requirements in units and the total for the quarter.

E8-5   Direct Materials Budget

SKS, Inc. makes portable chess tables. Each table requires four units of plastics as material. The table production budget provides the following quarterly (Q1-Q4) information on units to produce:

		Year 2			Year 3
	Q1	Q2	Q3	Q4	Q1
Tables to produce	24,000	35,000	58,000	41,000	30,000

The cost of the plastics is $0.80 per unit. Since the demand for the tables fluctuates significantly, the company wants to maintain an equivalent of 25% of the following quarter's plastics needs to make sure that the materials are available. The beginning inventory of plastics of Year 2 is 24,000 units.

Required:

Present a materials budget for plastics, showing material purchases for each of the four quarters and the total for the year.

E8-6   Cash Budget

The information needed to prepare a company's cash budget for June of Year 5 is presented below:

a.   Actual and budgeted sales:

	Actual		Budgeted
	April	May	June
Cash sales	$ 25,000	$ 27,000	$ 32,000
Credit sales	150,000	210,000	250,000

Credit sales collection pattern:

Percentage	Collected in
30%	the month of sale
50%	the month following sale
15%	the second month following sale
95%	

The remaining 5% balance is uncollectible.

b. May inventory purchases amounted to $150,000. June inventory purchases are budgeted to be $110,000. Payment policy on purchases:

Percentage	Paid in
40%	the month of purchase
60%	the month following purchase
100%	

c. Other cash purchases and cash expenditures budgeted for June:

Plant equipment purchases	$30,000
Operating expenses	160,000
(Depreciation included in operating expenses is $25,000.)	
Dividends to be paid	4,000

d. The ending cash balance on May 31 is $15,000. The minimum cash balance required at all times is $10,000. Ignore interest on the borrowing, if there is a need for borrowing.

Required:

1. Present a cash receipts schedule for June.
2. Determine the amount of payment for inventory purchases to be made in June.
3. Present a cash disbursements schedule for June.
4. Present a cash budget for June.

E8-7   Sales and Budgeted Cash Collections

PLM Company's sales peak in June of each year for a seasonal product. The product's budgeted sales for the second quarter of this year are:

	April	May	June	Quarter Total
Budgeted sales	$60,000	$70,000	$80,000	$210,000

The cash collection pattern is:

- 60% in month of sale
- 30% in month following sale
- 7% in second month following sale
- 3% uncollectible

On March 31 this year, the accounts receivable balance is $23,000, which includes $5,000 of uncollected February sales and $18,000 of uncollected March sales. For payments made by customers during the month of sale, the company gives a 2% cash discount.

Required:

1. Compute the total sales for February and March separately.
2. Present a schedule of budgeted cash collections on credit sales, by month and in total for the second quarter.

E8-8 Cash Collections; Profit Plan

Birch Construction has the following historical pattern on its credit sales:

> 70% collected in month of sale.
> 15% collected in the first month after sale.
> 10% collected in the second month after sale.
> 4% collected in the third month after sale.
> 1% uncollectible.

The sales on open account have been budgeted for the first six months of Year 5 as shown below:

Month	Sales on Open Account
January	$ 70,000
February	90,000
March	100,000
April	120,000
May	100,000
June	90,000

Required:

1. Determine the estimated total cash collections during April from accounts receivable.
2. Compute the estimated total cash collections during the second quarter from the second-quarter sales.
3. One of the following is the foundation of a profit plan. Which one is it?
   a. capital budget.
   b. sales forecast.
   c. cost and expense budget.
   d. production plan.
   e. projected inventory turnover.

(CMA, adapted)

■ PROBLEMS

P8-9 Ethics in Budgeting

Nancy Corless is controller of JTW, Inc., a division of Trans-World International, a large business group, located in Atlanta. JTW manufactures snowmobiles and all-terrain vehicles (ATVs). The sales of ATV's have been growing at a phenomenal rate of about 30% each year for the last three years.

The company is expanding its distribution system this year and is planning on increasing its sales next year by 40%. All managers have agreed that this is a reasonable growth expectation, and are excited about the future. The sales forecast has allowed the manufacturing department to plan on expanding its capacity, and the vice president-manufacturing is particularly happy about the prospect of seeing his area expand and hire more people.

On Friday last week, Nancy was having lunch with Robert Jump, division president, who has been her close friend since the college days. Robert asked Nancy if she could adjust the next year's expected sales increase upwards to 60% from the already agreed 40%. "The recent increases have been about 30% per year, and we are expanding our distribution system this year. That would make our sales jump considerably. I believe our 40% projection is too conservative," Robert said.

Nancy knows that Robert is being considered for a top executive position at a large company in Florida, and the higher sales forecast would make him look even more impressive to the board of directors of the potential new employer. Since the "60% increase" scenario has already been suggested as a possibility, albeit not as a highly probable outcome, at the meeting of vice presidents, Nancy could talk to vice president-sales about changing the forecast and budget. The situation, however, is making Nancy think again about the whole budgeting process and other things also.

Required:

Explain what Nancy Corless has to do at this point as controller, considering professional ethics.

 P8-10   Production Budget and Materials Budget

Tijuana Manufacturing Company makes various packaging items and sells them to shipping companies. One of the manufactured items is called TJ Box. The production of each unit of TJ Box requires 4 units of a material called Caper.

The company is preparing a production budget and a materials budget for the third quarter of Year 4. The monthly sales forecasts in units of TJ Box for the second half of Year 4 are as follows:

July	August	September	October	November	December
5,000	8,000	12,000	10,000	8,000	7,000

The company maintains a TJ Box ending inventory that is equivalent to 20% of the forecasted sales for the following month. All units of TJ Box that are started in each month are completed in the same month. The company carries a Caper ending inventory that is equivalent to 10% of the following month's material needs. The July 1 inventories of TJ Box and Caper meet the 20% and 10% requirements, respectively.

Required:

1. Present a TJ Box production budget for the third quarter of Year 4, showing the monthly units to be produced and the total for the quarter.

2. Present a materials budget for Caper for the third quarter of Year 4, showing the monthly units to be purchased and the total for the quarter.

P8-11 Production Budget; Material Purchase Budget

One of the products of THC, Inc. is a special pencil, called C-Pencil, which is used for corrective makeup. The company is preparing production and materials purchase budgets for the first quarter of Year 5.

The budgeted sales in units of C-Pencil for the first 6 months of Year 5 are presented below:

First quarter:

| January | 30,000 | February | 38,000 | March | 45,000 |

Second quarter:

| April | 26,000 | May | 13,000 | June | 11,000 |

Inventory information:

The ending inventory of C-Pencil consists of the basic level of 2,000 units plus 10% of the following month's expected sales. The expected C-Pencil inventory on January 1 is 5,000 units. There is no beginning or ending work in process.

Each unit of C-Pencil requires 4 units of material W. The ending inventory of material W in each month is the equivalent of 30% of the following month's material needs. The expected material W inventory on January 1 is 40,000 units.

Required:

1. Present a production budget for C-Pencil for January, February, March, and April of Year 5.
2. Present a materials budget for the first quarter of Year 5, showing the units of material W to be purchased in January, February, and March, and the total for the quarter.

P8-12 Cash Budget

The data needed to prepare Closter Company's cash budget for the second quarter are presented below.

a. Sales data:

Month	Actual Sales	Budgeted Sales
February	$240,000	
March	290,000	
April		380,000
May		570,000
June		300,000

b. Collection on sales:

Percentage   *Collected in*
30%   the month of sale
60%   the month following sale
 5%   the second month following sale
95%

The remaining 5% balance is uncollectible.

c. Expected merchandise purchases:

April $220,000   May $280,000   June $180,000

100% of the merchandise purchases are paid in the month following purchase. The March merchandise purchase was $200,000.

d. Budgeted expenses for the second quarter:

	April	May	June
Office expenses.	$ 40,000	$ 52,000	$41,000
Depreciation	15,000	15,000	15,000
Salaries.	100,000	120,000	90,000
Office rent	10,000	10,000	10,000

Computers will be purchased for $20,000 in cash in April.

e. The cash balance on April 1 is expected to be $45,000. The company is expected to borrow a short-term loan of $38,500 on April 1. The interest payment of $1,000 will be made at the time the loan is repaid. The loan will be repaid on June 30, if possible. A minimum cash balance of $10,000 is to be maintained at the end of every month.

Required:

1. Present a schedule of budgeted cash receipts for the second quarter, showing cash collections for April, May, and June, and the total for the quarter.
2. Present a cash budget for the second quarter, showing the monthly amounts and the total for the quarter.

 P8-13   Preparing a Master Budget

Fargo Company is preparing various budgets for July, Year 2. On June 30, Year 2, Fargo Company presented the following balance sheet:

Fargo Company
Balance Sheet
June 30, Year 2

Assets:

Cash	$ 10,000
Accounts receivable	60,000
Inventory	40,000
Plant and equipment, net	130,000
Total assets	$240,000

Liabilities and Stockholders' Equity:

Accounts payable	$ 70,000
Note payable	15,000
Capital stock	140,000
Retained earnings	15,000
Total liabilities and equity	$240,000

Other data items:

a. Budgeted sales for July:

Cash sales	$ 70,000
Credit sales	112,500

b. Collections on credit sales:

Percentage	Collected in
40%	the month of sale
60%	the month following sale
100%	

c. Expected July inventory purchases amount to $100,000. The July 31 inventory balance is expected to be $30,000. Payment policy on purchases:

Percentage	Paid in
30%	the month of purchase
70%	the month following purchase
100%	

d. The June 30 balance of note payable will be paid during July. The July interest to be paid on the note payable will be $150.

e. Cash operating expenses for July will be $60,000. The July depreciation is expected at $1,200.

f. A new computer will be purchased for $5,900 cash during July.

g. New borrowing from the company's bank will be $10,000 during July. A one-year note will be given to the bank for the amount. No interest will be paid in July on this note.

Required:

1. Present a schedule of budgeted cash collections on sales for July.
2. Present a schedule of budgeted cash payments for July.
3. Present a cash budget for July. For those items appearing in the above two schedules, just show the total receipts and the total disbursements.
4. Present a budgeted income statement for July.
5. Present a budgeted balance sheet as of July 31, Year 2.

P8-14   Sales Budget, Production Budget, and Materials Budget

Pitzer Company produces a disc that is sold at $15 per unit to companies in the metal-working industry. The company is in the process of preparing budgets for the second quarter. The following information is related to the budget preparation:

a.   Budgeted disc sales in units:

Second quarter:

| April | 40,000 | May | 60,000 | June | 54,000 |

Third quarter:

| July | 30,000 | August | 20,000 | September | 18,000 |

Actual dollar sales for March totaled $420,000.

b.   Collections on credit sales:

Percentage	Collected in
40%	the month of sale
55%	the month following sale
95%	

There are no cash sales. The remaining 5% are uncollectible.

c.   Payment policy on purchases of materials:

Percentage	Paid in
60%	the month of purchase
40%	the month following purchase
100%	

The accounts payable on April 1 for March material purchases will be $43,008. The material purchase cost is $1 per unit. The production of each disc requires three units of material.

d.   Desired disc ending inventory:
    20% of the following month's sales.
Desired materials ending inventory:
    40% of the following month's production needs.

Both requirements were met on March 31.

Required:

1.   Present a sales budget for the second quarter, showing units and dollars by month and in total for the quarter.
2.   Present a schedule of budgeted cash receipts, by month and in total for the second quarter.
3.   Present a disc production budget for April, May, June, and July.
4.   Present a materials budget for the second quarter, showing units and dollars by month and in total for the quarter.
5.   Present a schedule of budgeted cash payments for material purchases, by month and in total for the second quarter.

P8-15 Budgeted Cash Collections; Billing Practice

TPZ, Inc. is a retailer whose sales are all made on credit. Sales are billed twice monthly, on the 10th of the month for the last half of the prior month's sales and on the 20th of the month for the first half of the current month's sales. The terms of all sales are 2/10, net 30. Based upon past experience, the collection experience of accounts receivable is as follows:

Within the discount period	80%
On the 30th day	18%
Uncollectible	2%

The sales value of shipments for May and the forecasts for the next four months are:

May (actual)	$500,000
June	600,000
July.......................................	700,000
August	700,000
September..................................	400,000

The average markup on the products is 20% of the sale price. The company purchases merchandise for resale to meet the current month's sales demand and to maintain a desired monthly ending inventory of 25% of the next month's sales. All purchases are on credit with terms of net 30. The company pays for one half of a month's purchases in the month of purchase and the other half in the month following the purchase. All sales and purchases occur uniformly throughout the month.

Required:

1. How much cash can the company plan to collect from accounts receivable during July?
2. How much cash can the company plan to collect in September from sales made in August?
3. The budgeted dollar value of the inventory on August 31 will be _____.
4. How much merchandise should the company plan to purchase during June?
5. The amount the company should budget in August for the payment of merchandise is _____.

(CMA, adapted)

P8-16 Cash Budget and Related Schedules

RDN Company is a wholesaler of do-it-yourself home improvement goods. It has been successful with innovative business practices. One such example is life-size tableaux that show small-town retailers how the new improvement would actually look upon completion. In order to determine when the company needs financing, the company is in the process of preparing a cash budget for Year 4. The following information has been gathered for that purpose:

a. Actual sales of the last quarter of Year 3 amounted to $300,000. During the same period, actual purchases were made in the amount of $190,000.

b. Budgeted quarterly sales and purchases for Year 4 are:

	Budgeted Sales	Budgeted Purchases
First quarter	$495,000	$270,000
Second quarter.	580,000	300,000
Third quarter	730,000	440,000
Fourth quarter	300,000	180,000

c. Collections on credit sales:

Percentage	Collected in
60%	the quarter of sale
35%	the quarter following sale
95%	

There are no cash sales. The remaining 5% are uncollectible.

d. Payment policy on merchandise purchases:

Percentage	Paid in
70%	the quarter of purchase
30%	the quarter following purchase
100%	

e. Quarterly operating expenses:

Variable expenses	20% of sales
Fixed expenses	$70,000
(including depreciation of $30,000)	

f. Other cash expenditures:

	Quarter			
	1	2	3	4
Equipment purchases	–	$90,000	$70,000	–
Others	$15,000	15,000	15,000	$15,000

g. Financing:
The minimum cash balance of $15,000 should be maintained. This requirement was met at the end of the last quarter of Year 3. Borrowings (repayments) will be made at the beginning (end) of a quarter, if there is such need, in multiples of $1,000. Interest will be paid when the principal is repaid at the rate of 12% per year.

Required:

1. Present a schedule of budgeted cash receipts, by quarter and in total for Year 4.
2. Present a schedule of budgeted cash payments for merchandise purchases, by quarter and in total for Year 4.
3. Present a cash budget, by quarter and in total for Year 4.

P8-17   Annual Budget Development

Blue Trail Company has sales in the range of $25 to $30 million, has one manufacturing plant, and employs 700 people, including 15 national account salesmen and 80 traveling sales representatives. The home office and plant is in Philadelphia, and the product is distributed east of the Mississippi River. The product is a line of pumps and related fittings used at construction sites, in homes, and in processing plants. The company has total assets equal to 80% of sales. Its capitalization is: accruals and current liabilities, 30%; long-term debt, 15%; and shareholders' equity, 55%. In the last two years, sales have increased 7% each year, and income after tax has amounted to 5% of sales.

Required:

1. Strategic decisions by top management on a number of important topics serve as a basis for the annual profit plan. Those topics include: the overall objectives of the firm; the markets served; the channels of distribution utilized; the form of organization structure; the basic financial structure employed; and the intensity of research and development planned. Why are they important?
2. What specific procedures will be followed each year in developing the annual profit plan?

(CMA, adapted)

 ## P8-18   Master Budget

HUT, Inc. is in the process of preparing its master budget for the second quarter. The account balances as of March 31 are given below:

	Debits	Credits
Cash..................................	$ 32,000	
Accounts receivable..................	126,000	
Inventory	44,550	
Plant and equipment	246,000	
Accounts payable....................		$ 62,000
Capital stock		313,550
Retained earnings....................		73,000
	$448,550	$448,550

During March, the actual sales were $180,000. The following sales are budgeted for the next four months:

April	$270,000
May..	420,000
June	200,000
July..	150,000

The following data have been compiled for the master budget preparation:

a. Of all monthly sales, 30% are cash sales and 70% are credit sales. All credit sales made in one month are collected in cash in the following month.

b. Desired ending inventory of merchandise is 30% of the cost of the following month's expected sales.

c. The company's gross margin ratio is 45% of sales.

d. Payment policy on merchandise purchases:

Percentage	Paid in
40%	the month of purchase
60%	the month following purchase
100%	

e. Monthly operating expenses:

Office expenses	$18,000
Wages and salaries	48,000
Depreciation.............................	10,000
Selling expenses	8% of sales
Other expenses	5% of sales

f. Other cash expenditures:

Purchase of new printers in May................	$1,500
Purchase of other equipment in June............	56,000
Payment of dividends made in April.............	30,000

g. The company maintains a minimum cash balance of $20,000. Borrowings will be made at the beginning of the quarter, and repayments will be made at the end of the quarter, in multiples of $1,000. The interest rate is 12% per year. Interest will be paid when the principal is repaid.

Required:

1. Present a schedule of budgeted cash receipts, by month and in total for the second quarter.

2. Present a merchandise purchases budget in the following format:

	April	May	June	Quarter Total
Budgeted cost of sales				
Desired ending inventory				
Total needs				
Beginning inventory				
Purchase requirement				

3. Present the following schedules, by month and in total for the second quarter:
   a. Cash payments for merchandise purchases
   b. Cash operating expenses

4. Present a cash budget, by month and in total for the second quarter.

5. Present a budgeted income statement for the second quarter.

6. Present a budgeted balance sheet as of June 30.

P8-19 Production Budget, Direct Materials Budget, and Direct Labor Budget

C Division of Seed Corporation produces an intricate component part used in Seed's major product line. The division manager has been concerned recently by a lack of coordination between purchasing and production personnel and believes that a monthly budgeting process would improve the system.

C Division manager has decided to develop budget information for the third quarter of the current year as a trial before the budget system is implemented for an entire fiscal year. In response to the division manager's request for data which could be used to develop budget information, the division controller accumulated the following data:

Sales

Sales through June 30, the first six months of the current year, are 24,000 units. Actual sales in units for May and June and estimated unit sales for the next four months are detailed as follows:

May (actual).....................................	4,000
June (actual)	4,000
July (estimated)................................	5,000
August (estimated).............................	6,000
September (estimated)	7,000
October (estimated)...........................	7,000

C Division expects to sell 60,000 units during the year ending December 31.

Direct Labor

Data regarding the materials used in the component are shown in the schedule below. The desired monthly ending inventory for all direct materials is to have sufficient materials on hand to produce the next month's estimated sales.

Direct Material	Units of Direct Materials per Finished Component	Cost per unit	Inventory Level June 30
#201..........	6	$2.40	35,000 units
#252..........	4	3.60	30,000 units
#303..........	2	1.20	14,000 units

Direct Labor

Each component must pass through three different processes to be completed. Data regarding the direct labor is presented below:

Process	Direct Labor-Hours per Finished Component	Cost per Direct Labor-Hour
Forming..........	.80	$8.00
Assembly........	2.00	5.50
Finishing........	.25	6.00

Finished Goods Inventory

The desired monthly ending inventory in units of completed components is 80% of the next month's estimated sales. There are 5,000 finished units in the inventory on June 30.

Required:

1. Prepare a production budget in units for C Division for the third quarter ending September 30.
2. Without prejudice to your answer in requirement 1, assume that C Division plans to produce 18,000 units during the third quarter ending September 30, and 60,000 units for the year ending December 31.
   (a) Prepare a direct materials purchase budget in units and dollars for the third quarter ending September 30.
   (b) Prepare a direct labor budget in hours and dollars for the third quarter ending September 30.

(CMA, adapted)

P8-20   Cash Budget

School Supplies, Inc. sells academic goods. The sales are highly seasonal, and peak sales occur during August when "back to school" sales take place. The company is in the process of preparing a cash budget for the upcoming third quarter, and has gathered the following information:

a. Actual and budgeted sales:

	Actual			Budgeted	
May	June	July	August	September	October
$300,000	$400,000	$510,000	$720,000	$475,000	$320,000

b. Gross margin ratio is 35% of sales. This applies to every month.
c. Cash sales are 30% and credit sales are 70% of all monthly sales.
d. Credit sales collection pattern:

Percentage	Collected in
20%	the month of sale
50%	the month following sale
30%	the second month following sale
100%	

e. Merchandise inventory at the end of each month should be equal to 20% of the merchandise to be sold in the following month. The ending inventories of merchandise are: $52,000 for May, and $66,300 for June.
f. Fifty percent of a month's merchandise purchases are paid for in the month of purchase, and the other 50% are paid in the month following purchase.
g. Administrative expenses, which include depreciation expense of $15,000 each month, are budgeted as follows for the next four months:

July	August	September	October
$55,800	$72,600	$53,000	$40,600

h. Each month's selling expenses are 15% of the month's sales.
i. Cash bonuses of $75,000 will be paid in July.
j. Computers will be purchased for $26,000 in cash during August.
k. The company maintains a minimum cash balance of $30,000 at the end of each month. The June 30 cash balance is $41,000. Borrowings are made at the beginning of a month and repayments are made at the end of a month, in multiples of $1,000. The interest rate is 12% per year.

Required:

1. Present a schedule of budgeted cash receipts for the third quarter, by month and for the quarter in total.
2. Present a merchandise purchases budget, by month and for the quarter in total in the following format:

	July	August	September	Quarter Total
Budgeted cost of sales.....				
Desired ending inventory ..				
Total needs..............				
Beginning inventory.......				
To be purchased..........				

3. What is the accounts payable balance at June 30 for merchandise purchases made during June?
4. Present a schedule of budgeted cash payments for merchandise purchases, by month and for the quarter in total.
5. Present a cash budget for the third quarter, showing amounts by month and for the quarter in total.

P8-21 Cash Budget

Alpha-Tech, a rapidly growing distributor of electronic components, is formulating its plans for Year 5. Carol Jones, the firm's marketing director, has completed the sales forecast presented below.

Alpha-Tech
Year 5 Forecasted Sales
(in thousands)

Month	Sales	Month	Sales
January	$ 9,000	July	$15,000
February	10,000	August	15,000
March	9,000	September	16,000
April	11,500	October	16,000
May	12,500	November	15,000
June	14,000	December	17,000

Phillip Smith, an accountant in the Planning and Budgeting Department, is responsible for preparing the cash flow projection. The following information will be used in preparing the cash flow projection.

a. Alpha-Tech's excellent record in accounts receivable collection is expected to continue. Sixty percent of billings are collected the month after the sale and the remaining 40% two months after.

b. The purchase of electronic components is Alpha-Tech's largest expenditure and is estimated to be 40% of sales. Seventy percent of the parts are received by Alpha-Tech one month prior to sale and 30% are received during the month of sale.

c. Historically, 75% of accounts payable have been paid one month after receipt of the purchased components, and the remaining 25% is paid two months after receipt.

d. Hourly wages and fringe benefits, estimated to be 30% of the current month's sales, are paid in the month incurred.

e. General and administrative expenses are projected to be $15,620,000 for the year. The breakdown of these expenses is presented below. All expenditures are paid uniformly throughout the year, except the property taxes which are paid at the end of each quarter in four equal installments.

Year 5 Forecasted General and Administrative Costs
(in thousands)

Sales and fringe benefits	$ 3,200
Promotion	3,800
Property taxes	1,360
Insurance	2,000
Utilities	1,800
Depreciation	3,460
Total	$15,620

f. Income tax payments are made at the beginning of each calendar quarter based on the income of the prior quarter. Alpha-Tech is subject to an effective income tax rate of 40%. Alpha-Tech's operating income for the first quarter of Year 5 is projected to be $3,200,000.

g. Alpha-Tech maintains a minimum cash balance of $500,000. If the cash balance is less than $500,000 at the end of each month, the company borrows amounts necessary to maintain this balance. All amounts borrowed are repaid out of subsequent positive cash flow. The projected April 1, Year 5 opening balance is $500,000.

h. Alpha-Tech has no short-term debt as of April 1, Year 5.

i. Alpha-Tech uses a calendar year for both financial reporting and tax purposes.

Required:

1. Prepare a cash budget for Alpha-Tech by month for the second quarter of Year 5. Ignore any interest expense associated with borrowing.

2. Discuss why cash budgeting is important for Alpha-Tech.

(CMA, adapted)

P8-22 Production Budget; Materials Budget; Budgeted Income Statement

KD Diet Food, Inc. manufactures and sells a low-calorie syrup, called Katie, which the company markets as an alternative to maple syrup for diet-conscious consumers. The company is in the process of preparing various budgets for the next period, and has compiled the following data:

a. The company sells Katie in a pretty plastic container. The budgeted sales of Katie will be 150,000 units at a selling price of $8 per unit.

b. The beginning inventory of Katie is 60,000 units and the ending inventory is planned to be only 60% of the beginning inventory.

c. Three units of material K and 2 units of material T are required to produce each unit of Katie. The estimated cost and inventory levels of the materials are as follows:

Material	Cost Per Unit	Beginning Inventory	Ending Inventory
K	$0.15	45,000 units	65,000 units
T	0.50	100,000	70,000
Plastic container	0.20	50,000	48,000

d. Five minutes of direct labor time are required to produce one unit of Katie, at the rate of $12 per hour.

e. Manufacturing overhead costs: $0.12 per unit, variable, and $240,000 for the period, fixed.

f. Variable selling expenses are 5% of sales, and fixed selling and administrative expenses are $260,000 for the period.

Required:

1. Compute the variable manufacturing cost per unit of Katie.
2. Present a production budget for Katie for the period.
3. Present a materials budget for materials K and T, and the plastic container, showing the units to be purchased and the cost of purchase.
4. Present a budgeted income statement, using the contribution approach, for the period.

P8-23 Nonprofit Organization's Budget

MDS, Inc. is a nonprofit organization which sponsors a wide variety of management seminars throughout the United States. In addition, it is heavily involved in research into improved methods of educating and motivating business executives. The seminar activity is largely supported by fees. The research program is supported by member dues.

MDS operates on a calendar year basis and is in the process of finalizing the budget for Year 7. The following information has been taken from approved plans which are still tentative at this time.

b. Fifty percent of sales are cash sales and the other 50% are credit sales. Credit sales are collected in cash in the month following sale. The accounts receivable at December 31, Year 4 are related to the December sales.

c. The gross margin ratio to sales is 30%. The desired inventory at the end of each month is 40% of the following month's cost of sales.

d. Each month's inventory purchases are paid for as follows:

> 60% paid in the month of purchase.
>
> 40% paid in the month following purchase.

The accounts payable at December 31, Year 4 are related to the December purchases.

e. Monthly cash operating expenditures:

Rent	$1,800
Wages and salaries.	15% of sales
Office expenses	5% of sales

f. A computer will be purchased for $2,000 cash in January. Depreciation of all plant and equipment assets is $1,000 per month.

g. The company requires a minimum cash balance of $5,000. Any necessary borrowing is made at the beginning of a month, and repayment is made at the end of a month, in multiples of $1,000. The interest rate is 12% per year, and interest is paid only when the principal is repaid.

Required:

1. Present the following schedules or budgets for the first quarter of Year 5, by month and in total for the quarter:
    a. Schedule of expected cash receipts.
    b. Merchandise purchases budget.
    c. Schedule of budgeted cash payments for merchandise purchases.
    d. Cash budget.
2. Present a budgeted income statement for the first quarter of Year 5.
3. Present a budgeted balance sheet as of March 31, Year 5.

P8-25   Cash Budget; Related Schedules

It is now December, Year 5, and Hollywood Publications, Inc. is in the process of preparing a cash budget for next month, January, Year 6. The following data have been compiled for the budget preparation:

a. The budgeted sales for January are $650,000. All of the sales are credit sales. Fifty percent of the credit sales that will be collected in January will qualify for 2% discount that is allowed for the payments made within 15 days after the end of the month of sale.

b. Accounts receivable as of December 31, Year 5 represent the following:

From the sales of	Accounts Receivable	Percentages of Original Sales
September	$ 2,500	1%
October	45,000	10%
November	144,000	30%
December	600,000	100%
Total	$791,500	

The above collection pattern will continue in January, Year 6.

c. Budgeted manufacturing costs for January:

Direct materials..........................		$289,000
Direct labor		76,000
Manufacturing overhead:		
Utilities	$ 1,520	
Indirect labor.........................	28,800	
Property taxes.......................	1,600	
Depreciation	10,000	
Other overhead costs.................	20,000	61,920
Total manufacturing costs		$426,920

d. Budgeted selling and administrative expenses for January:

Promotion and advertising..........................	$80,000
Salaries...	40,000
Rent..	3,000
Others..	27,000

e. Equipment costing $36,000 will be purchased for cash during January.

f. The company pays for 40% of the material purchases in the month of purchase and 60% in the following month. Accounts payable for material purchases as of December 31, Year 5 will be $170,000.

g. The cash balance at December 31, Year 5 will be $60,000. The company requires a minimum cash balance of $60,000 at all times. Borrowings from banks are made in multiples of $1,000.

Required:

Present the following for January, Year 6:
1. Schedule of expected cash receipts
2. Schedule of budgeted cash payments for material purchases
3. Schedule of budgeted cash payments for manufacturing overhead
4. Cash budget

C8-26 Comprehensive Budget Preparation Using Spreadsheet

Refer to the data involving Budget Stores, Inc. in the text of this chapter. Assume the following changes in the situation:

1. Sales:

	Year 6 Actual		Year 7 Estimated				
	Nov.	Dec.	Jan.	Feb.	Mar.	Apr.	May
Units	10,000	12,000	13,000	16,150	14,000	16,000	12,000

The selling price is $70 per unit.

2. Cash collection policy: Cash sales are 20% of total sales and credit sales are 80%. Of the credit sales, the company collects 30% in the month after the month of sales and 70% in the month following that.

3. Production policy: The desired inventory at the end of each month is equal to 20% of the next month's sales. At December 31, Year 6, the finished inventory was 3,500 units at a cost of $47.18 each.

4. Raw materials purchasing policy: In each month the company purchases materials to meet that month's production requirements and to keep raw materials at the end of the month equivalent to 25% of the next month's production requirements. Each unit of finished product requires three pounds of raw materials. Raw materials are purchased at a cost of 40 cents per pound. On December 31, Year 6, there was enough raw materials inventory to meet 25% of Year 7's January production requirements.

    The company pays 60% of the cost of raw materials purchased in the month of purchase and the remaining 40% in the following month. The accounts payable balance of $15,190 on December 31, Year 6 represents 40% of purchases made in December, Year 6 to be paid in January, Year 7.

5. Manufacturing overhead: The company applies variable manufacturing overhead to production at the rate of 80% of direct labor cost. In addition, the company has the following fixed overhead expenses per month:
    Factory supervisor's salary $30,000
    Factory rent 8,000
    Factory insurance 1,000
    Depreciation of factory equipment 700

6. Selling and administrative expenses:

    Variable selling expenses include:
    Freight out . . . . $2 per unit
    Sales commission . . . . 8% of sales

    Fixed selling and administrative expenses per month:
    Salaries $4,200
    Rent 1,800
    Advertising 500
    Insurance 400
    Depreciation, excluding depreciation of
    personal computers to be purchased in
    January, Year 7. See below 5,000

7. Capital expenditures: The company expects to buy new personal computers for use in the administrative and sales offices at a cost of $140,000 which will be paid for by the end of January, Year 7. The monthly depreciation expense will be $5,000 for these PCs.

8. Financing policy: On March 31, Year 7, the company is scheduled to pay $250,000 of the long-term notes payable plus the interest expense. The minimum cash balance of $20,000 is required at the end of each month.

Other data remain unchanged. Budget Stores must prepare the following budgets and schedules again based on the above changes:

  1. Sales budget.
  2. Production budget.
  3. Direct materials budget.
  4. Direct labor budget.
  5. Manufacturing overhead budget.
  6. Cost of goods sold and ending finished goods inventory budget.
  7. Selling and administrative expenses budget.
  8. Cash receipts schedule.
  9. Cash disbursements schedule.
  10. Cash budget.

Required:

Using a spreadsheet, present the above 10 budgets and schedules for the first quarter of Year 7, by month and in total for the quarter. (Hint: First, program your spreadsheet to duplicate the budgets and schedules listed in the chapter. Then, replace those items that have changed with the new figures.)

STANDARD COSTS AND FLEXIBLE BUDGETS

After studying this chapter, you should be able to:

1. Understand the characteristics of mass-production as one of the two dominant production methods.

2. Explain how the costs of materials and labor can be managed.

3. Compute and explain price, quantity, rate, and efficiency variances for materials and labor.

4. Differentiate between static budgets and flexible budgets and explain the importance of flexible budgets in evaluating performance.

5. Explain the importance of choosing an appropriate activity base and discuss the characteristics of the most appropriate activity base.

6. Use different methods to compute variable overhead spending and efficiency variances, and prepare a performance report containing one or both of these variances.

7. Compute and explain the meaning of fixed overhead budget and volume variances.

8. Interpret overhead variances within a standard-cost system and mass-production environment.

9. Understand the implications of different levels of capacity used in flexible budgeting.

After managers have completed the budgeting process, discussed in Chapter 8, they would want to know how well the plans in the budgets were implemented. The accounting system records actual results of activities. Comparison of actual with budgeted performance provides managers with information necessary to make future decisions. In this chapter, we discuss the evaluation of financial results.

In order to evaluate performance, managers need certain performance benchmarks, called **standards,** against which actual results can be compared. We will first look at standards and issues related to direct materials and direct labor, which are more straightforward than overhead costs. Then, we will discuss standards and issues surrounding overhead costs.

In recent years, standard costing has been criticized for losing relevance as a performance evaluation and motivation mechanism in the new environment. Some practitioners and academicians have tried to modify standard costing to satisfy the needs for relevant management accounting information in the new environment.

The overwhelming trend, however, is to entirely depart from standard costing when the environment changes from mass-production to a new method, as discussed in Chapter 10. This is because it is more effective and economical to adopt a new planning and control technique than to try to improve standard costing to suit the needs of the new environment. Accordingly, we discuss standard costing in a basic format in this chapter.

The number of customers is a level of activity at Olive Garden Restaurant. A flexible budget uses a range of activity levels.

STATIC BUDGETS AND FLEXIBLE BUDGETS

The master budgets we discussed in Chapter 8 are **static budgets.** They reflect the budgeted costs at one level of activity. These static budgets are used for resource allocation, before the actual level of activity is known. Actual costs are compared to that static budget level, regardless of the actual level of output.

A **flexible budget** reflects the costs at a range of activity levels. Actual costs at the actual level of activity are compared to the budgeted costs at the corresponding level of activity. If the static budget is prepared for an activity level of 100,000 units and the actual level of activity is only 92,500 units, comparing the actual costs of 92,500 units to the budgeted costs of 100,000 units would not be meaningful for control purposes.

We will first discuss materials and labor costs, and then we will look at overhead costs, all within the flexible-budget environment. Before we discuss standard costs, however, we need to know the two dominant production methods.

MASS-PRODUCTION

We find in human history two dominant production methods: **craft production** and **mass-production.** The **craft producer** relies on highly skilled workers and simple, flexible tools to produce a custom product, such as an antique automobile or violin, in small quantities at high costs. The **mass-producer** relies on narrowly skilled designers and engineers to design products to be made by workers with a narrow specialization operating expensive, single-purpose machines, which turn out standardized products in large volumes.

In mass-production, there are certain characteristics that define the mode of production. Those characteristics are listed below:

Products:	Standardized
Workers:	Specialized
Machines:	Expensive, single-purpose
Production volume:	Large
Designers and engineers:	Narrowly skilled

The mass-producer's single-purpose machines cost less when they are run without disruption. Since the high acquisition cost of the machines represents a fixed cost, the more units produced on the machines, the lower the product cost per unit. In addition, when machine operation is disrupted, workers become idle. Since the workers must be paid regardless of whether they are engaged in production activities or are waiting for the production line to start again, idle time is costly to the company. Also, additional costs must usually be incurred when the production line starts again.

Accordingly, the mass-producer should keep the expensive machines running without disruption. Also, it is better to produce as many units as possible in large batches while the expensive machines are running.

Suppose you are a mass-producer. How should you keep production running without interruption? You need to have an abundant supply of raw materials and parts, so that you do not run out of stock. You need enough work-in-process inventories between different workers and workstations, so that a faster worker will not use up all the subassemblies before the preceding station's worker could replenish them.

Although the popularity of mass-production has declined recently because of the reasons explained in Chapter 10, there are still many manufacturers and service organizations that take advantage of the benefits of mass-production. We discuss managerial accounting and control for the mass-production environment in the following sections.

BUDGETS AND STANDARDS

In mass-production of standardized products, such as machine parts, it is practical to compute the standard time, say one minute, for the production line to take to fabricate a machine part. If the total number of units to be produced has been budgeted, the corresponding amount of time and cost required can be computed.

Standards and budgets are very closely related to each other. A **standard** is usually a *unit* amount, whereas a **budget** is usually a *total* amount. If it takes one minute of standard time to fabricate a machine part, a total budgeted time of 100 minutes would be required to process 100 units. Standards are used to control the quantity of materials and the number of labor hours needed to produce a product or service as well as the price per unit of materials or the rate per labor hour that should be paid. If the quantity actually used is greater than the standard quantity allowed, this may indicate inefficiency on the part of the manufacturing department. If the price actually paid per unit of materials or per hour of labor is greater than the standard price or rate, this may indicate lack of control on the part of the person who authorized the payment of such a higher price or rate. Managers investigate the causes of such deviations from standards to determine what actions should be taken to prevent further deviations.

Standards may be classified into the following three types: **Loose standards,** those that are set very low, do not challenge workers to perform well and may not reveal inefficiencies. **Perfect (ideal** or **strict) standards** are those that can only be attained by the most skillful and most efficient persons who work under the best conditions and circumstances. Accordingly, they discourage even the most hard-working and efficient persons. Most organizations use **attainable (practical) standards** that allow for specified breaks or rest periods, machine break-downs, materials shortages or waste, and other minor distractions that customarily occur in the work place. They require hard and highly efficient effort by the average person, and are useful because they are reasonable, fair, and can be used to measure the performance of the majority of the group under consideration.

VARIANCE ANALYSIS FOR DIRECT MATERIALS AND DIRECT LABOR

For purposes of managing the costs of direct materials and direct labor, managers compute the difference between actual performance and standards previously set for such performance. This difference, called **variance,** is analyzed, and the likely causes for these variances are identified and investigated. Corrective actions are taken, if necessary, for unfavorable variances.

Exhibit 9-1 illustrates a model for the computation of the variances for direct materials. If we subtract the amount of Box A from the amount of Box B, we obtain the **price variance.** If we subtract the amount of Box B from that of Box C, we obtain the **quantity variance.** And if we subtract the amount of Box A from the amount of Box C, we obtain the total variance.

Let's assume that a company has set the following standards of inputs for producing one unit of output:

Direct materials:	5 pounds	@$ 3.00	=	$15
Direct labor:	3 hours	@$10.00	=	$30

During October, Year 7, the company produced 20,000 units of output at the following actual costs:

Direct materials:	105,000 pounds	@$ 2.80	=	$294,000
Direct labor:	58,000 hours	@$10.50	=	$609,000

Direct Materials Variances

Using the above data, the direct materials price variance, direct materials quantity variance, and direct materials total variance may be computed as shown in Exhibit 9-1. If the company actually pays $2.80 per unit instead of the standard allowed price of $3.00, there is a favorable price variance of $0.20 per unit.

The materials quantity variance is $15,000, and it is negative and unfavorable. This unfavorable variance may be explained as follows: The company actually produced 20,000 units of output, and it should have used 100,000 pounds of raw materials (20,000 output units × 5 pounds standard input allowed per unit of output), rather than the actual usage of 105,000 pounds. At the standard price of $3 per unit, this extra usage of 5,000 pounds results in an unfavorable quantity variance of $15,000 (5,000 pounds × $3).

We computed the price variance on the total amount of material purchased (105,000 pounds). We also computed the quantity variance assuming that all of the material purchased was used in production. How should we compute the quantity variance if the actual output was only 18,000 units and only 91,000 pounds of material was used? In such a case, we should compute the variances as presented in Exhibit 9-2.

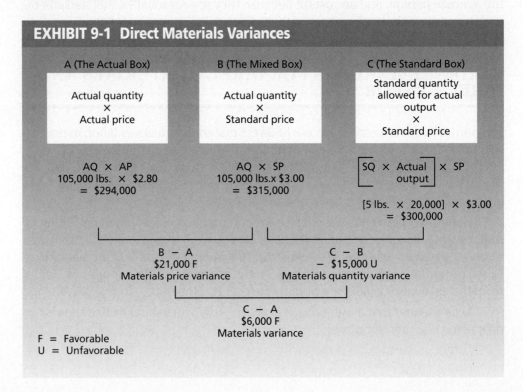

EXHIBIT 9-1 Direct Materials Variances

A (The Actual Box)

Actual quantity
×
Actual price

AQ × AP
105,000 lbs. × $2.80
= $294,000

B (The Mixed Box)

Actual quantity
×
Standard price

AQ × SP
105,000 lbs.x $3.00
= $315,000

C (The Standard Box)

Standard quantity allowed for actual output
×
Standard price

SQ × Actual output × SP

[5 lbs. × 20,000] × $3.00
= $300,000

B − A
$21,000 F
Materials price variance

C − B
− $15,000 U
Materials quantity variance

C − A
$6,000 F
Materials variance

F = Favorable
U = Unfavorable

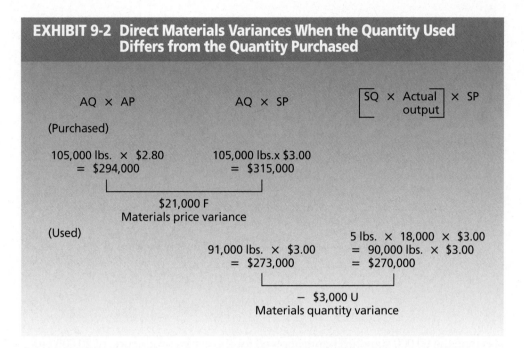

EXHIBIT 9-2 Direct Materials Variances When the Quantity Used Differs from the Quantity Purchased

AQ × AP

(Purchased)

105,000 lbs. × $2.80
= $294,000

AQ × SP

105,000 lbs.x $3.00
= $315,000

$\boxed{\text{SQ} \times \text{Actual output}} \times \text{SP}$

$21,000 F
Materials price variance

(Used)

91,000 lbs. × $3.00
= $273,000

5 lbs. × 18,000 × $3.00
= 90,000 lbs. × $3.00
= $270,000

− $3,000 U
Materials quantity variance

The exhibit shows that the quantity variance of $3,000 (unfavorable) is computed only on the quantity used (91,000 pounds) in production. The material of 14,000 pounds still remaining in inventory (105,000 pounds purchased − 91,000 pounds used) would be used in a future period. Only then would the quantity variance on that 14,000 pounds of material be computed.

In our computations of materials variances, we compute price variances when the materials are purchased, instead of waiting until they are used. This is because materials prices are influenced by external forces, such as general economic and specific industry conditions. When price variances are isolated, management can better focus on the efficiency in materials usage. This is accomplished by comparing the actual quantity of materials used to the standard materials quantity that was allowed for the actual output produced.

Direct Labor Variances

Using the above data, direct labor variances may be computed as illustrated in Exhibit 9-3. If we subtract the amount of Box A from the amount of Box B, we obtain the **rate variance.** If we subtract the amount of Box B from that of Box C, we obtain the **efficiency variance.** And if we subtract the amount of Box A from the amount of Box C, we obtain the total variance. The $29,000 labor rate variance is negative and unfavorable. The company paid an actual rate per hour of $10.50 which is $0.50 higher than the standard labor rate of $10 per hour. The total actual labor hours spent is 58,000, and the unfavorable labor rate variance is $29,000 ($0.50 × 58,000 hours). Exhibit 9-3 also shows that the direct labor efficiency variance is $20,000. It is positive and favorable. The actual labor hours spent of 58,000 is 2,000 hours

Direct labor associates at work in Timken Company's "clean room." The room is 10,000 times cleaner than a typical manufacturing area.

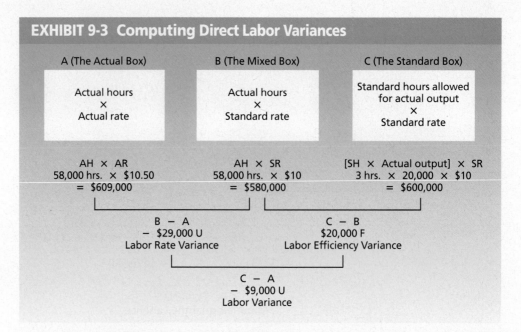

EXHIBIT 9-3 Computing Direct Labor Variances

less than the 60,000 standard hours allowed for the actual production of 20,000 units (20,000 units × 3 standard hours allowed per unit). At the standard labor rate of $10 per hour, this results in a $20,000 favorable variance (2,000 hours × $10 rate).

RESPONSIBILITY FOR VARIANCES

The basic purpose of analyzing variances is to identify the causes of such variances. This identification is the first step in the control process. The second step is to find ways to eliminate or minimize such causes. Some causes of variances are nothing more than trade-offs with other variances. For example, buying low-quality materials at low prices may produce a favorable materials purchase price variance, but may also result in unfavorable materials quantity variance and/or unfavorable labor efficiency variance. The lower-quality materials may be hard to handle, or may break or shrink during the manufacturing process, causing the production department to use more materials and/or more labor hours.

Similarly, using unskilled or untrained workers at low wage rates may result in a favorable labor rate variance as well as an unfavorable labor efficiency variance and/or unfavorable materials quantity variance. The unskilled workers would most likely take more time than skilled workers to produce a given quantity of products, and may use or waste more materials.

Such trade-offs among variances should not be made intentionally without top management's approval. A competitive company known for its high quality products cannot allow such trade-offs by individual managers even if this will result in some overall savings in total cost in the short run.

No manager should be held responsible for an unfavorable variance that he or she has no control over. The purchasing manager would be responsible for the materials price variance. The production manager would be responsible for the materials quantity variance and labor efficiency variance. The manager who approves the hiring and the wage rates for workers (the personnel manager or the production manager) would be responsible for the labor rate variance. Poor scheduling or use of overtime (demanding an overtime premium) could also cause a labor rate variance which would be the responsibility of a production manager or other operating managers.

STANDARDS FOR SERVICE ORGANIZATIONS

Many service organizations use standard costs when their activities can be standardized. Auto service centers, professional tax preparation firms, banks, fast food chains, hotels, hospitals, universities, governmental units and other non-manufacturing organizations may use standard costs and variance analysis.

The following illustrates what could be standardized in the operations of service organizations:

Auto service center: Standard labor time for changing oil and filter, or changing tires.

A tax preparer: Standard time for completing a short-form tax return or a long-form tax return.

Bank: Standard time for performing banking transactions, such as deposit, withdrawal, or usage of a safety deposit box.

Fast food chains: Standard quantity of cheese used in making pizza, or standard time it takes to serve a customer.

Hospitals: Standard charge for food and laundry per occupied room or bed per day.

Universities: Standard ratio of students per full-time faculty.

Governmental agencies: Standard labor time to complete a social welfare case, read a water meter, or write a ticket for a parking violation.

Standard costs and variance analysis can be applied to each of the above service operations in exactly the same way as they are applied to manufacturing operations.

Pizza Hut

MIX VARIANCE IN MANUFACTURING AND SERVICE

Many companies use a mix of more than one type of input (materials or labor) to produce a final product. If the actual mix of inputs differs from the standard mix of such inputs, a mix variance will result even if there is no price or quantity variance for each type of input. Assume that ABC Company has set the following standard mix and costs of materials per unit of Product C:

10 pounds of material A	@$2	=	$20
5 pounds of material B	@$3	=	15
			$35

Assume that ABC can deviate from the standard mix and still produce Product C. ABC used the following quantities of materials at the actual costs shown below to produce the actual output of 1,000 units of Product C:

Material A: 8,000 pounds	@$2	=	$16,000
Material B: 7,000 pounds	@$3	=	21,000
Total			$37,000

There is no materials purchase price variance for either type of material, since the actual price per pound is the same as the standard price per pound for each type of material. There is no quantity variance either because the actual quantity used of 15,000 pounds (8,000 pounds + 7,000 pounds) equals the total standard quantity of materials allowed (10,000 pounds + 5,000 pounds = 15,000 pounds), representing the standard quantity of material A allowed of 10,000 pounds (10 pounds × 1,000 units of output) plus the standard quantity of material B allowed of 5,000 pounds (5 pounds × 1,000 units of output).

Exhibit 9-4 shows that the actual cost of materials used is $37,000, which is $2,000 higher than the standard cost ($35,000) of materials allowed for the actual output. This difference is caused by a **mix variance,** which results from using an actual mix of materials A and B which is different from the standard mix. The unfavorable mix variance results from using a higher than standard proportion of the more costly material (B).

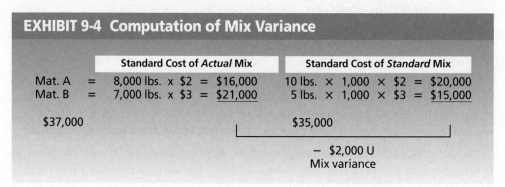

EXHIBIT 9-4 Computation of Mix Variance

		Standard Cost of *Actual* Mix	Standard Cost of *Standard* Mix
Mat. A	=	8,000 lbs. × $2 = $16,000	10 lbs. × 1,000 × $2 = $20,000
Mat. B	=	7,000 lbs. × $3 = $21,000	5 lbs. × 1,000 × $3 = $15,000
		$37,000	$35,000

− $2,000 U
Mix variance

The mix variance fits within the overall materials (or labor) variance analysis as follows:

Total materials variance
  = Price variance + **mix variance** + quantity variance
Total labor variance
  = Rate variance + **mix variance** + efficiency variance

The mix variance can be used in service and nonprofit organizations as well. Assume that an audit engagement by a CPA firm is normally performed using 100 hours of partners' time at $100 per hour and 400 hours of staff time at $50 per hour (a total of 500 hours). If that engagement was actually performed using 200 hours of partners' time and 300 hours of staff time (a total of 500 hours), an unfavorable mix variance will result even if there is no labor rate variance. Also, a patient in a hospital may normally require 10 hours of doctors' time at $120 an hour and 30 hours of nurses' time at $30 an hour (a total of 40 hours). If the patient actually used 5 hours of doctors' time and 35 hours of nurses' time (a total of 40 hours), a favorable mix variance will result even if there is no labor rate variance.

FLEXIBLE BUDGETS AND OVERHEAD COSTS

At the beginning of this chapter, we explained that a static budget shows actual costs compared to a static budget level, regardless of the actual level of output. Exhibit 9-5 shows ABC Company's variable overhead static budget for the planned production of 1,200 units during April.

EXHIBIT 9-5 Variable Overhead Static Budget For April

Planned production in units	1,200
Budgeted variable overhead:	
Supplies	$ 600
Indirect labor	1,200
Utilities	1,800
Total	$ 3,600

During April, only 1,100 units were produced and the actual variable overhead costs incurred are shown in the first column of Exhibit 9-6. The comparison made between actual costs and the static budget is inadequate for control purposes, because it compares the actual costs at one level of activity against the budgeted costs at another. The favorable cost variances are misleading, because the actual

EXHIBIT 9-6

ABC Company
Actual vs. Static Budget For April

	Actual	Budget	Variance
Production in units	1,100	1,200	100 U
Variable overhead costs:			
Supplies	$ 410	$ 600	$190 F
Indirect labor	820	1,200	380 F
Utilities	1,685	1,800	115 F
Total	$2,915	$3,600	$685 F

level of activity was 100 units lower than the budgeted level, and the lower costs were expected. Indeed, the only variance that is correct is the unfavorable variance of 100 units, which indicates that actual production was below planned production.

Management focuses on whether output was produced at the least possible cost, given that quality standards are met. The problem with using the static budget in a performance report is that it fails to distinguish between the responsibility for production level and the responsibility for cost incurrence.

Relevance of the Flexible Budget

At the beginning of this chapter, we explained that a **flexible budget** reflects the costs at a *range* of activity levels. A performance report based on flexible budget produces relevant information for control purposes, because it compares actual costs to budgeted costs at the *same* level of activity.

The flexible budget for a 1,100-unit level of activity is presented in Exhibit 9-7. To simplify the presentation, we do not include direct material and direct labor. Remember, however, that the flexible budget concept applies to *all* costs. We assume that these variable overhead components are truly variable, and derive the standard variable overhead per unit as follows:

	Costs	Units Produced	Cost Per Unit
Supplies	$ 600	1,200	$0.50
Indirect labor	1,200	1,200	1.00
Utilities	1,800	1,200	1.50
Total	$3,600		$3.00

EXHIBIT 9-7

ABC Company
Performance Report
Based on Flexible Budget For April

	A	B	C	D
		Actual	Budget	Variance
Production in units		1,100	1,100	0
	Standard Cost Per			
Variable overhead costs:	*Unit*		(1,100 × A)	(C − B)
Supplies..........................	$0.50	$ 735	$ 550	− $185 U
Indirect labor	1.00	1,470	1,100	− $370 U
Utilities	1.50	1,835	1,650	− $185 U
Total	$3.00	$4,040	$3,300	− $740 U
		(AQ × SP)		

All variances are unfavorable, because the actual costs are greater than the budgeted costs for each component of variable overhead, given the actual level of production.

Choosing the Right Activity Base

In the above example, we used the number of output units to measure the level of activity. We can also use other cost drivers, such as direct labor hours, machine hours, number of occupied beds in a hospital or a hotel, or number of orders processed, as discussed in Chapter 6. The appropriate activity base to use may vary from one firm to another, from one department to another within the same firm, and from one cost type to another within the same department.

The most appropriate activity base is the one that is simple and easy to understand, and has a causal relationship with the overhead costs. For example, in a machine-intensive shop, most overhead costs would vary with the fluctuations in the number of machine hours operated. In a labor-intensive service center, overhead costs would vary most with the changes in the number of labor hours. In an environment where both machines and labor are equally significant, the most appropriate activity base would be a combination of cost drivers.

OVERHEAD ANALYSIS

Analysis of Variable Overhead Variances

Variable overhead variances are computed in exactly the same way as direct materials and direct labor variances were computed. The price or rate variance for variable overhead is called the **variable overhead spending variance**, as it represents the rate at which variable overhead has actually been spent in comparison to the standard rate of spending. The difference between actual and standard activity, priced at the standard variable overhead rate, is called the **variable overhead efficiency variance.**

Assume that ABC Company budgets its variable overhead based on operating hours. The rate for every variable overhead component is usually developed based on the long-run historical relationship between the component and the number of operating hours. The variable overhead cost budgeted for ABC Company is as follows:

Variable overhead costs:	Cost Per Operating Hour
Supplies..	$0.10
Indirect labor	0.20
Utilities	0.30
	$0.60

According to the production budget, one unit of output requires five operating hours. For the month of October, the company planned to produce 1,200 units, and it budgeted 6,000 operating hours. During October, only 1,000 units of output were produced, and 5,500 actual hours were worked. The actual variable overhead costs during the month were as follows:

Supplies...	$ 715
Indirect labor	1,045
Utilities	1,760
Total	$3,520

Exhibit 9-8 illustrates the computation of variable overhead spending and efficiency variances during October.

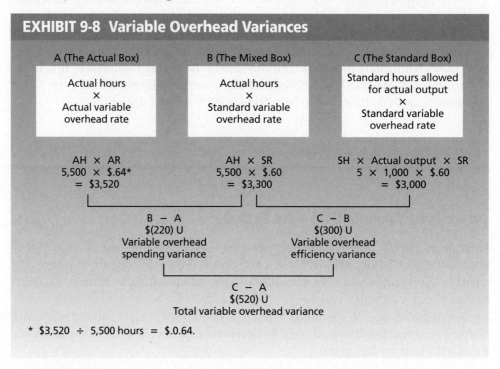

EXHIBIT 9-8 Variable Overhead Variances

Exhibit 9-8 shows the following three levels of costs:

(A)	(B)	(C)
Actual costs incurred when the company operated for 5,500 hours	Standard costs budgeted for 5,500 hours of operations = AH × SR = flexible budget	Standard costs budgeted for 5,000 hours that were allowed for actual output of 1,000 units

The spending variance (B − A) reflects the rate at which variable overhead was actually spent when 5,500 hours were worked. The efficiency variance (C − B) represents the effect of the difference between the 5,500 hours that production department actually worked and the 5,000 hours that it was allowed to work to produce 1,000 units of output.

Flexible Budget and Fixed Overhead

Exhibit 9-9 illustrates an overhead flexible budget for ABC Company based on the information provided thus far. Fixed overhead costs are the same regardless of the level of activity, since fixed overhead costs (rent, insurance, property taxes, etc.) remain unchanged for a given time period (lease period, insurance policy term, etc.) despite the variation in the level of activity, as long as the variation in the level of activity is within the relevant range.

EXHIBIT 9-9

ABC Company
Flexible Budget For Overhead

	Standard Per Hour	Operating Hours		
		4,000	5,000	6,000
Variable overhead costs:				
Supplies	$0.10	$ 400	$ 500	$ 600
Indirect labor.................................	0.20	800	1,000	1,200
Utilities..	0.30	1,200	1,500	1,800
Variable overhead total	$0.60	$2,400	$3,000	$3,600
Fixed overhead costs:				
Factory rent		$3,000	$3,000	$3,000
Factory insurance		1,200	1,200	1,200
Factory property taxes		900	900	900
Fixed overhead total		$5,100	$5,100	$5,100
Total overhead costs		$7,500	$8,100	$8,700

This raises an interesting question: if these fixed overhead costs do not vary from one level of activity to another, why are they included in the flexible budget? There are two reasons for this. First, the production manager is usually responsible for both variable and fixed overhead costs incurred in his/her department. Second, a single, predetermined overhead rate may have to be established for cost allocation to products and for pricing purposes. Thus, it is convenient to have both categories of overhead in one place, although the analysis of fixed overhead variances is quite different from the analysis of variable overhead variances.

Fixed Overhead Rates and Capacity

Based on what we learned about the predetermined overhead rate in Chapter 4, we compute the predetermined fixed overhead rate using the same formula:

$$\text{Predetermined fixed overhead rate} = \frac{\text{Budgeted fixed overhead}}{\text{Budgeted activity level}}$$

If we use 6,000 operating hours as the budgeted activity level for the $5,100 budgeted fixed overhead costs, then we get $0.85 per hour as the predetermined fixed overhead rate to apply to production as follows:

$$\text{Predetermined fixed overhead rate} = \frac{\$5,100}{6,000 \text{ hours}} = \$0.85 \text{ per hour}$$

Fixed overhead costs do not change from month to month, but the output level does. Thus, if the company budgets to work longer hours and produce more units of output, then the overhead rate per hour and per unit will be lower. For example, if the company budgets to work 6,375 operating hours, 375 more hours than the above, then the predetermined overhead rate decreases to $0.80 per hour, as shown below:

$$\text{Predetermined fixed overhead rate} = \frac{\$5,100}{6,375 \text{ hours}} = \$0.80 \text{ per hour}$$

We learned in Chapter 4 that as the *level of capacity (activity level)* decreases, the fixed cost per unit increases. We confirm here that as the level of activity increases from 6,000 hours to 6,375 hours, the fixed overhead rate decreases from $0.85 per hour to $0.80 per hour. This reduction in fixed overhead rate per hour (or per unit of product) as the activity level goes up reflects the **economy of scale** we learn in economics. *Mass-production takes advantage of the economy of scale*, lowering, among others, the fixed overhead cost per unit.

Analysis of Fixed Overhead Variances

Since ABC Company planned to produce 1,200 units, and each unit requires five operating hours, the original plan called for 6,000 operating hours. Now, we compute the predetermined fixed overhead rate per operating hour as follows:

The fabrication process at Harnischfeger Industries, Inc. As the level of activity increases, the fixed overhead rate decreases.

Fixed overhead costs:	Costs	Operating Hours	Rate Per Hour
Factory rent	$3,000	6,000	$0.50
Factory insurance	1,200	6,000	0.20
Factory property taxes	900	6,000	0.15
Total	$5,100		$0.85

The actual fixed overhead costs for October are given below:

Factory rent	$3,000
Factory insurance	1,500
Factory property taxes	1,000
Total...	$5,500

From the other data provided in the previous variable overhead analysis, we know the following: actual production of 1,000 units; actual hours of 5,500; and actual variable overhead of $3,520.

Now we compute the fixed overhead variances as shown in Exhibit 9-10.

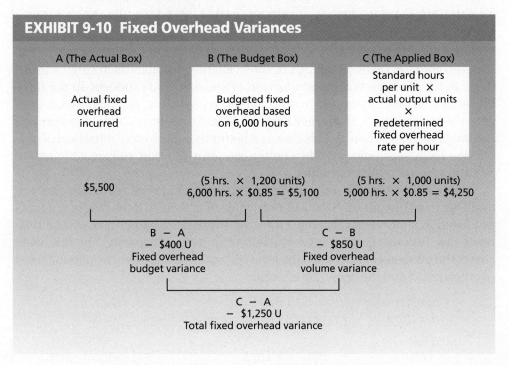

EXHIBIT 9-10 Fixed Overhead Variances

A (The Actual Box) — Actual fixed overhead incurred — $5,500

B (The Budget Box) — Budgeted fixed overhead based on 6,000 hours — (5 hrs. × 1,200 units) 6,000 hrs. × $0.85 = $5,100

C (The Applied Box) — Standard hours per unit × actual output units × Predetermined fixed overhead rate per hour — (5 hrs. × 1,000 units) 5,000 hrs. × $0.85 = $4,250

B − A — $400 U — Fixed overhead budget variance

C − B — $850 U — Fixed overhead volume variance

C − A — $1,250 U — Total fixed overhead variance

Using this analysis, we can compute the difference between actual fixed overhead and fixed overhead applied to actual output, and observe how much of this difference is due to changes in the level of activity, which we call **volume variance,** and how much is due to other factors, which we call **budget variance.**

Exhibit 9-10 presents the following three levels of costs:

(A)	(B)	(C)
Actual costs incurred when the company operated for 5,500 hours	Standard costs budgeted for 6,000 hours of operations originally planned (see flexible budget)	Standard costs budgeted for 5,000 hours that were allowed for *actual* output of 1,000 units

Please note that the predetermined fixed overhead rate of $0.85 per hour is used in both (B) and (C). The volume variance (C − B) represents the effect of the difference between the 5,000 standard hours allowed for actual output and the 6,000 hours of operations that were originally planned (5 hours × 1,200 = 6,000 hours). The volume variance is unfavorable because the actual output level (1,000 units) is below the orginally budgeted output level (1,200 units). This implies that the production facilities were not fully utilized as planned.

The budget variance (B − A) represents the difference between actual fixed overhead costs ($5,500) incurred during the period and budgeted fixed overhead costs ($5,100) which we used in the flexible budget. The fixed overhead budget variance reflects the effect of all other factors such as price increases and property tax hikes.

MASS-PRODUCTION, CAPACITY UTILIZATION, AND VARIANCES

Mass-production takes advantage of the availability of manufacturing facilities that can handle large-volume production of standardized products. In the flexible budget variance examples in this chapter, we saw that, at a higher-than-budgeted level of activity, the larger number of units produced would generate a favorable volume variance. This means a better-than-budgeted utilization of production facilities would provide a better economy of scale, reducing the manufacturing cost per unit of product.

Appendix 4A discussed capacity. Capacity includes all resources that are available to an organization in its performance of activities. If the number of units produced in a month is relatively large, the overhead cost per unit will be relatively low, because there was an efficient utilization of capacity. The following shows the relationships between the level of capacity utilization, the per-unit fixed overhead rate, and the economy of scale:

Capacity Utilization	Per-Unit Fixed Overhead Rate	Economy of Scale
High	Low	Exists
Low	High	Does not exist

With a predetermined overhead rate, the amount of overhead allocated to each unit of product remains the same throughout the year. From this basis, we can analyze the difference between actual fixed overhead and fixed overhead applied to actual output, and observe how much of this difference is due to changes in the *level of activity* (production volume variance), and how much is due to *other factors* (budget variance). Production volume variance measures capacity utilization to some extent.

E-BUSINESS AND VARIANCES

The nature of efficiency that affects variances we discuss in this chapter changes as e-business is introduced. The efficiency improvements that e-businesses have made have led to mixed results. The widely publicized efficiency-enhancing changes General Electric has made in its procurement procedures to the completely Inter-

Usefulness of Standard Costing Questioned

The usefulness of standard costing has been questioned by many managers and accounting professionals in recent years. Some of the criticisms leveled against standard costing are shown below:

"Standard costing is a convenient and economical vehicle for supporting financial reporting. It is harmless as long as it is not used for real cost management purposes."

*A comment made by a
Caterpillar accounting executive*

"The elaborate standard cost variances simply do not translate what workers do into easy-to-understand performance measures."

*A comment from a
Japanese auto company executive*

"Standards place unnecessary ceilings on future performance and actually form a barrier to constant improvement."

*A comment from a
Borg-Warner accounting executive*

Chapter 10 discusses the reasons for such criticisms.

net-based procurement have produced company-wide savings of hundreds of millions of dollars. For most e-businesses, however, efficiency improvements have not been converted into better operating results showing favorable variances.

Why haven't efficiency improvements turned into better operating results for so many e-businesses? Businesses derive their higher-than-normal profits from market information asymmetry: Many service businesses, including investment advisors, accountants, and knowledge-based professionals charge high fees for providing valuable information and knowledge their customers do not have. Neighborhood banks and auto dealerships have been able to charge high prices for their services and goods because customers did not have enough information about the availability of like-kind services and goods in the vicinity.

There is no such information asymmetry anymore. In the Internet era, customers can log on and get the information and knowledge on the goods and services for almost zero cost. This easy access to market information eliminates higher-than-normal profits for the providers of goods and services. A group of small publishers with their own network can procure typesetting, printing, and distribution services at about the same costs as big publishing giants have paid, using B2B exchanges to even out the differences in bargaining power. Car buyers can get the information on car options and prices before they visit their neighborhood auto dealerships. The efficiency gained from e-business has not translated into better operating results because of this change in the business environment.

SUMMARY

In this chapter, we have discussed planning and control in the mass-production environment. We first discussed the use of standards to control the costs of materials and labor. Standards are benchmarks against which actual performance is measured. The level at which standards are set will affect their motivational influence. If set too low or too high, efficient performance may be discouraged. Standards which represent efficient, attainable performance will be better motivators.

Total variances from standards are broken down into a price (or rate) variance and a quantity (or efficiency) variance. The price variance is equal to the difference in price per unit times the actual quantity used, whereas the quantity variance is equal to the difference in quantity used times the standard price per unit.

Standards may be used by any organization interested in controlling costs whose activities can be standardized. Thus, while standards are used most often in manufacturing organizations, they may also be used in service, governmental, and nonprofit organizations.

In the second part of this chapter, we discussed flexible budgets and how they are used in controlling overhead. A flexible budget differs from a static (master) budget with respect to relevant range of activity levels. The flexible budget has the advantage of allowing actual costs incurred at a given level of activity to be compared against budgeted costs at that same level of activity. The static budget does not have that advantage. Thus, comparing actual costs against the static budget produces inadequate and perhaps misleading variances.

The calculation of variable overhead variances is very similar to the analysis of direct materials and direct labor variances. The differences that exist are in the name of the variances, their interpretation, responsibility for the variances, and corrective actions necessary.

The analysis of fixed overhead variances is different from that of variable overhead variances. The total variance between actual fixed overhead and fixed overhead applied to actual output is broken down to the production volume variance (due to changes in the *level of activity*) and the budget variance (due to *other factors*). Production volume variance measures capacity utilization to some extent.

BASIC CONCEPTS AND TERMS

Attainable standards	Flexible budget
Direct labor efficiency variance	Ideal standards
Direct labor rate variance	Practical standards
Direct materials price variance	Static budget
Direct materials quantity variance	Strict standards
Economy of scale	Variable overhead efficiency variance
Fixed overhead budget variance	Variable overhead spending variance
Fixed overhead volume variance	

■ SELF-REVIEW PROBLEM: COMPREHENSIVE

The Sunshine Co. of Florida has a plant in a Caribbean territory which operates as a mass-producer of a single product using low-skilled, low-wage local workers. The budget for August provided for the production and sale of 10,000 units of output. The standard variable production cost per unit is as follows:

Two pounds of direct materials @ $5 per pound	$10
Five hours of direct labor @ $4 per hour	20
Variable overhead @ $1 per direct labor hour	5
Total variable cost per unit	$35

The budgeted fixed overhead per month is $300,000 for an activity level of 50,000 direct labor hours (10,000 units × 5 hours).

During August, the actual results were as follows:

Units produced and sold......................................	9,000
Costs:	
Direct materials purchased and used	$ 76,000
(19,000 pounds)	
Direct labor (44,000 hours)................................	220,000
Variable overhead incurred	35,200
Fixed overhead incurred	290,000

Required:

a. Compute the following variances during August, indicating whether each is favorable (F) or unfavorable (U):

   - Direct materials price variance.
   - Direct materials quantity variance.
   - Direct labor rate variance.
   - Direct labor efficiency variance.
   - Variable overhead spending variance.
   - Variable overhead efficiency variance.
   - Fixed overhead budget variance.
   - Fixed overhead volume variance.

b. What was the amount of over- or underapplied overhead during August?

c. Comment on the manufacturing performance of August.

SOLUTION

(a)

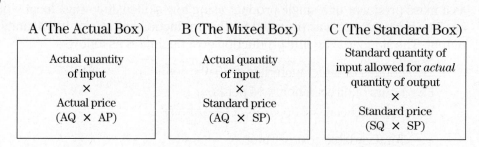

Direct Materials

19,000 lbs. × $4   19,000 lbs. × $5   (2 lbs. × 9,000 units)
= $76,000   = $95,000   18,000 lbs. × $5
                                              = $90,000

Price Variance   Quantity Variance
$19,000 F $5,000 U

Direct Labor

44,000 hrs. × $5   44,000 hrs. × $4   (5 hrs. × 9,000)
= $220,000   = $176,000   45,000 hrs. × $4
                                              = $180,000

Rate Variance   Efficiency Variance
$44,000 U $4,000 F

Variable Overhead

44,000 hrs. × $.80   44,000 hrs. × $1   45,000 hrs. × $1
= $35,200   = $44,000   = $45,000

Spending Variance   Efficiency Variance
$8,800 F $1,000 F

Fixed overhead

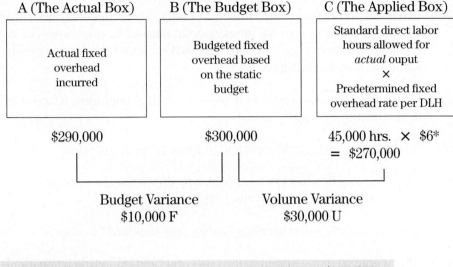

A (The Actual Box)	B (The Budget Box)	C (The Applied Box)
Actual fixed overhead incurred	Budgeted fixed overhead based on the static budget	Standard direct labor hours allowed for *actual* ouput × Predetermined fixed overhead rate per DLH
$290,000	$300,000	45,000 hrs. × $6* = $270,000

Budget Variance
$10,000 F

Volume Variance
$30,000 U

* Budgeted fixed overhead	$300,000
Budgeted direct labor hours	÷ 50,000
Budgeted fixed overhead rate (per hour)	$ 6

(b) Underapplied overhead was $10,200 calculated as follows:

Overhead

Actual	325,200	315,000	Applied
Underapplied overhead	10,200		

Actual:
  $35,200 variable overhead + $290,000 fixed overhead = $325,200
Applied:

9,000 units × 5 hrs. =	45,000 hrs.
Budgeted overhead rate ($1 variable + $6 fixed)	× $7
	$315,000

(c). Manufacturing performance of the period:

Materials were purchased at a lower price than budgeted. This, however, may have contributed to the use of extra materials. The company probably employed better-skilled workers in production who were paid at higher rates than budgeted, because their labor efficiency was better than budgeted. This favorable labor efficiency has produced favorable variable overhead efficiency also. There was savings in the usage of actual variable overhead items. Fixed overhead variances just indicate an unfavorable performance caused by a lower than budgeted production volume.

■ REVIEW QUESTIONS

9-1 In a mass-production environment, a company can effectively use standards and standard costs for cost management. Standard costs, however, are not compatible with craft production. What is the reason? (Hint: Consider the possibility of standardizing products.)

9-2 Why would a mass-producer insist on running machines, without disruption, to minimize cost?

9-3 Why would a mass-producer tend to favor large inventories?

9-4 If mass-production has lost its appeal, why do we discuss managerial accounting and control for mass-production?

9-5 What is the difference between budget and standard?

9-6 Why would so many organizations use practical standards when ideal standards would make their members strive for higher standards?

9-7 "Some causes of variances are nothing more than trade-offs with other variances." Do you agree? Why or why not?

9-8 When can a service organization use standard costs? Give some examples.

9-9 "At a higher-than-budgeted level of activity, the larger number of units produced would generate a favorable volume variance." Is this statement true? Why or why not?

9-10 Why is a performance report based on a flexible budget supposed to produce more relevant information for control purposes than a report based on a static budget?

9-11 What would be the most appropriate activity base to use to derive the numbers in a flexible budget?

9-12 The variable overhead spending variance is very similar to the price or rate variance for materials and labor. Why is this variance called a *spending* variance as opposed to a *price* or *rate* variance?

9-13 If fixed overhead costs do not vary from one level of activity to another, why are they included in the flexible budget?

9-14 Without a predetermined overhead rate, the amount of overhead allocated to one unit of product would vary from month to month. Why would it vary?

9-15 Where in the income statement would you find variable and fixed overhead variances?

INTERNET PROJECT

Web 9-1:

Websites: www.pncbank.com
              www.bankofny.com

The websites listed above represent two famous companies. Search the sites for information on their operating characteristics.

Required:

1.   Where would you apply standard costing? Why?

2.   What would be the hardest part in the implementation of standard costing for the two companies?

Web 9-2:

Websites: www.schwab.com
              www.bearstearns.com

The websites listed above represent two famous companies. Search the sites for information on their operating characteristics.

Required:

1.   Consider the e-business the companies have started or will have soon. What variances would you find there?

2.   How different would those variances be compared to the variances the companies would have for other businesses they have maintained for many years?

■ EXERCISES

E9-1   Mass-Production and Standard Costs

Mass-production provides a compatible setting for standard costs. The following list contains production characteristics for different production methods. Please indicate whether each item represents mass-production (M) or craft production (C) by placing "M" or "C" next to the item.

   a.   Relies on narrowly skilled designers and engineers.
   b.   Relies on highly skilled workers.
   c.   Uses workers with narrowly specialized skills.
   d.   Uses simple, flexible tools.
   e.   Produces a custom product.
   f.   Operates expensive, single-purpose machines.
   g.   Produces small quantities at high costs.
   h.   Turns out standardized products in large volumes.

E9-2 Material Variances; Output Concept

GXC, Inc. produces a chemical product, called GLN, that is used to convert black-and-white movies to color. The direct material standards for producing a unit of GLN follow:

	Standard Quantity	Standard Price	Standard Cost
Direct materials	3 units	$4 per unit	$12

During the last month, 5,000 units of materials were purchased at a cost of $4.10 per unit. All of the materials purchased were used to produce 1,500 units of GLN.

Required:

1. Compute the direct materials price and quantity variances for the last month.
2. Assume that the company produced only 1,200 units of GLN, using 3,720 units of direct materials in the manufacturing process last month. What is the direct materials quantity variance for the last month?

E9-3 Material Variances

Medox Company manufactures MDX, which is used to sterilize surgical gloves. During the last month, the company manufactured 4,000 units of MDX, using 8,200 units of direct materials. The materials cost the company $12,300. The direct material standards for producing a unit of GLN follow:

	Standard Quantity	Standard Price	Standard Cost
Direct materials	2 units	$1.40	$2.80

Required:

1. What is the standard cost of materials for producing 4,000 units of MDX?
2. Compute the materials price and quantity variances.

E9-4 Labor Variances; Output Concept

JDS, Inc. produces a perfume called Esther. The direct labor standards for producing one unit of Esther are presented below:

	Standard Hours	Standard Rate	Standard Cost
Direct labor	0.4 hours	$15 per hour	$6

During the last month, 1,500 units of Esther were produced. A total of 640 direct labor-hours were recorded at a total labor cost of $10,240.

Required:

1. Present a flexible budget for overhead costs at 30,000, 35,000, and 40,000 machine-hours.
2. Compute the predetermined overhead rate per hour. Specify the variable and fixed portions.
3. Determine the standard hours allowed for the actual output for the period.
4. Compute the variable overhead spending and efficiency variances and the fixed overhead budget and volume variances for the period.

E9-14 Fixed Overhead Variances

TDS, Inc. uses standards for planning and control. The following relates to operations for the last period, in which 9,600 units of output were produced:
a. The denominator activity level is 25,000 operating hours. It takes 2.5 operating hours to make one unit of output.
b. A total of $182,000 fixed overhead costs were incurred during the period. The fixed overhead budget variance was $5,500, favorable.
c. Overhead costs are applied to output based on operating hours.

Required:

1. Compute the standard hours allowed for the actual output of the period.
2. Compute the budgeted fixed overhead for the denominator activity level of 25,000 operating hours.
3. What was the fixed overhead application rate per operating hour?
4. Compute the fixed overhead volume variance for the period.

E9-15 Mix Variance

MAX, Inc. has adopted standards for measuring its performance in the production of its single product, called MX. MAX uses two types of materials, J and K. For the most recent period, there was no price or quantity variance for either type of materials used. The controller of the company, however, says that the total cost of materials actually used was less than the standard materials cost for the actual output of 1,000 units for the period.

Max's standard mix and costs of materials per unit of MX are as follows:

20 units of material J @$5	$100
20 units of material K @$6	120
	$220

MAX used the following quantities of materials at the actual costs shown below:

Material J, 24,000 units, @$5	$120,000
Material K, 16,000 units, @$6	96,000
	$216,000

Required:

1. How is it possible that "the total cost of materials actually used was less than the standard materials cost" when there was no price or quantity variance? Explain.
2. Compute the materials mix variance for the period.

■ PROBLEMS

P9-16   Ethics and the Actions of Managers

J&B Shelves, Inc. produces and sells steel shelves used in grocery stores. The line manager of a board-cutting operation sees a high likelihood that one of his machines needs servicing due to loose specification one afternoon. If not serviced promptly, the machine will be likely to turn out poor-quality panels that are used in subsequent operations. If the line is stopped for preventive maintenance, however, the manager's area cannot meet the target production level.

The line manager knows that actual labor and overhead costs will exceed the standards assigned to his area if his workers are left idle and the target is not met. (If the target is met, actual output will be equal to or higher than the budgeted level of output.) He decides to wait until the next scheduled maintenance date. He meets the target, and his costs are controlled within the standards.

Ten working days pass, and subsequent lines find themselves coping with newly arriving defective panels that are out of specification. Subsequent lines' operations are disrupted, and their actual labor and overhead costs exceed the standards.

Required:

1. Discuss the ethical implications of the action taken by the line manager of board-cutting operation.
2. Has the standard costing system caused the line manager to take such action? Explain how much of the responsibility belongs to the system.

P9-17   Variance Analysis; Variable Costs

Excel Inc. produces a filter that auto makers install in luxury cars to purify car indoor air. The company uses a standard cost system for planning and control, and applies overhead based on direct labor-hours. The company set the following standards for the normal activity level of 5,250 direct labor-hours per month, at which 3,500 filters are expected to be produced:

	For Total Output	Per Unit of Filter
Direct materials.....................	$115,500	$33.00
Direct labor	63,000	18.00
Variable overhead..................	15,750	4.50
		$55.50

The standard quantity of 3 units of materials are required in the production of one unit of filter. During the last month, the company recorded the following actual activity and costs:

Actual output..........................	3,600 filters
Direct materials, 11,000 units used	$122,400
Direct labor, 5,100 hours	94,350
Variable overhead........................	15,120

Required:

1. Compute the following variances:
   Materials price and quantity.
   Labor rate and efficiency.
   Variable overhead spending and efficiency.
2. Evaluate the manufacturing performance for the last month. Explain why labor efficiency and variable overhead efficiency variances are both favorable. Do the two variances always move in the same direction? Why or why not?

 P9-18 Standard Costs and Variance Analysis; Comprehensive

FTS, Inc. uses a standard cost system, which set the following standards per unit of output:

	Standard Quantity(Hours) of Input	Standard Price(Rate) of Input	Standard Cost
Direct materials.....	2.5 units	$ 3.20	$ 8.00
Direct labor	1.2 hours	14.00	16.80
Overhead	1.2 hours	7.55	9.06
			$33.86

Actual costs incurred during the last period were as follows:

Materials purchased, 20,000 units at $3.50	$70,000
(19,000 units of materials were issued to production.)	
Direct labor, 9,400 hours at $15........................	141,000
Variable overhead.......................................	16,920
Fixed overhead..	59,700

The following additional data relate to the operations of the last period:

a. The denominator activity level was 10,000 direct labor-hours. Overhead costs are applied to production at predetermined rates on the basis of direct labor-hours.

b. Standard variable overhead cost is $1.75 per hour. Budgeted fixed overhead was $58,000 for the period.

c. Actual output was 7,500 units for the last period.

Required:

1. What is the fixed portion of the overhead rate of $7.55 per hour?
2. Compute the materials price and quantity variances.
3. Compute the labor rate and efficiency variances.
4. Compute the variable overhead spending and efficiency variances.
5. Compute the fixed overhead budget and volume variances.

P9-19   Fixed Overhead Cost Analysis

CFP, Inc. uses a standard cost system, and applies overhead on the basis of operating hours. The following data relate to the actual operations of the company during the last period:

Actual output	6,400 units
Actual hours worked.	18,000 hours
Fixed overhead costs incurred	$141,000
Fixed overhead budget variance	5,000, unfavorable

Standard costs for producing a unit of output are as follows:

Direct materials, 2 units at $5	$10
Direct labor, 2.5 hours at $14.	35
Overhead, 2.5 hours at $10.	25
Total cost per unit of output	$70

The variable portion of the standard overhead costs is 20% of total overhead cost.

Required:

1. What is the fixed overhead rate applied per operating hour?
2. What was the denominator activity level which the company used for determining the fixed overhead rate for the period?
3. How many hours were allowed for producing the actual output?
4. What is the fixed overhead volume variance?

 ## P9-20   Comprehensive Variance Analysis

LHU, Inc. produces home-arrest monitoring devices that are used to relieve prison overcrowding, and relies on a standard cost system for planning and control. The following are the standards for producing one unit of ANB, a tamperproof ankle bracelet:

	Standard Quantity(Hours) of Input	Standard Price(Rate) of Input	Standard Cost
Direct materials	2 units	$15	$30
Direct labor	0.5 hours	14	7
Variable overhead. . . .	0.5 hours	6	3
Fixed overhead.	0.5 hours	20	10
Total standard cost per unit of ANB			$50

During the last period, the company recorded the following activity in connection with the production of ANB:

a. The actual output produced was 2,400 units.
b. Materials purchased were 5,500 units at a cost of $77,000. A total of 5,000 units of materials were used.
c. A total of 1,280 hours of labor time were recorded at an average rate of $15 per hour.
d. The flexible budget of overhead costs shows that a denominator activity level of 1,300 direct labor-hours was used to determine the overhead application rates. Actual overhead costs incurred were $7,450, variable, and $26,500, fixed.

Required:

1. Compute the material price and quantity variances.
2. Compute the labor rate and efficiency variances.
3. Compute the variable overhead spending and efficiency variances.
4. Compute the fixed overhead budget and volume variances.
5. Evaluate the company's manufacturing performance based on the computed variances.

P9-21   Incomplete Data and Variance Analysis

Bio-Products, Inc. produces Roid, an anabolic steroid that helps AIDS patients build up muscle strength to cope with weight loss, and uses a standard cost system for materials and labor cost management. During the last period, the company applied standard costs to production, and recognized variances as follows:

	Standard Costs Applied	Total Variance
Direct materials...............	$16,000	$500, unfavorable
Direct labor....................	24,000	$766, unfavorable

The standards for producing one unit of Roid are as follows:

	Standard Quantity(Hours) of Input	Standard Price(Rate) of Input	Standard Cost
Direct materials	2 units	?	?
Direct labor........	1.5 hours	$8	$12

During the period, the actual materials price of $4.02 per unit and the actual labor rate of $8.12 were paid. All materials purchased were actually used in production.

Required:

1. How many units of actual output were produced?

2. What was the actual cost of materials incurred?
3. What was the actual cost of labor incurred?
4. How many units of materials were purchased?
5. How many hours of labor were actually worked for production?
6. What was the standard price per unit of materials?
7. Compute the materials price and quantity variances.
8. Compute the labor rate and efficiency variances.

 P9-22   Comprehensive Variance Analysis

LPJ, Inc. produces a series of medical products. The company uses a standard cost system for planning and control. Direct labor-hours is the basis of applying overhead costs. The following data relate to the standard and actual variable costs of producing one of the company's products during the last period:

	Hours		Cost Rate Per Hour	
	Standard	Actual	Standard	Actual
Variable costs:				
Direct materials	2.5	2.6	$ 2.00	$ 2.10
Direct labor	0.5	0.6	14.00	12.00
Variable overhead	0.5	0.6	6.00	5.00

Fixed overhead costs of $38,000 were actually incurred, and the budgeted fixed overhead rate was $18 per direct labor-hour. The denominator activity for determining the fixed overhead rate was 2,200 direct labor-hours. The company produced 4,000 units of output for the period.

Required:

1. Compute the direct material price and quantity variances.
2. Compute the direct labor rate and efficiency variances.
3. Compute the variable overhead spending and efficiency variances.
4. Compute the fixed overhead budget and volume variances.
5. Evaluate the manufacturing performance of the company for the period.

P9-23   Overhead Variances; Per-Unit and Per-Hour Standards

CNA, Inc. developed its overhead application rate from the current annual budget. The budget is based on an expected actual output of 720,000 units requiring 3.6 million direct labor-hours (DLH). The company is able to schedule production uniformly throughout the year.

A total of 66,000 units requiring 315,000 DLH was produced during May. Actual overhead costs for May amounted to $375,000. The actual costs as compared to the annual budget and one-twelfth of the annual budget are shown below:

	Annual Budget				Actual
	Total Amount	Per Unit	Per DLH	Monthly Budget	Costs for May
Variable:					
Indirect Labor	$ 900,000	$1.25	$ .25	$ 75,000	$ 75,000
Supplies	1,224,000	1.70	.34	102,000	111,000
Fixed:					
Supervision	648,000	.90	.18	54,000	51,000
Utilities	540,000	.75	.15	45,000	54,000
Depreciation	1,008,000	1.40	.28	84,000	84,000
Total	$4,320,000	$6.00	$1.20	$360,000	$375,000

Required:

Calculate the following amounts for May:
a. Total overhead costs applied.
b. Variable overhead spending variance.
c. Variable overhead efficiency variance.
d. Fixed overhead budget variance.
e. Fixed overhead volume variance.

(CMA, adapted)

 P9-24 Comprehensive Variance Analysis

MJB, Inc. manufactures parts used by printing companies, and uses a standard cost system. The following standards are used for the production of a fold roller:

	Standard Quantity(Hours) of Input	Standard Price(Rate) of Input	Standard Cost
Direct materials ..	2.5 units	$ 3 per unit	$ 7.50
Direct labor	0.5 hours	12 per hour	6.00
Variable overhead.	0.25 hours	8 per hour	2.00
Fixed overhead...	0.25 hours	14 per hour	3.50
Total standard cost..................................			$19.00

Overhead costs, both variable and fixed, are applied to production on the basis of machine-hours. The fixed overhead rate of $14 per machine-hour is based on the denominator activity level of 1,600 machine-hours. Additional data on the operations of the last period are presented below:

a. The actual output for the period was 6,000 units.
b. Materials purchased, 18,000 units at a cost of $2.80 per unit. Materials used, 16,500 units.
c. Direct labor recorded, 3,400 hours at $13 per hour.
d. A total of 1,450 machine-hours was recorded.

e. Variable overhead costs incurred, $12,800. Fixed overhead costs incurred, $20,300.

Required:

1. Compute the following variances:
   a. Material price and quantity.
   b. Labor rate and efficiency.
   c. Variable overhead spending and efficiency.
   d. Fixed overhead budget and volume.
2. Evaluate the manufacturing performance of the company for the period.

 P9-25   Labor Variances for a Hospital

Mountain View Hospital has adopted a standard cost accounting system for evaluation and control of nursing labor. Diagnosis Related Groups (DRGs), instituted by the U.S. government for health insurance reimbursement, are used as the output measure in the standard cost system. A DRG is a patient classification scheme that perceives hospitals to be multiproduct firms, where inpatient treatment procedures are related to the numbers and types of patient ailments treated within a time period.

The nursing unit on the fourth floor treats patients with four DRG classifications. The unit is staffed with registered nurses (RNs), licensed practical nurses (LPNs), and aides. The standard nursing hours and salary rates are as follows:

	Fourth Floor Nursing Unit Standard Hours		
DRG Classification	*RN*	*LPN*	*Aide*
1	6	4	5
2	26	16	10
3	10	5	4
4	12	7	10

	Standard Hourly Rates
RN	$12.00
LPN	8.00
Aide	6.00

For the month of May, the results of operations for the fourth floor nursing unit are presented below.

Actual number of patients:

DRG 1	250
DRG 2	90
DRG 3	240
DRG 4	140
	720

	RN	LPN	Aide
Actual hours	8,150	4,300	4,400
Actual salary	$100,245	$35,260	$25,300
Actual hourly rate	$12.30	$8.20	$5.75

The accountant for Mountain View Hospital calculated the following standard times for the fourth floor nursing unit for May:

DRG Classification	Number of Patients	Standard Hrs./DRG RN	LPN	Aide	Total Standard Hours RN	LPN	Aide
1	250	6	4	5	1,500	1,000	1,250
2	90	26	16	10	2,340	1,440	900
3	240	10	5	4	2,400	1,200	960
4	140	12	7	10	1,680	980	1,400
					7,920	4,620	4,510

The hospital calculates labor variances, using a flexible budgeting approach, for each reporting period by labor classification (RN, LPN, Aide), since the hospital does not have data to calculate variances by DRG. The variances are used by nursing supervisors and hospital administration to evaluate the performance of nursing labor.

Required:

Calculate the total flexible budget variance for the fourth floor nursing unit of Mountain View Hospital for May, indicating how much of this variance is attributed to
1. labor efficiency, and to
2. rate differences.

(CMA, adapted)

P9-26 Overhead Cost Analysis

CWC, Inc. produces a machine tool, and uses a standard cost system for planning and control. Overhead, variable and fixed, is applied to production on the basis of machine-hours. The company's flexible budget shows the following:

Denominator activity in machine-hours............	25,000
Normal activity in output units....................	62,500
Variable overhead................................	$112,500
Fixed overhead	200,000
Total overhead at the denominator level	$312,500

During the last period, the company recorded the following hours and costs for the actual operations:

Machine-hours operated	22,000 hours
Variable overhead cost incurred	$105,600
Fixed overhead cost incurred.	180,400
Total overhead incurred.	$286,000

The company applied a total of $250,000 in manufacturing overhead for the period.

Required:

1. What is the standard machine time for producing one unit of output?
2. What is the standard variable overhead cost per machine-hour? What is the standard fixed overhead cost per machine-hour?
3. How many standard hours were allowed for the actual output during the period?
4. How many units were produced during the period?
5. Compute the variable overhead spending and efficiency variances.
6. Compute the fixed overhead budget and volume variances.
7. What was the under- or overapplied overhead for the period? Explain the under- or overapplied overhead in terms of overhead variances.

P9-27 Variance Analysis; Multiple Processes

EJ Max, Inc. produces a product that goes through two processes, and uses a standard cost system for planning and control. The product uses the following materials and labor according to the standards established per unit of output:

Materials	Unit Cost	Quantity Needed
T	$3.30 per unit	1.5 units
Q	1.00 per unit	2.2 units

Labor	Rate per Hour	Hours Needed
Process 1	$12	0.1 hours
Process 2	14	1.2 hours

Actual output during the last month was 5,800 units of the product. Data on the actual usage of materials and labor during the last month are provided below:

Materials	Cost	Quantity Purchased	Quantity Used
T	$34,100	11,000 units	9,000 units
Q	16,200	18,000 units	13,000 units

Labor	Cost	Hours Worked
Process 1	$ 7,500	600 hours
Process 2	100,820	7,100 hours

Required:

1. Compute the material price and quantity variances for the last month.
2. Compute the labor rate and efficiency variances for the last month.

P9-28 Variance Analysis; Comprehensive

The Sandberg Corporation manufactures and sells a single product and uses a standard cost system. The standard cost per unit of output is shown below:

Direct materials (1 pound plastic at $2 per pound)	$ 2.00
Direct labor (1.6 hours at $4 per hour)	6.40
Variable overhead cost	3.00
Fixed overhead cost	1.45
	$12.85

The overhead cost per unit was calculated from the following annual overhead cost budget for a 60,000-unit volume:

Variable overhead cost:	
Indirect labor (30,000 hours at $4 per hour)	$120,000
Supplies - oil (60,000 gallons at $.50 per gallon)	30,000
Allocated variable service department costs	30,000
Total variable overhead cost	180,000
Fixed overhead cost:	
Supervision	27,000
Depreciation	45,000
Other fixed costs	15,000
Total fixed overhead cost	87,000
Total budgeted overhead cost at 60,000 units	$267,000

The charges to the manufacturing department for November, when 5,000 units were produced, are given below:

Direct materials (5,300 pounds at $2 per pound)	$10,600
Direct labor (8,200 hours at $4.10 per hour	33,620
Indirect labor (2,400 hours at $4.10 per hour)	9,840
Supplies - oil (6,000 gallons at $.55 per gallon)	3,300
Allocated variable service department costs	3,200
Supervision	2,475
Depreciation	3,750
Other	1,250
Total	$68,035

The purchasing department normally buys about the same quantity as is used in production during a month. In November, 5,200 pounds were purchased at a price of $2.10 per pound.

Required:

Calculate the following variances from standard costs:
a. Materials price.
b. Materials quantity.

c. Direct labor rate.

d. Direct labor efficiency.

e. Variable overhead spending.

f. Fixed overhead budget.

g. Fixed overhead volume.

(CMA, adapted)

P9-29   Mix Variance; Service Industry; Materials and Labor

H-O Connect, Inc. is a consulting firm specializing in the installation of switchboards for small businesses, and has adopted standards for measuring its performance. The installation service is provided to the small business clients who want to bail out of the problems created by multiple additions of phone lines, cellular phones, faxes, answering machines, and computer modems. When a client buys a mini-switchboard from one of several vendors, H-O Connect helps install it.

H-O Connect uses two types of materials, R and T, in the switchboard installation. For the most recent period, there was no price or quantity variance for either type of the materials used. H-O Connect serviced 410 clients for the same period.

H-O Connect's standard mix and costs of materials and labor per each installation are as follows:

Materials:

4 units of material R @ $6	$24
5 units of material T @ $8	40
	$64

Manpower:

3 hours of consultant's time at $50 per hour	$150
4 hours of assistant's time at $30 per hour	120
	$270

H-O Connect used the following quantities of materials at the actual costs shown below:

Material R — 1,570 units @$6	$ 9,420
Material T — 2,120 units @$8	16,960
	$26,380

For the same period, H-O Connect's actual labor costs recorded were as follows:

Consultant's time, 1,450 hours @ $50	$72,500
Assistant's time, 1420 hours @ $30	42,600
	$115,100

Required:

1. According to the accountant's variance analysis report, the total cost of materials and labor actually used was higher than the standard costs of materials and labor for the actual output. The same report also indicates that there was no price or quantity variance for materials and there was no rate or efficiency variance for labor. Did the accountant make an error in the report? Explain whether it is possible to make both statements regarding the performance of the same period.

2. Compute the materials mix variance for the period.

3. Compute the labor mix variance for the period.

P9-30   Multiple Cost Drivers; Standard Costs vs. Activity-Based Costs (This problem is related to Chapter 7 also.)

Alyssa Manufacturing produces two items in its Trumbull Plant; Tuff Stuff and Ruff Stuff. Since inception, Alyssa has used only one manufacturing overhead pool to accumulate costs. Overhead has been allocated to products based on direct labor hours.

Until recently, Alyssa was the sole producer of Ruff Stuff and was able to dictate the selling price. However, last year Marvella Products began marketing a comparable product at a price below the standard costs developed by Alyssa. Market share has declined rapidly, and Alyssa must now decide whether to meet the competitive price or to discontinue the product line. Recognizing that discontinuing the product line would place additional burden on its remaining product, Tuff Stuff, Alyssa is using activity-based costing to determine if it would show a different cost structure for the two products. The two major indirect costs for manufacturing the products are power usage and set-up costs. Most of the power usage is used in fabricating, while most of the set-up costs are required in assembly. The set-up costs are predominantly for the Tuff Stuff product line.

A decision was made to separate the Manufacturing Department costs into two activity centers.

Fabricating: using machine hours as the cost driver (activity base).
Assembly: using the number of set-ups as the cost driver (activity base).

Manufacturing Department
Annual Budget Before Separation of Overhead

	Total	Product Line	
		Tuff Stuff	*Ruff Stuff*
Number of units		20,000	20,000
Direct labor per unit*		2 hours	3 hours
Total direct labor	$800,000		
Direct material per unit		$5.00	$3.00
Budgeted overhead:			
Indirect labor	$ 24,000		
Fringe benefits	5,000		
Indirect material	31,000		
Power	180,000		
Set-up	75,000		
Quality assurance	10,000		
Other utilities	10,000		
Depreciation	15,000		

*Direct labor is the same in both departments.

Manufacturing Department
Cost Structure After Separation of Overhead Into Activity Pools

	Fabrication	Assembly
Direct labor	75%	25%
Direct material (no change per product)	100%	0%
Indirect labor	75%	25%
Fringe benefits	80%	20%
Indirect material	$ 20,000	$11,000
Power	$160,000	$20,000
Set-up	$ 5,000	$70,000
Quality assurance	80%	20%
Other utilities	50%	50%
Depreciation	80%	20%

Activity base:	Product Line	
	Tuff Stuff	*Ruff Stuff*
Machine hours per unit	4.4	6.0
Number of set-ups	1,000	272

Required:

1. By allocating overhead based on direct labor hours, calculate the
   a. total budgeted cost of the Manufacturing Department.
   b. unit standard cost of Tuff Stuff.
   c. unit standard cost of Ruff Stuff.
2. After separation of overhead into activity pools, compute the total budgeted cost of the
   a. Fabricating Department.
   b. Assembly Department.
3. Using activity-based costing, calculate the unit standard costs for
   a. Tuff Stuff.
   b. Ruff Stuff.
4. Discuss how a decision by Alyssa Manufacturing regarding the continued production of Ruff Stuff will be affected by the results of your calculation in Requirement 3.

(CMA)

C9-31 Analysis of Overhead Variances

The Mason plant of Zast Corporation has been in operation for 15 months. Mason employs a standard cost system for its manufacturing operations. The first six months' performance was affected by the usual problems associated with a new operation. Since that time, the operations have been running smoothly. Unfortunately, however, the plant has not been able to produce profits on a consistent basis. As the production requirements to meet sales demand have increased, the profit performance has deteriorated.

The plant production manager commented at a staff meeting in which the plant general manager, the corporate controller, and the corporate budget director were in attendance, that the changing production requirements make it more difficult to control manufacturing costs. He further noted that the budget for the plant, included in the company's annual profit plan, was not useful for judging the plant's performance because of the changes in the operating levels. The meeting resulted in a decision to prepare a report which would compare the plant's actual manufacturing cost performance with a budget of manufacturing cost based on actual direct labor-hours in the plant.

The plant production manager and the plant accountant studied the cost patterns for recent months, and volume and cost data from other Zast plants. Then they prepared the following flexible budget schedule for a month with 200,000 planned production-hours which at standard would result in 50,000 units of output. The corporate controller reviewed and approved the flexible budget.

	Amount	Per Direct Labor-Hour
Manufacturing costs:		
Variable:		
Indirect labor..................	$160,000	$ .80
Supplies	26,000	.13
Power	14,000	.07
		$1.00
Fixed:		
Supervisory labor	64,000	
Heat and light	15,000	
Property taxes..................	5,000	
	$284,000	

The manufacturing cost reports prepared for the first three months after the flexible budget program was approved were pleasing to the plant production manager. They showed that manufacturing costs were in line with the flexible budget allowance. This was also reflected by the report prepared for November, which is presented below, when 50,500 units were manufactured. However, the plant was still not quite producing an adequate profit because the variances from standard costs were quite large.

MASON PLANT
Manufacturing Costs
November
(220,000 actual direct labor production-hours)

	Actual	Allowed	(Over) Under Budget
Variable:			
Indirect labor	$177,000	$176,000	$(1,000)
Supplies..................	27,400	28,600	1,200
Power....................	16,000	15,400	(600)
Fixed:			
Supervisory labor	65,000	64,000	(1,000)
Heat and light.............	15,500	15,000	(500)
Property taxes	5,000	5,000	0
	$305,900	$304,000	$(1,900)

Required:

1. Explain the advantages of using a flexible budget over a static budget for cost control purposes.
2. Calculate the excess amount over standard spent on manufacturing cost items during November. Analyze this excess amount into those variances due to:
   (a) Efficiency.
   (b) Spending.
3. Explain what the management of Mason plant should do to reduce:
   (a) The efficiency variance.
   (b) The spending variance.

(CMA, adapted)

PERFORMANCE IN THE NEW ENVIRONMENT

After studying this chapter, you should be able to:

1. Know the concept and application of the balanced scorecard as a measurement system.

2. Understand the implication of the lean production paradigm for manufacturing and service organizations.

3. Distinguish between mass-production and lean production in different aspects of operations.

4. Know the basic concepts and applications of the methods used to achieve lean production.

5. Analyze why the relevance of standard costing is lost in a lean production environment.

6. Understand how management accounting information needs change in a lean production environment.

7. Explain the value-added perspective in management accounting.

8. Define and apply target costing, kaizen costing, backflush costing in a lean production environment.

9. Understand the meanings and applications of nonfinancial performance measures such as cycle time, quality, and productivity.

10. Explain the changes in product costing when lean production is used.

11. Understand value chain analysis and apply it in a numerical setting for manufacturing and service.

In the last decade, organizations in the world, regardless of whether they are in manufacturing or in service, have undergone drastic changes in the way they operate. **Lean** organizations practicing lean production have replaced traditional organizations. **Lean production** includes programs such as customer satisfaction, just-in-time (JIT), total quality management (TQM), employee empowerment, and other organizational learning and improvement activities. Many organizations have not survived, or have seen their competitive positions eroded, when they did not adopt lean production while their competitors did.

The traditional financial performance measures that rely on standards are not compatible with the new management practices in today's environment as we learned in Chapter 9. In recent years, managers have adopted various performance measures that are more conducive to the new paradigm in the global business environment. In this chapter, we learn those new concepts and practices. They include balanced scorecard, value added, target costing, kaizen costing, life cycle costing, backflush costing, value-chain analysis, and nonfinancial measures such as cycle time, quality, and productivity.

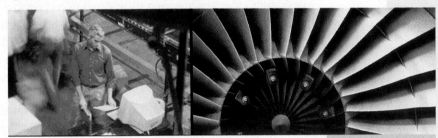

At CISCO SYSTEMS, INC. multi-measure performance evaluation is well understood by employees and managers. "The most expensive box of anything is the one sitting still."

MULTI-MEASURE PERFORMANCE EVALUATION: BALANCED SCORECARD

Multiple Measures of Performance

Managers must be aware of the pitfalls of relying on traditional financial performance measures. An organization has its priorities, and a single measure cannot capture various attributes of performance. For example, suppose Microsoft has set up a performance evaluation system that rewards its work teams based only on how fast the team launches a new software product. Work teams then would focus only on the speed of the product launch. They would not take into account the reliability of new software, its linkage with other software, and the environmental impact, thus subjecting Microsoft to future risks. We remember what has happened to Microsoft in federal courts for not having considered the full impact of its Internet-related products on other competitors' products. Individuals are motivated to score well on the measure the organization uses for evaluation. The use of only one performance measure may lead individuals to engage in dysfunctional behavior.

As organizations reorganize to deal with increasing pressures from global competition, they have eliminated the traditional hierarchy based on functional areas such as development, manufacturing, marketing, accounting, and finance. Instead, individuals in organizations usually work in cross-functional teams. For example, at Ford Motor Company's Premier Automotive Group, based now in California, the new product development teams have designers, engineers, and cost accountants working together on new models of Jaguar and Volvo. Accordingly, competitive organizations are increasingly reliant on a mix of quantitative and qualitative measures that include nonfinancial variables discussed later in this chapter.

BALANCED SCORECARD

The **balanced scorecard** is a measurement system that focuses on the vital signs of the company, and translates an organization's top-level visions into individual performance measures at every level. The balanced scorecard was born because of the following reasons: Financial performance measures focus on short-term accounting-oriented performance results, and ignore performance with respect to customers and competitors. Nonfinancial performance measures are hard to reconcile with financial measures across functions. Traditional measures also focus on outcomes rather than processes, not allowing management to identify bottlenecks that slow the organization's progress toward strategic goals. Lower-level employees also find it difficult to relate their performance to the strategic goals.

The balanced scorecard takes a systematic and balanced approach to operational performance measures, incorporating both tangible and intangible factors. It empowers everybody in the organization to contribute to the accomplishment of the strategic goals.

The balanced scorecard translates an organization's strategy into transparent objectives, measures, targets, and initiatives. The framework of the balanced scorecard is comprised of four measurement perspectives that are presented in Exhibit 10-1.

External Financial Perspective

Financial performance measures are needed to address an organization's strategy and objectives related to financial bottom-lines. Financial measures include operating income, economic value added (discussed in Chapter 12), return on equity, and growth in sales and profit.

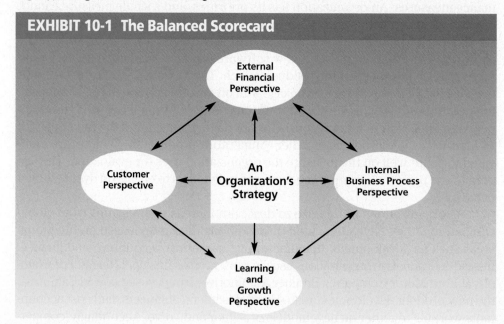

EXHIBIT 10-1 The Balanced Scorecard

Customer Perspective

Each business unit's customer perspective addresses its performance in targeted customer and market segments and uses measures such as customer satisfaction, market share, new customer addition, customer retention, and customer profitability.

Internal Business Process Perspective

The internal business process perspective focuses on improving existing processes and developing new processes to enhance customer value and financial performance.

Learning and Growth Perspective

Organizational learning and growth is related to personnel, systems, and procedures. People-related measures include employee training, satisfaction, and retention. Systems-related measures should address information accuracy, reliability, and consistency. Procedure-related measures should focus on what would indicate a successful performance has been made for learning and development before rewards are considered.

An Example

The Balanced Scorecard for Borough Finance Company, New York City
Area: Commercial Loan

Measures for Each Perspective	Targets	Results	% Improvement
External Financial:			
1. Operating profit to loan amount	25%	28%	12
2. Loan portfolio growth	20%	22%	10
3. Non-performing loans	2%	1.5%	25
4. Profit growth	10%	11%	10
Customer:			
1. Percentage of new customers	15%	18%	20
2. Percentage of failed customers	3%	4%	(33)
3. Loan applications	160	189	18
4. Withdrawn applications	12%	10.8%	11
Internal Business Process:			
1. Loan evaluation cycle time	6 days	6.9 days	(15)
2. Analysts' work cycle	3 days	3.6 days	(20)
3. Applications returned by loan committee	10%	9%	10
Learning and Growth:			
1. Analysts' ratings	4.5	4.3	(5)
2. Assistants training (hours)	20	22	10
3. Analysts turnover	17%	28%	65

CEO's evaluation of the manager of this area: 82 ↓

0	25	50	75	100
Very Poor	Poor	Average	Very Good	Excellent

Before JIT
In the mass-production environment (before 1987), Tellabs used a push system, as shown in this photo, a clear and good contrast with the previous page photo of Tellabs' after-JIT operation.

After JIT
Workers operate in well-organized product groups, as shown in this photo of Tellabs. The U-shaped work areas allow excellent communication and coordination among workers who "own" the process and solve problems as they arise.

THE LEAN PRODUCTION PARADIGM

Up until the mid-1980s, the auto industries of North America and Europe were relying on manufacturing and related operating techniques based largely on the concepts of Henry Ford's mass-production system. These techniques simply were not as efficient or effective as a new paradigm developed and practiced by the Japanese auto makers. American and European auto makers could not compete, in product cost and quality, with the Japanese counterparts, who subsequently gained considerable share in the global market.

Ultimately, American and European auto makers have transformed their manufacturing and related operating systems into more competitive ones based on the new paradigm, which an MIT program subsequently named **lean production.** The lean production paradigm soon became the standard of operations and guiding philosophy in all sorts of manufacturing industries. Manufacturers around the world are now trying to apply lean production, if appropriate, to their operations.

Lean production combines the strengths of craft production and mass-production which we discussed in Chapter 9. In order to understand lean production, we revisit the traditional mass-production concept below. This will allow us to compare the two for a better understanding of lean production.

Mass-Production Revisited

The mass-producer's single-purpose machines cost least when they are run without disruption. This is because the more units the expensive machines produce, the less the products cost per unit. In addition, when machine operation is disrupted, workers become idle and the assembly line must be restarted. Both of these factors are costly. Accordingly, the mass-producer should keep the expensive machines running without disruption.

Suppose you are a mass-producer. How can you keep production running without interruption? You need to have an abundant supply of raw materials and parts, so that you will not run out of stock. You need enough work-in-process inventories between different workers and workstations, so that a faster worker will not use up

all the subassemblies before the preceding station's worker could replenish them. High levels of work-in-process inventories also shield one workstation from the delays caused by production bottlenecks at another, at least temporarily.

What have you just created? Buffers of raw materials and work-in-process inventories. As a matter of fact, the mass-producer creates buffers in workers and space also. And problems, such as defective materials, defective parts, defective finished products, production bottlenecks, and so forth, are hidden. This is because buffers hide problems. When a part supplied by a vendor is defective, throw it away. Pick up another part that works from the pile of buffer inventories. Nobody else notices it. The defective part problem, accordingly, is hidden from the eyes of plant management.

The mass-producer aims to produce a product which is "good enough." There are a certain "acceptable" number of defects. If a finished product is defective, it is sent back to preceding processes for rework. Rework is a fact of life. Striving for a level of quality which exceeds the normal, acceptable level, the mass-producer believes, would simply cost too much.

Lean Production

The lean producer combines the advantages of craft production and mass-production, while avoiding the high cost of craft production and the inflexible nature of mass-production. In a lean producer's plant, teams of multiskilled workers use flexible, automated machines to produce a variety of products in small volumes. The flexibility comes from the ability to perform a wide range of activities across many product lines in a timely fashion.

Lean production consumes less labor, less inventory, less capacity and space, and less machine and operating time to produce products with fewer defects. The lean producer does not recognize an "acceptable" level of defects, and aims to achieve perfection in operations. In various efforts to achieve perfection, the lean producer practices **continuous improvement** in quality, cost, and inventory and production management. Exhibit 10-2 shows the differences between lean production and mass-production.

METHODS USED TO ACHIEVE LEAN PRODUCTION

The power of lean production is awesome. The dominance of the lean production paradigm as the guiding production and management philosophy in the global context of the 1990s proves it. Now we see the emergence of various managerial jargon, such as value-added, lean organization, lean finance, corporate restructuring, and reengineering. These are all based on the lean production paradigm, to which their conceptual origin can easily be traced.

Despite the appeal of lean production, companies have had mixed experiences in practicing it. General Motors, for example, found itself with too many workers, too many managers, and too many plants to adopt lean production in

EXHIBIT 10-2 Lean Production versus Mass-Production: A Comparison

		Lean Production	Mass-Production
1.	Workers	Multiskilled, teams	Specialized, individuals
2.	Machines	Flexible, multi-purpose	Inflexible, single-purpose
3.	Products	Diversified, in small volumes	Standardized, in large volumes
4.	Buffer inventory	No	Yes
5.	Quality goal	Perfection	Acceptable
6.	Defects	Zero	Acceptable number
7.	Production run	Short	Long
8.	Batch size	Small	Large
9.	Setups	Many	Few
10.	Production problems	Exposed	Hidden
11.	Rework	Not acceptable	Acceptable

its early stage. Other auto makers in U.S. and overseas, as well as numerous large corporations in other industries, have had similar problems.

How do companies actually practice lean production? There is no set formula. Lean production consists of various organizational operating and improvement concepts and activities, such as just-in-time (JIT), total quality management (TQM), customer satisfaction, employee empowerment, and others. In the following sections, we will look at these methods of practicing lean production. But first, we need to understand the value-added concept that is the underlying theme of lean production.

Value Added: Underlying Theme of Lean Production

The underlying theme of JIT and TQM is to maximize the **value added** to the organization and eliminate waste and inefficiency. Value-adding activities are those activities that are essential to the accomplishment of the organization's objectives.

The value added represents the following for the organization:

Value added = Final value received − Initial value purchased

For the *organization:*

Value added = Sales − Purchases

For a *unit* within an organization:

Value added = Final value created − Initial value given

Extra inventory and idle time, for example, reduce value added to the organization. Various types of value-adding and nonvalue-adding activities are discussed in this chapter.

Just-in-Time (JIT)

Just-in-time, or **JIT,** means buying, delivering, producing, or receiving a good or service only when the user, customer, or manufacturer needs it. Management of a company practicing JIT is devoted to the elimination of waste that is present anywhere in its activities. A JIT company believes that every activity should **add value.**

JIT, contrary to what some people claim, is not confined to just a JIT inventory system. It is a managerial concept that encompasses purchasing, receiving, inventory management, production, and delivery. It can help companies eliminate waste or inefficiency in service or administrative functions also.

If a company practices **JIT purchasing,** it directs attention toward reducing waste in the entire procurement process. Waste can be found in delays in receiving and inspecting materials, idle materials inventory, and defective materials. A manufacturer needs JIT purchasing to make sure that there is no waste created by purchased materials in the entire production process.

JIT manufacturing requires a continuous flow of production once materials and parts are put into the production process. In order to have workpieces (materials, parts, and work-in-process units) flow without delay or stoppage, well-trained workers use good-quality materials to produce products in small lot quantities in a plant with a reliable and efficient layout. Producing in small lots prevents inventories from piling up between processes or workstations.

In JIT manufacturing, continuous flow of workpieces is achieved by a **JIT pull** system. Production takes place in a particular department or workstation only if the units produced are required by the next workstation. The JIT pull system is in contrast with the conventional **push** system of flow control, where the objective is to keep the machines busy, regardless of whether the units are needed further down the line. The striking differences between the two systems exist as illustrated in Exhibit 10-3.

In a JIT pull system, the manufacturer can promptly respond to necessary schedule adjustments caused by product demand changes or production trouble by having the final process make the adjustment. The needed adjustments at the pre-

EXHIBIT 10-3 Conventional Push System versus JIT Pull System: A Comparison

	Conventional Push System	JIT Pull System
Production is initiated by:	First assembly process	Final assembly process
When and how much to produce is informed by:	Monthly production schedules provided to each process	Final process pulling the chain of production
Production flows as:	Preceding process pushes workpieces forward to subsequent process	Subsequent process pulls workpieces from preceding process
Each process produces as much as:	Each process can produce under the schedule	Subsequent process demands (only to replace)
Adjustment in production schedule is made by:	All processes simultaneously	Final process which initiates change

ceding processes will be pulled by the final process as it withdraws the workpieces it needs. The immediately preceding process then produces to replace only those workpieces withdrawn. The same routine takes place all the way down to the first process. Accordingly, there is no need for backup inventory to make adjustments smooth. If you play the simple "JIT Game" as presented at the end of the chapter, you will be able to feel the effects of the JIT pull system clearly.

Total Quality Management (TQM)

The lobby lounge of Ritz-Carlton Schlosshotel, Berlin. Ritz-Carlton's TQM employs most common defects and defects as a percentage of occupancy by day of week and by keyword.

Total quality management, or **TQM,** is an organized approach to instill a zero defects philosophy in the minds of people. If JIT is about how to improve work structure, TQM is about how to improve mind structure. TQM emphasizes the importance of doing everything right the first time people do them. Preventing an error or defect from occuring in the work is preferred to detecting and correcting it. Since manufacturing processes in a JIT-using plant operate with a minimum level of inventory, it is crucial that materials delivered by a supplier and workpieces produced at various processes be defect-free. Even a small number of defects can stop a whole assembly line. Accordingly, JIT and TQM are usually practiced together.

In a TQM environment, the focus of management is on the needs of a customer, which could be the next production process, the buyer of finished product, or any person or organizational unit one is supposed to serve. The performance in such an organization is measured from the perspective of the customer, rather than the service provider. Thus, **customer satisfaction** takes on a very important meaning in a TQM environment. How do organizations achieve customer satisfaction? They do it by promoting a self-managed team spirit among employees and by empowering them with appropriate authority and responsibility.

RELEVANCE OF STANDARD COSTING IS LOST IN LEAN PRODUCTION

In Chapter 9 we discussed standard costing and variances as a performance evaluation system. Standard cost variances based on a budget are relevant for a massproducer. The relevance of standard cost variances, however, becomes lost as a manufacturer becomes a lean producer. In this section, we will look at how standard costing loses relevance as an organization goes lean. This will help us understand how performance measurement can be adjusted to support a lean production environment.

Material Standards and Variances

In Chapter 9, we calculated the material price variance as follows:

$$\text{Materials price variance} = (\text{SP} - \text{AP}) \times \text{AQ or}$$
$$(\text{difference in price}) \times \text{actual quantity}$$

For a lean producer, this price variance becomes irrelevant for the following reasons:

First, in order to improve performance and show a favorable materials price variance, a manufacturer and its purchasing agent would like to lower the actual price paid (AP) by making large-volume purchases to get price discounts. Excess materials, which would result from large-volume purchases, as you know by now, are not permitted in lean production. Second, a favorable price variance may result if cheaper materials of poor quality are acquired. But the negative consequence of acquiring poor-quality materials may far outweigh the benefit of the small savings in prices paid if the whole plant must stop because of defective materials entering the production process. Accordingly, measuring performance using the material price variance loses relevance in lean production. Furthermore, wrong motivations result when variances actually become detrimental to the organization.

Labor Standards and Variances

In Chapter 9, we calculated the direct labor efficiency variance as follows:

$$\text{Direct labor efficiency variance} = (\text{SH} - \text{AH}) \times \text{SR or}$$
$$(\text{difference in hours}) \times \text{standard rate per hour}$$

As a mass-producer changes to a lean producer, this labor variance cannot maintain the same relevance it enjoyed in a mass-production environment for the following reason:

For a manufacturer to show a favorable labor efficiency variance, standard hours allowed for the actual output (SH) should exceed actual hours worked (AH). If you examine SH, you will notice that the standard hours allowed for each unit of output is fixed, say 2 hours per unit. Accordingly, the only way to attain a larger number of SH is to increase actual output. If you produce more, you are allowed a larger number of SH.

This provides production managers with an incentive to produce as many units of product as possible, or at least, to make the weekly or monthly quota assigned to them. Unless the quota is met, the production manager is faced with an unfavorable labor efficiency variance. Hence, the production manager comes under pressure to make the quota, whether the items produced are needed or not. This is relevant and encouraged in mass-production, but goes against the concept of lean production.

Overhead Standards and Variances

Labor is not usually the appropriate driver for overhead in a lean manufacturing environment. However, if a company budgets its variable and fixed overhead costs based on direct labor hours, as many companies actually do, the resulting overhead variances contain the same problem which we observed regarding the labor efficiency variance.

In Chapter 9, we calculated the variable overhead efficiency variance as follows:

$$\text{Variable overhead efficiency variance} = (\text{SH} - \text{AH}) \times \text{SR}$$
$$\text{or (difference in hours)} \times \text{standard rate per hour}$$

Remember that SH represents standard direct labor hours allowed for actual output. As we saw in the labor standards discussion, the amount of actual output plays an important role here too. For a manufacturer to show a favorable variable overhead efficiency variance, standard hours allowed for the actual output (SH) should exceed actual hours worked (AH). The only way to attain a larger number of SH is to increase actual output. If you produce more, you are allowed a larger number of SH. This provides production managers with an incentive to produce as many units of products as possible. We know this is not desirable in a lean production environment.

We calculated the fixed overhead volume variance in Chapter 9 as follows:

$$\text{Fixed overhead volume variance} = \text{Difference in}$$
$$\text{standard hours allowed} \times \text{predetermined rate per hour}$$

The difference between standard hours allowed for actual output and standard hours allowed for budgeted output times the predetermined fixed overhead rate per hour is the volume variance. If actual output is greater than budgeted output, the variance is favorable, implying that production facilities have been more fully utilized. Here again, a company's standard cost system encourages organizational units to produce as much as possible. This, we know, is not what lean production intends to accomplish.

PLANNING AND CONTROL FOR LEAN PRODUCTION

As an organization changes from a mass-producer to a lean producer, its management accounting information needs change accordingly. This is because the goals and objectives of the two types of production are different, as we discussed earlier in this chapter. We now take a look at how management accounting information needs change, and how organizations can satisfy those needs.

Lean Production and Budgeting

In Chapter 8, we discussed budgeting in a mass-production environment. A mass-producer's budgeting process starts with the product demand forecast. All other budgets depend, more or less, on the sales budget. The number of units to be produced in the production budget is determined based on the product demand forecast and desired ending inventory level. A mass-producer manufactures products to desired levels of inventory, and stores them for future shipments. This is exactly what a traditional push inventory system is designed for. In an algebraic form, the production requirement is calculated as follows:

> **Production requirement** (in mass-production)
>
> = Sales forecast + Desired ending inventory − Beginning inventory

In such a system, the reliability of the cycle of operations and budgets depends heavily on the accuracy of the demand forecast. If the demand forecast is larger than actual demand, the manufacturer will produce more than necessary. This will leave excess inventories in storage. If the demand forecast is smaller than actual demand, the manufacturer will produce less than is needed. Stockouts will result, and contribution margins will be lost.

A lean producer manufactures based on actual demand, not based on the demand forecast. It may seem impossible to accomplish this. How can a company plan manufacturing in such a way? It can plan by minimizing the total time the company takes to make the product, which is called **cycle time.** The best way to understand this implication is to use an extreme case. Imagine a manufacturer with a cycle time of one second. It takes only one second to get materials, process them, and move finished products out of the plant. In such a case, a company does not need any sales forecast or buffer inventory. Of course, no manufacturer can achieve a cycle time of one second, and appropriate planning has to be done.

But in a lean manufacturing environment, cycle time is reduced to a level where it is not necessary to rely on an extended demand forecast. Instead, the production requirement can be based on average actual demand, and will fluctuate weekly or even daily, depending on the plant's cycle time and efficiency.

> **Production requirement** (in *lean production*) = average actual demand

Lean production focuses on cycle time to manage the manufacturing process's self-response to the changes in actual demand. Lean producers accomplish this by using a well-coordinated physical flow control system.

LEAN PRODUCTION AND COST MANAGEMENT

We have discussed why and how standard cost variances are not compatible with lean production. Using standard cost variances for a lean producer's performance measurement would lead organizational units to produce results and behaviors that are detrimental to the objectives of lean production.

How should a lean producer manage costs and measure performance? First, activity-based costing (ABC), which we discussed in Chapter 6 and Chapter 7, is very conducive to measuring a lean producer's performance. Second, there are new operations cost management techniques, which have been used by Japan-

JIT at Tellabs

Tellabs is a manufacturer of sophisticated equipment for telecommunications networks. The company's 1987 conversion from a push system to a JIT-pull system has enabled its largest production facility to triple the output in less than 18 months. The increases in efficiency and quality included a 20% improvement in product quality, a 55% reduction in defects, a 96% decrease in production lead time, a 95% decline in work-in-process inventory, a 50% shrinkage in manufacturing floor space, and a 54% drop in labor costs. Those improvements have also increased the company's manufacturing capacity and improved its customer service. Compared to the remarkable successes, the costs of implementing JIT were small, less than $100,000. The basis of JIT implementation at Tellabs was the relentless elimination of waste and the streamlining of manufacturing. The company reorganized its manufacturing approach and the shop floor. (See the three photos in this chapter.)

In the previous push system, Tellabs used a batch system, manufacturing large quantities of one product at a time. The large batches of inventory would sit idle between and during the various stages of processing, inspection, and shipment.

In addition to wasting labor and time and creating bottlenecks, the large batches

would postpone inspection until the end of the manufacturing process. Accordingly, if one unit of product had a defect, the probability of hundreds or thousands having the same defect was high. Defective units had to be reworked or scrapped at a significant waste.

JIT made the difference. JIT made one group or product team responsible for the total manufacturing of one product. Instead of sitting along an assembly line as a typical mass-production system would dictate, workers are now organized in product groups. They build entire products by themselves.

Product groups are rewarded for producing the highest-quality product in the most efficient way possible. Each group member is responsible for inspecting her work and assuring the quality of the work performed at the preceding station. Defects are detected immediately and fixed.

ese lean producers thus far, that would be useful for any lean producer. Last, a lean producer can focus on **nonfinancial measures** to evaluate and improve performance. Nonfinancial measures of performance represent the attributes of performance that are not expressed in monetary terms. Cycle time, quality, and productivity are significant nonfinancial measures for most organizations. We will look at these performance measurement methods in the following sections.

Lean Production and Activity-Based Costing

Activity-based costing (ABC) can help companies measure the resources spent and financial contributions made by various activities which are involved in lean production. A linkage is developed between a lean producer's operations improvement programs and financial results if an ABC system is used. This is because ABC employs in its framework various activity measures such as setup, quality assurance, engineering, and design that become the focuses of lean production.

Of course, many have claimed that costs and profits will take care of themselves if a company improves quality and productivity, and reduces cycle time. There is, however, documented evidence that significant improvements in quality, productivity, and cycle time may not always produce profit increases. A lean producer can benefit from the use of ABC by being able to measure how much progress is made in its performance.

TARGET COSTING

Target costing, as popularized by world-class Japanese lean producers, is a cost management technique born out of the market-driven strategy. Target costing focuses on managing costs at the development and design stages of a product, although its concept is used throughout the product life cycle. This is because, once a product is developed and designed, the characteristics of manufacturing processes and routines are already determined, and there is a limit to how much cost reduction a company can accomplish in the manufacturing stage.

The technique is based on the price-down, cost-down strategy, and is closely connected with the company's long-term profit and product planning process. The main theme in the target costing process is, "What should the new product cost?" It is in direct contrast to a typical U.S. manufacturer's practice, in which the question is, "What does it cost?" Traditionally, a company would develop and design a product, calculate costs, price the product based on the desired markup, and market the product. In the target costing process, this process is reversed.

Target Costing Process

Target costing is practiced according to the following process:

1. Establish the target sales price for the newly planned product based on market research.
2. Determine the desired profit based on the company's desired return on sales.
3. Subtract the desired profit from the target sales price. This is the allowable cost, which becomes the goal. It is a target which is difficult or impossible to attain in the short run.
4. Calculate the estimated cost based on current standards for the materials, labor, and overhead components of the product.
5. Compare the allowable cost with the estimated cost, and calculate the difference.
6. Identify areas where estimated cost might be reduced without reducing the marketability of the product.
7. Develop a cost reduction target based on the analysis in step 6.

8. Subtract the cost reduction target from the estimated cost. This is the **target cost,** and is attainable in the short run.

9. Decompose the target cost into each cost element, and determine the necessary materials and production processes.

10. Perform cost improvement activities to achieve the target cost.

Chrysler's pilot manufacturing operation. Target costing helps Chrysler manage costs well before new vehicles are launched.

Target Costing: A Numerical Example

The following example helps us understand the target costing process better:

ETech, Inc., a Silicon Valley manufacturer of electronic products, is offered $50 per unit for 10,000 units of a product called ET-1 by a Los Angeles movie studio. ETech's usual return on sales rate is 30%. The estimated costs of producing a unit of this product are materials $28, labor $5, and overhead $9. A cost study reveals that 80% of the difference between the allowable cost and the estimated cost is possible to achieve in the short run.

Below, we show calculations related to the target cost determination:

The desired profit on this offer:

Desired return on sales	30%
Amount of the offer	× $50
Profit per unit	$15
Number of units	× 10,000 units
Desired profit	$150,000

The allowable cost for this production of 10,000 units of ET-1:

Sales price	$50
Desired return............................	(15)
Allowable cost............................	$35
	× 10,000 units
Total allowable cost......................	$350,000

The estimated cost for this production of 10,000 units of ET-1:

Materials.................................	$28	
Labor.....................................	5	
Overhead	9	$42
		× 10,000 units
Total estimated cost......................		$420,000

The cost reduction target:

Short-run cost reduction target rate.........	80%

Cost difference:

Estimated cost	$420,000	
Allowable cost	(350,000)	× $70,000
Cost reduction target		$56,000

The target cost:

Estimated cost	$420,000
Cost reduction target	(56,000)
Target cost	$364,000

As we can see, the target cost of $364,000 is still higher than the allowable cost of $350,000. Management, however, can accept the target cost, because the efforts of those who are involved in reducing costs would be substantial.

KAIZEN COSTING

Kaizen costing, which aims at reducing actual costs to below standard costs, functions in a fashion similar to a budgetary control system. The company develops manufacturing cost reduction targets and managers must attain the targets. While target costing is used in the product development and design stage, kaizen costing supports continuous improvement activities in the manufacturing phase. Accordingly, combined with target costing, kaizen costing helps manufacturers reduce costs throughout the development-manufacturing cycle, as follows:

Target costing: Design and development stage

↓   ↓

Kaizen costing: Manufacturing stage

Since the cost reduction target amounts are translated into specific improvement activities, each employee knows what to do to achieve the assigned targets.

Kaizen Costing Process

Kaizen costing and its cost reduction process follow the annual budgeting process. Each organizational unit prepares projections and plans as a part of its annual profit budget. A variable costing approach is used to calculate the budgeted operating profit as follows:

Sales forecast	$121,000,000
Expected variable costs	(40,000,000)
Budgeted contribution margin	81,000,000
Expected increases in variable costs	(2,000,000)
Adjusted contribution margin	79,000,000
Expected fixed costs	(65,000,000)
Budgeted operating profit	$ 14,000,000

The performance indicator for each department is the following difference in the two profit figures:

Profit difference (as the performance indicator)
= Actual operating profit realized
− Annual budgeted operating profit

The expected costs in the above illustration are calculated as follows:

Expected costs = Actual production costs of the previous year
− Target reductions of the current year

Since the target reductions are subtracted from the previous year's actual costs, those expected costs represent a more stringent performance than the usual standard costs. Annual target reductions are translated into monthly target reductions. The aggressive nature of target reductions leads kaizen costing to exert enormous amounts of pressure onto workers.

Kaizen Costing and Standard Costing: A Comparison

We can compare kaizen costing to standard costing in various ways. The following illustrates the differences between the two concepts:

	Standard Costing	**Kaizen Costing**
Goal:	Meet cost performance standards.	Achieve cost reduction targets.
Focus:	Cost control.	Cost reduction.
Manufacturing condition:	Stable manufacturing processes.	Continuous improvement in manufacturing.
Timing:	Set standards semi-annually or annually.	Set reduction targets monthly.
Variance analysis:	Compare actual to standard costs.	Compare actual cost reduction amounts to target kaizen costs.

Under kaizen costing, workers who are closest to the process provide inputs to the kaizen costing process, from target setting to feedback. Under standard costing, managers and engineers play the major role throughout the process.

LIFE CYCLE COSTING

Life cycle costing consists of various revenue-enchancing and cost-reducing activities that are designed to maximize profits during the life cycle of products and services. Life cycle costing relies on a revenue-oriented viewpoint of marketing life cycle, a cost-oriented viewpoint of product life cycle, and a customer-value oriented viewpoint of consumption life cycle.

Marketing life cycle is comprised of the following stages of a product or service:

| Introduction | → | Growth | → | Maturity | → | Decline |
| stage | | stage | | stage | | stage |

Sales revenue is created as production starts in the introduction stage, and increases until the peak of the maturity stage, and starts decreasing after that.

Product life cycle focuses on the three stages of activities in a product's life cycle: R&D activities, manufacturing activities, and logistical (moving products) activities. **Consumption life cycle** uses the four stages of a consumer's activities: purchasing, operating, maintaining, and disposal.

Life cycle costing provides a comprehensive perspective on cost management. In relationship to target costing and kaizen costing, life cycle costing adds the after-sale service stage and disposal as follows:

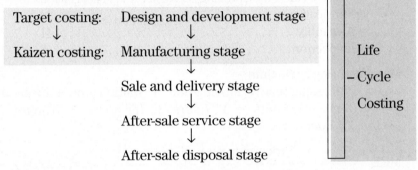

The interactive analysis using the three viewpoints of life cycle is very useful in evaluating an organization's overall strategies related to products and consumers. Life cycle costing, however, is not intended to serve as a cost accounting vehicle, and relies on cost and activity information that a good cost management system can provide. This is why an application example of life cycle costing is not presented here.

NONFINANCIAL PERFORMANCE MEASURES

Cycle Time

Manufacturing cycle time, the total time a company takes to make a product or create a service, is one of the most important elements of a lean producer's performance, and is composed of the following:

Manufacturing cycle time
= Working time + Waiting time
= Value-adding activities time + Non-value-adding activities time

Working time includes both value-adding and non-value-adding activities time. Waiting time, of course, is non-value-adding time. Value-adding activities time represents time for processing, such as fabrication and assembly. All others, such as moving, storing, and inspecting materials and finished goods, are non-value-adding activities. Those activities may be needed, but they are not indispensable in making products. The lower the proportion of the non-value-adding activities time, the higher the efficiency of manufacturing.

Manufacturing cycle time is also called **throughput time** or **production velocity,** which measures how fast materials are put through the whole process and turned into finished products. This process efficiency, called **manufacturing cycle efficiency (MCE),** is measured by the following formula:

$$MCE = \frac{\text{Value-adding activities time (Processing time)}}{\text{Manufacturing cycle time}}$$

The following is a simple numeric example of MCE for a manufacturer:

Data on hours taken to perform activities in a period:
Material handling 32
Waiting (including storing). 185
Fabrication. 39
Assembly 41
Inspection. 8

Manufacturing cycle time
 = Processing time + Moving time + Waiting time + Inspecting time
 = (39 + 41) hours + 32 hours + 185 hours + 8 hours
 = 305 hours

$$MCE = \frac{\text{Processing time, 80 hours}}{\text{Manufacturing cycle time, 305 hours}} = 0.262$$

The value-adding activities time consists of fabrication time of 39 hours and assembly time of 41 hours, which amount to 80 hours of processing time.

The ratio of non-value-adding activities time to manufacturing cycle time
 = (305 − 80) hours ÷ 305 hours = 0.738
or
 1 − MCE = 1 − 0.262 = 0.738

It is hard to believe that, for most industries, the MCE's are less than 10%. With a high level of work-in-process inventories, the major portion of the manufacturing cycle time in mass-production is waiting time. Workpieces just sit idle between processes and other activities. Many lean producers, however, have increased MCE to over 70%.

Quality as a Performance Measure

Quality is a measure of how satisfied a customer is about a product or service. Every product or service has a certain level of expectations to meet, and quality is a measure of how well the product or service meets the customer's expectations. Quality is a relative concept, because it is judged based on the product's (or service's) expectations. The expectations a customer has about a notebook computer are different from the expectations a customer has about a mainframe computer. The expectations a customer has about a five-star hotel are different from the expectations a customer has about a two-star motel.

Every product or service has certain functions to perform, and the assessment of quality is made about how well the functions are performed. For a product manufacturer or service-provider, performance is measured in terms of quality and cost. A manufacturing line of a defect-free product may not receive a very high performance appraisal if the line has to incur a prohibitively high cost to accomplish zero defects.

Quality has cost, and every organizational unit influences quality and cost in one way or another. But it is difficult for an organization to isolate the cost of achieving a certain level of quality. Most companies have no idea how much they spend on quality planning and control, with the exception of the cost reported by the quality control department. Accordingly, the costs of quality, which we will discuss here, do not come from a company's chart of accounts. Quality costs are rather conceptual, and are related to every aspect of a company's performance. Overall, some specialists estimate that quality costs amount to about 20-40% of sales revenue.

The total cost of quality can be categorized as shown in Exhibit 10-4. **Prevention costs** are costs, such as new product review costs, that are incurred to plan the product or process to minimize defects. **Appraisal costs** are associated with product inspections. **Internal failure costs** are caused by defects discovered before products reach customers, and include costs of scrap, rework, spoilage, and downtime. **External failure costs** result when defective products reach customers, and include costs associated with returned products, such as repairs, allowances, refunds, and warranty adjustments.

Marriott's quality assurance programs help ensure that food served is fresh and delicious.

Companies try to minimize quality costs by focusing on the relationship between control costs and failure costs. Low defects mean that the degree of conformance to customer expectations is high. In this case, the failure costs are low

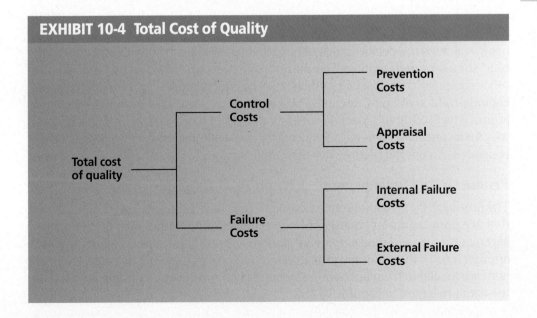

EXHIBIT 10-4 Total Cost of Quality

Total cost of quality
- Control Costs
  - Prevention Costs
  - Appraisal Costs
- Failure Costs
  - Internal Failure Costs
  - External Failure Costs

but the control costs are high. High defects represent a low degree of conformance, high failure costs, and low control costs. Companies look for an optimal level of conformance where total quality costs are minimized.

Productivity as a Performance Measure

Productivity measures the following:

$$\text{Productivity} = \frac{\text{Units of output}}{\text{Units of inputs}}$$

At many companies, productivity is defined as labor productivity. This preoccupation with labor cost originated from the measurement of national productivity by the Bureau of Labor Statistics. Cost accountants have also contributed to this thinking. While direct labor costs account for less than 10% of the total product cost at many manufacturing firms, cost reduction primarily has meant decreasing direct labor costs, as we have seen in variance analysis, for example. Productivity should focus on overall capabilities of a company, not just labor cost. It should be related to all the variables and strategies.

There are different productivity measures available for different purposes. For example, the following productivity measures can be calculated to compare the efficiency in using three cost elements between two competitors:

$$\text{Material productivity} = \frac{\text{Units of output}}{\text{Units of material used}}$$

$$\text{Labor productivity} = \frac{\text{Units of output}}{\text{Hours of labor used}}$$

$$\text{Overhead productivity} = \frac{\text{Units of output}}{\text{Units of overhead used}}$$

When managers use productivity, they need to be aware of the possibility that organizational units may substitute one input for another. For example, if a bank evaluates the performance of branch managers based on labor productivity only, then a branch manager could improve her performance by buying more office equipment to boost labor efficiency. This will increase labor productivity, but capital productivity may decline. Furthermore, the result may not help the bank improve its profitability because of higher equipment costs. Accordingly, it is not wise for an organization to push for increases in specific, narrowly defined productivity measures. An overall perspective is more desirable.

Productivity Measurement: A Numerical Example

The productivity measurement example we use here is based on actual practices that are popular among many U.S. companies. Many companies prefer a measurement approach that is relevant and easy to understand. We can apply the approach to both manufacturing and service companies. All the data we need here are available from accounting systems. Our numerical example is based on the data presented in Exhibit 10-5.

EXHIBIT 10-5

Input and Output Data for Base Year (Year 1) and Current Year (Year 2)

	Year 1			Year 2		
	Units	Prices	Values	Units	Prices	Values
Product A	100	$1,000	$100,000	120	$1,200	$144,000
Product B	50	1,500	75,000	70	$1,650	115,500
Output total (sales)			$175,000			$259,500
Material E	500	$110	$ 55,000	600	$120	$ 72,000
Material C	80	40	3,200	64	40	2,560
Material total			$ 58,200			$ 74,560
Labor-Office	100	$45	$ 4,500	110	$52	$ 5,720
Labor-Fabrication	250	26	6,500	240	28	6,720
Labor-Assembly	400	22	8,800	380	24	9,120
Labor total			$ 19,800			$ 21,560
Overhead-1	70	$65	$ 4,550	90	$ 75	$ 6,750
Overhead-2	120	80	9,600	180	100	18,000
Overhead total			$ 14,150			$ 24,750
Input total			$ 92,150			$120,870

Productivity indices are developed for the purpose of monitoring performance, identifying operating problems, and tracking long-term trends. A company's *profitability* improvements include the following two components:

> Profitability improvements = Price increases × Productivity increases

A company can increase its profitability by just increasing its product prices for the given output (sales) quantity. The effect of price increases should be removed to isolate the real productivity increases from profitability improvements.

Base-period weights: In our numerical example, we use Year 1 as the base period. The **base period** is the normal period against which to gauge the performance of a period. The period can be a week, month, quarter, or year, depending on the frequency of measurement a company needs. In order to combine products A and B into the total output, and materials E and C and different types of labor and overhead into each input total, base period weights are used.

The respective values of Year 1 are used to develop those weights. For example, the base-period weights for products A and B are:

Product	Sales	Base-Period Weight
A	$100,000	0.5714
B	75,000	0.4286
	$175,000	1.0000

The base-period weights for material E and material C are:

Material	Value	Base-Period Weight
E	$55,000	0.9450
C	3,200	0.0550
	$58,200	1.0000

The rest of the base-period weights are calculated in the SELF-REVIEW PROBLEM at the end of this chapter.

Base period-current period change ratios: These ratios show the percentage changes in units of outputs and inputs of the current period over those of the base period. For example, Year 2 *unit change ratios* are:

	Product A	Product B
Year 2 units	120	70
Year 1 units	÷ 100	÷ 50
	1.20	1.40

The unit change ratio for *output total* is:

	Product A	Product B	Output Total
Unit change ratio	1.20	1.40	
Weight	× 0.5714	× 0.4286	1.0000
Weighted ratio	0.69	0.60	1.29

The Year 2 unit change ratio for *material C* is:

Year 2 units	64
Year 1 units	÷ 80
	0.80

Productivity index: Productivity indices reflect the relative changes in output units compared to the changes in input units. The benchmark index is the base-period index of 1.00. For example, Year 2 productivity index for *material C* is 1.61, as calculated below:

Output unit change ratio	1.29
Material C unit change ratio	÷ 0.80
	1.61

The Meaning of Productivity Indices

Unlike standard cost variances, productivity indices help us explain the long-term trend of a company's performance. This is because standards change over time, and the magnitudes of favorable or unfavorable variances cannot be used for meaningful multi-year comparisons. Various indices, which we have discussed in this chapter, can also portray the nature of a certain period's performance in a concise manner.

Consider the Year 2 productivity indices which are presented in Exhibit 10-6.

EXHIBIT 10-6 Year 2 Productivity Indices

Material E	1.08
Material C	1.61
Material total	1.10
Labor-office	1.17
Labor-fabrication	1.34
Labor-assembly	1.36
Labor total	1.31
Overhead-1	1.00
Overhead-2	0.86
Overhead total	0.90
Input total	1.10

Based on the given productivity data, we can explain the company's performance as follows:

Productivity increases were mostly in manufacturing (indices of 1.34 and 1.36), although office (white-collar) productivity (index of 1.17) showed a healthy increase also. The use of material C, the cheaper one, was more efficient (index of 1.61) than the use of the more expensive material E (index of 1.08). The use of overhead resources was not very productive (index of 0.90). Overall, the company realized a healthy improvement (of 10%) in productivity of input total for the period (index of 1.10) over the base period.

LEAN PRODUCTION AND PRODUCT COSTING

When a manufacturer becomes a lean producer, its product costing process becomes simplified also. A simplified costing system is made possible by the attributes of lean production, such as a smaller number of suppliers, reduced inventory level and cycle time, and improved quality of work.

Cell Manufacturing

In a mass-producer's factory, the production and equipment layouts are focused on products. In a typical assembly-line operation, for example, as the product moves down the assembly line, necessary parts are attached and required processing is done. In lean production, the focus changes to a focus on process, called cell manufacturing.

A **cell** is a clustering of multiple machines which as a group perform the processing requirements for a product or product line. A lean producer's product flow line may consist of one or more cells, and may or may not include stand-alone machines. In cell manufacturing many indirect costs become directly linked to the product, requiring less arbitrary allocations because it is very clear now which process is dedicated to the production of which product.

Simplified Product Costing: Backflush Costing

In a traditional manufacturing environment, as we learned in our discussion of job-order costing in Chapter 4, work orders serve as the primary device for driving production schedules and for tracking costs. Costs of materials, labor, and overhead attach at various workstations and processes, as products move through the factory.

In lean production, product costing becomes more simplified, although the basic process remains the same as for mass-production. The simplification is attributed to the impact of simplified operations of lean production on product costing, as described below:

1. Shorter cycle times and lower inventory levels of lean production lead a substantial portion of manufacturing costs to become costs of goods manufactured and sold, rather than ending inventory costs of work in process or finished goods. In other words, there are not too many inventory items to count at the end of each accounting period. Materials and parts become finished goods very fast in lean production.

2. Due to the substantially lower levels of inventory, some lean producers merge the Raw Materials Inventory account with the Work in Process inventory account. The newly created account is called **Raw and In-Process Inventory.** Merging the two accounts into one simplifies the record-keeping part of accounting, but this is not acceptable, unless a truly lean production makes it unnecessary to separately recognize raw materials and work in process.

3. Some lean producers have adopted a radical practice called **backflush costing,** which eliminates cost tracking through job cost sheets or other means entirely. They "flush" costs out of the Raw and In-Process Inventory account and the Conversion Cost (labor and overhead) account and charge them to the Finished Goods Inventory account when they complete products. They do not charge any costs when they *use* materials and parts. The practice is based on the simple reasoning that, if a certain number of units have been completed, a certain amount of costs must have been spent in the process. Unless frequent physical counts of inventory can be performed at a minimal cost, back-

flush costing creates problems in allocating costs to ending inventories and costs of goods sold. Accordingly, only those companies that truly have minimal inventories should use backflush costing.

4. A lean producer uses a smaller number of suppliers and fewer cost classifications. Accordingly, managing accounts receivable and other purchase-related accounts is simpler.

Backflush Costing: An Illustration

A plant uses a JIT process for its one and only manufacturing cell. The following information relates to the company's performance for one week in the cost accounting period:

Beginning inventories:		
Raw materials and parts		$ 0
Work in process		0
Finished goods		0
Actual costs:		
Raw materials and parts purchased		
in the current period	$28,000	
Labor	16,800	
Overhead	68,000	
Standard costs:		
Raw materials and parts per		
unit of finished goods		$ 34
Conversion costs per hour:		
Labor cost per hour	$ 420	
Overhead cost per hour	1,700	2,120

(Standard costs are used here only for product costing as a part of financial reporting, not for cost management purposes.)

An actual output of 800 units was produced. Accordingly, the standard materials cost for the actual output is $27,200 ($34 × 800). The cycle time is 3 minutes. This is translated into an output of 20 units per hour (60 minutes ÷ 3 minutes), 160 units per an 8-hour day, or 800 units per a 5-day week.

Journal entries:

1. Raw materials and parts are purchased:

Raw and In-Process (RIP) Inventory	$28,000	
Accounts Payable.....................		$28,000

In a JIT setting, frequent deliveries are made in small quantities. Recording each delivery becomes impossible. Journal entries for JIT deliveries can be made on a weekly basis for all deliveries for the week.

2. Raw materials and parts are used in production:

No entry.

Raw materials and parts may be brought directly to the production floor, bypassing the stockroom altogether.

3. Finished goods (800 units) are produced:

Finished Goods..........................	27,200	
RIP Inventory		27,200
($34 × 800 units = $27,200)		

Raw materials costs are charged as finished goods are reported by the manufacturing cell. The RIP inventory account on-hand balances gradually decrease.

Finished Goods..........................	84,800	
Conversion Cost....................		84,800

Standard hours allowed for the actual output		
= 800 × 0.05 hour (cycle time)......		40 hours
Conversion cost per hour		× $2,120
Conversion cost for the standard hours		$84,800

(Debits to Conversion Cost are assumed to have been made when labor and overhead costs were incurred.)

The variances between actual costs and standard costs are closed to Cost of Goods Sold at the end of the period.

SERVICE ORGANIZATIONS AND LEAN PRODUCTION

As is true with almost every topic in managerial accounting, by replacing "produce goods" with "generate services," the concept is applied to service organizations. As a matter of fact, all businesses have service components. For large corporations, for example, it is not practical to classify them into manufacturing or service anymore. It is a matter of the **extent** of the service component of a business, rather than the **kind** that determines whether a business is in manufacturing or service.

Lean production was originated from and is practiced in manufacturing on a large scale. Its use, however, is not confined to manufacturing. At Hewlett-Packard's direct marketing division, for example, the process improvement efforts, which focused on applying the lean production concept to service functions, reduced the rate of overdue receivables from the second highest in the company to the 49th. The division also improved the lead time in its shipment of products from 48 hours to 24 hours. The California State Department of Motor Vehicles used the lean production concept, and reduced the errors in its vehicle registration process by over 60%.

The cycle time for operations of a service function is measured in the same way as in manufacturing. For example, the cycle time in a loan evaluation and approval process at a finance company is measured as the time from the receipt of a loan application to the approval or rejection of the loan application.

These service organizations practice lean production primarily by reducing time wasted for nonvalue-adding activities. Management accounting information on the costs of performing value-adding and nonvalue-adding activities is useful in the implementation of lean production at these organizations.

VALUE-CHAIN ANALYSIS

In order to survive and grow in the global environment of today, companies need to achieve a competitive advantage in the long run. Successful companies use **strategic cost management** for that purpose, employing cost data to support winning strategies. Value-chain analysis is the major part of strategic cost management.

Customer Value

When a customer buys a product or service, the customer receives something (realization) and gives up something (sacrifice). **Customer value** is the excess of realization over sacrifice. The ingredients of realization and sacrifice are as follows:

Realization: Product features, brand name, quality, reputation, before- and after-service, user instructions, and other values the customer desires.

Sacrifice: Product purchase cost, time and effort spent buying the product and learning to use it, costs of actually using, maintaining, and disposing of the product.

Competitive Advantage

A company creates competitive advantage by increasing customer value through either of the following two strategies:

Differentiation strategy: Maximize realization.
Low-cost strategy: Minimize sacrifice.

Each strategy focuses on the following:

$$\text{Customer Value} \quad = \quad \text{Realization} \quad - \quad \text{Sacrifice}$$

$\uparrow$ $\uparrow$

Differentiation   Low-cost
strategy   strategy

FedEx uses a differentiation strategy to provide a high-quality delivery service for which a higher price can be charged.

IBM and Toshiba use a differentiation strategy to produce and sell top-of-the-line notebook computers other competitors cannot provide. America Online uses a low-cost strategy to provide Internet services to a large number of Internet users at low cost.

Value-Chain Analysis

In order to successfully implement differentiation or low-cost strategies, companies must analyze their **value chain,** the linkage of value-creating activities. We call this analysis **value-chain analysis.**

The industrial value chain ranges from the supplier's extracting of raw materials to the end-user's discarding of the final product. The strategically relevant activities comprise the value chain, which includes internal and external linkages. **Internal linkages** link activities a company performs within the company, and includes development, design, manufacturing, marketing, distribution, sales and service. **External linkages** link value-chain activities a company performs with its external suppliers and customers.

Internal Linkage Analysis: An Example

We use the following example to illustrate internal linkage analysis:

SWI, Inc. manufactures steering wheels for various types of vehicles. The engineering team has advised management that a new plant layout would provide the following improvements in operations:

Activity	Cost Driver	Cost Rate Per Driver	Activity Level Present	Expected
Material handling	Number of movements	$4 per move	80,000	60,000
Plant maintenance	Square footage	$5 per sq.ft.	9,000	8,000
Process engineering	Engineering hours	$50 per hour	3,000	2,000

Direct costs of changing the layout would be $40,000, and interruptions in operations during the layout change would cost $30,000.

Analysis of internal linkages provides the following information:

Activity	(a) Cost Rate	(b) Reduction in Activity	(a × b) Cost Savings
Material handling	$ 4	20,000	$80,000
Plant maintenance	$ 5	1,000	5,000
Process engineering	$50	1,000	50,000
Total			$135,000

Since the cost of exploiting the internal linkage is only $70,000 ($40,000 plus $30,000), management would select the layout change strategy which would save $135,000. *The decision adds value* (of $65,000) because *the net impact on all aspects of the value chain would be positive.* As we see in this illustration, value chain analysis relies heavily on activity-based costing (ABC) for cost and activity information.

External Linkage Analysis: An Example

We use a service organization as an example to illustrate external linkage analysis. Westchester Finance Company has two classes of loan customers: small merchants and corporations. The following is the information on loans and costs:

	Customer Class			
	Small Merchants		**Corporations**	
	Per Unit	**Total**	**Per Unit**	**Total**
Number of customers		100		5
Total loans		$25,000,000		$10,000,000
Loan fees charged	1%	250,000	1%	100,000
Loan service cost	$ 1,000	100,000	$ 1,000	5,000
Credit analysis cost	200	20,000	2,000	10,000

The company charges loan fees of 1% of the loan amount. Recently, corporate customers have complained about the large amounts of loan fees they have to pay, and some have hinted at the possibility of switching to another lender if the same policy of charging 1% of the loan amount is continued.

The company's ABC information reveals the same $1,000 cost of servicing each loan customer, regardless of the loan size. However, the credit analysis cost for corporate customers is much higher, $2,000 compared to $200 per customer for small merchants. The high credit analysis cost is attributed to complex financial analysis needed for corporate customers.

Management has performed the following comparison of loan service cost and loan fee charged:

	Customer Class			
	Small Merchants		**Corporations**	
Average loan size		$250,000		$2,000,000
Loan fee (1%)		2,500		20,000
Costs:				
Loan service	$1,000		$1,000	
Credit analysis	200	1,200	2,000	3,000
Margin		$1,300		$17,000
Percentage of cost		108%		567%

The company earns an average margin of $17,000 on each corporate customer, which represents 567% of its cost. This compares very favorably to the $1,300 margin it earns on an average small customer, which represents only 108% of the company's cost. Based on this information, and also considering the importance of maintaining business with corporate customers, management selects the strategy of charging flexible percentages of loan fees to corporate customers.

What about the decreasing loan fee revenue from this change in strategy? The company could recover the lost revenue by charging higher loan fees to small customers. The higher fee could be justified by the relatively higher cost of doing business with small customers. The example illustrates how exploiting the external linkages will help the company and its customers through the re-examination of the cost-activity relationships. Again, we can see that value chain analysis relies heavily on ABC information on cost-activity relationships.

Value chain analysis involves looking at the financial impact of any decision on all aspects of the value chain. For example, a decision to add a particular feature to a product may increase production costs, but may add value because it reduces the customer's cost of disposal, thereby justifying a higher price.

SUMMARY

In this chapter, we discussed how accounting for managerial decisions is influenced by an organization's move to lean production. We revisited the traditional mass-production concept in order to compare mass-production with lean production. The lean producer combines the advantages of craft production and mass-production.

How do companies actually practice lean production? Lean producers use various combinations of organizational operating and improvement concepts and activities, such as JIT, TQM, customer satisfaction, employee empowerment, and others. When a company practices those lean production techniques, the traditional standard costing system becomes incompatible and irrelevant.

Cost management and other planning and control methods change as a company becomes a lean producer. As we have learned, ABC, target costing, and kaizen costing can be useful in a lean production environment. Nonfinancial performance measures, such as cycle time, quality, and productivity, are meaningful and effective performance measures to use in such an environment also. Lean production simplifies product costing. Lean production can be applied to service functions as well.

BASIC CONCEPTS AND TERMS

Appraisal costs	Total quality management
Balanced Scorecard	Backflush costing
Cell	Continuous improvement
Customer satisfaction	Cycle time
External failure costs	Internal failure costs
Just-in-time	JIT pull system
Kaizen costing	Lean production
Manufacturing cycle time	Manufacturing cycle efficiency
Mass-production	Nonfinancial measures
Prevention costs	Production velocity
Productivity index	Push system
Quality	Raw and in-process inventory
Target costing	Throughput time

■ SELF-REVIEW PROBLEM

TARGET COSTING: Tech House, Inc., a manufacturer of computer parts, is offered $40 per unit for 20,000 units of a part it has developed. The company's usual rate of return on sales is 25 percent. The estimated production costs are materials $16, labor $4, and overhead of $13 per unit. A cost study indicates that 60 percent of the difference between the allowable cost and the estimated cost can be achieved in the short run.

Required:

1. What is the desired profit on this offer?
2. What is the allowable cost for the production of 20,000 units of the part?
3. What is the estimated cost for the production of 20,000 units of the part?
4. What is the cost reduction target?
5. What is the target cost for the production of 20,000 units of the part?

Solution:

1. Desired profit

   $$= \text{(Desired rate of return 25\%} \times \text{Amount of the offer \$40)} \times 20,000 \text{ units}$$
   $$= \$10 \times 20,000 \text{ units}$$
   $$= \$200,000$$

2. Allowable cost

   $$= \text{(Sales price \$40} - \text{Desired return \$10)} \times 20,000 \text{ units}$$
   $$= \$30 \text{ per unit} \times 20,000 \text{ units} = \$600,000$$

3. Estimated cost

   $$= \text{Materials \$16} + \text{Labor \$4} + \text{Overhead \$13} = \$33$$
   $$\$33 \times 20,000 = \$660,000$$

4. Cost reduction target

   $$= 60\% \times (\$660,000 - \$600,000)$$
   $$= 60\% \times \$60,000 = \$36,000$$

5. Target cost

   $$= \text{Estimated cost \$660,000} - \text{Cost reduction target \$36,000} = \$624,000$$

CYCLE TIME: The above company's data on hours taken to perform various activities in a period are provided below:

Material handling	26
Waiting	127
Storing	38
Fabrication	31
Assembly	54
Inspection	9

Required:

1. Calculate the manufacturing cycle time.

2. Calculate the manufacturing cycle efficiency (MCE).

3. Calculate the ratio of non-value-adding time to manufacturing cycle time.

Solution:

1. Manufacturing cycle time = Processing time + Moving time + Waiting time (including storing time) + Inspecting time = (31 + 54) hours + 26 hours + (127 + 38) hours + 9 hours = 285 hours

2. MCE = Processing time (85 hours) ÷ Manufacturing cycle time (285 hours) = 0.298

3. Ratio of non-value-adding time to manufacturing cycle time
   = (285 − 85) hours ÷ 285 hours = 0.702, or
   1 − MCE = 1 − 0.298 = 0.702

PRODUCTIVITY INDEX: Refer to the data in Exhibit 10-5 in the chapter. We will use the data to calculate productivity indices and related values here and in the end-of-the-chapter exercises.

Required:

Calculate the following:

1. Base-period weights for various labor and overhead items.

2. Year 2 material E productivity index.

Solution:

1. Base-period weights are calculated based on the respective "values" of Year 1, the base period.

	Year 1 Value	Base-Period Weights
Labor-office	$ 4,500	0.2273
Labor-fabrication	6,500	0.3203
Labor-assembly	8,800	0.4444
	$19,800	1.0000
Overhead-1	$ 4,550	0.3216
Overhead-2	9,600	0.6784
	$14,150	1.0000

2. Material E productivity index:

Output unit change ratio	1.29
Material E unit change ratio (600/500)	÷ 1.20
	1.08

REVIEW CASE

"ALPHA-TOY": A Just-in-Time (JIT) Game

This game, a simulation of a JIT assembly line operation, is designed to help you understand (1) the concept of JIT, and (2) the managerial accounting implications of JIT. You can play this game in the classroom with minimum preparation.

The Product: You will manufacture a product in this simulation. The product is a simple toy, called "ALPHA-TOY." Exhibit 10-6 shows the picture of the toy. It is made of two paper cups, one cup placed upside down on top of the other. The inside of ALPHA-TOY is empty, and it can float on water.

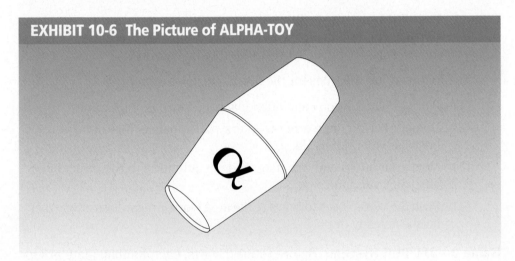

EXHIBIT 10-6 The Picture of ALPHA-TOY

Materials and Parts: The following materials and parts are needed for the production of 40 units of ALPHA-TOY:

	Number of Units
Paper cups (small size)	80
Masking tape	1
Stickers (small)	80
Brown grocery bags	5

Labor: Direct and indirect labor consist of the following:

	Number of People
Material handler	1
Direct labor workers	3
Packaging person	1

Facility and Tools: Two tables and three chairs (for three direct labor workers) serve as the fixed facility for the plant. A color marker and a stapler serve as tools. Four sheets of letter-size construction paper (to be placed between each worker), called the Kanban plate, are needed as fixtures.

Manufacturing Process: The operations are initiated as the material handler takes the paper cups out of the vinyl bags and feeds them into the production process. The three direct labor workers process them into finished ALPHA-TOY's as follows:

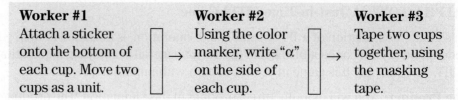

Worker #1
Attach a sticker onto the bottom of each cup. Move two cups as a unit.

→

Worker #2
Using the color marker, write "α" on the side of each cup.

→

Worker #3
Tape two cups together, using the masking tape.

The packaging person puts eight units of ALPHA-TOY's in each grocery bag, and seals the bag with a staple.

Game 1 - Push System: The push system production starts as the material handler feeds two cups to direct labor worker number one. Use two tables, because you need enough space between workers to store inventories.

The following are the rules for the first game, push system:

(1) Work as hard as you can. Individual excellence is important.

(2) Do not interfere with other workers' performance. It is none of your business what others do.

(3) Meet your quota and due date, and pay attention to the direct labor efficiency variance.

(4) Push the workpieces forward to the next worker regardless of whether he/she is ready or not.

Game 2 - JIT Pull System: Before Game 2 starts, each Kanban plate is supposed to have two units of work in process, consisting of 4 cups. (The two units represent the uniform work load on this assembly line.) The JIT pull system production starts as the packaging person withdraws two units of work in process from the Kanban plate, which is located between him/her and direct labor worker #3. Use only one table, because you do not need extra space for inventories.

The following are the rules for the second game:

(1) Each worker should produce to replenish the two units withdrawn from the Kanban plate.

(2) Produce only when your Kanban plate is empty.

(3) Work as a group, and pay attention to any other worker's trouble. Your performance is evaluated as a group.

(4) Stop the line if you spot any defect.

Required:

While playing each game, measure the following items. Compare the measurements between the two systems.

1. Operate for 10 minutes after the production is started. Stop the assembly line.

a. How many units of work-in-process inventory do you have on the line?

   b. Assume that the packaging person detected a defect. You want to check other units, and rework if there are additional defects. What is your rework quantity?

2. The material handler marks one cup with a long red line across it. How long does it take for the cup to travel from direct labor worker #1 to the packaging person? This is the manufacturing cycle time.

3. Each table represents the plant space. Charge $1,000 to each table for costs of rent, utilities, cleaning, and moving distances. What is the cost of space in each system?

4. Observe what has happened to direct labor worker #3, who tapes the two cups into one finished unit of toy. Which system is more conducive to finding and correcting production problems?

■ REVIEW QUESTIONS

10-1 How does a lean producer combine the strengths of craft production and mass-production?

10-2 What is the conceptual origin of corporate restructuring and reengineering?

10-3 Does Just-in-time refer only to inventory management?

10-4 To what kinds of waste does JIT purchasing direct attention?

10-5 Why does production occur in small lots when JIT manufacturing is implemented?

10-6 Why is it so crucial that materials delivered by a supplier to JIT manufacturing processes are defect-free?

10-7 Who are the "customers" as used in "customer satisfaction" in a TQM environment?

10-8 Why does the material price variance motivate the wrong behavior in lean production?

10-9 Why does the direct labor efficiency variance motivate the wrong behavior in lean production?

10-10 Comment on the relevance of variable overhead efficiency variance in lean production.

10-11 Would the pressure to show a favorable fixed overhead volume variance work as an incentive for a manufacturing department to produce excess inventories? Why or why not?

10-12 Consider the formula used to determine the budgeted production requirement in a mass-production environment. What information has the most significant influence on the reliability of the whole budgeting process? Why?

10-13 Does a lean producer rely on a demand forecast in the budgeting process as much as a mass-producer does? Why or why not?

10-14 How does a lean producer determine the production requirement in the budgeting process?

10-15 How does a lean producer manage costs and measure performance? Name three ways of doing this.

10-16 Why does target costing focus on managing costs at the development and design stages of a product?

10-17 The main theme in target costing is, "What should the new product cost?" How does this compare to a traditional practice, in which the question is, "What does it cost?"

10-18 What is the major difference between target costing and kaizen costing?

10-19 What is the major difference between kaizen costing and standard costing in terms of motivating behavior?

10-20 Consider the components of cycle time. Is working time always equal to value-adding time? Why or why not?

10-21 Consider a mass-producer with a high level of work-in-process inventories. What is the most significant portion of the manufacturing cycle time?

10-22 Why is quality regarded as a relative concept?

10-23 Is it wise for an organization to push for increases in certain, specific productivity measures? Why or why not?

10-24 What is the reason for calculating base-period weights first in the process of constructing productivity indexes?

10-25 What is the most serious weakness of backflush costing?

10-26- What are the four perspectives used in a balanced scorecard?

10-27- Hewlett-Packard has about 50 divisions in the continental U.S. What would be the advantages of using the balanced scorecard in the evaluation of those division heads by HP's CEO? What would be the CEO's expected problems in using the balanced scorecard?

INTERNET PROJECT

Web 10-1:

Websites: www.winn-dixie.com
www.kroger.com

The websites listed above represent two famous companies. Search the sites for information on their operating characteristics.

Required:

1. Prepare a balanced scorecard for the CEO of the first company.

2. Based on the website information, how would you change the balanced scorecard you prepared in (1) to suit the second company? Why?

Web 10-2:

Websites: www.ti.com
www.intel.com

The websites listed above represent two famous companies. Search the sites for information on their operating characteristics.

Required:

1. How would you use target costing for the first company?

2. Which cost items you used for (1) would change if you would like to apply the same target costing to the second company?

■ EXERCISES

E10-1 Balanced Scorecard

The following are performance measures that belong to one of the four measurement perspectives of the balanced scorecard used by Vickie's Secret, a ladies' apparel company. Please indicate your choice using the number: (1) financial perspective, (2) customer perspective, (3) internal business process, or (4) learning and growth perspective.

a. Shopper's program rating
b. Growth in sales dollars
c. Average employment period of sales people
d. Frequency of merchandise returns to suppliers
e. Shoppers' satisfaction index
f. Operating profit ratio to sales
g. Markdown frequency observed
h. Repeat sales
i. Business reengineering applied to existing stores
j. Hours of computer training

E10-2 Conventional Push System versus JIT Pull System

Indicate whether each of the following represents a conventional push system or a JIT pull system by designating "push" or "pull."

a. Production is initiated by the final assembly process.
b. When and how much to produce is informed by monthly production schedules provided to each process.

c. Production flows as the subsequent process withdraws workpieces from the preceding process.

d. Each process produces as much as it can produce under the schedule.

e. Adjustment in production schedule is made by all processes simultaneously.

f. Adjustment in production schedule is made by the final process which initiates change.

g. There is no need for backup inventory.

 ### E10-3 Lean Production and Standard Cost Variances

The following are the standard cost variances typically used by mass-producers for performance measurement. If the mass-producer becomes a lean producer, which variances become the most irrelevant? Why?

Materials price variance

Materials quantity variance

Labor rate variance

Labor efficiency variance

Variable overhead spending variance

Variable overhead efficiency variance

Fixed overhead budget variance

Fixed overhead volume variance

E10-4 Cost of Quality

Part 1. The total cost of quality consists of prevention costs (P), appraisal costs (A), internal failure costs (IF), and external failure costs (EF). Indicate which cost (P, A, IF, or EF) each of the following items represents:

  a. New product review cost

  b. Quality inspection supervisor's salary

  c. Returned product repair cost

  d. Process planning cost

  e. Rework cost

  f. Cost of quality inspection tools

  g. Cost of downtime caused by defective work

  h. Allowances granted for returned products

  i. Warranty adjustments made

Part 2. Refer to part 1. Now the company increases the overall level of quality control activities to a much higher level than before, so that the degree of conformance to customer expectations is higher. What effect does that have on the items (a) through (i)? Indicate whether, in general, the cost of each item increases (I) or decreases (D).

E10-5   Target Costing

TVP, Inc., a manufacturer of TV parts, is offered $20 per unit for 10,000 units of part #119, which it has just developed. The company's usual rate of return on sales is 30%. The estimated production costs are as follows:

	Per Unit
Materials	$7
Labor	2
Overhead	6

Cost accounting department's study reveals that 80% of the difference between the allowable cost and the estimated cost can be achieved in the short run.

Required:

1. What is the desired profit on this offer?
2. What is the allowable cost for the production of 10,000 units of part #119?
3. What is the estimated cost for the production of 10,000 units of part #119?
4. What is the cost reduction target?
5. What is the target cost for the production of 10,000 units of part #119?

E10-6   Kaizen Costing

The following are various stages of a manufacturer's product cycle. Which of the stages is kaizen costing used for?
a. Design stage
b. Development stage
c. Manufacturing stage
d. Forecasting stage

E10-7   Manufacturing Cycle Efficiency

Data on hours taken to perform various activities in the last period:

Material handling	21
Waiting	109
Storing	42
Fabrication	26
Assembly	44
Inspection	8

Required:

1. Calculate the manufacturing cycle time.
2. Calculate the manufacturing cycle efficiency (MCE).
3. What is the ratio of non-value-adding activities time to manufacturing cycle time?

E10-8   Productivity Indices for Labor

Refer to the data in Exhibit 10-5 of this chapter. Calculate (1) the base period-current period unit change ratio and (2) the productivity index for each of the following:

	(1)	*(2)*
a. Labor-office		
b. Labor-fabricaton		
c. Labor-assembly		

E10-9   Productivity Indices for Overhead

Refer to the data in Exhibit 10-5 of this chapter. Calculate (1) the base period-current period unit change ratio and (2) the productivity index for each of the following:

	(1)	*(2)*
a. Overhead-1		
b. Overhead-2		

E10-10   Productivity Indices for Each Input Category

Refer to the data in Exhibit 10-5 of this chapter. The following base-period weights were calculated:

	Year 1 Values	*Base-Period Weights*
Material E	$55,000	0.9450
Material C	3,200	0.0550
	$58,200	1.0000
Labor-office	$ 4,500	0.2273
Labor-fabrication	6,500	0.3203
Labor-assembly	8,800	0.4444
	$19,800	1.0000
Overhead-1	$ 4,350	0.3216
Overhead-2	9,600	0.6784
	$14,150	1.0000

Required:

Based on the Exhibit 10-5 data and the given base-period weights, calculate (1) the base period-current period unit change ratio and (2) the productivity index for each of the following:

	(1)	*(2)*
a. Material total		
b. Labor total		
c. Overhead total		

E10-11   Productivity Index for Input Total

Refer to the data in Exhibit 10-5 of this chapter.

Required:

Calculate (1) the base period-current period unit change ratio and (2) the productivity index for the Year 2 input total.

E10-12   Lean Production and Management Accounting

Part 1. Assume that the cycle time is reduced 50% in a lean producer's plant. Give your one-sentence answer to each of the following questions on lean production:
   a.   What is the impact on the work-in-process inventory level and cost of goods completed?
   b.   What happens to rework cost?

Part 2. Work-in-process inventory is piling up at a production bottleneck in a mass-producer's plant. Assume that you are the cost accountant at the plant, trying to find a solution for the problem. Would your solution include an increase in direct labor at the bottleneck? Why or why not?

Part 3. Lean Production versus Mass-Production. The following are production characteristics which belong to either lean production (L) or mass-production (M). Please indicate your choice using L or M.
   a.   Flexible, multi-purpose machines.
   b.   Standardized products in large volumes.
   c.   Buffer inventory.
   d.   "Good enough" as quality goal.
   e.   Zero defects.
   f.   Short production run.
   g.   Large batch size.
   h.   Few setups.
   i.   Exposed production problems.
   j.   Rework is acceptable.

■ PROBLEMS

P10-13   Ethics and Departmental Performance

Hercules, Inc. is a manufacturer of physical exercise equipment. One such equipment is Yoga Headstand. The equipment helps people practice yoga easily, because the two-piece equipment requires no special strength, agility, or balance. The user's shoulders rest comfortably on a cushion and the neck stretches naturally and the head is prevented from touching the ground due to a sturdy steel frame.

One Friday morning, Eric Karros, the line manager of steel-frame operations sees a high likelihood of defective production in one of his machines. Eric knows that if the machine is not serviced promptly, the machine would turn out poor-quality steel frames that are used in the subsequent assembly operation. Eric informs his supervisor of the problem, but the supervisor tells him to ignore it because the actual labor and overhead costs will exceed standards if the line is stopped for preventive maintenance.

"You know how important it is to meet the production quota," says the supervisor. "We can wait until the next scheduled maintenance date. You must keep in mind what our performance will look like for this week if the line is stopped."

Five working days pass, and the subsequent assembly operation finds itself coping with newly arriving defective frames that are out of specification. Subsequent lines' operations are disrupted, and unfavorable performance results are reported by the subsequent lines. While this is going on, Eric's line keeps reporting its on-schedule performance.

Required:

1. How does "meeting the production quota" affect the performance of a production line such as Eric's? Discuss the cost implications.
2. Is there any ethics-related issue involved in the above situation? What would you do if you were Eric?

P10-14   Kaizen Costing

Leisure Mobiles, Inc. of Westwood, California manufactures watercraft and snow-mobiles. The recent popularity of its products and surging sales have increased the size of the company. Combined with the bigger size and the higher sales, the company's costs have also increased very fast. The cost increase has caused management to worry about its control over the entire operations.

In an effort to control its operations and costs, the company has introduced kaizen costing. It is now January 1, Year 5. The information on kaizen costing for the current year is provided below:

Cost reduction target for the current year:

Variable costs	$ 50,000
Fixed costs	40,000
Total	$ 90,000
Sales forecast for the year	$950,000

Actual production costs for Year 4:

Variable costs	300,000
Fixed costs	520,000

It is the company's policy to develop manufacturing cost reduction targets which managers must attain. Continuous improvement activities are supported by managers.

Required:

1. Compute the budgeted contribution margin and budgeted operating profit for Year 5 under kaizen costing.
2. The Watercraft Production Group accounts for 40% of the total sales and profit of the company. Assume that this ratio applies to the current year also. If the manager of the group wants to achieve a performance indicator (profit difference) of 105% (compared to the average performance), how much profit should the manager's group actually realize this year?
3. How is kaizen costing different from standard costing from the following perspectives of an organizational unit?
   a. Cost goal.
   b. Focus of the technique.
   c. Underlying manufacturing condition.
   d. Timing of standard (target) setting.
   e. Variance analysis.

P10-15   Target Costing

BRG, Inc. has just developed Back Soothe, a special exercise machine designed to decompress the spine to ease painful disc pressure and relax supporting muscles. The technology is based on gravity traction that would undo damage caused by the daily grind of standing, sitting, or driving. The target sales price for Back Soothe is $240 per unit. Pat LePone, a national fitness chain, has offered to buy 5,000 units of Back Soothe at $240 per unit. The company estimates the following costs for producing one unit of Back Soothe:

Materials	$ 96
Labor	44
Overhead.	52
Total cost per unit.	$192

The company uses target costing. The company's usual return on sales rate is 30%. A cost study reveals that 80% of the difference between the allowable cost and the estimated cost is possible to achieve in the short run.

Required:

1. What would be the desired profit on the offer from Pat LePone?
2. What would be the allowable cost for the production of 5,000 units of Back Soothe?
3. What would be the estimated cost for the production of 5,000 units of Back Soothe?
4. Determine the cost reduction target for 5,000 units of Back Soothe.
5. Determine the target cost for 5,000 units of Back Soothe.

P10-16   Life Cycle Costing; Target Costing; Kaizen Costing

Earth and Water, Inc. is a manufacturer of various personal water purification products. The company has just developed a new product called Desal, a hand-held, manually operated desalinator. Desal works like a bicycle pump, making seawater flow through a semipermeable membrane that eliminates the salt from seawater.

The new product has bright prospects, judging from the early feedback from potential consumers who are environmentally conscious. The target sales price of the product is $545. Based on estimated sales of 40,000 units of Desal over its life cycle, the company estimates the following percentages of costs in various stages of activities that have already been performed or are scheduled to be performed in the product's life cycle:

Design stage	7%
Development stage	4%
Manufacturing stage	70%
Sale stage	8%
Delivery stage	2%
After-sale service stage	6%
Disposal stage	3%
Total for the life cycle	100%

The company wants to use the concepts of life cycle costing, target costing, and kaizen costing for cost management.

Required:

Determine the percentages of costs that would be managed by each of the following cost management concepts:
a.   Life cycle costing
b.   Target costing
c.   Kaizen costing

P10-17   Cost of Quality

MBM, Inc. of Phoenix, Arizona is a manufacturer of mountain bikes. Competing against several foreign competitors, MBM, Inc. has been producing top-of-the-line mountain bikes with aluminum frames and unique suspensions. Thanks to its manufacturing flexibility, the company has been able to adjust its production to actual demand very quickly. This is the main reason for its survival as one of the few U.S. makers of mountain bikes.

In its efforts to improve quality and reduce costs, the company has hired quality consultants to perform an in-depth study of its quality costs, the costs that do not usually appear on the company's chart of accounts. The following is a list of some selected items of cost which are related to quality:

a. Direct costs of inspecting shock-smoothing
   suspensions $54,000
b. Costs incurred by the in-house team reviewing
   the new bike frame production plan to reduce
   defects.   67,000
c. Costs of bike frame scraps   29,000
d. Repairs performed on the returned bikes   18,000
e. Engineering costs incurred to plan changes to
   the frame fabrication process to reduce
   defects.   31,000
f. Rework cost for the period.   25,000
g. Costs incurred while waiting for the engineers
   to fix the disabled robot.   46,000
h. Costs of warranty adjustments   33,000

Required:

Determine the amount of the following costs:
1. Prevention costs
2. Appraisal costs
3. Internal failure costs
4. External failure costs
5. Control costs
6. Failure costs

P10-18   Lean Production and Budgeting

LPB, Inc. is a manufacturer of a line of laser printers. Its laser printers send paper through a nearly straight path while conventional laser printers have paper winding around rollers. The direct paper path reduces the probability of paper jams which users experience frequently on conventional laser printers. The simpler paper path also enables users to print envelopes easier and use papers of varying sizes.

The company is capitalizing on the strength of its product and its lower production costs based on new technology. It has switched from mass-production to lean production to improve flexibility, lower the level of inventory, and reduce defects.

In connection with the switch to lean production, Janet Lys, controller of the company, is considering the necessary changes and adjustments her department has to make. The following is a summary of what her staff used to do in connection with budgeting in the old mass-production environment:

a. The budgeting process was started with the demand forecast her staff received from the sales department on laser printers.
b. All other budgets were prepared based on the sales budget.
c. The laser printer production requirement in the production budget was determined on the basis of the laser printer demand forecast and desired ending inventory level.
d. The production department manufactured laser printers to desired levels of inventory and stored them for future shipments.

Required:

1. Show how the laser printer production requirement was computed in the old mass-production environment. Use an algebraic form.
2. What is the single most important figure in the old budgeting process that determines the reliability of the whole budget cycle? Why?
3. Indicate how lean production would change each item Janet's staff used to do (a, b, c, and d) in the mass-production environment.

P10-19 Target Costing

AWA, Inc. is a manufacturer of premium aluminum wheels. The company's wheels are popular among car buffs. Sales have grown at an average rate of 15% a year for the last several years. The company has recently developed a new set of wheels called GX Wheels. The designer has stated that GX Wheels will excite many Gen-X car buffs who like to add instant style and prestige to the cars they drive.

The target sales price for GX Wheels is $300 per unit. Tet Boys, a national chain specializing in car accessories and custom-made tires, has offered to buy 2,500 units of GX Wheels at $300 per unit. AWA's usual return on sales is 30%. The following are estimated costs of producing one unit of GX Wheels:

Materials	$120
Labor.	55
Overhead	65
Total cost per unit	$240

A cost study reveals that 75% of the difference between the allowable cost and the estimated cost is possible to achieve in the short run. The company uses target costing.

Required:

1. What would be the desired profit on the offer from Tet Boys?
2. What would be the allowable cost for the production of 2,500 units of GX Wheels?
3. What would be the estimated cost for the production of 2,500 units of GX Wheels?
4. Determine the cost reduction target for 2,500 units of GX Wheels.
5. Determine the target cost for 2,500 units of GX Wheels.

P10-20 Target Costing; Process and Order of Tasks

Target costing is practiced in different steps. The following is a list of those steps:
a. Review the difference between estimated and allowable cost based on various dimensions of the product's attributes and market expectations.
b. Determine the desired profit based on the company's desired return on sales.
c. Establish the target sales price for the newly planned product based on market research.

d. Decompose the target cost into each cost element within the production process.

e. Adopt the cost reduction target from the difference between estimated and allowable cost.

f. Calculate the estimated cost based on the current standards of materials, labor, and overhead.

g. Perform cost improvement activities to achieve the target cost.

h. Compare the allowable cost with the estimated cost, and calculate the difference.

i. Subtract the desired profit from the target sales price. This is the allowable cost.

j. Subtract the cost reduction target from the estimated cost. This is the target cost, and is attainable in the short run.

Required:

Rearrange the order of the above steps so that a company can follow those steps in a proper sequence.

P10-21 Manufacturing Cycle Efficiency

HEW, Inc. manufactures Healthy Showerhead, a showerhead which ensures shower water to be free of chlorine. The product removes the toxic irritant by using a unique turbo action and a granulated purifier.

The production consists of two processes: fabrication and assembly. Management of the company is very serious about quality inspection to ascertain that the product meets standards set by the in-house health professionals.

Management is currently in the process of studying the effects of cycle time on manufacturing efficiency. In the process, management wants to see how much "fat" the company has, by isolating non-value-adding activities from value-adding activities. For that purpose, management has compiled the following data on hours taken to perform various activities in the last period:

Material handling	32
Waiting	124
Storing	46
Fabrication	25
Assembly	42
Inspection	7

Required:

1. Calculate the manufacturing cycle time.
2. Calculate the manufacturing cycle efficiency (MCE).
3. What is the ratio of non-value-adding time to manufacturing cycle time?

P10-22 Backflush Costing

Milacron, Inc. has five plants in the U.S. Its Toledo plant uses a JIT process for its one and only manufacturing cell. The plant is going to adopt backflush costing in the current period. The following information relates to the company's performance for one week in the current cost accounting period:

Beginning inventories:

Raw materials and parts....................	$ 0
Work in process	0
Finished goods..............................	0

Actual costs:

Raw materials and parts purchased in the current period.....................	$44,000
Labor......................................	20,000
Overhead...................................	60,000

Standard costs:

Raw materials and parts per unit of finished goods	$ 40
Labor cost per hour.........................	500
Overhead cost per hour	1,400

Actual output	700 units
Cycle time	6 minutes

Before the company decided to adopt backflush costing, the company performed a cost study, investigating how much it actually costs to maintain each and every account on the cost accounting system. The following information discloses the numbers of subsidiary accounts belonging to each control account and the costs of maintaining each subsidiary account per month: (Disregard the costs of maintaining control accounts.)

	Subsidiary Account Cost
Raw materials and parts (25 accounts)	$120
Labor (30 accounts)................................	100
Overhead (40 accounts)	100
Work in process (25 accounts)......................	120
Finished goods (20 accounts)	90

Required:

1. The plant will use the following accounts for the appropriate transactions in its backflush costing: Raw and In-Process Inventory, Accounts Payable, Finished Goods, and Conversion Cost. Make the journal entry for each of the following transactions under backflush costing:
    a. Purchase of materials and parts.
    b. Use of materials and parts in production.
    c. Completion of 700 units of finished goods.

2. How many accounts would be reduced when the plant adopts backflush costing? Assume that the plant will use only 20 subsidiary accounts for each control account in the new system.

3. What would be the plant's total annual savings in record-keeping costs when it switches from traditional cost accounting to backflush costing? Assume that the same per-account cost will be incurred in the new system.

P10-23 Value-Chain Analysis; Internal Linkage Analysis

ALS, Inc. manufactures components used in metal halide lamps. Metal halide makes brighter light than incandescent bulbs, but consumes less than 25% of the energy. The components manufactured by ALS, Inc. have been used to light many U.S. airports. As various auto makers begin to use metal halide headlights on their luxury models, the company's sales will continue to grow.

The company uses value-chain analysis, and its activity-based costing system indicates that a new processing sequence in its plant would provide the following improvements in operations if implemented:

Activity	Cost Driver	Cost Rate Per Driver	Activity Level Present	Expected
Setup	Number of setups	$1,800 per setup	800	700
Mfg. support	Machine hours	$ 25 per hour	4,000	3,000
Process engineering	Engineering hours	$ 60 per hour	2,600	2,200

The company estimates that direct costs of changing the processing sequence would be $58,000, and interruptions in operations during the sequence change would cost $40,000.

Required:

1. What would be the cost of exploiting the internal linkages?
2. What would be the savings from exploiting the internal linkages?
3. Select the proper strategy based on the value-chain analysis.

P10-24 Value-Chain Analysis; External Linkage Analysis; Service Industry

Out-of-This-World, Inc. operates a virtual-reality arcade and cappuccino corner on the Promenade of Redondo Beach. Most older patrons just use the popular cappuccino corner while enjoying the fantastic ocean view.

The company charges $2 per entry to the arcade area. The use of the virtual-reality equipment for each hour requires a coupon that sells for $9. A cup of cappuccino sells for $3. The following is the information on the number of customers and costs for the most recent period:

	Customers	
	Arcade Users	Cappuccino Sippers
Numbers sold............	9,000 coupons	4,200 cups
Service cost.............	$2 per hour	$0.50 per cup

Recently a new virtual-reality arcade opened in a shopping mall in the vicinity. The new arcade charges $8 per hour. In order to compete with the new arcade that charges less, Out-of-This World is considering lifting the $2 entry charge for the arcade patrons (when they buy the arcade coupons). A customer survey indicates that, if the $2 entry charge is lifted, the number of patrons will increase 20% from the current level despite the higher coupon price because the Promenade looks "cool" to even the younger generation.

If the entry charge continues, 25% of the younger patrons surveyed have stated, they would switch to the new arcade in the mall. For each percentage decrease in the number of noisy arcade patrons, however, there would be a corresponding percentage increase in the number of cappuccino sippers, according to the same survey.

It is estimated that 50% of the arcade patrons stay for one hour (1 coupon) and the other 50% stay for two hours (2 coupons). Most cappuccino customers buy one cup.

Required:

Perform the external linkage analysis on whether to continue to charge the $2 entry fee to the virtual-reality arcade patrons or lift it. Select the proper strategy based on the value-chain analysis.

P10-25   Lean Production and "Relevance" of Standard Costing

Comsound, Inc. is a manufacturer of an ultra-compact audio set designed to coax high-fidelity sound from any office computer. The mini-desktop speakers are powered by a black box that contains an amplifier and a bass driver users can hide under their desks. The product is popular among the computer users who are tired of the usual speakers that sound like a clock radio and hope for some good music from multimedia PCs.

The company has recently switched from mass-production to lean production. Now management wants some useful information on the company's manufacturing performance based on the existing standard costing system before it considers adopting a new performance measurement system. The following is a summary of the results of the company's variance analysis for the most recent cost accounting period:

Materials price variance	$ 6,000 F
Materials quantity variance	(800) U
Labor rate variance	(9,400) U
Labor efficiency variance	(5,600) U
Variable overhead spending variance	(470) U
Variable overhead efficiency variance	(700) U
Fixed overhead budget variance	(1,700) U
Fixed overhead volume variance	(5,800) U

Required:

1. Which of the two material variances is more irrelevant to performance evaluation in a lean production environment? Why?
2. Which labor variance loses relevance in a lean production environment? Why?
3. Which variable overhead variance loses relevance in a lean production environment? Why?
4. Which of the two fixed overhead variances is more irrelevant to performance evaluation in a lean production environment? Why?

P10-26 Value-Chain Analysis; Internal Linkage Analysis

HAD, Inc. manufactures tamperproof ankle bracelets equipped with radio transmitters. The products, used as home-arrest monitoring devices, monitor the presence of their homebound wearers. The company believes the sales of the ankle bracelets will continue to be strong as more municipalities try to ease prison overcrowding. The company uses value-chain analysis, and its activity-based costing system indicates that a new engineering routine in its plant would provide the following improvements in operations if implemented:

Activity	Cost Driver	Cost Rate Per Driver	Activity Level Present	Expected
Process engineering	Engineering hours	$ 80 per hour	1,900	1,600
Setup	Setup hours	$700 per hour	1,100	950
Material handling	Number of moves	$ 20 per move	7,000	6,500

The company estimates that direct costs of changing the engineering routine would be $39,000, and interruptions in operations during the engineering routine change would cost $60,000.

Required:

1. What would be the cost of exploiting the internal linkages?
2. What would be the savings from exploiting the internal linkages?
3. Select the proper strategy (changing to the new routine or not) based on the value-chain analysis.

P10-27 Target Costing; Missing Numbers

Clean-Air-Cabin, Inc. has developed a new air filter. Once installed on a car, the air filter will purify the air flowing into the car cabin. An auto maker has offered to buy 5,000 units of the filter. Based on the current technology and manufacturing conditions, Clean-Air-Cabin can produce the filter at the following cost per unit:

Materials	$ 9
Labor	15
Overhead	8
Manufacturing cost per unit	$32

Clean-Air-Cabin wants to reduce filter manufacturing costs through target costing. According to its internal cost study, Clean-Air-Cabin can achieve a 75% cost reduction target rate in the short run. Accordingly, a target cost of $152,500 has been determined.

Clean-Air-Cabin desires to make a profit of $10 per unit of filter. In determining the target cost, Clean-Air-Cabin uses the rate of return on sales.

Required:

1. What is the allowable cost for the production of 5,000 units of the air filter?
2. What is the price the auto maker has offered to pay for a unit of the filter?
3. What rate of return on sales does Clean-Air-Cabin use to determine target costs?

VARIABLE COSTING, ABSORPTION COSTING AND SEGMENTED REPORTING

After studying this chapter, you should be able to:

1. Explain the essential difference between variable costing and full absorption costing, and compute the unit product cost under each method.

2. Describe the effect of change in production and inventory on operating income under the two methods.

3. Prepare an income statement under the two methods and explain the difference in operating income.

4. Explain the significance of activity-based costing in the relationships between the two methods.

5. Understand the impact of lean production on the two methods.

6. Prepare segmented income statements using variable costing and explain the benefits of such statements.

In Chapter 3, we learned that the contribution margin is the difference between sales and *variable* costs. If we prepare an income statement based on the contribution margin concept, we may consider it to be based on the **variable costing** concept.

In Chapters 4 and 5, we did not differentiate between variable manufacturing expenses and fixed manufacturing expenses. *All* manufacturing expenses were assigned to a job (in job-order costing) or to a department (in process costing). Assigning all manufacturing expenses to jobs or departments is based on what we will henceforth call the **full absorption costing** concept.

We compare variable costing with full absorption costing in this chapter. First, we will identify the basic difference between the two concepts and the underlying philosophy, uses, advantages and disadvantages of each concept. Then, we will look at numerical examples illustrating the differences between the two concepts with respect to their effects on the financial statements. We will also discuss the use of variable costing in segmented reporting. Last, we will examine the effect of changes in the business environment on variable costing and full absorption costing.

COMPARISON OF VARIABLE AND FULL ABSORPTION COSTING

Variable costing, also known as *direct costing* or the *contribution approach*, is different from **full absorption costing,** also known as *functional costing* or the *traditional approach*, with respect to the way fixed manufacturing overhead is recognized. Fixed manufacturing overhead is excluded from the production cost under variable costing, but included in the production cost under full absorption costing.

The balancing operation in the manufacturing process of Baldor Electric Co. Under variable costing, fixed manufacturing overhead costs are period expenses rather than a part of inventory costs.

Underlying Philosophy

What are the philosophical arguments supporting each concept? These arguments stem from the definition of an asset. Under full absorption costing, fixed manufacturing overhead is a part of the total cost of production. It is recognized as an asset until the units produced are sold and become cost of goods sold. Under variable costing, however, fixed manufacturing overhead is not a part of the total cost of production and thus is not recognized as an asset. It is treated as a period cost and is expensed immediately on the income statement whether units are sold or not.

The proponents of full absorption costing believe that fixed manufacturing overhead meets the definition of an asset, whereas the proponents of variable costing believe that it does not. The proponents of full absorption costing define an asset as something that has future benefit potential. In their view, fixed manufacturing overhead, such as rent, depreciation, property taxes, and the manufacturing manager's salary, is needed for production just like other costs of production, such as materials, hourly labor, and variable manufacturing overhead, e.g., electricity. Since unsold units have the potential to be sold in the future, they have future benefit potential.

On the other hand, the proponents of variable costing believe that a cost incurred is an asset only if a future cost is avoided. For example, the cost of material used in production this period is an asset if some of the units produced in this period are not sold. The company can avoid payment for that material in the next period. However, a manufacturing manager's salary in the current period is not an asset, even if some units produced in this period are not sold. This is because the company cannot avoid payment of the manager's salary in the next period. Thus, the proponents of variable costing claim that all fixed manufacturing overhead should be immediately recognized as an expense on the income statement.

Intended Uses of the Two Methods

Variable costing is used for the purposes of making internal decisions, such as (a) to accept or reject a special order at a special price, (b) to buy or to produce certain parts, (c) to open up a new branch or to close down an existing one, (d) to expand or contract a product line, and (e) other similar decisions that can be made using the contribution approach, which is the essence of variable costing.

Variable costing may also be used in evaluating departmental or divisional performance since it classifies costs into variable and fixed components where the former are usually controllable by department heads or division managers and the latter are not usually controllable at these managerial levels. Sales planning by product lines, territories, sales teams, and classes of customers is another area where variable costing may be used. All of these decision situations may be considered to be *short run* with respect to their financial consequences.

On the other hand, full absorption costing may be used for other internal decisions, such as pricing. This is so because prices charged must cover both variable and fixed costs, and generate profits in the *long run*. Full absorption costing must also be used in external financial reporting to shareholders and in reporting to the IRS.

Advantages and Disadvantages

Table 11-1 summarizes the advantages of variable costing and full absorption costing. Since the two methods have strengths of their own, managers should look at them as complementary rather than as competing methods.

TABLE 11-1 Advantages of Variable Costing and Full Absorption Costing

Variable Costing Advantages	Full Absorption Costing Advantages
1. If the income statement is prepared using the variable costing method, it will provide information needed for cost-volume-profit analysis.	1. The only method acceptable for external reporting to stockholders as well as reporting to the IRS.
2. Variable costing may make it easier for management to focus on the effect of fixed costs on profits since fixed costs are treated as a period cost and reported in one place on the income statement.	2. It may not mislead users to believe that variable costs are recovered first, fixed costs are recovered next, then income is realized. Both variable and fixed costs have to be recovered before income is realized.
3. It forces managers to evaluate the cost behavior pattern of every cost item, thus they become aware of how changes in the level of activity may affect costs.	3. There is no need to classify costs into variable and fixed components which may be difficult and arbitrary.
4. Under variable costing, operating income is a function of sales, and not a function of both sales and production. This follows management's thinking about operating results.	4. Full absorption costing shows the inventory cost on the balance sheet at a higher level than variable costing, because the cost of inventory under full absorption costing includes both fixed and variable manufacturing overhead.
5. Variable costing may provide a ready-to-use basis for the preparation of flexible budgets, discussed in Chapter 9.	

NUMERICAL ILLUSTRATIONS

Units Sold Equal to Units Produced

If a company sells all the units it produces during a period and has no beginning or ending inventories, there is no difference between variable costing and full absorption costing income. This is because, if all production is sold, fixed production costs appear on the income statement whether as cost of goods sold or as part of fixed expenses.

ILLUSTRATION 11-1

The Directfull Company produces a single product. The following data for Year 7 are available:

Number of units in inventory, 1/1/x7	0
Number of units produced during year	10,000
Number of units sold during year	10,000
Selling price per unit................................ $	23
Variable cost per unit:	
Direct materials .... $	5
Direct labor	3
Variable manufacturing overhead	2
Variable selling expenses	1
Fixed costs per year:	
Manufacturing overhead......................... $40,000	
Selling and administrative expenses 30,000	

1. No Beginning or Ending Inventories

We now (a) compute cost of production per unit, and (b) prepare an income statement for Year 7 under the two methods.

(a) Cost of Production Per Unit	Variable Costing	Full Absorption Costing
Direct materials	$ 5	$ 5
Direct labor	3	3
Variable manufacturing overhead	2	2
Fixed manufacturing overhead	—	4 *
Cost of production per unit	$10	$14

*Fixed manufacturing overhead ÷ Number of units produced
= $40,000 ÷ 10,000 units = $4.

There were no beginning or ending inventories, and cost of sales equals variable cost of production (10,000 units × $10) under variable costing. Similarly, under full absorption costing, cost of goods sold equals cost of goods manufactured (10,000 units × $14). The difference of $4 in the unit cost is due solely to the fixed manufacturing overhead which is included under full absorption costing but excluded under variable costing. Because all units produced in Year 7

(b)

EXHIBIT 11-1

Directfull Company
Income Statement for Year 7

Variable Costing

Sales (10,000 units x $23)		$230,000
Variable expenses:		
Variable costs of sales		
(10,000 units x $10)	$100,000	
Variable selling expenses		
(10,000 units x $1)	10,000	
		110,000
Contribution margin		120,000
Fixed expenses:		
Manufacturing overhead	40,000	
Selling and administrative expenses	30,000	
		70,000
Operating Income		$ 50,000

Full Absorption Costing

Sales (10,000 units x $23)		$230,000
Cost of goods sold (10,000 units x $14)		140,000
Gross profit		90,000
Selling and administrative expenses:		
Variable (10,000 units x $1)	$ 10,000	
Fixed	30,000	
		40,000
Operating Income		$ 50,000

---

were sold during the same year, operating income is the same ($50,000) under both methods.

2. Beginning and Ending Inventories Exist

ILLUSTRATION 11-2

Even when beginning and ending inventories exist, operating income will still be the same under both methods, if there is no change in the inventory cost during the period. This means that the cost of production per unit in the current period is equal to the cost per unit in the beginning inventories under either method.

Let us assume the same facts as in Illustration 11-1 except that Directfull Company has a beginning inventory of 1,000 units with a cost of $10,000 under variable costing and a cost of $14,000 under full absorption costing. Let us also assume that the cost of production per unit in the current period is the same as in the last period. Since the company produced and sold 10,000 units during the year the income statement under both methods would be as shown in Exhibit 11-2.

EXHIBIT 11-2

Directfull Company
Income Statement for Year 7

Variable Costing

Sales (10,000 units x $23)		$230,000
Variable expenses:		
Beginning inventory (1,000 units x $10)	$ 10,000	
Variable cost of production		
(10,000 units x $10)	100,000	
Goods available for sale	110,000	
Ending inventory (1,000 units x $10)	(10,000)	
Variable cost of goods sold.	100,000	
Variable selling expenses		
(10,000 units x $1)	10,000	110,000
Contribution margin		120,000
Fixed expenses:		
Manufacturing overhead.	40,000	
Selling and administrative expenses	30,000	70,000
Operating income		$ 50,000

Full Absorption Costing

Sales (10,000 units x $23)		$230,000
Cost of goods sold:		
Beginning inventory (1,000 units x $14)	$ 14,000	
Cost of goods manufactured		
(10,000 units x $14)	140,000	
Cost of goods available for sale	154,000	
Ending inventory (1,000 units x $14)	(14,000)	140,000
Gross profit.		90,000
Selling and administrative expenses:		
Variable (10,000 units x $1)	10,000	
Fixed	30,000	40,000
Operating income		$ 50,000

Even though beginning and ending inventories exist, the operating income is the same ($50,000) under both methods. This is because the cost of ending inventory is equal to the cost of beginning inventory.

We simplified the illustration by assuming that the current period unit cost of production is equal to the beginning inventory unit cost. If we did not make that assumption, the ending inventory cost might be different from the beginning inventory cost, despite the same number of units in beginning and ending inventories. Operating income, accordingly, may be different under the two methods.

Units Sold Unequal to Units Produced

If units produced do not equal units sold during a period, both operating income and inventory will be different under the two methods. If units sold are *less* than units produced, fixed manufacturing overhead charged on the income statement under full absorption costing will be *less* than under variable costing. Hence, full absorption costing will produce a higher income.

At the same time, the ending inventory under full absorption costing will be greater than under variable costing by the amount of fixed manufacturing overhead cost included in that inventory. If units sold are greater than units produced, the opposite will happen.

1. Units Sold Are Less than Units Produced

ILLUSTRATION 11-3

Refer to ILLUSTRATION 11-1. Now, the number of units sold is 9,000 instead of 10,000. Exhibit 11-3 presents the income statement under variable costing and full absorption costing.

EXHIBIT 11-3

Directfull Company
Income Statement for Year 7

Variable Costing

Sales (9,000 units x $23)		$207,000
Variable expenses:		
Beginning inventory.	$ 0	
Variable cost of production		
(10,000 x $10)	100,000	
Goods available for sale	100,000	
Ending inventory		
(1,000 units x $10)	(10,000)	
Variable cost of goods sold	90,000	
Variable selling expenses		
(9,000 units x $1).	9,000	99,000
Contribution margin		108,000
Fixed expenses:		
Manufacturing overhead.	40,000	
Selling and administrative expenses	30,000	70,000
Operating income		$ 38,000

Full Absorption Costing

Sales (9,000 units x $23)		$207,000
Cost of goods sold:		
Beginning inventory.	$ 0	
Cost of goods manufactured		
(10,000 units x $14)	140,000	
Cost of goods available for sale	140,000	
Ending inventory (1,000 x $14)	(14,000)	126,000
Gross profit.		81,000
Selling and administrative expenses:		
Variable (9,000 units x $1)	9,000	
Fixed	30,000	39,000
Operating income		$42,000

The difference of $4,000 in operating income between the two methods is the same difference in ending inventory under the two methods. The cost of ending inventory is $10,000 under variable costing and $14,000 under absorption costing. This $4,000 difference is due to the fixed manufacturing overhead of $4 per unit, which is included in cost of production under full absorption costing, times the 1,000 units in ending inventory. See Exhibit 11-4 for a graphical illustration of this point.

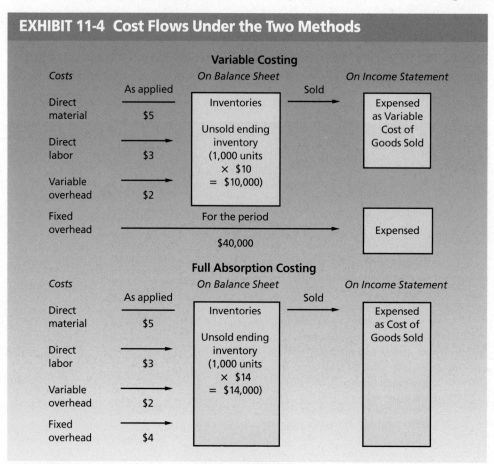

EXHIBIT 11-4 Cost Flows Under the Two Methods

Again, if all units produced during a period are sold during the same period and no beginning or ending inventories are kept, operating income will be the same under both methods. The difference between the two methods will arise only when there is a change in the inventory cost from the beginning to the end of the period.

2. Units Sold Are Greater Than Units Produced
ILLUSTRATION 11-4
Let us assume the following changes from ILLUSTRATION 11-1:

    a. The beginning inventory of 1,000 units costs $10,000 under variable costing and $14,000 under full absorption costing.

    b. During Year 7, 10,400 units were sold.

Exhibit 11-5 presents the income statement under the two methods.

EXHIBIT 11-7

Directfull Company
Income Statement Under the Two Methods
(Constant Production, Fluctuating Sales)

	Year 7	Year 8	Year 9	Total Three Years
Units in beginning inventory	0	1,000	500	0
Units produced	10,000	10,000	10,000	30,000
Units sold	9,000	10,500	10,000	29,500
Units in ending inventory	1,000	500	500	500

Variable Costing

	Year 7	Year 8	Year 9	Total Three Years
Sales ($23 per unit)	$207,000	$241,500	$230,000	$678,500
Variable expenses:				
Beginning inventory ($10 per unit)	$ 0	$ 10,000	$ 5,000	$ 0
Variable cost of units produced ($10 per unit)	100,000	100,000	100,000	300,000
Variable cost of goods available for sale	100,000	110,000	105,000	300,000
Ending inventory ($10 per unit)	(10,000)	(5,000)	(5,000)	(5,000)
Variable cost of goods sold	90,000	105,000	100,000	295,000
Variable selling expenses ($1 per unit)	9,000	10,500	10,000	29,500
Total variable expenses	99,000	115,500	110,000	324,500
Contribution margin	108,000	126,000	120,000	354,000
Fixed expenses:				
Manufacturing overhead	40,000	40,000	40,000	120,000
Selling and administrative expenses	30,000	30,000	30,000	90,000
Total	70,000	70,000	70,000	210,000
Operating income	$ 38,000	$ 56,000	$ 50,000	$144,000

Full Absorption Costing

	Year 7	Year 8	Year 9	Total Three Years
Sales ($23 per unit)	$207,000	$241,500	$230,000	$678,500
Cost of goods sold:				
Beginning inventory ($14 per unit)	$ 0	$ 14,000	$ 7,000	$ 0
Cost of goods produced ($14 per unit)	140,000	140,000	140,000	420,000
Cost of goods available for sale	140,000	154,000	147,000	420,000
Ending inventory ($14 per unit)	(14,000)	(7,000)	(7,000)	(7,000)
Cost of goods sold*	126,000	147,000	140,000	413,000
Gross profit	81,000	94,500	90,000	265,500
Selling and administrative expenses:				
Variable	9,000	10,500	10,000	29,500
Fixed	30,000	30,000	30,000	90,000
Total	39,000	40,500	40,000	119,500
Operating income	$ 42,000	$ 54,000	$ 50,000	$146,000

* Production is constant at the normal level of activity, and there is no under- or overapplied fixed manufacturing overhead.

The sales level fluctuates each year, and neither contribution margin nor operating income is the same for all three years under variable costing. The higher the sales, the higher the contribution margin and operating income. Under full absorption costing, the higher the sales, the higher the gross profit and operating income. Note, however, that in Exhibit 11-6, even though sales were the same every year, gross profit and operating income varied from year to year under full absorption costing, as a result of the fluctuations in production.

(3) Fluctuating Production and Sales

If both production and sales fluctuate from year to year, contribution margin (under variable costing), gross profit (under full absorption costing), and operating income (under both methods) will fluctuate from year to year. However, if fixed manufacturing overhead is applied to production at the same rate each year, and over- or underapplied overhead is closed out to cost of goods sold, the following will still be true:

1.   If inventory *increases*, operating income under full absorption costing will be *higher* than under variable costing.

2.   If inventory *decreases*, operating income under full absorption costing will be *lower* than under variable costing, and

3.   If inventory remains *unchanged*, operating income will be the *same* under both methods.

Exhibit 11-8 is based on the same data as Exhibit 11-6 except that both production and sales fluctuate from year to year:

EXHIBIT 11-8

Directfull Company
Income Statement Under the Two Methods
(Fluctuating Production and Sales)

	Year 7	Year 8	Year 9	Total Three Years
	Inventory Increases	Inventory Increases	Inventory Decreases	Inventory Increases
Units in beginning inventory	0	1,000	3,000	0
Units produced	10,000	10,500	8,500	29,000
Units sold	9,000	8,500	10,500	28,000
Units in ending inventory	1,000	3,000	1,000	1,000
Variable Costing				
Sales ($23 per unit)	$207,000	$195,500	$241,500	$644,000
Variable expenses:				
Beginning inventory	0	10,000	30,000	0
Variable cost of units produced*	100,000	105,000	85,000	290,000
Variable cost of goods available for sale	100,000	115,000	115,000	290,000
Ending inventory*	(10,000)	(30,000)	(10,000)	(10,000)
Variable cost of goods sold	90,000	85,000	105,000	280,000

(continued)

EXHIBIT 11-8 Cont.

Variable selling expenses**	9,000	8,500	10,500	28,000
Total variable expenses	99,000	93,500	115,500	308,000
Contribution margin	108,000	102,000	126,000	336,000
Fixed expenses:				
Manufacturing overhead	40,000	40,000	40,000	120,000
Selling and administrative expenses	30,000	30,000	30,000	90,000
Total	70,000	70,000	70,000	210,000
Operating income	$ 38,000	$ 32,000	$ 56,000	$126,000

* At $10 per unit
**At $1 per unit sold

Full Absorption Costing

Sales ($23 per unit)	$207,000	$195,500	$241,500	$644,000
Cost of goods sold:				
Beginning inventory[a]	0	14,000	42,000	0
Cost of goods produced[a]	140,000	147,000	119,000	406,000
Cost of goods available for sale	140,000	161,000	161,000	406,000
Ending inventory[a]	(14,000)	(42,000)	(14,000)	(14,000)
Subtotal	126,000	119,000	147,000	392,000
Under(over)-applied overhead[b]	0	(2,000)	6,000	4,000
Cost of goods sold	126,000	117,000	153,000	396,000
Gross profit	81,000	78,500	88,500	248,000
Selling and administrative expenses:				
Variable ($1 per unit)	9,000	8,500	10,500	28,000
Fixed	30,000	30,000	30,000	90,000
Total	39,000	38,500	40,500	118,000
Operating income	$ 42,000	$ 40,000	$ 48,000	$130,000

[a] At $14 per unit.
[b] Under(over)-applied overhead = Actual fixed manufacturing overhead
 − fixed manufacturing overhead applied to production.
For Year 8: $40,000 − (10,500 units × $4) = ($2,000)
For Year 9: $40,000 − (8,500 units × $4) = $6,000

Despite the fluctuations in both production and sales, full absorption costing produces higher income than variable costing when inventory increases (as in Year 7, Year 8, and all three years), and produces lower income when inventory decreases (as in Year 9).

Reconciling the Income Differences Between the Two Methods

In Exhibit 11-8, the difference in operating income between the two methods equals the increase (from the beginning to the end of the period) in inventory units times the $4 fixed manufacturing overhead per unit. In general, we can reconcile the income difference between the two methods using the following format:

	Year 7	Year 8	Year 9
Variable costing operating income	$38,000	$32,000	$56,000
Fixed manufacturing overhead deferred in inventory,			
$4 × (1,000 − 0) units.	4,000		
$4 × (3,000 − 1,000) units		8,000	
$4 × (1,000 − 3,000) units			(8,000)
Absorption costing operating income.	$42,000	$40,000	$48,000

The numbers in the parentheses represent (ending inventory − beginning inventory).

VARIABLE COSTING AND SEGMENTED REPORTING

A company that carries multiple products produced in multiple divisions and sold in various geographical locations, will find the use of variable costing very helpful. In reporting about these products, divisions, and sales territories, the company can show a contribution margin as well as a segment margin for each of these different segments of the company. Exhibit 11-9 presents a sample segmented income statement for Conglomerate International, Inc., a multi-division, multi-product, multi-national company.

The segmented income statements start with the major divisions that make up the total company and go down to smaller segments. In Exhibit 11-9, we start with divisions A, B and C; then Division A, segmented into products X, Y, and Z; Product Y, segmented into U.S. and International; and finally U.S., segmented into three regions, Eastern, Central, and Western. Of course, the other divisions, products, geographical territories, and regions would be segmented in a similar fashion.

Each segmented income statement in Exhibit 11-9 includes major subtotals as follows: We subtract total variable expenses from sales to obtain *contribution margin*. We then subtract *traceable fixed expenses* from contribution margin to obtain *segment margin*. Finally, we subtract *common fixed expenses* from segment margin to obtain *operating income*. *Traceable* fixed expenses are those that can be directly traced to a particular segment and can be avoided if the segment is eliminated. *Common* fixed costs are those that cannot be directly traced to a particular segment, and cannot be eliminated even if a particular segment is discontinued.

Segmented income statements are used for companies such as UPS, the world's largest integrated package delivery company. UPS has many subsidiaries providing not only package delivery services, but also supply chain solutions and e-commerce solutions.

As to the company as a whole, common fixed expenses may include, for example, the president's compensation or advertising expenses promoting the company's name. As to Division A, they may include the salary of Division A's manager or advertising expenses promoting Division A's products.

As we move from larger to smaller segments, a part of traceable fixed expenses becomes common fixed expenses. For example, the $40,000 traceable fixed expense for Division A is broken down into $30,000 in fixed expenses traceable to Products X, Y and Z and $10,000 in fixed expenses for Division A. This process is repeated as we move down from products to sales territories and further down to regions.

EXHIBIT 11-9

Conglomerate International, Inc.
Segmented Income Statements

Defining Segments as Divisions

	Segments			Total
	Division A	Division B	Division C	Company
Sales	$400,000	$600,000	$500,000	$1,500,000
Variable expenses:				
Variable cost of goods sold	200,000	450,000	300,000	950,000
Variable selling expenses	50,000	60,000	40,000	150,000
Total	250,000	510,000	340,000	1,100,000
Contribution margin	150,000	90,000	160,000	400,000
Traceable fixed expenses	40,000	50,000	60,000	150,000
Divisional segment margin	$110,000	$40,000	$100,000	250,000
Common fixed expenses				100,000
Operating income				$ 150,000

Defining Segments as Product Lines

	Segments			Total
	Product X	Product Y	Product Z	Division A
Sales	$100,000	$125,000	$175,000	$400,000
Variable expenses:				
Variable cost of goods sold	50,000	65,000	85,000	200,000
Variable selling expenses	5,000	25,000	20,000	50,000
Total	55,000	90,000	105,000	250,000
Contribution margin	45,000	35,000	70,000	150,000
Traceable fixed expenses	9,000	15,000	6,000	30,000
Product line segment margin	$ 36,000	$ 20,000	$ 64,000	120,000
Common fixed expenses				10,000
Operating income				$110,000

(continued)

EXHIBIT 11-9 Cont.

Defining Segments as Sales Territories

| | Segments | | Total |
	United States	International	Product Y
Sales	$100,000	$25,000	$125,000
Variable expenses:			
Variable cost of goods sold	55,000	10,000	65,000
Variable selling expenses	15,000	10,000	25,000
Total	70,000	20,000	90,000
Contribution margin	30,000	5,000	35,000
Traceable fixed expenses	7,000	3,000	10,000
Geographical segment margin	$ 23,000	$ 2,000	25,000
Common fixed expenses			5,000
Operating income			$ 20,000

Defining Segments as Regions of a Territory

| | Segments | | | |
	Eastern Region	Central Region	Western Region	Total U.S.
Sales	$45,000	$40,000	$15,000	$100,000
Variable expenses:				
Variable cost of goods sold	25,000	20,000	10,000	55,000
Variable selling expenses	6,000	5,000	4,000	15,000
Total	31,000	25,000	14,000	70,000
Contribution margin	14,000	15,000	1,000	30,000
Traceable fixed expenses	2,100	1,400	1,500	5,000
Regional segment margin	$11,900	$13,600	$ (500)	25,000
Common fixed expenses				2,000
Operating income				$ 23,000

Benefits of Using Variable Costing in Segmented Reporting

The most significant benefit of using variable costing in segmented reporting is that it allows management to attribute specific expenses to those particular segments that are responsible for the expenses. Thus, management can identify those segments that cannot generate sufficient revenues to cover their variable expenses and their traceable fixed expenses.   Management loses such tracking ability if full absorption costing is used in segmented reporting. That is, when a segment shows losses, management cannot identify the reasons for such losses as clearly as it can under variable costing. The losses may have resulted from fixed expenses that have been allocated arbitrarily to the segment under full absorption costing.

Variable Costing and Activity-Based Costing (ABC)

Variable costing is useful for various managerial decisions, as we have seen in this chapter. Managers should exercise extreme caution, however, in applying variable costing when the cost behavior of certain elements of business functions is not very clearly understood. Costs of production, production support, distribution, customer relations, etc. may not behave in a strictly variable or fixed manner with respect to the volume of production. As we discussed in Chapters 6 and 7, activity-based cost analysis shows that costs may have many different cost drivers.

Let's use the following example in Exhibit 11-1 to discuss this issue:

Selling price per unit		$23
Variable cost per unit:		
Direct materials.......................	$ 5	
Direct labor	3	
Variable manufacturing overhead........	2	
Variable selling expenses	1	11
Contribution margin per unit		$12

In this analysis, we asssumed that all other costs were fixed. What does that really mean? We assumed that the product price is fixed at $23; there is one product to sell; the product design is fixed; the market for this product is established; the company's relationships with suppliers and customers are known and fixed; and product distribution channels are known and fixed.   Only when the above assumptions hold true, can the variable cost of $11 per unit and the contribution margin of $12 per unit be used to make product and pricing decisions. In the real world, however, we must understand that none of the above assumptions may hold true. They can all change. As a matter of fact, in Chapters 6 and 7 we saw that, in the last several decades the costs that have changed the most were fixed overhead costs.

As the company increases production and adds more products to the existing product lineup, the costs that have been regarded as fixed will start to increase. The company will need more inventory-handling people to manage more materials and parts, more quality assurance people to handle the larger production volume and more variety in products, more engineers to write and rewrite processing routines in the plant, and so forth. All these personnel, you remember, create fixed (not variable) overhead costs in the traditional cost classifications.

It is very difficult for managers to estimate all relevant variable costs for decision making. We cannot estimate precisely what impact a manager's decision will have on the demands for fixed resources. When a manager accepts a special order for the production of 5,000 cases of blue markers, it is not possible to estimate how this decision will affect all those fixed resources, unless an ABC system is in place to measure an action's demand for all resources.

What lessons do we learn from this discussion? Variable costing is very useful in *short-term* decision making involving cost estimation or resource utilization. Variable costing loses its relevance as the time horizon is extended. Also, we confine our analysis to the *volume* decision: how many units of a single product do we produce and sell primarily. Variable cost information is not as useful in evaluating the financial effects of adding products, customer classes, and distribution channels.

Lean Production and the Two Methods

In Chapter 10, we discussed lean production and its impact on managerial accounting. When a company becomes a lean producer, the difference in operating income that arises from the different production and sales levels under variable costing and absorption costing becomes insignificant, as explained below.

We understand that lean producers operate with low levels of inventory. Accordingly, the change in inventory levels from the beginning to the end of the period would be smaller in lean production, compared to mass production. This means that the difference in operating income under variable costing and absorption costing would be smaller also.

We will use the following example taken from Exhibit 11-6 to explain the above observation:

	Year 7	Year 8	Year 9
Beginning inventory in units	0	1,000	500
Number of units produced	10,000	8,500	9,000
Number of units sold	9,000	9,000	9,000
Ending inventory in units	1,000	500	500
Change in inventory from beginning to end	1,000	(500)	0
Operating income under *variable costing*	$38,000	$38,000	$38,000
Operating income under *absorption costing*	$42,000	$36,000	$38,000
Difference in income	($4,000)	$2,000	$0

We have learned in this chapter that the difference in operating income is caused by the fixed overhead contained in inventory. When the change in inventory from the beginning to the end is zero (Year 9), there is no income difference. When the change in inventory is 500 units (Year 8), there is an income difference of $2,000. The income difference is the largest ($4,000) when the inventory changes most, by 1,000 units (Year 7).

For a lean producer, there would be a very small difference in inventory from the beginning to the end of a period, since the absolute level of inventory is low anyway. This means that the difference in operating income under variable costing and absorption costing would be smaller for a lean producer. Variable costing is still relevant in a lean production environment, because variable costing separates out those costs that change versus those that don't, with respect to a particular decision to be made.

SUMMARY

This chapter covered two different costing methods: variable (or direct) costing and full absorption (functional or traditional) costing. Under variable costing, only variable manufacturing expenses (direct materials, direct labor, and variable manufacturing overhead) are considered in computing production cost per unit.

All fixed expenses (manufacturing overhead, selling, and administrative expenses) are treated as period costs and charged immediately to the income statement in the period they are incurred. However, under full absorption costing, all manufacturing costs, whether they are variable or fixed, are applied to production. Thus, the only difference in the production cost per unit between the two methods is the fixed manufacturing overhead per unit.

Proponents of variable costing believe that fixed manufacturing overhead should not be applied to production because it does not qualify as an asset. They define an asset as a cost which will result in future cost avoidance. Proponents of full absorption costing define an asset as a cost which has a potential future benefit. They believe that production is not fully costed until all costs spent or incurred, whether variable or fixed, are included. Inventory costs assessed in this way have potential future benefit and thus fixed manufacturing overhead is an asset.

Provided that the cost of production per unit in the current period is equal to the cost per unit in beginning inventory, a comparison of the two methods reveals that: (1) if inventory *increases*, full absorption costing will show *higher* profits than variable costing; (2) if inventory *decreases*, full absorption costing will show *lower* profits; and (3) if inventory remains constant, from beginning to end of the period, both methods will show the *same* profit for the period.

Variable costing may be used in short run product planning. It may also be used in evaluating divisional performance and in sales planning by product lines, sales territories, salespersons, or customer classes. Full absorption costing is used in external financial reporting to stockholders and in reporting to the IRS. It may also be used for long-run production planning and product pricing. Variable costing is very helpful in segmented reporting because it helps management to identify segments that cannot generate enough revenues to cover their variable costs and their traceable fixed costs. Variable costing is very useful in *short-term* decision making involving cost estimation or resource utilization.

BASIC CONCEPTS AND TERMS

Activity-based costing

Common fixed costs

Direct costing

Full absorption costing

Functional costing

Future benefit potential

Future cost avoidance

Lean production

Traceable fixed costs

Traditional costing

Variable costing

■ SELF-REVIEW PROBLEM

Susan Manufacturing Company manufactures and sells a single product. Following are the data related to the first two years of operations:

Units	Year 1	Year 2
In beginning inventory	0	2,000
Produced.	20,000	25,000
Sold.	18,000	26,000
In ending inventory	2,000	1,000
Costs		
Manufacturing:		
Direct materials per unit	$ 10	$ 10
Direct labor per unit	5	6
Variable overhead per unit.	3	3
Fixed overhead per year	100,000	100,000
Selling and administrative expenses:		
Variable expense per unit	$ 3	$ 3
Fixed expenses per year	200,000	200,000

Additional information:
1. The company's normal production capacity is 25,000 units per year. Fixed manufacturing overhead is applied to production at a predetermined overhead rate per unit based on normal capacity. Any over- or under-applied overhead is charged to cost of goods sold.
2. Selling price per unit: $40 in Year 1 and $42 in Year 2.
3. The company uses the FIFO cost flow assumption.

Required:

(a) Prepare a schedule of cost of production per unit for Year 1 and Year 2 under variable costing and full absorption costing.
(b) Prepare an income statement for Year 1, Year 2, and the two years together under variable costing and full absorption costing.
(c) Comment on the difference in operating income between the two methods in each of the two years and for the two years together.

Solution

(a) Cost of production per unit:

	Variable Costing		Absorption Costing	
	Year 1	Year 2	Year 1	Year 2
Direct materials	$10	$10	$10	$10
Direct labor	5	6	5	6
Variable manufacturing overhead	3	3	3	3

			4*	4*
Fixed manufacturing overhead	–	–		
Total cost per unit	$18	$19	$22	$23

* Applied at the rate of $4 per unit ($100,000 ÷ 25,000 units of normal capacity).

(b) Income statements:
Information:

	Year 1	Year 2	Total Two Years
Units in beginning inventory	0	2,000	0
Units produced	20,000	25,000	45,000
Units sold	18,000	26,000	44,000
Units in ending inventory	2,000	1,000	1,000
Selling price per unit	$ 40	$ 42	

SUSAN MANUFACTURING COMPANY
Income Statements Under the Two Methods
Variable Costing

Sales	$720,000	$1,092,000	$1,812,000
Variable expenses:			
Beginning inventory	0	36,000	0
Cost of goods manufactured	360,000	475,000	835,000
Cost of goods available for sale	360,000	511,000	835,000
Ending inventory	(36,000)	(19,000)	(19,000)
Manufacturing cost of goods sold	324,000	492,000	816,000
Variable selling expenses	54,000	78,000	132,000
Total variable expenses	378,000	570,000	948,000
Contribution margin	342,000	522,000	864,000
Fixed expenses:			
Manufacturing	100,000	100,000	200,000
Selling and administrative	200,000	200,000	400,000
Total fixed expenses	300,000	300,000	600,000
Operating income	$ 42,000	$ 222,000	$ 264,000

Costs of goods manufactured:
$18 × 20,000 units = $360,000
$19 × 25,000 units = $ 475,000
Ending inventory costs:
$18 × 2,000 units = $ 36,000
$19 × 1,000 units = $ 19,000
Variable selling expenses:
$3 × 18,000 units = $ 54,000
$3 × 26,000 units = $ 78,000

Full Absorption Costing

Sales	$720,000	$1,092,000	$1,812,000
Cost of goods sold:			
Beginning inventory	0	44,000	0
Cost of goods manufactured	440,000	575,000	1,015,000
Cost of goods available for sale	440,000	619,000	1,015,000
Ending inventory	(44,000)	(23,000)	(23,000)
Subtotal	396,000	596,000	992,000
Underapplied overhead	20,000	0	20,000
Cost of goods sold	416,000	596,000	1,012,000
Gross profit	304,000	496,000	800,000
Selling and administrative expenses:			
Variable	54,000	78,000	132,000
Fixed	200,000	200,000	400,000
Total	254,000	278,000	532,000
Operating income	$ 50,000	$ 218,000	$ 268,000

Costs of goods manufactured:
$22 × 20,000 units = $440,000
$23 × 25,000 units = $ 575,000
Ending inventory costs:
$22 × 2,000 units = $ 44,000
$23 × 1,000 units = $ 23,000

Underapplied manufacturing overhead:

Actual   *Applied*
$100,000 − ($4 × 20,000 units) = $ 20,000
$100,000 − ($4 × 25,000 units) =   0

    Note to students: If the underapplied overhead is not additionally charged, only $80,000 of fixed overhead ($4 × 20,000) has been charged to Year 1. Remember that the actual overhead of $100,000 needs to be charged per year.

(c) Comments on the difference in operating income between the two methods:

    1. Inventory increased in Year 1, from zero to 2,000 units, and full absorption costing showed a higher operating income. Inventory decreased in Year 2, from 2,000 to 1,000 units, and full absorption costing showed a lower operating income. For the two years together, inventory increased by 1,000 units, and thus, full absorption costing showed a higher operating income than variable costing.

    2. The difference in operating income between the two methods: Change in inventory × Applied fixed manufacturing overhead per unit.
      For Year 1: 2,000 units × $4 = $8,000
      For Year 2: (1,000) units × $4 = ($4,000)
      For the two years together: 1,000 units × $4 = $4,000

■ REVIEW QUESTIONS

11-1   Why would the proponents of variable costing believe that fixed manufacturing overhead is not a part of a company's assets?

11-2   If all units produced are sold during the same year, which method, variable costing or absorption costing, generates a higher income? Why?

11-3   "Even when sales fluctuate from year to year, a constant level of production would generate the same operating income under variable costing." Would you agree with this statement? Why or why not?

11-4   Under full absorption costing, is the fixed manufacturing overhead included in ending inventory deferred or released when inventory increases?

11-5   Assume that fixed manufacturing overhead is applied to production at the same rate each year and over- or underapplied overhead is closed out to cost of goods sold. If inventory decreases, which method of alternative product costing would produce a higher operating income?

11-6   Why is variable costing particularly useful in segmented reporting?

11-7   Why does management lose the ability to track specific expenses to those particular segments that are responsible for those expenses under full absorption costing?

11-8   Why should managers exercise extreme caution in applying variable costing to the estimation of cost-activity relationships?

11-9   "Variable costing is very useful in short-term decision making involving cost estimation or resource utilization. When the time horizon is extended to long term, variable costing loses its relevance." Do you agree? Why or why not?

11-10 When a company becomes a lean producer, what happens to the difference in operating income that arises from the different production and sales levels under variable costing and absorption costing? Does the difference become more significant or less significant? Why?

⊕ INTERNET PROJECT

Web 11-1:

   Websites: www.cocacola.com
                    www.pepsico.com
The websites listed above represent two famous companies. Search the sites for information on their operating characteristics.

Required:
1.   Based on the website information, which company do you think would want to use variable costing more? Why?

2. Which CEO would be more reluctant to use variable costing? Why?

Web 11-2:

Websites: www.lucent.com
              www.motorola.com

The websites listed above represent two famous companies. Search the sites for information on their operating characteristics.

Required:

1. Based on the website information, which company do you think would need segmented reporting more? Why?

2. Which company's segmented income statement would look more complicated? Why?

■ EXERCISES

E11-1   Uses of Variable Costing and Absorption Costing

The following is a listing of various uses of variable costing and absorption costing information. Indicate whether variable costing (V) or absorption costing (A) is appropriate for each situation.

a. Accept or reject a special order for a short-term purpose.
b. Determine the initial price for a new product. The company should generate a long-term profit on product sales.
c. Decide whether to buy or produce a part using idle capacity.
d. Evaluate departmental performance when expenses include variable and fixed components which are controllable and noncontrollable at the department level.
e. Budget for sales of product lines in the short run.

E11-2   Advantages of Variable Costing and Full Absorption Costing

The advantages of using variable costing and absorption costing are listed below. Indicate whether each advantage is for using variable costing (V) or full absorption costing (F).

a. It will provide information needed for volume-profit analysis.
b. It is used for reporting to stockholders.
c. It facilitates management's analysis of the effect of fixed costs on profits.
d. It will never mislead users to believe that variable costs are recovered first and then fixed costs are recovered.
e. There is no need to arbitrarily classify costs into variable and fixed components.
f. It will provide a basis for preparing flexible budgets.

E11-3   Unit Cost under Variable Costing and Absorption Costing

VAT, Inc. manufactures and sells a single product, and shows the following information on its operations for Year 4:

Beginning inventory.	0 units
Production in the current period	15,000 units
Sales in the current period	12,000 units
Ending inventory	3,000 units

Variable costs:	Per Unit
Direct materials	$5
Direct labor	3
Variable overhead	2
Variable selling expenses	1

Fixed costs:	Per Year
Manufacturing overhead	$90,000
Selling and administrative expenses	60,000

Required:

1. Compute the unit cost of product, using variable costing.
2. Compute the unit cost of product, using absorption costing.

E11-4   Income Statements under Variable Costing and Absorption Costing

Refer to the information in E11-3. The company provides the following additional information:

Selling price per unit of product.	$25

Required:

1. Present an income statement for Year 4, using the variable costing method.
2. Present an income statement for Year 4, using the absorption costing method.

E11-5   Inventory Cost under Variable Costing and Absorption Costing

For the last year, STS, Inc. reports the following operating results on the single product it produces and sells:

Units produced	16,000
Units sold	14,000

Costs:	
Variable costs:	Per Unit
Direct materials	$ 6

Direct labor	14
Manufacturing overhead.	4
Selling expenses	2
Fixed costs:	*Per Year*
Manufacturing overhead.	$128,000
Selling and administrative expenses	360,000

There was no inventory at the beginning of the year.

Required:

1. Compute the ending inventory amount under variable costing.
2. Compute the ending inventory amount under full absorption costing.

E11-6 Income Statement under Variable Costing

MTW, Inc. presents the following absorption costing income statement for Year 1:

Sales, 17,000 units x $30		$510,000
Cost of goods sold:		
Beginning inventory	$ 0	
Cost of goods manufactured, 20,000 units x $19 =	380,000	
Goods available for sale	380,000	
Ending inventory, 3,000 units x $19 = ...	(57,000)	323,000
Gross margin		187,000
Selling and administrative expenses.		101,000
Operating income		$ 86,000

Additional information:

1. Manufacturing cost per unit:

Direct materials.		$ 4
Direct labor		8
Manufacturing overhead:		
Variable.	$2	
Fixed ($100,000 ÷ 20,000 units)	5	7
Unit cost		$19

2. Selling and administrative expenses:

Variable.	$3 per unit sold
Fixed	$50,000 per year

Required:

1. Present the income statement using variable costing.
2. Reconcile any difference between the absorption costing operating income and the variable costing operating income.

E11-7 Income Statements under Variable Costing and Absorption Costing

LJC, Inc. manufactures and sells a toy. The company presents the following information on its costs and operations for Year 1:

Units produced.	18,000
Units sold	15,000
Selling price	$45 per unit
Costs:	
Manufacturing:	
Direct materials.	$5 per unit
Direct labor.	8 per unit
Variable overhead	2 per unit
Fixed overhead	$270,000 per year
Selling and administrative expenses:	
Variable	$3 per unit
Fixed	$100,000 per year

Required:

1. Present an income statement using absorption costing.
2. Present an income statement using variable costing.
3. Reconcile any difference between the absorption costing net income and the variable costing net income.

E11-8 Income Statement Segmented By Product

HST, Inc. presents the following information on its two product lines for a typical year:

	Product Line	
	A	B
Units sold.	20,000	30,000
Unit selling price.	$7	$9
Expenses:		
Variable expense per unit.	3.80	5.40
Traceable fixed expenses per year	$38,000	$22,000
Common fixed expenses per year	$25,000	

Required:

Present an income statement for a typical year segmented by product lines, for the company in total and for each of the two product lines.

E11-9 Segmented Income Statement

Monterey Resort & Spa, Inc. has two business segments, Segment A and Segment B. The company presents the following income statement for Year 8:

	Company Total Amount	%	Segment A Amount	%	Segment B Amount	%
Sales	$560,000	100%	$140,000	100%	$420,000	100%
Variable expenses	182,000	32.5	35,000	25	147,000	35
Contribution margin	378,000	67.5	105,000	75	273,000	65
Traceable fixed expenses	266,000	47.5	56,000	40	210,000	50
Segment margin	112,000	20.0	$ 49,000	35	$ 63,000	15
Common fixed expenses	84,000	15.0				
Net income	$ 28,000	5.0				

Required:

1. Restate the segmented income statement, assuming that Segment A's sales were $40,000 higher. Fixed costs would not change. Use the same format as above.
2. Assume that Segment A's sales increase was $80,000. Other conditions remain unchanged. What would be the amount of the net income increase for the company?

■ PROBLEMS

P11-10 Ethics and Inventory Buildup under Absorption Costing

It is December 2, Year 6, and you are employed by TGY, Inc. , a division of Westech Company, as its assistant division controller. The sales are slow, but the budgeted sales goal for the year seems to be within reach even at the current pace. This afternoon, you have been requested to gather information on the operations of the year, and you have compiled the following information:

Beginning inventory, January 1	1,200 units
Production to date, Year 6	24,000 units
Sales to date, Year 6	21,000 units
Expected sales in December, Year 6	1,500 units

Since the inventory on hand is more than adequate for the expected sales in December, you assume that the Production Department would cut down on its activity significantly, thus allowing the inventory to be consumed in an orderly fashion. The year-end inventory, however, is expected to be higher than the normal level.

On your way back from a staff conference, you notice that the plant personnel continue to be busy. As you check further, you find out that the Production Department has been instructed to "maximize the use of the production facility for the rest of the year." You also hear from the division controller that the division president wants to maximize the division's absorption costing earnings which the company's top management uses as a basis of evaluating managers' performance.

Required:

1. What connection do you see between the division president's desire to maximize the division's absorption costing earnings and the Production Department's high activity level?
2. What is your assessment of any excess inventory that the division does not need? Assume that the ending inventory of Year 5 was at a reasonable level, and the production rate in December is the same as the rate the division has seen thus far this year.
3. Do you see any ethics-related implication in the inventory buildup? Explain.
4. What should the company do to prevent its divisions from unnecessarily building up their inventory near the end of the year?

P11-11   From Absorption Costing Income Statement to Variable Costing Income Statement

KJM, Inc. manufactures and sells a graphic-enhancing device used on lap-top computers. For the first two years of operations, the company reports the following results using absorption costing:

	Year 1	Year 2
Units sold	5,000	6,000
Sales, at $35 per unit	$175,000	$210,000
Cost of goods sold:		
Beginning inventory	0	9,500
Cost of goods manufactured, at $19	104,500	104,500
Goods available for sale	104,500	114,000
Ending inventory, at $19	(9,500)	0
Cost of goods sold	95,000	114,000
Gross margin	80,000	96,000
Selling and administrative expenses:		
Variable, $1 per unit	(5,000)	(6,000)
Fixed	(60,000)	(60,000)
Net income	$15,000	$30,000

The production and cost data are presented below:

	Year 1	Year 2
Units produced	5,500	5,500
Units sold	5,000	6,000

Product cost per unit:

Direct materials..	$ 5
Direct labor..	8
Variable manufacturing overhead	2
Fixed manufacturing overhead, $22,000 ÷ 5,500 = ...	4
Total product cost per unit	$19

Required:

1. a. What is the unit production cost under variable costing?
   b. Present an income statement using variable costing.
2. Reconcile the variable costing net income to the absorption costing net income.

 P11-12 Variable Costing and Absorption Costing; Income Statement

Hexato, Inc. manufactures and sells optical-quality, fog-free vanity mirrors. The following data are presented for the most recent month of its operations:

Inventory data:

Beginning inventory	0
Units produced.....................................	12,000
Units sold...	10,000
Ending inventory	2,000
Selling price per unit...................................	$ 80

Manufacturing costs:

Direct materials per unit	16
Direct labor per unit	12
Variable overhead per unit...........................	3
Fixed overhead total................................	120,000

Selling and administrative expenses:

Variable per unit....................................	7
Fixed total..	140,000

Required:

1. Compute the unit cost of production under variable costing and under absorption costing.
2. Present an absorption costing income statement for the period.
3. Present a variable costing income statement.
4. Reconcile the variable costing net income to the absorption costing net income.

P11-13 Unit Cost and Net Income; Variable Costing and Absorption Costing

Biopro, Inc. manufactures and sells special magnets used in the production of various industrial products. The company presents the following data on its operations and costs for the most recent period:

Selling price per unit $130

Inventory data:
Beginning inventory . . . .   0 units
Units produced. . . . . 7,000 units
Units sold. . . . . 6,000 units

Manufacturing costs:
Direct materials per unit. . . . . $ 10
Direct labor per unit   12
Variable overhead per unit.   4
Fixed overhead total $280,000

Selling and administrative expenses:
Variable. . . . . 10% of sales
Fixed total $200,000

Required:
1. Compute the unit production cost under variable costing and under full absorption costing.
2. Present a full absorption costing income statement.
3. Present a variable costing income statement.
4. Reconcile the variable costing net income to the absorption costing net income.

P11-14 Variable Costing and Absorption Costing; Multiple Periods

The following data relate to CJV, Inc.'s manufacturing and sales of its single product for March and April of this year:

Product data:
Selling price per unit $80

	March	April
Beginning inventory	0	1,000
Units produced.	7,000	7,000
Units sold.	6,000	8,000

Cost data:
Manufacturing costs:
Direct materials per unit . . . . $ 6
Direct labor per unit   14
Variable overhead per unit.   5
Fixed overhead total per month   140,000

Selling and administrative expenses:

Variable per unit....................	2
Fixed per month....................	160,000

Required:

1. Compute the production costs per unit under variable costing and under full absorption costing.
2. Present the variable costing income statement for March.
3. Present the absorption costing income statement for March.
4. Reconcile the variable costing net income to the absorption costing net income for March.
5. Present the variable costing income statement for April.
6. Present the absorption costing income statement for April.
7. Reconcile the variable costing net income to the absorption costing net income for April.

P11-15 Changing a Variable Costing Statement to an Absorption Costing Statement

Xercise-Products, Inc. manufactures and sells a muscle-toning exercise product. The company presents the following income statement for the first month of its operations:

Xercise-Products, Inc.
Income Statement
For the First Month, Year 1

Sales, $50 × 7,000 units = ...		$350,000
Variable expenses:		
Beginning inventory......,............	$ 0	
Variable cost of production	128,000	
Goods available for sale	128,000	
Ending inventory	(16,000)	
Variable cost of goods sold.............	112,000	
Variable selling expenses	7,000	119,000
Contribution margin......................		231,000
Fixed expenses:		
Manufacturing overhead................	80,000	
Selling and administrative expenses	160,000	240,000
Operating income.......................		$ (9,000)

The management did not expect to see profit in the first month of its operations, and appreciates the contribution approach used in preparing the income statement, which shows the cost-volume-profit aspects of operations. The company, however, is in the process of applying for a bank loan, and wants to see if a different format of income statement would portray the results of operations in a more favorable light.

The additional data on operations and costs are presented below:

Beginning inventory..........................	0 units
Units produced...............................	8,000 units
Units sold.....................................	7,000 units

Variable cost of production includes the following:

Direct materials per unit.....................	$ 4
Direct labor per unit	10
Variable overhead per unit....................	2
Variable selling expenses per unit	1

Required:

1. Would an absorption costing income statement produce a higher operating income? Answer the question without preparing an actual income statement.
2. Compute the production cost per unit under variable costing and under absorption costing.
3. Present an absorption costing income statement.
4. Reconcile the variable costing net income to the absorption costing net income.
5. Assume that the company produced the same 8,000 units in the second month. The sales, however, reached 9,000 units, without increasing any fixed costs.
   a. Present a variable costing income statement for the second month.
   b. Present an absorption costing income statement for the second month.
   c. Reconcile the variable costing net income to the absorption costing net income.

P11-16 Changing an Absorption Costing Statement to a Variable Costing Statement

GST, Inc. manufactures and sells a showerhead that uses a granulated medium and turbo action to make shower water chlorine-free . Last year (Year 3), the company wanted to produce a higher-than-usual number of showerheads in anticipation of a strong market, which has not materialized to date.

The company pays bonuses based on actual earnings realized by the company, and the controller has prepared the following income statement for Year 3 which is shown in comparison with the income statement of Year 2:

	Year 2	Year 3
Sales, $19 x 50,000	$950,000	$950,000
Cost of goods sold	600,000	575,000
Gross margin............................	350,000	375,000
Selling and administrative expenses	260,000	260,000
Net income.............................	$ 90,000	$115,000

Ted Anson, the owner of the company who has no accounting background, cannot understand how the company can show a higher net income in Year 3 in which the company sold the same number of units as it did in Year 2. "It's not that I don't want to pay higher bonuses this year," remarked Mr. Anson. "I simply cannot understand how a fair accounting system can generate a higher net income when the sales stay the same."

The controller believes that, unless a good explanation can be given, the owner's confidence in the accounting system as a whole is at risk. In order to provide the explanation, she has compiled the following additional information:

	Year 2	Year 3
Beginning inventory.	0	0
Units produced	50,000	60,000
Units sold	50,000	50,000
Variable manufacturing cost per unit.	$ 9	$ 9
Fixed manufacturing overhead for the year .	150,000	150,000
Variable selling expenses per unit.	2	2

Fixed overhead is applied to production at a predetermined overhead rate per unit based on normal capacity (50,000 units). Any over- or underapplied overhead is charged to cost of goods sold.

Required:

1. Before attempting any calculation, how would you explain the higher net income shown for Year 3? Briefly explain.
2. Compute the production cost per unit under absorption costing for Year 2.
3. Present the income statement for Year 2 using variable costing. Compare the variable costing income to the absorption costing income presented above. Why is the net income the same amount?
4. Present the income statement for Year 3 using (a) variable costing and (b) absorption costing.
5. Reconcile the variable costing net income to the absorption costing net income for Year 3.

P11-17 Fluctuating Activity Levels and Income

DDX, Inc. manufactures and sells a cordless teeth-cleaner that does the job of string dental floss. The sales are made mostly to hospitals and nursing homes which buy the product in bulk. The company enjoys stable sales and the resulting stability in its operations. The absorption costing income statement of the company for Year 4 reflects the operations of a typical year:

Income Statement
For Year 4

Sales, $30 × 8,000 = ...		$240,000
Cost of goods sold:		
Beginning inventory.	$ 0	
Cost of goods manufactured	160,000	

Goods available for sale	160,000	
Ending inventory	(0)	160,000
Gross margin		80,000
Selling and administrative expenses:		
Variable, $2 × 8,000 = ...	16,000	
Fixed	55,000	71,000
Operating income		$ 9,000

At the beginning of Year 5, the company hired a new president who had impressed the owner of the company as an aggressive manager who would turn the company into a "real competitor." The president seemed to have great plans to move the company ahead, but his actual performance was disappointing. His abrasive style alienated some healthcare professionals at several hospitals which subsequently terminated their business relationships with DDX, Inc. It didn't take the owner even one year to realize that he had made a mistake of trying to become too aggressive in a field that didn't like overly aggressive people. At the end of Year 5, Mary Fleming, the nurse-turned manager who had managed DDX, Inc. previously, was called back.

After her return to her old job, Ms. Fleming made serious efforts to win the previous customers back and she succeeded. By the middle of Year 6, the company was back in the previous position. The company also made adjustment in its production schedule to deal with the inventory buildup, caused by the drop in sales in Year 5, so that the extra inventory units would be sold before the company gets back to the regular production pace. The operations went smoothly for the rest of Year 6.

The income statements for Year 5 and Year 6 are presented below:

Income Statements

	Year 5	Year 6
Sales	$216,000	$240,000
Cost of goods sold:		
Beginning inventory	0	16,000
Cost of goods manufactured	160,000	146,000
Goods available for sale	160,000	162,000
Ending inventory	(16,000)	(2,000)
Subtotal	144,000	160,000
Underapplied overhead	0	10,500
Cost of goods sold	144,000	170,500
Gross margin	72,000	69,500
Selling and administrative expenses	69,400	71,000
Operating income	$ 2,600	$ (1,500)

The owner, who was happy with the performance of Ms. Fleming, was confused after he looked at the operating income figures for the two years. "I don't understand it," said the owner. "I thought we were doing better in Year 6."

In order to explain what the figures meant, Ms. Fleming saw the need to restate the income statement using variable costing. The following additional data are available for the task:

a. Variable manufacturing costs are $5 per unit, and fixed manufacturing overhead costs are $120,000 for the year. The costs haven't changed for the three years.

b. The company uses a FIFO assumption of inventory flow.

c. Fixed overhead is applied to production at a predetermined overhead rate per unit based on normal capacity (8,000 units). Any over- or underapplied overhead is charged to cost of goods sold.

d. Selling and administrative expenses, both variable and fixed, haven't changed from Year 4.

Required:

1. a. Compute the predetermined fixed manufacturing overhead rate per unit.
   b. How many inventory units were there at the end of Year 5 and Year 6?
2. Restate the income statements for the three years as Ms. Fleming wants, using variable costing.
3. a. How many units were produced in Year 6?
   b. What was the fixed manufacturing overhead applied to production in Year 6?
4. Reconcile the variable costing net income to the absorption costing net income for Year 5 and Year 6.

P11-18 Changing Sales and Profits under Variable Costing and Absorption Costing

CSG, Inc. manufactures and sells an electronic coaching device that golfers can carry with them. For the first two quarters of its first-year operations, the following results have been observed:

Income Statements

	Quarter 1	Quarter 2
Sales	$360,000	$420,000
Cost of goods sold:		
Beginning inventory............	$ 0	$ 27,000
Cost of goods manufactured	189,000	170,100
Goods available for sale	189,000	197,100
Ending inventory	(27,000)	(8,100)
Subtotal	162,000	189,000
Underapplied overhead.........	0	12,600
Cost of goods sold	162,000	201,600

Gross margin		198,000		218,400
Selling and administrative expenses:				
Variable, $7 per unit	42,000		49,000	
Fixed	101,000	143,000	101,000	150,000
Operating income		$ 55,000		$ 68,400

The management of the company is happy that the product development has been a success. Thanks to the recent popularity of the sport of golf, the sales of the coaching device have been at a satisfactory level, and the profits looked even better. "The sales increased only 17%, but the profit increased 25%," remarked Bill Taylor, the president. "We will be O.K. , except for one problem. We reduced production 10% in the second quarter. Why didn't the cost of goods manufactured decrease 10%? If it had, we would have made even more profits. "

Jackie Tyler, the company's controller, has gathered the following information related to what the president referred to:

	Quarter 1	Quarter 2
Beginning inventory in units.	0	1,000
Units produced	7,000	6,300
Units sold	6,000	7,000
Ending inventory in units	1,000	300
Costs:		
Variable manufacturing costs per unit		$9
Fixed manufacturing overhead per quarter	126,000	

The company uses the FIFO inventory method. Fixed overhead is applied to production at a predetermined overhead rate per unit based on normal capacity (7,000 units). Any over- or underapplied overhead is charged to cost of goods sold.

Ms. Taylor, the controller, thinks the best way to explain the reason why costs did not decrease the way production decreased is to show the management the income statements using variable costing. Variable costing statements would show the variability of variable costs and the fixed nature of fixed costs.

Required:

1. Compute the predetermined fixed manufacturing overhead rate per unit.
2. Restate the income statements for the two quarters using variable costing.
3. Explain why the cost of goods manufactured, according to the absorption costing income statements, did not decrease the same way the production decreased in Quarter 2. Do the variable costing statements help in explaining the reason?
4. Reconcile the variable costing net income to the absorption costing net income for (a) Quarter 1 and (b) Quarter 2.

P11-19 Business Segments and Managerial Focus

Consider the following income statement for a resort and spa company for the most recent period:

	Company Total		Division A		Division B	
	Amount	%	Amount	%	Amount	%
Sales.....................	$560,000	100.0%	$140,000	100%	$420,000	100%
Variable expenses.........	182,000	32.5	35,000	25	147,000	35
Contribution margin........	378,000	67.5	105,000	75	273,000	65
Traceable fixed expenses ...	224,000	40.0	56,000	40	168,000	40
Segment margin	154,000	27.5	$49,000	35	$105,000	25
Common fixed expenses....	84,000	15.0				
Net income...............	$70,000	12.5				

Division B consists of Seaside Unit and Mountain Unit for which the following financial performance has been reported for the last period:

			Segments			
	Division B		Seaside Unit		Mountain Unit	
	Amount	%	Amount	%	Amount	%
Sales	$420,000	100.0	$168,000	100.0	$252,000	100.0
Less variable expenses	147,000	35.0	68,880	41.0	78,120	31.0
Contribution margin	273,000	65.0	99,120	59.0	173,880	69.0
Less traceable fixed expenses	105,000	25.0	34,440	20.5	70,560	28.0
Product-line margin	168,000	40.0	$ 64,680	38.5	$103,320	41.0
Less common fixed expenses	63,000	15.0				
Net income	$105,000	25.0				

The company is in the process of choosing either Seaside Unit or Mountain Unit to promote heavily in Southern California. Thus far, the promotional activities were confined to Northern California only. If it is successful, the company would be able to extend it to another unit also. Due to various limitations, the company cannot undertake the promotion for both units. According to a preliminary study, the promotion would cost $18,000, and would have the effect of increasing sales by $60,000 per period for Seaside Unit or increasing sales by $70,000 for Mountain Unit.

Required:

1. In order to maximize the company's profit which unit of the two should the company choose for promotion? Why?

2. If the decision made in (1) is implemented, what would be the new segment margin for Division B?

P11-20   Profit Performance of Segments

Los Serranos Golf Company's variable expenses average 40% of sales. Average quarterly fixed expenses are $920,000, which include traceable fixed expenses of $800,000. For the last quarter, the company's three business segments showed the following operating results:

	Segment		
	Coast	Inland	Desert
Sales......................	$450,000	$400,000	$650,000
Variable expense ratio	40.0%	42.5%	38.46%
Traceable fixed expenses......	240,000	230,000	330,000

Management believes that the only way for the company to grow in the golf business is to expand its operations in the Desert Segment. The coastal and inland regions are expected to see a glut in the services provided by competitors in the future.

Required:

1. Present the company's income statement. Do not segment the statement.
2. Present the income statement for the three segments. Instead of profit for the company, the segment margin should be shown for each segment.
3. An internal study forecasts a sales increase of 25% for the Desert Segment for its expanded operations. The sales increase, however, requires a $25,000 promotional campaign. Should the company expand its operations for the Desert Segment?

P11-21   Income Statements Segmented by Sales Regions and Product Lines

Quail Company has two sales regions, Northern Cal Region and Southern Cal Region. The data on the operating results of the two regions for the last quarter are provided below:

	Sales Regions	
	Northern Cal	Southern Cal
Sales.....................	$120,000	$180,000
Variable expenses to sales ratio	45%	35%
Traceable fixed expenses............	$42,000	$37,000
	Northern Cal's Product Lines	
	Qua	Qub
Sales............................	$20,000	$100,000
Variable expenses to sales ratio	22.0%	49.6%
Traceable fixed expenses...........	$10,000	$14,000

The company's total fixed expenses for the quarter amount to $131,000.

Required:

1. Compute the common fixed expenses for the company which include traceable fixed expenses of both regions.
2. Present the income statement segmented by sales region.
3. Compute the common fixed expenses for Northern Cal Region.
4. Present the income statement segmented by product line.
5. If management wants to expand its operations in one of the sales regions, which region should be the focus?
6. If an expansion is considered for the Northern Cal Region, which product line should be the focus?

P11-22 Format of a Segmented Statement; Absorption Costing and Variable Costing

LJC, Inc. is a maker of cranberry juice that is sold in three regions: West, Midwest, and Southwest. The juice is bottled in three separate plants in the three regions to minimize delivery expenses. Still, each region incurs sizeable delivery expenses for transporting juice to its customers. Although the sales increase has been modest thus far, recent studies showing positive health benefits of cranberry juice are expected to help increase future sales. LJC, Inc. is also counting on the fact that its juice is 100% juice, compared to at most 30% juice that is used by the market leader in the bottling process.

The company had not used segmented reporting before, but presents the following information on the head office and its three sales regions for the most recent month:

	Sales Regions		
	West	Midwest	Southwest
Sales..............................	$180,000	$320,000	$300,000
Region's own expenses:			
Cost of goods sold	57,000	98,000	131,000
Delivery expenses.................	5,000	11,000	9,000
Marketing........................	37,000	70,000	73,000
Personnel	31,000	30,000	47,000
Utilities	4,000	4,000	5,000
Depreciation	9,000	9,000	9,000
Region's own expenses total	143,000	222,000	274,000
Region's own income	$ 37,000	$ 98,000	$ 26,000

Head office expenses that are hard to allocate:		
Marketing		$ 28,000
Administrative expenses.............		$ 52,000

Among the expense items, only cost of goods sold and delivery expenses are variable. All others are mostly fixed.

Required:

1. Present an income statement segmented by sales regions for the month, using variable costing.
2. The company is considering a special promotion for its cranberry juice, focusing on the "pure" (100%) juice it sells. The budget for the promotion, however, is limited, and only one region can be targeted. Which region should the company target in order to maximize the profit for the company?
3. Which sales region's performance is the weakest? What are the reasons for the poor performance?

■ CASES

C11-23 Multi-Level Segmented Income Statement

Visions, Inc. manufactures and sells lenses and frames used by eyeglass stores and industrial customers. Eyeglass stores buy lenses and frames for sales to the general public, and dealers buy special lenses and frames for sales to industrial customers. The growth of the business has been limited in the past, especially in the general eyeglass sales, but the outlook is good with the aging of the baby-boom generation who will need eyeglasses.

The income statement segmented by divisions for the most recent month is presented below, using the variable costing format:

		Division	
	The Company	General	Industrial
Sales.......................	$420,000	$240,000	$180,000
Variable expenses	180,000	108,000	72,000
Contribution margin...........	240,000	132,000	108,000
Traceable fixed expenses:			
Marketing	69,000	42,000	27,000
General administration	25,000	16,000	9,000
Depreciation	68,000	32,000	36,000
Total.....................	162,000	90,000	72,000
Divisional margin	78,000	$ 42,000	$ 36,000
Common fixed expenses	48,000		
Net income...................	$ 30,000		

The General Division's sales are greater than the Industrial Division's by one-third. The profit margin of the General Division, however, is higher only by one-sixth. This low profit margin ratio has become the major focus of management's attention recently. Management believes that the major portion of future sales increase should come from the General Division, capitalizing on the aging baby-boomers' needs for eyeglasses. In order to lay the foundation for turning future sales increases into significant profit increases, management wants to establish a sound financial performance structure.

In an effort to find the reasons for the low profit margin of the General Division, management has asked the General Division's performance be further broken down to product models. The following information is available for segmenting the income statement by product model:

	Product Model		
	Model S	Model T	Model U
Sales............................	$100,000	$100,000	$40,000
Variable expenses to sales ratio ...	45%	39%	60%
Traceable fixed expenses:			
Marketing	$17,000	$16,000	$9,000
General administration	3,000	4,000	2,000
Depreciation.................	12,000	13,000	7,000

Expenses that cannot be attributed to specific product models are the division's common expenses.

Required:

1. Present an income statement for the General Division, segmented by product model. Use variable costing.
2. The General Division management wants to analyze the poor performance of Model U further. Model U is sold in the two regions, East and West. The model was first marketed in the East, but the sales in the two regions are the same for the month. The variable expenses to sales ratio is the same 60% for both regions, but the division spent $3,000 for the East and $6,000 for the West on regional marketing expenses. Marketing expenses are the only expense that can be traced to specific sales regions. Other expenses are common to all regions. Present an income statement for Model U, segmented by sales region. Use variable costing.

RESPONSIBILITY ACCOUNTING AND DECENTRALIZED OPERATIONS

After studying this chapter, you should be able to:

1. Differentiate between centralized and decentralized operations and discuss the advantages and disadvantages of the latter.

2. Differentiate among cost centers, profit centers, and investment centers.

3. Explain responsibility accounting and give an overview of how it works.

4. Explain how return on investment (ROI), residual income, and economic value added (EVA) are computed and discuss the impact on the management behavior of using each in measuring the performance of investment centers.

5. Explain how to measure and reward managerial performance, including the determination of executive incentive pay.

6. Discuss how an appropriate price may be established for output transferred between two segments of an organization.

7. Understand the international dimensions of decentralization and transfer pricing.

As organizations become larger in size and more complex in their operations, management finds it necessary to delegate decision-making authority to lower-level managers. We call this delegation of decision-making authority **decentralization.**

In this chapter, we discuss management control in decentralized organizations. First, we compare decentralized operations to centralized operations. Second, we define and illustrate responsibility accounting. Third, we discuss three tools for evaluating the performance of decentralized operations, return on investment, residual income, and economic value added. Fourth, we examine different methods for determining the prices at which output may be transferred from one division to another within the same organization. Last, we look at the international dimensions of the issues surrounding decentralization.

CENTRALIZED VS. DECENTRALIZED OPERATIONS

When operations are highly **centralized,** a few top executives make important decisions in the organization. Lower-level managers are not free to make any significant decisions without top management approval. When operations are highly **decentralized,** managers at all levels have the authority to make day-to-day key operating decisions.

Responsibility comes with authority. In a decentralized organization, each managerial level is held responsible for the results of decisions made at that level. Centralization or decentralization is a matter of *degree* with regard to various decisions. All large organizations are decentralized to some extent out of economic or physical necessity, and all small organizations are centralized simply because there is no need for delegation.

Sara Lee's top management is committed to a decentralized management structure and employs a global perspective to seek growth and extend geographic reach with emphasis on high-return businesses.

In essence, organizational structure depends on top management philosophy. Let us take a nationwide retail chain such as Target as an example. If Target top management adopts a centralization philosophy, store managers nationwide would not have the authority to make key decisions as to which items go on sale, what discount percentage to use, what items to add or drop, and what kinds of local advertising, such as newspaper or television, to undertake. Store managers would still have the authority to make minor day-to-day decisions, such as hiring or laying off cashiers or storage clerks or contracting with local business to paint or remodel an office.

On the other hand, if top management adopts a decentralization philosophy, store managers have the authority to make all the important decisions previously listed. Top management at the headquarters makes company-wide, long-range strategic decisions, such as issuing new stocks or bonds, paying dividends, acquiring another company, or disposing of an existing subsidiary. Most companies fall between the two extremes of totally centralized or totally decentralized. However, in recent years, there has been a pronounced tendency towards more decentralization. This is so because decentralization has significant advantages in today's competitive environment, as discussed below.

Advantages of Decentralization

Decentralization has the following advantages:

1. Giving more responsibility and decision making authority to all managerial levels leads to high job satisfaction and provides incentive to managers to make their best efforts.
2. The time needed to reach a final decision decreases, because of the proximity of managers to the relevant data for decisions.
3. Managers will try to make decisions that they feel will result in the greatest profit for their areas of responsibility. This usually produces higher profits for the company as a whole.
4. Delegation relieves top management of the burden of making many repetitive, day-to-day decisions, and allows top management to concentrate on company-wide, long-range, policy decisions.
5. As an organization diversifies into a wider range of products and services, it becomes difficult for top management to be knowledgeable about every type of product and service. Thus, top management will find it necessary to have experts in each area and delegate authority to them.
6. Decentralization provides an excellent training opportunity for managers, which helps the company to develop future key executives by allowing managers to practice managerial skills at the divisional level where the cost of making mistakes is not as high as at the company level.

Disadvantages of Decentralization

If not planned and implemented carefully, decentralization has the following disadvantages:

1. The most serious disadvantage is loss of control by top management.
2. The decisions made by one manager may affect other managers in such a way that the profitability of the company as a whole may suffer. For example, if two division managers compete with each other through price cutting, the company's profits may be less than if they did not compete in this way.
3. A certain amount of duplication in efforts, assets, and costs is inevitable. For example, each division has its own office, sales force and administrative staff. Also, the process of gathering and processing operating information may be repeated by different divisions.

If the disadvantages are excessive, profits of the company as a whole may suffer. Accordingly, even in a decentralized organization, certain functions may continue to be fully or partially centralized. Management must consider the disadvantages of decentralization against the advantages before the final organizational structure is decided.

EVALUATING MANAGERIAL PERFORMANCE

Responsibility Centers

Decentralization leads to the delegation of authority and responsibility from top management to all managerial levels in charge of a set of organizational activities, called a **responsibility center.** A responsibility center is any organization unit headed by an "in charge" manager. It could be a manufacturing cell in a computerized manufacturing plant or the whole plant. It could be a group of animators at a Hollywood studio or the whole studio.

Due to top management's delegation of authority and responsibility to various responsibility centers, a good system of measuring and evaluating managerial performance is crucial. Such a control system may differ depending on whether the responsibility center is viewed as a cost center, a profit center, or an investment center.

Cost, Profit and Investment Centers

A **cost center** is a responsibility center whose manager has control over cost incurrence. The manager of a cost center does not have control over the generation of revenue or the investment in various assets (receivables, inventories and equipment). A **profit center** is a responsibility center whose manager has control over both cost incurrence and revenue generation. An **investment center** is a responsibility center whose manager has control over costs, revenues, and investments in certain assets.

How is a responsibility center defined as a cost, profit, or investment center? A responsibility center is created to accomplish one or more *objectives.* These objectives are supposed to help achieve the overall *goals* of the organization. For a profit-oriented corporation (Disney, for example) with a goal of earning a satisfactory return on investment, the following explains how a responsibility center is defined:

Responsibility Center Defined		Objective
Investment center (Disney, the company)	→	Maximize the profit compared to the assets employed in earning it.
Profit center (ABC, the network)	→	Maximize the difference between revenues and expenses.
Cost center (News Production Department of ABC)	→	Maximize the quantity and quality of news output at the lowest possible costs

What is Responsibility Accounting?

Responsibility accounting means that every responsibility center is held accountable for the revenues, costs, and assets it is responsible for. With the authority to control the level of costs, for example, the manager should account for any major deviations from the budgeted costs. That is the essence of responsibility accounting.

Evaluating a Responsibility Center's Performance

If we define performance by financial measures (nonfinancial measures are discussed in Chapter 10), a responsibility center's performance is evaluated as follows:

Responsibility Center	Comparison
Cost center	Actual costs versus budgeted costs
Profit center	Actual profits versus budgeted profits
Investment center	Actual return on investment versus expected (target) return on investment

More realistically speaking, however, we may have to define costs, profits and investments differently from case to case and from company to company as discussed below.

Use of Costs to Evaluate a Cost Center's Performance

Costs are defined differently: direct or indirect, variable or fixed, and controllable or uncontrollable. Costs are controllable when the manager of the area in which the costs are incurred has authority over the cost incurrence. Direct and variable costs are more controllable than indirect and fixed costs, although some indirect and fixed costs are controllable also.

In evaluating the performance of a cost center's manager, controllable costs would be the most relevant to use. A cost item that a manager has no control over should not be included in a performance report. This is because the manager's actions and decisions do not affect such costs. A performance report for a cost center includes actual and budgeted controllable costs, and the variance between the two. The reasons for the variance should be identified, explained, and corrective actions taken.

PepsiCo's subsidiaries, such as Pizza Hut, KFC, and TACO BELL, operate as profit centers.

Use of Profits to Evaluate a Profit Center's Performance

Profits of a profit center may be defined in various ways. For example, we have gross profit (sales less cost of sales), contribution margin (sales less variable cost of sales), operating profit (earnings before interest and taxes), and net income before and after taxes. Which one of these definitions would be the most appropriate in evaluating the performance of a profit center?

The profits used to evaluate a profit center's performance should be the following profits:

> Controllable revenues
> − Controllable costs
> = A center's profits used for performance evaluation

Generally speaking, all sales and revenues generated by a profit center are controllable by that center's manager if he or she has full authority to set selling prices and to implement various discount policies. Some companies, however, try to allocate interest income and interest expense of the whole company to profit centers. That practice is not useful in evaluating the performance of a profit center's manager. The center's manager usually does not have authority over how much capital is to be borrowed and how much is to be raised through the issuance of stocks and bonds. Nor does the center's manager have authority over dividends or interest rates. Top management makes these financing decisions.

The profit term, such as gross profit, contribution margin, operating profit or net profit, to be used in performance reports will vary from company to company depending on the existing degree of decentralization. If profit center managers have no control over fixed costs, then contribution margin is the best index to use in evaluating performance. If they have control over these costs, then operating income would be the best index to use. Net profits should not be used in evaluating the centers' performance because they are net of interest expenses allocated to each center and net of taxes. Profit center managers have no control over interest expenses. These are the results of the amounts borrowed and the interest rates charged, none of which are controlled by profit center managers. Income taxes are the results of tax rates, tax credits, and tax planning activities that are affected by central management decisions.

RESPONSIBILITY ACCOUNTING: HOW IT WORKS

In order to make a responsibility accounting system function properly, top management must make sure that the following three basic criteria are met:

1. Revenues, costs, profits, and investments can be classified according to managerial levels.
2. Revenues, costs, profits, and investments can be controlled at each of these managerial levels.
3. Effective budget data can be generated and used for evaluating actual performance at each managerial level.

An Overview

We use a service firm to illustrate how the responsibility accounting system works. The firm is a major department store chain that has branches all over the United States. Exhibit 12-1 depicts a simplified organization chart. Each store is divided into departments: men's, women's, children's, shoes, home appliances, sporting goods, pharmacy, garden shop, and automotive. Each department is supervised by a

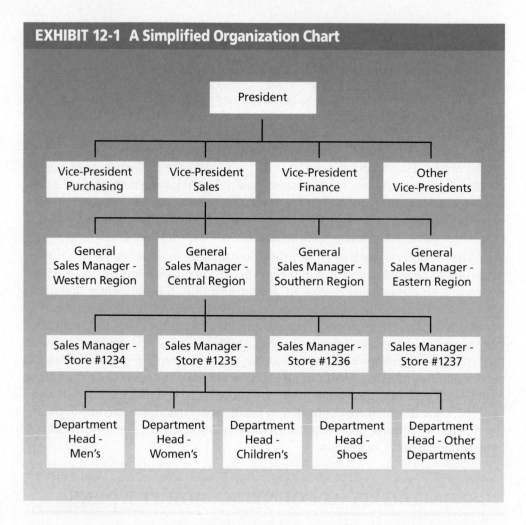

EXHIBIT 12-1 A Simplified Organization Chart

department head who reports to the store sales manager, who in turn reports to the general sales manager for the region.

Exhibit 12-1 assumes that the United States is divided into four regions, Eastern, Central, Southern and Western, each of which is headed by a general sales manager. All of the four general sales managers report to the Vice President-Sales who in turn reports to the President of the company.

Exhibit 12-2 provides an overview of the responsibility accounting system using the performance reports prepared by each level of responsibility for the level just above it. We can observe the following:

1. Information flows from the bottom up, i.e., from the lowest level of management to the president. Reports are summarized, and details are lost, as the reports move up the organizational chart.

2. While Exhibit 12-2 focuses on total sales, other reports may focus on variable costs, contribution margin, total cost, operating income or net income. Total sales is used as illustration because the sales figure is easier to understand than the other items mentioned above.

EXHIBIT 12-2

A Department Store Chain
An Overview of Responsibility Accounting
and Reports Generated by Each Level of Responsibility
(in Sales Dollars)
For July, Year 8

	Actual		Budget		Variance	
	This Month	Year to Date	This Month	Year to Date	This Month	Year to Date
Monthly Performance Report to the President						
Vice President-Purchasing	x	x	x	x	x	x
Vice President-Sales	11,120	72,360	10,500	71,400	620F	960F
Vice President-Finance	x	x	x	x	x	x
Other Vice Presidents	x	x	x	x	x	x
Total Company Operations	x	x	x	x	x	x
Monthly Performance Report to Vice President-Sales						
General Sales Manager-Western Region	x	x	x	x	x	x
General Sales Manager-Central Region	2,545	17,815	2,600	18,100	55U	285U
General Sales Manager-Southern Region	x	x	x	x	x	x
General Sales Manager-Eastern Region	x	x	x	x	x	x
	11,120	72,360	10,500	71,400	620F	960F
Monthly Performance Report to General Sales Manager						
Sales Manager-Store #1234	x	x	x	x	x	x
Sales Manager-Store #1235	180	1,344	190	1,365	10U	21U
Sales Manager-Store #1236	x	x	x	x	x	x
Sales Manager-Other Stores in Central Region	x	x	x	x	x	x
Total Central Region	2,545	17,815	2,600	18,100	55U	285U
Monthly Report to Sales Manager-Store #1235						
Department Head-Men's	29	208	30	210	1U	2U
Department Head-Women's	53	352	50	350	3F	2F
Department Head-Children's	38	291	40	285	2U	6F
Department Head-Shoes	9	72	10	70	1U	2F
Department Head-Other Departments in Store	51	421	60	450	9U	29U
Total Store #1235	180	1,344	190	1,365	10U	21U

F: Favorable
U: Unfavorable

3. These reports are not standards that are used by every company. The format of such reports may vary from company to company. For example, the actual results column or the budget column may be eliminated. Other columns, such as a percentage variance column, may be added.

4. The details by product line may be prepared for each department head. For example, the Men's Department Head in Store #1235 may require a breakdown by product line (pants, shirts, socks, etc.) of the $29 million actual sales during the month of July, Year 8. Similarly, any responsibility level higher than the Men's Department Head may require the same detailed report for each department sales.

5. In manufacturing companies, these responsibility reports may include only costs (for cost centers), revenues, costs, and profits (for profit centers), or revenues, costs, profits, and investments (for investment centers). In such manufacturing companies, lower levels of management benefit from detailed reports that include not only total, but also unit costs and physical volumes of inputs and outputs. Upper levels of management generally prefer summary reports.

ROI and Investment Center's Performance

The manager of an investment center does not only have control over the revenues and costs of the center but also over the amount of capital to be invested in the center. Accordingly, we need a performance evaluation index which incorporates not only the amount of profit generated but also the amount of funds invested in the center. Such an index is called **return on investment (ROI).** The ROI is calculated by dividing the return (profit) by the capital invested in the center as follows:

$$\text{ROI} = \frac{\text{Profit}}{\text{Investment}}$$

"Profit" and "investment" may be defined differently by different companies. For example, profit may be defined as operating profit or net profit. Also, investment may be defined as operating assets, total assets, or stockholders' equity. To measure operating performance, operating profits divided by operating assets would be the most appropriate ROI to use. It is called **operating ROI** as shown below:

$$\text{Operating ROI} = \frac{\text{Operating profit}}{\text{Operating assets}}$$

Analysis of Operating ROI

An investment manager's performance is evaluated by comparing his or her center's *actual* operating ROI against its *expected* operating ROI, the performance potential under the relevant conditions. But what if the actual operating ROI is lower than the expected or budgeted operating ROI? What can the manager do to improve the actual operating ROI? To answer these questions, the operating ROI must be analyzed to identify the problem areas that might have caused the actual operating ROI to be lower than expected.

Sempra Energy Solutions finances, owns, and operates the Venetian Resort-Hotel-Casino's $70 million (investment) energy system. This joint venture reduces energy-system operating costs by 20% (return) at the posh mega-resort in Vegas. The ROI reflects the performance of the venture.

The first step in this analytical process is to break down the operating ROI into two components as shown below:

$$\text{Operating ROI} = \frac{\text{Operating profit}}{\text{Sales}} \times \frac{\text{Sales}}{\text{Operating assets}}$$

$$= \text{Operating profit margin}$$
$$\times \text{Operating asset turnover}$$

The above equation is still correct since sales cancels itself out. The first component (operating profits ÷ sales) is called **operating profit margin.** The second component (sales ÷ operating assets) is called **operating asset turnover.**

The second step in the analysis of operating ROI is to determine whether the low operating ROI is caused by a low operating profit margin or a low operating asset turnover. In rare occasions both may be low. Managers do this by comparing *actual* operating profit margin against *expected* (budgeted) operating profit margin, and *actual* operating asset turnover against *expected* (budgeted) operating asset turnover. If operating profit margin seems to be causing the problem of low operating ROI, the investment center manager may have to reduce costs or increase unit selling price or do a little bit of both. This should increase operating profit margin. One way of determining which costs to reduce is to look at each expense item as a percentage of sales and compare this to budget or prior years' results.

Residual Income and Investment Center Performance

The use of operating ROI to measure performance has pitfalls. For example, it encourages some managers to reject some investment opportunities that may increase the profits of the whole company while lowering the center's ROI. For example, a center's manager whose ROI is 18% will probably reject any new investment opportunity that promises an ROI of less than 18%, although the company's overall ROI may be well below 18%. To avoid this pitfall, companies can use a concept known as residual income.

Residual income is the amount of income generated by a center in excess of the cost of capital (or a desired minimum ROI). For example, assume that a company has three centers with the data shown below and the cost of capital is 10%.

	Center A	Center B	Center C
Net operating profit (R)	$ 50,000	$ 80,000	$ 140,000
Average operating assets (I)	$250,000	$500,000	$1,000,000
ROI (R ÷ I)	20%	16%	14%

We can calculate the residual income for each center as follows:

	Center A	Center B	Center C
Net operating income	$50,000	$80,000	$140,000
Cost of capital (10%)	(25,000)*	(50,000)	(100,000)
Residual income	$25,000	$30,000	$ 40,000

* Cost of capital for Center A = 10% × $250,000 = $25,000

E-Business and Operating Profit

In the pre-Net era, efficiency improvements usually translated into higher operating margins for the corporations that implemented efficiency-enhancing methods. The efficiency improvements that e-businesses have made have led to mixed results. The efficiency-enhancing changes GE has made in its procurement procedures to the completely Internet-based procurement have produced company-wide savings of hundreds of millions of dollars. For most e-businesses, however, efficiency improvements have not been converted into higher operating margins.

Why haven't efficiency improvements turned into higher operating margins for so many e-businesses? Businesses derive their higher-than-normal profits from market information asymmetry: Many service businesses, including neighborhood banks and auto dealerships, have been able to charge high prices for their services and goods because customers did not have enough information about the availability of like-kind services and goods in the vicinity.

Not anymore. In the Internet era, customers can log on and get the information and knowledge on the goods and services for almost zero cost. This easy access to market information eliminates higher-than-normal profits for the providers of goods and services.

Based on the residual income concept, Center C's performance is better than those of Centers A and B. The problem with the residual income concept, however, is that it cannot be used to measure the performance of divisions of significantly different sizes. With respect to the average operating assets, Center C is twice as big as Center B, and Center B is twice as big as Center A. Thus, the fact that Center C's residual income is the highest does not necessarily mean that it is the most efficiently managed center. The result may be due only to the size of Center C.

Indeed, suppose we use ROI for comparison. We find that Center C's ROI is only 14% whereas Center B's ROI is 16% and Center A's ROI is 20%. Thus, the residual income concept should only be used as a performance measure when centers or divisions are of comparable sizes. The residual income, however, provides a measure of how much each center adds to the total company value.

ROI versus Residual Income

ROI is useful in evaluating the performance of divisions that have significantly different sizes. A basic disadvantage of using ROI in evaluating divisional performance is that it tends to discourage the company's growth, since projects that show relatively low ROI's but are still profitable for the company may be rejected.

On the other hand, the use of residual income to evaluate divisional performance will produce different results from those produced by the use of ROI. All divisions, regardless of their ROI expectations, would have the same incentive to invest in new projects based on the profitability of the projects after the cost of capital is considered.

Consider the following situation. A project, that will earn 18% or $45,000 per year on a $250,000 investment, is proposed to the Centers A, B, and C. The cost of capital is still 10% per year. Now, which center, do you think, will undertake the project?

First, let's see what would happen if each center decided to invest $250,000 in the project:

	Center A	Center B	Center C
Net operating income (R)	$95,000	$125,000	$ 185,000
Average operating assets (I)	500,000	750,000	1,250,000
Cost of capital (C = 10% × I)	50,000	75,000	125,000
ROI (R ÷ I)	19%	16.7%	14.8%
Residual income (R − C)	$45,000	$50,000	$60,000

The manager of Center A, the most profitable, would see her ROI decrease from 20% to 19%. The ROI of Center B increases from 16% to 16.7%; and the ROI of Center C increases from 14% to 14.8%. The less profitable investment centers (B and C) see more incentive to invest in the new project than does the most profitable investment center (A), when the company uses ROI for performance evaluation.

What would the residual income tell the managers of the investment centers? The residual income would increase $20,000 for each center with the addition of the new project, from $25,000 to $45,000, from $30,000 to $50,000, and from $40,000 to $60,000. Every investment center sees the same incentive to invest in the new project which is attractive to the company as a whole, when the return is compared to the cost of capital.

Overall, the use of residual income leads the company to avoid incongruent decisions between investment centers. Despite this merit of residual income as the performance measure, most companies still use ROI, because it is very easy and convenient to be able to digest everything down to percentages for comparison across investment centers. Many companies, however, rely on both ROI and residual income to promote goal congruence.

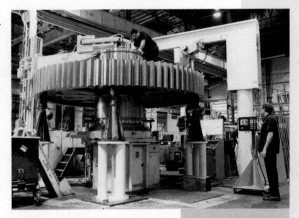

Harnischfeger Industries, Inc. uses the EVA concept, focusing on product cost reduction and efficiency improvement. Innovative welding and assembly processes, such as the one shown here, have shortened lead times, reduced costs and raised quality levels.

Economic Value Added (EVA)

In addition to ROI and residual income, there is another measure of investment center performance. **Economic value added (EVA®)** was originally designed by Stern Stewart, a consulting firm, to determine how much shareholder wealth a company created, and is computed as follows:

EVA = Operating income after tax − Actual cost of capital

Actual cost of capital

= Weighted-average capital cost (%) × Total capital used

Unlike ROI and residual income, EVA uses the *actual* cost of capital which is not based on accounting book values, and is popular among investors for that reason. The computation of weighted-average capital cost (%) requires the details of all sources of capital invested: borrowed funds and equity funds. In the computation of residual income, the cost of capital is the *desired* rate of return. In the computation of EVA, the *actual* cost of capital is used.

EVA Computation

We use the following example to illustrate the computation of EVA for an investment center:

Operating income after tax	$175,000
Sources of capital invested:	
Bonds payable (7% interest)	300,000
Common stock	600,000
Total	$900,000

The tax rate is 30%, and tax-deductible bond interest expense is reduced for the tax break. The company computes the cost of common stock as 10% (long-term treasury bond rate of 6% plus a premium of 4%), which represents the investors' opportunity cost.

Weighted-average capital cost (%):

	(a)	(b)	(c)	(d)	(e = c − d)	(b × e)
	Amount	Weight	Cost Rate	30% Tax Break	Cost Rate After Tax	Weighted Cost Rate
Bonds	$300,000	1/3	7%	2.1%	4.9%	1.633%
Stock	600,000	2/3	10%	−	10.0%	6.667%
	$900,000	1				8.300%

The *actual cost of capital* is:

Weighted-average capital cost (%) × Total capital used
= 8.3% × $900,000 = $74,700.

We can compute the EVA as follows:

Operating income after tax	$175,000
Actual cost of capital	74,700
EVA	$100,300

The computation shows a positive EVA, which indicates that the company creates shareholder wealth.

Effect of EVA on Divisional Managers' Behavior

The effect of subtracting actual cost of capital from operating income after tax on divisional managers is significant and healthy. If divisional managers know that their performance measure, EVA, reflects the cost of capital they use, they make investments with return greater than the cost of capital used.

Performance and Compensation of Divisional Managers

Companies need to develop a compensation plan for divisional managers which is closely tied to their performance, and encourages goal congruence, providing incentive to managers so that they perform in the company's best interests. Many companies use a combination of cash and stock-based compensation.

Cash compensation includes salaries, which stay at a certain level, and bonuses, which are tied to divisional profits that are controllable by divisional managers. *Stock-based compensation* is often in the form of *stock options*, the rights to purchase certain number of shares, at a certain price, after a certain period of time. Since stock options can be changed to actual shares at a pre-set price, a higher future stock price provides more earnings to the managers who hold stock options. This encourages managers to think about the company's long-term health and competitive position.

Companies also provide *noncash compensation* to divisional managers. Perquisites in terms of title, staff support, office, expense accounts, rights to use company airplane, etc. serve as important noncash compensation for managers.

New York Stock Exchange. Equity funds (common stocks) usually carry higher costs compared to borrowed funds for investment centers. A positive EVA indicates a creation of shareholder wealth.

TRANSFER PRICING

In decentralized organizations, problems may arise when a segment or a division of an organization buys certain products or services of another segment or division of the same organization. The problem simply is this: At what price should these products or services be transferred between segments or divisions? The internal price used for such transfer is called **transfer price.**

The transfer price makes no difference in overall company performance, since it is sales revenue to the selling division and expense to the buying division. Indeed, under generally accepted accounting principles, all these interdivisional sales and costs are eliminated in external financial reporting. So, why are we concerned about it in managerial accounting? We discuss some possible answers to this question below.

The Importance of Transfer Pricing

The transfer pricing issue is important because the transfer price used will affect the operating results of both the selling and the buying divisions and the performance evaluations of their managers. Transfer pricing affects the profits of the company as a whole. In today's global environment, multinational companies use transfer pricing to make optimal decisions regarding duties, tariffs, and taxes paid.

Transfer prices should guide divisions and their managers to make the most appropriate decisions on whether to buy or sell products and services internally (from and to other divisions) or externally (from and to other companies). Alternative transfer prices have different effects on the choices made by divisional managers.

Consider a division that is forced to sell products to other divisions at prices that are lower than what the division would charge outside customers. The company, in this case, does not provide the selling division and its manager with an environment in which they can make the best possible decisions. In order to maximize the potential, the divisions (profit centers) should be free to buy and sell products and services inside or outside the company if they are evaluated as separate centers. This is necessary to achieve the **goal congruence** that aligns the interests of top management with those of division managers in the same direction. Otherwise, the profits of the company as a whole suffer.

Setting the Right Transfer Prices

What transfer price should be used? The answer depends on existing circumstances, such as (a) whether the selling division can sell its products to outside customers, (b) whether the buying division can buy its products from outside suppliers, and (c) whether the selling division is operating at full capacity or whether it has some idle capacity.

There is no one best transfer price that can be used in all circumstances. Transfer prices are set at cost, at market price, or at some price in between, as discussed below.

Transfer Prices at Cost

Some companies set transfer prices between divisions at cost, whether it is variable cost, total cost, or standard cost. Proponents of setting transfer prices at cost argue that this approach is simple to apply, avoids wasting time to arrive at credible market prices or fair negotiated prices, and sometimes is the only objective price to use when market prices do not exist.

This approach has major disadvantages that may outweigh its advantages. First, it provides no incentive to the manager of the selling division to control costs, since all costs are simply passed on to the buying division. Second, the buying division manager bears all the responsibility for the waste and inefficiency that may exist in the selling division. Third, if the selling division's products have no outside market, the division will show no profit or loss, and only divisions that sell to outside customers will show profit or loss. Thus, it is not possible to use ROI or residual income to evaluate performance.

Negotiated Transfer Prices

A *negotiated* transfer price is whatever transfer price the selling and buying divisions agree to based on arms' length negotiations without any pressure from or inter-

ABC as Disney's Megaphone: The Changing Concept of Business Segment

Network executives won't quite admit it, but they do not regard the networks as reliable moneymaking profit centers of big parent companies any longer. They now view the networks as "the lifeblood of the global, vertically integrated entertainment giants that own them." The networks deliver programming to the affiliated TV stations and promote other more profitable operations. This is like looking at "ABC as Disney's megaphone, to be used by Michael Eisner & Co. to tell the masses about Disney movies, theme parks, and toys," and "Fox as the engine that drives the value of Fox's TV stations, cable networks, and owned shows like The X-Files and The Simpsons." Then, what happens to the concept of responsibility accounting?

From "What's Wrong with This Picture?" *Fortune*, January 12, 1998, p.108.

ference by top management. The divisions usually follow company-wide established procedures to avoid unnecessary impediments or delays in negotiations. This method of transfer pricing is based on the belief that only the buying and selling divisions have the best information and knowledge about the products and services that are bought and sold.

In general, companies that are fiercely committed to divisional autonomy would permit divisions to negotiate transfer prices. When there are outside markets from which the buying division can buy and to which the selling division can sell, it is easier to negotiate transfer prices.

Transfer Prices at Market

Companies can use the prices at which the selling division's products are sold to outside customers. *Market-based* transfer prices are usually used in highly decentralized organizations where each division is run as if it were a completely independent and separate company. Division managers must be completely free to make whatever decisions they please even to the point of refusing to buy from a sister division at prevailing market prices.

The following conditions are required for the use of market-based transfer prices:

First, there exists an intermediate market for the selling division's products, where the selling division can immediately sell its products in their present form. If such an intermediate market does not exist, and the selling division has no choice but to sell its products to another division, true market-based transfer prices cannot be set. Either a cost-based or a negotiated transfer price must be used.

Second, there is enough demand by outside customers for the product of the selling division to have it operating at full capacity. If the selling division has satisfied all the demand by outside customers and still has some idle capacity, insisting on charging the market price is not reasonable. This is because there is no outside customer who pays the market price anymore. Transfers made at market prices in such a situation unfairly favor the selling division.

Alternative Transfer Prices: Profit Implications for Divisions and the Company

Alternative transfer prices have different profit implications for the buying and selling divisions and the whole company. Assume that the Two-Division Company has two divisions, A and B, with data as shown below:

	Division A	Division B
Number of units sold per year	10,000	10,000
Market price per unit sold to outside customers	$10	$40
Variable cost per unit	$6	$20*

Fixed costs are related to corporate headquarters and are not allocated between divisions.

*This excludes the cost of Division A's output.

Division A can sell its products in the outside market and can also sell them internally to Division B. Division B can buy Division A's output or can buy the same units from outside for $9 per unit.

Should the transfer price for Division A's output be set at the variable cost of $6? At the market price of $10 or $9? Or should Division A's output not be transferred at all to Division B? If Division A has idle capacity to produce the entire 10,000 units needed by Division B in addition to the 10,000 units that it now sells to the outside market, what transfer price should be used?

Exhibit 12-3 shows the results for each division and for the whole company under various conditions.

As Exhibit 12-3 illustrates, each of the first three alternatives provides the same contribution margin of $140,000 for the company as a whole. A transfer made at a variable cost favors the buying division (alternative 1). The selling division fares better when transfers are made at market prices (alternatives 2 and 3).

The company as a whole makes a higher contribution margin if the selling division sells to outside customers at the market price of $10 and the buying division can buy from an outside supplier at a lower price of $9 (alternative 4). The company as a whole makes the highest contribution margin when the selling division sells to outside customers at the market price and to the buying division at the variable cost (alternative 5).

Why does the company make a higher contribution margin under alternative 5, compared to alternative 4? The company earns a higher margin because there is an extra profit made when the business is kept within the company. The higher margin represents the difference between $9 (paid to outside suppliers under alternative 4) and $6 (paid to Division A under alternative 5). As long as the price paid is higher than the cost, there is a profit to be made by the seller, and the profit is kept within the company under alternative 5.

EXHIBIT 12-3

Two-Division Company
Results Under Alternative Transfer Pricing Decisions

Alternative 1: Set transfer price at the *variable cost* of $6.

	Division A	Division B	Total Company
Sales	$60,000a	$400,000b	$460,000
Variable costs	(60,000)c	(260,000)d	(320,000)
Contribution margin	$ 0	$140,000	$140,000

(a) 10,000 units × $6 transfer price per unit.
(b) 10,000 units × $40 selling price per unit.
(c) 10,000 units × $6 variable cost per unit.
(d) 10,000 units × $26 ($20 variable cost per unit in Division B
     + $6 transfer price per unit for Division A's output).

Alternative 2: Set transfer price at the *market price* of $10.

	Division A	Division B	Total Company
Sales	$100,000a	$400,000	$500,000
Variable costs	(60,000)	(300,000)b	(360,000)
Contribution margin	$ 40,000	$100,000	$140,000

(a) 10,000 units × $10 transfer price per unit.
(b) 10,000 units × $30 ($20 variable cost per unit in Division B
     + $10 transfer price per unit for Division A's output).

Alternative 3: Set transfer price at the *market price* of $9.

	Division A	Division B	Total Company
Sales	$90,000a	$400,000	$490,000
Variable costs	(60,000)	(290,000)b	(350,000)
Contribution margin	$30,000	$110,000	$140,000

(a) 10,000 units × $9 transfer price per unit.
(b) 10,000 units × $29 ($20 variable cost per unit in Division B
     + $9 transfer price per unit for Division A's output).

Alternative 4: Do *not transfer* products at all between divisions. Let Division A sell to outside customers for $10 and let Division B buy from outside suppliers at $9.

	Division A	Division B	Total Company
Sales	$100,000a	$400,000	$500,000
Variable costs	(60,000)	(290,000)b	(350,000)
Contribution margin	$40,000	$110,000	$150,000

(a) 10,000 units × $10 market price per unit.
(b) 10,000 units × $29 ($20 variable cost per unit in Division B
     + $9 purchase price per unit paid to outside suppliers).

Alternative 5: Sell 10,000 units to outside customers at $10 and set transfer price of $6 for the 10,000 units transferred to Division B.

	Division A	Division B	Total Company
Sales	$160,000a	$400,000	$560,000
Variable costs	(120,000)	(260,000)b	(380,000)
Contribution margin	$40,000c	$140,000	$180,000

(a) (10,000 units sold to outside customers × $10 market price per unit)
     + (10,000 units transferred to Division B × $6 transfer price).
(b) 10,000 units × $26 ($20 variable cost per unit in Division B
     + $6 transfer price per unit paid to Division A).

Computing the Appropriate Transfer Price

The five alternatives in the preceding section provide important lessons on setting transfer prices. If the selling division can sell a product to outside customers at $10 per unit, and the buying division can buy the same product from outside suppliers at less than $10 per unit, the company as a whole will benefit if each division did so and no products are transferred between divisions. This assumes that freight-in and freight-out and other variable selling expenses are included in the prices quoted.

Indeed, if each division manager has complete autonomy, and is free to sell to outside customers or buy from outside suppliers, no transfers between the two divisions would take place. This is so, because Division A's manager would accept the transfer only at $10 (the price at which he can sell to outside customers), and Division B's manager would not accept any price over $9 (the price at which he can buy from outside suppliers).

In general, an appropriate transfer price is determined within the following range:

> Maximum: Market price
> $\updownarrow$
> Minimum: Variable cost of the selling division

No division would want to sell at below the variable cost. Also if there is any possible contribution margin lost because of the internal transfer, rather than outside sales, the lost margin should be recovered. Accordingly, we can summarize what we have seen in the following transfer pricing formula:

Appropriate Transfer Price

= Per-unit variable cost to the selling division
+ Per-unit contribution margin lost by the selling division
   on outside sales

Applying this formula to the Two-Division Company example, we obtain:

Appropriate Transfer Price
= $6 Per-unit variable cost to Division A
+ $4 Per-unit contribution margin lost by Division A on outside sales
= $10

Since this transfer price is higher than the price, $9, at which Division B's manager can buy the products from outside suppliers, Division B's manager will not accept it, and no transfers between the two divisions will take place. Of course, we assume the availability of outside markets for Division A's products and competitive market conditions.

What about the higher margin for the company as a whole when the business is kept within the company? Under alternative 5 in the preceding section, the company as a whole makes a contribution margin of $180,000 ($30,000 more, compared to alternative 4). If at all possible, divisions must work together to achieve *goal congruence* and keep business within the company. Divisions, however, should not be forced to buy or sell internally. Otherwise, decentralization does not work. The benefit of maintaining the *autonomy* of its divisions (profit centers) should be weighed against the cost of losing business to outside companies.

Variable-Cost Pricing

What if there are no outside markets for Division A's products? What if Division B cannot buy those products from outside suppliers? In these cases, transfer prices may be based on cost. The question, then, is this: Which cost should be used when there is no ready market? Should it be variable cost, total cost, standard cost, or some other cost?

Some argue that the best cost to use for transfer pricing is *standard variable cost*. The use of standard cost eliminates the problem of transferring the waste and inefficiency of the selling division to the buying division. The use of variable cost eliminates the problem of contaminating the transfer price with fixed costs which do not vary with production volume. This assumes the same level of fixed costs regardless of whether the products transferred are produced or not.

Idle Capacity

When the selling division has idle capacity, its production capacity is greater than the current demand for its products. If idle capacity exists, the decision to produce units for transfer to a buying division does not create any lost contribution margin for the selling division. The selling division can meet outside customers' demands for its products fully, and still produce enough to transfer to the buying division.

Managers can still use the *same* formula to determine transfer price when idle capacity exists. This is so because the second component of the formula, per-unit contribution margin lost on outside sales, would be equal to zero. The products transferred would be produced using the idle capacity that was not used because of lack of demand from outside customers. That is, no contribution margin from additional outside sales would have been made anyway.

Applying the formula to the Two-Division Company example, we obtain the following when idle capacity exists:

Appropriate Transfer Price
= $6 Per-unit variable cost to Division A
+   0 Per-unit contribution margin lost by Division A on outside sales
= $6

Most likely, however, even when Division A has idle capacity, its manager may ask for a transfer price somewhere between its variable cost of $6 and the price which Division B would have had to pay to obtain the products from outside suppliers ($9). A transfer price of $6 or any other price between $6 and $9 would produce the same contribution margin for the company as a whole. This is so, because whatever price included as sales in one division is included as cost in the other division. The only difference created by different transfer prices will be in the contribution margins of the buying and selling divisions.

Summary of Transfer Pricing

The following guidelines summarize the transfer pricing rules:

1. Intermediate markets for the selling division's output exist, and the selling division has no idle capacity: The transfer price should be the market price for the selling division's output.

2. The selling division has idle capacity: The transfer price should be negotiated, with the standard variable cost as the lower limit and the price at which the buying division can buy these same products from outside suppliers as the upper limit.

3. No intermediate markets for the selling division's output exist: The transfer price should be standard variable cost for the selling division or a negotiated price between the divisions.

THE INTERNATIONAL DIMENSION OF TRANSFER PRICING

Multinational Companies

Managers of multinational companies must consider the international dimension of transfer pricing when products are transferred between divisions in different countries. **Multinational companies** are those companies that are headquartered in a country, such as the U.S., and have subsidiaries operating in foreign countries, that are called host countries.

Management control systems for foreign operations are similar to those established for domestic operations. When problems related to managerial control, including performance evaluation and transfer pricing, arise in foreign operations, however, companies experience more difficulties in dealing with those problems. The difficulties are attributed to the fact that headquarters managers do not have the intimate knowledge about their foreign operations required to solve those problems.

Multinational Transfer Pricing

The difficulties with foreign operations are most pronounced in transfer pricing. When we discussed transfer pricing in the previous section, *goal congruence* was very important. This was because, without insuring goal congruence in transfer pricing, the interests of divisional managers do not coincide with the overall interests of the company. In multinational transfer pricing, however, there are other significant factors that *interfere* with goal congruence. The significant factors include: different income tax rates; different rates of tariff, interest, foreign exchange, and inflation; and host countries' government regulations.

In order to see the effects of income tax rate and tariff on transfer pricing, we can relate each factor to the level of transfer price as follows:

If the selling division transfers a product at a *high* price, the operating cost of the buying division is increased, and this reduces the profit of the buying division. When this transfer is made

To a country with	Effect on the company is
High income tax rate	Lower overall tax
High tariff	Higher tariff

Income tax and tariff have opposite effects as seen in the above. If the transfer price is *low*, the operating cost of the buying divison decreases, and its profit goes up. The host country's income tax goes up accordingly. The low transfer price, however, would make the host country levy low tariffs on the products imported.

As we saw in the above discussion, income tax and tariff are just two factors to consider in multinational transfer pricing. Managers must consider all other factors such as interest, foreign exchange, inflation, and host countries' government regulations also to insure that the net effect is positive for transfer pricing.

SUMMARY

This chapter covers how a responsibility accounting system is used to control decentralized operations. The concept of responsibility accounting means that a person who has control over a certain item (revenue or expense) should be held accountable for that item. For this concept to work, any person held responsible or accountable for an item must have the full authority and freedom of action to control that item. Such a responsibility accounting system is beneficial in highly decentralized operations where every division of the organization is run by the division manager as a totally separate and independent company.

To implement a responsibility accounting system an organization may have to be divided into cost centers, profit centers, or investment centers. Each center is run by a manager who has full control over the costs, profits, or investments related to his or her center. The performance of the manager of a cost or a profit center may be evaluated by comparing actual results to budgeted performance. The performance of an investment center's manager may be evaluated by return on investment (ROI), residual income, or economic value added (EVA). Unlike ROI and residual income, EVA uses the actual cost of capital which is not based on accounting book values, and is popular among investors for that reason.

One problem that may affect the performance evaluation tools discussed above is the problem of setting transfer price, the price at which the output of one division is transferred to another division. Transfer prices may be set at cost (variable, or total; actual or standard), at market, or at a negotiated price. In general, the appropriate transfer price is variable cost plus the contribution margin lost by the selling division.

The difficulties with foreign operations are most pronounced in transfer pricing. Without insuring goal congruence in transfer pricing, the interests of divisional managers do not coincide with the overall interests of the company.

In multinational transfer pricing, however, there are other significant factors that interfere with goal congruence. Those significant factors managers must consider in multinational transfer pricing are: Different income tax rates; different rates of tariff, interest, foreign exchange, and inflation; and host countries' government regulations.

BASIC CONCEPTS AND TERMS

Centralization	Multinational transfer pricing
Cost centers	Operating asset turnover
Decentralized operations	Operating profit margin
Economic value added (EVA)	Profit center
Executive performance	Residual income
Incentive pay	Return on investment (ROI)
Intermediate markets	Suboptimization
Investment centers	Transfer price
Multinational companies	

■ SELF-REVIEW PROBLEM

BT Company has two divisions: a Battery Division which produces AA batteries and a Toy Division that produces one type of toy. During Year 8, both divisions sold their outputs to outside customers, and no interdivision sales took place between the two divisions.

The following are the pertinent data on the two divisions:

	Battery Division	Toy Division
Number of units sold	20,000	10,000
Selling price per unit	$ 3	$ 16
Variable cost per unit	$ 1	$ 8
Fixed costs per year	$ 16,000	$ 25,000
Operating assets	$100,000	$250,000

Required:

1. Compute the operating ROI for each division. Determine which division outperforms the other based on operating ROI.
2. Assume that the minimum desired rate of return is 18%. Determine which division outperforms the other based on the residual income concept.
3. Based on your answers to 1 and 2 above, discuss the advantages and disadvantages of ROI and residual income as a tool for measuring divisional performance.
4. The Toy Division's manager is considering buying batteries from the Battery Division.

a. Assume that the Toy Division is currently purchasing 10,000 packages of AA batteries from outside suppliers at $2.80 per package, and that the Battery Division has no idle capacity. Determine the transfer price between the two divisions. Will any transfers be made at that price?

b. Assume the same situation as in (a) above, except that the Battery Division can save $0.40 per unit in shipping costs if it sells 10,000 packages to the Toy Division. Determine the transfer price. Will any transfers be made at that price?

c. Assume the same situation as in (a) above, except that the Battery Division has idle capacity to produce 10,000 packages of batteries. Determine the transfer price. Will any transfers be made at that price?

d. Assume that the Toy Division is contemplating the production of 5,000 units of a new toy each of which will require one unit of C battery. The Battery Division will incur a unit variable cost of $0.75 to produce C batteries, and, since it has no idle capacity, give up the production of 4,000 packages of AA batteries. If the Battery Division decides to produce C batteries, what transfer price should it charge per battery? Will any transfers be made at that price?

Solution

	Battery Division	Toy Division
1. Operating ROI:		
Sales:		
20,000 units × $3	$ 60,000	
10,000 units × $16		$160,000
Variable costs:		
20,000 units × $1	20,000	
10,000 units × $8		80,000
Contribution margin	40,000	80,000
Fixed costs	16,000	25,000
Operating income (R)	$ 24,000	$ 55,000
Operating assets (I)	$100,000	$250,000
Operating ROI (R ÷ I)	24%	22%

The Battery Division outperforms the Toy Division based on operating ROI.

2. Residual Income:

	Battery Division	Toy Division
Operating income (per 1 above)	$ 24,000	$ 55,000
Minimum desired ROI:		
$100,000 × 18% =	18,000	
$250,000 × 18% =		45,000
Residual income	$ 6,000	$ 10,000

Based on the residual income concept, the Toy Division outperforms the Battery Division.

3. Comparison of ROI and Residual Income:

If the ROI is used, the manager of the Battery Division is likely to reject any project that would earn less than 24% even though such a project may indeed increase residual income. Furthermore, the Toy Division's manager will probably look for projects that will earn over 24% to compete with the Battery Division manager. Thus, the advantage of ROI is that it will tend to push the overall return on investment upward. Its main disadvantage is that projects with returns that are lower than the costs of capital are rejected.

The use of residual income as a tool for measuring performance will produce opposite results. The ROI may decrease, but expansion may be achieved faster. This is so, because the Battery Division manager would be willing to accept additional projects that promise an ROI of above 18%. This will increase the residual income, but may reduce the Division's ROI down to below 24% if the additional projects earn returns of below 24%.

4. Transfer Pricing:

a. Since the Battery Division has no idle capacity, it will lose contribution margin from outside sales if it sells to the Toy Division. Accordingly,

$$\text{Transfer price} = \text{Variable cost per unit}$$
$$+ \text{ lost contribution margin per unit}$$
$$= \$1 + \$2^* = \$3$$
$$^*\text{Lost CM per unit} = \text{Selling price to outside customers}$$
$$- \text{ variable cost per unit}$$
$$= \$3 - \$1 = \$2.$$

Since the Toy Division is purchasing batteries at $2.80 per unit, no transfers will be made at the transfer price of $3.

b. This is the same situation as in (a) above, except that variable cost is $0.40 less per unit. Thus, the transfer price will be $0.40 less.

$$\text{Transfer price} = \$0.60 + \$2 = \$2.60$$

Since the Toy Division is purchasing from outside suppliers at $2.80 per unit, the company as a whole will gain if the Toy Division buys from the Battery Division at $2.60 per package.

c. Since the Battery Division has idle capacity to produce 10,000 additional units, lost contribution margin will be zero.

$$\text{Transfer price} = \text{Battery Division's variable cost of } \$1.$$

This $1 is the minimum transfer price that the Battery Division will accept. Since the Toy Division is paying $2.80 to outside suppliers, the actual transfer price will be negotiated. The lower limit is $1, and the upper limit is $2.80. If one manager's position is not relatively stronger or weaker than the other's, they will probably split the difference and agree on a transfer price of $1.90. This is also the average of the lower and upper limits [($1.00 + $2.80) ÷ 2].

d. Since the Battery Division has to give up the CM on 4,000 packages of AA batteries, the total CM lost on outside sales will be $8,000 (4,000 packages × $2). Thus, on a per-unit basis for the C batteries, the lost CM will be $1.60 per battery ($8,000 ÷ 5,000 batteries). Thus,

Transfer price = $0.75 Variable cost + $1.60 lost CM

$$= \$2.35$$

At the transfer price of $2.35, the Battery Division will just recover $8,000 ($1.60 × 5,000 C batteries) of the lost CM of $8,000 ($2 × 4,000 AA batteries). Therefore, the Battery Division itself has nothing to gain by selling to the Toy Division, unless more than $2.35 is charged. How much more should be charged depends on the price at which the Toy Division can purchase the C batteries from outside suppliers.

■ REVIEW QUESTIONS

12-1 What is the responsibility accounting concept?

12-2 Differentiate among a cost center, a profit center, and an investment center.

12-3 What is the major difference between centralization and decentralization?

12-4 What are the major advantages of decentralization?

12-5 Give a brief overview of how a responsibility accounting system really works.

12-6 How is performance measured in a cost center, a profit center, and an investment center?

12-7 Suppose the actual ROI is lower than the budgeted ROI. What techniques can the division manager use to increase the ROI in the future?

12-8 Both ROI and residual income have advantages and disadvantages as measures of performance. What are they?

12-9 How is economic value added (EVA) different from ROI and residual income from the perspective of cost of capital?

12-10 How is EVA different from ROI and residual income with respect to divisions' asset buildup?

12-11 What is the transfer pricing problem? Why is it considered a problem?

12-12 Transfer prices may be based on costs, market prices, or negotiated prices. Why are they all used in practice?

12-13 "Under no circumstances should top management intervene to impose a certain transfer price between two divisions even if lack of intervention will lead to suboptimal profits for the organization as a whole." Do you agree? Why or why not?

12-14 If the selling division has idle capacity, does the decision to produce units for transfer to a buying division create any lost contribution margin? How does the transfer pricing formula change when there is idle capacity?

12-15 Difficulties in management control arise in multinational companies' foreign operations. What difficulties arise due to transfer pricing?

12-16 Assume that the host country, in which a multinational company's buying division is located, has a high income tax rate. If the selling division transfers a product to this buying division at a high price, what would be the effect on the overall tax burden of the company? Why?

⊕ INTERNET PROJECT

Web 12-1:

Websites: www.berkshirehathaway.com
             www.gm.com

The websites listed above represent two famous companies. Search the sites for information on their operating characteristics.

Required:

1. The first company is known for its outstanding investment performance. Where on the website do you find such performance?

2. Compare the performance of the two companies for the last ten years. Which company would prefer the use of ROI for evaluating the performance of its divisional managers? Why?

Web 12-2:

Websites: www.wellsfargo.com
             www.bankofamerica.com

The websites listed above represent two famous companies. Search the sites for information on their operating characteristics.

Required:

1. Compare the performance of the two companies for the last ten years.

2. Which company would prefer the use of ROI for evaluating the performance of its divisional managers? Why?

■ EXERCISES

E12-1   Return on Investment (ROI); Residual Income; Economic Value Added (EVA)

Consider the following statements:

a. Is useful in evaluating the performance of divisions that have significantly different sizes.

b. Uses the actual cost of capital in the computation.
c. Provides all divisions with the same investment incentive based on the project profitability after the cost of capital is considered.
d. Tends to discourage the company's growth, because projects that show relatively low return but are still profitable for the company may be rejected.
e. Is the easiest to compute.
f. Uses a predetermined cost of capital in computation.

Required:

Indicate whether the statement refers to return on investment (ROI), residual income (RI), or economic value added (EVA).

E12-2 ROI Computation

GRD, Inc. shows the following operating data on its two divisions for the most recent year:

	K Division	L Division
Operating income....................	$ 150,000	$ 250,000
Sales...............................	2,500,000	3,000,000
Operating assets (average)............	1,000,000	1,000,000
Plant assets (net)....................	450,000	350,000

Required:

1. Compute the rate of return on investment (ROI) for each division.
2. What is your assessment on the performance of each division?

E12-3   ROI, Profit Margin, and Asset Turnover

KLM, Inc. shows the following information on its three divisions for the most recent year:

	K Division	L Division	M Division
Sales......................	$ –	$5,000,000	$ –
Operating income...........	–	450,000	250,000
Operating assets (average)....	600,000	–	–
Operating profit margin.......	5%	–	5%
Operating asset turnover	8	–	–
ROI	–	10%	10%

Required:

1. Compute the missing numbers.
2. Both K Division and M Division show the same (5%) operating profit margin ratio. If you had a choice between the two divisions, which division would you choose for investment? Why?

3. Both L Division and M Division show the same ROI of 10%, despite L Division's higher operating income of $450,000 versus M Division's $250,000. Assume that the sales of both divisions are the same $5,000,000, regardless of the computations in (1). How could M Division achieve the same ROI? No calculation is necessary.

E12-4   ROI and Residual Income

DHI, Inc. has two divisions, K and L, and requires a minimum return of 18% from the divisions. The company shows the following data on its divisions:

	K Division	L Division
Operating income....................	$ 120,000	$ 560,000
Sales	2,000,000	8,000,000
Operating assets (average)............	800,000	3,000,000

Required:

1. Compute the ROI for each division.
2. Compute the residual income for each division.
3. Which division met the minimum required rate of return?

E12-5   Comparison of ROI and Residual Income Among Companies

Three companies show the following data:

	Company		
	K	L	M
Operating income..............	$ 150,000	$ 280,000	$ 150,000
Sales	3,000,000	4,000,000	2,500,000
Operating assets (average).......	1,200,000	1,400,000	1,000,000
Minimum required rate of return ..	14%	15%	18%
(cost of capital)			

Required:

1. Compute the ROI for each company.
2. Compute the residual income for each company.
3. In order to determine whether a company met the minimum required rate of return, we can use ROI or residual income. Which company met the minimum required rate of return? Show computations.

E12-6   Computation of ROI and Residual Income

Three companies, P, Q, and R, show the following data:

	Co. P	Co. Q	Co. R
Operating income	$ 200,000	$ 240,000	$ 300,000
Sales.	5,000,000	4,000,000	8,000,000
Operating assets (average)	2,000,000	1,200,000	2,000,000
Minimum required rate of return .	11%	14%	15%
(cost of capital)			

Required:

1. Compute the ROI for each company.
2. Compute the residual income for each company.
3. Would Company P be able to meet the minimum required rate of return if the operating income were $300,000? Use the results of (2) to answer the question.

E12-7   Components of ROI

Data on three companies are presented below:

	Co. A	Co. B	Co. C
Operating income.	$ 27,000	$ 25,000	$ –
Sales	200,000	150,000	–
Operating assets (average). . . .	120,000	–	400,000
Operating profit margin.	–	–	5.0%
Operating asset turnover	–	–	1.5
ROI	–	6.0%	–

Required:

1. Compute the missing numbers.
2. Which company shows the highest profit margin per sales dollar? Why then does the company show the lowest ROI? What should the company do to improve its ROI?

E12-8   Economic Value Added (EVA)

PTF, Inc. uses economic value added (EVA) to measure its performance from the perspective of creating shareholder wealth. The company shows the following data for the most recent period:

Operating income after tax	$130,000
Sources of invested capital:	
6% Bonds payable	200,000
Common stock	400,000
Tax rate	30%

The company computes the investors' opportunity cost as 11%, representing the long-term treasury bond rate of 6% plus a premium of 5%.

Required:

1. Compute the weighted-average cost of capital for the period.
2. Compute the EVA for the company.

E12-9   Responsibility Centers - Multiple Choice

1. A segment of an organization is referred to as a profit center if it has
   a. Authority to make decisions affecting the major determinants of profit, including the power to choose its markets and sources of supply.
   b. Authority to make decisions affecting the major determinants of profit, including the power to choose its market and sources of supply and significant control over the amount of invested capital.
   c. Authority to make decisions over the most significant costs of operations, including the power to choose the sources of supply.
   d. Authority to provide specialized support to other units within the organization.
   e. Responsibility for combining the raw materials, direct labor, and other factors of production into a final output.
2. A segment of an organization is referred to as an investment center if it has
   a. Authority to make decisions affecting the major determinants of profit, including the power to choose its markets and sources of supply.
   b. Authority to make decisions affecting the major determinants of profit, including the power to choose its market and sources of supply and significant control over the amount of invested capital.
   c. Authority to make decisions over the most significant costs of operations, including the power to choose the sources of supply.
   d. Authority to provide specialized support to other units within the organization.
   e. Responsibility for developing markets for and selling of the output of the organization.
3. A segment of an organization is referred to as a cost center if it has
   a. Responsibility for developing markets for and selling of the output of the organization.
   b. Authority to make decisions affecting the major determinants of profit, including the power to choose its markets and sources of supply.
   c. Authority to make decisions over the most significant costs of operations, including the power to choose the sources of supply.
   d. Authority to provide specialized support to other units within the organization.
   e. Responsibility for combining the raw materials, direct labor, and other factors of production into a final output.

(CMA, adapted)

E12-10 Responsibility Accounting and Transfer Pricing

Listed below are three charges found on the monthly report of a division which manufactures and sells products primarily to outside customers. Divisional performance is evaluated by the use of return on investment (ROI). You are to state which, if any, of the following charges are consistent with the "responsibility accounting" concept. Support each answer with a brief explanation.

1. A charge (at 10% of division sales) for the cost of operating general corporate headquarters.
2. A charge for goods purchased from another division. The charge is based upon the competitive market price for the goods.
3. A charge for the use of the corporate computer facility. The charge is determined by taking actual annual computer department costs and allocating an amount to each division on the ratio of its use to total corporate use.

(CMA, adapted)

E12-11 Transfer Price and Profit

KLC, Inc. has two divisions, K and L. Division K produces "Kandide," a product that is sold either to Division L or to outside customers. Division K's normal capacity is 1,000 units of Kandide per year, which the division sells to the following:

Sales of Kandide to:	
Division L...	200 units
Outside customers..................................	800
Total	1,000 units

The market price of Kandide is $60 and the manufacturing cost is $50 per unit. It is the company policy that all transfers between divisions be made at market price. Division L purchases Kandide, and processes it further at a cost of $70 per unit and then sells to outside customers for $150 each.

Required:

1. Compute operating income for Division K, Division L, and for the total company.
2. Assume Kandide is not available from any outside suppliers, and Division L wants to purchase an additional 200 units of Kandide from Division K. Which is more profitable from the perspective of the company as a whole, Division K selling the extra units to Division L or continuing to sell Kandide to outside customers?

E12-12 Transfer Pricing

PQC, Inc. has two decentralized divisions, P and Q. For the last eight years, Division P has purchased "Quanta," a product Division P uses in its production, from Division Q at $45 per unit. This year, Division Q has informed Division P of a price hike, to $50 per unit, due to the need to recover full costs of products. Division P, unhappy with the impending price hike, now wants to purchase these units from an outside supplier, which still charges $45 per unit.

Division Q produces 10,000 units of various products a year. Data on Division Q's costs follow:

Variable costs per unit of Quanta	$	40
Total fixed costs per year		100,000

If Division P buys from an outside supplier, the facilities that Division Q uses to manufacture Quantas will remain idle.

Required:

1. What should Division Q do in response to Division P's plan to buy from an outside supplier? Consider from the perspectives of Division Q and the whole company.
2. What impact does the proposed change in transfer price have on the overall profit of the company?

E12-13 Transfer Pricing

The Printed Circuit Board (PCB) Division of Pulitt-Hackard, Inc. produces PCB's for sales to other divisions and outside customers. One-third of the PCB Division's output is sold to the Office Products (OP) Division of Pulitt-Hackard; the remainder is sold to outside customers. The PCB Division's estimated sales and standard cost data for the fiscal year ending December 31, Year 9, are presented below:

	To OP Division	To Outsiders
Units sold	10,000	20,000
Sales	$450,000	$1,200,000
Variable costs	(300,000)	(600,000)
Fixed costs allocated.	(90,000)	(180,000)
Gross margin.	$ 60,000	$ 420,000

The OP Division has an opportunity to purchase 10,000 comparable-quality circuit boards from an outside supplier at a cost of $37 per unit on a continuing basis. Assume that the PCB Division's sales to outside customers are limited, and it cannot sell any additional products to outsiders in the foreseeable future.

Required:

Should the OP Division buy the circuit boards from the outside supplier? Why or why not? Discuss the issue from the perspective of the company as a whole.

■ PROBLEMS

P12-14   Ethics and Transfer Pricing

When a multinational finance company headquartered in Panama wanted to accumulate its funds in a no-tax country instead of a high-tax country, it actually did the following, according to its top management:

"We had our subsidiary in the no-tax country charge a higher-than-usual interest rate for the loan it extended to the subsidiary in the high-tax country. This no-nonsense practice has made the flow of our funds from the high-tax country to the no-tax country possible without any headache on our part in the short term."

Required:

1. How was it possible to make the funds flow between the two countries? Explain the process of fund flow in terms of income, expense, and profit.
2. How is this topic related to transfer pricing? What is the product in this case? What is the transfer price of the product?
3. Discuss the long-term effect of this practice on the company's future. Include, in your discussion, the ethical implications of the company's practice.

P12-15   Responsibility Accounting; Profit Center's Performance and Cost Allocation

Lark-Kent, Inc. is an electronics company headquartered in Salt Lake City, Utah. The company has five divisions: the two largest divisions located in Utah and three smaller divisions in Arizona, California, and New Mexico. The five divisions are operating as profit centers under the company's responsibility accounting system.

The operating performance of Division B in Utah and Division D in California for the year just ended is presented below:

	Division B	*Division D*
Sales	$55,000,000	$18,000,000
Cost of sales	30,000,000	9,000,000
Gross profit	25,000,000	9,000,000
Operating expenses	23,000,000	7,000,000
Operating profit	$ 2,000,000	$ 2,000,000

The general manager of Division B is concerned about the marginal profitability of the division's operations, and has asked the division controller to analyze the reasons for the high level of operating expenses. The division controller's analysis, however, has indicated that there is very little the division can do to improve the situation, because most of the operating expenses are allocations from the head office.

"It's really frustrating," the general manager said. "Look at the allocation of the president's airplane expenses. Last year the company bought a new business aircraft, and see what it has done to the allocation of depreciation expenses. There should be a better way to allocate corporate expenses to divisions. Nobody here has even seen the new aircraft."

The controller knows that the president uses the aircraft to fly faster to and from the three divisions located out of state. The total aviation expenses of $480,000 last year have been allocated based on each division's sales revenues. The total sales revenues of the whole company amounted to $220 million.

The general manager of Division B has asked the division controller to draft a letter to the corporate controller, suggesting a more equitable way of allocating corporate expenses to divisions. The allocation of the president's airplane expenses will be used as an example.

Required:

If you were the division controller, what would you write in the letter to the corporate controller?

P12-16   Computation of ROI and Residual Income

JLP, Inc. has three investment centers (A, B, and C). The company shows the following data for the most recent period:

	Investment Center		
	A	B	C
Operating income	$?	$96,000	$ 84,000
Sales.....................	360,000	?	?
Operating assets (average) .	?	?	180,000
Operating margin ratio.....	?	?	14%
Asset turnover	3	4	?
ROI	30%	48%	?
Minimum desired rate of return (cost of capital)...	18%	?	?
Residual income..........	?	60,000	46,200

Required:

Compute the missing numbers.

 ## P12-17   ROI and Residual Income: Performance Comparison

Data on three companies in the same industry are given below:

	Company		
	A	B	C
Operating income...........	$ 300,000	$ 270,000	$ 1,080,000
Sales	6,000,000	8,000,000	10,000,000
Operating assets (average)...	1,500,000	3,000,000	6,000,000
Minimum required ROI (cost of capital)...........	15%	12%	18%

Required:

1. Compute the ROI for each company.
2. Compute the residual income for each company.
3. Assume that there is an investment opportunity that would produce a return of 16%.
   a. If performance is measured by ROI, which companies would decide to invest? Explain.
   b. If performance is measured by residual income, which companies would decide to invest? Explain.

P12-18   ROI and Residual Income

DEPP, Inc. has three investment centers (D, E, and F). Incomplete data on the performance of the three investment centers are presented below:

	Investment Center		
	D	E	F
Operating income............	$?	$?	$?
Sales	?	400,000	600,000
Operating assets (average).....	240,000	200,000	?
Operating margin ratio	?	12%	15%
Asset turnover...............	3	?	?
ROI........................	36%	?	45%
Minimum desired rate of return..	20%	?	?
Residual income..............	?	10,000	34,000

Required:

Compute the missing numbers.

P12-19   Transfer Price

SPS, Inc. has two divisions, Chip Division and PC Division. Chip Division produces chips, and sells them to PC Division, as well as to outside customers. Chip Division charges less for the inter-division sales made to PC Division because some variable expenses it incurs for sales to outside customers are avoided in the internal sales. Operating data on Chip Division for Year 8 are given below:

Chip Division operating data:

	To PC Division	To Outsiders
Sales:		
150,000 units at $4	$600,000	
300,000 units at $5		$1,500,000
Variable expenses:		
150,000 units at $2	300,000	
300,000 units at $3		900,000

Contribution margin	300,000	600,000
Fixed expenses	187,500	375,000
Operating income	$112,500	$225,000

Recently, PC Division received an offer from an outside supplier to supply the same-quality chip at $3.25 each. Chip Division, however, is not willing to meet the $3.25 price because it would only cover the full cost and not generate any profit from sales to PC Division. Chip Division cannot find outside buyers for the 150,000 units, which are currently sold to PC Division, if PC Division goes outside for sourcing its materials.

Required:

1. Calculate the effect on Chip Division's profit if the $3.25 price is met.
2. If you were the Chip Division manager, would you meet the $3.25 outside price? Explain.

P12-20   Economic Value Added (EVA)

TGH, Inc., located in southern California, is in the business of providing cable TV services to the viewers in Latin American countries. The company has absorbed small cable operators in the region, and has developed them into a thriving network. Ted Croner, the CEO who was hired by the company's board three years ago, has a goal: turning the venture into an attractive takeover target for big cable and phone companies so that his shareholders could get the maximum return for the invested capital when the industry is deregulated by the governments in the region. The company uses economic value added (EVA) to measure its performance from the perspective of creating shareholder wealth. The company shows the following data for the most recent period:

Operating income after tax	$270,000
Sources of invested capital:	
Bonds payable	400,000
Common stock	400,000

The tax rate is 30%. The bonds carry a tax-deductible interest of 6% per annum. The company computes the investors' opportunity cost as 11%, representing the long-term treasury bond rate of 6% plus a premium of 5%.

Required:

1. Compute the weighted-average cost of capital for the period.
2. Compute the EVA for the company.

P12-21   Cost-Based vs. Market-Based Transfer Price

HPB, Inc. has two divisions, Fab Division and Sab Division. Both divisions operate as profit centers. The Fab Division produces "Faba," which it sells to outside customers. The data on Faba are presented below:

Selling price............................	$20 per unit
Costs:	
Variable..............................	$11 per unit
Fixed overhead......................	$60,000 per month
Normal output of Faba	10,000 units per month

The Sab Division currently purchases 3,000 parts that are equivalent to Fabas from an outside supplier, which allows the Sab Division to take advantage of the volume discount price of $18 per unit for purchases in excess of 1,000 units. The regular price charged by the outside supplier is $20 per unit.

Required:

1. Assume that Fab Division has no idle capacity, and can sell all of its output to outside customers at a price of $20.
   a. If the Sab Division purchases 2,000 units of Faba per month from the Fab division, what transfer price would the Fab Division demand?
   b. If the Fab Division charges the same price the outside supplier charges and sells 3,000 units to the Sab Division each month, what will be the effect on the profits of the company as a whole?
2. Assume that the Fab Division has an idle capacity of 4,000 units and sells only 6,000 units per month to outside customers at $20 per unit.
   a. If the Sab Division purchases 2,000 units of Faba per month from the Fab Division, what transfer price would be appropriate?
   b. Suppose the outside supplier cuts its price to $16 per part. Should the Fab Division meet the $16 price? What will be the effect on the profit of the Fab Division?
   c. If the Fab Division refuses to meet the $16 price, should the company force the Sab Division to purchase from the Fab Division at a higher price, for the good of the company as a whole?
   d. What is the minimum transfer price that the Fab Division could accept and still make a profit in the short run?
   e. What is the minimum transfer price that the Fab Division requires in the long run?

P12-22 Transfer Pricing and Overall Profit

BTX, Inc. has two divisions, A and B, which operate as investment centers. The company uses ROI in evaluating the performance of its investment centers. Division B produces "Bon," a standard product which Division A can use in production. Division B's normal capacity is 2,000,000 units, and the current activity level is 1,200,000 units per year. The market price for Bon is $15. Division B's cost data are presented below:

Direct materials	$6 per unit
Direct labor..................................	$2 per unit
Variable overhead	$1 per unit
Fixed overhead..............................	$2,400,000 per year

Division A purchases 600,000 units of the same product per year from an outside supplier at a volume discount price of $14 per unit. The supplier regularly charges $15 per unit.

Required:

1. Consider the current volume of 1,200,000 units of Bon a year.

   a. What would be the appropriate range of prices for internal transfers of Bon between Division A and Division B?

   b. If the transfer of Bon is made between the two divisions at a price of $14, what will be the effect on the profits of Division A, Division B, and the company as a whole?

   c. If the transfer price is $14, what will be the effect on the ROI of both divisions?

2. Assume that Division B is now selling 2,000,000 units a year.

   a. What transfer price would be appropriate? Why?

   b. If Division B decides to sell to Division A at the same $14 which the outside supplier charges, what would be the effect on the profits of Division B and the company as a whole?

P12-23   ROI and Residual Income

Johnson Industries has manufactured prefabricated houses for over 20 years. The houses are constructed in sections to be assembled on customers' lots.

Johnson expanded into the precut housing market several years ago when it acquired Lexington Company, one of its suppliers. In this market, various types of lumber are precut into the appropriate lengths, banded into packages, and shipped to customers' lots for assembly. Johnson decided to maintain Lexington's separate identity and therefore established the Lexington Division as an investment center.

Johnson uses return on investment (ROI) as a performance measure. Management bonuses are based in part on ROI. All investments in operating assets are expected to earn a minimum return of 15% before income taxes.

Lexington's ROI has ranged from 19% to 22% since it was acquired by Johnson. During the past year, Lexington had an investment opportunity that had an estimated ROI of 18%. Lexington's management decided against the investment because it believed the investment would decrease the division's overall ROI.

Last year's income statement for Lexington Division is given below. The division's operating assets employed were $15,500,000 at the end of the year, which represents a 24% increase over the previous year's year-end balance. (Several purchases of new equipment were made during the year.)

LEXINGTON DIVISION
Divisional Income Statement
For the Year Ended December 31, Year 7

Sales		$35,000,000
Cost of goods sold		24,600,000
Gross margin		10,400,000
Less operating expenses:		
Selling expenses	$5,700,000	
Administrative expenses	1,900,000	7,600,000
Net operating income		$2,800,000

Required:

1. Calculate the following performance measures for Year 7 for Lexington Division:
   a. Return on investment (ROI).
   b. Residual income.
2. Would the management of Lexington Division have been more likely to accept the investment opportunity it had in Year 7 if residual income were used as a performance measure instead of ROI? Explain.
3. The Lexington Division is a separate investment center within Johnson Industries. Identify the items Lexington Division must be free to control if it is to be evaluated fairly by either the ROI or residual income performance measures.

(CMA, adapted)

P12-24 Performance Evaluation Program; Proper Responsibility Centers

The ATCO Company purchased the Dexter Company three years ago. Prior to the acquisition, Dexter manufactured and sold plastic products to a wide variety of customers. Dexter has since become a division of ATCO and now only manufactures plastic components for products made by ATCO's Macon Division. Macon Division sells its products to hardware wholesalers.

ATCO's corporate management gives the Dexter Division management a considerable amount of authority in running the division's operations. However, corporate management retains authority for decisions regarding capital investments, price setting of all products, and the quantity of each product to be produced by the Dexter Division.

ATCO has a formal performance evaluation program for the management of all of its divisions. The performance evaluation program relies heavily on each division's return on investment. The income statement of Dexter Division presented below provides the basis for the evaluation of Dexter's divisional management.

The financial statements for the divisions are prepared by the corporate accounting staff. The corporate general services costs are allocated on the basis of sales dollars and the computer department's actual costs are apportioned among the divisions on the basis of use. The net division investment includes division fixed assets at net book value (cost less depreciation), division inventory, and corporate working capital apportioned to the divisions on the basis of sales dollars.

ATCO COMPANY
Dexter Division
Income Statement
For the Year Ended December 31, Year 5
(in thousands)

Sales		$4,000
Costs:		
Product costs:		
Direct materials	$500	
Direct labor	1,100	
Factory overhead	1,300	
Total	2,900	
Less: Increase in inventory................	350	2,550
Engineering and research.....................		120
Shipping and receiving		240
Division administration:		
Manager's office	210	
Cost accounting	40	
Personnel.................................	82	332
Corporate costs:		
Computer..................................	48	
General services..........................	230	278
Total costs		3,520
Divisional operating income		$ 480
Net plant investment		$1,600
ROI		30%

Required:

1. Discuss the financial reporting and performance evaluation program at ATCO Company as it relates to the responsibilities of the Dexter Division.
2. Based upon your response to requirement (1), recommend appropriate revisions of the financial information and reports used to evaluate the performance of Dexter's divisional management. If revisions are not necessary, explain why revisions are not needed.

(CMA, adapted)

P12-25 Target Income, Target ROI, and Transfer Pricing

SGN, Inc. has two divisions, PPV Division and DVD Division. The PPV Division manufactures graphic adapters that help create top-quality images for PC screens. The market potential for graphic adapters is excellent, due to the need for graphic adapters in the manufacture of future multimedia products, some of which DVD Division will develop in the near future. The current selling price of graphic adapters is $5 per unit. Fixed costs total $105,000 per month, and variable costs are $3 per unit. The division has a target ROI of 10%. Total assets of PPV Division are $150,000.

Required:

1. What will be the required sales of graphic adapters in order to achieve the desired ROI on the assets of PPV Division?
2. If the PPV Division drops the sales price to $4.75 per unit, the sales volume is expected to increase to 70,000 units per month. If this happens, what will be the new ROI?
3. Assume normal capacity for the PPV Division is 70,000 units per month, and the division is currently selling 60,000 units per month. DVD Division is developing a new multimedia product which requires 10,000 units of graphic adapters per month. PPV Division needs to increase its assets by $20,000 to meet the demand from DVD Division. DVD Division offers to pay a price of $4.50 per unit for the graphic adapters.
   a. Should the PPV Division accept the offer? Use ROI as the basis of making the decision to sell.
   b. Is ROI a good decision basis in (a)? Why or why not?

P12-26 Transfer Pricing: Capacity and Internal Sales

National Industries is a diversified corporation with separate and distinct operating divisions. Each division's performance is evaluated on the basis of total dollar profits and return on division investment.

The WindAir Division manufactures and sells air conditioner units. The coming year's budgeted income statement, based upon a sales volume of 15,000 units, appears below:

WindAir Division

Budgeted Income Statement for Year 8

	Per Unit	Total (in thousands)
Sales revenue	$400	$6,000
Manufacturing costs:		
Compressor	70	1,050
Other raw materials	37	555
Direct labor	30	450
Variable overhead	45	675
Fixed overhead	32	480

Total manufacturing costs............	214	3,210
Gross margin	186	2,790
Operating costs:		
Variable marketing	18	270
Fixed marketing.......................	19	285
Fixed administrative..................	38	570
Total operating costs	75	1,125
Income before taxes..................	$111	$1,665

WindAir's division manager believes sales can be increased if the unit selling price of the air conditioners is reduced. A market research study conducted by an independent firm at the request of the manager indicates that a 5% reduction in the selling price ($20) would increase sales volume 16%, or 2,400 units. WindAir has sufficient production capacity to manage this increased volume with no increase in fixed costs.

At the present time, WindAir uses in its units a compressor that it purchases from an outside supplier at a cost of $70 per compressor. The division manager of WindAir has approached the manager of the compressor division regarding the sale of a compressor unit to WindAir. The compressor division currently manufactures and sells a unit exclusively to outside firms which is similar to the unit used by WindAir. The specifications of the WindAir compressor are slightly different, which would reduce the compressor division's raw material cost by $1.50 per unit. In addition, the compressor division would not incur any variable marketing costs in the units sold to WindAir. The manager of WindAir wants all of the compressors it uses to come from one supplier and has offered to pay $50 for each compressor unit.

The compressor division has the capacity to produce 75,000 units. The coming year's budgeted income statement for the compressor division is shown below and is based upon a sales volume of 64,000 units without considering WindAir's proposal.

Compressor Division
Budgeted Income Statement for Year 8

	Per Unit	Total (in thousands)
Sales revenue	$100	$6,400
Manufacturing costs:		
Raw materials.........................	12	768
Direct labor..........................	8	512
Variable overhead	10	640
Fixed overhead	11	704
Total manufacturing costs...........	41	2,624
Gross margin	59	3,776

Operating costs:		
Variable marketing	6	384
Fixed marketing......................	4	256
Fixed administrative..................	7	448
Total operating costs	17	1,088
Income before taxes	$42	$2,688

Required:

1. Should WindAir Division institute the 5% price reduction on its air conditioner units even if it cannot acquire the compressors internally for $50 each? Support your conclusion with appropriate calculations.
2. Without prejudice to your answer to requirement (1), assume WindAir needs 17,400 units. Should the compressor division be willing to supply the compressor units for $50 each? Support your conclusions with appropriate calculations.
3. Without prejudice to your answer to requirement (2), assume WindAir needs 17,400 units. Would it be in the best interest of National Industries for the compressor division to supply the compressor units at $50 each to the WindAir Division? Support your conclusions with appropriate calculations.

(CMA, adapted)

P12-27   Transfer Price and Lost Contribution Margin

TLC, Inc. has two divisions, Division A and Division B, which operate as profit centers. Division A produces a component part which is sold to outside customers. Its income statement for the most recent month is given below:

	Total	Unit
Sales, 500 units	$125,000	$250
Variable manufacturing cost	65,000	130
Variable selling and administrative expenses..................	5,000	10
Fixed overhead...........................	10,000	20
Fixed administrative expenses..............	25,000	50
Total	105,000	210
Divisional net income	$ 20,000	$ 40

Division B is considering the purchase of 40 parts from Division A, provided that a somewhat different design can be used. Division A has estimated the incremental cost of production as $20 if the new design is used. In order to produce the new parts, Division A has to reduce production of its present output by 100 units per month. All variable selling and administrative expenses related to these 100 units could be avoided if production is actually reduced.

Required:

1. What transfer price would be appropriate for the new parts to be transferred between the two divisions?
2. Suppose Division B found an outside offer of $350 per unit for the same parts. If Division A meets this price, what will be the effect on the profits of the company as a whole?

P12-28   Transfer Pricing; Behavioral Issues Involving Division Managers

Duxbury Company is a decentralized organization containing six divisions. The Brake Division has asked the Electrical Division (which is operating at capacity) to supply it with a large quantity of electrical fitting 172. The Electrical Division sells this fitting to its regular customers for $7.50 each. The Brake Division, which is operating at 50% of capacity, wants to pay $5 each for the fittings. The Brake Division will put the fittings into a brake unit that it is manufacturing and will sell on essentially a cost basis to a large commercial airplane manufacturer.

The Electrical Division has a variable cost of producing fitting 172 of $4.25. The cost of the brake unit being built by the Brake Division follows:

Purchased parts (from outside vendors)	$22.50
Electrical fitting 172	5.00
Other variable costs	14.00
Fixed overhead and administration	8.00
Total cost per brake unit	$49.50

Although the $5 price for electrical fitting 172 represents a substantial discount from the regular $7.50 price, the manager of the Brake Division believes that the price concession is necessary if his division is to get the airplane manufacturer job.

The company uses ROI and dollar profits in the measurement of division and division-manager performance.

Required:

1. Assume that you are the division controller of the Electrical Division. Would you recommend that the Electrical Division supply fitting 172 to the Brake Division as requested? Why or why not? (Ignore any tax issues.)
2. Would it be to the short-run economic advantage of the Duxbury Company for the Electrical Division to supply the Brake Division with the fittings at $5 each? Explain your answer. (Ignore any tax issues.)
3. Discuss the organizational and manager behavior difficulties, if any, inherent in this situation. As the Duxbury Company controller, what would you advise the Duxbury Company president to do in this situation?

(CMA, adapted)

■ CASES

Case 12-29   Transfer Pricing in a Multinational Company

The Company and Its Three Foreign Subsidiaries

Global Tech, Inc. is a laptop computer manufacturer located in southern California. The company imports its computer parts from various Pacific-Rim countries; assembles laptop computers in its plant in Los Angeles; and sells them in the domestic market, as well as to Australia, Indonesia, and Japan. The company also assembles its computers at its Australian and Indonesian subsidiaries.

The cost of assembling laptop computers is the highest in its U.S. plant, and the lowest in its Indonesian plant. After the cost of shipping computers from Australia to southern California is added, however, the total cost of computers imported to the U.S. from its Australian subsidiary is about equal to the cost of U.S.-assembled computers.

Accordingly, the proportion of the computers assembled by the Indonesian subsidiary among all the computers sold by the company in its U.S. and foreign markets has been steadily increasing. The Japanese subsidiary, which does not have its own assembly operation, buys mostly from Australian and Indonesian subsidiaries, and sells to the Japanese market.

Sourcing Decision and Transfer Price

In this month, the company's top management is faced with a difficult decision to make regarding the transfer of 2,000 units of its laptop computer to its subsidiary in Japan. It started when Patrick Hogan, the Australian Division's manager, called and appealed to David Johnson, the company's president, as follows:

"The Japanese subsidiary is about to award the contract to the Indonesian subsidiary for the purchase of 2,000 laptop computers. We know the transfer price the Indonesian subsidiary is charging is well below our price, but we believe all our business units, wherever they may be, should make decisions which would benefit the company as a whole.

We have some idle capacity here in Australia, and the Japanese subsidiary should help us utilize our fixed facilities to the maximum. The Indonesian plant is operating at full capacity, we have heard, and they could easily sell the 2,000 units to some other buyers. This deal may not mean too much to the Indonesian operations, but it would be a significant boost for our operations here. Please help us with this."

Additional Information

In connection with this appeal, David Johnson has collected the following information:

	Produced in	
	Indonesia	*Australia*
Number of units	2,000	2,000
Transferred to	Japan	Japan
Transfer price	$700	$900
Out-of-pocket costs	$500	$600
Host country's income tax rate	0%*	40%

* Indonesian government provides a temporary income tax exemption on export sales.

Required:

Consider only out-of-pocket costs in your answers to questions 1, 2, and 3.
1. Compute the selling subsidiary's after-tax profit on the proposed sales, assuming
   a. The Japanese subsidiary buys from the Indonesian subsidiary.
   b. The Japanese subsidiary buys from the Australian subsidiary.
2. The Japanese subsidiary sells the imported computers for $1,500 per unit. The appropriate income tax rate in Japan is 30%. Compute the Japanese subsidiary's after-tax profit on the final sales of the 2,000 computers, assuming
   a. The computers were bought from the Indonesian subsidiary.
   b. The computers were bought from the Australian subsidiary.
3. Compute the total after-tax profit for the company as a whole, assuming
   a. The Japanese subsidiary buys from the Indonesian subsidiary.
   b. The Japanese subsidiary buys from the Australian subsidiary.
4. If you were David Johnson, president, what action would you take? Explain your decision, including a discussion on the idle capacity in Australia. You do not need any additional calculations for this answer.

C12-30   Negotiated Transfer Price

Drexel Products is a divisionalized furniture manufacturer. The divisions are autonomous segments, with each division being responsible for its own sales, costs of operations, working capital management, and equipment acquisition. Each division serves a different market in the furniture industry. Because the markets and products divisions are so different, there have never been any transfers between divisions.

The Commercial Division manufactures equipment and furniture that is purchased by the restaurant industry. The division plans to introduce a new line of counter and chair units that feature a cushioned seat for the counter chairs. Joe Mellia, the division manager, has discussed the manufacture of the cushioned seat with Tom Jones of the Office Division. They both believe that a cushioned seat currently made by the Office Division for use on its deluxe office stool could be modified for use on the new counter chair. Consequently, Mellia has asked Jones for a price for 100-unit lots of the cushioned seat. The following conversation took place about the price to be charged for the cushioned seats.

Jones: Joe, we can make the necessary modifications to the cushioned seat easily. The raw materials used in your seat are slightly different and should cost about 10% more than those used in our deluxe office stool. However, the labor time should be the same because the seat fabrication operation is basically the same. I would price the seat at our regular rate - full cost plus 30% markup.

Mellia: That's higher than I expected, Tom. I was thinking that a good price would be your variable manufacturing costs. After all, your capacity costs will be incurred regardless of this job.

Jones: Joe, I'm at capacity. By making the cushion seats for you, I'll have to cut my production of deluxe office stools. Of course, I can increase my production of economy office stools. The labor time freed by not having to fabricate the frame or assemble the deluxe stool can be shifted to the frame fabrication and assembly of the economy office stool. Fortunately, I can switch my labor force between these two models of stools without any loss of efficiency. As you know, overtime is not a feasible alternative in our community. I'd like to sell it to you at variable cost, but I have excess demand for both products. I don't mind changing my product mix to the economy model if I get a good return on the seats I make for you. Here are my standard costs for the two stools and a schedule of my manufacturing overhead. (See the following tables.)

Mellia: I guess I see your point, Tom, but I don't want to price myself out of the market. Maybe we should talk to corporate to see if they can give us any guidance.

OFFICE DIVISION
Standard Costs and Prices

	Deluxe office stool		*Economy office stool*
Raw materials:			
Framing	$8.15		$9.76
Cushioned seat:			
Padding	2.40		–
Vinyl	4.00		–
Molded seat (purchased)	–		6.00
Direct labor:			
Frame fabrication (0.5 × $7.50/DLH)	3.75	(0.5 × $7.50/DLH)	3.75
Cushion fabrication			
(0.5 × $7.50/DLH)	3.75		–
Assembly* (0.5 × $7.50/DLH) . . .	3.75	(0.3 × $7.50/DLH)	2.25
Manufacturing:			
Overhead (1.5 DLH x $12.80)	19.20	(0.8 DLH × $12.80)	10.24

Total standard cost.............	$45.00	$32.00
Selling price (30% markup).......	$58.50	$41.60

* Attaching seats to frames and attaching rubber feet.

Manufacturing Overhead Budget

Overhead Item	Nature	Amount
Supplies.............	Variable, at current market prices	$420,000
Indirect labor........	Variable	375,000
Supervision..........	Nonvariable	250,000
Power..............	Use varies with activity; rates are fixed	180,000
Heat and light........	Nonvariable, same regardless of production	140,000
Property taxes and ... insurance	Nonvariable, any change in amounts or rates is independent of production	200,000
Depreciation........	Fixed dollar total	1,700,000
Employee benefits....	20% of supervision; direct and indirect labor	575,000
Total overhead.....		$3,840,000
Capacity in DLH......		300,000
Overhead rate/DLH...		$12.80

Required:

1. Assume that you are the corporate controller. What transfer price would you recommend for a 100-unit lot of seats? Show all computations.
2. Which alternative transfer pricing system - full cost, variable manufacturing cost, or variable cost plus lost contribution margin - would be best as the underlying concept for an intracompany transfer pricing policy? Explain your answer.

(CMA, adapted)

CHAPTER 13

CAPITAL BUDGETING

After studying this chapter, you should be able to:

1. Explain the concept of capital budgeting and the nature of capital investment decisions.

2. Determine whether a capital investment project should be accepted or rejected using (a) the net present value method, (b) the internal rate of return method, (c) the payback method, and (d) the accounting rate of return method.

3. Determine the net present value for two alternatives using either the differential approach or the total approach.

4. Discuss the factors that managers should consider for use of the discounted cash flow models.

5. Explain why the payback and the accounting rate of return methods are conceptually inferior to the net present value and the internal rate of return methods for making capital budgeting decisions.

6. Define the cost of capital and explain how to compute it.

7. Discuss how capital budgeting techniques can be used in nonprofit organizations.

Capital budgeting refers to the planning and financing of a firm's capital expenditures. This includes the purchase of new equipment or the replacement of old equipment; the expansion of plant facilities or the acquisition of a new plant; and the enterance into a new market or the introduction of a new product line. Expenditures for such purposes usually require significant amounts of money and the returns usually are generated over several years.

These capital budgeting projects are considered long-term investments. To make appropriate long-term investment decisions, management needs to set a minimum return on investment criterion, say 15 or 20%, that any proposed capital investment project must meet before it can be approved. This minimum criterion then is used to screen all capital investment proposals.

Frequently, several capital investment projects will pass the screening test. However, these projects will require more funds than those available to the firm. As a result, in addition to the screening tools described above, some preference device or ranking criterion are needed to help management select, from among all acceptable projects, only those that are the most favorable. This chapter deals with the use of various screening tools, whereas the following chapter discusses various preference tools.

A heavy-equipment plant of Harnischfeger Industries, Inc. Planning on an investment in a plant like this requires a good capital budgeting analysis.

NATURE OF CAPITAL INVESTMENT DECISIONS

In making capital investment decisions, managers try to maximize the return on investment given the degree of risk they are willing to assume. For ease of comparisons among various investment opportunities, the annual return is usually computed as a percentage of the original investment. The risk is defined as the possible loss of the original investment and the uncertainty of the amount and timing of future returns from the investment.

The higher the risk managers are willing to take, the higher the returns they expect to realize. Managers differ as to how much risk they are willing to take. Short-term investments generally have less risk than long-term investments because of the time frame. It is more difficult to predict the outcome of a project several years in the future than in the next few months. As a result, the return on long-term investments is expected to be higher than the return on short-term investments.

Capital budgeting decisions are long term in nature. In determining the minimum acceptable return on a capital investment project, a prudent manager should consider the relative degrees of risk. In our discussion of the various tools of screening capital budgeting projects in this chapter, we will assume that the degree of risk of each project has been evaluated and accepted by management.

Examples of Capital Budgeting Decisions

Capital budgeting projects are assumed to improve the profitability of the firm. This may be attributed to reduced costs, increased revenues, or both. The reduction in costs means a decrease in variable cost per unit or total fixed costs for the period, or both. The increase in revenues may result from a higher product selling price per unit or larger volume of units sold, or both. Accordingly, capital budgeting decisions take the following forms:

Cost Reduction Decisions:
   a. Should new labor-saving equipment be purchased?
   b. Should existing equipment be replaced with new, more efficient equipment?
   c. Should the new equipment or facility be leased or purchased?

Revenue Enhancement Decisions:
   a. Should a new product line or new facility be acquired to increase capacity and sales?
   b. Should the firm enter a new market or expand an already existing business?
   c. Should the current product be improved to warrant a higher selling price or a greater number of units sold?

DISCOUNTED CASH FLOW MODELS

Discounted cash flow (DCF) **models** consider the two important characteristics of capital investment projects: the time value of money and the true return on investment. The two most commonly used DCF techniques are (1) the net present value (NPV) method, and (2) the internal rate of return (IRR) method. Both are based on compound interest and present value concepts, which are discussed in Appendix 13A at the end of this chapter.

The Net Present Value Method

Under the **net present value** (NPV) **method,** management sets a minimum required rate of return (also called cutoff rate, hurdle rate, or discount rate), which is used to compute the present value of the cash flows from the proposed project. If the present value of cash inflows is greater than the present value of cash outflows, the NPV will be positive and the project is accepted. If the present value of cash inflows is less than the present value of cash outflows, the NPV will be negative and the project is rejected. If the present value of cash inflows is exactly equal to the present value of cash outflows, which will happen only by coincidence, the NPV will be zero and the project would still be accepted. This is because a zero NPV means that the project will earn exactly the required return.

If the NPV is positive, the project will earn a return higher than the required rate of return. Thus, a positive NPV may be considered as an additional safety margin over and above the required return. This represents an amount that the NPV could be reduced before the project is rejected. It can be used as a preference device and is explained in the following chapter.

Net Present Value Illustrations

Even Cash Inflows: Assume that ABC Company is considering the purchase of new equipment that costs $10,000 but can save $3,000 in operating costs per year. The equipment is expected to last for five years after which it will have no salvage value. Management decides that it will buy this equipment only if the return on the $10,000 investment is at least 14% per year. Should the equipment be purchased?

The decision to buy the equipment will depend on whether the NPV of the $3,000 annual savings in operating costs discounted at a rate of 14% will be positive or negative. That is, whether the present value of an annuity of $3,000 for five years discounted at 14% will be greater or less than $10,000.

To simplify the computations, assume that the $3,000 annual savings occur at the end of each year although such savings would occur throughout the year. We will also ignore income taxes. Thus:

Present value of cash inflows
= Annual cash inflow x 14% factor from Table 13A-2 (present value of an annuity of $1) for 5 years

= $3,000 x 3.4331 =	$10,299
Present value of cash outflows	(10,000)
NPV	$ 299

Since the NPV is greater than zero, the equipment should be purchased. If the equipment is purchased and the annual savings in operating costs amount to $3,000 as expected, the $10,000 investment will earn 14% plus a cushion of $299.

Uneven Cash Inflows: Assume the same data as above, except that the cash savings in operating costs (cash inflows) is not the same in each of the five years, but varies as follows: Year 1, $2,400; Year 2, $2,600; Year 3, $2,900; Year 4, $3,000; and Year 5, $4,100. Should the equipment be purchased?

The answer will depend on whether the NPV is positive or negative. Even though the gross amount of all cash inflows during the five years is the same, $15,000 in both cases, we cannot assume that the NPV will be positive as in the previous illustration. Because the cash flows are uneven, we cannot use the annuity table (13A-2). Instead, each year's cash flow must be treated as a single sum. We have to discount each year's cash flow separately, using factors from the present value of $1 at the end of each year (Table 13A-1) as shown below:

Year	Annual Cash Inflow	Present Value of $1 (Table 13A-1) at Yearend at 14%	Present Value of Cash Inflow
1	$2,400	.8772	$2,105
2	2,600	.7695	2,001
3	2,900	.6750	1,958
4	3,000	.5921	1,776
5	4,100	.5194	2,130
Total	$15,000	3.4332	$9,970

PV of cash inflows	$9,970
PV of cash outflow (initial investment)	(10,000)
Net present value	$(30)

This analysis indicates that the equipment should not be purchased because the NPV is negative. The investment of $10,000 in this equipment will not earn the minimum required rate of return of 14% per year. A comparison of the results of the two illustrations demonstrates the importance of the time value of money. Even though the total amount of cash inflows over the five-year period is the same $15,000, and the total of the present value factors over the five years is also the same 3.4332 (rounding difference), most of the cash inflows in the second case occur in later years.

Additional Items: Now refer to the original example and assume that the equipment will need an overhaul at the end of the third year. The overhaul will cost $2,000, and the equipment will have a salvage value of $800 at the end of the fifth year. Should the equipment be purchased?

The $2,000 overhaul at the end of the third year is a cash outflow in addition to the $10,000 original investment. The $800 salvage value is a cash inflow at the end of the fifth year in addition to the annual cash savings of $3,000 in operating costs. The PV of these additional items of cash outflows and inflows must be computed and factored into the NPV calculation, as shown below:

PV of Cash Inflows:

	Amount	**Factor**	**PV**
Annual savings in operating costs	$3,000	3.4331[a]	$10,299
Salvage value at the end of 5th year	800	.5194[b]	416
Total (A)			$10,715

PV of Cash Outflows:

Initial investment	$10,000	1.0000	$10,000
Overhaul at the end of 3rd year	2,000	.6750[c]	1,350
Total (B)			$11,350
NPV = A − B =			$ (635)

[a] From Table 13A-2 (for five years at 14%).
[b] From Table 13A-1 (at the end of 5th year at 14%).
[c] From Table 13A-1 (at the end of 3rd year at 14%).

Because the NPV is negative, the equipment would not be purchased.

Working Capital, Sale of Old Equipment, and Salvage Value: Let us assume the same data as in the above illustration, except that the new equipment will replace old equipment. The old equipment has a remaining useful life of five years, but can be sold now for $1,900, or at the end of the five years for $300. If the old equipment is kept, it will need an overhaul at the end of two years costing $1,000. The new equipment will require additional working capital of $2,500, over and above the $1,500 now required by the old equipment. This working capital will be released at the end of the fifth year. The $3,000 annual cost savings mentioned earlier will result from replacing the old equipment with the new. Should the old equipment be replaced?

In this illustration, the $1,900 proceeds from the sale of the old equipment is considered a reduction of the initial investment of $10,000 in the new equipment. The $300 salvage value of the old equipment in five years will be foregone if the new equipment is purchased. Since the company will receive a salvage value of $800 from the new equipment in five years, the difference in salvage value caused by the replacement decision is only $500. The $2,500 commitment of working capital is considered as an additional investment (cash outflows) now and as additional cash inflow when released at the end of the fifth year. The detailed calculations are shown below:

PV of Cash Inflows:

	Amount	Factor	PV
Annual savings in operating expenses	$ 3,000	3.4331	$10,299
Cost of overhauling old equipment			
at end of year 2 saved	1,000	.7695	770
Salvage value at end of year 5	800	.5194	416
Salvage value of old equipment			
at end of year 5 lost	(300)	.5194	(156)
Working capital released at end			
of year 5	2,500	.5194	1,299
Total(A)			$12,628

PV of Cash Outflows:

	Amount	Factor	PV
Initial investment	$10,000	1.0000	$10,000
Additional working capital committed	2,500	1.0000	2,500
Proceeds from sale of old equipment	(1,900)	1.0000	(1,900)
Overhaul of new equipment at end of			
year 3	2,000	.6750	1,350
Total (B)			$11,950
Net present value = A − B =			$678

Since the NPV is positive, the old equipment should be replaced with the new equipment.

Total Approach and Differential Approach

In the above solution, we used the **differential (incremental) approach,** because it considers only the difference between keeping the old equipment and buying the new equipment. We asked, "What difference does that replacement make?" Under the **total approach,** the question is, "What are the results if we keep the old equipment and what are the results if we buy the new equipment?"

We illustrate the total approach below using the same data as in the previous illustration and the following additional data:

	Keep Old Equipment	Replace Old With New Equipment
Total cash revenues per year	$10,000	$10,000
Total cash operating costs per year	6,000	3,000
Net annual cash inflows	$ 4,000	$ 7,000

The solution, based on the total approach, is shown in Exhibit 13-1. Also shown is a sketch of cash flows at the end of the relevant years. We compare the differential approach presented earlier with the total approach.

Note that the results of the total approach are exactly the same as the differential approach, a positive NPV of $678 in favor of replacing the old equipment. Some managers prefer the differential approach because it highlights only the differences. Other managers prefer the total approach because they can see the entire picture.

Recovery of Investment and Return on Investment

Suppose that XYZ Company is undecided about whether to purchase equipment that costs $32,743 and will last for five years. The equipment will increase revenue by $10,000 a year. XYZ will purchase the equipment only if it earns at least 16% (rate of return on common stock funds) per year for five years. The equipment will be worthless at the end of five years. The present value of an annuity of $10,000 for five years is calculated below:

	Annual cash inflow	Factor at 16% for 5 years	Present value
Increased revenue =	$10,000 ×	3.2743 =	$32,743

Since the present value is exactly equal to the original investment, the NPV is equal to zero and the equipment earns exactly 16% per year. Exhibit 13-2 illustrates how the $10,000 annual cash inflow is broken down into a portion representing the return on investment and a portion representing the recovery of investment.

As shown in Exhibit 13-2, the total cash inflows during the five-year period is made up of two portions: (1) $17,257 representing return on investment at 16% per year, and (2) $32,743 representing recovery of the original investment.

Kodak vs. Fuji: The Difference a Low Cost of Capital Makes

With a net cash position of about $4.5 billion and access to cheap borrowing (an annual interest of around 2.5% in Japan), Fuji has been able to make acquisitions like the estimated $400 million purchase in 1996 of Wal-Mart's six wholesale photo labs. The move "in one swoop gave it about 15% of the U.S. photo-processing market." Fuji's financial strength provides more flexibility to cut prices also. Kodak, however, still dominates the $2.7 billion U.S. amateur film market. Worldwide, Kodak and Fuji are neck and neck, with about a third of the market each.

From "What's Ailing Kodak? Fuji," *Fortune*, October 27, 1997, pp.185–192.

EXHIBIT 13-2

XYZ Company

Breakdown of Cash Inflows Into Two Components:
Return on Investment and Recovery of Investment

Year	(1) Balance of Investment at Beginning of Year	(2) Annual Cash Inflow	(3) Return on Investment at 16% (1) × 16%	(4) Recovery of Investment (2) − (3)	(5) Balance of Investment at End of Year (1) − (4)
1	32,743	$10,000	$ 5,239	$ 4,761	$27,982
2	27,982	10,000	4,477	5,523	22,459
3	22,459	10,000	3,594	6,406	16,053
4	16,053	10,000	2,568	7,432	8,621
5	8,621	10,000	1,379	8,621	0
Totals		$50,000	$17,257	$32,743	

Discount Rate

The NPV method requires the choice of a discount rate to apply to future cash flows. If the rate chosen is too low, most, if not all, capital investment projects would be accepted. If it is too high, most, if not all, projects would be rejected. Thus, firms carefully choose a discount rate that is either equal to their cost of capital or is based on that cost.

To increase profits, firms try to find investment projects that will earn more than the cost of capital. However, projects that earn far more than the cost of capital may be not available or may be too risky. This is the reason that the discount rate chosen for capital investment projects is usually close to the cost of capital. The cost of capital is not just the interest rate that a firm pays on its borrowed funds. It is a weighted-average cost that a firm pays on all its sources of funds including long-term debt, preferred stock, and common stock.

Assume that NRM Company has the following capital structure and after-tax cost of funds:

Source of Funds	Amount	After-Tax Cost*
Long-term debt	$ 4,000,000	8%
Preferred stock	1,000,000	10%
Common stock	5,000,000	16%

* Equity funds usually cost more than borrowed funds.

The cost of capital would be computed as follows:

Source of Funds	Amount	Percent of Total	After-Tax Cost	Weighted Average Cost of Capital
Long-Term Debt	$ 4,000,000	40%	8%	3.2%
Preferred Stock	1,000,000	10%	10%	1.0%
Common Equity	5,000,000	50%	16%	8.0%
	$10,000,000	100%		12.2%

Thus, the cost of capital would be 12.2%. NRM Company may decide to set the required rate of return for its capital investment projects at its cost of capital of 12.2% or at a slightly higher rate to compensate for such factors as inflation and risk.

The Internal Rate of Return Method

The **internal rate of return** (IRR), also called the time-adjusted rate of return, is the rate of return that will produce a NPV of zero. It is the discount rate that makes the present value of cash inflows equal to the present value of cash outflows. In the previous illustration, XYZ Company required at least a 16% return on the investment of $32,743 in equipment that will increase cash inflows by $10,000 a year for five years. Using the NPV method, the present value of an annuity of $10,000 for five years at 16% is exactly equal to $32,743. That is, the NPV is zero. Thus, the 16% is also the IRR.

What if the discount rate of 16% was not known? Indeed, under the IRR method, we do not know in advance what the rate is. Usually, management will set a minimum required IRR for a project to be accepted. Given a set of cash outflows and inflows for the project, the IRR can be computed. If the computed IRR is equal to or greater than the minimum rate of return required by management, the project is accepted. Otherwise, it is rejected.

IRR Calculations: Even Cash Inflows

Assume the same data as the above illustration, except that the 16% discount rate is not known. Also assume that management has decided not to invest in any project unless it has an IRR of at least 17%. Would the project be accepted?

Since the IRR is the rate that will make the present value of cash inflows equal to the present value of cash outflows, we first must determine the present value factor that, if multiplied by the annual cash inflows of $10,000, will produce the original investment of $32,743, as follows:

$$\frac{\text{Original investment}}{\text{Annual cash inflow}} = \frac{\$32,743}{\$10,000} = 3.2743$$

We look for this factor along the 5-period line in Table 13A-2, the present value of an annuity of $1. The discount rate under which this factor is listed is the IRR for the project. The factor 3.2743 is listed under 16%. Since the computed IRR for the project is 16%, and the desired IRR is 17%, the project would not be accepted.

Even Cash Inflows and Interpolation

We found 3.2743 listed under 16%. However, if the exact present value factor is not listed in the table, interpolation can be used to find the exact IRR. Assume the same data as in the first illustration, except that the discount rate of 14% is not given. What is the IRR?

$$\text{Factor} = \frac{\text{Original investment}}{\text{Annual cash inflow}} = \frac{\$10,000}{\$3,000} = 3.3333$$

Look for 3.3333 along the 5-period line in Table 13A-2. It lies between 3.4331 (14%) and 3.2743 (16%). The exact rate can be computed by interpolation as follows:

14% Factor 3.4331	True IRR Factor 3.3333	16% Factor 3.2743
.0998	.0590	

Difference = .1588

$$\text{IRR} = 14\% + (\frac{.0998}{.1588} \times 2\%) = 14\% + 1.257\% = \underline{15.257\%}$$

or

$$\text{IRR} = 16\% - (\frac{.0590}{.1588} \times 2\%) = 16\% - .743\% = \underline{15.257\%}$$

Thus, the IRR is 15.257%. If the desired rate of return is 15% or less, the project will be accepted. If it is greater than 15.257%, the project will be rejected.

Uneven Cash Inflows: Trial and Error

If the cash inflows are uneven, a trial-and-error approach must be used. That is, select a discount rate at random and compute the PV using it. If the PV of cash inflows is higher than the PV of cash outflows, select a higher discount rate. If the PV of cash inflows is lower than the PV of cash outflows, try a lower rate. When two rates resulting in two PV amounts of cash inflows that are very close to the PV of cash outflows are found, interpolate between the two as explained in the above illustration.

Assume the same data as in the second illustration (uneven cash inflows) in this chapter. What is the true IRR?

Rather than starting with a random rate that may be too far from the true rate, compute an annual average of cash inflows, and use it to derive a PV factor as shown below:

Annual average of cash inflows
= ($2,400 + $2,600 + $2,900 + $3,000 + $4,100) ÷ 5 years = $3,000
The PV factor = $10,000 ÷ $3,000 = 3.3333

From the previous illustration, we know that the IRR for the PV factor of 3.3333 is close to 16%. Thus, we try 16% and compute the PV as shown below:

Year	Cash Inflow	16% Factor (Table 13A-1)	Present Value
1	$ 2,400	.8621	$2,069
2	2,600	.7432	1,932
3	2,900	.6407	1,858
4	3,000	.5523	1,657
5	4,100	.4761	1,952
Totals	$15,000	3.2744	$9,468

Since the present value of $9,468 calculated using 16% is less than the $10,000 original investment, we must select a lower rate because the lower the discount rate, the higher the present value. Since there is no 15% rate in the table, we use 14%. Using a 14% discount rate results in a present value of $9,970 calculated in the same way as shown above. Although this is still lower than $10,000, it is very close, and we know the actual IRR is slightly below 14%. We could interpolate between 14% and 12%, as illustrated above. These trial-and-error calculations are time consuming, but can be done in seconds, using available canned computer software programs, or using spreadsheets on personal computers.

Comparison of NPV and IRR Methods

The NPV and IRR methods are similar DCF methods, but they differ in the application of the decision rule. Under the NPV method, the required rate of return is used to compute the NPV. If the NPV is zero or positive, the project is accepted. Under the IRR method, the computed IRR is compared to the desired rate of return. If the computed IRR is equal to or greater than the desired rate of return, the project is accepted.

The NPV method has some advantages over the IRR method. First, the dollar amount of the NPV allows it to be used as a preference criterion for evaluating several competing projects. Many managers consider the excess dollar amount of NPV to be more useful than IRR in decision making. Second, some managers consider the NPV method to be easier to use, since it does not require a trial-and-error procedure as does the IRR method. Last, the NPV method allows for adjusting the discount rate every few years to compensate for the risk associated with cash flows projected to occur in the distant future. The discount rate used can be changed during the project life. A lower discount rate can be used for cash inflows occurring in earlier years, and a higher rate may be used in later years. Such flexibility is not available under the IRR method.

Despite the above advantages of the NPV method, the IRR method is more widely used in practice because managers like to think in terms of rates. It is easy to understand that a proposed project has a rate of return of 18% compared to a cost of capital of 15%. The project simply looks acceptable.

Simplifying Assumptions of the DCF Models

We have made the following simplifying assumptions regarding the two DCF models:

First, we assumed that the future cash flows occur at the end of the period. Normally, cash flows occur somewhat uniformly throughout the period, or at any given date during the period. Second, we assumed that the portion of the initial investment recovered from a project will be immediately reinvested in another project earning the same rate of return. In reality, this may not be true. Funds recovered from a project may sit idle for some time before they are reinvested, or may be reinvested in a less profitable project. Last, we assumed a world of certainty in which predicted future cash flows will occur. In reality, these predictions are just expectations.

OTHER CAPITAL BUDGETING MODELS

The DCF models are the most commonly used techniques of large corporations because of their theoretical superiority. However, other capital budgeting models, that do not consider the time value of money, are also used by some firms, in addition to the DCF models. These other models are perceived to be simpler than the DCF models or more compatible with financial reporting. The two most commonly used non-DCF models are the payback method and the accounting rate of return method.

The Payback Method

The payback method simply measures the payback time or payback period during which a given project will recover its original investment from the cash inflow that it generates. This method does not measure the profitability of a project. If the annual cash inflows are even, and there is only one initial investment at the beginning, we can calculate the payback period as follows:

$$\text{Payback Period} = \frac{\text{Initial Investment}}{\text{Annual Cash Inflow}}$$

For example, assume that Glenview Hospital is considering the purchase of X-ray equipment for $20,000. The equipment will save $4,000 per year in operating costs over six years. The general policy of hospital management states that the investment must pay for itself in four years or less. Would this investment be accepted?

The payback period is five years for the investment, calculated as follows:

$$\text{Payback period} = \frac{\$20,000}{\$4,000} = 5 \text{ years}$$

Since the calculated payback period is longer than the four years hospital policy requires, the investment will not be accepted.

Measuring the payback time, not the profitability of capital investment projects, is a major weakness of the payback method, because a project that recovers its initial outlay fast is not necessarily the most profitable.

Consider the following example:

LMN Company is undecided about purchasing machine A or machine B. Either machine can save $5,000 a year in operating costs, but the machines' purchase costs and useful lives are different as shown below:

	Cost	Useful life
Machine A	$20,000	5 years
Machine B	25,000	10 years

According to the payback method, machine A is more desirable because its payback period is shorter than machine B's:

$$\text{Payback period for machine A} = \frac{\$20,000}{\$5,000} = 4 \text{ years}$$

$$\text{Payback period for machine B} = \frac{\$25,000}{\$5,000} = 5 \text{ years}$$

A major defect in the conclusion based on the payback calculations is that it ignores the cash inflow that will be generated by each machine beyond the payback period. While machine A generates $5,000 cash inflow for one additional year beyond its payback period, machine B generates $5,000 cash inflow for six additional years. Indeed, if the company needs the machine for ten years it would have to make two purchases of machine A for $40,000 (2 x $20,000), instead of one purchase of machine B for $25,000.

The Problem of Uneven Cash Inflows: If cash inflows are uneven, we must reduce the initial investment by each successive year's cash inflows until the entire initial investment is recovered, as shown in the following example:

Year	Net Cash Inflows	Balance of Unrecovered Investment
0	$ 0	$10,000
1	2,400	7,600
2	2,600	5,000
3	2,900	2,100
4	2,100	0

The $2,100 cash inflow listed for year 4 is the amount needed to recover the remaining balance of the unrecovered initial investment. If the total cash inflow for year 4 is $3,000, the payback period is less than 4 years. If we interpolate within year 4, we get a payback period of 3.7 years as follows:

$$\text{Payback Period} = 3 \text{ years} + [1 \text{ year} \times \frac{\$2,100}{\$3,000}] = 3.7 \text{ years}$$

Additional Cash Outflows: If extra cash outflows, in addition to the original investment, are needed during the life of the project, they can be netted against the cash inflows in the respective years. For example, if the equipment in the above example needed an overhaul in the third year at a cost of $1,000, net cash inflow for the third year would only be $1,900 ($2,900 − $1,000). The payback period will then be slightly over 4 years (4.024 years to be exact).

If the new equipment replaces old equipment, and there is salvage value from selling the old, the salvage value should be netted against the initial investment in the new equipment. The payback period emphasizes cash flow and not operating income. Accordingly, depreciation expense is not deducted from cash operating revenues.

The Accounting Rate of Return Method

The **accounting rate of return** (ARR) **method,** also known as the simple rate of return method, unadjusted rate of return method, financial statement method, and book value model, is similar to the payback method in that both do not involve DCF's. They are dissimilar in two respects, however. First, the payback method emphasizes cash flow but the ARR method uses accounting income. Under the payback method, depreciation expense is not deducted from cash operating revenues, but it is deducted under the ARR method. Second, the ARR method attempts to measure ROI or profitability, but the payback method does not.

One reason the ARR method is called the simple rate of return method is that it is simple to compute. The ARR equals accounting net income from the income statement (more precisely, the expected average annual net income from a project) divided by the book value of the investment from the balance sheet (the initial investment), as follows:

$$\text{ARR} = \frac{\text{Expected average annual net income from a project}}{\text{Initial investment in the project}}$$

Assume that Tri-State, Inc. is contemplating the purchase of $100,000 of new equipment that is expected to increase revenue by $40,000 each year. Its operating costs, excluding depreciation, will be $15,000 a year. The useful life of the equipment is 10 years. No salvage value is expected at the end of the 10 years. The company uses straight-line depreciation. The company's accounting rate of return is currently 16%. The company's policy is to purchase any needed equipment, provided that it does not reduce the current accounting rate of return. Would the company purchase the equipment? (Ignore income tax effects.)

$$\text{Accounting rate of return for the new equipment} = \frac{\text{Incremental income}}{\text{Initial investment}} =$$

$$\frac{\text{Increase in revenue } - \text{ Increase in cash operating expenses } - \text{ Depreciation}}{\text{Initial Investment}}$$

$$= \frac{\$40,000 \ - \ \$15,000 \ - \ \$10,000^*}{\$100,000} = 15\%$$

$* \$100,000 \div 10 \text{ years.}$

Since the ARR for the equipment (15%) is lower than the current ARR (16%), the company would not purchase the equipment.

Some firms use the average investment instead of the entire initial investment in the denominator. In the above example, the average investment is calculated as follows:

Average investment
 = (The balance of the investment at beginning of year 1
     + the balance of the investment at end of year 10) $\div$ 2
 = ($100,000 + 0) $\div$ 2 = $50,000.

Drawbacks of Accounting Rate of Return

The ARR method has two major drawbacks. The most significant drawback of the ARR method is that it does not consider the time value of money. A dollar of income realized in the first year of the project is weighted equally with a dollar of income realized in the last year of the project. Another drawback of the ARR method is that it does not emphasize cash flow. Depreciation expense is deducted from net cash inflows from operations even though depreciation expense does not require cash outlay. This usually leads to understating the rate of return on the project, because income (the numerator) is less than cash inflow.

Assume that PQR, Inc. must choose between two projects, each of which requires an $80,000 initial investment and will last for four years, with no salvage value at the end. As Exhibit 13-3 illustrates, the basic difference between the two projects is in the pattern of cash inflows before depreciation.

According to the ARR method, project X is more desirable than project Y. If we consider the time value of money and use the IRR, however, project Y is more desirable than project X. The IRR for project X is 9.18% and the IRR for project Y

EXHIBIT 13-3

PQR, Inc.

ARR for Two Projects with Different Cash Inflow Patterns

	Project X	Project Y
Cash inflows before depreciation:		
Year 1	$ 10,000	$ 40,000
Year 2	20,000	30,000
Year 3	30,000	20,000
Year 4	44,000	10,000
Total (A)	$104,000	$100,000
Average annual cash inflows (A ÷ 4)	$ 26,000	$ 25,000
Straight-line depreciation ($80,000 ÷ 4)	20,000	20,000
Increase in average annual income (B)	$ 6,000	$ 5,000
Accounting rate of return (B ÷ $80,000)	7.50%	6.25%
Internal rate of return (for reference)	9.18%	12.17%

is 12.17%. (These IRR's can be computed using the trial-and-error method discussed previously.) The ARR is lower than the IRR for each project.

POST-AUDIT OF INVESTMENT PROJECTS

Management should subject all approved investment projects to a periodic, follow-up review, known as a **post-audit.** The purpose of a post-audit is to determine whether there are major variances between actual results and expected results. Post-audits should be conducted using the same capital budgeting techniques originally used when the project was approved. A project, which was approved based on a DCF model, for example, should not be post-audited using an ARR method. This would distort performance evaluation results, because the ARR method usually shows lower rates of return than the DCF models.

A post-audit should be considered as an integral part of the capital budgeting decision process. It provides management with valuable information for control and decision making purposes. Such information may enable management to (1) identify projects encountering difficulty and strengthen them or terminate them before losses become too great, (2) identify projects that surpass the initial expectations and reinforce investment in them to reap even greater profits, and (3) review the overall capital budgeting process to see if the acceptance criteria should be modified or replaced by new criteria. The simple existence of the post audit process forces managers to submit realistic proposals, since they know that the plans will be carefully scrutinized later and compared against actual results.

The Issue of Uncertainty

Capital investment projects entail risk, and the degree of risk differs from one project to another. When managers apply capital budgeting techniques to projects perceived to be too risky, they should consider: (1) using a relatively high required minimum rate of return, (2) adjusting downward the initially estimated cash inflows, (3) adjusting upward the initially estimated cash outflows, and/or (4) adjusting downward the initially estimated useful life of the project.

All these adjustments are designed to reduce the attractiveness of the project. If some or all of the hurdles are placed in front of the project and the project still passes them, perhaps the risk inherent in the project is worth taking. The ultimate decision depends on the risk attitude of the person making the final decision.

Sensitivity analysis is another way to deal with risk. Managers should use more than one estimate for each variable in the capital budgeting model: cash outflow, cash inflow, useful life, salvage value, and discount rate. In this way, before making the final capital budgeting decision, the manager will review different results for the same project ranging from the most optimistic to the most pessimistic. Managers may also want to apply multiple capital budgeting techniques to the same set of projections.

CAPITAL BUDGETING IN NONPROFIT ORGANIZATIONS

Nonprofit organizations, such as hospitals, universities, churches, and federal, state and local government agencies, use capital budgeting techniques. While governments can impose taxes to raise the funds needed for investment in any capital projects desired, there are economic, political and practical factors that limit the amount of taxes that can be imposed. Thus, well-organized government agencies implement control systems that insure the selection of the least costly projects for a given set of objectives.

The financial resources of other religious, educational, and health care organizations are obtained through contributions, government support and/or their own revenues generated. In order to maximize the value of the limited resources, these organizations select capital projects based on the cost-benefit approach.

One problematic issue in implementing capital budgeting techniques in nonprofit organizations is the discount rate to be used. Profit-oriented organizations may use their cost of capital as a hurdle rate, but the cost of capital for some nonprofit organizations may be quite low, such as a church that raises most of its needed resources through contributions. Accordingly, a nonprofit organization can use a discount rate that is two or three percent above the rate of return on federal government securities.

Some other nonprofit organizations may want to use the bank prime rate or the average interest rate on AA-rated corporate bonds, both of which are published regularly by banks, Moody's or Standard & Poor's. While DCF models are used by some federal agencies, such as the U.S. Postal Service, these models are less frequently used by state and local governments.

SUMMARY

Capital budgeting refers to the planning and financing of capital expenditures for long-term projects. Screening tools are available to select capital investment projects that meet a specified required rate of return. The discounted cash flow models are conceptually superior to other tools, such as the payback method and the accounting rate of return, that do not take the time value of money into consideration.

Under the NPV method, the present value of expected future cash inflows from a proposed project is computed using a desired minimum rate of return. This present value is then compared to the present value of the cash outflows for the project using the same desired rate of return. If the present value of cash inflows are equal to or greater than the present value of cash outflows, the project is accepted; otherwise, it is rejected.

Under the IRR method, the rate of return that makes the present value of cash inflows equal to the present value of cash outflows is calculated and compared to a minimum desired rate of return. If the project's IRR is equal to or greater than the required rate of return, the project is accepted; otherwise it is rejected.

The payback method measures the time, in years, during which a project will recover its original investment. This payback period is compared to a maximum desired payback period. If the project's payback period is equal or less than the desired payback period, the project is accepted. Otherwise, it is rejected.

The accounting rate of return is equal to the expected average annual increase in net income resulting from a project divided by the increase in investment caused by the project. If the project's ARR is equal to or greater than a minimum required rate of return, the project is accepted. Otherwise it is rejected.

Both the payback and the accounting rate of return methods, even though widely used because of their relative simplicity, do not take the time value of money into consideration, and this may lead to suboptimal economic decisions.

All accepted capital projects should be post-audited to identify those projects that need modification or elimination and those that need expansion or reinforcement. In implementing capital budgeting techniques, the risk of the projects should be considered and some sensitivity analysis may be required to assess the relative risk of each project. Capital budgeting techniques can, and should, be used by nonprofit organizations whenever possible.

BASIC CONCEPTS AND TERMS

Accounting rate of return
Annuity
Capital budgeting
Compound interest

Net present value method
Payback method
Payback period
Post-audit

Cost of capital

Cut-off rate

Differential approach

Discount rate

Discounted cash flow models

Hurdle rate

Internal rate of return

Interpolation

Preference tools

Present value

Required rate of return

Sensitivity analysis

Simple rate of return

Time-adjusted rate of return

Total approach

■ SELF-REVIEW PROBLEM

The Diagnostic Lab, Inc. is considering the purchase of a $115,000 piece of diagnostic equipment for its research laboratory to replace old equipment. The new equipment will save $30,000 a year in cash operating costs. Its estimated useful life is five years, and it will have a salvage value of $10,000 at the end of its useful life. The company uses the straight-line depreciation method.

If a decision is made to replace the old equipment, the old equipment can be sold now for $5,000. It will have no salvage value in five years. The new equipment will need a $2,000 overhaul at the end of the third year. The old equipment has a book value of $40,000, and a remaining useful life of five years. If the old equipment is kept, it will need an overhaul at the end of the second year that will cost $1,000.

Required:

Determine whether the old equipment should be replaced in each of the following individual cases. Assume all cash inflows occur at the end of each year. Ignore income taxes.

a. Use the NPV method. Assume a required rate of return of 12%.

b. Use the IRR method. Assume a target IRR is 13%.

c. Use the payback method. Assume a maximum payback period of three years.

d. Use the accounting rate of return method. Assume a minimum required ARR of 16%.

SOLUTION

Preliminary Calculations

Initial investment:

Purchase price of new equipment	$115,000
Proceeds from sale of old equipment	(5,000)
Net	$110,000

Annual cash inflows:

	Year				
	1	**2**	**3**	**4**	**5**
Savings in cash operating expenses	$30,000	$30,000	$30,000	$30,000	$30,000
Saving of overhaul expenses (old equipment)		1,000			
Overhaul expenses for new equipment			(2,000)		
New equipment salvage value					10,000
Annual cash inflows	$30,000	$31,000	$28,000	$30,000	$40,000

Annual depreciation expenses

$$= \frac{\text{Purchase price} - \text{Salvage value}}{\text{Useful life}}$$

For new equipment: $\dfrac{\$115,000 - \$10,000}{5 \text{ years}} = \$21,000$

For old equipment: $\dfrac{\$40,000 - 0}{5 \text{ years}} = \underline{\$8,000}$

Difference in depreciation: $\underline{\$13,000}$

(a) The NPV Method

Since the cash inflows are uneven, we must use present value factors from Table 13A-l to compute the present value of cash inflows as shown below:

Year	Cash Inflow	PV Factor at 12% (Table 13A-l)	PV of Cash Inflow
1	$ 30,000	.8929	$ 26,787
2	31,000	.7972	24,713
3	28,000	.7118	19,930
4	30,000	.6355	19,065
5	40,000	.5674	22,696
Total	$159,000		$113,191

Alternative NPV calculation: Since the expected reduction in cash operating expenses is even at $30,000 a year, the PV factor for an annuity of $1 (from Table 13A-2) may be used to discount this annual $30,000 to the present. The PV of the other three uneven cash inflows and outflows may be computed using factors from Table 13A-l, as follows:

		12%	
	Amount	Factor	PV
Cost reduction of $30,000 a year for 5 years	$30,000	× 3.6048 =	$108,144
Saving of old equipment overhaul expenses at end of year 2	1,000	× .7972 =	797
New equipment overhaul expenses at end of year 3	(2,000)	× .7118 =	(1,424)
New equipment salvage value at end of year 5	10,000	× .5674 =	5,674
Total			$113,191

NPV: $113,191 − $110,000 = $3,191

Since the NPV is positive, the old equipment should be replaced with the new equipment.

(b) The IRR Method

We need to derive, by trial and error, the rate that will make the PV of all the cash inflows exactly equal to the $110,000 initial investment. Since we already know from solution (a) above that a 12% discount rate results in a PV amount ($113,191) that is over $110,000, we could start with 14%.

		14%	
	Amount	Factor	PV
Cost reduction of $30,000 a year for 5 years	$30,000	× 3.4331 =	$102,993
Saving of old equipment overhaul expenses at end of year 2	1,000	× .7695 =	770
New equipment overhaul expenses at end of year 3	(2,000)	× .6750 =	(1,350)
New equipment salvage value at end of year 5	10,000	× .5194 =	5,194
Total			$107,607

Since the PV of cash inflows is less than $110,000, we know that the IRR must be lower than 14%. The true IRR for the new equipment must be somewhere between 12% and 14%. We derive that rate by interpolation as shown below:

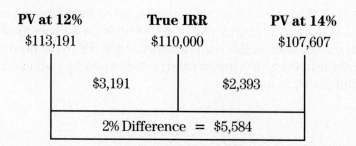

PV at 12%	True IRR	PV at 14%
$113,191	$110,000	$107,607
$3,191		$2,393
	2% Difference = $5,584	

$$\text{IRR} = 12\% + (\frac{\$3,191}{\$5,584} \times 2\%) = 13.14\%$$

or

$$\text{IRR} = 14\% - (\frac{\$2,393}{\$5,584} \times 2\%) = 13.14\%$$

Since the new equipment's IRR of 13.14% is greater than the required IRR of 13%, the old equipment should be replaced.

(c) The Payback Period

Since the cash inflows are uneven, we must reduce the initial investment by the cash inflow generated each year, until the entire initial investment is recovered:

Year	Net Cash Inflow	Remaining Unrecovered Investment
0	0	$110,000
1	$ 30,000	80,000
2	31,000	49,000
3	28,000	21,000
4	21,000	0

Since total cash inflow for year 4 is $30,000, and we only needed $21,000 to recover the remaining balance of the initial investment, the payback period is:

$$3 \text{ years} + (\frac{\$21,000}{\$30,000} \times 1 \text{ year}) = 3.7 \text{ years}$$

Since the actual payback period (3.7 years) is longer than the maximum payback period required (3 years), the old equipment should not be replaced.

(d) The ARR Method

We already calculated the incremental depreciation expense related to the new equipment that must be subtracted from the average annual increase in cash operating revenues.

Average annual incremental cash inflow (before depreciation)
= ($30,000 + $31,000 + $28,000 + $30,000 + $40,000) ÷ 5 years
= $31,800

ARR = (Incremental cash inflow − Incremental depreciation)
÷ Initial investment
= ($31,800 − $13,000) ÷ $110,000 = 17.1%

Since the calculated ARR (17.1%) is higher than the minimum required ARR (16%), the new equipment should be purchased to replace the old one.

APPENDIX 13A

Interest, Future Value, and Present Value

People prefer a dollar today to a dollar tomorrow, because the value of a dollar today is greater than the value of a dollar tomorrow. There is the uncertainty that the dollar will indeed be received tomorrow. There is inflation that lowers the purchasing power of the dollar. Also, a dollar received today can be deposited in a bank to earn interest at a certain rate per period. We can compute the interest in two ways, as explained below.

1. Simple Interest

Assume you have $5,000 available for three years. You have decided to deposit this at your bank at an interest rate of 10% per year. You will withdraw the annual interest income of $500 ($5,000 × 10%) at the end of each year. Your total interest income will be $1,500 for the three years. The total of the principal and the interest income at the end of the three-year period would be $6,500:

$$Total = The\ principal + Interest\ income$$
$$= \$5,000 + (\$500\ per\ year \times 3\ years)$$
$$= \$5,000 + \$1,500 = \$6,500$$

If you withdraw the interest annually, the principal of $5,000 will remain constant, and the annual interest of $500 will also remain constant. This is called simple interest.

2. Compound Interest

If you do not withdraw the interest income of $500 at the end of each year, and ask the bank to add it to the principal of $5,000, the bank will have to pay interest on the interest that is not withdrawn. This process of paying interest on interest is called compounding. The interest itself is called compound interest.

The future value of your account at the end of the three-year period will be $6,655, computed as follows:

Year	Principal at Beginning of Year	Interest at 10% Per Year	Balance (Principal + Interest) at End of Year
1	$5,000	(5,000 × .10) = $500	$5,500
2	5,500	(5,500 × .10) = $550	6,050
3	6,050	(6,050 × .10) = $605	6,655

The difference of $155 ($6,655 − $6,500) is the interest on the interest accumulated during the last two years. Interest can be compounded annually, quarterly, monthly, or daily.

Future Value of an Amount for n Periods

In general, future value (F) of a principal amount (P) for n periods at a given interest rate (i) may be computed as follows:

$$F_n = P(1 + i)^n$$

The future values from the above example are:

For n = 1 year F_1 = $5,000(1 + .1)^1$ = $5,500
For n = 2 years F_2 = $5,000(1 + .1)^2$ = $6,050
For n = 3 years F_3 = $5,000(1 + .1)^3$ = $6,655

These are the same answers obtained under compound interest above. There are tables, called future value tables, that provide future values of $1 to be received after any number of periods at different interest rates. All we have to do to obtain the future value of any amount after a given period at a rate is multiply the future value of $1 for that period and rate as given in the table by the amount. Table 13A-3 provides these future values. We can easily calculate these future values using calculators or computers.

Future Value of an Annuity of an Amount for n Periods

Assume that you want to open a savings account in which you will deposit $1,000 at the beginning of each year for five years to earn interest at 10% per year compounded annually. How much would the balance in your account be after five years? This is an example of the future value of a series of annual payments, called an **annuity,** for n periods at a given interest rate.

We know that total payments, excluding compound interest, amount to $5,000 (5 payments × $1,000). The first deposit will remain for five years, the second will remain for four years, the third for three years, the fourth for two years, and the fifth deposit will remain only for one year.

Thus, the balance in the account will equal the future value of each of those five deposits added together, as follows:

$1,000(1.1)^5$ + $1,000(1.1)^4$ + $1,000(1.1)^3$ + $1,000(1.1)^2$ + $1,000(1.1)^1$ = $6,105.10

In general, the future value of an annuity (F_n) is computed as follows:

$$F_n = P(1+i)^n + P(1+i)^{n-1} + P(1+i)^{n-2} \ldots + P(1+i)^1$$

There are tables that provide the future value of an annuity of $1 for any number of periods at different interest rates. Table 13A-4 shows these future values. To compute the future value in the above example, we find that the factor in the future value table of an annuity of $1 (Table 13A-4) under 10% for five years is 6.10510. This factor of 6.10510 multiplied by the annuity of $1,000 results in $6,105.10.

Present Value

Present value is the value, in today's dollars, of a sum of money to be received one, two, or any number of periods from now. The present value depends on the future value, the date of expected receipt of a sum of money, and the interest rate.

The higher the degree of uncertainty and the higher the expected rate of inflation in the future, the higher the interest rate to be used. Obviously, the higher the amount to be received in the future, the higher the present value. However, the longer into the future the money will be received, and the higher the interest rate, the lower the present value. This occurs because present value is the inverse of future value.

Present Value of $1 To Be Received After n Periods

The PV of $1 to be received after n periods equals one divided by the future value of $1 after n periods given the same interest rate. If the future value of $1 after three years at 10% is 1.1^3, the present value of $1 to be received three years from now discounted at 10% is $1/1.1^3$.

From the compound interest example, we know that the future value of $5,000 after three years at 10% will be $6,655. Assume that we do not know the principal amount (P) of $5,000, which is the present value of $6,655. Can we compute it? Yes. Since F_3 = P × 1.1^3 = $6,655. P = $6,655/1.1^3 = $5,000.

In general, we obtain present value as follows:

$$P = \frac{F_n}{(1 + i)^n}$$

Using the compound interest example, we can compute the present value for each of the three years as follows:

Present value of $5,500 to be received after one year
   = $5,500/1.1^1$ = $5,000

Present value of $6,050 to be received after two years
   = $6,050/1.1^2$ = $5,000

Present value of $6,655 to be received after three years
   = $6,655/1.1^3$ = $5,000

The present value is the same for each of the above cases, because they refer to the same example we used earlier. There are present value tables that provide the present value of $1 to be received after n periods using a variety of interest rates. Table 13A-1 is an example of such tables.

To obtain the present value of any future amount, multiply the factor from Table 13A-1 by that future amount. Assume that you will receive $100,000 after 20 years from now. What is the present value of that $100,000 at a discount rate of 8% per year? The answer is $21,450 (= $100,000 × .2145).

Present Value of an Annuity of $1 for n Periods

The present value of an annuity of $1 for n periods is the inverse of the future value of an annuity of $1 for n periods, given the same interest rate. Assume that, starting a year from now, you will receive $1,000 a year for five years. What is the present value of this series of cash inflows assuming a discount rate of 10%?

We must obtain the present value of each future value using the particular period and rate. From Table 13A-1, we obtain the PV factors and calculate the following:

At End of Year	Future Amount	10% Factor (Table 13A-1)	Present Value
1	$1,000	.9091	$ 909.1
2	1,000	.8264	826.4
3	1,000	.7513	751.3
4	1,000	.6830	683.0
5	1,000	.6209	620.9
Total		3.7907	$3,790.7

There are tables that provide the present value of an annuity of cash inflow of $1. These tables, such as Table 13A-2, list present value of an ordinary annuity of $1. **Ordinary annuity** means that the payment is received at the end of the period, not at the beginning. It is also called **annuity in arrears.**

For present value calculations, we multiply the factor from Table 13A-2 by the amount of the annuity, $1,000 in the above example, as follows:

Present value $= \$1,000 \times 3.7908 = \$3,790.80$

The factor of 3.7908 is from Table 13A-2, under 10% for five periods.

TABLE 13A-1 Present Value of $1

Year	2%	4%	6%	8%	10%	12%	14%	16%	18%	20%	22%	24%	26%	28%	30%	32%	34%	36%	38%	40%
1	0.9804	0.9615	0.9434	0.9259	0.9091	0.8929	0.8772	0.8621	0.8475	0.8333	0.8197	0.8065	0.7937	0.7812	0.7692	0.7576	0.7463	0.7353	0.7246	0.7143
2	0.9612	0.9246	0.8900	0.8573	0.8264	0.7972	0.7695	0.7432	0.7182	0.6944	0.6719	0.6504	0.6299	0.6104	0.5917	0.5739	0.5569	0.5407	0.5251	0.5102
3	0.9423	0.8890	0.8396	0.7938	0.7513	0.7118	0.6750	0.6407	0.6086	0.5787	0.5507	0.5245	0.4999	0.4768	0.4552	0.4348	0.4156	0.3975	0.3805	0.3644
4	0.9238	0.8548	0.7921	0.7350	0.6830	0.6355	0.5921	0.5523	0.5158	0.4823	0.4514	0.4230	0.3968	0.3725	0.3501	0.3294	0.3102	0.2923	0.2757	0.2603
5	0.9057	0.8219	0.7473	0.6806	0.6209	0.5674	0.5194	0.4761	0.4371	0.4019	0.3700	0.3411	0.3149	0.2910	0.2693	0.2495	0.2315	0.2149	0.1998	0.1859
6	0.8880	0.7903	0.7050	0.6302	0.5645	0.5066	0.4556	0.4104	0.3704	0.3349	0.3033	0.2751	0.2499	0.2274	0.2072	0.1890	0.1727	0.1580	0.1448	0.1328
7	0.8706	0.7599	0.6651	0.5835	0.5132	0.4523	0.3996	0.3538	0.3139	0.2791	0.2486	0.2218	0.1983	0.1776	0.1594	0.1432	0.1289	0.1162	0.1049	0.0949
8	0.8535	0.7307	0.6274	0.5403	0.4665	0.4039	0.3506	0.3050	0.2660	0.2326	0.2038	0.1789	0.1574	0.1388	0.1226	0.1085	0.0962	0.0854	0.0760	0.0678
9	0.8368	0.7026	0.5919	0.5002	0.4241	0.3606	0.3075	0.2630	0.2255	0.1938	0.1670	0.1443	0.1249	0.1084	0.0943	0.0822	0.0718	0.0628	0.0551	0.0484
10	0.8203	0.6756	0.5584	0.4632	0.3855	0.3220	0.2697	0.2267	0.1911	0.1615	0.1369	0.1164	0.0992	0.0847	0.0725	0.0623	0.0536	0.0462	0.0399	0.0346
11	0.8043	0.6496	0.5268	0.4289	0.3505	0.2875	0.2366	0.1954	0.1619	0.1346	0.1122	0.0938	0.0787	0.0662	0.0558	0.0472	0.0400	0.0340	0.0289	0.0247
12	0.7885	0.6246	0.4970	0.3971	0.3186	0.2567	0.2076	0.1685	0.1372	0.1122	0.0920	0.0757	0.0625	0.0517	0.0429	0.0357	0.0298	0.0250	0.0210	0.0176
13	0.7730	0.6006	0.4688	0.3677	0.2897	0.2292	0.1821	0.1452	0.1163	0.0935	0.0754	0.0610	0.0496	0.0404	0.0330	0.0271	0.0223	0.0184	0.0152	0.0126
14	0.7579	0.5775	0.4423	0.3405	0.2633	0.2046	0.1597	0.1252	0.0985	0.0779	0.0618	0.0492	0.0393	0.0316	0.0254	0.0205	0.0166	0.0135	0.0110	0.0090
15	0.7430	0.5553	0.4173	0.3152	0.2394	0.1827	0.1401	0.1079	0.0835	0.0649	0.0507	0.0397	0.0312	0.0247	0.0195	0.0155	0.0124	0.0099	0.0080	0.0064
16	0.7284	0.5339	0.3936	0.2919	0.2176	0.1631	0.1229	0.0930	0.0708	0.0541	0.0415	0.0320	0.0248	0.0193	0.0150	0.0118	0.0093	0.0073	0.0058	0.0046
17	0.7142	0.5134	0.3714	0.2703	0.1978	0.1456	0.1078	0.0802	0.0600	0.0451	0.0340	0.0258	0.0197	0.0150	0.0116	0.0089	0.0069	0.0054	0.0042	0.0033
18	0.7002	0.4936	0.3503	0.2502	0.1799	0.1300	0.0946	0.0691	0.0508	0.0376	0.0279	0.0208	0.0156	0.0118	0.0089	0.0068	0.0052	0.0039	0.0030	0.0023
19	0.6864	0.4746	0.3305	0.2317	0.1635	0.1161	0.0829	0.0596	0.0431	0.0313	0.0229	0.0168	0.0124	0.0092	0.0068	0.0051	0.0038	0.0029	0.0022	0.0017
20	0.6730	0.4564	0.3118	0.2145	0.1486	0.1037	0.0728	0.0514	0.0365	0.0261	0.0187	0.0135	0.0098	0.0072	0.0053	0.0039	0.0029	0.0021	0.0016	0.0012
21	0.6598	0.4388	0.2942	0.1987	0.1351	0.0926	0.0638	0.0443	0.0309	0.0217	0.0154	0.0109	0.0078	0.0056	0.0040	0.0029	0.0021	0.0016	0.0012	0.0009
22	0.6468	0.4220	0.2775	0.1839	0.1228	0.0826	0.0560	0.0382	0.0262	0.0181	0.0126	0.0088	0.0062	0.0044	0.0031	0.0022	0.0016	0.0012	0.0008	0.0006
23	0.6342	0.4057	0.2618	0.1703	0.1117	0.0738	0.0491	0.0329	0.0222	0.0151	0.0103	0.0071	0.0049	0.0034	0.0024	0.0017	0.0012	0.0008	0.0006	0.0004
24	0.6217	0.3901	0.2470	0.1577	0.1015	0.0659	0.0431	0.0284	0.0188	0.0126	0.0085	0.0057	0.0039	0.0027	0.0018	0.0013	0.0009	0.0006	0.0004	0.0003
25	0.6095	0.3751	0.2330	0.1460	0.0923	0.0588	0.0378	0.0245	0.0160	0.0105	0.0069	0.0046	0.0031	0.0021	0.0014	0.0010	0.0007	0.0005	0.0003	0.0002

TABLE 13A-2 Present Value of An Ordinary Annuity of $1

Year	2%	4%	6%	8%	10%	12%	14%	16%	18%	20%	22%	24%	26%	28%	30%	32%	34%	36%	38%	40%
1	0.9804	0.9615	0.9434	0.9259	0.9091	0.8929	0.8772	0.8621	0.8475	0.8333	0.8197	0.8065	0.7937	0.7812	0.7692	0.7576	0.7463	0.7353	0.7246	0.7143
2	1.9416	1.8861	1.8334	1.7833	1.7355	1.6901	1.6467	1.6052	1.5656	1.5278	1.4915	1.4568	1.4235	1.3916	1.3609	1.3315	1.3032	1.2760	1.2497	1.2245
3	2.8839	2.7751	2.6730	2.5771	2.4869	2.4018	2.3216	2.2459	2.1743	2.1065	2.0422	1.9813	1.9234	1.8684	1.8161	1.7663	1.7188	1.6735	1.6302	1.5889
4	3.8077	3.6299	3.4651	3.3121	3.1699	3.0373	2.9137	2.7982	2.6901	2.5887	2.4936	2.4043	2.3202	2.2410	2.1662	2.0957	2.0290	1.9658	1.9060	1.8492
5	4.7135	4.4518	4.2124	3.9927	3.7908	3.6048	3.4331	3.2743	3.1272	2.9906	2.8636	2.7454	2.6351	2.5320	2.4356	2.3452	2.2604	2.1807	2.1058	2.0352
6	5.6014	5.2421	4.9173	4.6229	4.3553	4.1114	3.8887	3.6847	3.4976	3.3255	3.1669	3.0205	2.8850	2.7594	2.6427	2.5342	2.4331	2.3388	2.2506	2.1680
7	6.4720	6.0021	5.5824	5.2064	4.8684	4.5638	4.2883	4.0386	3.8115	3.6046	3.4155	3.2423	3.0833	2.9370	2.8021	2.6775	2.5620	2.4550	2.3555	2.2628
8	7.3255	6.7327	6.2098	5.7466	5.3349	4.9676	4.6389	4.3436	4.0776	3.8372	3.6193	3.4212	3.2407	3.0758	2.9247	2.7860	2.6582	2.5404	2.4315	2.3306
9	8.1622	7.4353	6.8017	6.2469	5.7590	5.3282	4.9464	4.6065	4.3030	4.0310	3.7863	3.5655	3.3657	3.1842	3.0190	2.8681	2.7300	2.6033	2.4866	2.3790
10	8.9826	8.1109	7.3601	6.7101	6.1446	5.6502	5.2161	4.8332	4.4941	4.1925	3.9232	3.6819	3.4648	3.2689	3.0915	2.9304	2.7836	2.6495	2.5265	2.4136.
11	9.7868	8.7605	7.8869	7.1390	6.4951	5.9377	5.4527	5.0286	4.6560	4.3271	4.0354	3.7757	3.5435	3.3351	3.1473	2.9776	2.8236	2.6834	2.5555	2.4383
12	10.575	9.3851	8.3838	7.5361	6.8137	6.1944	5.6603	5.1971	4.7932	4.4392	4.1274	3.8514	3.6059	3.3868	3.1903	3.0133	2.8534	2.7084	2.5764	2.4559
13	11.348	9.9856	8.8527	7.9038	7.1034	6.4235	5.8424	5.3423	4.9095	4.5327	4.2028	3.9124	3.6555	3.4272	3.2233	3.0404	2.8757	2.7268	2.5916	2.4685
14	12.106	10.563	9.2950	8.2442	7.3667	6.6282	6.0021	5.4675	5.0081	4.6106	4.2646	3.9616	3.6949	3.4587	3.2487	3.0609	2.8923	2.7403	2.6026	2.4775
15	12.849	11.118	9.7122	8.5595	7.6061	6.8109	6.1422	5.5755	5.0916	4.6755	4.3152	4.0013	3.7261	3.4834	3.2682	3.0764	2.9047	2.7502	2.6106	2.4839
16	13.578	11.652	10.106	8.8514	7.8237	6.9740	6.2651	5.6685	5.1624	4.7296	4.3567	4.0333	3.7509	3.5026	3.2832	3.0882	2.9140	2.7575	2.6164	2.4885
17	14.292	12.166	10.477	9.1216	8.0216	7.1196	6.3729	5.7487	5.2223	4.7746	4.3908	4.0591	3.7705	3.5177	3.2948	3.0971	2.9209	2.7629	2.6206	2.4918
18	14.992	12.659	10.828	9.3719	8.2014	7.2497	6.4674	5.8178	5.2732	4.8122	4.4187	4.0799	3.7861	3.5294	3.3037	3.1039	2.9260	2.7668	2.6236	2.4941
19	15.678	13.134	11.158	9.6036	8.3649	7.3658	6.5504	5.8775	5.3162	4.8435	4.4415	4.0967	3.7985	3.5386	3.3105	3.1090	2.9299	2.7697	2.6258	2.4958
20	16.351	13.590	11.470	9.8181	8.5136	7.4694	6.6231	5.9288	5.3527	4.8696	4.4603	4.1103	3.8083	3.5458	3.3158	3.1129	2.9327	2.7718	2.6274	2.4970
21	17.011	14.029	11.764	10.017	8.6487	7.5620	6.6870	5.9731	5.3837	4.8913	4.4756	4.1212	3.8161	3.5514	3.3198	3.1158	2.9349	2.7734	2.6285	2.4979
22	17.658	14.451	12.042	10.201	8.7715	7.6446	6.7429	6.0113	5.4099	4.9094	4.4882	4.1300	3.8223	3.5558	3.3230	3.1180	2.9365	2.7746	2.6294	2.4985
23	18.292	14.857	12.303	10.371	8.8832	7.7184	6.7921	6.0442	5.4321	4.9245	4.4985	4.1371	3.8273	3.5592	3.3254	3.1197	2.9377	2.7754	2.6300	2.4989
24	18.914	15.247	12.550	10.529	8.9847	7.7843	6.8351	6.0726	5.4509	4.9371	4.5070	4.1428	3.8312	3.5619	3.3272	3.1210	2.9386	2.7760	2.6304	2.4992
25	19.523	15.622	12.783	10.675	9.0770	7.8431	6.8729	6.0971	5.4669	4.9476	4.5139	4.1474	3.8342	3.5640	3.3286	3.1220	2.9392	2.7765	2.6307	2.4994

TABLE 13A-3 Future Value of $1

Year	2%	4%	6%	8%	10%	12%	14%	16%	18%	20%	22%	24%	26%	28%	30%	32%	34%	36%	38%	40%
1	1.0200	1.0400	1.0600	1.0800	1.1000	1.1200	1.1400	1.1600	1.1800	1.2000	1.2200	1.2400	1.2600	1.2800	1.3000	1.3200	1.3400	1.3600	1.3800	1.4000
2	1.0404	1.0816	1.1236	1.1664	1.2100	1.2544	1.2996	1.3456	1.3924	1.4400	1.4884	1.5376	1.5876	1.6384	1.6900	1.7424	1.7956	1.8496	1.9044	1.9600
3	1.0612	1.1249	1.1910	1.2597	1.3310	1.4049	1.4815	1.5609	1.6430	1.7280	1.8158	1.9066	2.0004	2.0972	2.1970	2.3000	2.4061	2.5155	2.6281	2.7440
4	1.0824	1.1699	1.2625	1.3605	1.4641	1.5735	1.6890	1.8106	1.9388	2.0736	2.2153	2.3642	2.5205	2.6844	2.8561	3.0360	3.2242	3.4210	3.6267	3.8416
5	1.1041	1.2167	1.3382	1.4693	1.6105	1.7623	1.9254	2.1003	2.2878	2.4883	2.7027	2.9316	3.1758	3.4360	3.7129	4.0075	4.3204	4.6526	5.0049	5.3782
6	1.1262	1.2653	1.4185	1.5869	1.7716	1.9738	2.1950	2.4364	2.6996	2.9860	3.2973	3.6352	4.0015	4.3980	4.8268	5.2899	5.7893	6.3275	6.9068	7.5295
7	1.1487	1.3159	1.5036	1.7138	1.9487	2.2107	2.5023	2.8262	3.1855	3.5832	4.0227	4.5077	5.0419	5.6295	6.2749	6.9826	7.7577	8.6054	9.5313	10.541
8	1.1717	1.3686	1.5938	1.8509	2.1436	2.4760	2.8526	3.2784	3.7589	4.2998	4.9077	5.5895	6.3528	7.2058	8.1573	9.2170	10.395	11.703	13.153	14.758
9	1.1951	1.4233	1.6895	1.9990	2.3579	2.7731	3.2519	3.8030	4.4355	5.1598	5.9874	6.9310	8.0045	9.2234	10.604	12.166	13.930	15.917	18.151	20.661
10	1.2190	1.4802	1.7908	2.1589	2.5937	3.1058	3.7072	4.4114	5.2338	6.1917	7.3046	8.5944	10.086	11.806	13.786	16.060	18.666	21.647	25.049	28.925
11	1.2434	1.5395	1.8983	2.3316	2.8531	3.4785	4.2262	5.1173	6.1759	7.4301	8.9117	10.657	12.708	15.112	17.922	21.199	25.012	29.439	34.568	40.496
12	1.2682	1.6010	2.0122	2.5182	3.1384	3.8960	4.8179	5.9360	7.2876	8.9161	10.872	13.215	16.012	19.343	23.298	27.983	33.516	40.037	47.703	56.694
13	1.2936	1.6651	2.1329	2.7196	3.4523	4.3635	5.4924	6.8858	8.5994	10.699	13.264	16.386	20.175	24.759	30.288	36.937	44.912	54.451	65.831	79.371
14	1.3195	1.7317	2.2609	2.9372	3.7975	4.8871	6.2613	7.9875	10.147	12.839	16.182	20.319	25.421	31.691	39.374	48.757	60.182	74.053	90.846	111.12
15	1.3459	1.8009	2.3966	3.1722	4.1772	5.4736	7.1379	9.2655	11.974	15.407	19.742	25.196	32.030	40.565	51.186	64.359	80.644	100.71	125.37	155.57
16	1.3728	1.8730	2.5404	3.4259	4.5950	6.1304	8.1372	10.748	14.129	18.488	24.086	31.243	40.358	51.923	66.542	84.954	108.06	136.97	173.01	217.80
17	1.4002	1.9479	2.6928	3.7000	5.0545	6.8660	9.2765	12.468	16.672	22.186	29.384	38.741	50.851	66.461	86.504	112.14	144.80	186.28	238.75	304.91
18	1.4282	2.0258	2.8543	3.9960	5.5599	7.6900	10.575	14.463	19.673	26.623	35.849	48.039	64.072	85.071	112.46	148.02	194.04	253.34	329.48	426.88
19	1.4568	2.1068	3.0256	4.3157	6.1159	8.6128	12.056	16.777	23.214	31.948	43.736	59.568	80.731	108.89	146.19	195.39	260.01	344.54	454.68	597.63
20	1.4859	2.1911	3.2071	4.6610	6.7275	9.6463	13.743	19.461	27.393	38.338	53.358	73.864	101.72	139.38	190.05	257.92	348.41	468.57	627.45	836.68
21	1.5157	2.2788	3.3996	5.0338	7.4002	10.804	15.668	22.574	32.324	46.005	65.096	91.592	128.17	178.41	247.06	340.45	466.88	637.26	865.89	1171.4
22	1.5460	2.3699	3.6035	5.4365	8.1403	12.100	17.861	26.186	38.142	55.206	79.418	113.57	161.49	228.36	321.18	449.39	625.61	866.67	1194.9	1639.9
23	1.5769	2.4647	3.8197	5.8715	8.9543	13.552	20.362	30.376	45.008	66.247	96.889	140.83	203.48	292.30	417.54	593.20	838.32	1178.7	1649.0	2295.9
24	1.6084	2.5633	4.0489	6.3412	9.8497	15.179	23.212	35.236	53.109	79.497	118.21	174.63	256.39	374.14	542.80	783.02	1123.4	1603.0	2275.6	3214.2
25	1.6406	2.6658	4.2919	6.8485	10.835	17.000	26.462	40.874	62.669	95.396	144.21	216.54	323.05	478.90	705.64	1033.6	1505.3	2180.1	3140.3	4499.9

TABLE 13A-4 Future Value of An Ordinary Annuity of $1

Year	2%	4%	6%	8%	10%	12%	14%	16%	18%	20%	22%	24%	26%	28%	30%	32%	34%	36%	38%	40%
1	1.0000	1.0000	1.0000	1.0000	1.0000	1.0000	1.0000	1.0000	1.0000	1.0000	1.0000	1.0000	1.0000	1.0000	1.0000	1.0000	1.0000	1.0000	1.0000	1.0000
2	2.0200	2.0400	2.0600	2.0800	2.1000	2.1200	2.1400	2.1600	2.1800	2.2000	2.2200	2.2400	2.2600	2.2800	2.3000	2.3200	2.3400	2.3600	2.3800	2.4000
3	3.0604	3.1216	3.1836	3.2464	3.3100	3.3744	3.4396	3.5056	3.5724	3.6400	3.7084	3.7776	3.8476	3.9184	3.9900	4.0624	4.1356	4.2096	4.2844	4.3600
4	4.1216	4.2465	4.3746	4.5061	4.6410	4.7793	4.9211	5.0665	5.2154	5.3680	5.5242	5.6842	5.8480	6.0156	6.1870	6.3624	6.5417	6.7251	6.9125	7.1040
5	5.2040	5.4163	5.6371	5.8666	6.1051	6.3528	6.6101	6.8771	7.1542	7.4416	7.7396	8.0484	8.3684	8.6999	9.0431	9.3983	9.7659	10.146	10.539	10.946
6	6.3081	6.6330	6.9753	7.3359	7.7156	8.1152	8.5355	8.9775	9.4420	9.9299	10.442	10.980	11.544	12.136	12.756	13.406	14.086	14.799	15.544	16.324
7	7.4343	7.8983	8.3938	8.9228	9.4872	10.089	10.730	11.414	12.142	12.916	13.740	14.615	15.546	16.534	17.583	18.696	19.876	21.126	22.451	23.853
8	8.5830	9.2142	9.8975	10.637	11.436	12.300	13.233	14.240	15.327	16.499	17.762	19.123	20.588	22.163	23.858	25.678	27.633	29.732	31.982	34.395
9	9.7546	10.583	11.491	12.488	13.579	14.776	16.085	17.519	19.086	20.799	22.670	24.712	26.940	29.369	32.015	34.895	38.029	41.435	45.135	49.153
10	10.950	12.006	13.181	14.487	15.937	17.549	19.337	21.321	23.521	25.959	28.657	31.643	34.945	38.593	42.619	47.062	51.958	57.352	63.287	69.814
11	12.169	13.486	14.972	16.645	18.531	20.655	23.045	25.733	28.755	32.150	35.962	40.238	45.031	50.398	56.405	63.122	70.624	78.998	88.336	98.739
12	13.412	15.026	16.870	18.977	21.384	24.133	27.271	30.850	34.931	39.581	44.874	50.895	57.739	65.510	74.327	84.320	95.637	108.44	122.90	139.23
13	14.680	16.627	18.882	21.495	24.523	28.029	32.089	36.786	42.219	48.497	55.746	64.110	73.751	84.853	97.625	112.30	129.15	148.47	170.61	195.93
14	15.974	18.292	21.015	24.215	27.975	32.393	37.581	43.672	50.818	59.196	69.010	80.496	93.926	109.61	127.91	149.24	174.06	202.93	236.44	275.30
15	17.293	20.024	23.276	27.152	31.772	37.280	43.842	51.660	60.965	72.035	85.192	100.82	119.35	141.30	167.29	198.00	234.25	276.98	327.28	386.42
16	18.639	21.825	25.673	30.324	35.950	42.753	50.980	60.925	72.939	87.442	104.93	126.01	151.38	181.87	218.47	262.36	314.89	377.69	452.65	541.99
17	20.012	23.698	28.213	33.750	40.545	48.884	59.118	71.673	87.068	105.93	129.02	157.25	191.73	233.79	285.01	347.31	422.95	514.66	625.66	759.78
18	21.412	25.645	30.906	37.450	45.599	55.750	68.394	84.141	103.74	128.12	158.40	195.99	242.59	300.25	371.52	459.45	567.76	700.94	864.41	1064.7
19	22.841	27.671	33.760	41.446	51.159	63.440	78.969	98.603	123.41	154.74	194.25	244.03	306.66	385.32	483.97	607.47	761.80	954.28	1193.9	1491.6
20	24.297	29.778	36.786	45.762	57.275	72.052	91.025	115.38	146.63	186.69	237.99	303.60	387.39	494.21	630.17	802.86	1021.8	1298.8	1648.6	2089.2
21	25.783	31.969	39.993	50.423	64.002	81.699	104.77	134.84	174.02	225.03	291.35	377.46	489.11	633.59	820.22	1060.8	1370.2	1767.4	2276.0	2925.9
22	27.299	34.248	43.392	55.457	71.403	92.503	120.44	157.41	206.34	271.03	356.44	469.06	617.28	812.00	1067.3	1401.2	1837.1	2404.7	3141.9	4097.2
23	28.845	36.618	46.996	60.893	79.543	104.60	138.30	183.60	244.49	326.24	435.86	582.63	778.77	1040.4	1388.5	1850.6	2462.7	3271.3	4336.8	5737.1
24	30.422	39.083	50.816	66.765	88.497	118.16	158.66	213.98	289.49	392.48	532.75	723.46	982.25	1332.7	1806.0	2443.8	3301.0	4450.0	5985.8	8033.0
25	32.030	41.646	54.865	73.106	98.347	133.33	181.87	249.21	342.60	471.98	650.96	898.09	1238.6	1706.8	2348.8	3226.8	4424.4	6053.0	8261.4	11247.2

■ REVIEW QUESTIONS

13-1 Why are capital budgeting decisions considered long term?

13-2 Why are long-term investments considered riskier than short-term investments?

13-3 Is the return on long-term investments expected to be higher than the return on short-term investments? Why or why not?

13-4 What are the two key elements of discounted cash flow models?

13-5 The net present value of a project is equal to zero. Should management accept or reject the project? Why or why not?

13-6 "A positive net present value is an additional safety margin over and above the required return." Do you agree? Explain.

13-7 Why do some managers prefer a differential approach to a total approach in computing net present value?

13-8 How does a high discount rate affect the net present value analysis?

13-9 In order to increase profits, firms must find projects that will earn more than the cost of capital. The discount rate chosen for capital investment projects, however, is usually close to the cost of capital. Why?

13-10 Assume that a trial-and-error approach is used to determine the internal rate of return for a capital investment project. If the present value of cash inflows is higher than the present value of cash outflows, do you have to select a higher discount rate or a lower one? Explain.

13-11 Why do some managers prefer the net present value method to the internal rate of return method? Give three reasons.

13-12 Why is the internal rate of return method more widely used in practice, despite some advantages of the net present value method?

13-13 Managers make certain simplifying assumptions regarding the use of the two discounted cashflow methods, the net present value method and the internal rate of return method. What are the three primary assumptions?

13-14 In addition to disregarding the time value of money, the payback period also ignores some cash inflows. What cash inflows are ignored?

13-15 Both the payback period and the accounting rate of return methods do not involve discounted cash flows. How are the two dissimilar? Give two examples.

13-16 What would happen if a project, which was approved based on a discounted cashflow method, is post-audited using an accounting rate of return method?

13-17 What exactly would management gain from a post-audit of a capital budgeting project that has already been undertaken?

13-18   What should management consider doing when they apply capital budgeting techniques to a capital investment project that is deemed very risky?

13-19   How is sensitivity analysis related to the evaluation of a high-risk capital investment project?

13-20   What is the most problematic issue in implementing capital budgeting techniques in nonprofit organizations?

🌐 INTERNET PROJECT

Web 13-1:

Websites: www.disney.com
www.dreamworks.com

The websites listed above represent two famous companies. Search the sites for information on their product and operating characteristics.

Required:

1.   Find a recent investment project each company has undertaken. Can you construct a capital investment evaluation model for each company? Explain the results.

2.   Consider NPV and IRR for each company. Based on the website information, determine which method is easier to apply. Why?

■ EXERCISES

E13-1   Net Present Value; Internal Rate of Return

The following relates to either the net present value (NPV) method or the internal rate of return (IRR) method:

a.   The required rate of return is used in computation.
b.   In the capital investment decision making, the desired rate of return is used for comparison.
c.   A dollar amount is available for evaluation of competing projects.
d.   There is flexibility in adjusting the discount rate every few years.
e.   It requires a trial-and-error procedure.
f.   The discount rate can be different during the project life.
g.   Managers who like to think in terms of rates would prefer this.

Required:

Indicate whether the statement refers to NPV or IRR.

E13-2 Present Value

Each of the following situations refers to the computation of present value. Treat each situation as independent of others.

1. Patti Zamora wants to invest a lump-sum amount in a money market fund that yields a fixed return so that the amount will reach $7,000 at the end of the fourth year when her daughter goes to college. How much should Zamora invest now?

    a. Assume the fund pays an annual interest of 8%.

    b. Assume the fund pays an annual interest of 12%.

2. Management of GTX, Inc. has two investment projects. Investment P generates smaller amounts of cash flows in early years and larger amounts in later years. Actual cash inflows from investment P are: $4,000 in year 1, $5,000 in year 2, $8,000 in year 3, and $13,000 in year 4. Investment Q generates larger amounts of cash flows in early years and smaller amounts in later years. Actual cash inflows from investment Q are: $13,000 in year 1, $8,000 in year 2, $5,000 in year 3, and $4,000 in year 4. The required rate of return is 16%. Compute the total present value of investment P and the total present value of investment Q.

E13-3 Future Value; Present Value

Each of the following situations refers to the computation of present value or future value. Treat each situation independently.

1. It is January 1, Year 1. Eddie has just won a lottery, which allows the winner to take a lump sum of $200,000 now, or receive $18,000 at the end of each year for 20 years plus a lump sum of $70,000 at the end of Year 20. Eddie can earn 10% per year on his investment. Which is better?

2. Max's small engineering firm uses a robot in its operations. Robots-R-Us is selling a 6-year robot maintenance contract that would save $8,000 each year in maintenance costs. What would be the maximum purchase price of the maintenance contract Max would be willing to pay if Max requires a return of:

    a. 14%.

    b. 18%.

3. Joe Baker has just won this week's Lotto jackpot of $6.4 million. The jackpot is expected to pay $320,000 per year for 20 years. Baker can earn 10% on his investment. What is the present value of Baker's winnings?

4. JPM, Inc. has just reported annual earnings of $1.4 million for the last fiscal year. JPM wants to set aside a certain portion of its earnings so that it will be able to retire a long-term debt of $800,000 (principal plus accumulated interest) after 5 years. How much should JPM set aside now? Assume that the company can earn the following rates of return on its investments:

    a. 8%.

    b. 12%.

E13-4   Net Present Value; Internal Rate of Return

1. LPH, Inc. earns a 12% return on its investments. The company is considering the installation of an air purification system in one of its plants. The system costs $74,000 now, but will save $12,000 per year in terms of lower medical insurance premiums and reduced machine malfunction caused by dust in the air. The system will have a useful life of 12 years. Should the company install the system? Use the system's net present value as the single decision making criterion.

2. Hornblower Cruise Company is considering the purchase of a new boat which will be used for dinner cruise services around Marina Del Rey. The cruise services are estimated to generate cash inflows of $40,178 per year. The new boat costs $230,000 now and will have a useful life of 14 years. The company's cost of capital is 14%. Compute the internal rate of return for the investment in the boat. Should the company buy the boat?

3. Assume that the above Hornblower Cruise Company is facing the same situation, except that it has no information on annual cash inflows. What should be the annual cash inflows to earn a 14% annual return on the investment in the new boat?

E13-5   Net Present Value

Ken Gerg has been operating a travel services company for several years. Ellen Johnson invested $15,000 in the company's new tour business at the beginning of Year 3. Johnson received $500 at the end of each of the following three years. At the end of Year 5, Johnson wanted to withdraw her share so that she could pursue other investment opportunities. Gerg paid $18,000 to her. She believes that she usually earns 12% on her investments.

Required:

Did Johnson earn the usual return of 12% on the investment in the tour business? Use the net present value method to determine the result.

E13-6   Net Present Value; Internal Rate of Return and Interpolation

Fanta Cola, Inc. is considering the purchase and installation of new bottling equipment in its Cerritos bottling plant. The new equipment costs $92,778. The company estimates that the new equipment will save $20,000 in annual operating costs, wil last 8 years, and will have zero salvage value.

Required:

1. Compute the internal rate of return for the investment in the new equipment.
2. Compute the net present value for the investment in the new equipment, using a discount rate of 12%.

3. Compute the net present value for the above investment, using a discount rate of 8%.

4. Assume that the new equipment will save only $18,000 per year. Other conditions remain unchanged. What is the internal rate of return now? Use interpolation if needed.

E13-7   Amount of Cash Flows; Interpolated Internal Rate of Return

Ginkos, Inc. is in the business of providing photocopying and word-processing services to the general public. The company is considering the purchase of a new-generation photocopying machine that will cost $29,000 now, and will have a useful life of 6 years.. The new machine will reduce the company's labor costs by $5,508 per year. The new machine is also expected to generate new service and revenue by enhancing the company's graphics capability, which will produce a contribution margin of $2.11 per graphic design sold. Ginkos estimates that a total of 1,422 graphic designs will be produced and sold each year.

Required:

1. Determine the annual cash inflows from the investment in the new machine.
2. Compute the internal rate of return for the new investment in the machine. Use interpolation if needed.
3. Assume that the photocopier dealer promises to buy the machine back for $12,000 at the end of the 6-year useful life. Other conditions remain unchanged. What is the new internal rate of return? Use the trial-and-error approach.

E13-8   Alternative Investments; Net Present Value

Linda LeBlanc has received $45,000 in severance pay from her former employer. Since she will not need the money for the next 8 years until her retirement, she has been looking for a proper investment project. LeBlanc has two choices: one, she could invest the money in a project that pays $11,000 a year for the next 8 years; or two, she could invest the money in a fund that promises a lump-sum payment of $120,000 at the end of the eighth year. LeBlanc earns 14% on her other investments, and requires an investment that yields at least a comparable return.

Required:

Which investment project should LeBlanc choose? Use the net present value method to make the decision.

E13-9   Net Present Value; Investment in Equipment or Inventory

PST, Inc. faces a choice between an investment in new equipment or an investment in inventory buildup. Both require an immediate cash outlay of $150,000. The equipment investment is expected to generate annual cash inflows of $30,000 per year for the next 5 years. At the end of the 5-year useful life, the equipment will have a salvage value of $10,000. The inventory investment is expected to generate annual cash inflows of only $24,000 per year for the next 5 years, but the entire cash investment in inventory will be released in cash at the end of the 5-year period. The released capital will be available for another investment project. PST, Inc. has computed the cost of capital as 12% per year.

Required:

Which investment should PST choose? Use the net present value method to make the decision.

E13-10   Expected Cash Flows; Present Value

Consider each of the following exercises independently:

1. Mary Fleming has promised her mother that an investment of $123,000 in her friend's flowershop would yield at least a 10% return. In the first two years, Fleming's mother received cash returns of $35,000 (Year 1) and $48,000 (Year 2), respectively. The flowershop does not need the money beyond the three-year period. To keep the promise, Fleming's friend wants to pay the amount of return in the third year that will make the investment yield 10% for the three-year period. Calculate the third-year payment.
2. Western Division of Nicole's Food Company requires a minimum return of 18% on its investments. This year, the company has asked Western Division to penetrate the Hawaiian beverage market to establish Nicole's presence in Hawaii. Western Division estimates that the Hawaiian operation would require an initial investment of $1,800,000. The expected annual cash inflows will be $300,000 for the 12-year operation. The project will be reevaluated after 12 years about whether to continue or withdraw. Since the project entails a high level of risk, the head office will subsidize Western Division to guarantee at least an 18% return each year. What is the amount of subsidy the head office will have to pay each year for 12 years, assuming the estimates are correct?
3. Tom Peters is considering whether to open a neighborhood swimming pool in the Desert Springs area. The pool will require an initial investment of $124,300, and generate $22,000 in annual cash inflows. Peters requires a 12% on his investments. For how many years should Tom operate the pool to produce the 12% return?

E13-11   Payback Period; Accounting Rate of Return

Lights & Nights, Inc. sells various home-lighting items. The company is considering a proposal on the possible addition of a metal halide product line. This latest light technology, metal halide produces a brighter light than incandescent bulbs while using only 20% of the electricity. The initial investment required is $400,000, and the contract with the manufacturer stipulates the refund of $40,000 at the end of the 6-year contract. Lights & Nights, Inc. estimates the following annual sales and expenses for the metal halide product line:

Metal halide sales...................		$250,000
Operating expenses:		
Payments to the manufacturer..........	$120,000	
Depreciation..........................	38,000	
Insurance............................	8,000	
Other operating expenses	15,000	181,000
Operating income		$ 69,000

Required:

1. Lights & Nights, Inc. requires every new project to have a maximum payback period of 5 years. Should the company accept the proposal?
2. Compute the accounting rate of return for the new product line, using the initial investment as the denominator. The company's cost of capital is 10%. Should the company accept the proposal if the accounting rate of return is used as the decision criterion? Disregard the income tax.

E13-12   Payback Period; Accounting Rate of Return

MJP, Inc. is considering the purchase and installation of a water purification system. The system costs $450,000 to install, but would eliminate the need to buy bottled drinking water for the company's employees' consumption for the next 10 years. The annual cash savings from discontinuing the purchase of bottled drinking water would be $80,000. The company's cost of capital is 12%.

Required:

1. MJP requires a maximum payback period of 5 years. Should the company purchase the water purification system?
2. The company depreciates assets using the straight-line method. Should the company purchase the system? Use the accounting rate of return as the decision criterion.

■ PROBLEMS

P13-13   Ethics, Capital Budgeting Decisions, and Problems of Rapid Automation

Carey & Co., an automobile parts manufacturer, has scaled down its ambitious floor automation plan. Hailed as a panacea for all the problems in manufacturing, many companies in the industry had pushed for sophisticated automation, such as flexible manufacturing systems, up until the early 1990s. The push for rapid automation, however, has created a new set of problems, such as high costs, lack of compatibility with existing manufacturing systems of other areas, and friction among different areas.

"There is a new conservatism in the company," Ray Allen, the controller said. "Our competitors who had embraced computerized manufacturing too early have fared very poorly in terms of earnings growth, cost reduction, and even efficiency improvement. Their expectations about the benefits of automation have been unrealistic. In the meantime, we have done pretty well without any serious investment in automation. Our company's earnings growth has been as healthy as most competitors'. I am glad we have resisted the temptation to create fictitious cash inflows in our capital budgeting plan to justify the investment in flexible manufacturing systems. Thank God, we scrapped our previous capital budgeting plan."

The sentiment of Bill Andrews, a manufacturing manager, is a little different. Bill thinks that an investment in automation is an investment in the future. Trying to buy their way out of factory-floor inefficiencies has been a mistake for many of the company's competitors, but many other intangible benefits, such as enhanced flexibility and improved product quality, have started to materialize in those competitors' plants, according to the information he has obtained.

Required:

1. What must have been the reason for "the temptation to create fictitious cash inflows" in the controller's scrapped capital budgeting plan? Explain using the net present value method of capital budgeting. Include, in your explanation, a comment on the ethics consideration in such capital budgeting.
2. Is there a way to justify such investment in automation, even when the estimates of future cash inflows are not sufficient?

P13-14 Net Present Value; Differential Approach

Fun Desert Playground, Inc. is considering the purchase of a new fleet of all-terrain vehicles (ATVs) for its desert recreation facility. The new fleet of ATVs cost $150,000. The ATVs will have a useful life of 10 years with a reconditioning required at the end of Year 5 at a cost of $8,000. At the end of the tenth year, the ATVs will be sold for $6,800.

The current fleet of ATVs require operating costs of $35,000 per year. The new fleet will require operating costs of only $6,500 per year. In addition, the improved performance of the new ATVs will increase the number of rides by 5,000 a year. Each ride generates a contribution margin of $1.20. The company requires a return of 16% on its comparable investments.

Required:

1. Compute the incremental cash inflows per year generated by the new fleet of ATVs.

2. Compute the net present value of the investment in the new fleet of ATVs, using the differential approach.

P13-15   Net Present Value; Asset with a Limited Life

Jerry Arnold is considering a proposal to open a virtual-reality arcade on a lot adjacent to Jerry's Bar and Restaurant. The lot can be used only for 5 years until a proposed highway construction project starts at the end of Year 5. Tom Landry, a long-time friend of Jerry and computer wizard, has persuaded Jerry to consider the virtual-reality arcade. Landry thinks that the younger area residents would provide a huge customer base for the arcade.

The proposal includes the following information:

Total cost of investment in the facility..................	$240,000
Initial investment of working capital	
(to be released at the end of Year 5).................	90,000
Cost to upgrade software at the end of Year 4............	35,000
Annual cash inflows...................................	105,000

The facility will have to be abandoned at the end of Year 5, but some items could be sold to other arcades for about $50,000 at that time. Jerry's cost of capital is 16%.

Required:

Should Jerry accept or reject the investment proposal? Use the net present value method.

P13-16   Internal Rate of Return; Different Useful Lives

Century City Designs, Inc. is considering the replacement of its computer design facility. The replacement would upgrade its computer-aided design (CAD) capability to render impressive 3-D graphics and third-party plug-in applications. The new CAD facility, including software, would have a useful life of 10 years, and cost $250,000. Cash inflows would be increased by $35,000 per year through cost savings and increased revenue. If the replacement actually is made, the current design equipment could be sold to a smaller animation studio for $54,000.

Required:

1. Determine the net incremental cost of installing the new CAD facility, including software for use in capital budgeting analysis.
2. What is the internal rate of return on the new CAD facility?
3. The rapid advancement in computer graphics technology makes the estimate of the useful life of the CAD facility not very reliable. The useful life could be 2 years shorter or longer than the estimated life of 10 years. How will the internal rate of return change if the useful life were (a) 8 years or (b) 12 years?

P13-17   Net Present Value; Value of Intangible Benefits

Visions-O-U, Inc. manufactures and sells special lenses that can be surgically implanted in the eyes of cataract patients to replace the lost natural lenses. The company is considering a proposal for a showroom to demonstrate its state-of-the-art technology and products in downtown Los Angeles. The showroom would require $450,000 in construction costs and $75,000 in interior decorations. In addition, it would cost $2,500 every month to maintain the showroom. The place would have to be partially refurbished at the end of Year 5 at a cost of $40,000.

The showroom is expected to generate extra revenues of $97,000 per year. Additionally, the showroom would reduce the company's other advertising expenses by $6,000 per year. The company expects to receive a cash grant of $11,000 from the city's urban renewal program at the start of actual construction of the showroom. The salvage value of the equipment will be about $18,000 at the end of the estimated 10-year useful life. The cost of capital is 14%.

Required:

1.   Compute the net annual cash inflows from the showroom.
2.   Compute the net present value of the investment in the showroom. Should Visions introduce the showroom?
3.   The Marketing Department of the company sees some permanent value in the proposed showroom through increased exposure to the city residents, although it is difficult to quantify the value. How much should the annual benefit from the increased exposure be in order to make the showroom project attractive in capital budgeting?

P13-18   Accounting Rate of Return; Payback Period

PC-Hi-Fi Company manufactures and sells ultra-compact audio sets that coax high-fidelity sound from any personal computers. The audio sets are popular because the standard speakers do not provide high quality sound when users play compact disks in the CD-ROM drive of a multimedia PC. The company is considering a proposal to open a direct outlet in a shopping mall for a limited period of 12 years. The following information has been gathered on the proposed outlet:

Initial cost of readying the outlet facility for business . . .	$300,000
Expected salvage value of the equipment at the end of the 12-year life	20,000
Depreciation method	Straight-line
Estimated sales per year	$330,000
Monthly rent for the space in the mall.	$ 4,000
Variable cost of goods sold	31% of sales
Other operating expenses per year:	
Manpower expenses.	$ 80,000
Insurance.	3,800
Other	31,000
Cost of capital.	12%

Required:

1. Compute the contribution margin and the operating income from the outlet.
2. Compute the accounting rate of return on the investment, using the initial investment as the denominator. Should the company open the outlet?
3. Compute the payback period on the investment. If the company uses a maximum payback period of 5 years, what should be the decision?

P13-19 Cash Inflow; Net Present Value

Joan Kelly has $180,000 to invest, and is looking for an opportunity to operate a business for a period of 10 years until her retirement. A friend has advised her to consider a piercing service, which the friend is operating in a different town. Based on her own research and the information her friend has provided, Kelly has compiled the following:

a. Kelly's service will be unique, and confined to piercing ears. No sales of earrings, chains, and charms will be made. The neighboring department stores in the same mall sell those, and will refer customers to Kelly for piercing service if she does not sell those.

b. Prices and costs of piercing services:

	Price	Variable Cost
Piercing one ear	$1.80	$0.25
Piercing the second ear	0.30	0.12

Estimated revenue from piercing one ear is $1,500 per week. Kelly's friend says about 60% of the patrons have both ears pierced.

c. Costs and investments:

Monthly rent for a space in a suburban shopping mall (10-year lease)	$ 2,000
Cost of facility installation and decoration	180,000
Salvage value of the facility at the end of the tenth year	18,000
Initial investment of working capital needed for operation (to be released and available for other investments after 10 years)	3,000
Other monthly operating expenses:	
County Health Department compliance expenses	500
Insurance	100
Maintenance	400

d. Kelly requires a 12% return on her investments.

Required:

1. Compute the net annual cash inflows from operation. Assume a 52-week year. Exclude the initial cost of installing the facility, initial investment of working capital, and the salvage value from your computation.

2. Compute the net present value of the investment. Should Kelly accept the investment proposal?

P13-20 Internal Rate of Return; Varying Useful Lives

Safe Work, Inc. of Ann Arbor, Michigan, provides manufacturing companies with workstation diagnostic services that will prevent muscle strain in workers. The company uses a software that detects ergonomic problems before they cause health problems for factory workers. The service has helped many manufacturing companies reduce workers' health insurance premiums and other related costs significantly. The company is considering a proposal to open another operation in Danbury, Connecticut. The following information has been compiled:

a. The initial investment required would be $260,000 to have a facility ready for operation.
b. The project will be operated for 10 years, and a 10-year lease is available from the building owner.
c. The annual net cash inflows are estimated to be about $61,000.

Required:

1. Compute the internal rate of return on the investment in the Connecticut operation. Use interpolation if necessary.
2. Safe Work, Inc. requires a minimum return of 12%. What should be the net annual cash inflows that will satisfy this requirement for the $260,000 investment in the Connecticut operation?
3. Since the project duration is not certain, Safe Works, Inc. wants to test the investment potential with the different useful lives of (a) 8 years, and (b) 12 years. Compute the internal rate of return for the two selected durations.
4. Since the annual cash inflows are also uncertain, Safe Works, Inc. wants to test the investment potential with different cash inflows. Compute the internal rate of return, assuming that the annual cash inflows were (a) 10% less, and (b) 10% more, than the original estimate of $61,000.
5. It is possible that the Connecticut operation will not be successful and be discontinued before the 10-year lease expires. Assume that the Connecticut operation will generate annual cash inflows of only $40,000 for the first 9 years, and the company discontinues the operation at the end of Year 9. At that time, the facility will be sold for $98,542. Compute the internal rate of return for the 9-year investment.

P13-21 Accounting Rate of Return; Payback Period

J.T. Nolan, the owner of JT's Video Shop is considering an additional investment in a snack corner in a space adjacent to his video shop in the same shopping mall located in downtown Chicago. J.T. has gathered the following information on the investment in a snack corner:

a. Snack corner facility can be installed at a cost of $265,000. The space is available for a 10-year lease.
b. The facility will have a zero salvage value at the end of the 10-year period and be depreciated using the straight-line depreciation method.
c. The city of Chicago has an urban renewal grant program which would pay a cash grant of $45,000 for a small business investment like this. The grant will be available for use in connection with the facility installation.
d. The future traffic estimate puts the number of patrons who will use the snack corner at 50,000 per year. On an average, each person spends about $3 per visit.
e. Annual operating expenses estimated:

Manpower expenses	$70,000
Insurance	3,500
Utilities	10,000
Facility maintenance	8,000

f. J.T.'s cost of capital is 12%.

Required:

1. Compute the operating income from the snack corner operation.
2. Compute the accounting rate of return on the investment in the snack corner. Should J.T. invest in the proposed snack corner?
3. Compute the payback period for the snack corner. Should J.T. invest in the snack corner if his maximum payback period is 4 years?

P13-22 Total-Cost Approach; Incremental-Cost Approach

Chips-R-Us, Inc. manufactures and sells various chips which are used by manufacturers of lap-top computers. The company is currently considering the replacement of the etching equipment. The equipment is used in the process where selected portions of metal and oxide film are removed from a silicon wafer to make etches. The company has compiled the following information on the replacement:

	Current Etching Equipment	New Etching Equipment
Initial purchase cost	$30,000	$40,000
Salvage value, now	13,000	–
Salvage value, 6 years later	1,500	6,000
Reconditioning cost, now	10,000	–
Current book value	15,000	–
Annual operating costs	15,000	10,000

If the current etching equipment is reconditioned now for $10,000, it will be operational for 6 more years. The company intends to use the new etching equipment for only 6 years. At that time, new-generation equipment will be purchased. The company uses straight-line depreciation and earns 14% on its other investments.

Required:

1. Should Chips-R-Us, Inc. replace the etching equipment? Use the total-cost approach and compute net present value.
2. Use the incremental-cost approach and compute net present value. Is the net present value the same as in (1)?

P13-23 Accounting Rate of Return; Internal Rate of Return; Payback Period

Geological Survey, Inc. is considering the purchase of personal water purification kits for its employees in the field. The employees require a significant amount of drinking water in the field. The kits use microfilters to remove sediment and larger microorganisms from the water. The company has compiled the following information about the purification kits:

a. The current expenditure for drinking water used in the field is $18,000 per year.
b. The kits would cost $24,000 each.
c. According to the dealer, the kits would have a useful life of 8 years and no salvage value at the end of the 8-year period. Geological Survey, Inc. would depreciate the kits using the straight-line method.
d. The company's out-of-pocket expenses to operate the kits would be as follows:

Replacement of filters	$8,000
Batteries	2,100
Maintenance	1,100

e. The company's minimum required rate of return on investments is 18%.

Required:

1. Determine the annual savings from the purchase and use of water purification kits.
2. Should the company purchase the kits? Use the accounting rate of return to make the decision.
3. If the company's maximum payback period is five years, should the company purchase the kits?
4. Compute the internal rate of return on the investment in the kits, and compare it to the accounting rate of return computed in (2).

 ### P13-24 Net Present Value; Variation in Cash Flows

GTA, Inc. is considering the purchase and installation of virtual engineers in its manufacturing process. The technology is based on computer-aided production engineering (CAPE), which is an advancement from computer-aided design (CAD). CAPE actually incorporates CAD information to make human efforts unnecessary in the setup of the factory floor. The company has compiled the following information on the proposed investment:

Useful life of virtual engineers	8 years
Initial cost of purchasing virtual engineers	$2,000,000
Software and installation	1,000,000
Salvage value in 8 years	60,000
Annual savings in engineering costs	480,000
Annual savings in scheduling costs	230,000
Increase in utility and maintenance costs per year.......	33,600

In addition to the annual cost savings, the use of virtual engineers would generate a one-time benefit of $450,000 in the first year through the elimination of various existing inefficiencies. The benefit will be received throughout the first year. The company requires a minimum return of 18% on investments.

Required:

1. Determine the amount of net annual cost savings if the virtual engineers are installed.
2. Compute the net present value of the investment in the virtual engineers. Should the company install the virtual engineers?
3. The company is uncertain about the estimate of the annual cost savings in engineering costs, and wants to compute the net present value using a second version of the proposal. The second version assumes that the annual cost savings in engineering costs is only 90% of the original estimate and the software and installation cost $80,000 more than the original estimate. All other items remain unchanged. Compute the net present value of the investment using the second version. Should the company install the virtual engineers?
4. Refer to the net present value computed in (3). Determine the amount of additional cash inflows per year needed to earn the required rate of return of 18%.

 P13-25 Lease versus Purchase

Monterey Golf Course, Inc. (MGC) uses 20 golf carts on its 18-hole golf course. MGC has, in the past, purchased the golf carts from Degas Cart Manufacturing Co. and then sold the used carts to used-cart dealers. Golf carts are usually replaced after three years of use. This year, Golfcarts, Inc. , a different cart manufacturer, has proposed a lease option to MGC. MGC has compiled the following information comparing purchase and lease plans.

1. Purchase Plan:

    MGC could purchase 20 carts from Degas at $5,700 each. The costs of operating the 20 carts include:

Maintenance costs	$2,000
Repairs in Year 1.......................................	1,000
Repairs in Year 2.......................................	3,000
Repairs in Year 3.......................................	5,000

The used carts would be sold for about $38,000 at the end of Year 3.

2. Lease Plan:

   Golfcarts, Inc. would provide a three-year lease with payments of $39,000 per year at the beginning of each year which include maintenance and repairs. MGC would also make a security deposit of $7,000 at the beginning of the lease period. The deposit would be refunded at the end of the three-year period.

Required:

Compute the present value of the cash flows for each plan, using the total-cost approach. MGC's cost of capital is 14%. Which plan is better?

 P13-26   Net Present Value; Incremental-Cost Approach

TAG, Inc. is considering the purchase and installation of an automated material-handling system (AMHS) in its plant. The AMHS would replace the old material-handling equipment, improve efficiency, and reduce operating costs in the entire material-handling process. The company has compiled the following information on the proposed investment:

Useful life of AMHS	10 years
Initial cost of purchasing AMHS	$3,000,000
Software and installation	1,000,000
Salvage value of AMHS in 10 years	90,000
Annual savings in material moving costs	600,000
Annual savings in material-unloading costs	520,000
Increase in utility and maintenance costs per year	360,000
Salvage value of the old material-handling equipment	30,000

The AMHS not only is efficient in handling materials, but also would help reduce the permanent level of inventory in the entire inventory cycle. The one-time benefit from this inventory reduction would be $700,000 in the first year. This benefit would materialize throughout the first year. The company requires a minimum return of 16% on investments.

Required:

1. What is the amount of net annual cost savings if the AMHS is installed?
2. Compute the net present value of the investment, using the incremental-cost approach. Should the company install the AMHS?
3. The company is not sure about the annual cost savings and wants to compute the net present value using a second version of the proposal. The second version assumes that the annual cost savings in material-moving costs would be only $400,000 and the software and installation would cost $180,000 more than the original estimate. All other items remain unchanged. Compute the net present value of the investment using the second version. Should the company still make the same decision?

4. Refer to the net present value computed in (3). Determine the additional cash inflows per year needed to earn the required rate of return of 16%.

 P13-27   Lease versus Purchase; Total-Cost Approach

Biotech Berkeley, Inc. (BBI) manufactures and sells bio-medical products, including an anabolic steroid and a human-growth hormone. The anabolic steroid is used in the treatment of extensive weight loss of cancer and AIDS patients. BBI's steroid is different from other steroids that are sold on the market in that it produces scant liver toxicity. The products of BBI have been very successful and have made the company profitable. Now BBI wants to expand its operation beyond northern California, and establish a promotion center in Columbia, Maryland.

BBI has two choices in establishing the promotion center: purchase or lease a property. The details of the two choices have been compiled as follows:

Purchase Plan:

BBI could purchase a property in Columbia for $700,000, a payment of $200,000 now and a payment of $125,000 at the end of each year for the next four years. Annual cash operating costs of this property would be $14,000. The company would use the property for 10 years, and sell it at the end of the 10-year period. The resale value is expected to be about $300,000.

Lease Plan:

The property in Columbia is owned by a property management company, which is willing to lease it to BBI. The 10-year lease would require annual lease payments of $80,000 per year with the first lease payment due immediately. The remaining nine payments would be made at the end of each of the next nine years. (The second annual lease payment will be made at the end of the first year. The tenth annual lease payment will be made at the end of the ninth year.) Annual operating costs would be $5,000 per year under the lease plan. The lessor would require a security deposit of $12,000 now, and would return the deposit at the end of the tenth year.

Required:

Compute the present value of cash outflows under each plan, using the total-cost approach. BBI's cost of capital is 14%. Should BBI purchase or lease the property in Columbia?

■ CASES

C13-28   Product Decision; Net Present Value

V-Chips, Inc. is a manufacturer of chips used in computers and audio-visual products. V-Chips, Inc. has just developed a digital audio decoding chip for the sound system used in movie theaters. Manufacturers of products using digital versatile disks (DVDs) with state-of-the-art sound work with the company. The customers of V-Chips, Inc. include the manufacturers with famous brand names. Computer makers also buy the chips from the company because PC users demand state-of-the-art sound also.

The company needs to buy new equipment to produce the newly developed digital audio decoding chip. The equipment is needed for the important etching step in chip making. The etching step makes a chip's intricate pattern of circuitry. The equipment uses dry etch that performs with high precision. For example, the etch equipment can create details as fine as 0.35 microns in width (a micron is 0.01 of the diameter of a human hair).

The company is currently in the process of performing studies on the production and marketing aspects of the product. Management accountants have compiled the following information:

a. The new etching equipment would cost $252,000 and have a 10-year useful life. At the end of the tenth year, the equipment would have a salvage value of $10,000.

b. The company would need to inject working capital of $50,000 to support the production and sales of the new product now. The working capital would be released at the end of the 10-year period.

c. The new chip will be sold for $32 each. To establish the market, the company would promote the chip through aggressive advertising. The company projects the following sales and advertising over the 10-year period:

Year	Units to be Sold	Advertising Dollars
1	5,000	$140,000
2	11,000	140,000
3	14,000	120,000
4-10	15,000	100,000

d. Variable costs of manufacturing and variable selling and administrative expenses would total $15 per unit of product.

e. Fixed manufacturing costs and fixed operating expenses would total $110,000. The amount includes straight-line depreciation on the etching equipment based on acquisition cost minus salvage value.

f. The company targets a minimum return of 12% on new product lines.

Required:

1. Determine the net cash inflow from operations for each year over the 10-year period. (Year 4 through Year 10 could be represented by a single column in your table.)

2. Compute the net present value of the investment in the new product. Should the company proceed with the new product?

C13-29   Net Present Value; Total-Cost Approach; Sensitivity Analysis

Gen-X Ice Cream Shop in Santa Monica is considering a new investment utilizing an adjacent space in the same mall which has become available recently for a 12-year lease. The shop has two options: one, it could start an operation which would sell prepackaged ice cream; or two, it could open a virtual-reality arcade which has become very popular among the area's young population. The following information has been compiled on the two options:

The Prepackaged Ice Cream Option:

The shop estimates that the costs of having the facility ready for making and selling prepackaged ice cream would be $320,000. This option would require additional working capital of $6,000, which would be released for use elsewhere at the end of the 12-year lease. The facility would have a salvage value of $24,000 at the end of the lease period. The shop would be selling three different kinds of prepackaged ice cream:

Hearty-Delight: The shop's early choice, Hearty-Delight has been very popular among Santa Monica's population, regardless of age. The concoction contains 17% butterfat, however. The shop estimates that the sales of Hearty-Delight would be 6,300 cartons.

Gen-X Light: Although Hearty-Delight tastes good, it is a tad hard on the customers' heart and waistline. The shop has introduced Gen-X Light which contains 40% less fat and one-third the calories and cholesterol of Hearty-Delight. The estimated sales of Gen-X Light would be 10,500 cartons.

Super-Premium: The shop has developed this top-of-the-line ice cream to cater to Santa Monica's affluent customers. Super-Premium contains 55% less fat and two-thirds the calories and cholesterol of Hearty-Delight while it still tastes as good as Hearty-Delight. The estimated sales of Super-Premium would be 4,200 cartons.

Selling prices and production costs of ice cream are presented below:

	Selling Price	Production Cost
Hearty-Delight.	$6.40	$1.00
Gen-X Light	8.10	2.00
Super-Premium.	10.00	2.50

Other operating expenses per year are:

Space rent	$15,000
Manpower expenses	43,000
Utilities.	10,500
Insurance.	6,000

The Virtual-Reality Arcade Option:

According to the estimates, about 23,000 people would use the arcade and spend an average of $4 per person. In addition, the arcade would earn about $12,000 a year from sales of beverage to the patrons. The following additional information on the virtual-reality arcade is available:

Total cost of investment in the facility	$190,000
Initial investment of working capital	
(to be released at the end of Year 12)	3,000
Salvage value of the arcade facility at the end of Year 12	10,000
Other operating expenses per year:	
Space rent	15,000
Virtual-reality software	25,000
Manpower expenses	14,000
Utilities	4,400
Insurance	7,500

Required:

1. Determine the estimated net annual cash inflow from each option.
2. Compute the net present value of each option, using the total-cost approach. The shop's cost of capital is 12%. Which option should the shop choose?
3. The Shop is uncertain about the annual cash inflows from the virtual-reality arcade option. Assume that only 20,000 people used the arcade and spent $4 per person. The sales of beverage provided cash inflows of only $10,000 per year. All other items remain unchanged. Compute the net present value of the investment in the arcade using the new information. Should the shop still make the same decision?

 C13-30   Uneven Cash Flows; Total-Cost Approach; Incremental-Cost Approach

Luxury Checks, Inc. is a manufacturer of checkbooks. Despite ATMs, electronic banking, and debit cards, the check-printing company's business has been growing at a healthy rate. The company estimates that the demand for its checkbooks will increase in the future because of the following reasons: One, only about one-tenth of all checks are written for cash. Two, many Americans, especially the older ones, are still intimidated by teller machines. Three, several check-printers in the region have gone out of business. Four, many households would rather have a grace period before the checks written to pay bills are cleared than have electronic fund transfers zap their bank account balances.

To meet the higher demand for its checkbooks, the company wants to upgrade its printing capacity. The company is considering an investment in one of the two choices: one, buy another printer similar to the one currently in use; or two, buy a new model (X-10) which can print twice as fast as the current printer does. The existing printer will be kept as a back-up. More detailed information is provided below:

a. The existing printer cost $128,000 when it was purchased, and the same model (new printer) would cost $136,000 now. The accumulated depreciation on the existing printer is $38,400. It has a remaining life of 5 years.

b. The new model (X-10) would cost $240,000 to purchase and install. Both the existing model and the new X-10 have a useful life of 8 years. The salvage value of both printers is negligible. The printers would be depreciated using the straight-line method.

c. If the company buys the same model as the existing printer, the existing printer would have to be replaced in Year 6 at a cost of $160,000. The printer bought in Year 6 would have a market value of $112,000 at the end of Year 8.

d. Estimated number of units produced:

Year	Units Produced
1	32,000
2	48,000
3	64,000
4-8	72,000

e. Variable costs per unit produced would vary, depending on which printer is used, as follows:

	If Existing Model of Printer Is Used	If the New X-10 Printer Is Used
Direct materials.	$0.20	$0.32
Direct labor	0.39	0.13
Variable overhead.	0.05	0.03
Total variable cost per unit.	$0.64	$0.48

f. The total repairs and maintenance costs per year would be $4,000 for the two printers of the existing model, or $2,000 per printer (choice 1). The total repairs and maintenance costs per year would be $3,040 for the new model X-10 and the existing model as a back-up (choice 2).

g. The company's cost of capital is 18%.

Required:

1. Compute total production costs for each year for the two choices. Years 4-8 can be combined as a single column.
2. Compute the present value of cash outflows for each of the two choices and the net present value of the better choice. Use the total-cost approach.
3. Compute the net present value of purchasing the new model (choice 2). Use the incremental-cost approach.

CAPITAL BUDGETING: TAXES, INFLATION AND TECHNOLOGY

After studying this chapter, you should be able to:

1. Define and compute the after-tax cost and the after-tax benefit of cash flow items.

2. Explain the meaning of depreciation tax shield and give an example of how it is computed.

3. Explain how depreciation deductions affect net present value.

4. Perform capital budgeting decision analyses on an after-tax basis, considering the non-tax-deductible cash outflows and the non-taxable cash inflows.

5. Describe how capital investment projects may be ranked using the profitability index.

6. Explain why incorporating expected inflation rates in capital budgeting analysis is not important.

7. Explain how the technological advances affect capital budgeting decisions.

The previous chapter presented an introduction to capital budgeting. In that introduction, we omitted certain aspects of capital budgeting in order to simplify the concepts presented. In this chapter, we discuss the effects of income taxes, inflation, and technological advances on capital budgeting. We will also examine the ranking of capital investment projects.

INCOME TAXES AND CAPITAL BUDGETING

Tax Rate and Investment

Assume there are two investment projects. All items of cash inflow are taxable and all items of cash outflow are tax deductible at the same tax rate. For the two projects, it should not matter if the capital budgeting decisions are made with or without tax consideration. In most projects, however, different components of cash flows are taxable or deductible, and some are not.

Assume that $10,000 is available for one year. It can purchase either (a) federal government securities that pay 10% per year, or (b) municipal bonds that pay 8% per year. Assume that both are virtually risk-free, and you are guaranteed to recover your original investment of $10,000 plus its specific return after one year. The income from federal government securities is taxable, whereas the income from municipal bonds is not. Which investment would you choose?

Technology investment at Edison Development Corp. Capital budgeting changes when the project involves an investment in new technology.

The return of 10%, or $1,000, is better than the return of 8%, or $800, and, if you ignore income tax effects, investment (a) is better than investment (b). If you consider the income tax effect, however, the decision will depend on your tax bracket. Since the return from municipal bonds is $200 (20%) less than the return from the federal government securities, the decision will depend on the following:

If your tax rate is	Your decision will be
Below 20%	Choose investment (a).
20%	Indifferent as to (a) or (b).
Above 20%	Choose investment (b).

Exhibit 14-1 presents the results assuming tax rates of 15%, 20%, and 28%.

Tax and Method of Financing an Investment

Company A has discovered that a piece of land adjacent to its building is available for sale at $200,000. Management has been considering expansion, and decides to proceed with the land purchase. The Company does not have $200,000, but it has two financing alternatives available:

(a) Borrow the money at 10% interest per year.
(b) Issue preferred stock that pays a 10% dividend per year.

EXHIBIT 14-1 Taxable and Nontaxable Incomes at Different Tax Rates

	(a) Taxable Income	(b) Nontaxable Income
Tax Rate: 15%		
Pre-tax income	$1,000	$800
Income tax at 15%	150	—
After-tax income	$ 850*	$800
Tax Rate: 20%		
Pre-tax income	$1,000	$800
Income tax at 20%	200	—
After-tax income	$ 800	$800
Tax Rate: 28%		
Pre-tax income	$1,000	$800
Income tax at 28%	280	—
After-tax income	$ 720	$800*

*The better choice.

According to the company's investment banker, the preferred stock needs a mandatory annual dividend payment clause in its prospectus to attract buyers. Before an actual expansion starts, the company can rent the land to a local farmer for $36,000 a year, but the company would have to pay the annual property taxes of $6,000.

Which financing alternative is better for the company based on the net cash flow? Since interest expense is tax deductible, and dividend payments are not, we obtain the results presented in Exhibit 14-2.

EXHIBIT 14-2 Income and Cash Flow Under Two Methods of Financing

	(a) Financing with Debt	(b) Financing with Preferred Stock
Rent Income	$36,000	$36,000
Expenses:		
Property taxes	6,000	6,000
Interest expense ($200,000 x 10%)	20,000	—
	26,000	6,000
Pre-tax income	10,000	30,000
Income tax at 30%	3,000	9,000
After-tax income	7,000	21,000
Preferred stock dividends ($200,000 x 10%)	—	20,000
Net cash inflow	$ 7,000	$ 1,000

Alternative (a) with $7,000 net cash inflow is better than alternative (b) with $1,000 net cash inflow. The after-tax income under alternative (a) is lower than under alternative (b) by only $14,000 (= $21,000 − $7,000), and not by the entire interest expense of $20,000. The net annual cash inflow under alternative (a) is higher than under alternative (b) by $6,000 (= $7,000 − $1,000), although both the interest and dividends paid are the same $20,000.

The difference in net cash inflow is because of income tax. The interest expense is tax deductible, but the dividend payments are not. The $14,000 difference in net income represents the after-tax cost of interest expense, as follows:

The difference in net income
= Interest expense − Tax savings
= $20,000 − (30% × $20,000)
= $20,000 × (1 − 30% tax rate) = $14,000.

The $6,000 difference in net cash inflow is the tax savings (30%) of $20,000 interest expense. The tax rate is the same under both alternatives, and the choice between the two alternatives reduces to the tax deductibility of interest expense. If taxes were ignored, or if interest and dividends were both tax deductible, the company would be indifferent between the financing methods.

After-Tax Cost and After-Tax Benefit

Based on the above illustrations, the following after-tax concepts become evident:

After-tax cost   = Amount of tax-deductible expense × (1 − tax rate).
After-tax benefit = Amount of taxable revenue   × (1 − tax rate).

Cash outflows that are not tax-deductible, such as dividend payments, and non-taxable cash inflows, such as interest on municipal bonds, are not affected by tax. The after-tax amounts of these cash flows are the same as the before-tax amounts. This is very important in capital budgeting.

Income taxes are taxes on income and not on capital. The return on investment is income. The recovery of investment is not income. The original cost of an investment and the working capital committed to the project are outflows that are not tax deductible. The original cost of an investment is tax deductible through the annual depreciation of depreciable assets.

Tax Savings on Depreciation

Depreciation is a non-cash expense, and is not regarded as a cash outflow in capital budgeting. Depreciation expense is tax deductible, however, and reduces the amount of taxes paid. Since tax payments require cash outflow, the tax payments must be considered in capital budgeting.

Consider the following illustration.

The Funland Company is undecided about whether to buy a piece of land or a piece of equipment. Each can be purchased for $100,000. The equipment can generate a net cash inflow, before depreciation and taxes, of $30,000 a year for

SERVICE DEPARTMENT COST ALLOCATION

After studying this appendix, you should be able to:

1. Distinguish between operating and service departments in an organization and explain why we need to allocate service costs to operating departments.

2. Differentiate between the direct method and the step method of allocating service department costs and perform service cost allocations under each method.

3. Explain why service departments' variable costs should be allocated separately from their fixed costs and why their budgeted, rather than actual, costs should be allocated.

4. Discuss why certain central costs should not be allocated at all and why sales dollars should not be used as an allocation base.

Accelerated Depreciation

The depreciation expense can be different among projects if a different depreciation method is used for each project. Tax law allows the use of accelerated depreciation. We consider the effects of accelerated depreciation here.

Assume the above company uses an accelerated depreciation method, as shown in Exhibit 14-4.

EXHIBIT 14-4 Tax Savings on Depreciation Based on an Accelerated Depreciation Method

Year	(A) Depreciation Expense	(B) Tax Rate	(A x B) Depreciation Tax Savings	PV Factor	PV
1	$ 33,333	40%	$13,333	.9259	$12,345
2	26,667	40%	10,667	.8573	9,145
3	20,000	40%	8,000	.7938	6,350
4	13,333	40%	5,333	.7350	3,920
5	6,667	40%	2,667	.6806	1,815
Total	$100,000	40%	$40,000		$33,575

PV factors are from Table 13A-1 under 8%.

The total depreciation expense ($100,000) and total tax savings on depreciation ($40,000) for the five-year useful life of the equipment are the same as before. The PV of the tax savings on deprecation here is $33,575, compared to $31,941 ($28,131 + $3,810) from Exhibit 14-3, showing a difference of $1,634.

The difference is due to the use of different depreciation methods. Using an accelerated depreciation method could lead to the acceptance of a capital investment project that otherwise would be rejected if the straight-line depreciation method was used. This occurs because the higher depreciation expenses in earlier years using accelerated depreciation generate higher depreciation tax savings in early years. Accordingly, the PV of net cash inflows increases.

For this reason, most companies use accelerated depreciation methods for tax purposes, even though they may use a straight-line depreciation method for external reporting. The best-known accelerated depreciation method is the double-declining-balance (DDB) method. Under U.S. income tax laws, most assets acquired since 1987 are depreciated using the Modified Accelerated Cost Recovery System (MACRS), which is a variation of the DDB method. The computation of depreciation rates is not discussed here. We focus rather on the decision-making aspects of income tax implications in capital budgeting for managers who operate in the global environment.

Morton International, Inc.'s designers are working with Computer Aided Design (CAD) technology to create three-dimensional passenger module layouts in Ogden, Utah. Evaluating investments in technology such as this requires special considerations that have been disregarded in the past.

Depreciation and Cash Flow

The role of depreciation in capital budgeting must be understood properly. Depreciation itself is not a cash flow item. It only affects the amount of cash outflow for taxes. Accordingly, a project requiring a larger original investment and higher depreciation deductions is not necessarily better than another project with a smaller investment and lower depreciation deductions.

Consider the following two projects with a useful life of five years:

	Project A	Project B
Annual operating cost savings before depreciation and taxes	$180,000	$160,000
Original investment	$500,000	$400,000

Assume a tax rate of 30%, a minimum required rate of return of 12%, and straight-line depreciation with no salvage value for each project. Which project is better? Exhibit 14-5 presents the solution.

EXHIBIT 14-5 Effect of Depreciation on NPV

Project A	Before -Tax Amount	Tax Effect	After -Tax Amount	Years	PV Factor at 12%	PV
Operating cost savings	$180,000	(1 − 0.3)	$126,000	1-5	3.6048	$454,205
Depreciation	100,000	0.3	30,000	1-5	3.6048	108,144
Total						562,349
Investment	500,000	−	500,000	Now	1.0000	500,000
NPV						$ 62,349
Project B						
Operating cost savings	$160,000	(1 − 0.3)	$112,000	1-5	3.6048	$403,738
Depreciation	80,000	0.3	24,000	1-5	3.6048	86,515
Total						490,253
Investment	400,000	−	400,000	Now	1.0000	400,000
NPV						$ 90,253

While project A shows higher depreciation deductions of $100,000, the NPV of project B, with lower depreciation deductions of $80,000, is significantly higher than the NPV of project A. Accordingly, managers would prefer project B to project A. The lesson from this is that depreciation by itself is not relevant to the decision. Only the tax savings from depreciation, called **depreciation tax shield,** is relevant to the investment decision.

Gain (Loss) on Disposal of Equipment

When equipment is disposed of for cash, there is an income tax effect on the gain (loss) on disposal. Consider the following alternatives with a useful life of five years:

	Equipment A	Equipment B
Sold after 3 years for	$250,000	$100,000
Original cost	500,000	400,000

Total depreciation for 3 years	(300,000)	(240,000)
Book value	200,000	160,000
Gain (loss) on disposal	50,000	(60,000)
Tax saving at 30% tax rate		18,000
Tax paid at 30% tax rate	(15,000)	
Net cash inflow from sale	$235,000	$118,000

The $250,000 cash proceeds from the sale of equipment A *minus* the $15,000 tax paid on the gain generates a net cash inflow of $235,000. The $100,000 cash proceeds from the sale of equipment B *plus* the $18,000 tax saving provides a net cash inflow of $118,000.

A gain or loss does not have any cash flow significance. It is just an accounting gain or loss. Tax paid or tax saved on a gain or loss has cash flow significance. The $235,000 cash inflow is still favorably compared to equipment A's book value of $200,000, despite the tax payment. The $118,000 cash inflow is still below equipment B's book value of $160,000, despite the tax saving.

CAPITAL BUDGETING AND INFLATION

Thus far, we have assumed zero inflation throughout the project's life. In reality, however, managers should consider the effects of inflation on capital budgeting.

First, inflation affects the discount rate. If the rate of inflation is higher, the higher is the interest rate, or the required rate of return for a capital investment project. Thus, managers should predict the future inflation rate, and use it to adjust the required rate of return year after year. Future cash inflows should be discounted, using this annually adjusted rate of return.

Second, inflation affects both cash inflows and outflows. This is because price increases tend to inflate cash flows. But, if we adjust future cash flows by the same inflation rate used for adjusting the discount rate, the NPV will be exactly the same as before adjustment.

Consider the following. INFLATO CORPORATION is considering an investment in project Z, which requires an initial investment of $100,000 and promises an after-tax operating cost savings of $50,000 a year for three years. It will have no salvage value at the end of the three years. INFLATO predicts that the inflation rate will average about 10% in each of the next three years. If the company's required rate of return is 14%, should the company invest in project Z?

Without inflation, the NPV will be:

PV of an ordinary annuity of $50,000 for three years at 14%

= $50,000 × 2.3216 (From Table 13A-2 for 3 years) = $116,080

Original investment	(100,000)
NPV	$ 16,080

Adjustment for Inflation

If we consider inflation, both the required rate of return and future cash inflows require adjustments. The required rate of return must be adjusted by two factors: the inflation rate of 10% and the combined effect of the inflation rate and the required rate of return, as shown below:

Inflation-adjusted required rate of return	
= Required rate of return	14.0%
+ Inflation rate	10.0%
+ Combined effect (14% × 10%)	1.4%
	25.4%

The future cash inflows must be adjusted as follows:

Inflation-adjusted cash inflows
= Cash inflows × (1 + inflation rate)
For Year 1: $50,000 × 1.10 = $55,000
For Year 2: $55,000 × 1.10 = $60,500
For Year 3: $60,500 × 1.10 = $66,550

If we discount the inflation-adjusted cash inflows shown above at the inflation-adjusted required rate of return of 25.4%, the PV will be computed as follows:

Year 1: $55,000	×	.7974 =	$43,859
Year 2: 60,500	×	.6359 =	38,473
Year 3: 66,550	×	.5071 =	33,748
PV Total			116,080
Investment			(100,000)
NPV			$16,080

The NPV is the same $16,080 computed without considering inflation adjustments. Because the NPV is the same whether inflation is considered or not, most managers do not include inflation adjustments in their capital investment analysis. The only drawback of not considering inflation adjustments is that actual future cash flows will be inflated, whereas the required rate of return is not adjusted for inflation. Accordingly, the post-audit may indicate that the project's results are more favorable than they actually are.

For example, if everything has materialized as expected, the actual cash inflow for year 1, adjusted for inflation of 10%, would be $55,000 ($50,000 × 1.10). When these cash inflows are compared to the originally estimated $50,000 annual cash inflows, actual results will appear to be 10% more favorable than the projection. But, of course, the reason for the seemingly favorable results is the 10% inflation.

To overcome this problem, managers should adjust the actual results to remove the inflation effects. This is done by dividing the actual results by (1 + inflation rate). If the inflation rate is 10% per year as expected, the cash inflows excluding inflation effects for year 1 would equal $55,000/1.10, or $50,000. For year 2, the cash inflows of $60,500 must be divided by $(1.10)^2$, or 1.21, to obtain the projected results of $50,000, and so on.

RANKING OF CAPITAL INVESTMENT PROJECTS

We now discuss several **preference criteria** or **ranking techniques** that managers can use to select the most preferable project from several acceptable projects. Managers can also rank the projects on a preference order so that the available, but limited, funds would be used for the projects that rank at the top of this preference order.

All the screening techniques discussed in the previous chapter can also be used as ranking techniques as follows:

Ranking based on NPV, IRR, or ARR: The project with the highest NPV, IRR, or ARR would be ranked as the most preferable, the one with the second highest NPV, IRR, or ARR would be ranked as the second, and so on.

Ranking based on the payback method: The project with the shortest payback period would be ranked as the most preferable, the one with the second shortest payback period would be ranked as the second, and so on.

In the previous chapter, we discussed the shortcomings of the ARR and the payback method as screening devices. These shortcomings will continue to plague these methods as ranking criteria. Indeed, these shortcomings will become more serious, because the limited funds available for a firm may be invested in the projects that are not the most preferable. For this reason, prudent managers will discourage the use of the ARR and payback methods as preference devices.

Shortcomings of NPV As Screening Device

Although they do not have the shortcomings of the ARR and payback methods as screening devices, the use of the NPV or IRR methods as preference devices may also give results that are not the most desirable. The following example of three projects shows why the use of NPV as a ranking device may not be useful. All three projects produce the same NPV of $1,000.

	Project A	Project B	Project C
PV of cash inflows	$101,000	$51,000	$11,000
Required investment	(100,000)	(50,000)	(10,000)
NPV	$ 1,000	$ 1,000	$ 1,000

In this example, the projects cannot be ranked using NPV. Even if the NPV for each project is different, the project with the highest NPV is not necessarily the most desirable.

Consider the following data:

	Project A	Project B	Project C
PV of cash inflows	$102,000	$51,500	$11,000
Required investment	(100,000)	(50,000)	(10,000)

NPV	$ 2,000	$1,500	$1,000
Return on investment	2%	3%	10%

If the projects are ranked according to NPV, project A is the most desirable, project B the second, and project C the least desirable. Are we making the correct decision here?

If we use the cash return on investment, the preference order of these three projects will be reversed. Project C would be the most desirable whereas project A would be the least desirable. Project B remains as the second most desirable. A different ranking tool that captures this return on investment or profitability is needed.

Profitability Index

Most management accountants agree that the profitability index is such a ranking tool. The **profitability index** is the ratio of the PV of cash inflows to its required investment, as shown below:

$$\text{Profitability index (PI)} = \frac{\text{PV of cash inflows}}{\text{Required investment}}$$

The project with the highest PI is ranked the most desirable, the one with the second highest PI is ranked the second, and so on. If the PI is used to rank the above three projects, we obtain the following:

	Project A	Project B	Project C
PV of cash inflows	$101,000	$51,000	$11,000
Required investment	÷ 100,000	÷ 50,000	÷ 10,000
PI	1.01	1.02	1.10

Project C is the most desirable and project A is the least desirable. If a project's PI is less than 1, the project should be dropped because it fails the screening test. The PI can be used to rank projects that have unequal lives also.

We have determined the above preference order assuming that the funds available in excess of the $10,000 invested in project C will be invested in other projects that will also earn 10%. If the excess funds will remain idle or will be invested in projects that earn below 10%, then project C may not be the most desirable investment.

Profitability Index and IRR

We have shown earlier that the use of the IRR may lead to incorrect ranking. Now, assume a choice between two mutually exclusive projects. In other words, if you choose one project, you cannot choose the other. Project X requires a capital investment of $83,946, and will improve net operating cash inflows by $30,000 a year for four years. Project Y requires a capital investment of $87,636, and will improve net operating cash inflows by $15,000 a year for 13 years.

Conventional Cash Inflow Estimation Problem

In estimating future cash inflows, managers conventionally consider only operating cost savings, labor cost in particular. There are many other benefits managers must consider and use in estimating cash inflows in today's environment.

Tangible benefits:

Inventory savings. Work-in-process and finished-goods inventory levels are reduced substantially due to the increased flexibility, more stable product flow, better quality, and improved production scheduling.

Less floor space. The decrease in inventory and the installation of a smaller number of computer-controlled machines, which replace a larger number of conventional machines, release a substantial amount of floor space.

Improved quality. The new technology allows the company to conform to product specifications better, which reduces product defects and improves product uniformity.

Intangible benefits:

More flexibility. Machines can serve as backups for each other, and easily accommodate product changes. The same equipment handles both current high-volume models and discontinued models.

Shorter lead time. The new technology allows the company to respond to new customer demands more quickly.

Employee education. Technology advances at a fast pace, and a company that employs new technology will be able to educate the managers and employees much better when a new generation of technology is introduced.

In today's environment, the magnitude of the benefits from these new elements of capital budgeting may be even greater than labor cost savings. As a matter of fact, these benefits may be the very reason why the company wants to invest in new technology. Without these benefits incorporated in capital budgeting, the justification of investment in technology is not complete. Managers must try to quantify these benefits and use them in the estimation of future cash inflows.

SUMMARY

This chapter covered four topics: the effects of income taxes on capital budgeting, the effects of inflation on capital budgeting, the ranking of capital investment projects, and the effect of technological advances on capital budgeting.

Taxes are cash outflows and thus, all other things being equal, the higher the taxes the less attractive the capital investment projects. Capital investment projects should be analyzed on an after-tax basis. The role of depreciation in capital budgeting decisions is that it saves taxes by shielding an equal amount of revenue from being taxed. The gain on the sale of an old asset is taxable and the loss on the sale of an old asset provides a tax credit, which is treated as a cash inflow.

Capital budgeting projects may be ranked using the net present value, the internal rate of return, the accounting rate of return, or the payback method. Using the first three methods, the project with the highest score (NPV, IRR or ARR) is ranked as the most desirable and vice versa. Using the payback method, the project with the shortest payback period is ranked as the most desirable and the one with the longest payback period is ranked as the least desirable. However, all these methods, particularly the ARR and the payback methods, have major drawbacks. The most reliable ranking tool is the profitability index which is the ratio of the present value of net after-tax cash inflows from a project to the investment required for the project.

The projected inflation rate need not be incorporated in capital investment analysis because the process is somewhat complicated, but more importantly because if incorporated properly the net present value will be the same as the net present value without considering inflation adjustments. For post-audit purposes, actual cash inflows should be adjusted to exclude the effect of inflation.

Managers also face problems in the justification of investment in new technology, and how to use additional factors and new methodology to correct the deficiencies in capital budgeting. The major problems include the discount rate problem, the longer project life problem, and the conventional cash inflow estimation problem.

BASIC CONCEPTS AND TERMS

After-tax benefit	Profitability index
After-tax cash flow	Project ranking
After-tax cost	Tax saving on depreciation
Depreciation tax shield	Technology
Flexibility	

■ SELF-REVIEW PROBLEM

The SAS Company is undecided about whether to replace its conventional equipment with high-tech equipment. The high-tech equipment will increase the company's production capacity by 80%, without increasing other fixed expenses, except depreciation. The demand for the company's products is strong, and the company will have no problem selling the higher volume. The existing equipment does not have any cash value now, but, if rebuilt at a cost of $67,000, will be operational for another 5 years. The company's tax rate is 30% and its after-tax required rate of return is 14%.

The following data are available:

	High-Tech Equipment	Existing Equipment
Operating data:		
Units of output	18,000	10,000
Selling price per unit	$10	$10
Variable cash cost per unit	7	7

Equipment data:

Purchase cost	$160,000	—
Rebuilding cost	—	$67,000
Salvage value at end of year 5	12,000	2,000
Useful life	5 years	5 years

Depreciation:

    High-tech equipment: Accelerated depreciation deductions are taken. The depreciation rates (applied to the original cost of equipment) for the 5 years are 40%, 30%, 20%, 10%, and 0%, respectively.

    Existing equipment: Straight-line depreciation for each of the remaining 5 years is $13,000.

Required:

1. Determine which project is more desirable, using the NPV as the preference criterion.
2. Determine which project is more desirable, using the profitability index as the preference criterion.
3. Why is it so difficult to justify investment in the high-tech equipment?

Solution

Annual operating cash inflows (cash CM per unit $\times$ units):

    For high-tech machine: ($10 $-$ $7) $\times$ 18,000
                      = $3 $\times$ 18,000 = $54,000

    For existing machine: ($10 $-$ $7) $\times$ 10,000
                      = $3 $\times$ 10,000 = $30,000

Depreciation deductions for high-tech equipment:

Year	Cost	Depreciation Rate	Depreciation Deduction	Asset Book Value
1	$160,000	0.4	$64,000	$96,000
2	160,000	0.3	48,000	48,000
3	160,000	0.2	32,000	16,000
4	160,000	0.1	16,000	0
5	160,000	—	—	0
		1.0	$160,000	$160,000

Depreciation deductions for existing equipment:

    $13,000 $\times$ 5 years = $65,000

Book value of existing equipment after 5 years:

    $67,000 $-$ $65,000 = $2,000

Tax on the salvage value = (Cash received − Book value) × Tax rate
High-tech machine: ($12,000 −   0) × 0.3 = $3,600
Existing machine: ($ 2,000 − $2,000) × 0.3 = 0

Tax is paid only on the gain on disposal. The salvage value of the existing machine is equal to the book value, representing the portion that has not been deducted on the tax return. The high-tech machine would be fully depreciated by the end of Year 4, and the salvage value represents the gain on disposal.

1. NPV Computation:

	Years	Pre-Tax Cash Flow	Tax Effect	After-Tax Cash Flow	PV Factor at 14%	PV of Cash Flow
High-tech equipment:						
Investment cost	0	$(160,000)	—	$(160,000)	1.0000	$(160,000)
Annual cash inflows	1–5	54,000	1 − 0.3	37,800	3.4331	129,771
Depreciation:						
	1	64,000	0.3	19,200	0.8772	16,842
	2	48,000	0.3	14,400	0.7695	11,081
	3	32,000	0.3	9,600	0.6750	6,480
	4	16,000	0.3	4,800	0.5921	2,842
	5	—	—	—	0.5194	—
Salvage value	5	12,000	1 − 0.3	8,400	0.5194	4,363
NPV						$ 11,379
Existing equipment:						
Rebuilding cost	0	$ (67,000)	—	$ (67,000)	1.0000	$ (67,000)
Annual cash inflow	1–5	30,000	1 − 0.3	21,000	3.4331	72,095
Depreciation:	1–5	13,000	0.3	3,900	3.4331	13,389
Salvage value	5	2,000	—	2,000	0.5194	1,039
NPV						$ 19,523

Based on the NPV, rebuilding the existing equipment is better than investing in the high-tech equipment.

2. PI Computation:

$$\text{Profitability index (PI)} = \frac{\text{PV of cash inflows}}{\text{Required investment}}$$

	High-Tech	Existing
PV of cash inflows:		
Annual cash inflows	$129,771	$72,095
Total tax savings on depreciation ...	37,245	13,389
Salvage value	4,363	1,039
PV total	$171,379	$86,523
Required investment................	÷ $160,000	÷ $67,000
Profitability index	1.07	1.29

Based on the PI, rebuilding the existing equipment is better than investing in the high-tech equipment.

3. The tangible benefits, such as inventory savings, less floor space, and improved quality, and the intangible benefits, such as more flexibility, shorter lead time, and employee education have not been considered in the estimation of future cash inflows for the high-tech equipment. In today's environment, the benefits from these new elements of capital budgeting may be the very reason why the company wants to invest in new technology. Without these benefits incorporated in capital budgeting, the justification of investment in technology is very difficult.

■ REVIEW QUESTIONS

14-1 Assume that all items of cash inflow are taxable and all items of cash outflow are tax deductible at the same tax rate for two available investment projects. Does it make any difference whether we make capital budgeting decisions with or without tax consideration? Explain.

14-2 What is the major difference between financing through borrowing at a certain interest rate and financing through issuing a preferred stock paying the same rate of dividend?

14-3 How are after-tax costs computed?

14-4 How are after-tax benefits computed?

14-5 Are the after-tax amounts of dividend payments and interest on municipal bonds really the same as the before-tax amounts? Explain.

14-6 What is the difference between the income tax effect on return on investment and that on recovery of investment?

14-7 The original cost of an investment is the cash outflow that is not tax deductible. How does a company that invests in a machine used in production get a tax benefit on the investment?

14-8 Regardless of the depreciation method used, the total amount of depreciation taken over the useful life is the same. Why would the use of an accelerated depreciation method make a difference in investment decisions, compared to the straight-line depreciation method?

14-9 Precisely speaking, depreciation itself is not a cash flow item. Explain how depreciation affects capital investment decisions?

14-10 A gain or loss on disposal of production equipment is just an accounting item. Does it have any cash flow significance in capital budgeting?

14-11 Inflation affects the discount rate. Future cash inflows should be discounted using the annually adjusted rate of return. Price increases tend to inflate cash flows. But, if future cash flows are adjusted by the same inflation rate used for adjusting the discount rate, the net present value will be exactly the same as before adjustment. Then, why is the inflation issue considered in capital budgeting?

14-12 How should managers deal with the inflated cash flows that are observed during post-audit?

14-13 In the process of ranking various capital investment projects, is the project with the highest net present value the most desirable? What size project may yield the highest net present value under usual circumstances?

14-14 If the internal rate of return is the project ranking criterion, what types of projects are usually chosen as the most desirable?

14-15 How does the discount rate make the decision to invest in new technology difficult? Is the discount rate used by many companies related to the accounting rate of return in reality?

14-16 Why is the useful life of the capital investment in new technology an issue in justifying such investment?

14-17 What tangible benefits of new technology tend to be disregarded in the conventional capital budgeting analysis?

14-18 What intangible benefits of new technology tend to be disregarded in the conventional capital budgeting analysis?

🌐 INTERNET PROJECT

Web 14-1:

Websites: www.aa.com
             www.united.com

The websites listed above represent two famous companies. Search the sites for information on their operating characteristics.

Required:

1.   Consider NPV as a capital investment screening device. Which company would prefer the use of NPV? Why?

2.   Consider IRR as a capital investment screening device. Which company would prefer the use of IRR? Why?

■ EXERCISES

E14-1   Project-Ranking Criteria

Each of the following statements refers to the characteristic of one of the various project-ranking criteria. Indicate which criterion the statement refers to, among net present value (NPV), internal rate of return (IRR), accounting rate of return (ARR), profitability index (PI), or payback period (PB).

a.   Is a discounted cash flow technique, and favors projects that appear profitable in the short run.

b.   Is a discounted cash flow technique, and tends to indicate that the project involving the largest amount of capital investment cost is the most desirable.

c.   Considers the return on investment or profitability based on present values of cash flows.

d.   Disregards present values and does not consider cash flows that are generated after the cost of investment is recovered.

e.   Reflects the distortion in financial reporting convention.

E14-2   Concept of After-Tax Cash Flows

1.   MPG, Inc. wants to start a productivity improvement program in its plants. A series of workshops would cost $80,000 per year. What would be the after-tax cost of the workshops? The company's income tax rate is 25%.

2.   A series of productivity workshops that were started last year at an innovative supplier of MPG, Inc. have improved the employees' productivity awareness, and increased the company's taxable income by $50,000. What is the after-tax benefit (income increase) from the supplier's workshops? The supplier's income tax rate is 30%.

3.   HGS, Inc. has purchased a new machine at a cost of $160,000. The machine has a 10-year useful life, but the tax law allows the following yearly accelerated depreciation deductions for the machine: 14.3% (Year 1), 24.5% (Year 2), 17.5% (Year 3), 12.5% (Year 4), 8.9% (Year 5), 8.9% (Year 6), 8.9% (Year 7), and 4.5% (Year 8). Compute the yearly income tax savings from the depreciation tax shield. The company's income tax rate is 30%.

E14-3   Tax Savings from Accelerated Depreciation;
Net Present Value

PFS, Inc. is considering an investment in new equipment. The equipment costs $90,000 and has a salvage value of $8,200 at the end of its 4-year useful life. The tax law allows the following yearly accelerated depreciation deductions for the equipment: 33.3% (Year 1), 44.5% (Year 2), 14.8% (Year 3), and 7.4% (Year 4).

The new equipment would produce net cash inflows of $38,000 per year. It will require reconditioning at a cost of $15,000 at the end of Year 3. The company's tax rate is 30%. The after-tax cost of capital is 14%.

Required:

1. Compute the net present value of the investment in the equipment.
2. Should the company invest in the equipment?

E14-4   Net Present Value; Straight-Line Depreciation

PST, Inc. faces a choice between an investment in new equipment or an investment in inventory buildup. Both require a cash outlay of $150,000 now and both would generate annual cash inflows of $28,000 per year for the next 8 years. The equipment will have a salvage value of $14,000 at the end of the 8-year useful life. The entire cash investment in inventory will be released at the end of the 8-year period. The equipment will be depreciated at the following rates: 10% (Year 1), 20% (Years 2-5), and 10% (Year 6). The company requires an after-tax return of 12% on its investments. The company's tax rate is 25%.

Required:

Which investment should the company choose? Use the net present value method to make the decision.

E14-5   Profitability Index

A company has two investment choices: project P and project Q. Both projects require an initial investment of $150,000. The company has computed the following present values of cash inflows from the two projects:

	Present Values	
	Project P	*Project Q*
Net annual cash inflows	$104,320	$104,320
Tax savings from depreciation	25,587	–
Salvage value of the equipment.	4,241	–
Release of cash from investment	–	60,582

Required:

Which project should the company choose for investment? Use the profitability index in making your decision.

 ### E14-6   Net Present Value; Accelerated Depreciation

MRV, Inc. earns a 12% after-tax return on its investments. The company is considering the installation of an air purification system in one of its plants. The system costs $180,000 now, but will save $45,500 per year in terms of lower medical insurance premiums and reduced machine malfunction caused by dust in the air. The system will have a useful life of 10 years, but it will require a new set of filters in 5 years at a cost of $16,000. The system will have a salvage value of $8,000 at the end of the 10-year useful life. The tax law allows the following yearly accelerated depreciation deductions for the equipment: 14.3% (Year 1), 24.5% (Year 2), 17.5% (Year 3), 12.5% (Year 4), 8.9% (Year 5), 8.9% (Year 6), 8.9% (Year 7), and 4.5% (Year 8). The company's tax rate is 30%.

Required:

Should the company install the system? Use net present value as the single decision making criterion.

E14-7 Project Ranking; Profitability Index and Net Present Value

Max Sactor, Inc. has the following four investment projects under consideration:

	Project P	Q	R	S
Initial investment cost	$ 80,000	$70,000	$ 90,000	$100,000
Present value of cash inflows	110,000	60,000	100,000	135,000

Required:

1. Rank the projects according to profitability index.
2. Rank the projects according to net present value.
3. Compare the rankings of project S under the two different criteria. Explain the results.

E14-8 Gain (Loss) on Disposal of Equipment; Tax Effects

LJX, Inc. has just sold equipment items, P and Q, for $50,000 and $20,000, respectively. The following information is available on the cost and depreciation of the two:

	Equipment P	Q
Useful life	5 years	5 years
Original cost	$100,000	$80,000
Total depreciation for 3 years	60,000	48,000

The company's tax rate is 30%.

Required:

Compute the after-tax cash inflow from the disposal of each equipment for discounted cashflow analysis.

E14-9 Inflation Adjustment; Discount Rate

PTR, Inc. is in the process of making the following inflation adjustments for its discounted cash flow analysis:

1. The company requires a minimum return of 12% on its investments. In Year 1, the inflation rate is 10%. The company uses the inflation-adjusted discount rate in the discounted cash flow analysis. What is the inflation-adjusted discount rate the company would use in its discounted cash flow analysis for Year 1?

2. The company predicts that the inflation rate will average 10% in each of the following three years (Years 1-3). The annual cash inflows from a proposed investment project is $80,000 in constant dollars. What would be the annual inflation-adjusted cash inflows for each of the three years?

■ PROBLEMS

P14-10   Ethics; Justifying Investment in New Technology

"This is already the fourth defeat of this year for us. Our team worked hard on the proposal that has just been turned down by our prospective client. The project is an ambitious one, and it is within our expertise. It would have made us grow into the next decade." Ted Mazur, a project manager at TDX Consultants, Inc. continued his remarks, showing deep frustration on his face, to Megan Tyler, controller of the firm. "The primary, no, the only reason why we lost the bid was that our competition used far more advanced generation technology with 3-D perspectives. Our proposal didn't have any problem in terms of the quality of work and the cost quoted. Please do something, so that we can obtain the state-of-the-art technology which the president refused to give us two months ago."

Tyler could understand the frustration of the project manager. Yes, there was no problem justifying investment in new technology, as long as the technology meant small computers and equipment which saved labor costs in operations. The payback period on those small investments usually was under two or three years. If the investments, however, involved an extended period of time or a large sum of money, it was difficult to generate a positive net present value in the capital investment analysis.

The traditional elements alone have not been enough to produce a positive net present value. The labor cost savings and productivity gains cannot account for the big chunk of the present value of future cash inflows needed to justify investment in state-of-the-art technology. "Perhaps, the only solution may be your creativity." the project manager said. "How much present value of future cash inflows do you need to generate a positive net present value? Just come up with enough cash inflows as your estimates, for God's sake. I know this: having the new technology is the only way we can survive in the future."

Tyler is now faced with a difficult task. "I know he has a point. But the problem is how to come up with the number," she said to herself walking back to her office.

Required:

What are the ethical implications of "just coming up with enough cash inflows needed to generate a positive net present value"? Explain, based on the Standards of Ethical Conduct for Management Accountants.

P14-11   Net Present Value; Accelerated Depreciation

Desert Ride, Inc. is considering the purchase of a new fleet of all-terrain vehicles (ATVs) for its desert recreation facility. The new fleet of ATVs cost $300,000. The ATVs will have a useful life of 7 years with reconditioning required at the end of Year 5 at a cost of $48,000. At the end of the seventh year, the ATVs will be sold for $15,000.

The new fleet of ATVs will generate cash inflows of $95,000 per year. The old ATVs will be sold for $20,000 now if the new ATVs are purchased. The tax law allows the following yearly accelerated depreciation deductions for the new ATVs: 20.0% (Year 1), 32.0% (Year 2), 19.2% (Year 3), 11.5% (Year 4), 11.5% (Year 5), and 5.8% (Year 6). The company requires an after-tax return of 14% on its comparable investments. The company's tax rate is 30%.

Required:

Compute the net present value of the investment in new ATVs. Should the company invest in new ATVs?

P14-12   Net Present Value; New Operation

DTS, Inc. provides manufacturing companies with workstation diagnostic services that will prevent muscle strain in workers. The company uses special equipment and a software that detects ergonomic problems before they cause health problems for factory workers. The service has helped many manufacturing companies reduce workers' health insurance premiums and other related costs significantly. The company is considering a proposal to open another operation in Cedar Rapids, Iowa. The following information has been compiled:

a. The initial investment required would be $300,000 to equip and open the facility.

b. The project will be operated for 10 years. At the end of the tenth year, DTS, Inc. will have to spend $40,000 to refurbish and return the space.

c. The net cash inflows are estimated to be $65,000 per year for the 10-year project.

d. At the beginning of the project, DTS, Inc. must invest working capital of $60,000. This working capital will be released at the end of the tenth year for investment elsewhere.

e. The diagnostic equipment would have a salvage value of $30,000 at the end of the tenth year.

f. The tax law allows the following yearly accelerated depreciation deductions for the equipment: 14.3% (Year 1), 24.5% (Year 2), 17.5% (Year 3), 12.5% (Year 4), 8.9% (Year 5), 8.9% (Year 6), 8.9% (Year 7), and 4.5% (Year 8).

g. The company's tax rate is 30%, and the after-tax cost of capital is 12%.

Required:

Compute the net present value of the new operation. Should the company open the Cedar Rapids operation?

 P14-13 **Straight-Line Depreciation versus Accelerated Depreciation; Tax Effects**

Illusions, Inc. produces cartoons for motion picture studios in Burbank, California. The firm has been offered an 8-year contract to provide cartoons for movie projects undertaken by a major studio. The contract stipulates that special, state-of-the-art equipment be used in the production of cartoons. The information on the costs and cash flows is presented below:

a. The cost of the equipment is $480,000. The equipment would have a salvage value of only $7,000 at the end of the 8-year useful life.

b. The firm needs to invest working capital of $95,000. The total amount of the working capital will be released at the end of the eighth year, and be available for investment elsewhere.

c. The contract would generate net cash inflows of $130,000 per year.

d. The equipment will be depreciated at the following rates: 10% (Year 1), 20% (Year 2-Year 5), and 10% (Year 6).

e. The company requires an after-tax return of 14% on its investments.

f. The company's tax rate is 30%.

Required:

1. Compute the net present value of the investment in the equipment. Should Illusions, Inc. accept the offer from the major studio?

2. Now assume that the tax law allows the following yearly accelerated depreciation deductions on the new equipment: 20.0% (Year 1), 32.0% (Year 2), 19.2% (Year 3), 11.5% (Year 4), 11.5% (Year 5), and 5.8% (Year 6). Compute the net present value again, using the new depreciation rates. Would your answer in (1) change because of the new depreciation deductions?

P14-14 Alternative Investment Ranking Criteria

RPM, Inc. is in the process of evaluating five investment alternatives. The company's cost of capital is 12%. Detailed information on the five alternatives is provided below:

	Investment Alternatives				
	P	Q	R	S	T
Project life	5 years	4 years	6 years	10 years	5 years
Initial investment	$210,000	$360,000	$320,000	$280,000	$380,000
Present value					
of cash inflows	262,000	418,000	304,000	338,500	449,000

RPM has only $380,000 available to invest. The company has chosen to use the profitability index, net present value, and internal rate of return as the evaluation criteria.

Required:

1. Compute the profitability index for each investment alternative.
2. Compute the net present value for each investment alternative.
3. Determine the annual cash inflow from each investment alternative.
4. Determine the internal rate of return for each investment alternative.
5. Rank the five investment alternatives, according to:
   a. Profitability index
   b. Net present value
   c. Internal rate of return
6. Which investment should be selected?

P14-15   Net Present Value versus Profitability Index; Straight-Line and Accelerated Depreciation

C-Cola, Inc. is in the process of evaluating two investment alternatives. The company uses the net present value and the profitability index as the criteria for decision making. The following information on the two investment alternatives is available:

Alternative 1: The company could purchase and install new bottling equipment in its bottling plant. The new equipment costs $180,000 including installation. The company estimates that the new equipment will save $55,000 in annual operating costs from the current level. The new equipment is expected to last 7 years, and will have a salvage value of $10,000. The bottling equipment requires reconditioning in 4 years at a cost of $7,000. The equipment will be depreciated at the following rates: 10% (Year 1), 20% (Year 2-Year 5), and 10% (Year 6).

Alternative 2: The company could invest in a new fleet of delivery trucks. The new trucks cost $240,000 in total, and would save $70,000 in annual cash operating costs. The salvage value of the trucks would be $16,000 at the end of the 7-year useful life. The trucks would need parts replacement in 4 years at a cost of $8,000. The tax law allows the following yearly accelerated depreciation deductions on the new trucks: 20.0% (Year 1), 32.0% (Year 2), 19.2% (Year 3), 11.5% (Year 4), 11.5% (Year 5), and 5.8% (Year 6).

The company's after-tax cost of capital is 12%, and the applicable income tax rate is 30%.

Required:

1. Compute the net present value of each of the two alternatives. Which alternative should the company choose?
2. Compute the profitability index for each of the two alternatives. Which alternative should the company choose?

P14-16   Ranking Investment Alternatives

J. Fox, Inc. finances its investments with debt. The cost of borrowed funds is 12%. The company is in the process of evaluating various investment alternatives. The details of the investment alternatives are presented below:

	Investment Project				
	A	B	C	D	E
Project life	6 years	5 years	6 years	4 years	10 years
Investment cost......	$125,000	$100,000	$ 85,000	$130,000	$120,000
Present value of cash inflows	160,000	91,000	112,000	159,000	152,000

The company has a policy of examining the profitability index, net present value, and internal rate of return as the evaluation criteria before it finalizes the investment decision.

Required:

1. Compute the profitability index for each investment alternative.
2. Compute the net present value for each investment alternative.
3. Determine the annual cash inflow from each investment alternative.
4. Determine the internal rate of return for each investment alternative.
5. Rank the five investment alternatives, according to:
   a. Profitability index
   b. Net present value
   c. Internal rate of return

 ## P14-17   Effects of Accelerated Depreciation; Net Present Value

Recreation Business, Inc. is considering a proposal to open a virtual-reality arcade. The lot, which the company has available for opening the arcade, can be used only for 8 years until a proposed construction project by the city starts at the end of Year 8. The company has concluded its preliminary market study, and the outlook is good for the proposed arcade.

The proposal includes the following information on the virtual-reality arcade:

Initial cost of investment in the facility......................	$590,000
Initial injection of working capital (to be released at the end of Year 8)	8,000
Cost to upgrade software at the end of Year 5................	65,000
Annual cash inflows	150,000

The facility will have to be abandoned at the end of Year 8, but some items will be sold to other arcades for $59,000 at that time. The company's after-tax cost of capital is 14% and its tax rate is 30%. The equipment will be depreciated at the following rates: 10% (Year 1), 20% (Year 2-Year 5), and 10% (Year 6).

Required:

1. Assume that the company uses the net present value in making capital investment decisions. Should the company invest in the arcade? Justify your recommendation.
2. Now assume that the tax law allows the following yearly accelerated depreciation deductions on the arcade facility: 20.0% (Year 1), 32.0% (Year 2), 19.2% (Year 3), 11.5% (Year 4), 11.5% (Year 5), and 5.8% (Year 6). Compute the net present value of the investment in the arcade, using the accelerated depreciation rates. Does the recommendation you made in (1) change?
3. What is the reason for a higher net present value you obtained in (2)?

P14-18   Net Present Value; Uneven Cash Flows

Image & Color, Inc. provides unique photo services: It converts black-and-white movies to color. The company entered the field when a single company was monopolizing the market. Image & Color has colorized 31 movies thus far, including some very famous movies from the old Hollywood era. After some movie critics wrote very nasty articles two years ago in the entertainment section of major newspapers about putting a palette to classic films, the company has avoided business in the controversial area and started concentrating on old TV series.

At the present time, the company is considering the purchase of a new-generation photo-imaging machine that will cost $640,000 now, and will have a useful life of 10 years.. The new machine will require an injection of $60,000 of working capital at the beginning of the first year of operation. The total amount of the working capital will be released and be available for investment elsewhere at the end of the 10-year life. The equipment will have a salvage value of $64,000 at the end of the useful life. The company will also have to spend about $200,000 at the end of the 10-year life in order to clean up the environmentally hazardous photochemicals from the site.

The company estimates an operating loss of $90,000 in the first year of the new equipment operation because of the need to train and closely supervise its operators in the early stage of the use. The new equipment is expected to generate the following annual cash inflows after the first year:

	Year			
	2	3	4	5-10
Cash inflows	$60,000	$300,000	$390,000	$40,000

The tax law allows the following yearly accelerated depreciation deductions for the equipment: 14.3% (Year 1), 24.5% (Year 2), 17.5% (Year 3), 12.5% (Year 4), 8.9% (Year 5), 8.9% (Year 6), 8.9% (Year 7), and 4.5% (Year 8). The company's after-tax cost of capital is 16%, and tax rate is 30%.

Required:

Compute the net present value of the investment in the new equipment. Should the company invest in the equipment?

P14-19 Net Present Value; Incremental Cost Approach

Baja Cruise, Inc. is considering the replacement of its existing boat with a new boat that can be used for dinner cruise services around San Diego. The cruise services are estimated to generate cash inflows of $92,200 per year. The new boat costs $360,000 now and will have a useful life of 8 years. The new boat will have a salvage value of $12,000 at the end of the 8-year life. In order to maintain the new boat properly, the company will have to replace the boat engine in 5 years at a cost of $25,000.

If the new boat is purchased, the existing boat, which still has a remaining life of 4 years, will be sold for $80,000. The book value of the existing boat is $180,000, and the old boat will have a zero salvage value in four years. The depreciation on the existing boat over the remaining 4-year period will be:

	Year			
	1	2	3	4
Annual depreciation	$40,000	$40,000	$40,000	$20,000

The tax law allows the following yearly accelerated depreciation deductions on the new boat: 20.0% (Year 1), 32.0% (Year 2), 19.2% (Year 3), 11.5% (Year 4), 11.5% (Year 5), and 5.8% (Year 6). The company's after-tax cost of capital is 16%, and tax rate is 30%.

Required:

Compute the net present value of the investment in the new boat, using the incremental-cost approach. Should the company invest in the new boat?

P14-20 Net Present Value; Total-Cost and Incremental-Cost Approach

T. Chips, Inc. manufactures and sells various chips which are used by manufacturers of desk-top computers. The company is currently considering the replacement of the etching equipment. The equipment is used in the process where selected portions of metal and oxide film are removed from a silicon wafer to make etches. The company has compiled the following information on the replacement:

	Current Etching Equipment	New Etching Equipment
Initial purchase cost	$300,000	$500,000
Salvage value, now..................	68,000	–
Salvage value, 7 years later	12,000	50,000
Reconditioning cost for this year	130,000	–
Current book value	96,000	–
Annual operating costs..............	153,000	91,000

If the current etching equipment is reconditioned for $130,000 this year, it will be operational for 6 more years (a total of 7 years from now). The company intends to use the new etching equipment for only 7 years. At that time, new-generation equipment will be purchased.

The company would take depreciation deductions of $60,000 this year and $30,000 next year on the current etching equipment if it keeps the current equipment. The tax law allows the following yearly accelerated depreciation deductions on the new etching equipment: 20.0% (Year 1), 32.0% (Year 2), 19.2% (Year 3), 11.5% (Year 4), 11.5% (Year 5), and 5.8% (Year 6). The company's after-tax cost of capital is 14%, and tax rate is 30%.

Required:

1. Should T. Chips, Inc. replace the etching equipment? Use the total-cost approach and compute the net present value.
2. Use the incremental-cost approach and compute the net present value. Do you get the same net present value as in (1)?

P14-21   Incremental-Cost Approach; New Technology

TOP, Inc. is considering the purchase and installation of virtual engineers in its manufacturing process. The technology is based on computer-aided production engineering (CAPE), which is an advancement from computer-aided design (CAD). CAPE actually incorporates CAD information to make human efforts unnecessary in the setup of the factory floor. The company has compiled the following information on the proposed investment:

Useful life of virtual engineers	8 years
Initial cost of purchasing and installing	
virtual engineers	$3,600,000
Salvage value in 8 years	160,000
Annual savings in engineering costs	400,000
Annual savings in scheduling costs	600,000
Increase in utility and maintenance costs per year	40,000
Injection of working capital	
(to be released at the end of Year 8)	800,000
Cost to upgrade software at the end of Year 5	720,000

The virtual engineers would make the existing setup equipment obsolete for TOP, Inc., but the company could sell it to smaller manufacturers. The existing setup equipment was purchased four years ago at a total cost of $800,000, and may be sold for $80,000 now. It is being depreciated by an optional straight-line method, which provides depreciation deductions of $160,000 this year, $160,000 next year, and $80,000 the following year. The current book value of the existing setup equipment is $400,000.

The virtual engineers will be depreciated at the following rates: 10% (Year 1), 20% (Year 2-Year 5), and 10% (Year 6). The company's after-tax cost of capital is 12%, and tax rate is 30%.

Required:

1. What is the amount of net annual cost savings if the virtual engineers are installed?
2. Compute the net present value of the investment in the virtual engineers. Should the company install the virtual engineers?

■ CASES

C14-22   Make or Buy; Total-Cost Approach

GT Publications, Inc. has been a successful publishing company for the last 21 years. The company tries to appeal to younger readers with superb color pictures that are very compatible with the contents of the books. The company takes great pride in providing interesting but proper stories to young people in ways that are perceived as "not boring at all."

The company is considering the replacement of its computer design facility with new-generation computers and software. Since graphic design is a key component in the process of publishing books, the company regards maintaining a high-quality computer design facility as essential in its operations. The new facility, including software, will have a useful life of only 5 years due to rapid technological development, and costs $756,000. The tax law allows the following annual accelerated depreciation deductions: 33.3% (Year 1); 44.5% (Year 2); 14.8% (Year 3); and 7.4% (Year 4).

If the replacement is actually made, then the current design equipment will be sold to a smaller animation studio for $1,200. The current equipment has been fully depreciated. The new computer design facility will have a salvage value of $12,000 at the end of the 5-year useful life, and requires an injection of $16,000 of working capital now. The working capital will be released at the end of the 5-year life, and be available for investment elsewhere.

The size of the graphic design, which is used in books in a typical process, is such that each unit of graphic design requires the following production costs, according to the production records:

	Per Unit
Design materials.	$10.40
Design labor	3.20
Variable overhead	2.40
Fixed overhead.	8.00
Total cost per unit of graphic design	$24.00

According to the company's estimates, the following graphic designs will be needed for the next five years of operations:

	Year				
	1	2	3	4	5
Units of graphic design . . .	40,000	40,000	41,600	44,000	44,000

Recently, the company has been approached by Graphics, Inc., a graphic design studio in West Hollywood . Graphics, Inc., known for its effective and efficient operations that are well regarded in the industry, has offered to provide graphic designs to GT Publications, Inc. at a price of $23 per unit. Graphics, Inc. specializes in graphic designs, and would be able to create graphic designs at lower costs. If GT Publications, Inc. decides to buy graphic designs, rather than create its own graphic designs, it would be able to reduce $36,000 of fixed overhead per year, primarily through the reduction in indirect labor.

The company's after-tax cost of capital is 14%, and tax rate is 30%.

Required:

Should GT Publications, Inc. replace its computer design facility with a new one (and continue to create its own graphic designs) or purchase the graphic designs from Graphics, Inc.? Use the net present value method and the total-cost approach.

C14-23   Make or Buy; Incremental-Cost Approach

Eyetech, Inc. manufactures various types of lenses that are sold to eyeglass stores. One special type of lens Eyetech manufactures is Visionet, special lens surgically implanted in the eye. Visionet makes the old method of correcting for cataracts "look like a really ancient way of treating an eye problem." Eyetech is one of only several manufacturers of the special lens in the U.S. Visionet is not a very profitable product itself, but including it among the other lenses the company manufactures allows the company to be called a full-line manufacturer of lenses.

The manufacture of Visionet requires specialized lens-crafting machines which need to be replaced. The special lens-crafting machines cost $2,000,000 now and will have a useful life of only 4 years due to rapid technological advancement. Their salvage value will be $80,000 at the end of the 4-year useful life. The tax law allows accelerated annual depreciation deductions on the new lens-crafting machines as follows: 33.3% (Year 1); 44.5% (Year 2); 14.8% (Year 3); and 7.4% (Year 4).

The new lens-crafting machines require a working capital injection of $48,000 that will be released at the end of the 4-year useful life and be available for investment elsewhere. The existing machines have been fully depreciated and have no book value now. A small manufacturer of lenses is interested in buying the old machines at $36,000 if Eyetech decides to replace the machines.

Recently, another lens manufacturer has offered to supply the special lenses at $18 per unit. The quality of the special lenses would meet the high quality standards Eyetech has set for its products. The manufacturer has a large volume of business and the economy of scale would allow it to produce special lenses at lower costs.

Eyetech needs about 64,000 units of Visionet each year, and estimates of future demand would be about the same. Eyetech's production of Visionet has required the following costs:

	Per Unit
Direct materials	$ 1.60
Direct labor	2.00
Variable overhead	3.00
Fixed overhead	12.40
Total manufacturing cost per unit	$19.00

The company's after-tax cost of capital is 12%, and tax rate is 30%. Fixed overhead costs of the company are not avoidable in the foreseeable future.

Required:

1. Compute the amount of cost savings Eyetech, Inc. would realize if it decides to purchase the new equipment and continue to manufacture Visionet rather than buy the special lenses from the outside.
2. Should Eyetech, Inc. invest in the new lens-crafting machines and make Visionet? Use the net present value method and the incremental-cost approach.

C14-24   Net Present Value; Purchase of JIT Inventory System

Rosen Manufacturing Corporation produces office furniture equipment and sells it wholesale to furniture distributors. Rosen's management is reviewing a proposal to purchase a just-in-time inventory (JIT) system to better serve its customers. The JIT system will include a computer system and materials handling equipment. The decision will be based on whether or not the new JIT system is cost-beneficial to the organization over the next five years.

The computer system, for both hardware and software, will initially cost $1,250,000. Materials handling equipment, such as a new conveyor belt, will cost $450,000. Both groups of equipment are to be classified as five-year property for the purposes of using the Modified Accelerated Cost Recovery System (MACRS) for income tax purposes. The MACRS rates for five-year equipment are given below. At the end of the five years, the newly acquired equipment will be sold. It is estimated that at the time the computer system will have a projected market value of $100,000, while the materials handling equipment will have a projected market value of $50,000.

	MACRS Depreciation Rates for
Year	Five-Year Property
1	20.0%
2	32.0%
3	19.2%
4	11.5%
5	11.5%
6	5.8%

Other factors to be considered over the next five years for this proposal include the following:

a. Due to the service improvement resulting from this new JIT system, Rosen will realize a $600,000 sales increase in the first year. Rosen expects this initial $600,000 sales increase to continue to grow by 10% per year thereafter.
b. The contribution margin from sales is 60%.
c. Annual material ordering costs will increase $50,000 due to a greater level of purchase orders.

    d. There will be a one-time decrease in working capital investment of $150,000 at the end of the first year.

    e. There will be a 20% savings in warehouse rent due to less space being needed; the current annual rent is $300,000.

    Rosen uses an after-tax hurdle rate of 10% and has an effective income tax rate of 40%. Assume that all cash flows occur at year end for tax purposes except for any initial purchase amounts.

Required:

1. Prepare an analysis of the after-tax effects for the purchase of the just-in-time system at Rosen Manufacturing Corporation using the net present value method for evaluating capital expenditures. Be sure to show all of your calculations.
2. Determine whether or not Rosen Manufacturing Corporation should purchase the just-in-time inventory system. Explain your answer.

(CMA)

CONSTRAINTS AND RELEVANT COSTS

After studying this chapter, you should be able to:

1. Explain the meaning of constraints and scarce resources in managerial decision making, and show how a scarce resource may best be used to maximize the company's profits.

2. Compare the contribution-margin approach, activity-based costing (ABC), and Theory of Constraints (TOC) as to their approach to dealing with constraints and scarce resources.

3. Distinguish between relevant and irrelevant costs and factors in a variety of non-routine decision making situations.

4. Analyze available data to make a decision on inventory management or equipment replacement.

5. Prepare an analysis to show whether a product line or department should be added or dropped, or whether a company should make or buy a part for manufacturing.

6. Differentiate between joint products and by-products, and show how to make a decision on whether to sell products at the split-off point or after further processing.

7. Explain how to make a decision on whether to accept or reject a special sales order.

Every organization encounters **constraints** in its operations. It also faces the reality that its resources are limited. How to identify and maximize the use of its **scarce resources** sometimes determines the success or failure of an organization.

Managers make *routine* as well as non-routine or special decisions. *Non-routine* decisions include justifying an investment in a project, remodeling or discarding obsolete inventory, adding or dropping a product line or department, making certain subassembly parts or buying them from outside suppliers, accepting or rejecting a special sales order at a certain price, and selling some products at a certain stage in manufacturing or processing them further.

In making all these non-routine decisions, a manager must consider all costs and factors that are *relevant* to those decisions. The purpose of this chapter is to provide tools for distinguishing between relevant and irrelevant costs and factors, and show how managers can apply these tools in a variety of non-routine decision making situations.

CONSTRAINTS AND SCARCE RESOURCES

Every organization encounters **constraints** in its operations. Material, labor, and other resources required for manufacturing, sales, and services are also limited. In a particular firm, some resources may be more scarce than others. Labor hours, for example, may be adequate, but machine hours may be limited.

Managers must deal with the task of how best to utilize those scarce resources. For example, a firm may have a limited advertising budget for its products. How much money should be spent on each product? Another firm may have a limited number of machine hours needed for production of its products. Which product(s) should be produced? A department store may have a limited amount of floor space it can use either for expensive products with high profit margin and low turnover, or for inexpensive products with low profit margin and high turnover. Which products should it use the limited floor space for?

Non-routine decisions of Southwest Airlines include adding or dropping a flight route. Managers must consider relevant costs and factors for such decision-making needs.

There are three approaches that managers can use to deal with the problem of constraints or scarce resources. The contribution-margin approach is what we are already familiar with. The Theory of Constraints and activity-based costing are two other approaches that have become popular in recent years.

The Contribution-Margin Approach

Under the **contribution-margin (CM) approach,** managers take the course of action that will produce the highest CM per unit of the constraint or scarce resource, such as an advertising dollar, a machine hour, or a square foot of floor space. If the demand for the company's product is strong, this course of action will lead to the maximum overall CM for the company. Managers must be aware that the highest

CM per unit of scarce resource may not be the highest CM per unit of product, or the highest CM ratio per dollar of sales.

Consider the following illustration.

Casablanca Fan Company manufactures and sells two types of antique fans: ceiling fans and table fans. The relevant data are presented below:

	Ceiling Fan		Table Fan	
Selling price		$50		$30
Variable costs:				
Direct materials	$10		$7	
Direct labor	20		13	
Variable overhead	5	35	4	24
CM		$15		$ 6
CM ratio		30%		20%

Assuming that the demand for the company's fans is strong, and it has sufficient production capacity in terms of machine hours, which fan should the company produce and sell? The answer is obvious: The company should produce and sell only ceiling fans, since the CM per unit and the CM ratio for ceiling fans is higher.

Now assume that Casablanca's production capacity is limited to only 30,000 machine hours per month, and each ceiling fan requires three machine hours whereas each table fan requires only one machine hour. Which fans should Casablanca produce and sell?

Now that the production capacity is limited, the company should produce the product that will generate the higher CM per machine hour (the scarce resource), as shown below:

	Ceiling Fan	Table Fan
CM per unit	$15	$6
Machine hours required per unit	÷ 3	÷ 1
CM per machine hour (scarce resource)	$ 5	$6
Number of machine hours available	× 30,000	× 30,000
Total CM per month	$150,000	$180,000

The company should produce and sell only table fans, because they produce a higher CM per unit of scarce resource and a higher CM for the company as a whole.

We can also compute the total CM as follows:

	Ceiling Fan	Table Fan
Number of machine hours available	30,000	30,000
Machine hours required per unit	÷ 3	÷ 1
Number of fans that can be produced	10,000	30,000
CM per unit	× $15	× $6
Total CM per month	$150,000	$180,000

If one ceiling fan requires only two machine hours versus one machine hour a table fan requires, it would be better to produce ceiling fans only. You can use either of the above two formats to find out why.

The Theory of Constraints (TOC) Approach

The **Theory of Constraints (TOC),** developed by Goldratt and Fox, is a variable costing-oriented optimization technique which focuses on the system's constraints. The TOC approach is similar to the CM approach in that both focus on short-term optimization. The TOC approach, however, is comprehensive in nature, and can incorporate numerous constraints to provide a powerful solution to a company's operating problem.

The TOC approach uses **throughput** as the measure of profit the company needs to achieve. We can define throughput as follows using our above illustration:

	Ceiling Fan		Table Fan	
Selling price		$50		$30
Variable costs:				
Direct materials	$10		$7	
Energy	7	17	5	12
Throughput		$33		$18

Under the TOC, only variable costs of materials and energy are subtracted from revenue to compute throughput. Direct labor is not a variable cost under the TOC. Labor is a company's long-term commitment, and is not assumed to change in the short run. Overhead costs do not change in the short run either, under the TOC.

The TOC assumes that there is always at least one constraint on each product that limits the growth of the company's throughput. In our example, this constraint is machine hours. Since the production capacity is assumed to be fixed in the short run, under the TOC, the solution will be to produce table fans, as follows:

	Ceiling Fan	Table Fan
Throughput per unit	$ 33	$ 18
Machine hours required per unit	÷ 3	÷ 1
Throughput per machine hour (constraint)	$ 11	$ 18
Number of machine hours available	× 30,000	× 30,000
Total throughput per month	$ 330,000	$ 540,000

We are capturing only the basic structure of the TOC here. The TOC is a very sophisticated technique that employs three types of resources and the interactions between resources and products to focus on what constraints prevent throughput from increasing. The three types of resources are scarce bottleneck resources, nonbottleneck resources, and capacity constraint resources. It also considers statistical fluctuations and random events in order to accomplish the ultimate goal of increasing the rate at which throughput is generated.

Under the TOC, it is not necessary to analyze operating expenses in detail. The spirit is to identify constraints and exploit the constraints. The TOC advocates say, "If cost allocation has not been done properly, why do we waste time and money trying to fix the cost accounting problem? The goal is to make money now and in the future. Just emphasize maximizing throughput to make money."

The CM and TOC approaches are the *same*, except for the interpretation of *which costs change* with the decision. The CM approach assumes direct labor and variable overhead change with volume and the TOC approach does not. *Otherwise, the two approaches produce the same result.* Either approach may be valid, depending on the behavior of costs for the particular situation.

The ABC Approach

We discussed **activity-based costing (ABC)** in Chapter 7. The ABC approach to constraints and scarce resources is long-term oriented. Accordingly, the ABC's usefulness as a short-term operating decision making tool is limited.

ABC addresses the shortcomings of both the CM approach and the TOC approach with respect to the fundamental structure of costs. The TOC assumes that only materials and energy costs are variable, and all other costs are fixed. The CM approach assumes that the costs vary according to the number of units produced, and it is possible to determine what the variable costs will be in each situation.

Using the ABC approach, we realize that costs are not either variable with production volume or fixed (as under the CM approach), nor are most costs fixed (as under the TOC approach). Rather, different activities drive costs, and analysis of the effect of a special decision on these activities is necessary to predict the resulting change in costs.

Consider the costs of a table fan in our illustration. If the company decides to increase the production of table fans to 30,000 units a year, would the variable costs stay at $24 per unit?

The direct materials cost of $7 and the direct labor cost of $13 may remain unchanged. The unit overhead costs, however, would certainly change. As the company increases production to 30,000 units, the level of support activities would almost certainly have to rise. Fixed overhead costs, such as the costs of material handling, inventory management, engineering, and manufacturing support, would all increase as the larger size of materials, work-in-process, and finished-goods inventories move through the plant.

The ABC advocates claim that it is impossible to determine accurate variable costs when a particular decision situation arises. In the real world, management encounters such decision situations thousands, if not millions, of times. A thousand customers times a thousand products creates one million decision situations. Determining accurate costs, without the availability of a full absorption costing system, such as an ABC system, would be impossible. Furthermore, assuming that a company can measure how costs will vary in each situation, they claim, is unrealistic.

Multiple Constraints and Linear Programming

In the above example, we assumed that only one resource, machine hours, was scarce. But what should the company do if there are multiple constraints? It may have a limited number of machine hours available, a limited number of labor hours available, and a limited amount of money to buy the motors for each type of fan. If each type of fan requires a different number of machine hours, a different number of labor hours, and a different cost per motor, which fan should the company produce and sell?

The answer to such a problem of multiple constraints can only be obtained through the use of an analytical tool, called linear programing. It is an optimization technique that operations personnel use. It is beyond the scope of our discussion here, and is covered in operations research and production courses.

RELEVANT COSTS FOR DECISION MAKING

Managers must consider only relevant revenue and costs in decision making. What are relevant costs? **Relevant costs** are future costs that will differ among alternatives. Costs that have been incurred in the past are *sunk* and are irrelevant to the current decision. Similarly, costs that are the same regardless of the decision are irrelevant.

An underground line mechanic of American Electric Power. AEP must consider multiple constraints to determine what to do to accommodate new customers down the road.

Assume you bought a car for $30,000. A week later, you were offered an opportunity to get into a construction business that required a pick-up truck. You realize that you do not have enough money to buy the pick-up truck and also keep the car.

You can buy the truck if you sell the car. The truck costs $25,000. You can sell the car as a used one for only $26,000. Should you sell the car at a loss of $4,000 and buy the truck? Neither the original car cost nor the loss on the sale of the car is relevant to the decision on whether you should buy the truck and get into the construction business.

The reason for this is that the original car cost is a sunk cost that does not have any effect on future cash flows from the construction business. Even if you can sell the car at a profit and get into the business, this could be the wrong decision if the income expected from the business is less than what you could make by working for some other company.

Thus, relevant costs are costs that you will pay in the future, and differ among alternatives. We will focus on these two characteristics of relevant costs, *future costs that differ* among alternatives, as we discuss a variety of special non-routine decisions in the remainder of this chapter.

An Example Using Future Costs

Assume that a company has obsolete inventory that it could either discard or remodel and sell. What should the company do? We will use the following illustration:

The Lamp Gallery has 500 lamps with square shades that have gone out of style. These lamps, which were originally acquired at a cost of $50 each, can be (1) reshaped with round shades at a cost of $30 per lamp and then sold for $60 each, or (2) dumped to a swap-meet retailer at $5 per lamp. Which should be done?

The original acquisition cost of $25,000 (500 lamps at $50) is irrelevant to the decision on whether to reshape or dump. It is unfortunate that the Gallery will lose $25,000 because of the change in style. This $25,000, however, is a sunk cost that will not be saved by anything that the Gallery could do with the lamps now. The only relevant factors to consider in making the decision at hand are the *future* revenues and costs, as illustrated in Exhibit 15-1 below.

EXHIBIT 15-1

The Lamp Gallery
Obsolete Inventory and Relevant Factors

	Reshape	Dump	Difference
Future revenues	$30,000	$2,500	$27,500
Future costs	15,000	–	15,000
Relevant margin	$15,000	$2,500	$12,500

Only *future* revenues and costs are *relevant* to the decision to reshape or dump the inventory. The historical inventory costs ($25,000) are irrelevant. The decision: Reshape the lamps.

To Add or Drop a Product Line or Department

How do we determine what product line or department to add or drop? If we just look at the bottom line of the operating statement, and drop whatever product or department showing an operating loss, we may make a wrong decision. What if the operating loss for the product or department occurred because of certain fixed costs that were arbitrarily allocated to the product or department?

Let us look at the following illustration:

EXHIBIT 15-2

The Home Improvement Company
Operating Statement For Year 2

	Total	Departments Hardware	Lumber	Plumbing
Sales	$460,000	$100,000	$120,000	$240,000
Variable expenses	192,000	60,000	36,000	96,000
Contribution margin	268,000	40,000	84,000	144,000
Fixed expenses:				
Advertising	30,000	13,000	15,000	2,000
Depreciation	11,000	4,000	4,000	3,000
General administrative	59,000	11,000	18,000	30,000
Insurance	4,000	1,000	1,000	2,000
Rent	40,000	8,000	12,000	20,000
Salaries	100,000	15,000	25,000	60,000
Utilities	4,000	2,000	1,000	1,000
	248,000	54,000	76,000	118,000
Operating income (loss)	$ 20,000	$ (14,000)	$ 8,000	$ 26,000

The operating statement of The Home Improvement Company for one year is shown in Exhibit 15-2.

The hardware department shows an operating loss of $14,000. Should management eliminate the hardware department if the department continues to incur loss? Is it possible that some of the fixed expenses allocated to the hardware department will not be eliminated with the department?

We must carefully analyze all fixed expenses, and separate those that will be avoided if the hardware department is dropped.

Assume that our analyses reveal the following:

1. Of the advertising expenses, $20,000 was spent for the company as a whole, and $10,000 was spent for specific departments as follows: Hardware, $5,000; Lumber, $4,000; and Plumbing, $1,000.
2. Depreciation expenses relate to the store fixtures which cannot be sold or used for any other purposes.
3. General administrative expenses are unavoidable whether the hardware department is eliminated or not.
4. Insurance expenses relate to merchandise, and can be avoided if the hardware department is dropped.
5. Rent expense is allocated to departments based on floor space.
6. Salaries can be completely eliminated if the department is dropped.
7. Utilities represent gas heat and electricity for the company as a whole, and will not be eliminated or reduced when a department is dropped.

Comparison of avoidable expenses to contribution margin (CM): If the hardware department is dropped, its CM will be eliminated together with its avoidable expenses. Management should see if the company saves more avoidable expenses than the CM it loses by dropping the department. This method is illustrated in Exhibit 15-3.

EXHIBIT 15-3

The Home Improvement Company
Avoidable and Unavoidable Expenses

	Hardware Department		
	Total Fixed Expenses	Avoidable Fixed Expenses	Unavoidable Fixed Expenses
Advertising	$13,000	$5,000	$8,000
Depreciation — straight line	4,000		4,000
General administrative	11,000		11,000
Insurance	1,000	1,000	
Rent	8,000		8,000
Salaries	15,000	15,000	
Utilities	2,000		2,000
Total	$54,000	$21,000	$33,000

The company would save avoidable expenses of $21,000, but lose the CM of $40,000 it is making now. Accordingly, the company should not drop the hardware department. If the hardware department is dropped, the overall profit of the company as a whole will decrease $19,000, or the difference between its CM of $40,000 and its avoidable expenses of $21,000.

Comparison of the profits of the company as a whole if the hardware department is kept and if it is dropped: This method is illustrated in Exhibit 15-4.

EXHIBIT 15-4

The Home Improvement Company
Effect of Dropping Hardware Department on Profit

	Keep Hardware Department	Drop Hardware Department	Profit Increase (Decrease)
Sales	$460,000	$360,000	$(100,000)
Variable expenses	192,000	132,000	60,000
CM	268,000	228,000	(40,000)
Fixed expenses that will change:			
Advertising	30,000	25,000	5,000
Insurance	4,000	3,000	1,000
Salaries	100,000	85,000	15,000
Total	134,000	113,000	21,000
Operating profit (loss)	$134,000	$115,000	$ (19,000)

Dropping the hardware department will result in a $19,000 decrease in operating profit. We draw the same conclusion as we did under the first method.

Using a segment statement: In Chapter 11, we discussed the importance of segment margin. There, we defined segment margin as segment CM minus segment traceable fixed expenses. All allocated common fixed expenses are deducted from the company's total margin to arrive at the company's operating profit.

The segmental income statement can be used as a decision tool for management which reveals the income effect of dropping a product line or business segment. Exhibit 15-5 presents a segment margin statement for The Home Improvement Company.

If the company drops the hardware department, it will lose the department segment margin of $15,000. In addition, the $4,000 depreciation expense traceable to the hardware department will not be avoided in the future, since it is already a sunk cost. The sum of these two ($15,000 + $4,000 = $19,000) represents the expected decrease in operating profit if the hardware department is eliminated.

Alternative Uses of Idle Capacity After a Department is Dropped

In the above analysis, we assumed that if the hardware department is dropped, the sales for the remaining two departments will remain the same. In reality, this assumption may not be valid, because the vacated space may be used by the remaining departments to increase their sales. Alternatively, the space may be used to produce an additional product.

Assume that the space vacated by the dropped department will be used by the remaining two departments. The sales of each of the remaining two departments

EXHIBIT 15-5

The Home Improvement Company
Segmented Income Statement

| | | Departments | | |
	Total Company	Hardware	Lumber	Plumbing
Sales	$460,000	$100,000	$120,000	$240,000
Variable expenses	192,000	60,000	36,000	96,000
CM	268,000	40,000	84,000	144,000
Traceable fixed expenses:				
Advertising	10,000	5,000	4,000	1,000
Depreciation	11,000	4,000	4,000	3,000
Insurance expense	4,000	1,000	1,000	2,000
Salaries	100,000	15,000	25,000	60,000
Total	125,000	25,000	34,000	66,000
Department segment margin	143,000	$ 15,000	$ 50,000	$ 78,000
Common fixed expenses:				
Advertising	20,000			
General administrative	59,000			
Rent	40,000			
Utilities	4,000			
Total	123,000			
Operating income	$ 20,000			

will increase 20%. The CM ratio for each of the remaining two departments will remain unchanged. All fixed expenses, except the $5,000 hardware advertising expense (avoidable), will also remain the same for the company as a whole. Now, should the hardware department be dropped?

EXHIBIT 15-6

The Home Improvement Company
Effects of Alternative Uses of Vacated Space

| | | Departments | |
	Total Company	Lumber	Plumbing
Sales	$432,000	$144,000[a]	$288,000[a]
Variable expenses	158,400	43,200[b]	115,200[b]
CM	$273,600	$100,800	$172,800

(a) New sales = Existing sales × 120%
   Lumber: $120,000 × 120% = $144,000
   Plumbing: $240,000 × 120% = $288,000
(b) New sales × Existing ratio of variable expenses to sales
   Lumber: $144,000 × ($36,000/$120,000) = $ 43,200
   Plumbing: $288,000 × ($96,000/$240,000) = $115,200

Net effect of dropping the hardware department (when the vacated space is used):
  Increase in total CM:
    Drop the hardware department $273,600
    Keep the hardware department   268,000 $ 5,600

  Decrease in expenses:
    Advertising expense avoided   5,000
  Increase in operating income $10,600

Exhibit 15-6 presents the effects of alternative uses of the vacated space on the CM and the operating income of the company.

Since operating income will increase $10,600, the company should drop the Hardware Department and use the vacated space to increase the sales of the two remaining departments.

MAKE OR BUY DECISIONS

Managers often face the question whether the company should manufacture a part **(insourcing)** or buy it from outside suppliers **(outsourcing).** The relevant costs in this situation still need to have the same two characteristics: (1) they are future costs, and (2) they will differ among alternatives.

Consider the following example:

M Corporation manufactures subassembly parts for its final product. The cost of manufacturing part No. 300 is shown below:

	Total Cost of 10,000 Units	Cost Per Unit
Direct material	$60,000	$ 6
Direct labor	90,000	9
Variable manufacturing overhead	40,000	4
Fixed manufacturing overhead	50,000	5
Total	$240,000	$24

The same part can also be purchased from outside vendors. An outside supplier offered to sell 10,000 units of part No. 300 to M Corporation for $22 per unit. Should the company make or buy the part?

The **make-or-buy decision** requires the consideration of both qualitative and quantitative factors. If the company places significant importance on the quality of the parts, and is not sure if the purchased parts would be of the same qual-

EXHIBIT 15-7

M Corporation
Make or Buy
(If facilities remain idle)

	Make Per Unit	Make 10,000 Units	Buy Per Unit	Buy 10,000 Units
Direct material	$ 6	$ 60,000		
Direct labor	9	90,000		
Variable manufacturing overhead	4	40,000		
Total relevant costs	$19*	$190,000	$22	$220,000

* Fixed manufacturing overhead is not included. It is irrelevant since it will not differ with the decision to make or buy.

ity as those manufactured internally, the company will want to manufacture rather than buy the parts, regardless of the price.

Assuming that all qualitative factors have been considered, the decision depends on alternative uses for the facilities that are now being used in making the part. If such facilities will remain idle, making the part may be better than buying it. The company will save $19 per unit in internal manufacturing costs, but will spend $22 per unit, as illustrated in Exhibit 15-7.

The company will save $3 per unit or a total of $30,000, if it makes the part. This solution assumes that the facilities will remain idle even if the parts are purchased.

Now, assume that the facilities released as a result of buying the part could be eliminated, saving $40,000 of fixed overhead costs. If $40,000 can be saved, buying the parts would be better, as illustrated in Exhibit 15-8.

EXHIBIT 15-8

M Corporation
Make or Buy
(If facilities are eliminated, saving overhead)

	Make		Buy	
	Per Unit	10,000 Units	Per Unit	10,000 Units
Direct materials	$ 6	$ 60,000		
Direct labor	9	90,000		
Variable manufacturing overhead	4	40,000		
Fixed manufacturing overhead	4	40,000		
Total relevant costs	$23	$230,000	$22	$220,000

We show that making the part would require a differential fixed overhead of $40,000, which would be eliminated if the part is purchased. The company will save $1 per unit or $10,000 in total, if it buys. The make-or-buy decision is very common in today's market. For example, major automakers (General Motors and Ford) buy auto parts for their cars since outsourcing is less expensive than insourcing in many cases.

JOINT PRODUCTS AND BY-PRODUCTS

Joint products are two or more products that are jointly produced from one common input. They cannot be separately identified until the **split-off point.** For example, gasoline and kerosine are two products, among others, that are produced from one input: crude oil. Other examples of joint products include chemicals, perfume, flour, lumber, and meat-packing. **Joint product costs** are those costs that are incurred on the common input, until the individual products can be separately identified at the split-off point. Exhibit 15-9 illustrates the joint product costs, split-off point, additional processing costs after the split-off point, and individual products produced after additional processing.

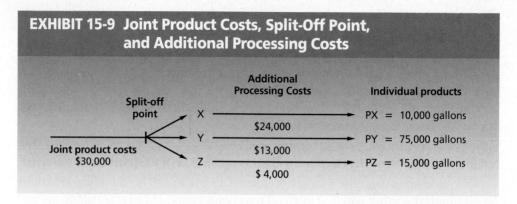

EXHIBIT 15-9 Joint Product Costs, Split-Off Point, and Additional Processing Costs

The joint product costs are $30,000. At the split-off point, we have three separate products: X, Y and Z. Each of the three products can be processed further, into PX at an additional cost of $24,000, into PY at $13,000, and into PZ at $4,000, respectively.

Sell or Process Further

Some products cannot be sold at the split-off point, and must be processed further if they are to be sold. Some products cannot be processed further, and must be sold at the split-off point. In these cases, the company does not have a choice as to whether to sell at the split-off point or to process further. Many products, however, can be sold either at the split-off point or after further processing. In these cases, companies have to make a decision as to which products should be sold at the split-off point and which products should be processed further. The company needs to make the decision that will maximize profit.

Let us refer to Exhibit 15-9, and assume that we have the following additional information:

	Selling Price Per Gallon	
Product	At Split-Off Point	After Processing Further
X	$0.90	$3.60
Y	$0.64	$0.80
Z	$1.20	$1.60

EXHIBIT 15-10 Sell or Process Further

	X	Y	Z
Number of gallons (A)	10,000	75,000	15,000
Selling price per gallon:			
After processing further (B)	$ 3.60	$ 0.80	$ 1.60
At the split-off point (C)	$ 0.90	$ 0.64	$ 1.20
Revenue after processing (A × B)	$36,000	$60,000	$24,000
Revenue at split-off point (A × C)	9,000	48,000	18,000
Incremental revenue	27,000	12,000	6,000
Additional processing costs	24,000	13,000	4,000
Incremental CM	$ 3,000	$ (1,000)	$ 2,000

Relevant Costs and the Owner of Miami Dolphins

When Wayne Huizenga, the owner of the Miami Dolphins and the Florida Marlins, created a nationwide network of used-car outlets, he must have considered relevant costs and made sell-or-process further decisions at various stages of his business. Dealers' profit margins are about 6% on new cars and about 11% on used cars. Huizenga leases a new car to a customer for 12 to 18 months from his new-car dealerships. At the end of the lease, he reconditions the car and uses it at Alamo or National, which he owns, as a rental car for about four months. Then he reconditions it again and sells it as a used car. His staff estimates that all of this provides Huizenga a $1,000-per-car advantage over conventional dealers. Differential costs? Make versus buy? Huizenga figures he saves $200 per car by supplying uses cars internally instead of buying them from used-car auctions.

For more details, see "Car Wars: Wayne Huizenga Vs. Everybody," *Fortune*, June 9, 1997, pp. 93–96.

Which product should be processed further and which should be sold at the split-off point? In making sell-or-process further decisions, we must observe the following:

(1) Ignore joint product costs.

(2) Process a product further, if its incremental revenue is greater than its additional processing costs.

We must ignore joint costs, because, by the time we get to the split-off point, they are *sunk costs*. Sunk costs are irrelevant costs for decision making. We incur the joint costs whether we process a product further or not. Incremental revenue from further processing a product is the revenue from selling this product after further processing minus the revenue that we can generate from selling this product at the split-off point. The company should process products X and Z further, but should sell product Y at the split-off point, as illustrated in Exhibit 15-10.

Opportunity Costs Revisited

In Chapter 2, we discussed the concept of opportunity costs. An **opportunity cost** is the benefit foregone when we choose another alternative. If we process a product further, we forego the revenue that can be achieved from selling that product at the split-off point. Thus, sales revenue at the split-off point is an opportunity cost of processing further. Exhibit 15-11 presents another format of reaching the decision as to which product to process further and which to sell at the split-off point.

Exhibit 15-11 presents exactly the same incremental CM figures for each product as Exhibit 15-10. In fact, we can make most of the decisions involving relevant costs in this chapter using the opportunity cost concept.

EXHIBIT 15-11 Sell or Process Further
Sales Revenue at Split-Off As Opportunity Cost

	X	Y	Z
Revenue after processing (Exh.15-10)	$36,000	$60,000	$24,000
Less:			
Additional processing costs	24,000	13,000	4,000
Opportunity costs (revenue at split-off point) (Exh.15-10)	9,000	48,000	18,000
Total costs	33,000	61,000	22,000
Incremental CM	$3,000	$(1,000)	$2,000

Allocation of Joint Product Costs

Some companies allocate joint product costs ($30,000 in Exhibit 15-9) among products. Managers should not use the resulting income for each product to decide whether they should process the product further or not. They allocate joint product costs for balance sheet (inventory valuation) purposes, and sometimes for product income statement purposes.

Joint product costs can be allocated using different bases, such as: (a) sales value at the split-off point, (b) final sales value after further processing, (c) physical volume, or (d) weight. Each allocation base will produce different results, as shown in Exhibit 15-12.

EXHIBIT 15-12 Allocation of Joint Product Costs
Using Different Bases

Product	(a) Sales Value After Processing			(b) Sales Value at Split-off Point			(c) Number of Gallons		
	Sales Value	%	Joint Costs	Sales Value	%	Joint Costs	Gallons	%	Joint Costs
X	$ 36,000	30	$ 9,000	$ 9,000	12	$ 3,600	10,000	10	$ 3,000
Y	60,000	50	15,000	48,000	64	19,200	75,000	75	22,500
Z	24,000	20	6,000	18,000	24	7,200	15,000	15	4,500
	$120,000	100	$30,000	$75,000	100	$30,000	100,000	100	$30,000

Exhibit 15-12 shows that every allocation base produces different amounts of joint product costs allocated to each product. However, all such allocations are completely arbitrary. The resulting profit figures are not useful for deciding which products to produce or which to process further. The proper analysis to use for such purpose is illustrated in Exhibit 15-10 or Exhibit 15-11.

By-Product Costs

By-products are those products that can be separately identified at the split-off point, but they are of insignificant sales value relative to the sales values of the joint products. All relevant cost concepts we discussed above also apply to by-products. The analysis of whether to sell or process further a by-product is the same as for a joint product.

We can allocate costs to by-products in exactly the same way as we allocated joint product costs. However, the insignificant sales value of by-products makes that allocation not worthwhile.

SPECIAL SALES ORDERS

The important lesson we have learned from various decision making exercises is that we should take the course of action that would maximize overall profit. We reinforce that lesson here in the special sales order situation.

Sara Corporation's condensed income statement for Year 7 is presented below:

Amoco Corporation's new wastewater treatment plant in Belgium produces a bio-gas as fuel for steam generation. The bio-gas is a byproduct, and its use saves the company about $500,000 of costs a year.

Sales (100,000 units at $5)		$500,000
Total costs:		
Variable costs	$200,000	
Fixed manufacturing overhead	80,000	
Fixed administrative expenses	100,000	380,000
Operating income		$120,000

Assume that the company sells all it produces daily, and keeps no inventory. A wholesaler has offered to buy 50,000 units from the company at a unit price of $2.50. This special order will not affect the company's present sales volume or fixed costs. The company has enough idle capacity to produce the 50,000 units. Furthermore, this special order would not result in any price discrimination lawsuits against the company (for charging different prices to different customers for the same product) nor would it encourage current customers, who buy small quantities, to ask for similar price cuts. Should the company accept this special order?

The answer will depend on whether its total profit will increase when it accepts this special order. Since the company keeps no inventory, the number of units produced is equal to the number of units sold (100,000 units). The variable cost per unit is $2 ($200,000 ÷ 100,000 units).

Since the $2.50 special purchase price offered per unit is greater than the $2 variable cost per unit, and since total fixed expenses will not increase, the company should accept the special order. Accepting this special order will increase total operating income by $25,000, as illustrated in Exhibit 15-13.

Had the company rejected the order on the basis that the price offered of $2.50 per unit is less than the total cost per unit of $3.80 (total cost $380,000 ÷ 100,000 units), the company would have lost $25,000. We note that the special price offered is greater than the variable cost per unit. The special order generates a positive CM per unit.

Based on the discussion we had at the beginning of the chapter on constraints, ABC advocates would say that some fixed costs would certainly increase without managers knowing about the increase. Again, the CM approach to decision making is short-term oriented, although it is very useful if adequate cost estimation is possible.

EXHIBIT 15-13

Sara Corporation
Effect of Accepting Special Order on Operating Income

	Without Special Order	With Special Order	Effect of Special Order Total	Effect of Special Order Per Unit
Sales	$500,000	$625,000[a]	$125,000	$2.50
Variable costs	200,000	300,000[b]	100,000	2.00
CM	300,000	325,000	25,000	0.50
Fixed expenses:				
Manufacturing	80,000	80,000	–	–
Administrative	100,000	100,000	–	–
	180,000	180,000	–	–
Operating income	$120,000	$145,000	$25,000	$0.50

(a) $500,000 + (50,000 units × $2.50) = $625,000
(b) 150,000 units × $2 per unit = $300,000

SUMMARY

In this chapter, we discussed constraints and scarce resources. There are three approaches that managers can use to deal with the problem of constraints or scarce resources. The CM approach is a short-term optimization technique. The Theory of Constraints (TOC) is a variable costing-oriented optimization technique which focuses on the system's constraints. The TOC approach is similar to the CM approach in that both focus on short-term optimization.

The ABC approach to constraints and scarce resources is long-term oriented. Accordingly, ABC's usefulness as a short-term operating decision making tool is limited. ABC notes the shortcomings of both the CM approach and the TOC approach with respect to the fundamental structure of costs. The TOC assumes that only materials and energy costs are variable, and all other costs are fixed. The CM approach assumes that the costs vary according to the number of units produced, and it is posssible to determine what the variable costs will be.

We distinguished between relevant and irrelevant costs and applied this distinction to a variety of non-routine decision making situations. Relevant costs are those future costs that differ among alternatives. Both relevant qualitative and quantitative factors must be considered in decision making.

Joint products are those products that have significant sales value and are produced jointly from one common input. The decision to sell a product at the split-off point or process it further is made by comparing its incremental revenue from further processing to its further processing cost. Allocated joint product costs should be completely ignored in that decision.

A special sales order decision is correctly made by comparing the sale price per unit to variable cost per unit. If the former is greater than the latter, the order should be accepted, and vice versa. It is incorrect to compare the sale price being offered per unit to total cost per unit, particularly if all fixed expenses and present sales volume will remain the same whether the special order is accepted or not.

BASIC CONCEPTS AND TERMS

By-products	Joint product costs
Constraints	Joint products
Contribution-margin approach	Outsourcing
Drop a product line	Relevant costs
Future costs	Scarce resources
Incremental costs	Split-off point
Incremental revenue	Theory of constraints (TOC)
Insourcing	Throughput
Irrelevant costs	Use of idle capacity

■ SELF-REVIEW PROBLEM

R Company is faced with the following decision-making situations. Each situation is independent.

1. One of its desk-top computers, which has a book value of $1,000, has a bad hard-disk drive. The company can either repair the disk drive at a cost of $500, or sell the computer as a junk for $100. Whether the disk drive is repaired or not, the computer is no longer suitable for the company's use. If the disk drive is repaired, the computer can easily be sold for $700. What should the company do?

2. The company's condensed income statement for its three products for the most recent year is shown below:

	Products			Company
	X	Y	Z	Total
Sales	$50,000	$ 60,000	$70,000	$180,000
Total costs	30,000	70,000	65,000	165,000
Operating income	$20,000	$(10,000)	$ 5,000	$ 15,000

The company is considering dropping product Y which is showing a loss. A further analysis indicated the following:

	Product		
Analysis of total costs:	X	Y	Z
Variable costs	$25,000	$40,000	$60,000
Allocated fixed costs — unavoidable	2,000	20,000	3,000
Allocated fixed costs — avoidable	3,000	10,000	2,000
Total	$30,000	$70,000	$65,000

Should the company drop product Y?

3. The company's own delivery cost averages $20 per customer. This $20 cost includes $3 allocated fixed costs that are not avoidable even if the company subcontracts the delivery service. An outside delivery service has offered to provide the delivery service to the 1,000 customers at an average delivery charge of $18 per customer. R Company could use its relieved delivery trucks and generate up to $1,500 in cash. Should R Company accept the outside delivery service company's offer? What if the extra $1,500 cash cannot be generated?

4. Refer to situation 2 above. Assume that the company currently produces 1,000 units of each of its three products. The labor required per unit is 4 hours for product X, 3 hours for Y, and 2 hours for Z. The company has 9,000 hours of labor available for the year. The company can sell as many units of any of its three products as it can produce. The company wants to allocate all the labor hours to the product that will maximize the company's total CM. Which product should be produced?

5. Refer again to situation 2 above. Assume that the three products are produced jointly from a common input. The total unavoidable fixed costs are the joint product costs. The total avoidable fixed costs and variable costs are additional processing costs. The sales values shown are the final sales values after further processing. Product X can not be sold at the split-off point but products Y and Z can be sold at split-off for $8,000 and $12,000, respectively. Which products should be sold at the split-off point? Which should be processed further?

6. Assume the same data as in situations 2 and 4, except that the company can obtain as many labor hours as it needs. A wholesaler has offered to purchase large quantities of each of the three products at the following prices:

	Product		
	X	Y	Z
Number of units ordered	500	400	600
Price offered	$27	$41	$58

Accepting this special sales order will not increase fixed expenses, nor will it affect the present sales volume.

(a) If the company should either accept the order or reject it as one deal (three products combined), should it accept the order?

(b) If the wholesaler is willing to buy any products the company is willing to sell, which products should the company sell?

7. Assume the same data as in situations 2 and 4, except for the changes mentioned in each of the following questions:

(a) The total market demand for a single product is limited to 2,000 units. The company wants to allocate the 9,000 labor hours to the products that will maximize the company's total CM. How many units of each product should be produced?

(b) The company has a contract to supply a minimum of 500 units of each product to a customer. The total market demand for a single product is limited to 1,500 units. How many units of each product should the company produce to maximize the company's total CM?

Solution

1. Compare the two alternatives:

	Repair disk drive and sell	Sell computer as a junk
Incremental revenue	$700	$100
Incremental cost	500	—
Relevant margin	$200	$100

The company should repair the disk drive and sell the computer. The $1,000 book value is completely irrelevant to this decision.

2. Prepare product segment margin income statement:

	Products			Company
	X	Y	Z	Total
Sales	$50,000	$60,000	$70,000	$180,000
Variable costs	25,000	40,000	60,000	125,000
CM	25,000	20,000	10,000	55,000
Avoidable fixed costs	3,000	10,000	2,000	15,000
Product segment margin	$22,000	$10,000	$ 8,000	40,000
Unavoidable fixed costs				25,000
Operating income				$ 15,000

The company should *not* drop product Y. Product Y contributes $10,000 to company profit.

3. Analyze the three alternatives, as follows:

	Reject the Offer	Accept the Offer, Extra Cash	Accept the Offer, No Extra Cash
Revenue	—	$ 1,500	—
Cost of delivery service	$(17,000)*	(18,000)	$(18,000)
Net cost of delivery	$(17,000)	$(16,500)	$(18,000)

* 1,000 customers × Relevant cost of $17 per customer ($20 − $3 unavoidable fixed cost)

If the extra cash can be generated, the offer should be accepted. Otherwise, it should not be accepted.

4. We want to maximize the CM per unit of the scarce resource, labor hours.

	Product		
	X	**Y**	**Z**
Labor hours available	9,000	9,000	9,000
Labor hours required per unit	÷ 4	÷ 3	÷ 2
Number of units that can be produced	2,250	3,000	4,500
CM per unit*	× $25	× $20	× $10
Total CM	$56,250	$60,000	$45,000

* Product CM (per situation 2) ÷ 1,000 units

Only product Y should be produced and sold, because it would generate the largest CM of $60,000.

5. Compare incremental revenue to additional processing costs, as follows:

	Product	
	Y	**Z**
Sales value	$60,000	$70,000
Sales value at split-off point	8,000	12,000
Incremental revenue	52,000	58,000
Additional processing costs*	50,000	62,000
Incremental margin	$2,000	$(4,000)

* Variable costs plus avoidable fixed costs

For Product Y = $40,000 + $10,000 = $50,000
For Product Z = $60,000 + $ 2,000 = $62,000

Thus, product Z should be sold at the split-off point. It is correct to process product Y further. The company has no choice but to process product X further.

6. Compute total product CM's and for the order as a whole, as follows:

	Product			Total
	X	**Y**	**Z**	**Order**
Number of units ordered	500	400	600	
CM per unit*	× $2	× $1	× $(2)	
Total CM	$1,000	$400	$(1,200)	$200

* Selling price less variable cost per unit.

For Product X: $27 − $25 = $2
For Product Y: $41 − $40 = $1
For Product Z: $58 − $60 = $(2)

(a) Yes. The company should accept the whole order. It will contribute a profit of $200.

(b) The company should sell only products X and Y.

7. Rank the products by CM per labor hour:

	Product		
	X	Y	Z
CM per unit	$ 25	$ 20	$ 10
Hours required per unit	÷ 4	÷ 3	÷ 2
CM per labor hour	$6.25	$6.67	$5.00
Ranking	2	1	3

(a) First, the company must produce 2,000 units (maximum) of product Y, using 6,000 hours of labor (3 hours × 2,000). The remaining 3,000 hours should be used to produce 750 units of product X (3,000 ÷ 4 hours). Product Z should not be produced.

(b) The company should first produce the minimum required volume (500 units) of each product consuming 4,500 total labor hours as shown below. Second, the company should produce 1,000 additional units of product Y to make the total of 1,500 units (maximum), using 3,000 labor hours. Last, the remaining 1,500 hours (4,500 hours − 3,000 hours) should be used to produce 375 additional units of product X (1,500 hours ÷ 4 hours).

	Product			Total
	X	Y	Z	Hours
Minimum production (units)	500	500	500	
Hours required per unit	× 4	× 3	× 2	
Hours used	2,000	1,500	1,000	4,500
Additional hours for product Y (1,000 units × 3)		3,000		3,000
Additional hours for product X	1,500			1,500
Total labor hours used	3,500	4,500	1,000	9,000
Units produced	875	1,500	500	

■ REVIEW QUESTIONS

15-1 How is a constraint in resource availability related to managerial decision making?

15-2 How is the Theory of Constraints (TOC) approach different from the contribution margin (CM) approach?

15-3 Evaluate the TOC approach from the perspective of ABC. Focus on the fundamental structure of costs.

15-4 Evaluate the CM approach from the perspective of ABC. Focus on the fundamental structure of costs.

15-5 Differentiate between qualitative and quantitative factors in decision making. Provide examples of each.

15-6 How can you tell if a certain cost is relevant or irrelevant to decision making? Provide an example of a relevant cost and an irrelevant cost.

15-7 "Any future cost is relevant to decision making." Do you agree? Why or why not?

15-8 "Historical or past cost is always irrelevant to decision making." Do you agree? Why or why not?

15-9 Why is a gain or loss on sale of old equipment irrelevant to the decision on whether to keep or replace that equipment, regardless of the tax consequence of the gain or loss?

15-10 What is the decision rule on accepting or rejecting special sales order decisions? What assumptions do you make in the process of making special sales order decisions?

15-11 Why is the cost of new equipment relevant, yet the original cost of existing equipment is irrelevant to the decision as to whether the old equipment should be replaced?

15-12 How would you make a decision on whether to remodel obsolete inventory or dump that inventory and write it off the books?

15-13 "Any department or product that shows an operating loss should be eliminated as soon as possible." Do you agree? Why or why not?

15-14 "The segmented income statement by product or department can be used as a basis for keeping or dropping a department or product." Do you agree? Why or why not?

15-15 What costs are relevant costs in make-or-buy decisions?

15-16 What are scarce resources?

15-17 How should a company utilize scarce resource in its efforts to maximize CM?

15-18 Differentiate between joint product costs and additional processing costs.

15-19 How can you use the opportunity cost concept in sell-or-process-further decisions?

🌐 INTERNET PROJECT

Web 15-1:

Websites: www.3m.com
www.gp.com

The websites listed above represent two famous companies. Search the sites for information on their operating characteristics.

Required:

Where would you find a need for a sell-or-process-further decision for each company? Why?

Web 15-2:

Websites: www.merck.com
www.pfizer.com

The websites listed above represent two famous companies. Search the sites for information on their operating characteristics.

Required:

What actual opportunity costs can you find if each company decides to use opportunity costs in its sell-or-process-further decisions? List them.

■ EXERCISES

E15-1 Constraints; Contribution-Margin Approach

Cell-Fon, Inc. produces and sells two types of cellular phones, Fon-A and Fon-B. The relevant data are presented below:

	Fon-A	Fon-B
Selling price per unit	$40	$25
Costs:		
Direct materials per unit	11	6
Direct labor per unit	12	9
Variable overhead per unit	5	3
Fixed costs (total)	$40,000	

The company has 8,000 machine hours available for the period. Each unit of Fon-A requires two hours, and each unit of Fon-B requires one hour of machine time.

Required:

1. How many units of Fon-A and Fon-B should the company produce and sell to maximize its profit for the period?
2. What will be the total profit for the company when you choose to produce the number of units determined in (1)?

E15-2 Constraints; Theory of Constraints (TOC) Approach Using Throughput

Refer to E15-1. Now, assume that 40% of variable overhead costs are energy costs, and the remaining 60% are not directly related to throughput. All other conditions remain unchanged.

Required:

Use the Theory of Constraints (TOC) approach to answer the following:
1. Compute the throughput per unit of Fon-A and Fon-B.
2. How many units of Fon-A and Fon-B should the company produce and sell to maximize throughput?

E15-3   Obsolete Inventory

College Bookstore has 80 photo albums bearing the logo of a campus sports team which has gone out of existence. The albums were originally acquired at a cost of $35 per album, and were to be sold at a price of $60 each. The bookstore manager has the following two options regarding the obsolete albums:

Option 1: The art department can replace the album cover at a cost of $15 each. The albums could then be sold at a price of $25 each.

Option 2: A student organization is planning a big garage sale, and has offered to buy the albums at $8 each.

Required:

1. Which option should the bookstore manager choose?
2. What is the sunk cost involved in the case?

E15-4   Dropping a Product Line

The Toy Store sells electronic toys and traditional toys. The relevant data for a recent period are provided below:

	Electronic Toys	Traditional Toys	Total
Sales	$450,000	$270,000	$720,000
Expenses:			
Variable	150,000	90,000	240,000
Fixed-Avoidable	170,000	120,000	290,000
Fixed-Unavoidable	80,000	70,000	150,000
Total	400,000	280,000	680,000
Profit	$ 50,000	$(10,000)	$ 40,000

The store owner wants to eliminate the traditional toy department since it has incurred losses in recent periods.

Required:

1. Do you think the owner should eliminate the traditional toy department? Show supporting computations for your conclusion.

2. Assume that the owner eliminates the traditional toy department. What will be the effect on operating profit?

E15-5   Make or Buy: Idle Facility

AST, Inc. manufactures subassembly parts needed for its final product. One critical part, part no. 101, is required in assembling the final product. The company produces 20,000 units of the product in each period.

The cost of manufacturing part no.101 is presented below:

	Per-Unit Cost
Direct materials	$ 7
Direct labor.	5
Variable manufacturing overhead	4
Fixed manufacturing overhead allocated.	3
Total	$19

An outside supplier offered to sell 20,000 units of part 101 for $17 per unit.

Required:

Should AST, Inc. make or buy the part? Assume that the part-manufacturing facilities will remain idle even if the company buys the part.

E15-6   Make or Buy: Alternative Uses for the Facility

Refer to E15-5. Now, assume that the released facility, if part no. 101 is bought from the outside supplier, can be rented out to another company for $35,000 per period. All other conditions remain unchanged.

Required:

Should AST, Inc. make or buy the part?

 ## E15-7   Sell or Process Further; Opportunity Cost

J Company produces three products which come out of a joint processing operation costing $28,000 up to the split-off point per period. Selling prices of the three products are given below:

| | Selling Price Per Unit | |
| | At Split-Off | After Processing |
Product	Point	Further
X	$1.10	$2.20
Y	1.20	1.60
Z	1.50	2.50

The joint product costs are allocated on the basis of their sales value at the split-off point. Total output and costs of additional processing after split-off are as follows:

Product	Output	Additional Processing Costs
X	20,000 units	$16,000
Y	30,000	15,000
Z	10,000	12,000

Required:

1. Which product(s) should be processed further and which should be sold at the split-off point?
2. In making your decision in (1), why did you, or didn't you, allocate joint processing costs to the products?
3. Your computation can be presented using the sales revenue at the split-off point as opportunity cost. The opportunity cost becomes a part of total costs in making your decision. Using this form of analysis, which product(s) should be processed further and which should be sold at the split-off point?

E15-8   Optimal Product Mix; Contribution Margin; Scarce Resource

OPM, Inc. shows the following income statement for its three products for the most recent year:

	Products			Company
	A	B	C	Total
Sales	$180,000	$200,000	$220,000	$600,000
Total costs	154,000	165,000	181,000	500,000
Operating income	$26,000	$ 35,000	$ 39,000	$100,000

A further analysis of costs indicated the following:

	Products		
	A	B	C
Variable costs	$144,000	$148,000	$165,000
Fixed costs allocated	10,000	17,000	16,000
Total costs	$154,000	$165,000	$181,000

OPM, Inc. produced 2,000 units of each of its three products for the year. The machine time required per unit is 1.5 hours for product A, 2 hours for B, and 2.5 hours for C. The cost structure is expected to remain unchanged for the foreseeable future.

Required:

1. For the current year, OPM has 15,000 machine hours available. The total market demand for a single product is limited to 4,000 units. How many units of each product should be produced to maximize the company's total contribution margin?

2. Assume the same data as in (1), except that OPM has a contract to supply a minimum of 1,000 units of each product per year to a customer. How many units of each product should be produced to maximize the company's total contribution margin?

■ PROBLEMS

P15-9 Ethics and Relevant Costs

Linda Evans and Susan Sampson graduated from a local college. Upon gradua-tion, Linda was employed by Security Products, Inc. (SPI) as a product specialist, and Susan joined a large accounting firm as a junior accountant. As former room-mates in the campus dormitory, the two have kept in touch and remained good friends. Four years later, Susan moved to Linda's company as cost accounting manager. By that time, Linda had been promoted to a product manager's position.

SPI produces various security-related products, which include automobile anti-theft security devices (Linda's product line). The company uses a merit-based sys-tem which uses the contribution margin from each product line as the performance indicator for each product-line manager.

In May of this year, an automobile dealers group in Japan offered to buy 30,000 units of an anti-theft security device from SPI for $35 per unit. Although the offered price is $30 below the regular selling price of $65 per unit, Linda is anxious to accept the offer for two reasons: one, the sale wouldn't affect the exist-ing market and the prices, because SPI has been selling in the domestic market, and the Japanese market is the only foreign market SPI will be exporting to; and two, the sale would double the quarterly sales volume and contribution margin of her product line, which would lead to a very favorable performance evaluation for the second quarter.

SPI has been using the contribution margin approach in most special sales decisions. If the special sales price is higher than the incremental costs of the deal, the decision is left to the product line managers. The $35 price offered is higher than the estimated variable costs of $32, which include direct materials, direct labor, variable overhead, and variable selling expenses per unit of product.

Susan, cost accounting manager, first computed the costs based on the tra-ditional procedures of SPI, looking at only the variable costs. Susan, however, knew that, even without a formal activity-based costing (ABC) system, there were some fixed cost items that will increase when the special order of 30,000 units is accepted. Inventory management team, for example, was operating at near the full capacity level, and in order to work on the special order, the team would certainly need to add at least two inventory handlers.

While having lunch at the company cafeteria, Susan asked: "Linda, do you really believe that the deal would increase the profit of your product line?" To this Linda replied: "I have seen your numbers, and I know the profitability on this deal is marginal. But look, according to the traditional way SPI has been analyzing special sales, no fixed cost has been entered in the analysis. Inventory management cost is a fixed cost, isn't it? Susan, you can't hurt me on this, using your new cost management concept. This sale is important to me. You know that. Don't you?"

Required:

1. If you were Susan, how would you handle the task of contribution margin analysis?
2. If the deal is approved, which stakeholders would be affected by the decision?

P15-10   Dropping a Product Line

The Computer Store sells computers and related products using six sales people. It also sells photocopying equipment, employing two additional salespeople and occupying one quarter of the total store space.

The relevant data on the store's operations in a recent period are provided below:

	Computers	Photocopiers	Total
Sales	$650,000	$100,000	$750,000
Expenses:			
Variable	330,000	30,000	360,000
Fixed-Salaries	60,000	20,000	80,000
Fixed-Others	187,500	62,500	250,000
Total	577,500	112,500	690,000
Profit	$72,500	$(12,500)	$60,000

Scott Cummings, the store owner, wants to eliminate the photocopier business, since it continues to incur operating losses which average about $12,500 in each period. The elimination would save only fixed salaries for each period. The released store space cannot be used for any other revenue-generating purposes. Fixed expenses are allocated between the two product lines according to the floor space.

Required:

1. Should Cummings eliminate the photocopier business? For the analysis, compare avoidable expenses to contribution margin.
2. Do the same analysis by comparing the profits of the whole store if the photocopier business is kept and if it is dropped.

P15-11   Relevant Costs; Multiple Choice

Choose the best answer.

1. A company's approach to a make-buy decision
    a. depends on whether the company is operating at or below breakeven.
    b. depends on whether the company is operating at or below normal volume.
    c. involves an analysis of avoidable costs.
    d. should utilize full absorption costing.
    e. should utilize activity-based costing.

2. Sunk costs
    a. are substitutes for opportunity costs.
    b. in and of themselves are not relevant to decision making.
    c. are relevant to decision making.
    d. are relevant to long-run decisions but not to short-run decisions.
    e. are fixed costs.

3. The term "relevant cost" applies to all the following decision situations **except** the
    a. acceptance of a special order.
    b. manufacture or purchase of component parts.
    c. determination of a product price.
    d. replacement of equipment.
    e. addition or deletion of a product line.

The following data apply to items 4 and 5.

Regis Company manufactures plugs used in its manufacturing cycle at a cost of $36 per unit that includes $8 of fixed overhead. Regis needs 30,000 of these plugs annually, and Orlan Company has offered to sell these units to Regis at $33 per unit. If Regis decides to purchase the plugs, $60,000 of the annual fixed overhead applied will be eliminated, and the company may be able to rent the facility previously used for manufacturing the plugs.

4. If Regis Company purchases the plugs but does not rent the unused facility, the company would
    a. save $3.00 per unit.
    b. lose $6.00 per unit.
    c. save $2.00 per unit.
    d. lose $3.00 per unit.
    e. save $1.00 per unit.

5. If the plugs are purchased and the facility rented, Regis Company wishes to realize $100,000 in savings annually. To achieve this goal, the minimum annual rent on the facility must be
    a. $10,000.
    b. $40,000.
    c. $70,000.
    d. $190,000.
    e. $280,000.

(CMA, adapted)

P15-12   Constraints; Best Product Mix

Gentech Pharmaceuticals, Inc. (GPI) manufactures a line of drugs that fight gingivitis by inhibiting the destructive enzyme that causes the disease. GPI's information on estimated sales for the following year is given below:

Product	Selling Price	Estimated Sales in Units
A1	$78	24,000
A2	65	35,000
B1	54	40,000
B2	58	30,000
B3	40	20,000

The estimated variable costs per unit of producing the five products are as follows:

Product	Direct Materials	Direct Labor	Variable Overhead
A1	$21	$18	$8
A2	13	15	7
B1	12	9	6
B2	19	12	9
B3	10	9	5

Due to the highly technical nature of manufacturing the drugs, the company cannot train additional direct labor workers in the near future, and its production is constrained by the available direct labor-hours. GPI has the current capacity of 50,000 direct labor-hours per year. The average labor cost is $30 per hour. Annual fixed costs are $2,200,000.

Required:

1. Compute the per-unit contribution margin for each product.
2. Compute the contribution margin per unit of constrained resources (direct labor-hour).
3. Show how many direct labor-hours each product's estimated sales for next year require.
4. How would you allocate the current capacity of 50,000 direct labor-hours to maximize the company's profit?

P15-13   Constraints; Contribution Margin vs.
Theory of Constraints (TOC)

Sterile Closure, Inc. (SCI) produces and sells sutures. The sutures made by SCI are popular, because they use a topical adhesive that forms a sterile, flexible seal over wounds, and does not require anesthesia for medical treatment of wounds. SCI produces two types of sutures, called SUT and TUT. The relevant data for each quarter are presented below:

	SUT	TUT
Selling price per unit	$65	$55
Costs:		
Adhesive per unit...........................	18	12
Other materials per unit.....................	10	9
Direct labor per unit	8	7
Energy cost per unit	3	2
Non-energy variable overhead per unit	6	5
Fixed costs (total).........................	$2,420,000	

The company could sell any number of sutures it can produce at the current selling prices for the time being, but its production is constrained by the limited supply of adhesives. Only 100,000 grams of adhesives are available per quarter. Adhesives cost $30 per gram.

Required:

1. Compute the contribution margin per unit of each product.
2. Compute the CM per gram of adhesive (constraint) used on each product.
3. How many units of SUT and TUT should the company produce and sell to maximize its profit for the period?
4. What will be the total profit for the company when you choose to produce the number of units determined in (3)?
5. Refer to (3). Assume the company has sufficient supply of adhesive to meet the production needs of the company for the foreseeable future. Now, what will be the answer to (3)?
6. Compute the throughput per unit of selling SUT and TUT.
7. How many units of SUT and TUT should the company produce and sell to maximize throughput?

P15-14 ABC's Criticism of the CM Approach and the Theory of Constraints (TOC) Approach

Refer to P15-13. All conditions remain unchanged. Assume you are an advocate of activity-based costing (ABC).

Required:

1. If you were an advocate of ABC, what would be your criticism of the contribution-margin approach used to find an answer to question 3? Be specific as to which items are inaccurate in using for the analysis.
2. What is your criticism of the Theory of Constraints (TOC) approach used to find an answer to question 7? Be specific as to which items are inaccurate in using for the analysis.

P15-15   Sell or Process Further

Winchester Chemicals uses a joint process to produce VX-4, a chemical used in the manufacture of paints and varnishes; HD-10, a chemical used in household cleaning products; and FT-5, a by-product that is sold to fertilizer manufacturers. Joint production costs are allocated to the main products on the basis of market value. The first-in, first-out (FIFO) inventory method is used to cost the main products. The by-product is inventoried at its market value less its disposal cost, and this value is used to reduce the joint production cost before allocation to the main products.

During the month of November, Winchester incurred joint production costs of $1,568,000. Data regarding Winchester's November operations are presented below.

	VX-4	HD-10	FT-5
November production in gallons	600,000	320,000	85,000
Sales value per gallon at split-off	none	$3.00	$.90*
Additional processing cost	$720,000	$920,000	none
Final sales value per gallon	$4.00	$6.375	none
Finished goods inventory in gallons at November 30	9,000	26,000	1,500

* Disposal costs of $.10 per gallon will be incurred in order to sell the by-product.

Required:

1. Winchester Chemicals has an opportunity to sell HD-10 for its sales value at the split-off point. Determine if Winchester should sell HD-10 at the split-off point or continue to process it further. Support your conclusion with appropriate calculations.
2. Are joint costs relevant to Winchester's decision making in (1)? Explain.

(CMA, adapted)

P15-16   Optimal Product Mix; Scarce Resource

Cran-Beverage, Inc. produces three beverage products and sells them to desert-area casinos owned and operated by native American tribes in California. The three products are: cranberry juice (100%), cran-apple juice, and cranberry juice cocktail. Thanks to favorable news reports on the medical benefits of cranberry drinks, Cran-Beverage's sales have been growing fast.

Cran-Beverage shows the following data on its three products, sold in 72-can cases:

	Products		
	Cranberry Juice (100%)	Cran-apple Juice	Cranberry Juice Cocktail
Selling price per case	$2.60	$2.20	$2.50
Variable costs per case	1.40	1.20	1.42
Cranberries required per case	3.0 pounds	2.0 pounds	2.4 pounds

The current cost structure is expected to remain unchanged for the foreseeable future and the company has sufficient production capacity to accommodate any reasonable increases in sales. Cran-Beverage, however, has recently been experiencing difficulty in procuring adequate quantities of cranberries. The materials sourcing problem is caused by the recent surge in the demand for cranberries by beverage manufacturers.

Cran-Beverage can purchase only 18,000 pounds of cranberries per month from its suppliers due to the limited supply. The total demand for Cran-Beverage's single product by the desert casinos is limited to 3,000 cases per month.

Required:

1. How many cases of each product should be produced per month to maximize the company's total contribution margin?
2. Cran-Beverage is under a long-term agreement with Desert Hot Springs Resort to supply a minimum of 2,000 cases of each product per month. How many cases of each product should be produced per month to maximize the company's total contribution margin?

P15-17 Alternative Uses of Idle Capacity After a Product Line is Dropped

The Video Shop, located in a residential neighborhood, has two departments: movie department and video game department. The movie department rents movies; and the video game department rents video games and operates a video game arcade which is popular among the young residents in the area.

The relevant data on the shop's operations for the last year are provided below:

	Movie Department	Video Game Department	Total
Revenues	$300,000	$400,000	$700,000
Expenses:			
Variable	120,000	100,000	220,000
Fixed-personnel	95,000	120,000	215,000
Fixed-facility	90,000	80,000	170,000
Total	305,000	300,000	605,000
Profit	$(5,000)	$100,000	$95,000

The movie-rental customers have complained about the noise the video game arcade generates, but another video shop is twelve blocks away and the customers continue to rent movies from The Video Shop. The movie-rental business was profitable, until a nationwide video rental chain opened a shop across the street several months ago. Many customers are using the nationwide chain shop now.

Thinking that the operating loss may not be a temporary phenomenon, the shop's owner is considering the elimination of the movie-rental business. The elimination would certainly save the fixed personnel expenses of the movie department.

Required:

1. Assume that the space and facility released by dropping the movie-rental business cannot be used for any other revenue-generating purposes, and the current level of revenue and expenses will continue for at least the foreseeable future. Should the owner drop the movie-rental business?

2. Assume that the released space can be used to expand the video game rental and arcade operations. The expansion would increase the video game department's revenues by 40% without increasing any fixed cost for the whole shop. The variable cost ratio for the video game department will stay unchanged. Should the owner drop the movie-rental business? Show your analysis clearly.

P15-18   Sell or Process Further

Sonimad Mining Company produces and sells bulk raw coal to other coal companies and exporters. Sonimad mines and stockpiles the coal; it is then passed through a one-step crushing process before being loaded onto river barges for shipment to customers. The annual output of 10 million tons, which is expected to remain stable, has an average cost of $20 per ton with an average selling price of $27 per ton.

Management is currently evaluating the possibility of further processing the coal by sizing and cleaning in order to expand markets and enhance product revenue. Management has rejected the possibility of constructing a large sizing and cleaning plant which would require a significant long-term capital investment.

Bill Rolland, controller of Sonimad, has asked Amy Kimbell, mining engineer, to develop cost and revenue projections for further processing the coal through a variety of contractual arrangements. After extensive discussions with vendors and contractors, Kimbell has prepared the following projections of incremental costs of sizing and cleaning Sonimad's annual output:

	Incremental Costs
Direct labor (employee leasing)	$600,000 per year
Supervisory personnel (employee leasing)	100,000 per year
Heavy equipment rental, operating, and maintenance costs	25,000 per month
Contract sizing and cleaning	3.50 per ton
Outbound rail freight (per 60-ton rail car)	240 per car

In addition to the preceding cost information, market samples obtained by Kimbell have shown that electrical utilities enter into contracts for sized and cleaned coal similar to that mined by Sonimad at an expected average price of $36 per ton.

Kimbell has learned that 5% of the raw bulk output that enters the sizing and cleaning process will be lost as a primary product. Normally, 75% of this product loss can be salvaged as coal fines. These are small pieces ranging from dust-like particles up to pieces two inches in diameter. Coal fines are too small for use by electrical utilities, but are frequently sold to steel manufacturers for use in blast furnaces.

Unfortunately, the price for coal fines frequently fluctuates between $14 and $24 per ton (F.O.B. shipping point), and the timing of market volume is erratic. While companies generally sell all their coal fines during a year, it is not unusual to stockpile this product for several months before making any significant sales.

Required:

1. Prepare an analysis to show whether it would be more profitable for Sonimad Mining Company to continue to sell the raw bulk coal or to process it further through sizing and cleaning. (Note: Ignore any value related to the coal fines in your analysis.)
2. a. Taking into consideration any potential value to the coal fines, prepare an analysis to show if the coal fines would affect the results of your analysis prepared in Requirement 1.
   b. What other factors should be considered in evaluating a sell-or-process-further decision?

(CMA)

P15-19 Special Order; Ethical Conduct

Award Plus Co. manufactures medals for winners of athletic events and other contests. Its manufacturing plant has the capacity to produce 10,000 medals each month; current monthly production is 7,500 medals. The company normally charges $175 per medal. Variable costs and fixed costs for the current activity level of 75% are shown below.

Variable costs:		
Manufacturing		
Labor	$ 375,000	
Material	262,500	
Marketing	187,500	$ 825,000
Fixed costs:		
Manufacturing	275,000	
Marketing	175,000	450,000
Total costs		$1,275,000
Unit variable costs		$ 110
Unit fixed costs		60
Average unit costs		$ 170

Award Plus has just received a special one-time order for 2,500 medals at $100 per medal. For this particular order, no variable marketing costs will be incurred. Cathy Senna, a management accountant with Award Plus, has been assigned the task of analyzing this order and recommending whether or not the company should accept or reject it. After examining the costs, Senna suggested to her supervisor, Gerard LePenn who is the controller, that they request competitive bids from vendors for the raw materials as the current quote seems high. LePenn insisted that the prices are in line with other vendors and told her that she was not to discuss her observations with anyone else. Senna later discovered that LePenn is a brother-in-law of the owner of the current raw materials supply vendor.

Required:

1. Identify and explain the costs that will be relevant to Cathy Senna's analysis of the special order being considered by Award Plus Co.
2. Determine if Award Plus Co. should accept the special order. In explaining your answer, compute both the new average unit cost for Award Plus and the incremental unit cost for the special order.
3. Discuss at least three other considerations that Cathy Senna should include in her analysis of the special order.
4. Based on the description of the "Standards of Ethical Conduct for Management Accountants" in Chapter 1, explain how Cathy Senna should try to resolve the ethical conflict arising out of the controller's insistence that the company avoid competitive bidding.

(CMA, adapted)

P15-20   Relevant Costs; Comprehensive

Electrovision, Inc. produces and sells CD-ROM-based videogames played on PCs. It has successfully made the transition from 16-bit to 32-bit and N-64 systems. Since 32-bit games on CD-ROM are more profitable to sell than cartridge games for the N-64, Electrovision has decided to produce only 32-bit games this year in its Burbank, California, plant. The videogames are sold for $75 per unit, and the normal production level is 50,000 units a year. The unit variable costs of the videogames are as follows:

Direct materials	$ 8
Direct labor	14
Variable overhead	5
Variable selling expenses	2
Total	$29

Fixed manufacturing overhead costs are $600,000, and fixed administrative expenses are $400,000.

Required:

Each of the following questions is independent.

1. Electrovision has 2,500 units of football videogames on hand that have been carried over from the last Christmas season. Due to the declining popularity of the contents, the company will not be able to sell those games at the $75

regular selling price. The company wants to clear space in the storeroom to be ready for a series of new products to be stored. What is the minimum price the company should charge for a clearance sale?

2. The sales manager projects a sales increase of 20% over the normal level with a special, one-time media blitz that will cost $350,000. Should the company launch the special promotion? All other conditions remain unchanged.

3. A foreign buyer has placed a special order for 3,000 games at a one-time price of $45 a unit. The acceptance of this offer would not require extra support of fixed resources. What will be the impact of accepting this offer on the company's profit?

4. The controller of the company is concerned about so many "special" orders salespeople bring in. They always claim that it is a one-time deal, but they keep coming up with special orders that require price concessions. In the current quarter alone, the salespeople have brought in 12 special orders. The addition of those orders to the normal capacity level does not increase the total fixed costs yet, but the controller believes somebody must pay for those fixed resources pretty soon. Finally, she decides to charge at least the full cost of operations at the normal activity level for even a special order. How much should she charge per unit?

5. Due to a series of "politically incorrect" remarks made by the company president, a large group of employees are going on a strike. They say that they want to "teach a lesson" to management and will continue the strike for 3 months. The company could operate at 40% of the normal level for 3 months with the non-striking workforce, or could shut the Burbank plant down for the period. A plant shutdown would reduce the fixed overhead costs by 25% and the fixed administrative expenses by 40%. What should the company do?

P15-21 Make or Buy; Scarce Resource

OmniSport Inc. is a wholesale distributor supplying a wide range of moderately priced sporting equipment to large chain stores. About 60% of OmniSport's products are purchased from other companies while the remainder of the products are manufactured by OmniSport. The company has a Plastics Department that is currently manufacturing the boot for in-line skates. OmniSport is able to manufacture and sell 5,000 pairs of skates annually, making full use of its machine capacity at available workstations. Presented below are the selling price and costs associated with OmniSport's skates.

Selling price per pair of skates		$98
Costs per pair:		
Molded plastic	$ 8	
Other direct materials	12	
Machine time ($16 per hour)	24	
Manufacturing overhead	18	
Selling and administrative cost	15	77
Profit per pair		$21

Because OmniSport believes it could sell 8,000 pairs of skates annually if it had sufficient manufacturing capacity, the company has looked into the possibility of purchasing the skates for distribution. Colcott Inc., a steady supplier of quality products, would be able to provide 6,000 pairs of skates per year at a price of $75 per pair delivered to OmniSport's facility.

Jack Petrone, OmniSport's product manager, has suggested that the company could make better use of its Plastics Department by manufacturing snowboard bindings. To support his position, Petrone has a market study that indicates an expanding market for snowboards and a need for additional suppliers. Petrone believes that OmniSport could expect to sell 12,000 snowboard bindings annually at a price of $60 per binding. Petrone's estimate of the costs to manufacture the bindings is presented below.

Selling price per snowboard binding		$60
Costs per binding:		
Molded plastic	$16	
Other materials	4	
Machine time ($16 per hour)	8	
Manufacturing overhead	6	
Selling and administrative cost	14	48
Profit per binding		$12

Other information pertinent to OmniSport's operations is presented below.

a. An allocated $6 fixed overhead cost per unit is included in the selling and administrative cost for all of the purchased and manufactured products. Total fixed and variable selling and administrative costs for the purchased skates would be $10 per pair.

b. In the Plastics Department, OmniSport uses machine hours as the application base for manufacturing overhead. Included in the manufacturing overhead for the current year is $30,000 of fixed, factory-wide manufacturing overhead that has been allocated to the Plastics Department.

Required:

In order to maximize OmniSport Inc.'s profitability, recommend which product or products should be manufactured and/or purchased. Prepare an analysis based on the data presented that will show the associated financial impact. Support your answer with appropriate calculations.

(CMA)

P15-22   Sell or Process Further; By-Product

Goodson Pharmaceutical Company manufactures three main products from a joint process: Altox, Lorex, and Hycol. Data regarding these products for the fiscal year ended May 31, Year 9, are shown below.

	Altox	Lorex	Hycol
Units produced	170,000	500,000	330,000
Sales value per unit at split-off	$ 3.50	–	$ 2.00
Allocation of joint costs*	$450,000	$ 846,000	$504,000
Separable costs	–	$1,400,000	–
Final sales value per unit	–	$ 5.00	–

* Joint costs are allocated on the basis of final sales value less costs of completion and disposal. The sales value of any by-product is deducted from the joint costs before allocation.

The president of Goodson, Arlene Franklin, is reviewing an opportunity to change the way in which these three products are processed and sold. Proposed changes for each product are described below.

a. Altox is currently sold at the split-off point to a manufacturer of vitamins. Altox can also be refined for use as a medication to treat high blood pressure; however, this additional processing would cause a loss of 20,000 units of Altox. The separable costs to further process Altox are estimated to be $250,000 annually. The final product would sell for $5.50 per unit.

b. Lorex is currently processed further after the split-off point and sold by Goodson as a cold remedy. The company has received an offer from another pharmaceutical company to purchase Lorex at the split-off point for $2.25 per unit.

c. Hycol is an oil product from the joint process and is currently sold at the split-off point to a cosmetics manufacturer. Goodson's Research Department has suggested that the company process this product further and sell it as an ointment to relieve muscle pain. The additional   processing would cost $75,000 annually and would result in 25% more units of product. The final product would be sold for $1.80 per unit.

The joint process currently used by Goodson also produces 50,000 units of Dorzine, a hazardous chemical waste product. The company must pay $.35 per unit to properly dispose of the Dorzine. Dietriech Mills Inc. is interested in using the Dorzine as a solvent; however, Goodson would have to refine the Dorzine at an annual cost of $43,000. Dietriech would purchase all the refined Dorzine produced by Goodson and is willing to pay $.75 for each unit.

Required:

1. Identify which of the three main products Goodson Pharmaceutical Company should sell at the split-off point in the future and which of the three main products the company should process further in order to maximize profits. Be sure to support your decisions with appropriate calculations.

2. Assume that Goodson Pharmaceutical Company has decided to refine the waste product Dorzine for sale to Dietriech Mills Inc. and will treat Dorzine as a by-product of the joint process in the future.

   a. Evaluate whether or not Goodson made the correct decision regarding Dorzine, supporting your answer with appropriate calculations.

   b. Explain whether or not the decision to treat Dorzine as a by-product will affect the decisions reached in Requirement 1 above.

(CMA, adapted)

CHAPTER 16

STATEMENT OF CASH FLOWS

After studying this chapter, you should be able to:

1. Describe the objectives and uses, both internal and external, of the statement of cash flows.

2. Explain cash flows and differentiate among the three categories of cash flows: operating, investing, and financing.

3. Determine cash flows from operating activities using the direct method and the indirect method.

4. Prepare a statement of cash flows using a simple technique, the worksheet technique, or the T-account technique.

5. Analyze and interpret the statement of cash flows of a given enterprise.

In the Supplement

FINANCIAL STATEMENT ANALYSIS

After studying this chapter, you should be able to:

1. List the major objectives of financial statement analysis.

2. Explain the major tools and techniques of financial statement analysis.

3. State the ratios used for assessing the short-term liquidity, the long-term solvency, or the profitability of a company.

4. Explain how managers use selected market measures or ratios in making investment decisions.

5. Discuss the benchmarks used for financial statement analysis.

In the Supplement

SERVICE DEPARTMENT COST ALLOCATION

After studying this appendix, you should be able to:

1. Distinguish between operating and service departments in an organization and explain why we need to allocate service costs to operating departments.

2. Differentiate between the direct method and the step method of allocating service department costs and perform service cost allocations under each method.

3. Explain why service departments' variable costs should be allocated separately from their fixed costs and why their budgeted, rather than actual, costs should be allocated.

4. Discuss why certain central costs should not be allocated at all and why sales dollars should not be used as an allocation base.

Most organizations have two types of departments: operating and service. **Operating departments** are those that perform the central functions of the organization. **Service departments** provide service and support to operating departments, but do not themselves produce any products or services for sale to outside customers.

A manufacturer's production departments, such as cutting, fabricating, or assembly, are operating departments, whereas cafeteria, information systems, and personnel are service departments. In a university, academic departments, such as Engineering, Language, and Philosophy, are operating departments, whereas the office of admissions and records, campus security, and building and grounds are service departments.

Why Do We Allocate Service Department Costs?

Service departments do not produce any products. Yet, they incur costs. Operating departments incur costs, but they produce products or services for sale to outside customers. We cannot compute the product cost per unit using only the costs incurred in production departments. To do so would yield inaccurate production costs for inventory valuation, cost of sales determination, and pricing decisions.

Without including service department costs in the unit production cost computation, manufacturers would underestimate the cost of inventory and cost of sales and overestimate gross profit. Service firms would underestimate their operating costs and overestimate their operating profit. Eventually, this miscosting may lead the manufacturing and service firms to make improper pricing decisions.

Although selling, general, and administrative expenses must be factored into pricing and other managerial decisions, they are not allocated to production departments for financial reporting purposes. Under generally accepted accounting principles, manufacturers should not include selling and general administrative expenses in inventory valuation.

Avis Rent A Car learning and development department personnel. This department is a service department whose costs should eventually be assigned to operating departments that produce services for sale to car rental customers.

The costs to allocate to production departments are the costs of the service departments that provide support services to production departments during the production process. This service cost, accordingly, is an integral part of the cost of production. If there are multiple production (operating) departments and multiple service departments, an organization must find some equitable process to allocate the cost of service departments to the production (operating) departments.

The Allocation Process and Cost Drivers

First, an organization must define which service departments and which operating departments are involved. Distinguishing between operating and service departments may be straightforward in some organizations and may be confusing in others. For example, is the X-ray department in a hospital a service or an operating department? While we may define the X-ray department as a service department serving the hospital's operating departments, the definition may change if we look at the X-ray department's out-patient services which it provides for charges. The out-patient service is not a service activity, but an operating activity for which the department charges outside customers.

After service and operating departments have been defined, the organization should allocate the total costs of each service department to operating departments based on service usage. The measure of each operating department's service usage may be straightforward or confusing. For example, the utility used by each department and measured by a meter may be exact. The compensation paid to the factory's general manager, the cost of the cafeteria, or the cost of the maintenance department are not easy to allocate among the production departments in the factory.

The organization must find proper cost drivers for such allocation of service department costs. For more details of cost drivers and activities, please refer back to Chapter 6.

SERVICE DEPARTMENT COST ALLOCATION METHODS

The two most commonly used methods of allocating service department costs to operating departments are the direct method and the step-down method.

Direct Method

Under the **direct method,** we allocate each service department's costs directly to operating departments. No portion of any service department's costs is allocated to any other service department. The advantage of this method is its simplicity. The disadvantage of this method is that, since we ignore **reciprocal services** between service departments, this method is less accurate than the step-down method we discuss below.

Step-down Method

Under the **step-down method,** we allocate service department costs as follows:

First, we allocate the costs of the service department that serves the greatest number of other departments. Then, we allocate the costs of the service department that serves the second greatest number of other departments. We follow this until we allocate all service departments' costs to other departments.

Once we have allocated the costs of a service department, we do not allocate other departments' costs back to that department. The advantage of this method is that it considers the reciprocal services among the service departments. Its disadvantages are: (1) It is somewhat difficult to implement. (2) It requires arranging the service departments, according to which department has served a greater number of other departments.

The widespread use of personal computers has simplified the implementation of the step-down method. With respect to the second disadvantage, if two service departments serve an equal number of other departments, we need to break the tie. There is no principle we can use to determine which service department's costs should be allocated first. Each company must find an equitable way of determining the order of allocation. For example, we can allocate the costs of the service department with higher total costs first.

A Numerical Example

Gen-X Gum Company has two production departments (Mixing and Shaping & Packaging) and two service departments (Factory Administration and Custodial Services). Exhibit A-1 presents the budgeted overhead costs traceable to each of these four departments for Year 3.

Management allocates service department costs to production departments using the following cost drivers:

EXHIBIT A-1

Gen-X Gum Company
Budgeted Costs for Year 3

	Factory Adm.	Custodial Services	Mixing	Shaping & Packaging	Total
Variable expenses	$40,000	$15,000	$ 95,000	$33,000	$183,000
Fixed overhead	20,000	15,000	15,000	7,000	57,000
Total costs before allocation	$60,000	$30,000	$110,000	$40,000	$240,000

Service Departments	Cost Drivers
Factory Administration	Number of employees
Custodial Services	Square feet

The number of employees and square footage for all departments are shown below:

	Factory Adm.	Custodial Services	Mixing	Shaping & Packaging	Total
Number of employees	10	5	60	15	90
Square feet (000)	150	270	432	648	1,500

To apply the step-down method, management allocates the costs of Factory Administration first. Exhibits A-2 and A-3 present the allocation of service department costs to production departments using the direct method and the step-down method.

In Exhibit A-2, we allocate the costs of Factory Administration and Custodial Services directly between the two production departments, using the two cost drivers. Even though Custodial Services and Factory Administration provide and receive some service to and from each other, the proportionate cost of such a service is ignored completely under the direct method.

As Exhibit A-3 illustrates, we consider the interdepartmental services provided between service departments under the step-down method. When we allocate the new total cost of $33,750 ($30,000 + $3,750) of the Custodial Services department, we do not re-allocate any portion of it back to the Factory Administration department.

EXHIBIT A-2

Gen-X Gum Company
Service Department Cost Allocation
Direct Method

Departments	Service		Production		
	Factory Adm.	Custodial Services	Mixing	Shaping & Packaging	Total
Costs before allocation (Exhibit A-1)	$60,000	$30,000	$110,000	$40,000	$240,000
Factory Administration costs allocated[a]	(60,000)		48,000	12,000	0
Custodial Services costs allocated[b]		(30,000)	12,000	18,000	0
Total	0	0	$170,000	$70,000	$240,000

(a) Allocation of Factory Administration costs to production departments based on the number of employees:

Production Department	Number of Employees	% of Total	Factory Administration Costs
Mixing	60	80%	$48,000
Shaping & Packaging	15	20%	12,000
Total	75	100%	$60,000

(Allocated costs = $60,000 × 80%, 20%)

(b) Allocation of Custodial Services costs to production departments based on square feet:

Production Department	Square Feet	% of Total	Factory Administration Costs
Mixing	432	40%	$12,000
Shaping & Packaging	648	60%	18,000
Totals	1,080	100%	$30,000

(Allocated costs = $30,000 × 40%, 60%)

Allocating Variable Costs and Fixed Costs Separately

Whenever possible, we need to allocate service departments' variable costs separately from their fixed costs. This will help avoid any possible inequities in allocation. Variable costs vary proportionately with the amount of service used by the consuming departments. Fixed costs remain fixed regardless of the amount of service.

Accordingly, it is more equitable to allocate the variable costs based on the *actual* level of service used, and allocate fixed costs based on a *predetermined*, lump-sum amount. If we combine the variable and fixed costs of a service department and allocate the total based on the level of actual service usage, we would be treating fixed costs as variable costs.

For example, the College of Business, City University, has a word-processing center (WPC) serving its three academic departments: Accounting, Management, and Marketing. The budgeted fixed costs (salaries for two operators and a supervisor) of the WPC for the year are $120,000. Variable costs, such as diskettes, paper, and other supplies, of the WPC average about $2 per hour of operator's actual time on the machines.

EXHIBIT A-3

Gen-X Gum Company
Service Department Cost Allocation
Step-Down Method

Departments	Service		Production		
	Factory Adm.	Custodial Services	Mixing	Shaping & Packaging	Total
Costs before allocation (Exhibit A-1)	$60,000	$30,000	$110,000	$40,000	$240,000
Factory Administration costs allocated[a]	(60,000)	3,750	45,000	11,250	0
Custodial Services costs allocated[b]		(33,750)	13,500	20,250	0
Total	0	0	$168,500	$71,500	$240,000

(a) Allocation of Factory Administration costs to all other departments based on the number of employees.

Department	Number of Employees	% of Total	Factory Administration Costs
Custodial Services	5	6.25%	$ 3,750
Mixing	60	75.00%	45,000
Shaping & Packaging	15	18.75%	11,250
Totals	80	100.00%	$60,000

(b) Allocation of Custodial Services costs to production departments based on square footage:

Production Department	Square Feet	% of Total	Custodial Services Costs
Mixing	432	40%	$13,500
Shaping & Packaging	648	60%	20,250
Total	1,080	100%	$33,750

The College charges the departments the actual rate per hour of service for their use of the WPC. The most equitable way of allocating the WPC costs would be to allocate the $120,000 budgeted fixed costs among the three departments on the basis of *long-run average* needs of each department and allocate the variable costs using the $2 budgeted rate per hour times the number of actual hours used by each department.

Why would it be the most equitable way? We spend the fixed costs to have a certain level of *capacity* available for long-run needs. That's why we use budgeted fixed costs. But the departments should pay for variable costs based on the actual usage.

The academic departments have the following long-run average needs:

WPC Operators' Hours	
Accounting	160 hours
Management	100
Marketing	140
	400 hours

The following represents the actual data for the month of October:

Variable costs		$ 660
Fixed costs		10,000
Actual hours used:		
	Accounting	75 hours
	Management	90
	Marketing	135
		300 hours

Exhibit A-4 presents the allocation of the total cost of the WPC for October among the three academic departments.

EXHIBIT A-4 Allocation of Variable and Fixed Costs

Departments	(1) Long-Run Average Needs	(2) %	(3) Fixed Costs Allocated	(4) Actual Hours Used	(5) Variable Costs Allocated	(6) Total Costs Allocated
Accounting	160 hours	40%	$ 4,000	75	$150	$4,150
Management	100	25	2,500	90	180	2,680
Marketing	140	35	3,500	135	270	3,770
Totals	400 hours	100%	$10,000	300	$600	$10,600

Columns (1) and (4) are given.
(3) = $10,000 budgeted fixed costs × Column (2)
(5) = $2 budgeted rate per service hour × Column (4)
(6) = Column (3) + Column (5)

Although the accounting department actually used the WPC for the smallest number of hours during October, we charge it with the largest proportion (40%) of fixed costs. This is because it has the greatest long-run average need for the word-processing capacity. It is fair to charge variable costs to every department for actual hours used at the budgeted rate of $2.

Actual Usage Rate or Budgeted Usage Rate?

Assume the following actual data for November:

Actual variable costs	$ 540
Actual fixed costs	10,000
Hours Used	
Accounting	45 hours
Management	90
Marketing	135
	270 hours

If we allocate the WPC's service costs based on an average actual rate per hour, we would have the results as shown in Exhibit A-5.

EXHIBIT A-5 Allocation of Service Costs

	Actual Rate	October		November	
Actual costs (variable and fixed)		$10,660		$10,540	
Actual hours of use		÷ 300		÷ 270	
Average rate per hour		$ 35.53		$ 39.04	

Allocation:

		October		November	
	Hours	Actual Costs	Hours	Actual Costs	
Accounting	75	$ 2,665	45	$ 1,757	
Management	90	3,198	90	3,513	
Marketing	135	4,797	135	5,270	
Totals	300	$10,660	270	$10,540	

The management and marketing departments used the WPC in November for the same number of hours they used in October (90 hours and 135 hours). The two departments, however, were charged about 10% more in November than in October because the accounting department used the WPC very little in November. The high fixed costs, incurred to have the capacity for the long-run needs for word processing, was charged mostly to the management and marketing departments.

The above presentation demonstrates that the actual rate is not a fair measure of the cost burden each operating department has to bear. We show a more equitable way of allocating the WPC costs for November in Exhibit A-6.

We allocate the same variable costs, fixed costs, and total costs to the management and marketing departments for November as for October. This is fair, since they used the WPC for the same number of hours in each month. We allocate $60 less to the accounting department for variable costs in November ($90) than in October ($150), representing $2 variable cost per hour times 30 hours of less use. The fixed costs we allocate to the three departments are the same for the two months, because the fixed costs do not vary with the changes in the level of activity.

EXHIBIT A-6 Allocation of Service Costs

Departments	(1) Long-Run Average Needs	(2) %	(3) Fixed Costs Allocated	(4) Actual Hours Used	(5) Variable Costs Allocated	(6) Total Costs Allocated
Accounting	160 hours	40%	$ 4,000	45	$ 90	$4,090
Management	100	25	2,500	90	180	2,680
Marketing	140	35	3,500	135	270	3,770
Totals	400 hours	100%	$10,000	270	$540	$10,540

Columns (1) and (4) are given.
(3) = $10,000 budgeted fixed costs per month × Column (2)
(5) = $2 budgeted rate per hour of service × Column (4)
(6) = Column (3) + Column (5)

Since fixed costs are allocated based on the long-run average needs, it may tempt some departments to underestimate their predicted use of the service department. To discourage this, some companies monitor predictions and material discrepancies. Other companies reward accurate predictions and penalize low-demand predictions. Such penalties include charging higher rates or delaying the service for additional hours in excess of predicted hours.

Should We Allocate All Service Department Costs?

If managers believe that allocating certain service department costs will produce undesirable behavioral response from user departments, then they should not allocate such costs. Consider the costs of the overall systems design at a company. While the services of such a department are essential in the long run, operating departments' managers may opt not to use the services in the short run, especially if they must cut costs fast.

Some costs that are related to the central administration, such as the expenses of the offices of the president, public relations, legal counsel, income tax planning, basic research, and company-wide advertising, are very difficult to allocate to the operating departments. Management may not want to allocate these expenses at all because finding proper cost drivers that show a cause-and-effect relationship is often difficult. Similarly, management does not need to include such expenses in overhead rates or inventory costs.

Actual or Budgeted Costs of Service Departments

Generally speaking, we should allocate *budgeted* costs, not *actual* costs, of service departments to operating departments. This applies to both variable and fixed costs. If we allocate actual costs of service departments, service departments' managers would have no incentive to control their costs or improve their efficiency. They may just incur costs and allocate them to the operating departments. If, however, they can allocate only budgeted costs, any actual costs in excess of budget (unfavorable variances) remain in the service departments.

The managers of the service departments would make every effort to eliminate those unfavorable variances which top management uses in measuring their performance. These variances can be carried over from month to month, favorable variances offsetting unfavorable variances. Any remaining balance may be closed out at year-end against the cost of goods sold.

SUMMARY

We can allocate service departments' costs to operating departments using either the direct method or the step-down method. Under the direct method, we allocate service department costs directly to operating departments and ignore all reciprocal services among service departments. Under the step-down method, we allocate some service departments a portion of other service departments' costs.

Whenever possible, we need to allocate service departments' variable costs and fixed costs separately. Variable costs should be allocated based on actual level of needs times the budgeted rate. Fixed costs should be allocated in lump sum amounts based on long-run average needs of operating departments. Budgeted, not actual, costs should be allocated.

If a service department provides services to other service departments, such reciprocal services should be recognized in cost allocation. Cost allocations that may result in undesirable behavioral response need not be performed. Central administration costs should not be allocated at all.

BASIC CONCEPTS AND TERMS

Direct method   Reciprocal services
Interdepartmental services   Service departments
Operating departments   Step-down method

◼ REVIEW QUESTIONS

A-1 What is the basic difference between service departments and operating departments with respect to customers?

A-2 Why do we allocate service departments' costs?

A-3 Is there anything wrong with allocating each service department's costs directly to the operating departments using the direct method?

A-4 Would the step-down method lead to accurate product costing with respect to the allocation of reciprocal services provided between service departments?

A-5 Why would there be an issue regarding separate allocation of variable costs and fixed costs? How would you deal with any inequity resulting from the separate allocation?

A-6 Should we use the actual rate of service department costs or budgeted rate for allocation to operating departments?

A-7 Should we allocate all service department costs to operating departments? Give examples of some service departments' costs that are not appropriate to allocate.

A-8 Which should we allocate: actual or budgeted costs of service departments?

◼ EXERCISES

E(A)-1 Direct Method

Diverdisk, Inc. produces digital versatile disks (DVD) in two manufacturing departments, labeled M1 and M2. Two service departments, S1 and S2, provide support services to M1 and M2. Costs and proportions of services provided and used by each department are given below:

Department	Own Costs	Proportion of Services Provided to Departments			
		S1	S2	M1	M2
M1	$80,000				
M2	46,000				
S1	24,000	–	70%	20%	10%
S2	32,000	10%	–	50%	40%

Required:

Allocate service department costs to manufacturing departments, using the direct method.

E(A)-2   Step-down Method

Refer to the data for Diverdisk, Inc. in E(A)-1.

Required:

Allocate service department costs to manufacturing departments, using the step-down method.
1.   Allocate the costs of S1 first.
2.   Allocate the costs of S2 first.

E(A)-3   Service Department Cost Allocation to Jobs

Ansonia Manufacturing Company has two manufacturing departments, M1 and M2. The two departments worked on two jobs: Job D-1 and Job F-3. Costs are allocated to jobs based on machine-hours in M1 and based on labor-hours in M2. The data on work hours in each department are provided below:

		M1	M2
Job D-1:	Machine-hours	60	70
	Labor-hours	35	50
Job F-3:	Machine-hours	40	85
	Labor-hours	65	30

Assume that service department costs allocated are $52,000 for M1 and $48,000 for M2.

Required:

How much of the service department costs allocated to M1 and M2 would be allocated to each of the two jobs?

E(A)-4 Dual Rates for Variable and Fixed Costs

The computer services department of WHR Precision Manufacturing Company provides services to all three manufacturing departments: Machining, Connecting, and Finishing. The budgeted monthly costs of the computer services department are $150,000 fixed and $90,000 variable. The budgeted service hours for a typical month are shown below:

	Service Hours Demanded	
Manufacturing Departments	Based on Practical Capacity Available	Based on Expected Monthly Needs
Machining	12,000	9,000
Connecting	15,000	11,000
Finishing	13,000	10,000
Total	40,000	30,000

Required:

1. Compute the costs to be allocated to each manufacturing department. The company allocates variable costs and fixed costs separately. Fixed costs are incurred to have a certain level of computer service capacity available. Variable costs are more closely related to expected monthly needs for computer services.
2. Another company combines variable and fixed costs of operating its computer services department and allocates the total costs to manufacturing departments based on expected monthly needs. Is this a sound approach? Explain.

■ PROBLEMS

 ## P(A)-5 Service Department Cost Allocation

Sunset Hotel has two operating units, guest lodging and conference center. These two operating units are supported by three service units: administration, housekeeping, and accounting.

The following data relate to the activities of the five units for a recent month:

	Service Units			Operating Units		
	Administration	Housekeeping	Accounting	Guest Lodging	Conference Center	Total
Number of employees	120	70	280	420	630	1,520
Square feet occupied	30,000	20,000	40,000	200,000	80,000	370,000
Number of guests (per day)				15,000	30,000	45,000
Overhead costs	$280,000	$210,000	$96,000	$860,000	$550,000	$1,996,000

The hotel allocates the costs of the service units in the following order using the cost drivers:

Order	Service Units	Cost Drivers
1	Administration	Number of employees
2	Housekeeping	Square feet of space
3	Accounting	Number of guests per day

Required:

Determine how much overhead costs should be charged to each operating unit using
1. The direct method.
2. The step-down method.

P(A)-6 Service Department Cost Allocation—Step Method

Exam Review Institute has two operating units, SAT Unit and Language Unit. Two service units, facility maintenance and administrative office, provide support services to the operating units. The institute allocates the fixed costs of the two service departments on the following bases:

Service Department	**Basis for Allocation**	
Facility Maintenance	*Square footage of space occupied*	
		Square Footage
	Administrative office	4,000
	SAT Unit	66,000
	Language Unit	20,000
Administrative Office	*Average usage*	
		Average Usage
	SAT Unit	55%
	Language Unit	45%

Fixed costs in each year:

Facility Maintenance.......................	$30,000
Administrative Office	$80,000

Required:

Allocate the fixed costs of Facility Maintenance and Administrative Office to the operating units, using the step-down method of allocation.

P(A)-7 Actual or Budgeted Costs of Service Departments (Variable and Fixed Costs)

Campus Writing Center of Midwest College administers the writing proficiency test to the incoming students of the college's three schools: Arts and Sciences (A&S), Engineering, and Business. The College allocates the variable costs of the Writing Center according to the number of tests administered for each school.

The Center budgeted $28 as the unit variable cost of the test, but the actual variable cost of the tests administered during Year 8 was $30 per test. The budgeted and actual number of tests administered for each school during Year 8 are shown below:

	Schools		
	A&S	**Engineering**	**Business**
Budgeted..................	7,000	5,000	12,000
Actual.....................	9,000	6,000	15,000

The college's Facility Maintenance department provides maintenance services to all units on campus. The fixed costs of Facility Maintenance are allocated based on the square footage of each unit occupying spaces as follows:

Writing Center	9,000 sq.ft.
A&S..	45,000
Engineering.................................	36,000
Business....................................	135,000

The Writing Center's fixed costs are allocated according to the long-run average test needs of each school as shown below:

A&S..	13,500 tests
Engineering.................................	9,000
Business....................................	22,500

Budgeted and actual fixed costs in the two service departments for Year 8 follow:

	Facility Maintenance	**Writing Center**
Budgeted fixed costs................	$750,000	$1,200,000
Actual fixed costs..................	760,000	1,220,000

Required:

1. Allocate the variable costs of the Writing Center to each of the three schools at the end of Year 8.
2. Did you use the budgeted or actual rate for the variable cost allocation? Why?
3. If you didn't allocate the Writing Center's total costs incurred in (1), who is responsible for the remaining costs that have not been allocated?
4. Allocate, using the step-down method, the fixed costs of the two service departments at the beginning of Year 8 to the three schools so that each school can compute its own overhead rate.
5. Allocate, using the step-down method, the fixed costs of the two service departments at the end of Year 8 to the three schools for performance evaluation purposes.

P(A)-8   Service Cost Allocation; Sales Dollars as a Basis

KPM, Inc. has used sales amounts of its divisions as a basis for allocating the expenses of the central administration. The company allocated the central administration's expenses of $1,000,000 in Year 6 as follows:

Division A	Division B	Division C	Total
$400,000	$375,000	$225,000	$1,000,000

The total sales of the company amounted to $20,000,000 in Year 6.
In Year 7, the company's sales increased $5,000,000 from the Year 6 level due to the increase of Division B's sales by two-thirds. The sales of the other two divisions remained unchanged. The central administration's expenses in Year 7 remained unchanged at $1,000,000.

Required:

1. Compute the sales of each division for Year 6.
2. Determine the sales of each division for Year 7.
3. Allocate the Year 7 central administration's expenses to the three divisions.
4. Examine the cost allocations to Division B for Year 6 and Year 7. Evaluate the merits of using sales dollars as a cost allocation basis.

P(A)-9 Allocation of Selling and Administrative Expenses; Revenue as a Basis

NYS, Inc. has a policy of allocating all costs to its divisions. The allocated costs include head office administrative expenses and product marketing expenses. Since most of these costs are hard to attribute to individual divisions that benefited from the expenses incurred, the company uses the actual revenue of each of the divisions as the allocation basis.

In Year 3, the following allocations were made to the company's three divisions (in thousands):

	Albany Division	Buffalo Division	Syracuse Division	Total
Revenue..................	$20,000	$16,000	$4,000	$40,000
Expenses allocated on the basis of revenue.........	2,400	1,920	480	4,800

The revenues of Albany Division and Buffalo Division stayed at the same level in Year 4. Syracuse Division's revenue, however, increased significantly to $12 million because of the division's successful change in sales strategy to direct outreach to the community. The actual selling and administrative expenses of the head office in Year 4, due largely to the cost management efforts of the new corporate controller, remained at the same level as Year 3.

Required:

1. Determine the head office selling and administrative expenses allocated to each of the three divisions in Year 4.
2. Comment on the fairness of allocating the head office expenses on the basis of divisions' revenues.

B

PRICING PRODUCTS AND SERVICES

After studying this appendix, you should be able to:

1. Explain how cost-plus prices can be set based on different cost bases.

2. Distinguish between market penetration and skimming pricing polices and explain when each can be used.

3. Compute the selling price that would achieve a desired dollar amount of profit or a given percentage return on investment.

4. Explain time and material pricing and derive target selling prices using these pricing polices.

The U.S. auto industry has claimed quite often in the past that the wholesale prices Japanese auto makers charge U.S. dealers are lower than the prices they charge Japanese dealers. The difference is called "dumping margin." The Japanese auto makers, it was claimed, were using profits from their protected home market to subsidize predatory pricing to gain market share in the U.S.

How do managers set prices? How do we know certain prices are set deliberately low? What kind of a pricing strategy would enable a company to increase its market share in a certain geographical area? In this appendix, we discuss pricing of products and services.

REGULAR PRICING OF PRODUCTS AND SERVICES

Managers must first consider the company's target return on investment in pricing. Other factors to consider include customer demand, competitors' prices, cost of production or purchase, the company's position in the market, the availability of substitutes for the company's products, and whether the product is price-elastic. The price also reflects a company's pricing strategies. The company may want to penetrate a new market, increase its market share in an existing market, or skim the market for a newly invented product. We will look at the most common pricing strategies.

A Marriott Hotel lounge. The hotel's position is very strong in the business travelers market. Market position is one of the factors considered in pricing.

COST-PLUS PRICING

Cost-plus pricing (markup pricing) uses a cost base of a product or service and adds a certain percentage of the cost base as a markup to determine a selling price. If one unit of a product costs $20 and the markup is 50%, management will set the selling price at $30 ($20 plus 50% of $20). We now look at the markup percentage and cost base.

Markup Percentage

Managers determine the markup percentage so that it will cover operating expenses, taxes, and the desired profit margin. The markup could be a percentage of the selling price, rather than the cost of the product. Depending on whether the percentage is based on the cost or on the selling price, the results could be quite different.

If the product cost is $20 and the markup percentage is 50% of the selling price (P), the selling price will be $40, as calculated below:

$$
\begin{aligned}
\text{Selling price } P &= \text{Cost of the product } + \text{ Markup} \\
&= \$20 + 0.5P \\
P - 0.5P &= \$20 \\
0.5P &= \$20 \\
P &= \$20 \div 0.5 = \$40
\end{aligned}
$$

The 50% markup on the selling price is actually 100% of the cost.

Determining the Cost Base and Markup

The cost base may include only variable costs or full costs (variable costs plus fixed costs). Some firms may even include fixed administrative expenses in the cost base. If we use variable costs as a base for the markup percentage, the percentage should be high enough to cover fixed manufacturing overhead, fixed administrative expenses, income taxes, and the desired profit. If full costs are used as a base for the markup percentage, such a percentage should be sufficient to cover fixed administrative expenses, income taxes, and the desired profit.

We will use the following data to illustrate the determination of markup and cost base using variable costs, full absorption costs, and total operating costs:

Data:
Annual output	10,000 units
Per-unit manufacturing cost:	
Direct materials	$ 5
Direct labor	4
Variable overhead	2
Fixed manufacturing overhead	$40,000 per year
Variable selling expenses	$ 1 per unit
Fixed administrative expenses	$60,000 per year
Target operating profit before taxes	$20,000

Variable Cost Base:

Variable cost per unit:
Direct materials	$5
Direct labor	4
Variable overhead	2
Variable selling expenses	1
	$12

Total variable costs for 10,000 units:
$$10,000 \times \$12 = \qquad \$120,000$$

Total fixed expenses:
Fixed overhead	$ 40,000
Fixed administrative expenses	60,000
	$100,000

Total sales required
= Variable costs + Fixed costs + Target operating profit
= $120,000 + $100,000 + $20,000 = $240,000.

Selling price per unit = $240,000 ÷ 10,000 units = $24.

Markup over variable costs = Selling price − Variable costs
= $24 − $12 = $12.

Markup percentage = Markup ÷ Variable costs
= $12 ÷ $12 = 100%.

Full Absorption Cost Base:

Total manufacturing cost per unit:

Direct materials	$ 5
Direct labor	4
Variable overhead	2
Fixed overhead ($40,000 ÷ 10,000 units)	4
	$15

Total manufacturing costs 10,000 × $15 = $150,000

Selling and administrative expenses:

Variable selling expenses 10,000 × $1 =	$10,000
Fixed administrative expenses	60,000
	$70,000

Total sales required = $150,000 + $70,000 + $20,000
= $240,000

Desired selling price = $240,000 ÷ 10,000 units = $24

Markup over full absorption cost = $24 − $15 = $9

Markup percentage = $9 ÷ $15 = 60%

Total Operating Cost Base:

Target profit = Sales − Total operating costs
Total operating costs = Sales − Target profit
= $240,000 − $20,000 = $220,000
Markup percentage = Target profit ÷ Operating costs
= $20,000 ÷ $220,000 = 9.09%

Although we use the same target profit and the same desired selling price, the markup percentages are different because the three cost bases are different. Few companies use total operating expenses as a cost base to compute the markup because of the difficulty in allocating general administrative expenses to units of product.

Most companies use full absorption costs as a base for determining the markup percentage. Some firms use the variable cost base, but do so primarily in pricing special sales orders as we discussed in Chapter 15.

The markup percentages we computed above will be correct only if the number of units produced during the year is exactly 10,000 units. If the actual output level differs, the markup percentage will differ accordingly. This is because all fixed expenses will be allocated among a different number of output units, producing different fixed costs per unit.

TARGET ROI PRICING

Target return-on-investment (ROI) pricing is similar to cost-plus pricing, but uses the target percentage ROI to obtain the target operating profit. The following example demonstrates this pricing method.

A company plans to produce 50,000 units, the normal capacity, during next year. Other projections include:

Variable production costs (per unit)	$ 12
Variable selling expenses (per unit)	3
Fixed manufacturing overhead	100,000
Fixed administrative expenses	190,000
Total assets	300,000

If the company's target ROI is 20%, what markup percentage should it add on the full absorption cost per unit and on the variable cost per unit? We will proceed as follows:

Variable production costs $= 50,000$ units $\times$ $12 =$	$ 600,000
Fixed manufacturing overhead	100,000
Variable selling expenses $= 50,000$ units $\times$ $3 =$	150,000
Fixed administrative expenses	190,000
Target ROI $= \$300,000 \times 20\% =$	60,000
Total desired sales	$1,100,000

Selling price $= \$1,100,000 \div 50,000$ units $= \$22$

Full absorption cost of production per unit:

Variable costs	$12
Fixed overhead $= \$100,000 \div 50,000$ units $=$	2
	$14

Markup on full absorption cost $= \$22 - \$14 =$	$8
Markup percentage (based on full absorption cost)	
$= \$8 \div \$14 =$	57.14%
Markup on variable cost per unit $= \$22 - \$12 =$	$10
Markup percentage based on variable cost $= \$10 \div \$12 =$	83%

MATERIAL AND TIME PRICING FOR SERVICES

Many service organizations, such as automobile, computer, and appliance repair shops and accounting, law, and engineering firms, use **material and time pricing** (parts and labor pricing). They set two prices (rates): one for the materials used and the other for the labor time consumed in completing the job. Each of these two rates includes a markup percentage to cover overhead, selling and administrative expenses, and the target profit or ROI.

Material Pricing

Managers set the price for materials or parts used by adding a **material loading charge** to the invoice price of the materials. Such a loading charge is added to cover the costs of ordering, handling and storing the materials, in addition to a profit margin on such materials.

Time Pricing

Similar to materials pricing, **time pricing,** which is usually expressed as a rate per direct labor hour, is determined by adding an *allowance* to the direct labor cost of the employee, including fringe benefits. Such an allowance is added to cover a proportionate share of selling and administrative expenses and a target profit per hour of employee time. In some organizations, such as accounting, law, and engineering firms, the rate may vary, depending on who is assigned to the job.

The following example illustrates a material and time pricing:

Import Car Service uses parts and labor pricing for all auto repairs. In addition to the invoice cost of the parts ordered, the shop incurs the following costs each year in ordering, handling and storing parts:

Utilities	$ 30,000
Wages (including fringe benefits)	60,000
Property taxes	5,000
Other fixed expenses (rent, insurance, etc.)	15,000
	$110,000

The invoice cost of parts totals $550,000 per year.
The mechanics work a total of 20,000 hours per year.
The shop desires a 10% profit margin on parts used and a $4 profit margin per hour of mechanics' time.
The average direct labor cost per hour of mechanics' working time is $15 (including fringe benefits).

In addition to direct labor cost and fringe benefits paid to mechanics, the shop incurs the following expenses related to the repair shop:

Supervisory salaries (including fringe benefits)	$100,000
Receptionist and cashiers salaries	70,000
Other (depreciation, utilities, etc.)	30,000
	$200,000

Based on the above data, we can compute the parts loading charge and labor rate per hour as follows:

Parts Loading Charge:

Charge for ordering, handling and storing parts, $110,000 ÷ $550,000 =	20% of invoice cost
Target profit margin on parts	10% of invoice cost
Parts loading charge	30% of invoice cost

Labor Rate Per Hour:

Average pay per mechanic's hour.............................	$15
Proportionate share of other shop expenses,	
$200,000 ÷ 20,000 hours = ...	10
Target profit margin per hour of mechanic's time	4
Labor rate per hour..................................	$29

COMPETITION-BASED PRICING AND TARGET COSTING

Competition-based pricing allows managers to set prices so that their firm can compete with a competitor's price. The price may reflect a slight difference in the product features or after-sale service.

In Chapter 10, we discussed target costing. **Target costing,** as popularized by world-class Japanese lean producers, is a cost management technique born out of a market-driven strategy. Target costing focuses on managing costs at the development and design stages of a product, although its concept is used throughout the product life cycle.

Target costing is based on the price-down, cost-down strategy, and is therefore connected with the company's long-term profit and product planning process. Accordingly, target costing is closely linked with competition-based pricing. The main theme in the target costing process is, "What should the new product cost?" It is in direct contrast to a typical U.S. manufacturer's practice, in which the question is, "What does it cost?"

Traditionally, a company would develop and design a product, calculate costs, price the product based on the desired markup, and market the product. In the target costing process, a company follows a different practice, starting from setting the competitive price first.

After setting the competitive price, the company will determine how to manufacture the product at a certain cost that will provide a satisfactory return. We must realize here that such a pricing policy may not allow the company to achieve its normal markup or target ROI percentage.

Consider Cleaner Inc., which is trying to decide whether to enter the market with a new glass cleaning liquid. A can of a similar liquid is selling for $2 in the market. Considering the competition, the company decides to charge the same price for its product. For an expected sales volume of 250,000 cans per year, selling and administrative expenses will amount to $150,000. The company's target return is 25% on its investment of $1,000,000 net assets.

To achieve this return, the company computes the allowable manufacturing costs as follows:

Expected sales (250,000 cans × $2)	$500,000
Less:	
Selling and administrative expenses	150,000
Target return on net assets = $1,000,000 × 25% =	250,000
	400,000
Allowable manufacturing costs	$100,000
Allowable manufacturing cost per can = $100,000 ÷ 250,000 cans =	$0.40

The company must now determine how to manufacture the cans at $0.40 per can. If this is not possible, the company must choose either to accept a return rate that is less than 25% or not enter the market at all. We use the concept of return on investment here for our discussion of pricing, but the concept of return on sales is more appropriate for target costing. Refer to Chapter 10 for more details of target costing.

OTHER PRICING METHODS

Demand-Oriented Pricing and the Robinson-Patman Act

Demand-oriented pricing requires setting a high price when demand is high and setting a low price when demand is low. Firms such as airlines, hotels, and restaurants regularly use demand-oriented pricing. For example, an airline usually charges more for an air ticket during the summer than it does during the winter. Similarly, a restaurant may charge less for the same meal at lunch than it does at dinner.

Manufacturers who use demand-oriented pricing must be careful not to violate the **Robinson-Patman Act** of 1936. This Act prohibits price discrimination among the same class of customers—all airline summertime travelers, all lunchtime patrons, all wholesalers, and all retailers. The only exception is when the discrimination is justified by the differential in marketing and administrative costs. The cost differential in manufacturing does not apply.

Market Penetration Pricing

A firm that wants to capture a large share of a market or penetrate a new market may decide to set the price relatively low to achieve these objectives. We refer to this as a **market penetration pricing** policy. Such a pricing policy is usually used when there are many competitors who find it relatively easy to enter the market. These competitors usually show high fixed costs and require a relatively high sales volume to break even.

Skimming Pricing

If a company invents a new product, it may decide to set the price for the product extremely high to "skim the cream" off the market. Many bio-medical products companies use this strategy when they develop a new product. The **skimming pricing** strategy provides the company with a cushion against the high risk involved in developing a new product. With a relatively high profit margin, the company can quickly recover the R&D costs. The company can gradually lower the price to attract more customers and expand production. The skimming policy will be most effective when it is difficult for competitors to enter the market.

SUMMARY

This appendix covers pricing policies and strategies. Pricing strategies include the following:

(a) cost-plus pricing: add to the product cost a markup (%);

(b) target ROI pricing: add to the product cost a target profit derived from the ROI;

(c) material and time pricing: add a material loading charge and an allowance;

(d) Competition-based pricing: set prices equal or very close to those set by competitors;

(e) market penetration pricing: set prices relatively low to enable the company to penetrate a new market (or increase its market share in an existing market);

(f) skimming pricing: set prices relatively high at the beginning and reduce gradually; and

(g) demand-oriented pricing: set prices high when demand is high and low when demand is low.

BASIC CONCEPTS AND TERMS

Competition-based pricing	Material and time pricing
Cost-plus pricing	Robinson-Patman Act
Demand-oriented pricing	Target costing
Market penetration pricing	Target ROI pricing
Markup pricing	Skimming pricing

■ SELF-REVIEW PROBLEM

Sunset Hotel has two operating units, guest lodging and convention center.

The following data relate to the activities of the two operating units for a recent month:

| | Operating Units | | |
	Guest Lodging	Convention Center	Total
Number of guests (average per day)	15,000	30,000	45,000
Direct costs (materials and labor)	$ 600,000	$400,000	$1,000,000
Overhead and allocated service			
department costs	$1,154,000	$842,000	$1,996,000

Required:

1. The hotel wants to add a fixed markup to cover selling and administrative expenses of $300,000 and to earn an operating profit of $200,000 before tax. Management wants to allocate the $300,000 equally between the two operating units and allocate the $200,000 operating profit in the ratio of the direct costs of materials and labor. What price per guest per day should the hotel charge for guest lodging and for convention center?

2. Refer to (1). Assume that management wants to set the price per guest per day for each operating unit at a markup of 30% (instead of a flat amount of $200,000) over total costs including allocated selling and administrative expenses. What price should the hotel charge per guest per day for each operating unit? How much is the operating profit before tax for each operating unit and for the hotel as a whole?

Solutions

1. Setting prices for operating units to earn a fixed amount of profit:

	Guest Lodging	Convention Center
Direct costs (materials and labor)	$ 600,000	$ 400,000
Overhead costs	1,154,000	842,000
Markup to cover selling and administrative expenses (equally)	150,000	150,000
Desired operating profit before tax (in ratio of direct costs)	120,000	80,000
Total	$2,024,000	$1,472,000
Number of guests	÷ 15,000	÷ 30,000
Price per guest per day	= $134.93	= $49.07

2. Setting prices for operating units to earn a given markup on total costs:

	Guest Lodging	Convention Center
Direct costs (materials and labor)	$ 600,000	$ 400,000
Overhead costs	1,154,000	842,000
Selling and administrative expenses (allocated equally)	150,000	150,000
Total costs	1,904,000	1,392,000
Markup at 30% of total costs	571,200	417,600
Total	$2,475,200	$1,809,600
Number of guests	÷ 15,000	÷ 30,000
Price per guest per day	= $165.01	= $60.32

■ REVIEW QUESTIONS

B-1   Assume that a manager wants to use cost-plus pricing for a product. What items should be covered by the markup?

B-2   Refer to B-1. What types of cost base can be used in cost-plus pricing? Which cost base would lead the manager to use the highest markup percentage?

B-3   Why would the markup percentage change if the actual output level changes?

B-4   What is the difference between cost-plus pricing and target ROI pricing?

B-5   Material pricing is used by many service organizations. Is material pricing used by manufacturing companies also? Why or why not?

B-6   If there is a direct labor rate per hour already established, why would a company need time pricing?

B-7   Is target costing related to competition-based pricing?

B-8   What is a company supposed to do if the allowable product manufacturing cost, which has been determined based on target costing and competition-based pricing, is too low for the company to realize?

B-9   How does the Robinson-Patman Act affect demand-oriented pricing?

B-10   Is it possible to use market penetration pricing when expected sales volume is limited?

B-11   When can a company use skimming pricing?

■ EXERCISES

E(B)-1 Relationship between Markup, Product Cost, and Sales Price

Each of the following cases presents product cost and the required markup percentage of the selling price:

	Product Cost	Markup Percentage
(1)	$40	50% of the selling price
(2)	60	40% of the selling price
(3)	30	25% of the selling price

Required:

For each of the cases, determine (a) the selling price that would provide the required markup and (b) the percentage of the markup to the product cost.

E(B)-2 Cost-Plus Pricing; Full Absorption Costing

SAC, Inc. is in the process of determining the sales price of a newly developed product. The relevant information is presented below:

Annual production volume (in units)...................	20,000
Unit production cost.................................	$ 20
Expected selling and administrative expenses per year ...	$ 75,000
Investment in the product	$525,000
Desired return on investment	20%

The company uses cost-plus pricing.

Required:

Compute the following, assuming that the company uses the absorption costing method:
1. Required markup percentage based on production cost.
2. Target selling price per unit.

E(B)-3 Time and Materials Pricing

DBC, Inc. of Hollywood makes animated movies. The Company's costs incurred in its operations for a recent period are presented below:

Animators:

Annual animation time	25,000 hours
Desired profit per hour of animators' time	$ 6
Wages paid per hour............................	26
Other employee benefits per hour	1
Selling and administrative expenses for the year ...	200,000

Animation materials loading charge:

	Percentage
For cost of handling materials	20%
For cost of storing materials........................	5%
Desired profit on materials	25%

Required:

1. The company uses time and material pricing. Compute the time rate and the material loading charge that should be used to bill animation jobs.
2. Two of the animators have completed a small job that required 5 hours and $70 in materials. Compute the amount that should be billed for the job.

E(B)-4   Cost-Plus Pricing; Full Absorption Costing

EZX, Inc. uses the full absorption costing method for product costing and pricing. The company determines its selling price based on the expected sales volume in units. The following information is related to a new product the company has developed:

Desired markup on the new product	70% of the
	manufacturing cost

Variable costs per unit:

Manufacturing...............................	$	20
Selling and administrative....................		5

Fixed costs:

Manufacturing..............................	500,000
Selling and administrative....................	540,000

Required:

1. Compute the target selling price per unit for the following expected sales volume in units:
   a. 32,000 units
   b. 50,000 units
2. Will the company make a profit if the target prices computed in (1) are used?

E(B)-5   Cost-Plus Pricing; Variable and Full Absorption Costing

ESC Inc. uses cost-plus pricing to determine target selling price for its products. It uses a markup of 50% of total manufacturing cost or a markup of 75% of total variable expenses for pricing purposes. The following are the data on the costs of a new product:

	Per Unit	Total
Direct materials	$ 9	
Direct labor	11	
Variable overhead	4	
Fixed overhead		$350,000
Variable selling expenses	2	
Fixed administrative expenses		200,000

The normal production volume of 50,000 units is used to compute per-unit costs.

Required:

1. Compute the target selling price, using variable costing.
2. Compute the target selling price, using full absorption costing.

E(B)-6   Target ROI Pricing

Patech Inc. is in the process of launching a new product. The company uses cost-plus pricing and variable costing. The following information relates to the new product:

Desired rate of return on the investment	10%
Required investment	$400,000
Variable manufacturing costs per unit	15
Fixed overhead costs	180,000
Variable selling expenses per unit	3
Fixed selling and administrative expenses	140,000

The company wants to achieve the target ROI of 10%.

Required:

Determine the percentage markup and the selling price per unit assuming
1. 50,000 units of expected sales volume a year.
2. 30,000 units of expected sales volume a year.

E(B)-7 Cost-Plus Pricing; Variable Costing; Target ROI

PDI, Inc. is in the process of pricing a new product. The relevant information on the new product is presented below:

Variable costs per unit:	
Production...	$ 10
Selling...	2
Fixed costs:	
Production...	135,000
Selling and administrative	95,000
Target markup.......................................	60%
Expected annual sales volume	50,000 units

The company uses variable costing for pricing purposes.

Required:

1. Compute the target selling price for the new product.
2. If the desired ROI is 20% and the investment in the assets employed totals $500,000, what markup percentage would be required on the new product to earn the desired ROI?

E(B)-8   Varying Markup Percentages

NKS, Inc. is in the process of pricing a new product. The relevant information on the product is provided below:

	Per Unit	Total
Direct materials	$4	
Direct labor.	2	
Variable overhead	1	
Variable selling expenses.	2	
Fixed overhead		$500,000
Fixed administrative expenses.		300,000

The normal level of production and sales is 100,000 units a year. The company uses a markup of 120% based on full absorption costing.

Required:

1. Compute the full absorption cost of the product.
2. Compute the selling price using a markup of 120% based on full absorption costing.
3. Compute the markup percentage assuming the selling price in (2) is based on variable manufacturing costs.
4. Compute the markup percentage assuming the selling price in (2) is based on total variable costs.

E(B)-9   Markup Percentages; Income Tax; Full Absorption Costing

AMD, Inc. is in the process of pricing a new product and wishes to earn an after-tax target return of 14% on it. The following information is available:

Variable manufacturing costs per unit	$ 6
Variable selling expenses per unit	$ 1
Fixed manufacturing costs	$ 400,000
Fixed selling and administrative expenses	$ 300,000
Investment in employed assets	$1,000,000
Income tax rate	30%

The firm uses a markup percentage based on full absorption costing.

Required:

1. Compute the unit selling price for each of the following projected sales volumes:
   (1) 50,000 units.
   (2) 60,000 units.
   (3) 70,000 units.

2. For each of the above sales volumes, compute the markup percentage based on full absorption costing.

P(B)-10   Changes in Price and Volume

K&M, Inc. is considering changing its price of Salien, which presently sells for $15. The changes being considered include increases and decreases of both 10% and 25%. Currently, it produces and sells 130,000 units per year. The estimated results from the changes are presented below for Year 8 and Year 9:

Price Change	Estimated Unit Sales		Estimated Advertising and Promotion Expenditure	
	Year 8	Year 9	Year 8	Year 9
−25%	190,000	200,000	$200,000	$200,000
−10%	180,000	190,000	250,000	250,000
No change	160,000	170,000	300,000	300,000
+10%	140,000	150,000	400,000	450,000
+25%	130,000	140,000	450,000	550,000

The Company has the necessary flexibility in its production capacity to meet these volume levels. The variable manufacturing cost per unit of Salien is estimated to be $7.25 in Year 8 and $7.80 in Year 9.

Required:

What should the recommended sales price be in Year 8 and Year 9?

(CMA, adapted)

P(B)-11   Target Costs; Target ROI Pricing

Dentart, Inc. of Ohio is developing a new dental product, which will be marketed domestically and internationally. Art Dentos, the president of the company, is a very aggressive businessman who inspires his employees by saying things such as, "Our market size is 140 billion. That's the number of teeth in people's mouths worldwide." In his efforts to manage costs and price efficiently, the president has made the employees use the concepts of target costs and target returns. The company has determined the following target costs of one unit of the new product, based on the normal production level of 22,000 units a year:

	Target Costs	
	Per Unit	Per Year
Direct materials	$20.00	
Direct labor	4.00	
Variable overhead	3.00	
Fixed overhead		$154,000
Variable selling	2.00	
Fixed selling and administrative		150,000

The required investment of funds for the new product development is:

For working capital	$275,000
For equipment	175,000
Total investment	$450,000

The company requires a 17% target return on investments and uses cost-plus pricing.

Required:

1. Compute (a) the markup percentage and (b) the selling price needed for the company to earn its target ROI of 17% of the investment in the new product, assuming that the company uses absorption costing.
2. Repeat (1) assuming that the company uses variable costing.

P(B)-12   Markup Percentage and Competition

HAP, Inc. is considering the development of a new product. The development requires an investment of $1,500,000. The industry average markup is 30% of manufacturing cost. The cost information on the new product is presented below:

Direct materials per unit..............................	$ 8
Direct labor per unit	25
Variable manufacturing overhead per unit...............	3
Variable selling expenses per unit	7
Fixed manufacturing overhead per year.................	300,000
Fixed administrative expenses per year	221,400

The expected production and sales is 30,000 units per year. The company requires a 20% target return on investment. The company uses absorption costing for product costing and pricing.

Required:

1. Determine the markup percentage (based on manufacturing cost) necessary to earn the company's target ROI.
2. Do you think the company's product will be competitive in the market? Assume that the quality of the new product would be comparable to other competing products.

absorption costing (455) A costing approach that includes fixed manufacturing overhead in the production cost.

account analysis (229) A cost estimation approach that relies on a review of each cost item to identify it as either fixed or variable.

accounting rate of return (565) A capital budgeting method that measures the rate of return computed by dividing accounting net income by the book value of the investment.

activity analysis (257) A part of activity-based costing that entails surveying the personnel and analyzing the work performed by each support department.

activity-based costing (ABC) (8, 255) A costing concept that views organizational costs through a prism of organizational activities rather than departments.

activity center (262) An area of operations for which a meaningful collection of activities is separately identified and reported.

activity cost pool (262) A cost pool created to house all the costs incurred while a certain activity is performed.

appraisal costs (418) A part of the total cost of quality that is incurred for product inspection.

attainable standards (357) Standards that allow for specified breaks or rest periods, machine break-downs, materials shortages or waste, and other minor distractions that customarily occur in the work place.

backflush costing (424) A radical product costing practice that eliminates cost tracking through job cost sheets entirely and flushes costs to the finished goods account when products are completed.

balanced scorecard (8, 402) A measurement system that focuses on the vital signs of the company and translates an organization's top-level visions into individual performance measures at every level.

beta (727) A ratio that indicates the degree of risk inherent in a company's stock relative to all other stocks on the market.

bill-of-material (210) A document that shows the components and the quantity of each required for a finished product unit.

break-even point (61) The point at which revenues exactly equal expenses.

budget (303, 357) A plan of future activities, expressed in quantities and/or monetary values.

budget variance (369) The difference between actual costs and budgeted costs.

budgetary control (303) The use of budgets as a part of a control process.

budgeting (303) The actual preparation of a budget.

by-products (652) Those products that can be separately identified at the split-off point, but are of insignificant sales value relative to the sales values of the joint products.

capacity fixed costs (33) *See* committed fixed costs.

capital budget (306) A budget that relates to long-term investment projects.

capital budgeting (551) The planning and financing of a firm's capital expenditures.

capital investment budget (306) *See* capital budget.

cash budget (319) A budget that shows a combination of the cash receipts schedule, the cash disbursements schedule, any financing results, and the beginning and ending cash balances.

cash equivalents (668) Short-term highly liquid investments that can easily be converted into cash.

cell (424) A clustering of multiple machines which as a group perform the processing requirements for a product or product line.

committed fixed costs (33) Costs an organization must incur if it is to have the capacity to be in business.

common costs (37) Costs that cannot be directly traced to any one segment or any one product of the organization.

competition-based pricing (701) A method of pricing that allows managers to set prices so that their firm can compete with a competitor's price.

continuous budget (306) A budget prepared in a continuous fashion to which one future period is added as the period just ended is dropped.

continuous improvement (405) An approach to operations management that focuses on new ways of performing tasks.

contribution approach (67) An internal reporting method that emphasizes the classification of costs as variable and fixed.

contribution margin (62) The unit sales price less the unit variable cost.

control (303) The process of monitoring performance and taking corrective action.

controllable costs (34) Costs over which the manager has complete authority whether to incur or not.

controller (3) The chief accountant who belongs to top management and is responsible for maintaining data and reporting information needed in decision making.

conversion costs (21) Costs of direct labor and manufacturing overhead. Costs of converting direct material into finished goods.

cost (19) Resources given up to generate some services or to obtain goods.

cost-benefit concept (4, 28) The concept used in the choice of accounting information methods and systems in which management considers estimated costs against expected benefits.

cost center (261,503) A manufacturing or service unit where costs are accumulated and the unit has control over the costs it incurs.

cost driver (26, 123, 209) The factor that will be the best indicator of the cost increase or decrease.

cost hierarchy (216) A hierarchy of manufacturing and service costs that contain unit, batch, product, and facility-level costs.

cost-plus pricing (696) A pricing method that uses a cost base of a product or service and adds a certain percentage of the cost base as a markup to determine a selling price.

cost-volume-profit analysis (61) The study of the relationships between output volume, costs, revenue, and profit.

craft producer (356) A producer who relies on highly skilled workers and simple, flexible tools to produce a custom product in small quantities at high costs.

customer satisfaction (403) An organized approach that focuses on the needs of a customer.

customer value (427) The excess of realization a customer receives over sacrifice when a product or service is bought.

decentralization (501) The delegation of decision-making authority to lower-level managers.

demand-oriented pricing (702) A method of pricing that requires setting a high price when demand is high and setting a low price when demand is low.

differential approach (555) An approach that considers only the difference between alternatives by computing cash flows and their present values.

differential costs (35) Differences in the costs of alternative courses of action.

direct costing (455) *See* variable costing.

direct costs (20) Costs that can be easily traced to the final product manufactured or service generated.

direct method (682) A method for allocating service department costs that ignores any portion of service department's services provided to any other service departments.

direct-labor costs (20,315) Costs of labor that can be easily traced to the final product or service created.

direct-material costs (20,314) Costs of materials that can be easily traced to the final product or service created.

discounted cash flow (DCF) models (552) Capital budgeting models that consider the time value of money and the true return on investment.

discretionary fixed costs (33) Costs over which management has some choice as to whether they should be incurred during a short period of time.

economic value added (511) A measure of shareholder wealth that a company creates over the actual cost of capital employed.

economy of scale (368) The reduction in cost rate per hour or per unit of product that results from a higher level of activity.

efficient capital market (729) A capital market where stock prices are supposed to fully reflect all information about a company and its stock.

efficiency variance (359, 365) The labor or variable overhead variance that represents the difference between actual hours at the standard rate and standard hours allowed for actual output at the standard rate.

engineering approach (229) A cost estimation approach that involves a systematic study of materials, labor, services, and facilities needed at varying activity levels.

engineering change notice (ECN) (210) A document that is used to notify the appropriate personnel that an engineering drawing is modified.

engineering drawing (209) A drawing that illustrates the dimensions, materials, and finishes of the components that comprise a manufactured product.

equivalent units (176) The number of units that could have been produced from all materials, labor, and overhead used in production.

external failure costs (420) A part of the total cost of quality that results when defective products reach customers.

external linkages (428) Linkages of value-chain activities a company performs with its external suppliers and customers.

financial accounting (1, 4) The field of accounting that provides persons outside the organization such as investors, creditors, etc. with information that is useful in making decisions about the organization.

financial budget (306) A budget that relates to an organization's financial activities.

financial leverage (728) A ratio that refers to a company's ability to raise funds at a fixed rate of interest or return and earn a higher rate of return on the investment of the funds.

financial statement analysis (715) The process of applying analytical tools and techniques to the financial statements of an entity to derive useful information.

first-in, first-out (FIFO) process-costing method (183) The process-costing method under which the work done in the current period is distinguished from the work done in the prior period and the two are not averaged.

fixed cost (28, 33) A cost that remains constant regardless of the changes in the cost driver.

flexible budget (306, 355, 364) An operating budget presented at various possible levels of activity.

full absorption costing (455) *See* absorption costing.

functional costing (455) *See* absorption costing.

future costs (35) Costs that are expected or projected to be spent in the future for a specific purpose.

high-low method (212) A method of estimating cost-activity relationship based on the highest and lowest levels of activity.

historical costs. *See* sunk costs.

horizontal analysis (717) The comparison of multiple years' financial data.

hybrid-costing system (171) A system that blends features from one costing system, such as job costing, with another costing system, such as process-costing system.

ideal standards (357) *See* perfect standards.

imputed costs (36) Costs that are not obvious, stated, or paid directly for a specific purpose even though they exist.

incremental analysis (65) The analysis of the effect of an increment in a factor on final results.

indirect costs (20) Costs that can be traced to the final product only at a great cost and inconvenience.

insourcing (648) Manufacturing a part in the company.

internal audit (4) Audit of internal control systems and procedures to determine whether they are appropriate and functioning properly.

internal failure costs (418) A part of the total cost of quality that is caused by defects discovered before products reach customers.

internal linkages (428) Linkages of activities a company performs within itself.

internal rate of return (560) The rate of return that will produce a net present value of zero.

investment center (503) A responsibility center whose manager has control over costs, revenues, and investments in certain assets.

job costing. *See* job-order costing.

job-cost record. *See* job-cost sheet (114).

job-cost sheet (114) A document that contains cost information about an individual job, product, or batch of products.

job-order costing (113) The method of costing jobs, products, or batches of products that are individually identified based on job orders.

joint products (649) Two or more products that are jointly produced from one common input.

just-in-time (JIT) (407) Buying, delivering, producing, or receiving a good or service only when the user, customer, or manufacturer needs it.

just-in-time pull system (407) An operating system in which production takes place in a particular department or workstation only if the units produced are required by the next workstation.

kaizen costing (415) A cost management technique that focuses on continuous improvement activities in the manufacturing phase.

lean production paradigm (9, 401) A new paradigm in production that combines the strengths of craft production and mass-production.

learning curve (31) The concept on the decreasing variable cost per unit as activity level increases and employees become more efficient with experience.

least-squares method (227) A method of estimating cost-activity relationships that uses a cost estimation line where the sum of the squared differences between each point and that line is the least possible.

life cycle costing (416) A cost management technique that focuses on maximizing profits during the life cycle of products and services.

line authority (3) Authority exerted directly over subordinates.

loose standards (357) Standards that are set very low and do not challenge workers to perform well.

managerial accounting (1, 4) The process of providing managers of all levels inside the organization with information that is useful to them in making all kinds of decisions.

manufacturing cycle efficiency (418) The process efficiency that focuses on the proportion of the value-adding activities time within the manufacturing cycle time.

manufacturing cycle time (416) The total time a company takes to make a product or create a service.

manufacturing overhead (20) The total of all the indirect cost elements associated with the manufacturing process.

margin of safety (71) The excess of a given sales level over the break-even point.

market penetration pricing (702) A pricing method used by a firm that wants to penetrate a new market or capture a large share of a market by usually setting the price relatively low.

markup pricing (696). *See* cost-plus pricing.

mass-producer (356) A producer who relies on narrowly skilled designers and engineers to design products to be made by workers with a narrow specialization operating expensive, single-purpose machines, which turn out standardized products in large volumes.

master budget (306) A master plan that incorporates all operating, financial, and capital budgets.

material and time pricing (699) A method of pricing used by service organizations that sets two prices, one for the materials used and the other for the labor time consumed in completing the job.

mix variance (362) The variance that results from using an actual mix of a resource which is different from the standard mix.

multinational companies (520) The companies that are headquartered in a country and have subsidiaries operating in foreign countries.

multiple regression analysis (229) A regression analysis that incorporates multiple explanatory variables in the model.

net present value (NPV) method (552) A discounted cash flow method that compares the present value of future cash inflows from the proposed project to the required investment.

nonfinancial performance measures (417) The attributes of performance that are not expressed in monetary terms.

normal costing (125) The method of costing products using actual direct materials, actual direct labor, and normal applied overhead.

operating budget (306) A budget that relates to an organization's operating activities.

operating department (681) A department that performs the central functions of the organization.

operating leverage (68) The ratio of fixed costs to variable costs.

operating return on investment (508) A performance evaluation index calculated by dividing operating profits by operating assets.

operation costing (186) A method of costing different batches of like products that go through individual and common processing stages called operations.

opportunity cost (36, 651) The benefit sacrificed as a result of choosing one alternative compared to another.

outsourcing (648) Buying a part from outside suppliers.

overapplied overhead (122) The excess of overhead applied to products or services over actual overhead incurred.

parts and labor pricing (699) *See* material and time pricing.

payback method (563) A capital budgeting method that measures the period during which a given project will recover its original investment from the cash inflow generated.

perfect standards (357) Standards that can only be attained by the most skillful and most efficient persons who work under the best conditions and circumstances.

period costs (20, 22) Costs incurred during the period, not directly related to the creation of the products.

perpetual budget (306) *See* continuous budget.

post-audit (567) A periodic, follow-up review of approved capital budgeting projects.

practical standards (357) *See* attainable standards.

prevention costs (418) A part of the total cost of quality that is incurred to plan the product or process to minimize defects.

price variance (357) The materials variance that represents the difference between actual quantity at actual price and actual quantity at standard price.

prime cost (20, 19) Direct materials cost plus direct labor cost.

process costing (114, 171) The method of costing many like units that are completed by going through various processing stages or departments in a continuous fashion.

product costs (20, 22) Costs incurred in the creation of the products.

product mix (79) The relative proportion of each product to total sales of the firm.

production velocity (417) *See* manufacturing cycle time.

productivity (420) A measure that compares the units of output generated to the units of inputs used.

profit center (503) A responsibility center whose manager has control over both cost incurrence and revenue generation.

profit plan (303) A budget showing how much profit is expected in a future period.

profit planning (303) Budgeting of future profits.

profitability index (614) The ratio of the present value of cash inflows to the required investment in capital budgeting.

quality (418) A measure of how satisfied a customer is about a product or service.

quantity variance (357) The materials variance that represents the difference between actual quantity at standard price and standard quantity allowed for actual output at standard price.

rate variance (359) The labor variance that represents the difference between actual hours at the actual wage rate and actual hours at the standard rate.

ratio analysis (718) An analytical method that uses computed ratios to focus on a specific decision at hand or specific area that requires attention.

regression line (227) A cost estimation line where the sum of the squared differences between each point and that line is the least possible.

relevant costs (643) Future costs that will differ among alternatives.

residual income (509) The amount of income generated by an investment center in excess of the cost of capital (or a desired minimum rate of return).

responsibility accounting (504) A control concept that holds every responsibility center accountable for the revenues, costs, and assets it is responsible for.

return on investment (508) A performance evaluation index calculated by dividing the profit by the capital invested in the investment center.

responsibility center (503) A managerial level in charge of a set of organizational activities.

Robinson-Patman Act (702) A 1936 act that prohibits price discrimination among the same class of customers.

semi-variable costs (30) Costs that include both fixed and variable portions.

service department (681) A department that provides service and support to operating departments.

skimming pricing (703) A method of pricing that allows a firm to set the price of a new product extremely high to quickly recover the R&D costs incurred in product development.

spending variance (365) The price or rate variance for variable overhead.

split-off point (649) The juncture of production where common inputs are processed into separately identified joint products.

staff authority (3) Authority used to give guidance, consultation, or advice.

statement of cash flows (667) A statement that highlights the major sources and uses of cash during a period of time.

static budget (355) A budget that reflects the budgeted costs at one level of activity.

step-down method (682) A method for allocating service department costs that considers the services provided by service departments for other service departments as well as for operating departments.

step-variable costs (30) Costs that vary with production in steps.

strategic cost management (9, 427) A cost management concept that relies on managerial accounting information to develop and choose organizational strategies that will ensure a long-term competitive advantage for the organization.

strict standards (357) *See* perfect standards.

sunk costs (34) Costs that have already been spent.

target costing (412) A cost management technique born out of the market-driven strategy that focuses on managing costs at the development and design stages of a product.

target return-on-investment (ROI) pricing (699) A pricing method that relies on the concept of cost-plus pricing, but uses the target percentage ROI to obtain the target profit.

Theory of Constraints (641) A variable costing-oriented optimization technique which focuses on the system's constraints.

throughput (641) A measure of profit under the Theory of Constraints calculated by subtracting variable costs of materials and energy from revenue.

throughput time (417) *See* manufacturing cycle time.

time-adjusted rate of return (560) *See* internal rate of return.

total approach (555) An approach that considers the impact of each investment alternative on cash flows and their present values and compares them.

total quality management (TQM) (408) An organized approach to instill a zero defects philosophy in the minds of people.

transfer price (513) The internal price used for products or services transferred between segments or divisions.

trend analysis (717) *See* horizontal analysis.

uncontrollable costs (34) Costs that cannot be authorized by a particular managerial level.

underapplied overhead (120) The excess of actual overhead incurred over the overhead applied to products or services.

value-adding activity (405) An activity that is essential to the accomplishment of the organization's objectives.

value chain (9, 428) The linked set of value-creating activities ranging from material procurement to product and service delivery to customers.

variable cost (28) A cost that varies in the same percentage of variation in the cost driver.

variable costing (455) A costing approach that relies on the contribution margin concept and excludes fixed manufacturing overhead from the production cost.

vertical analysis (718) An analytical method that transforms a given financial statement into a common-size statement.

volume variance (369) The fixed overhead variance that is caused by changes in the level of activity.

weighted-average process-costing method (181) The process-costing method under which the cost of production in the current period is averaged with, and added to, the cost of production in the previous period.

zero-base budget (323) A budget prepared from scratch every year.

INDEX